Online Resources for Criminal Justice

Wadsworth Cengage Learning
Criminal Justice Resource Center
academic.cengage.com/criminaljustice

Designed with both instructors and students in mind, this website features information about Wadsworth Cengage Learning's technology and teaching solutions, as well as several features created specifically for today's criminal justice student. Supreme Court updates, timelines, and hot-topic polling can all be used to supplement in-class assignments and discussions. You'll also find a wealth of links to careers and news in criminal justice, book-specific sites, and much more.

Careers in Criminal Justice Website
Accessible at academic.cengage.com/criminaljustice/careers

Helping students investigate and focus on criminal justice career choices that are right for them, the site includes:

▶ Career Profiles: video testimonials from a variety of practicing professionals

▶ Interest Assessment: helping students decide which CJ careers are suited for them

▶ Career Planner: resumé writing tips and successful job search strategies

▶ Links for Reference to federal, state, and local agencies (where students can get contact information)

Students: A card with a code allowing access to this site may have come with your text. If not, you may purchase access at **www.ichapters.com**.

INTRODUCTION TO PRIVATE SECURITY

KÄREN M. HESS, Ph.D.
Normandale Community College

with contributions by **Christine Hess Orthmann, M.S.**

WADSWORTH
CENGAGE Learning™

Australia • Brazil • Japan • Korea • Mexico • Singapore • Spain • United Kingdom • United States

WADSWORTH
CENGAGE Learning™

Introduction to Private Security,
Fifth Edition

Kären M. Hess

Senior Acquisitions Editor,
   Criminal Justice: Carolyn Henderson
   Meier

Senior Development Editor: Bob Jucha

Assistant Editor: Meaghan Banks

Technology Project Manager: Bessie Weiss

Marketing Manager: Michelle Williams

Marketing Communications Manager:
   Tami Strang

Project Manager, Editorial Production:
   Jennie Redwitz

Creative Director: Rob Hugel

Art Director: Maria Epes

Print Buyer: Linda Hsu

Permissions Editors: Bob Kauser, John Hill

Production Service: Sara Dovre Wudali,
   Buuji, Inc.

Photo Researcher: Terri Wright

Copy Editor: Linda Ireland

Illustrator: Jill Wolf, Buuji, Inc.

Cover Designer: Yvo Riezebos, Riezebos
   Holzbaur Design Group

Cover Image: Center: © Brand X Pictures/
   FotoSearch

Compositor: Newgen

For product information and technology assistance, contact us at **Cengage Learning Customer & Sales Support, 1-800-354-9706**.

For permission to use material from this text or product, submit all requests online at **cengage.com/permissions**. Further permissions questions can be e-mailed to **permissionrequest@cengage.com**.

Library of Congress Control Number: 2008923199

ISBN-13: 978-0-534-63204-5

ISBN-10: 0-534-63204-1

Wadsworth
10 Davis Drive
Belmont, CA 94002-3098
USA

Cengage Learning is a leading provider of customized learning solutions with office locations around the globe, including Singapore, the United Kingdom, Australia, Mexico, Brazil, and Japan. Locate your local office at **international.cengage.com/region**.

Cengage Learning products are represented in Canada by Nelson Education, Ltd.

For your course and learning solutions, visit **academic.cengage.com**.

Purchase any of our products at your local college store or at our preferred online store **www.ichapters.com**.

Printed in Canada
1 2 3 4 5 6 7 12 11 10 09 08

Brief Contents

Contents

SECTION II

 BASIC SECURITY GOALS AND
RESPONSIBILITIES 119

Chapter 5: Risk Management: The Foundation of Private Security 119

Chapter 8: Preventing Losses from Accidents, Emergencies and Natural Disasters   211

SECTION III

 CHALLENGES FACING SECURITY   303

Chapter 11: Information Technology (IT) Security   303

Preface

Welcome to *Introduction to Private Security*, Fifth Edition. This text was written to present an overview of the private security field and the numerous complexities within it. It also seeks to instill an appreciation for those who protect 85 percent of our critical infrastructure.

Space does not permit a thorough discussion of all the topics presented in the text; however, ample references are provided at the end of each chapter should the reader wish to explore any of the topics in greater depth. Most of the chapter topics could, if covered in depth, constitute entire texts in themselves.

When we wrote the last edition of this text, private security seemed more predictable and faced different challenges than today. This was before September 11, 2001, which had a profound impact on not only private security but also every segment of society. This was also before the emergence of information technology (IT) security as one of the greatest challenges facing the profession. And yes, private security has now come into its own as a true profession with tremendous opportunities for those entering this exciting and challenging field.

Context Themes

Three themes run through this text. First, as mentioned, private security has become a profession and is being appreciated as such. The former image of security as consisting of the three Gs—guards, gates and guns—has been all but eliminated, replaced by the image of well-educated individuals certified in many different areas.

Second is the convergence and integration of many areas formerly separate from security, such as the IT department and the safety department, with interoperability becoming crucial.

The third theme is the vital need for private security to partner with the public police in many areas, as explained throughout the text. The historical friction between these two entities is disappearing as each perceives what the other can provide in keeping our country strong and safe.

Organization of the Text

Not unexpectedly, the text begins with chapters that provide background needed to understand the current status of private security (Section I). Private security has evolved slowly, shaped by numerous factors, including social and political influences. Chapter 1 traces its beginnings in ancient times through contemporary private security, including types of private security services and personnel. Chapter 2 describes the private security profession, including what constitutes professionalism and how different types of certification contribute to this status. It also describes the administrative and managerial responsibilities of the chief security officer (CSO). Chapter 3 explains how private security and the public police interface and collaborate in keeping our country safe. Chapter 4 concentrates on legal and ethical issues that affect how private security functions and how private security professionals can avoid costly lawsuits. The general overview presented in Section I should provide the reader with an understanding of why private security functions as it does today.

Section II describes the basic goals and responsibilities of security professionals. Chapter 5 focuses on risk management, which is the heart of private security and an important element in every chapter that follows. Chapter 6 describes basic physical security measures. Chapter 7 describes procedural controls to enhance security. Chapter 8 explains how losses from accidents, emergencies and natural disasters can be prevented or at least mitigated. Chapter 9 looks at preventing losses from criminal actions. The last chapter in this section, Chapter 10, examines what private security professionals need to do when prevention fails, including investigating, reporting and perhaps testifying in court.

Section III explores other important challenges to the profession in the twenty-first century. It begins with a discussion in Chapter 11 of the challenge of information technology (IT) security and the vast array of new technologies that security professionals must understand. Another major challenge, dealing with drugs and violence in the workplace, is discussed in Chapter 12. Chapter 13 explores a relatively new challenge: fulfilling responsibilities relating to homeland security.

The final section, Section IV, pulls together the basic concepts from Sections II and III by describing how the pieces fit together in various applications including infrastructure security (Chapter 14), institutional security (Chapter 15) and commercial security (Chapter 16).

New to This Edition

The fifth edition has been streamlined: several chapters have been combined, moving from 23 chapters to a total of 16 chapters. More specific examples have been added, and all references have been updated. Following are the major additions or changes to each chapter.

- **Chapter 1, The Evolution of Private Security** (formerly Chapters 1 and 2): The initial parallel evolution of private security and the public police.
- **Chapter 2, The Private Security Professional** (formerly Chapters 10 and 22): The various types of ASIS certification; the chief security officer and the chief information officer; enterprise security.
- **Chapter 3, The Public/Private Interface**: The growth of private security due in part to the shortage of applicants in law enforcement; privatization of public justice; controversy surrounding privatization.
- **Chapter 4, Legal and Ethical Considerations** (formerly Chapters 4 and 21): Common civil lawsuits brought against private security; common defenses against such lawsuits; surviving a lawsuit.

- **Chapter 5, Risk Management: The Foundation of Private Security** (formerly Chapter 14): This content has been moved earlier in the text to reflect risk management's place as the first and most important security responsibility. The chapter also touches on reactive versus proactive risk management; quantitative and qualitative risk assessment; the Enterprise Risk Management Model; security as a business center.

- **Chapter 6, Enhancing Security through Physical Controls** (formerly Chapter 5): Advances in locks, lighting, alarms and surveillance systems; future systems.

- **Chapter 7, Enhancing Security through Procedural Controls** (formerly Chapter 6): Restricting use of cameras and video equipment; insurance and bonding.

- **Chapter 8, Preventing Losses from Accidents, Emergencies and Natural Disasters** (formerly Chapter 7): Preparing for pandemics; business continuity guidelines; lessons learned from Hurricane Katrina; risk analysis for extreme events.

- **Chapter 9, Preventing Losses from Criminal Activity** (formerly Chapter 8): Greatly expanded discussion of computer crime; legislation related to computer crime; recommendations for a computer security program.

- **Chapter 10, When Prevention Fails: Investigating, Reporting and Testifying** (formerly Chapters 11, 12 and 13): The Professional Certified Investigator; investigating specific crimes.

- **Chapter 11, Information Technology (IT) Security** (formerly Chapter 9 but with over half new information): How IT projects can effect change; why some IT projects fail; new technologies, including IP video surveillance systems, Voice over Internet Protocol, universal serial bus, mesh networks, computer telephony interface and net-centric security; dangers in implementing new technologies including spyware, adware and bots; competitive intelligence; IT and lawsuits.

- **Chapter 12, Drugs and Violence in the Workplace** (formerly Chapter 20): Drugs are now covered as is school security; the increase in violent crime; the impact of domestic violence in the workplace; school shooters and the massacre at Virginia Tech; preparing for a school takeover by a terrorist.

- **Chapter 13, Terrorism and Homeland Security Responsibilities** (new chapter): Brief chronology of terrorism; the threat of terrorism; classification of terrorist acts; knowing the enemy; preventing terrorism at the local level; methods used by terrorists; responding to terrorist attacks and investigating them; concerns related to the war on terrorism.

- **Chapter 14, Securing the Infrastructure** (formerly Chapter 15): Security at food producing facilities, at chemical plants, at U.S.-based oil companies, in the utilities industry, at drinking water facilities and in the transportation system.

- **Chapter 15, Institutional Security** (formerly Chapter 18): New information on security at libraries, museums, art galleries, religious facilities, financial institutions, hospitals and healthcare facilities and at educational institutions.

- **Chapter 16, Commercial Security** (formerly Chapter 16): New information on retail security, including the threat of organized retail crime (ORC);

lodging and hospitality establishments; casinos, racetracks and sporting events; office buildings including high-rises such as the Sears Tower and the Burj Dubai public and private housing.

How to Use This Text

Introduction to Private Security is more than a text. It is a learning experience requiring your active participation to obtain the best results. You will get the most out of the book if you first familiarize yourself with the total scope of private security: Read and think about the subjects listed in the Contents. Then follow five steps for each chapter to achieve triple-strength learning.

1. Read the objectives at the beginning of each chapter, stated in the form of "Do You Know. . ." questions. This is your *first* exposure to the key concepts of the text. The following is an example of this format:

 Do You Know. . .

■ Into what status private security has evolved in the twenty-first century?

   Also review the key terms and think about their meanings in the context of private security.

2. Read the chapter, underlining or taking notes if that is your preferred study style. Pay special attention to all information within the highlighted areas identified by the security shield icon. This is your *second* exposure to the chapter's key concepts. The following is an example of this format:

 Private security has evolved into a multibillion-dollar-a-year business employing more than a million people.

   The key concepts of each chapter are emphasized in this manner. Also pay attention to all words in bold print—these are the key terms when they are first used and defined.

3. Read the summary carefully. This will be your *third* exposure to the key concepts. By now you should have internalized the information.

4. When you have finished reading a chapter, reread the list of objectives given at the beginning of that chapter to make certain you have learned the information and can answer each question. If you find yourself stumped, locate the appropriate material in the chapter and review it. Often these questions will be used as essay questions during testing.

5. Review the key terms to make sure you can define each. These also are frequently used as test items.

Note: The material we've selected to highlight using the triple-strength learning instructional design includes only the chapter's key concepts. Although this information is certainly important in that it provides a structural foundation for understanding the topics discussed, do not expect to master the chapter by simply glancing over the "Do You Know. . ." questions and the highlighted material and summaries. You are also responsible for reading and understanding the material that surrounds these basics—the meat around the bones, so to speak.

The text also provides an opportunity for you to apply what you have learned or to go into specific areas in greater depth through discussion questions and application assignments. Complete these activities as directed by the text or by your instructor. Be prepared to share your findings with the class. Good reading and learning!

Ancillaries

A number of supplements are provided by Wadsworth to help instructors use *Introduction to Private Security*, Fifth Edition, in their courses. Supplements are available to qualified adopters. Please consult your local sales representative for details.

For the Instructor

- **Instructor's Resource Manual with Test Bank** Fully updated and revised, the *Instructor's Resource Manual with Test Bank* includes detailed chapter outlines, key terms and figures, class discussion exercises and a complete test bank. Each chapter's test bank contains multiple-choice, true-false, fill-in-the-blank and essay questions, and a full answer key.
- **Book Companion Website** The book-specific website at academic.cengage .com/cj/hess offers students a variety of study tools and useful resources such as outlines, objectives, glossary, flash cards and quizzing.
- **Microsoft® PowerPoint® Slides** Available on the book companion website and for download (contact your representative), these slides assist in your day-to-day preparation for lectures.
- **Classroom Activities for Criminal Justice** This valuable booklet, available to adopters of any Wadsworth criminal justice text, offers you the best of the best in criminal justice classroom activities. Containing both tried-and-true favorites and exciting new projects, its activities are drawn from across the spectrum of criminal justice subjects, including introduction to criminal justice, criminology, corrections, criminal law, policing and juvenile justice, and can be customized to fit any course. Novice and seasoned instructors alike will find it a powerful tool to stimulate classroom engagement.
- **Internet Activities for Criminal Justice** In addition to providing a wide range of activities for any criminal justice class, this useful booklet helps familiarize students with Internet resources they will use both as students of criminal justice and in their criminal justice careers. *Internet Activities for Criminal Justice* allows you to integrate Internet resources and addresses important topics such as criminal and police law, policing organizations, policing challenges, corrections systems, juvenile justice, criminal trials and current issues in criminal justice. Available to adopters of any Wadsworth criminal justice text and prepared by Christina DeJong of Michigan State University, this booklet will bring current tools and resources to the criminal justice classroom.
- **Distance Learning Instructor's Resource Manual for Criminal Justice** Your best guide for setting up a distance learning course in criminal justice, this manual features coverage of the pedagogy of distance education, tips

and strategies for managing an online course, purposes/objectives, grading policy, how to post assignments and much more.

For the Student

- **Careers in Criminal Justice Website: academic.cengage.com/login** This unique website gives students information on a wide variety of career paths, including requirements, salaries, training, contact information for key agencies and employment outlooks. Several important tools help students investigate the criminal justice career choices that are right for them.
  - *Career Profiles*: Video testimonials from a variety of practicing professionals in the field as well as information on many criminal justice careers, including job descriptions, requirements, training, salary and benefits and the application process.
  - *Interest Assessment*: Self-assessment tool to help students decide which careers suit their personalities and interests.
  - *Career Planner*: Résumé-writing tips and worksheets, interviewing techniques and successful job search strategies.
  - *Links for Reference*: Direct links to federal, state and local agencies where students can get contact information and learn more about current job opportunities.
- **Writing and Communicating for Criminal Justice** Provides students with a basic introduction to academic, professional and research writing in criminal justice. This text contains articles on writing skills, a basic grammar review and a survey of verbal communication on the job that will benefit students in their professional careers.

Acknowledgments

First, we must acknowledge Henry M. Wrobleski (1922–2007), the original lead author for the first two editions of this text. Henry was the coordinator of the Law Enforcement Program at Normandale Community College. He was a respected author, lecturer, consultant and expert witness with 30 years of experience in law enforcement and security. He was also the Dean of Instruction for the Institute for Professional Development and a graduate of the FBI Academy. Other Wadsworth texts Wrobleski contributed to were *Introduction to Law Enforcement and Criminal Justice* and *Police Operations*. He is very much missed.

We would like to thank the following individuals for their reviews of previous editions of the text and for their numerous helpful suggestions: Robert Wyatt Benson, Jacksonville State University; Terry A. Biddle, Cuyahoga Community College; William Bopp, Florida Atlanta University; Robert Camp; R. B. J. Campbelle, Middle-Tennessee State University; Vincent DeCherchio, Bryn Mawr College; Jerry Dowling, Sam Houston State University; Robert Fischer, Western Illinois University; James Fyke, Illinois Central College; Edmund Grosskopf, Indiana State University; Leo C. Hertoghe, California State University at Sacramento; Susan Hinds; Robert Ives, Rock Valley College; Stephen Jones, Crown Academy; Ernest Kamm, California State University, Los Angeles; Robert LaRatta, LaSalle University; Hayes Larkins, Community College of Baltimore; David MacKenna, University of Texas at Arlington; Donald Mayo, Loyola University; Janet McClellan, Park College; Michael D. Moberly, Southern Illinois University at Carbondale; Merlyn Moore, Sam Houston State University; Mahesh K. Nalla, Northern Arizona University; Robert L. O'Block, Appalachian State University; Bill Riley, Albuquerque Technical and Vocational Institute; Norman Spain, Ohio University; David Steeno, Western Illinois University; Bill Tillett, Eastern Kentucky University; Michael J. Witkowski, University of Detroit; and Diane Zahm, Florida State University.

The reviewers for the fifth edition faced the challenge of updating the very outdated fourth edition. Thanks so much to these reviewers:

Norm Allen
Trident Technical College

Emmanuel N. Amadi
Mississippi Valley State University

Michael Boyko
Cuyahoga Community College

Russ Cheatham
Cumberland University

Geary M. Chiebus
James Sprunt Community College

Robert Edwards
Champlain College

Salih Hakan
Pennsylvania State
University, Schuylkill

Tom Hughes
University of Louisville

Patrick D. Otto
Mohave Community College

Banyon Pelham
Florida State University, Panama City

Lisa Petentier
Carl Sandburg College

Jim Schumann
St. Cloud State University

James Showers
Pensacola Christian College

Denise M. Strenger
Metro State University DCTC
and University of St. Thomas

Michael R. Summers
Erie Community College,
North Campus

Cort Tanner
Western Texas College

Corey Tinsman
University of North Texas

Dean Van Bibber
Pierpont Community College

Patrick D. Walsh
Loyola University, New Orleans

Thomas Wuennemann
Sacred Heart University

Loren Zimmerman
Chadron State College

In addition to the reviewers, special thanks go to Craig Orthmann, who provided invaluable information for the IT chapter, and to J&B Innovative Enterprises, Inc., which provided security surveys, charts and diagrams. Another big thank-you goes to Bobbi Peacock, our photo consultant. Thanks also to our editors, Carolyn Henderson Meier and Bob Jucha; our production editor, Jennie Redwitz; and to Sara Dovre Wudali at Buuji, the production house for the text.

A very special acknowledgment and thanks go to Christine Hess Orthmann whose contributions to this text were monumental. As content researcher and writer, she incorporated the most current information into the text while preserving the core components of previous editions. Her skill in reorganizing and streamlining the previous edition was invaluable. A heartfelt thanks, Christine.

About the Author

Kären M. Hess, Ph.D., has written extensively in law enforcement, criminal justice and private security. She was a member of the English department at Normandale Community College as well as the president of the Institute for Professional Development. She is also a member of the American Association of Industrial Security, the Academy of Criminal Justice Sciences (ACJS), the American Correctional Association (ACA), the International Association of Chiefs of Police (IACP), the Police Executive Research Forum and the Text and Academic Authors' Association (TAA), of which she is a fellow and a member of the TAA Foundation Board of Directors.

Other Wadsworth texts Dr. Hess has co-authored are *Constitutional Law*, Fourth Edition; *Corrections in the 21st Century: A Practical Approach*; *Criminal Investigation*, Eight Edition; *Criminal Procedure*; *Juvenile Justice*, Fourth Edition; *Management and Supervision in Law Enforcement*, Fifth Edition; *Community Policing: Partnerships for Problem Solving*, Fifth Edition; *Police Operations: Theory and Practice*, Fourth Edition; *Introduction to Law Enforcement and Criminal Justice*, Ninth Edition; and *Careers in Criminal Justice and Related Fields: From Internship to Promotion*, Sixth Edition.

The Evolution of Private Security

The field of private security in the United States has evolved considerably since its humble beginnings during colonial times. Today it is a multibillion dollar industry that continues to grow faster than most other professions.

Do You Know . . .

■ Why private security evolved?

■ What security measures were used in ancient times? In the Middle Ages? In eighteenth-century England? In early colonial America?

■ What security measures were established by the Statute of Westminster?

■ What contributions to private security were made by Henry Fielding, Sir Robert Peel, Allan Pinkerton, Washington Perry Brink, William J. Burns and George Wackenhut?

■ What role the railroad police played in the evolution of private security?

■ What impact the world wars had on the evolution of private security?

■ Into what status private security has evolved in the twenty-first century?

■ What entry-level, mid-level and top-level security positions typically are?

■ How proprietary private security differs from contractual private security?

■ How private security services might be regulated?

■ How private investigators and detectives are regulated?

■ What the requirements usually are for becoming a private investigator?

Can You Define?

alarm respondent	courier	outsourcing	Statute of
assize of arms	hybrid services	private security	Westminister
Bow Street Runners	hue and cry	proprietary services	watch and ward
contract services	licensing	registration	

Introduction

Since September 11, 2001, the word *security* has taken on new meaning and unprecedented importance to most Americans. Its significance was captured in the creation of an entirely new government agency, the Department of Homeland Security (DHS).

A trend that was well underway before the terrorist attacks of 9/11, private security *is* big business and a protective presence that continues to get bigger every year. Private security is a multifaceted industry that has made great advances since the day of the lone watchman or the single guard in a guardhouse. As a profession, it has truly come into its own, as evidenced by the development and proliferation of college degree programs in security and state and national efforts to license and register security professionals. The variety of functions performed by private security personnel and the vast array of security equipment and procedures developed in the past decades offer the potential for more security than ever before.

The American Society for Industrial Security (ASIS) (n.d., p.2) notes that all businesses, regardless of size, have numerous security concerns relating to fraud, theft, computer hacking, industrial espionage, workplace violence and, now, terrorism: "Security is one of the fastest growing professional careers worldwide. A career in the security field provides a multitude of opportunities. These opportunities range from entry level security officer positions to investigators specializing in specific areas and managers and directors of security at major corporations and organizations around the world."

This chapter begins by defining security and private security, and then reviews the influences on the evolution of private security from ancient times to the twenty-first century. This is followed by a description of contemporary private security, including a discussion of the types of services and personnel that might be used as well as the advantages and disadvantages of using proprietary and contract private security services. The chapter concludes with a discussion of the regulation of private security.

Security and Private Security Defined

Before looking at a definition of private security, consider first the importance of *security*. Over 60 years ago Abraham Maslow set forth a theory in psychology that as humans meet basic needs, they seek to satisfy successively higher needs that occupy a set hierarchy. This hierarchy can be illustrated as a pyramid (see Figure 1.1). At the base of the pyramid are the physiological needs of food, water, shelter and the like. Next in importance is safety or security, including self, employment, resources and property. **Private security**, aimed at this level of need, is a profit-oriented industry that provides personnel, equipment and procedures to prevent losses caused by human error, emergencies, disasters or criminal actions.

As the name implies, private security meets the needs of individuals, businesses, institutions and organizations that require more protection than is afforded by public police officers. The consumer of private security services might be any individuals, public or private, large or small. Wealthy individuals may hire a private security patrol for their residences or sprawling estates; col-

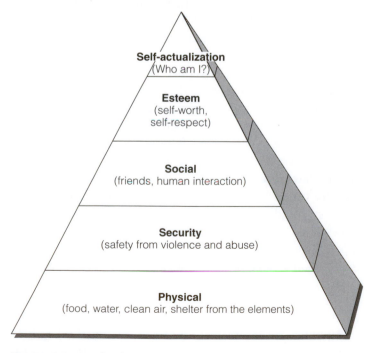

Figure 1.1   Maslow's Hierarchy of Needs

SOURCE: J. Scott Harr and Kären M. Hess, *Careers in Criminal Justice and Related Fields: From Internship to Promotion*, 5th ed. (Belmont, CA: Thomson/Wadsworth, 2006) p.3.

leges often hire security patrols; a bank, a shopping center, an office building—almost any conceivable business, organization or agency—might use private security services.

Consumers of private security services seek protection against many types of natural and human-made risks, with emphasis on the human-made risks of accidents; theft and pilferage; fraud; employee disloyalty and subversion; espionage; sabotage; strikes, riots and demonstrations; and violent crimes, including terrorist acts. Although the duties assumed by private security personnel may vary greatly, most private security officers spend the majority of their time in nonenforcement, nonpolice functions. In addition to protecting assets and property, private security seeks to provide a stable, safe environment in which employees may pursue their work without disruption or harm and to which others may safely visit. Furthermore, private security personnel may provide valuable public relations services.

Before looking at the personnel involved and the types of services provided, consider the historical context of security as a way to understand why private security looks like it does in the twenty-first century.

Influences on the Evolution of Private Security

Since the beginning of recorded time, people have sought *security*—safety, protection, freedom from fear and danger. They have armed themselves, built barriers around their dwellings and made rules and laws that they have tried to enforce individually, as a group and through others.

Reith (1975, pp.13–15) outlines four phases in the evolution of the quest for security. First, individuals or small community groups came together in search of collective security, to ease food finding or to satisfy other mutually felt individual needs. Second, they discovered the need for rules or laws. Historically people believed that passing "good" laws was sufficient; the ruler's army could enforce them. Third, they inevitably discovered that some community members would not obey the rules. Even the best laws people can devise are useless, and rulers and governments are powerless, if the laws are not obeyed. Fourth, in one form or another, means to compel the observance of rules were found and established. Sometimes they worked, but frequently they did not.

Reith's main premise is that past civilizations fell because no police mechanism existed between the ruler's army and the people. Without such a police mechanism to enforce the laws, the country fell into anarchy. When this occurred, armed troops were called in to restore order, but, as a form of force divorced from the law, they could secure only temporary relief. Thus, the dispatching of troops to restore order became: "as often as not, a pouring of oil on flames" (Reith, 1940, p.105).

Early civilizations relied on a ruler and the ruler's army to govern and protect the people. During the Middle Ages, loosely organized experiments were devised with evolving forms of public law enforcement and isolated instances of private security when public law enforcement was ineffective. Not until the nineteenth century did public law enforcement and private security begin to clearly separate. To that point, the history of private security is intertwined with that of public law enforcement. With the acceptance of public police officers, private individuals and organizations began to seek further protection as a means of preventing access to themselves or their property.

 Private security evolved from the human desire for additional, individual protection for themselves and their property.

Influences from Ancient Times

Throughout history, people have erected physical barriers for security, and certain individuals, notably rulers, have demanded special security. The objective then, as it is today, was to prevent others from gaining access to them or their property.

 In ancient times people relied on physical security measures such as weapons, lake or cliff dwellings, walls and gates.

Lake dwelling was one popular means of achieving security. Healy (1968) describes some 300 such lake sites discovered in Switzerland alone, all simple homes, some single units, some entire villages able to house more than 1,000 people, built with meager tools on sunken pilings. Access to these lake dwellings was controlled by drawbridges or boats.

Some prehistoric Americans, surrounded by unfriendly tribes, moved into natural caves high on cliffs. Their security came from isolating themselves high in the air with ladders that could be pulled up to make their homes impregnable (Healy, p.1).

The most elaborate security system in ancient times was the Great Wall of China, built 20 centuries ago by Emperor Chin to guard China from the Mongols. Requiring 15 years and half a million workers to build, the Wall was long enough to stretch from New York to Mexico.

Rome also emphasized physical security in the form of broad, straight roads patrolled by legions and bridges controlled by iron gates and guards. Frequently, however, rulers went beyond mere physical controls, designating armed guard forces to enhance security over the region's property and citizenry.

 Rulers often appointed individuals to assist them in enforcing the laws, protecting not only the general welfare (public security), but also the safety of the ruler (private security).

Influences from England

It was in England that the public and private means to achieve security clearly separated.

The Middle Ages (476–1453)

Early in the Middle Ages feudalism held sway, with the lowliest workers (serfs) laboring for a nobleman who answered to the king. The nobleman provided food and security for the serfs who worked the land; the serfs, in turn, provided arms for the king and fought in his wars. Castles with moats and drawbridges afforded additional security.

The Anglo-Saxons brought with them to England the acceptance of mutual responsibility for civil and military protection of individuals, with groups of

The Great Wall of China—actually an interconnected series of walls, watchtowers, passes and garrison towns—stretches more than 4,000 miles. Built to protect the country from northern invaders, the wall required tremendous effort to construct, maintain and repair. At the peak of the Ming Dynasty, as many as 1 million soldiers guarded the wall.

A modern-day equivalent of the Great Wall of China, the Mexico-U.S. border fence is an effort to keep illegal immigrants from easily entering the United States. Securing the nearly 2,000 mile stretch of our country's southern border is a considerable challenge.

families banding together for security, thus providing an informal collective responsibility for maintaining local law and order. The **Statute of Westminster**, issued by King Edward in 1285, formalized much of England's practice in criminal justice and apprehension by requiring ordinary citizens to act on behalf of the community and its safety: "Not only was it the right of any person to apprehend offenders; there was also a positive duty to drop all work when the hue and cry was raised, and to join immediately in pursuit" (Hall, 1952, p.166).

 The Statute of Westminster established three practical measures: (1) the watch and ward, (2) hue and cry and (3) assize of arms.

The **watch and ward** provided town watchmen to patrol the city during the night to supplement the traditional duties of the constable during the day (ward). Watchmen, stationed at every gate of the walled town between sunset and sunrise, were given power to arrest strangers during darkness and hand them over to the constable in the morning. All men in the town were placed on a roster for regular service. Those who refused to serve were placed in the stocks.

The **hue and cry** revived the ancient Saxon practice for dealing with those who resisted the watchman's arrest. When resistance occurred, the watchman cried out and all citizens pursued the fugitive and assisted in his capture. To enforce the hue and cry, the Statute of Westminster also established the **assize of arms**, which required every male between ages 15 and 60 to keep a weapon in his home as a "harness to keep the peace."

Merchants of England, however, were often dissatisfied with the protection afforded them by this system. Furthermore, the middle class was rebelling against compulsory watch service, insisting on paying deputies to take their places. Unfortunately, the hired deputies frequently did not protect them, forcing the merchants to take matters into their own hands.

 Some English merchants in the Middle Ages hired private police to guard their establishments, to investigate crimes against them and to recover property stolen from them.

Early attempts at security and protection reveal two common themes. First was division into geographic sections and the rotation of duties among the citizens. Second, citizens' dissatisfaction with their duties resulted in the hiring of others to take their place. (Even up to the American Civil War one could hire another to serve in one's place.)

The Eighteenth Century

Extensive social and economic changes during the Industrial Revolution brought about the mechanization of production systems and resulted in a change from home or cottage industries to large factories located in cities. A primary reason for the shift from cottage work to factories and shops was the growing problem of shrinkage, although it had yet to be defined as such. This shift was an effort to control workers' production and inventory in the textile industry, as too much material was being diverted for personal use.

During this same period, famine struck the rural areas, causing thousands to move from the country into the towns to seek work in the mills and factories. As people left the rural areas for jobs in the cities, the problem of protection from crime gained new impetus and created employment opportunities for private security forces.

Rural eighteenth-century England also used private policing in reaction to increasing rural crime (Critchley, 1967, p.28). The wealthy paid gamekeepers to protect their property and slept with arms close by, and the middle-class tradesmen formed voluntary protection societies.

 During the eighteenth century English private citizens carried arms for protection and banded together to hire special police to protect their homes and businesses. The military was used to suppress riots.

Because of prejudices toward those responsible for upholding the law, no serious reform was advocated until the late eighteenth century. The policy was to encourage law-abiding citizens' participation in criminal justice with rewards and to discourage law-breaking citizens with severe punishments.

Henry Fielding (1707–1754) In 1748 Henry Fielding, lawyer, novelist and playwright, became Chief Magistrate of Bow Street in policeless London. Sympathetic to the injustices that abounded in the city, Fielding fought for social and criminal reform and defied the law by discharging prisoners convicted of petty theft. He gave reprimands in place of the death penalty and exercised general leniency (Reith, 1975). Fielding advocated that all magistrates be paid a salary, making them independent of fees and fines as their source of income. He also suggested that magistrates be given power to inflict light sentences when advisable.

During this time thieves and robbers moved freely in the streets, and no one interfered with looting and rioting. Although riots inevitably brought soldiers, the response sometimes took two or three days. Law-abiding citizens looked after their own safety: "The rich surrounded themselves with armed servants and were comparatively safe and independent. . . . The less affluent saw to it that their houses were protected as strongly as possible by bars and bolts and heavy doors and shutters, and that blunderbusses and pistols were always close at hand" (Reith, 1975, p.134).

Fielding conceived the idea that citizens might join forces, go into the streets, trace the perpetrators of crime and meet the instigators of mob gatherings *before* they assembled a following and caused destruction.

 Henry Fielding was one of the earliest and most articulate advocates of crime *prevention*.

Fielding selected six honest, industrious citizens to form an amateur volunteer force. With his advice and direction, they "swept clean" the Bow Street neighborhood. Many criminals were arrested, and many others fled from the area. Several years after Henry Fielding's death, the Bow Street volunteer force turned professional and was known as the **Bow Street Runners**, the first detective agency in England. Unfortunately, the practical results of Fielding's preventive ideas achieved in the Bow Street neighborhood were ignored for 30 years, and nationwide hostility against a police force persisted in England.

Nineteenth-Century England

In the beginning of the nineteenth century, inadequate law enforcement over much of England required a further supplementation of security by private enterprise. Industrial firms that employed large numbers of unruly workers established their own police. The railway companies, in particular, employed a private police force to maintain order. Similar forces were hired by the ironmasters of the Tredegar Works in Monmouthshire and Lancashire. For the most part, however, collective responsibility for repression of disturbances, the employment of special constables and the formation of the armed associations remained the major forms of law enforcement until the reforms proposed by Sir Robert Peel.

Sir Robert Peel (1788–1850)   Public opposition to a police department was still strong when Sir Robert Peel became Home Secretary in 1821. Six years later Peel became a member of a parliamentary committee on criminal matters. This committee's second report, published in 1828, asserted: "The art of crime, if it may be so called, has increased faster than the art of detection." Based on the committee's report, Peel proposed a return to the Anglo-Saxon principle of individual community responsibility for preserving law and order, but also said that London should have a body of civilians appointed and paid by the community to serve as police officers. Parliament agreed and in 1829 organized the Metropolitan Police of London.

 Robert Peel's Metropolitan Police Act created the London Metropolitan Police, whose principal objective was to be prevention of crime.

The First Order of the Metropolitan Police read:

> IT SHOULD BE UNDERSTOOD, AT THE OUTSET, THAT THE PRINCIPAL OBJECTIVE TO BE ATTAINED IS THE PREVENTION OF CRIME.

Unfortunately, this emphasis on crime prevention did not last. The public police became more and more occupied with investigating crimes and apprehending criminals, and prevention efforts decreased proportionately. Thus, the need for private security as a means to *prevent* crime continued to exist.

The Evolution of Private Security in the United States

The American colonists brought with them the English system of law enforcement and its reliance on collective responsibility.

 Constables and night town watchmen were the primary means of security in the United States until the establishment of full-time police forces in the mid-1800s.

Out West, following the Civil War, crime was rampant. It was the era of outlaw gangs such as the James Gang and the Wild Bunch. Stagecoaches carrying mail, money and passengers were prey to holdups by road agents. The professionals who went up against these road agents rode shotgun on the stagecoaches. Stage line companies responded by building their own security forces and hiring detective agencies to track down outlaws. Other industries saw the need to form protective services, especially those industries vulnerable to strikes, such as coal and iron mining.

Violence in the West increased with the discovery of gold in 1848. Cities in the East and South fared little better. Even in Washington, DC, members attending Congress had to carry arms. Because transporting goods was so fraught with risk, express companies were created. In 1850 Henry Wells and William Fargo joined to form the American Express, which operated east of the Missouri River. In 1852 Wells Fargo and Company was established to serve the country west of the Missouri. These companies had their own private detectives and shotgun riders.

Roads were not the only vulnerable avenue of transportation. The rails were also becoming increasingly dangerous.

Railroad Police

With the westward expansion in the United States during the 1800s, railroad lines moved into sparsely settled territories that had little or no public law enforcement. Trains were attacked by Indians and roving bands of outlaws who robbed passengers, stole cargos, dynamited tracks and disrupted communications.

 Because of problems of interstate jurisdiction and lack of public police protection, many states passed railway police acts, allowing private railroads to establish proprietary security forces, with full police powers, to protect their goods and passengers.

As noted by Gough (1977, p.19): "The railroad special agent was a colorful part of the old Wild West. Being able to shoot fast and ride hard were important skills in the late 1800s. In addition to train robbers, there were also station holdup crooks, pickpockets, con men and bootleggers to contend with."

 In many parts of the country, the railroad police provided the only protective services until governmental units and law enforcement agencies were established.

Dewhurst (1955) observes: "A railroad agent who could hold his own in a gun battle with train robbers was considered an asset to the railroad. In this era of the smoking six-shooters, tact and investigative intelligence placed second to the ability to handle physical contact with those who preyed upon the railroad. . . . It was the general custom simply to hand the newly appointed man a badge, a revolver and a club and send him out to work without further instructions as to the laws or how to enforce them, or even how to make an arrest." Nevertheless, the railroad police made a significant contribution to the evolution of private security. In 1921 the Association of American Railroads was formed to help coordinate mutual problems, particularly security.

Allan Pinkerton (1819–1884)

Allan Pinkerton was a key figure in the development of the railroad police as well as in the development of contract security forces. Born in Scotland, he joined the radical Chartist group as a young man and was forced to flee from Scotland or face imprisonment. He and his young wife fled to America, where Pinkerton set up his trade of coopering (making barrels) in Chicago. Soon after, they moved to Dundee, Illinois, where his cooperage became a way station for the Underground Railroad, a secret network that assisted escaping slaves.

One day Pinkerton accidentally found the hideout of a group of counterfeiters and helped the local sheriff capture them. He eventually sold his shop and

© Bettmann/CORBIS

Allan Pinkerton, President Lincoln and Major General John A.
McClernand photographed during the Civil War at Antietam,
Maryland, in October 1862.

was appointed deputy sheriff of Cook County. In 1843 he was appointed Chicago's first detective. Pinkerton resigned his position in 1850 because of economic pressures and took two private clients, the Rock Island and the Illinois Central railroads. The next year he formed the Pinkerton National Detective Agency. Its slogan was "We Never Sleep," and its logo was an open eye, often hypothesized as the origin of the term "private eye." His agency concentrated on catching train robbers and setting up security systems for the railroads.

 Allan Pinkerton was the first law enforcement officer hired to protect railroads. He also established the first private security contract operation in the United States.

Pinkerton's services were important to his clients mainly because public enforcement agencies either were inadequate or lacked jurisdiction. When the Civil War broke out in 1861, President Lincoln called Pinkerton to Washington to discuss establishing a secret service department to "ascertain the social, political, and patriotic relations of the numerous suspected people in and about Washington" (Lavine, 1963, p.33). Using the name E. J. Allen, Pinkerton did intelligence work for the Union army.

In the 1860s and 1870s the Pinkerton National Detective Agency gained national stature by capturing train robbers and bandits. They chased murderous gangs of bank robbers and such notorious criminals as the Dalton Boys, the Hole in the Wall Gang and Jesse James. Gough (p.17) notes: "Pinkerton encouraged the use of burglarproof safes in all railroad express cars. By using such a heavy safe, any outlaws intending to rob the train had to use a large charge of black powder or dynamite to blow it open. The resulting blast's magnitude usually destroyed the contents of the safe, as well as the roof and sides of the express car. Pinkerton also recommended the employment of express guards heavily armed with high-powered rifles." One reason the Pinkerton Agency became so famous was that they were virtually the only agency to offer national enforcement. The company became a public corporation in 1965 and changed its name to Pinkerton's, Inc.

Other Security Advances

In 1853 August Pope patented one of the first electric burglar alarm systems. The system had electromagnetic contacts mounted on doors and windows and then wired to a battery and bell. He sold his invention to Edwin Holmes who took it to New York City and sold alarms to wealthy homeowners. In 1858 Holmes established the first central burglar alarm service in the country. His operation evolved into Holmes Protection, Inc. Pope also installed electrified metal foil and screens still widely used by many alarm companies. In addition, he built the first central communications center wired to bank and jewelry vaults (Kaye, 1987, p.243).

By the 1870s and 1880s mansions and businesses were being protected against fire with heat sensors. William Watkins established a company called AFA Protection and was first to use such sensors in a central monitoring station. Other companies followed suit, adding burglar systems to the fire protection systems. The use of alarms and detection devices grew to provide protective services through the use of messengers and telegraph lines. By 1889 the use of such alarms and detection devices in industrial and commercial enterprises was well established. In 1901 Western Union consolidated several of these local alarm companies into American District Telegraph Company (ADT) (Kaye, p.243).

In 1858 Washington Perry Brink founded Brink's, Inc., as a freight and package delivery service. He began by shuttling trunks and packages around Chicago in a one-horse dray. At first Brink concentrated on transporting goods for travelers passing through Chicago. Abraham Lincoln used Brink's services when he was in Chicago attending a Republican convention.

Bonded courier and express delivery services flourished partly because provisions in the common law made it risky to use employees or servants as couriers (Hall, 1935, pp.31–32):

> The common law recognized no criminality in a person who came legally into possession of property and later converted it. Apparently it was thought that the owner should have protected himself by selecting a trustworthy person. Since, presumably, this could readily be done, the owner must have been negligent if he delivered his property to a person who absconded with it.

In 1891, Brink's carried its first payroll for Western Electric Company. In the early days Brink's tried to be inconspicuous, using standard buggies and wrapping cash in newspapers or overalls. But in 1917, when "Ammunition" Wheed and his gang killed two Brink's men in a holdup, the armored car was born.

 Washington Perry Brink established armored car and courier services in the United States.

Advancements in security continued and accelerated in the twentieth century. In 1909 William J. Burns, a former Secret Service investigator and head of the Bureau of Investigation (forerunner of the FBI), started the William J. Burns' Detective Agency.

 William J. Burns founded the sole investigating agency for the American Banking Association. It grew to become the second-largest contract guard and investigative service in the United States.

For all practical purposes, the Pinkerton's agency and Burns' were the only national investigative bodies concerned with nonspecialized crimes in the country until the advent of the FBI in 1924.

The World Wars

Before and during World War I, concern for security intensified in American industry because of fear of sabotage and espionage. Private security forces were used to protect war industries and the docks against destruction by saboteurs. Security services expanded to meet the demands but tapered off after the war, reaching a low point during the Depression.

World War II was a significant catalyst in the growth of the private security industry. This conflict was considered "a watershed event with regard to security's role in society, as manufacturing industries were mobilized to produce tanks, jeeps, ammunition" (Davidson, 2005, p.101). Before awarding national defense contracts, the federal government required munitions contractors to implement stringent, comprehensive security measures to protect classified materials and defense secrets from sabotage and espionage. The FBI assisted in establishing these security programs. Additionally, the government granted the status of auxiliary military police to more than two hundred thousand plant security guards whose primary duties were protecting war goods and products, supplies, equipment and personnel. Local law enforcement agencies were responsible for training them.

 The world wars heightened emphasis on security in the government and made industry increasingly aware of the need for plant security.

Private Security Comes into Its Own

By the middle of the twentieth century, the use of private security services had expanded to encompass all segments of the private sector. Increases in government regulations and the inability of the public police to respond to every private need further promoted the growth of private security. In 1954 George R. Wackenhut and three other former FBI agents formed the Wackenhut Corporation as a private investigative and contract security firm. In five short years the Wackenhut Corporation had more than tripled its business, from revenues of $300,999 in 1954 to more than $1 million in 1959.

In only 20 years Wackenhut established itself as the third-largest contract guard and investigative agency in the country.

Other businesses began to form their own in-house security services rather than contracting for services from private agencies. However, whether the security personnel were proprietary or contracted, private security provided industry and private businesses with individual protection for people and homes; guard services for construction sites and business property when they were closed; security services for large shopping centers; advice on internal and external security systems for homes, businesses and factories and private investigations. In fact, by 1963, United States businesses and industries were spending between $250 and $300 million annually for private protection (Davidson, 2005 p.104).

The American Society for Industrial Security (ASIS)

In January 1955 the American Society for Industrial Security (ASIS) was officially incorporated and, two months later, 257 individuals signed on as charter members. From the start, principles were stressed, and one of the first orders of business was the drafting of an ASIS Code of Ethics. ASIS founders recognized that chapters would be an essential component to bring members together and allow them to participate in local committees and undertakings. They divided the country into seven regions and established the position of regional vice president (RVP) to promote formation of chapters in each region. These chapters became a magnet for networking among security contemporaries. By the end of 1959, 48 chapters had been formed, including the first international chapter in Europe (Davidson, 2000, p.52).

In July 1957 the inaugural issue of the society-sponsored magazine *Industrial Security*, which became *Security Management* in 1972, debuted. By the end of the twentieth century, ASIS revenues had surpassed $17 million with membership topping 30,000. In 2002 ASIS changed its name to ASIS International and had, at that time, 35,000 members worldwide.

The Globalization of Security

The second half of the twentieth century found the security industry and the profession responding to evolving legislation, technology, societal issues and world events. The Cold War and Cuban Missile Crisis resulted in a thriving civil defense industry, with fallout shelters and emergency evacuation plans at industrial sites. Terrorist acts of such diverse groups as Basque separatists, Irish nationalists and Marxist cabals in Latin American spread fear, as did the murder of eleven Israeli athletes at the 1972 Munich Olympics. The fall of the Berlin Wall in 1989 symbolized the end of the Cold War and the beginning of globalization, creating new challenges for business and security professionals.

As Davidson (2005, p.107) notes: "For the founding fathers of ASIS, the world changed with the outbreak of WWII. For security professionals 50 years later, the world changed on September 11, 2001. The specter of terrorism reached into every corner of society after that attack." And the emphasis on prevention continues into the twenty-first century.

The *preventive* philosophy underlying the private security field has influenced other areas as well. Notably, it is influencing architecture and building codes, as noted by C. Ray Jeffery in his classic *Crime Prevention through Environmental Design* (CPTED) (1972): "Criminal behavior can be controlled primarily through the direct alteration of the environment of potential victims. . . . Crime control programs must focus on crime before it occurs, rather than afterward. As criminal opportunity is reduced, so will be the number of criminals." CPTED is discussed in Chapter 6.

Perhaps even more significant, the preventive approach to crime is now being stressed by many public law enforcement agencies, as evidenced by the creation of the National Crime Prevention Institute (NCPI), established in 1971 as a division of the University of Louisville's School of Police Administration. This does not mean, however, that the need for private security officers and measures will lessen. Rather, it means that the full importance of preventive measures has become apparent. The public police will likely never attain sufficient levels of personnel to meet all private needs, and government regulations regarding security will doubtless continue to proliferate.

Contemporary Private Security

The attacks on the United States on September 11, 2001, dramatically changed and increased the role of private security in protecting all aspects of America. The role of private security in homeland security is the focus of Chapter 13.

From two hundred thousand plant security guards in World War II to more than one million private security personnel today, the private security force has experienced tremendous growth. With increased technology and needed protection for sophisticated, delicate machinery, private security employment will increase even more rapidly in the future.

 Private security has evolved to a multibillion-dollar-a-year business employing more than a million people.

Harowitz (2003) observes:

> Security is now a rising star in the corporate firmament. The people responsible for security "have become much more visible to the top of the business," says [AT&T CEO Mike] Armstrong, "and much more important to the business itself." The shift in business attitudes is also evident in a market report on the security industry by Lehman Brothers. In that report, analyst Jeffrey Kessler writes that the global security industry "has moved from a peripheral activity to center stage."

A further sign of the maturing nature of corporate security is that Boyden Global Executive Search saw a market need for a formalized "Chief Security Officer" (CSO) job description.

The leading security company in 2008 is Niscayah Group AB, previously known as Securitas Security Services, U.S.A., Inc. Niscayah (Securitas Group) entered the market in 1999 by acquiring Pinkerton's, Inc., and by 2001 had acquired seven more U.S. guarding companies, including Burns International. In July 2003, the combined American acquisitions became Securitas and then, in May 2008, Niscayah. Niscayah Group operates in more than 30 countires, primarily in Europe and North America. They have anual sales of approximately

$6 billion; more than 200,000 employees who work to carry out the mission of protecting homes, workplaces and community; and work with more than 80 percent of the Fortune 1000 companies.

Types of Private Security Personnel and Services

The continuously evolving complexity of our society necessitates specially trained private security officers in all phases of life. Businesses need individuals who can effectively use high-tech surveillance equipment. They rely on private suppliers of search dogs and strike/civil disobedience response teams. Some businesses need 24-hour surveillance.

Because of ever-tightening government budgets, law enforcement also has come to rely on private security for several of its traditional services. Services commonly identified as candidates for privatization include animal control, court security, funeral escorts, parking enforcement, patrolling of public parks, prisoner transport, public building security, public housing development patrol and special event security. Privatization is discussed in Chapter 3.

With the enhanced function of private security has come the opportunity for specialization. As the private security profession has expanded, so too have the kinds of jobs available. ASIS lists the following as security specialties with career opportunities (www.asisonline.org):

Corporate security	Loss prevention
Cyber security	Physical security
Executive protection	Private security management
Financial services security	Risk assessment
Government security	Strategic intelligence
Healthcare security	Terrorism (including bioterrorism and agro-terrorism)
High rise facilities security	
IT security	Workplace violence & legal liability

Regardless of the specific security discipline or specialty, opportunities in the private sector are typically categorized as entry-level, mid-level and top-level positions.

Entry-Level Positions

 The most common entry-level positions are the security guard and the security patrol officer.

Private Security Guards

A common, highly visible position is the security guard, who is usually in uniform and is sometimes armed. Premises may be guarded 24/7, only during the day, only during the night or only during peak periods such as sporting events or holidays. Private security officers control access to private property; protect against loss through theft, vandalism or fire; enforce rules; maintain order and lower risks of all kinds.

These officers may work inside or outside or both, patrolling the interior of buildings or the exterior grounds. They may be stationed at a desk to monitor security cameras and to check the identification of people coming and going. As with many other jobs, a typical guard shift lasts eight hours, although many guards work at night and on weekends, and many work alone. The *Occupational Outlook Handbook* [1] (2006–2007) states:

> Guards, who are also called *security officers*, patrol and inspect property to protect against fire, theft, vandalism, terrorism and illegal activity. These workers protect their employer's investment, enforce laws on the property, and deter criminal activity and other problems. They use radio and telephone communications to call for assistance from police, fire, or emergency medical services as the situation dictates. Security guards write comprehensive reports outlining their observations and activities during their assigned shift. They also may interview witnesses or victims, prepare case reports, and testify in court.
>
> Although all security guards perform many of the same duties, their specific duties vary with whether the guard works in a "static" security position or on a mobile patrol. Guards assigned to static security positions usually serve the client at one location for a specified length of time. These guards must become closely acquainted with the property and people associated with it and must often monitor alarms and closed-circuit TV cameras. In contrast, guards assigned to mobile patrol duty drive or walk from location to location and conduct security checks within an assigned geographical zone. They may detain or arrest criminal violators, answer service calls concerning criminal activity or problems, as discussed shortly.
>
> The security guard's job responsibilities also vary with the size, type and location of the employer. In department stores, guards protect people, records, merchandise, money and equipment. They often work with undercover store detectives to prevent theft by customers or employees, and they help apprehend shoplifting suspects prior to the arrival of the police. Some shopping centers and theaters have officers who patrol their parking lots to deter car thefts and robberies. In office buildings, banks, and hospitals, guards maintain order and protect the institutions' property, staff, and customers. At air, sea, and rail terminals and other transportation facilities, guards protect people, freight, property, and equipment. Using metal detectors and high-tech equipment, they may screen passengers and visitors for weapons and explosives, ensure that nothing is stolen while a vehicle is being loaded or unloaded, and watch for fires and criminals.
>
> Guards who work in public buildings such as museums or art galleries protect paintings and exhibits by inspecting people and packages entering and leaving the building. In factories, laboratories, government buildings, data processing centers, and military bases, security officers protect information, products, computer codes, and defense secrets and check the credentials of people and vehicles entering and leaving the premises. Guards

---

[1]SOURCE: *Occupational Outlook Handbook*, 2006–07 Edition. U.S. Department of Labor, Bureau of Labor Statistics (Washington, DC: U.S. Government Printing Office, 2006).

working at universities, parks and sports stadiums perform crowd control, supervise parking and seating, and direct traffic. Security guards stationed at the entrance to bars and places of adult entertainment, such as nightclubs, prevent access by minors, collect cover charges at the door, maintain order among customers, and protect property and patrons.[2]

Some security guards are responsible for preventing and detecting embezzlement, as well as misappropriation or concealment of merchandise, money, bonds, stocks, notes or other valuable documents. Some security guards protect individuals rather than premises and property. The rising incidence of executive kidnappings and hostage situations has resulted in a dramatic increase in bodyguard service since the mid-1970s. Likewise, escort services increased in demand in the 1980s. Several major corporations are concerned about protecting their chief corporate executives from terrorism or from kidnapping for ransom. Larger companies may carry corporate executive kidnap and ransom insurance policies or may provide armed bodyguards to protect top executives.

Security guards are sometimes also responsible for property control, energy conservation, sign-in log maintenance, opening and closing, escort service and emergency response and support during medical, fire or weather emergencies. The trend is to replace the term *security guard* with *security officer* as they do much more than "guard."

Private Patrol Officers

Patrol has been the "backbone" of the public police force because it is the primary means of preventing or detecting criminal activity. Private patrol officers perform the same function. Moving from location to location on foot or in a vehicle, they protect the property of specific employers rather than that of the general public. They are, in essence, an extension of the public patrol, because many people do not readily differentiate between the vehicles of public police officers and private patrol officers. Thus, the private security patrol officers may prevent criminal activity while en route to an assigned area.

This type of security was employed by an upscale Los Angeles neighborhood after it had experienced a number of drive-by shootings and armed robberies. In response to the violence, the neighbors organized and hired a private armed patrol service. The results were extremely successful, with the neighborhood going from a serious crime every week before the involvement of the security patrol to only one carjacking in the 12 months the patrol service was involved.

Security patrols are sometimes also responsible for opening and closing facilities, conducting interior and exterior inspections, checking on facilities and equipment, providing escort service, transporting equipment or documents and responding to alarms.

Some private patrol officers have one employer who is responsible for an establishment with very large premises requiring patrol. Other private patrol officers work for several employers, moving from place to place, sometimes going inside the premises, sometimes not. Some wealthy neighborhoods may employ a private patrol officer to maintain surveillance of the neighborhood and

---

[2]SOURCE: *Occupational Outlook Handbook*, 2006–07 Edition. U.S. Department of Labor, Bureau of Labor Statistics (Washington, DC: U.S. Government Printing Office, 2006).

to routinely check homes and property. Likewise, a group of business people or merchants within a neighborhood or within a shopping center may hire a private officer to patrol their establishments. Many communities have established special patrol service agencies.

Mid-Level Positions

 Mid-level positions in private security include private investigators and detectives, armed couriers, central alarm respondents and consultants.

Private Investigators and Detectives

Private investigators and detectives may freelance or may work for a specific employer. Often the work involves background checks for employment, insurance and credit applications, civil litigation and investigation of insurance or workers' compensation claims. Sometimes investigators are brought in to work undercover to detect employee dishonesty, shoplifting or illegal drug use. According to the *Occupational Outlook Handbook*:

> Private detectives and investigators use many methods to determine the facts in a variety of matters. To carry out investigations, they may use various types of surveillance or searches. To verify facts, such as an individual's place of employment or income, they may make phone calls or visit a subject's workplace. In other cases, especially those involving missing persons and background checks, investigators often interview people to gather as much information as possible about an individual. In all cases, private detectives and investigators assist attorneys, businesses and the public with legal, financial and personal problems.
>
> Private detectives and investigators offer many services, including executive, corporate, and celebrity protection; pre-employment verification; and individual background profiles. They investigate computer crimes, such as identity theft, harassing e-mails, and illegal downloading of copyrighted material. They also provide assistance in civil liability and personal injury cases, insurance claims and fraud, child custody and protection cases, missing persons cases, and premarital screening. They are sometimes hired to investigate individuals to prove or disprove infidelity.
>
> Most detectives and investigators are trained to perform physical surveillance. They may observe a site, such as the home of a subject, from an inconspicuous location or a vehicle. They continue the surveillance, which is often carried out using still and video cameras, binoculars, and a cell phone, until the desired evidence is obtained. This watching and waiting often continues for a long time.
>
> Detectives also may perform computer database searches or work with someone who does. Computers allow investigators to quickly obtain massive amounts of information on individuals' prior arrests, convictions, and civil legal judgments; telephone numbers; motor vehicle registrations; association and club memberships; and other matters.
>
> The duties of private detectives and investigators depend on the needs of their clients. In cases for employers that involve fraudulent workers' compensation claims, for example, investigators may carry out long-term covert

observation of subjects. If an investigator observes a subject performing an activity that contradicts injuries stated in a worker's compensation claim, the investigator would take video or still photographs to document the activity and report it to the client.

Private detectives and investigators often specialize. Those who focus on intellectual property theft, for example, investigate and document acts of piracy, help clients stop illegal activity, and provide intelligence for prosecution and civil action. Other investigators specialize in developing financial profiles and asset searches. Their reports reflect information gathered through interviews, investigation and surveillance, and research, including review of public documents.

Legal investigators specialize in cases involving the courts and are normally employed by law firms or lawyers. They frequently assist in preparing criminal defenses, locating witnesses, serving legal documents, interviewing police and prospective witnesses, and gathering and reviewing evidence. Legal investigators also may collect information on the parties to the litigation, take photographs, testify in court, and assemble evidence and reports for trials.

Corporate investigators conduct internal and external investigations for corporations. In internal investigations, they may investigate drug use in the workplace, ensure that expense accounts are not abused, or determine whether employees are stealing merchandise or information. External investigations are typically done to uncover criminal schemes originating outside the corporation, such as theft of company assets through fraudulent billing of products by suppliers.

Financial investigators may be hired to develop confidential financial profiles of individuals or companies that are prospective parties to large financial transactions. These investigators often are certified public accountants (CPAs) who work closely with investment bankers and other accountants. They search for assets in order to recover damages awarded by a court in fraud or theft cases.[3]

Popular television series have glamorized the vocation of private investigator (PI), but in reality, criminal investigation is only a small part of a private investigator's work.

Armed Couriers

Most private armed courier services use armored cars, vans or trucks, but they may use airlines and trains as well. A **courier** is uniformed and armed to ensure the protection of money, goods, documents or people as they are transported from one location to another. The public police seldom become involved with armed courier deliveries unless there is a high probability that a crime will be attempted during the delivery.

Armored car guards protect money and valuables during transit. In addition, they protect individuals responsible for making commercial bank deposits from

[3]SOURCE: *Occupational Outlook Handbook*, 2006–07 Edition. U.S. Department of Labor, Bureau of Labor Statistics (Washington, DC: U.S. Government Printing Office, 2006).

theft or bodily injury. When the armored car arrives at the door of a business, an armed guard enters, signs for the money and returns to the truck with the valuables in hand. Carrying money between the truck and the business can be extremely hazardous; because of this risk, armored car guards usually wear bulletproof vests.

Managers considering using armored car services should be aware that regulations to ensure the protection of assets simply do not exist. Brink's, a large, well-established armed courier service, has built a credible service record while it carries billions of dollars a day. The armored car specialist has been called on to move diamonds, Picasso paintings, the original Gettysburg Address, 15 tons of rare coins, and special materials for the World War II's Manhattan Project—the atomic bomb.

Central Alarm Respondents

Some intrusion detection systems simply sound an alarm when an intrusion is detected, thus relying on an employee or a passerby to notify the police. Other alarm systems are connected directly to police headquarters, so the police are automatically notified. However, because the false-alarm rate is greater than 95 percent for many currently used systems, some cities have banned direct connection of alarms to police equipment because so much public effort is expended in responding to these private false alarms. Consequently, private central alarm services, dominated by American District Telegraph (ADT), have become a popular, effective alternative.

The false-alarm problem has long been recognized. Given the extremely high percentage of false alarms, a central alarm system improves relationships with the police, but it also poses considerable hazard to the **alarm respondent**, that is, the individual sent to investigate the alarm. An intruder may still be on the premises and may pose a direct threat to anyone answering the alarm. Chapter 3 discusses the false-alarm problem.

Consultants

As private security expands and becomes professionalized, the need for expertise on security problems also expands. The expansion has given rise to a variety of specialists who provide consultation in areas such as electronic surveillance; protective lighting, fencing and barricading; alarm systems; access control; key control and security training.

Some individuals have become experts in polygraph examination and psychological stress evaluation (PSE) and may be used as consultants to private enterprise. Since polygraph ("lie detector") tests were first submitted as evidence in an Illinois court in 1964, their use in the private sector has been controversial.

Using the polygraph for pre-employment became strictly regulated through the Employee Polygraph Protection Act (EPPA) signed into law in 1988. This law prohibits use of all mechanical lie detector tests in the workplace, including polygraphs, psychological stress evaluators and voice stress analyzers. Subject to restrictions, the act permits polygraph tests to be administered to certain job applicants of security service firms (armored car, alarm and guard) and of pharmaceutical manufacturers, distributors and dispensers. Subject to restrictions, the act also permits polygraph testing of certain employees of private firms who are reasonably suspected of involvement in a workplace incident (theft, embezzlement, etc.) that resulted in specific economic loss or injury to the employer.

In addition to doing background checks on employees, consultants also can provide advice on risk management, loss prevention and crime prevention systems design and evaluation, architectural liaison and security ordinance compliance.

When selecting a consultant, security directors should make sure the consultant is not affiliated in some way with a vendor or equipment supplier, being in reality a salesperson. One way to avoid this hazard is to seek advice from the International Association of Professional Security Consultants (IAPSC), an organization whose primary purpose is to establish and maintain the highest set of standards for professionalism and ethical conduct in the industry. Its members are independent of affiliation with any product or service they may recommend while on a job, ensuring their services are in the client's best interests. Furthermore, IAPSC members represent the best talent available.

Another organization, the International Professional Security Association (IPSA), was formed 49 years ago to ensure professionalism in managing security operations. This worldwide professional organization operates within the framework of 14 regions, including many overseas. The association has no trade union or political connections.

Top-Level Positions

 Top positions in security include loss prevention specialists, security directors, risk managers and chief security officers (CSOs).

Top jobs in security include managing a private security company or heading up security for a private concern. Common titles include loss prevention specialist, security director, risk manager and chief security officer (CSO). Higher-level security positions are most likely to exist in urban regions with higher populations. International jobs are also available in security, but obtaining them is not easy. Many businesses and establishments, such as hotels, are opening facilities in foreign countries. Often the security director of such businesses and establishments are sent to set up the security system.

While top jobs in security involve managing people and budgets, companies are not necessarily looking to hire MBAs to fill their CSO slots. Many corporate executives are looking for CSOs who have intelligence capabilities or experience and investigative skills. As a result, many top jobs go to people from federal law enforcement, the intelligence community, certain areas of the military and investigative areas within an agency like the U.S. Department of Treasury. For example, Larry L. Cockell was hired as senior vice president and CSO at AOL/ Time Warner, Inc., a business with 90,000 employees and seven distinct global companies. In the aftermath of 9/11, management wanted someone with strong international experience and a strategic approach to structuring the security function. They did not put the emphasis on business skills.

The remainder of this text focuses on the skills and knowledge required to fill a top-level position and to manage those in lower-level positions.

Proprietary versus Contract Private Security Services

At the heart of sound security are individuals—people at all levels of the security hierarchy. An important management decision is whether to use professionals who are employees of the entity seeking the services or to hire employees of a security agency that contracts out the services.

 Proprietary services are *in-house*, directly hired, paid and controlled by the company or organization. In contrast, **contract services** are *outside* firms or individuals who provide services for a fee. **Hybrid services** combine the two.

Proprietary Services

Many companies prefer to have their own security personnel because they are likely to be more loyal, more motivated due to promotion possibilities, more knowledgeable of the specific operation and personnel of the organization, more courteous and better able to recognize VIPs, and more amendable to training and supervision. In addition, having proprietary security personnel is seen as a status symbol among many employers, and there is usually less turnover.

Important disadvantages to proprietary security services are cost, lack of flexibility and administrative burdens. In addition, proprietary security personnel may become *too* familiar with the organization and become ineffective or even corrupt. Also, they may go on strike with the company union members. Because of such reasons, many business executives seek to contract with outside agencies or individuals to receive security services.

Contract Services

A *Security Director News* "Newspoll" (2005, p.23) found that 68 percent of U.S. organizations used contract services, with nearly half of respondents using contracted security officers. A survey of 158 senior executives from a variety of companies found that 83 percent of respondents were currently or actively considering using external security providers, or ESPs (Hamilton, 2006). "World Security Services" by the Freedonia Group (2005) reported that the world market for private contract security services was expected to expand more than 7 percent annually to $137 billion in 2008. Among the most commonly provided contract security services are guard services, private patrol services and investigative services, and armored car and courier services.

Reasons given for using ESPs or **outsourcing** included cost savings (37 percent), time savings (24 percent), lowered liability (18 percent) and other (21 percent), including the ability to cover the staffing needs of 24/7 shifts and holidays. Another survey conducted by *Security Director News* reported nearly 70 percent of respondents said they outsourced physical security functions, with guard services being the most commonly outsourced (57 percent) (Daniels, 2007, p.1). Other outsourced security functions included system maintenance (23 percent), employee screening (23 percent), central monitoring of facilities (20 percent) and security staff training (15 percent). Forty-six percent reported cost savings and 17 percent reported labor savings.

One of the most important factors behind the rise in contract services is the cost: "Converting from a proprietary work force to a contract security team can provide immediate and significant savings" (Somerson, 2005, p.73). The cost may be 20 percent less than in-house services, *not counting* administrative savings on such items as insurance, pensions, social security, medical care, vacation time and sick days, supervision, training and administrative functions—all assumed by the contract service.

However, cost is not always, nor should it be, the foremost factor in the decision to outsource security. Piazza (2006, p.46) reports: "Senior executives are ready and willing to pay a premium for an outsourcing partner that emphasizes tight security." The top three factors in their selection of a partner were services, pricing and security capabilities.

Another distinct advantage of contract services is their flexibility; more or fewer personnel are available as needs change, and many contract services can provide a variety of services and equipment unavailable to in-house security. In addition, contract security personnel are likely to be more objective, having no special loyalty to the employer or contractor.

Although outsourcing security services has many advantages, with benefit comes risk. The top risks of outsourcing, as reported by senior executives, were service disruption (94 percent), loss of sensitive information (94 percent), brand or reputation damage (92 percent) and loss of customer trust (91 percent) (Piazza, p.46). Other disadvantages of contracting services include a high turnover in guards due to frequent reassignment; diminished job satisfaction for guards because of a lower level of job security; and the possibility for a conflict of loyalties to develop. Umanskly (2006, p.44) points out that security directors should help their organizations assess the reliability of ESPs even if the ESPs are not providing a security service because outsourcing could bring risks to an organization.

In addition, the image of the contracted private security officers is not always the most favorable. Management may equate low wages with lack of training or skill. If not adequately informed about the scope of security officers' authority, executives may also mistakenly think they are getting more than they are paying for, as seen in the phrase "rent-a-cop," for clients often believe their security officers have enforcement powers that they simply do not possess. Nonetheless, as Adler et al. (2005, p.65) predict: "Outsourcing will continue to be a favored business strategy." They recommend that security managers who use outsourcing follow a Contract Lifecycle Management (CLM) model, which consists of four primary components: (1) contract governance and oversight, (2) request for proposal (RFP), (3) due diligence and (4) contract negotiation and execution.

Once the decision is made to outsource specific functions, a choice must be made between security services provided by a one-stop shop or by a specialty service provider. Friedrick (2005, p.18) contends that using a single ESP can blur the contractor-client relationship, which can be difficult if a problem arises or a lawsuit occurs: "If you're unhappy with one aspect, it's hard to fire them because you rely on them so much for other things." He recommends that organizations avoid overly binding themselves to one contractor and rather seek multiple contractors with expertise in specific areas. Table 1.1 compares the numerous advantages and disadvantages of proprietary and contract services.

Table 1.1 Comparison of Proprietary and Contract Security Services

Proprietary	Contract
Advantages	*Advantages*
Loyalty	Selectivity
Incentive	Flexibility
Knowledge of internal operation	Replacement of absenteeism
Tenure (less turnover)	Supervision (at no cost)
Control stays in-house	Training at no cost
Supervision stays in-house	Objectivity
Training geared to specific job	Cost (20% less, not counting administrative costs)
Company image improved	Quality
Morale	Administration and budgeting taken care of
Courtesy to in-house personnel	Little union problems
Better law enforcement liaison	Variety of services and equipment
Selection controlled	Hiring and screening (at no cost)
Better communication	Better local law enforcement contacts
	Sharing expertise and knowledge
Disadvantages	*Disadvantages*
Unions	Turnover (extremely high industrywide)
Familiarity with personnel	Divided loyalties
Cost	Moonlighting (may be tired and not alert)
Inflexibility	Reassignment
Administrative burdens	Screening standards (may be inadequate)
	Insurance

Hybrid Services

The choice between a contractual or proprietary service need not be an either/or situation. The appropriate solution is often a combination, with proprietary security functioning in a management role and an ESP providing personnel for line staff. Performance quality can be obtained by seeking qualified contract security officers—not automatically going for the low bid. Company loyalty is also tied to wages and fair treatment.

Security Compensation

The 2007 ASIS International U.S. Security Salary Survey reported that "overall, security professionals fared well in 2007, with the average compensation of U.S. security professionals rising to $117,000 for 2007 from $87,900 in 2006—a 33 percent increase. Median salaries rose 6 percent, the fourth straight year of increases." Performance bonuses were received by 54 percent of security personnel (Moran, 2007, p.67). Figure 1.2 shows the compensation for top-level positions by industry. These industries are discussed later in the text. Figure 1.3

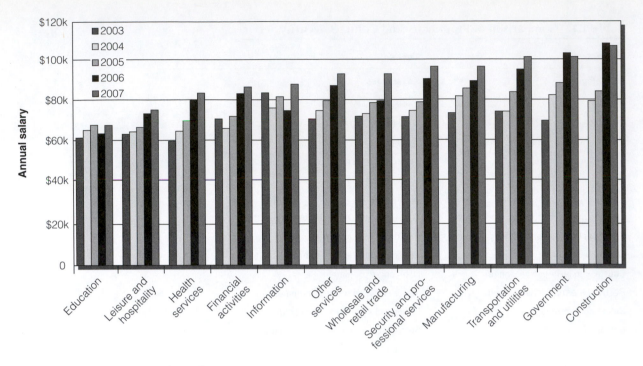

Figure 1.2 Compensation by Industry Sector

SOURCE: From "What Are You Worth?" by Mike Moran. © 2007 ASIS International, 1625 Prince Street, Alexandria, VA 22314. Reprinted by permission from the August 2007 issue of *Security Management* magazine.

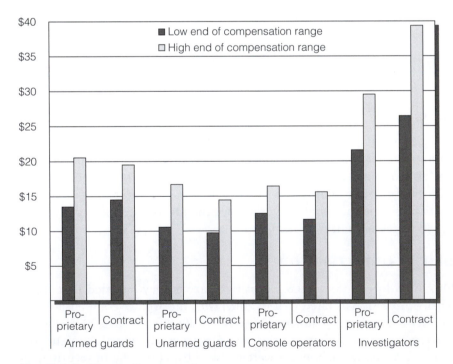

Figure 1.3 Hourly Compensation

SOURCE: From "What Are You Worth?" by Mike Moran. © 2007 ASIS International, 1625 Prince Street, Alexandria, VA 22314. Reprinted by permission from the August 2007 issue of *Security Management* magazine.

depicts hourly compensation for security personnel who have not reached a top-level position.

Regulation of Private Security

Private security is joining the trend of other fields that stress the importance of achieving certain basic professional requirements. Employers with proprietary forces usually set their own standards for security officers. Contractual security companies often are regulated by state law. Individuals who wish to provide security services on their own may need to be licensed by their state. Requirements vary.

Anderson (2007, p.88) reports: "State legislatures around the country have enacted dozens of security-related laws during the past year. Some provisions reflect a state's need to respond to local incidents, as when a crime occurs and the state passes laws to prevent future attacks, such as requiring background screening of certain groups of people; others reflect a state's desire to act in the absence of direction from the federal level, such as has occurred with identity theft."

While some states require few, if any, qualifications be met by those seeking work in private security, other states are very strict as to who may practice in this field, either as an individual or a company supplying security services. A majority of states now recognize that some controls must be in place to ensure responsible involvement by those operating in this field: "Most states require that guards be licensed. To be licensed as a guard, individuals must be at least 18 years old, pass a background check, and complete classroom training in such subjects as property rights, emergency procedures and detention of suspected criminals. Drug testing is often required, and may be random and ongoing" (*Occupational Outlook Handbook*).

Some county and city governments also require certification or licensure of those working in private security positions within their jurisdiction. Because many duties of private security officers can have consequences as substantial as those of the law enforcement officer—for example, using firearms, K-9s and other weapons, arresting people, rendering emergency medical assistance and the like—it is prudent to have basic requirements in place.

 Nearly every state now has licensing or registration requirements for contract service agencies and their personnel as well as for individuals who work in the security field. Some states have a residency requirement, and many states have regulations concerning autos and uniforms.

Licensing is the process of being granted permission from a competent authority to carry out the business of providing security services on a contractual basis. **Registration** is the process of being granted permission from a state authority before being employed as an investigator or detective, guard, security patrol officer, courier, alarm system installer or repairer, or alarm respondent.

Training requirements and other qualifications vary among different agencies; however, some applicant qualities are fairly common. Most employers prefer officers who are high-school graduates. Some jobs require a driver's license. Some employers seek individuals who have had experience in the military police or in state and local police agencies. Furthermore: "Applicants are expected to have good character references, no serious police record, and good health.

They should be mentally alert, emotionally stable and physically fit in order to cope with emergencies" (*Occupational Outlook Handbook*).

Various departments are responsible for regulating private security at the state level, including state troopers and state police, departments of public safety, boards of examiners and departments of commerce. These state regulatory bodies establish licensing and registering requirements and a mechanism for resolving consumer complaints.

Grounds for revocation of a license include violations of license laws, false statements, felony convictions, dishonesty/fraud, impersonating a police officer, insolvent bond, release of confidential information, failure to render service, violation of a court order, false advertising and incompetence.

Regulation of Private Investigators and Detectives

Most states and many cities provide some degree of government regulation of the formation and operation of private investigation agencies, but only a few states have enacted laws controlling the investigative employees of private contract agencies. In addition, state laws regulating security, private investigators and related enterprises vary in content and application. For example, Minnesota statutes stipulate who needs to be licensed as a private investigator in the state, what the application consists of and what must accompany the application, including:

- A surety bond for $5,000.
- Verified certificates of at least five citizens not related to the signer who have known the signer for more than five years, certifying that the signer is of "good moral character."
- Two photographs and a full set of fingerprints for each signer of the application.

The *Occupational Outlook Handbook* reports:

> There are no formal education requirements for most private detective and investigator jobs, although many private detectives have college degrees. . . .
>
> The majority of the states and the District of Columbia require private detectives and investigators to be licensed. Licensing requirements vary widely, but convicted felons cannot receive a license in most states and a growing number of States are enacting mandatory training programs for private detectives and investigators. Some states have few requirements, and 6 States—Alabama, Alaska, Colorado, Idaho, Mississippi, and South Dakota—have no statewide licensing requirements while others have stringent regulations. For example, the Bureau of Security and Investigative Services of the California Department of Consumer Affairs requires private investigators to be 18 years of age or older; have a combination of education in police science, criminal law, or justice, and experience equaling 3 years (6,000 hours) of investigative experience; pass an evaluation by the Federal Department of Justice and a criminal history background check; and receive a qualifying score on a 2-hour written examination covering laws and regulations. There are additional requirements for a firearms permit.[4]

---

[4]SOURCE: *Occupational Outlook Handbook*, 2006–07 Edition. U.S. Department of Labor, Bureau of Labor Statistics (Washington, DC: U.S. Government Printing Office, 2006).

Most states that regulate the private investigative business require the licensing of individuals, partnerships and corporations providing private contract investigative services, and most have established a variety of standards to obtain a license.

The cost of such a license and the provisions for renewing it vary from state to state.

In addition to state and city statutes and regulations, federal laws such as the Fair Credit Reporting Act affect private investigators and their activities. Although the act was passed originally to regulate and control mercantile credit, insurance, employment and investment agencies, interpretations of this law have resulted in its being applied to many facets of the private investigative function.

 Requirements for a private investigator's license usually include state residency, U.S. citizenship, training and/or work experience as a police officer or investigator, a clean arrest record, passing a background investigation and passing an oral or written examination.

SUMMARY

- Private security is a profit-oriented industry that provides personnel, equipment and procedures to *prevent* losses caused by human error, emergencies, disasters or criminal actions.

- Private security evolved from the human desire for additional, individual protection and the desire to prevent crimes against one's person or property.

- In ancient times people relied on physical security such as weapons, lake or cliff dwellings, walls and gates. In addition, rulers appointed individuals to protect the general safety as well as their own personal safety.

- During the Middle Ages, King Edward issued the Statute of Westminster to "abate the power of felons" by establishing the watch and ward, which provided town watchmen to patrol the city during the night; reviving the hue and cry, which required all citizens to assist in the capture of anyone resisting arrest; and instituting the assize of arms, which required that every male between the ages of 15 and 60 have a weapon in his home.

- Some English merchants hired private police to guard their establishments, to investigate crimes against them and to recover property stolen from them.

- During the eighteenth century in England, private citizens carried arms for protection and banded together to hire special police to protect their homes and businesses. The military was used to suppress riots.

- Midway through the eighteenth century, Henry Fielding became one of the first and most articulate advocates of crime prevention.

- Sir Robert Peel's Metropolitan Police Act, passed in 1829, created the London Metropolitan Police, whose principal objective was to be *prevention* of crime.

- In colonial America, constables and town watchmen were the primary means of security until the establishment of full-time police forces in the mid-1800s.

- Because of problems of interstate jurisdiction and lack of public police protection, many states passed railroad police acts, allowing private railroads to establish proprietary security forces, with full police powers, to protect their goods and passengers. In many parts of the country, the railroad police provided the only protective services until governmental units and law enforcement agencies were established.

- Allan Pinkerton was the first law enforcement officer hired to protect the railroads. He also established the first private security contract operation in the United States. About the same time,

Washington Perry Brink established armored car and courier services in the United States. In the twentieth century, William J. Burns founded the sole investigating agency for the American Banking Association. It grew to become the second-largest contract guard and investigative service in the United States.

- The world wars heightened emphasis on security in the government and made industry increasingly aware of the need for plant security.

- George R. Wackenhut's corporation, in only 20 years, established itself as the third-largest contract guard and investigative agency in the country.

- Private security has evolved into a multibillion-dollar-a-year business employing more than a million people.

- Typical entry-level positions include private security guards and private patrol officers. Mid-level positions include private investigators and detectives, armed couriers, central alarm respondents, consultants and Internet specialists. Top security positions include loss prevention specialists, security directors, risk managers and chief security officers (CSOs).

- Security services may be proprietary or contracted. Proprietary services are in-house, directly hired, paid and controlled by a company or an organization. In contrast, contract services are outside firms or individuals who provide security services for a fee. Both arrangements present advantages and disadvantages to the security manager. Some security managers elect to use hybrid services, combining proprietary and contract services to meet their needs.

- Private security is regulated at the state level through a regulatory board and staff that require licensing of contract security services and registration of all persons specifically performing private security functions.

- Most states that regulate the private investigative business require the licensing of individuals, partnerships and corporations providing private contract investigative services, and most have established a variety of standards to obtain a license. Requirements usually include state residency, U.S. citizenship, training and/or work experience as a police officer or investigator, a clean arrest record, the passing of a background investigation and the passing of an oral or written examination.

APPLICATIONS

1. You have been asked to speak to a college class on "The Evolution of Private Security." What facts will you include in your talk? What will you stress most?

2. You have been asked to speak to a class at the local police academy on the historical role of private security as it related to early public law enforcement. What facts will you include? What will you stress most?

3. Consult your Yellow Pages. What security listings are given? Is there a listing for *polygraph services? Lie detection services? Surveillance?*

DISCUSSION QUESTIONS

1. What features of ancient security systems still exist?

2. What relationship exists between the ancient assize of arms and our Constitution's Second Amendment right of the people "to keep and bear arms" for the necessity of a "well-regulated militia"?

3. Throughout history there has been hostility to the establishment of public police. Why were people so opposed to an organization that could have benefited them so greatly?

4. In the absence of effective public law enforcement, what parallel functions did the Pinkerton Detective Agency and the railroad police perform?

5. Why might a nuclear plant use contract services and a hospital use proprietary services?

REFERENCES

Adler, Steven I.; Robertson, Prentice; and Dickson, Kort L. "The Inside Story on Outsource Planning." *Security Management*, August 2005, pp.61–65.

American Society for Industrial Security (ASIS). Online: http://www.asisonline.org

ASIS International. *Career Opportunities in Security*. Alexandria, VA: ASIS International, no date.

Anderson, Teresa. "Legal Reporter." *Security Management*, January 2007, pp.88–93.

Critchley, T. A. *A History of Police in England and Wales*, 2d ed. Montclair, NJ: Patterson Smith, 1967.

Daniels, Rhlanna. "Opinions Vary on Outsourcing." *Security Director News*, February 2007, pp.1, 10.

Davidson, Mary Alice. "A Time to Remember." *Security Management*, January 2000, pp.48–60.

Davidson, Mary Alice. "Fifty Years of Advancing Security." *Security Management*, December 2005, pp.101–107.

Dewhurst, H. S. *The Railroad Police*. Springfield, IL: Charles C. Thomas, 1955.

Friedrick, Joanne. "Security Services—Simplifying the Selection Process." *Security Director News*, December 2005, p.18.

Gough, T. W. "Railroad Crime: Old West Train Robbers to Modern-day Cargo Thieves." *FBI Law Enforcement Bulletin*, February 1977, pp. 16–25.

Hall, J. *Theft, Law and Society*. Indianapolis, IN: Bobbs-Merrill, 1935.

Hall, J. *Theft, Law and Society*, 2d ed. Indianapolis, IN: Bobbs-Merrill, 1952.

Hamilton, Booz Allen. *Outsourcing Security: Concerns Growing*. ASIS Online, March 21, 2006.

Harowitz, Sherry L. "The New Centurions." *Security Management Online*, January 2003. http://www.security management.com/ library/001363.html

Healy, R. J. *Design for Security*. New York: John Wiley and Sons, 1968.

Jeffrey, C. Ray. *Crime Prevention through Environmental Design*. Beverly Hills, CA: Sage Publications, 1972.

Kaye, Michael S. "Residential Security in the Year 2000." In *Security in the Year 2000 and Beyond*, by Louis A. Tyska and Lawrence J. Fennelly. Palm Springs, CA: ETC Publications, 1987.

Lavine, S. A. *Allan Pinkerton: America's First Private Eye*. New York: Dodd, Mead, and Company, 1963.

Moran, Mike. "What Are You Worth?" *Security Management*, August 2007, pp.67–73.

"Newspoll: Do You Use Contract Services?" *Security Director News*, June 2005, p.23. *Occupational Outlook Handbook*. 2006–2007 Edition. U.S. Department of Labor, Bureau of Labor Statistics, Washington, DC: U.S. Government Printing Office, 2006.

Piazza, Peter. "Looking for Secure Outsource Partners." *Security Management*, July 2006, pp.46–48.

Reith, C. *Blind Eye of History*. Montclair, NJ: Patterson, Smith, 1975.

Reith, C. *Police Principles and the Problems of War*. London: Oxford University Press, 1940.

Somerson, Ira S. "Insight about Outsourcing." *Security Management*, March 2005, pp.73–77.

Umanskly, Ilya A. "Security's Input on Outsourcing." *Security Management*, October 2006, pp.44–48.

"World Security Services." The Freedonia Group, 2005.

CHAPTER 2

The Private Security Professional

© Kim Kulish/Corbis

Debbie Bazan, Director of Security at San Mateo County Hospital, stands with Niscayah officers John Garcia (L) and Jeffrey Edralin (C). The County partners with Securitas, an international private security company, to better use its resources to protect its citizens.

DO YOU KNOW . . .

- ■ Where in an establishment's organizational structure private security fits?
- ■ What primary roles a security director fills?
- ■ What administrative responsibilities a security director has?
- ■ What the ultimate goal of a private security system is?
- ■ How employees and management can be educated about their security and safety system?
- ■ What the managerial responsibilities of security directors are?
- ■ What pre-employment qualifications should be met by private security personnel?
- ■ How effective job performance of security officers can be increased?
- ■ When training of security officers should occur?
- ■ What a Certified Protection Professional (CPP) is?
- ■ What role security personnel have in public relations?

CAN YOU DEFINE?

andragogy	Certified Protection Professional (CPP)	due diligence	prerequisites
bona fide occupational qualification (BFOQ)	convergence	enterprise security	SMART objectives
		pedagogy	vicarious liability

Introduction

"The past few years have seen a fundamental shift in the security industry. As security is becoming increasingly globalized, it is being transformed into complex systems of interconnections and interdependencies. Unprecedented recent events have increased the demand for heightened security to protect people, facilities, assets, and data. This new security landscape presents both opportunities and challenges for today's security practitioner" (*ASIS International Security Certifications*, 2007, p.1).

This chapter begins with a discussion of private security professionalism and the sociological elements of professionalism. Then the position of security in an organization's structure is addressed. Next the key competencies and the responsibilities of the security professional are described, followed by a review of the specific responsibilities of most security professionals. The chapter concludes with a discussion of certification and its role in professionalizing the field as well as how security professionals can contribute to an organization's public relations efforts.

Private Security Professionalism

Throughout this text private security is referred to as a profession; however, whether it technically qualifies as a profession is controversial. Part of the problem is that definitions of professionalism vary. To some, *professional* means simply an important job or one who gets paid, as opposed to an *amateur*. Sociologists, however, have identified certain key elements that qualify an occupation as a profession. The three key elements of professionalism are (1) specialized knowledge, (2) autonomy and (3) a service ideal.

Specialized Knowledge

As technology advances and as criminals become more sophisticated, security providers are expected to have more knowledge and training. Because private security is a rapidly changing field, it is important to communicate with others in the field, to read professional journals, to join professional associations and to maintain outside contacts with other private security practitioners. A college education is also becoming more beneficial. In 2005, among top-level security executives, 37 percent had an undergraduate degree, 26 percent held a master's degree and 2 percent had a doctorate (Harowitz, 2005, p.45). By 2007 those figures had risen slightly, with 43 percent having an undergraduate degree and 28 percent having a master's degree. Those with doctorate degrees remained steady at 2 percent (see Figure 2.1).

Autonomy

Professional autonomy refers to the ability to control entrance into the profession, to define the content of the knowledge to be obtained and to be responsible for self-monitoring and disciplining. In addition the autonomy of a profession is usually authorized by the power of the state; for example physicians, dentists, lawyers and teachers are licensed by the state. These professions are, in effect, legalized monopolies. Private security does fit the criterion of professional autonomy in that requirements to be a security officer are usually set by a state's legislature.

A Service Ideal

The third element of a profession, a service ideal, requires that members of the profession follow a formal code of ethics and be committed to serving the

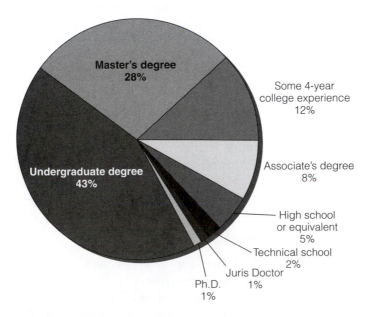

Figure 2.1 Educational Attainment

SOURCE: From "What Are You Worth?" by Mike Moran. © 2007 ASIS International, 1625 Prince Street, Alexandria, VA 22314. Reprinted by permission from the August 2007 issue of *Security Management* magazine.

Code of Ethics for Private Security Employees

In recognition of the significant contribution of private security to crime prevention and reduction, as a private security employee, I pledge:

I   To accept the responsibilities and fulfill the obligations of my role: protecting life and property; preventing and reducing crimes against my employer's business, or other organizations and institutions to which I am assigned; upholding the law; and respecting the constitutional rights of all persons.

II   To conduct myself with honesty and integrity and to adhere to the highest moral principles in the performance of my security duties.

III To be faithful, diligent, and dependable in discharging my duties, and to uphold at all times the laws, policies, and procedures that protect the rights of others.

IV   To observe the precepts of truth, accuracy and prudence, without allowing personal feelings, prejudices, animosities or friendships to influence my judgments.

V   To report to my superiors, without hesitation, any violation of the law or of my employer's or client's regulations.

VI   To respect and protect the confidential and privileged information of my employer or client beyond the term of my employment, except where their interests are contrary to law or to this Code of Ethics.

VII To cooperate with all recognized and responsible law enforcement and government agencies in matters within their jurisdiction.

VIII To accept no compensation, commission, gratuity, or other advantage without the knowledge and consent of my employer.

IX   To conduct myself professionally at all times, and to perform my duties in a manner that reflects credit upon myself, my employer, and private security.

X   To strive continually to improve my performance by seeking training and educational opportunities that will better prepare me for my private security duties.

Figure 2.2   Code of Conduct for Security Officers

SOURCE: From *Private Security: Report of the Task Force on Private Security,* National Advisory Committee on Criminal Justice Standards and Goals, Washington, DC, 1976. Reprinted with the written permission of ASIS International, Alexandria, VA.

community. Figures 2.2 and 2.3 provide such a code for security officers and for security managers.

Both codes have as the first responsibility protecting life and property. In this area security personnel may qualify as professionals, provided the organization stresses the public service aspect of security work.

Does Private Security Qualify as a Profession?

Private security has certainly increased in status since September 11, 2001, as its criticality to homeland security became apparent. However, the answer to the question of whether private security qualifies as a profession is currently provided on a case-by-case basis, by examining each individual and organization. Some individuals and organizations meet all three criteria, but many others do not. As security becomes progressively more professionalized, its status within organizations also increases.

The Place of Private Security in the Organizational Structure

In many establishments the security function evolved primarily in response to losses that occurred, growing from a simple reliance on locks and alarms into

---

Code of Ethics for Private Security Management

As managers of private security functions and employees, we pledge:

I   To recognize that our principal responsibilities are, in the service of our organizations and clients, to protect life and property as well as to prevent and reduce crime against our business, industry, or other organizations and institutions; and in the public interest, to uphold the law and to respect the constitutional rights of all persons.

II   To be guided by a sense of integrity, honor, justice and morality in the conduct of business; in all personnel matters; in relationships with government agencies, clients, and employers; and in responsibilities to the general public.

III   To strive faithfully to render security services of the highest quality and to work continuously to improve our knowledge and skills and thereby improve the overall effectiveness of private security.

IV   To uphold the trust of our employers, our clients, and the public by performing our functions within the law, not ordering or condoning violations of law, and ensuring that our security personnel conduct their assigned duties lawfully and with proper regard for the rights of others.

V   To respect the reputation and practice of others in private security, but to expose to the proper authorities any conduct that is unethical or unlawful.

VI   To apply uniform and equitable standards of employment in recruiting and selecting personnel regardless of race, creed, color, sex, or age, and in providing salaries commensurate with job responsibilities and with training, education, and experience.

VII   To cooperate with recognized and responsible law enforcement and other criminal justice agencies; to comply with security licensing and registration laws and other statutory requirements that pertain to our business.

VIII   To respect and protect the confidential and privileged information of employers and clients beyond the term of our employment, except where their interests are contrary to law or to this Code of Ethics.

IX   To maintain a professional posture in all business relationships with employers and clients, with others in the private security field, and with members of other professions; and to insist that our personnel adhere to the highest standards of professional conduct.

X   To encourage the professional advancement of our personnel by assisting them to acquire appropriate security knowledge, education, and training.

Figure 2.3   Code of Conduct for Security Managers

SOURCE: From *Private Security: Report of the Task Force on Private Security,* National Advisory Committee on Criminal Justice Standards and Goals, Washington, DC, 1976. Reprinted with the written permission of ASIS International, Alexandria, VA.

a complex, comprehensive protective system. This reactive response often resulted in a disorganized security approach rather than in an integrated service department. The need for a security system as an integral component of the organizational structure has been recognized by growing numbers of establishments. Usually such departments are headed by a specialist in security.

Effective management practices are integral to private security, whether it is proprietary or contractual, and whether regulated by the state or not. Management decides what money to spend where, what rules and procedures to establish *and* enforce, and who has specific responsibilities for given assignments. Finally, management is responsible for ensuring security. If an organization has a security problem, it has a management problem.

 Private security should be a priority concern for top-level management of businesses, industries and institutions.

Those in charge of security must be given the requisite authority to fulfill their responsibilities and must have access to top-level management. Lines of communication must be kept open. Planning, evaluating and updating must be continuous to ensure the full benefits of private security personnel, equipment and procedures.

Heads of security departments have varying titles, including Chief Security Officer, Chief of Security, Director of Security, Executive Security Officer, Security Director, Security Manager and Security Supervisor. Whatever the title, to be effective, security directors must have a position of authority within the organization, and they must have the support of top management. Whether this top manager is the president or a vice president will depend on the availability of these executives. Although ideally the security director would report directly to the president, in large organizations the president may be too busy to effectively communicate security needs and concerns to the security director. In such organizations, a vice president may be designated the responsibility.

If security is to be effective, the cooperation of all departments is essential. This can best be accomplished by private security directors who are not only knowledgeable in their field, but also innovative, who can deal forcefully yet tactfully, objectively yet imaginatively, flexibly yet systematically with people and with security problems.

The Chief Security Officer and the Chief Information Officer

Telders (2004, p.18) describes the overlap in responsibilities when an organization has a Chief Security Officer (CSO) and a Chief Information Officer (CIO), two positions that have traditionally been separate, but which now appear to be merging: "Some companies are leading the change, while some are struggling to adapt, and other are actively resisting the change." He explains that changing technology has transformed both positions in the last 20 years, and now convergence is beginning to draw them closer. **Convergence**, meaning to come together and unite in a common interest or focus, is a trend affecting security in many ways, as will be seen throughout this text.

According to Telders (p.19) the traditionally distinct CIO and CSO positions seem set up for conflict. The CIO focuses on system and network availability, system and network throughput, system response times and innovative uses of new technology to enhance and support business objectives. The CIO often has a level of responsibility for the security of the corporation's information as well, but only indirectly or through the influence of other resources, like the CSO. The CSO, in contrast, is responsible for the security of the information and assets of the corporation. Telders illustrates the difference in functions by the following example involving theft of a laptop:

> The CSO is responsible for preventing theft and investigating it when it occurs. If the laptop has sensitive information on it, the CSO must consider the safety of trade secrets, privacy issues, company confidential information and the recovery of that information. The CIO may also have an interest in the lost information; however, if the information is recoverable from a backup, the CIO is often done at that point. The CSO has to answer questions such as how many thefts have occurred this year, their cost, and what the company is doing about it.

The growth in information technology (IT) and companies' ever-increasing reliance on electronic systems and the data contained therein have presented new challenges for security practitioners: "The shifting dynamic between IT and physical security divisions makes their interdependence a sometimes sticky subject" (Plante and Craft, 2005a, p.44). Prior to the explosion of global Internet connections, security-related responsibilities were clearly defined and clearly separated from IT. Corporate security focused on the physical world; IT security focused on the logical world. Security and IT competed for an organization's limited resources. Plante and Craft note: "Bridging two such distinct disciplines together is not easy. The personality types of corporate and IT security directors can be very different, simply [because] of the roles they're hired to fill. And even though skills and competencies for both disciplines are evolving, the technical expertise required by each security discipline is still quite unique."

The convergence of the two functions is in part a result of the demands placed on security resources by terrorism: "The physical security domain suffers the threat of domestic and international terrorism; the information technology domain suffers the threat of cyberterrorism" (Fay, 2004a, p.50). This convergence has led to a new form of security leadership with the title *chief security officer*, a position responsible for both physical security and IT security. Fay (p.50) contends that when the two functions are merged, the IT executive is winning the CSO contest, with only about 10 percent of CSOs coming up through the physical security ranks. Most executive managers believe that the IT security professional can learn physical security more quickly and easily than the physical security professional can learn information technology. The skills required for information security are the focus of Chapter 11. Another source of potential conflict is between the CSO and the human resources department.

The CSO and Human Resources Department

In many organizations, screening potential employees is the responsibility of the Human Resources (HR) Department. In others it is the responsibility of the CSO. Yet in others, HR and the CSO share the responsibility. However, as a president of a background information service said: "The goal of HR is to get someone hired quickly, while the goal of security is to get the safest person" (Friedrick, 2004, p.19). Friedrick reports that the trend among companies with 500 or more employees is to outsource the screening process, with 82 percent of surveyed companies outsourcing this function in 2003, up from 70 percent in 2001. In addition to IT and HR departments, security is now being affected by laws requiring organizations to provide security in other departments as well.

The CSO and the Entire Enterprise

Plante and Craft (2005a, p.45) note: "In the United States, legislative initiatives, most notably Sarbanes-Oxley (SOX) and the Health Information Portability and Accountability Act (HIPAA), are awakening CEOs to the enterprise security risks their corporations face. The Sarbanes-Oxley Act directly affects the financial department. The HIPPA directly affects the Health and Safety Department. All must collaborate to effectively manage risks for the entire enterprise." **Enterprise security** encompasses overseeing *all risks* an organization may face.

Unity of command is important. Although the CEO is the ultimate authority in the organization, he or she will seldom have an understanding of technology to the degree necessary for security decision purposes. Thus it is recommended that an enterprise designate one person—the CSO, perhaps working with a consensus-based council if necessary—to be responsible for enterprise security and be granted authority equal to that responsibility (Plante and Craft, 2005b, p.54). As an element of such authority, security directors must be given access to top management. They must also communicate with and coordinate the security efforts of all departments within the enterprise.

The security director must not only build a team to ensure a secure environment, but must also manage and lead that team. Fay (2004b, p.50) observes that leadership can exist by itself, but effective management cannot exist without leadership.

The CSO as a Leader

Leadership has been defined as "working with and through individuals and groups to accomplish organizational goals" (Hersey and Blanchard, 1977). Centuries ago, Lao Tsu observed: *The good leader is he who the people revere. The great leader is he whose people say, "We did it ourselves."* President and World War II Commanding General Dwight Eisenhower defined leadership as: "The art of getting someone else to do something you want done, because he wants to do it."

- Leaders create a compelling vision for subordinates to follow. Managers deal with challenges and obstacles to daily performance.
- Leaders achieve higher levels of performance. Managers keep things in balance and stay focused on organizational goals.
- Leaders are innovative. Managers reduce risks.
- Leaders focus on articulating strategy. Managers execute tactics.

A basic difference between managers and leaders is that managers focus on things, whereas leaders focus on people. Manage things; lead people. Table 2.1 presents some other differences between management and leadership.

Depending on the situation, effective CSOs must be able to function in either capacity. They must also possess several key competencies.

Key Competencies of the Chief Security Officer

Chief Security Officer (CSO) Guideline[1] (2006, pp.9–10) describes several key competencies required of CSOs. They need both business and interpersonal skills as well as a high degree of emotional security. They must also be able to explain security's value to senior executives. These competencies are likely to be of more importance than the CSO's technical skills. In addition, the CSO should be able to:

- Relate to and communicate with senior executives, the Board of Directors, and its operating committees.
- Understand the strategic direction and goals of the business and how to intertwine security needs with the goals and objectives of the organization. This implies the ability to establish a vision for the global and individual business security programs and to build support for their implementation and ongoing development.

---

[1]SOURCE: From *Chief Security Officer (CSO) Guideline* (Arlington, VA: American Society for Industrial Security, 2006) pp.9–10. Reprinted with the written permission of ASIS International, Alexandria, VA.

Table 2.1   Management versus Leadership

Management	Leadership
Does the thing right	Does the right thing
Tangible	Intangible
Referee	Cheerleader
Directs	Coaches
What you do	How you do it
Pronounces	Facilitates
Responsible	Responsive
Has a view of the mission	Has a vision of mission
Views world from inside	Views world from outside
Chateau leadership	Front-line leadership
What you say	How you say it
No gut stake in enterprise	Gut stake in enterprise
Preserving life	Passion for life
Driven by constraints	Driven by goals
Looks for things done wrong	Looks for things done right
Runs a cost center	Runs an effort center
Quantitative	Qualitative
Initiates programs	Initiates an ongoing process
Develops programs	Develops people
Concerned with programs	Concerned with people
Concerned with efficiency	Concerned with efficacy
Sometimes plays the hero	Plays the hero no more

SOURCE: From Bill Westfall, "Leadership: Caring for the Organizational Spirit" in *Knight Line USA*, May–June 1993, p.9. Reprinted with permission of Executive Excellence Publishing, Provo, Utah.

- Understand and assess the impact of changes in the areas of economics, geopolitics, organizational design and technology, and how they relate to potential threats and risks to the organization.
- Ensure security incidents and related ethical issues are investigated and resolved without further disrupting operations, and are conducted in a fair, objective manner in alignment with the organization's values and code of business conduct.
- Facilitate the use of traditional and advanced scenario planning techniques in assessing risks and threats to the organization.
- Understand how to successfully network and develop working relationships with key individuals in staff and line positions throughout the organization.
- Promote organizational learning and knowledge sharing through internal and external information resources in line with the culture of the organization.
- Be politically astute but not politically motivated.

- Be realistic and comprehend the need to assess the financial, employee, or customer implications of any plan or recommendation.
- Function as an integral part of the senior management team with regard to planning and capital expenditures.
- Develop organization-wide security awareness as appropriate for the business and the culture of the organization (pp.9–10).

These key competencies will allow security directors to fulfill the numerous responsibilities the position entails.

Responsibilities of the Security Director

Whether proprietary or contractual, security managers have a vast array of responsibilities to meet and, consequently, must wear a variety of hats. CSOs should provide liaison with other managers, the CEO, union representatives, auditors, personnel department, engineers and architects, city inspectors, local police, the fire department, health officials, insurance companies and the press, as needed. Security directors also must establish rapport with top management and with other departments, enlisting their cooperation by helping each meet their own objectives. A positive attitude toward the budgetary and personnel problems of each department helps foster such rapport.

 A security director's primary roles are those of administrator, manager and loss prevention specialist.

Security directors must also understand and function not only within the formal structure depicted in the corporate organizational chart, but also within the informal organization that exists in any establishment.

Administrative Responsibilities

 Security directors are responsible for security goals; policies, procedures and daily orders; financial controls and budgets; educational programs and the image of security within the organization.

Establishing Security Goals and Objectives

Management's philosophy and the desired overall atmosphere greatly influence the security goals that are established. Some managements strive for a very open environment; others, for a very rigid one. Security goals are easier to set if a proper balance is maintained between openness and rigidity.

 The ultimate goal of private security is loss prevention resulting in maximum return on investment.

Security measures are aimed at protecting people, deterring crime, reducing risks and making the establishment a less-attractive target to would-be criminals. Different establishments obviously have different needs that must be discussed with top management before specific security goals can be established.

The goals should be measurable—for example, reducing shrinkage by a certain percent, or eliminating a certain number of risks identified during a security survey. Once the goals are stated, specific steps to accomplish the goals can be listed, prioritized and set into a time frame. According to Blanchard (1988, p.14), **SMART objectives** can ensure that goals are met. SMART objectives are:

- Specific
- Measurable
- Attainable
- Relevant
- Trackable

For example, to establish an objective of eliminating *all* accidents on the job is probably unrealistic. However, to establish an objective of reducing accidents by 50 percent might be reasonably attainable.

Establishing Policies, Procedures and Daily Orders

Managers also use three kinds of instructions: policies, procedures and daily orders. *Policies* are general guidelines or underlying philosophies of the organization. They help ensure that an organization runs efficiently and effectively and meets its goals and objectives. They are the basic rules of the organization and are seldom changed without a basic change in organizational philosophy. For example: All visitors must check in at the reception area.

Procedures are the general instructions detailing how employees are to conduct various aspects of their job. Most procedures are aimed at achieving a reasonable, acceptable level of security as unobtrusively and cost-effectively as possible. For example: When visitors check in at the reception area, they will sign in, including who they are representing, who they are visiting and the time. They will be given badges. The person they are visiting will be called to escort them to his or her office. Visitors will be instructed to return the badges and sign out at the conclusion of the visit.

Daily orders are temporary instructions or informational items. They are usually dated and last for only a few days. For example: A list may be provided to the receptionist indicating specific individuals who may be allowed to go directly to the person they are visiting without an escort on a specific day or days.

Establishing Financial Controls and Budgets

One of the most difficult administrative responsibilities is establishing a budget, including costs of equipment, equipment maintenance and security personnel. Cost for security personnel should be carefully considered.

Ideally, security directors are allowed to prepare their own budgets for management's consideration. Justifying expenses for security is extremely difficult if results cannot be proven. Ironically, if security efforts are effective, nothing happens. This may lead top management to the erroneous conclusion that security efforts are no longer critical. Baseline data illustrating what existed before specific security measures were instituted will help to justify security expenses.

Security directors must also be realistic in their budget preparations. Security is one department among many, all vying for limited resources. Priorities must be set because everything cannot be accomplished at once. Rather, an effective security system is built logically and systematically as resources become available.

Establishing Educational Programs

People are a company's most important asset, but they also can be a great threat to a company's other assets. Educational programs to promote safety, to implement security procedures and to reduce losses from internal theft are critical to an effective security system.

A security system is not established or operated in a vacuum. It requires the informed cooperation of management and all employees. Security directors are often directly or indirectly involved in such education. Sometimes they are given the responsibility to educate personnel on security equipment and procedures. At other times, especially in large companies, training departments are responsible for educating employees. Even in such instances, however, security directors may provide valuable assistance.

Education can enhance the image of private security by showing management and employees that the primary function of security is to ensure a safe place to work and to protect the company's assets so all can benefit. Losses from internal or external theft make raises and other benefits less likely. Safety programs can serve a positive public relations function as well. A cardiopulmonary resuscitation (CPR) program, for example, can make employees feel secure and prepared. Such a program can make them feel they are of value to the company and to one another. If someone does have a heart attack or need other basic first aid, those in the best position to help will be prepared.

Visitors and the public can also be educated as restrictions and safety procedures to be followed are explained. Effective educational programs can change the image that some people have of security officers from negative to positive.

 Personnel can be educated about the security and safety system through posters, signs, manuals, training sessions, drills and the suggestions and examples of security officers.

Signs and posters can be an effective educational tool and can also heighten awareness. Although permanent signs are cost-effective, they lose their impact after a time; therefore, they should be used only to give directions rather than to educate. Educational posters and displays should be bright, attractive and changed frequently.

Training manuals are helpful because management is forced to put the procedures into writing, which usually requires careful consideration of what is important. Although preparing a security and safety manual is a good idea, it is *not* sufficient by itself. Employees may not read it; they may not understand it; not wanting to appear ignorant, they may not ask questions or ask for clarification. The manual might also be simply put away and forgotten. Another hazard inherent in training manuals is that frequently they are not kept current.

Training programs or workshops are excellent means of educating. However, it is often hard to get the employees together at one time. In addition, turnover may leave some employees without needed training until the next training session is conducted.

Developing Employee Awareness Programs

The Department of Defense is a leader in mandatory security awareness programs to safeguard national energy and industrial secrets. Security managers in other areas should follow this lead, using such mechanisms as videotapes, newsletters, posters and safety and crime prevention activities to accomplish the following:

- Explain important security programs and help gain their acceptance.
- Stimulate employees to be aware of security measures directly in their control.
- Give the security department the additional eyes and ears needed to combat crime.
- Help reduce problems in high-crime areas such as computer rooms, parking areas, storage rooms or docks.

Information about "intellectual property" and property information security to preserve trade secrets should be an integral part of a security awareness program.

Establishing Image

Security directors also establish the image of the security department. Many security directors are retired police, FBI or military officers who once served in an apprehension function; that is, they were primarily reactive rather than preventive in their responsibilities. This difference in purpose and authority has posed problems for some security directors, making it difficult for them to become an integral, accepted part of the organization. An authoritarian image will perhaps deter a few dishonest employees, but it is also likely to make other employees resentful and uncooperative. The influence of security should be pervasive, but not suffocating. Security directors can set this tone by example.

Decisions must also be made as to whether security officers will be uniformed and whether they will be armed. Factors influencing these decisions include the product produced or sold, the type of security interest involved, the number and type of employees and the area in which the establishment is located. Other important considerations are the availability of local police, past experience and hazards inherent in foreign locations. If security officers are armed, strict regulations regarding the issuing, use and care of weapons must be established and enforced.

Managerial Responsibilities

Management is a complex relationship among employees of different levels, ranks, authority and responsibilities. It is often a person-to-person relationship, working within the organizational framework.

Security directors must support the development of *individual* responsibility, encouraging all personnel to achieve maximum individuality and potential while simultaneously supporting the organization's needs. The sum total of individual energy is transformed into organizational energy needed for success. Because management is an area in which many private security professionals have limited experience, a brief summary of the language it uses follows before specific managerial responsibilities are discussed.

The Language of Management

In addition to being expert and current in all areas of loss prevention and asset protection, security managers must also be familiar with the language of business management if they are to effectively interact with other business executives and overcome the stereotypical image of the "company cop." Most security managers must vie with other top executives for personnel and budget. To successfully compete, they must be familiar with "management jargon" such as:

- *Affirmative action*—actions to eliminate current effects of past discrimination.
- *Agenda*—items to be accomplished, usually during a meeting.
- *Authoritarian*—describes a manager who uses strong control over personnel; this type of manager also is called autocratic.
- *Authority*—right to give orders.
- *Bureaucratic*—reliance on rules and regulations.
- *Delegation*—assigning tasks to others.
- *Democratic*—describes a manager who involves personnel in decision making.
- *Dictatorial*—describes a manager who is close-minded and uses threats with personnel.
- *Discipline*—actions taken to get personnel to follow rules and regulations.
- *Equal Employment Opportunity Commission (EEOC)*—commission set up to enforce laws against discrimination in the workplace.
- *Goal*—end result desired.
- *Grievance*—a complaint, usually written, made to one's supervisor.
- *Hierarchy*—levels; management hierarchy goes from the CEO to vice presidents (managers) to supervisors to on-line personnel.
- *Hierarchy of needs*—human needs identified by psychologists, placed in order from lower-level needs (food, shelter, etc.) to higher-level needs (self-actualization).
- *Job description*—statement of duties and responsibilities for a specific position.
- *Management*—the "bosses" in an organization.
- *Management by Objectives (MBO)*—management and staff set goals and time lines within which to accomplish the goals.
- *Manager*—one who accomplishes things through others.
- *Mentor*—teacher, role model.
- *Morale*—how a person feels; the general mood of an organization or company (e.g., morale is high or low).
- *Motivate*—encourage, inspire.
- *Occupational Safety and Health Act of 1970 (OSHAct)*—makes employers responsible for providing a safe workplace.
- *On-line personnel*—those who do the work (e.g., security guards and patrols).
- *Performance appraisal*—evaluation of an employee's work.
- *Permissive*—describes a manager who has or exercises little control over personnel.
- *Span of management (or control)*—number of people for whom a manager is responsible.
- *Supervisor*—directly oversees the work of on-line personnel; usually reports to a manager.
- *Unity of command*—people have only one supervisor.

In addition to knowing the language of management, CSOs have numerous managerial responsibilities.

 Security directors are responsible for hiring, writing job descriptions, training, issuing equipment, scheduling, supervising, conducting inspections, taking corrective action and evaluating security personnel.

Hiring Security Personnel

"The key to limiting employee problems is to avoid hiring problem employees by conducting pre-employment screening" (Rosen, 2005, p.26). However, industries that hire large numbers of hourly employees are stuck in a catch-22: They know that without pre-employment screening and due diligence in hiring, which is expensive for employees who may be temporary, the company may leave themselves open to lawsuits (Rosen, 2004, p.36). **Due diligence** is the care a reasonable person exercises under the circumstances to avoid harm to other persons or their property. Liability for negligent hiring is discussed in Chapter 4.

The hiring process is so critical in private security in part because of **vicarious liability**, which refers to the legal responsibility one person has for the acts of another. *Vicarious* means "taking the place of another thing or person, substituting for something or someone." This concept refers to the fact that security directors and the entire organization that employs them may be legally responsible for the actions of a single officer.

Negligent hiring and retention have become major problems because of numerous court cases that have resulted in such significant judgments. Conducting background investigations, hiring qualified personnel and then developing them into permanent employees can help reduce such lawsuits. When security directors are responsible for hiring security officers, they should keep in mind the vicious circle shown in Figure 2.4.

 Private security personnel should meet the following minimum preemployment standards:

- Minimum age of 18
- High-school diploma or equivalent written examination
- No record of conviction (of a serious crime)
- Written examination to determine the ability to understand and perform the duties assigned
- Minimum physical standards:
  - Armed personnel—vision correctable to 20/20 (Snellen) in each eye; capable of hearing ordinary conversation at a distance of 10 feet with each ear without benefit of a hearing aid
  - Others—no physical defects that would hinder job performance

These are minimum requirements. Others may be established depending on the position to be filled.

Police departments have traditionally required that applicants be 21 years of age, a restrictive requirement that need not apply to private security. A mature 18-year-old, given proper training, can function effectively as a security officer, as evidenced by the military services, which have used people under age 21 for decades. The age requirement should be low enough that qualified

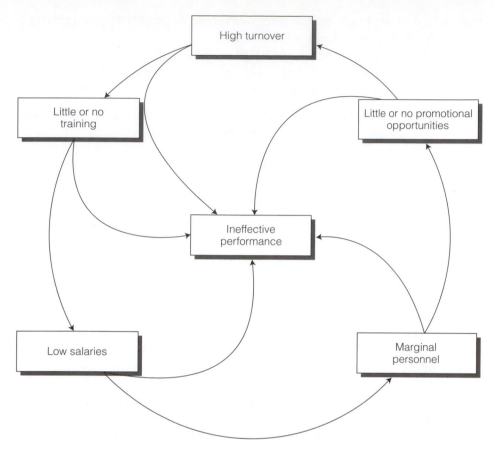

Figure 2.4   Private Security Vicious Circle

SOURCE: *Private Security Vicious Circle*

applicants can enter the field before they are committed to other careers. By the time a person is 21, he or she has often made a career decision that is not readily changed.

Applicants should demonstrate that they have mastered the basic skills taught in high school, either by having a high-school diploma or by having passed an equivalent written examination (GED). Additionally, a valid test should be given to assess the applicant's ability to learn the information required to effectively fill the role of security officer.

Because security officers are in a position of extreme trust, they should have a clean record. This means that criminal history records should be available to employers of private security officers, a key issue in many states today. Current rules and regulations do not authorize dissemination of nonconviction data to private security personnel, but do authorize release of conviction data. Additionally, criminal history record information, including arrest data on an individual currently being processed through the criminal justice system, may be restricted. It is up to individual states whether to allow other than criminal justice agencies to have access to such records. Therefore, private security professionals should encourage their state officials to specifically allow private security employers access to nonconviction data to assist in screening potential employees. An arrest or conviction record need not automatically exclude the person from being hired, but the employer should be provided this information so an informed decision can be made.

Physical requirements should be based on the specific type of job the person is expected to perform. Height and weight are often relevant, and vision and hearing are almost always relevant, especially if the person will be armed.

The Selection Process   The person wanting to be a security officer must usually go through several steps in the selection process. Although procedures differ greatly from organization to organization, several elements are common to most selection processes. The selection process is based on carefully speci-fied criteria and usually includes completing an application form, undergoing a series of tests and examinations, passing a background check and successfully completing an interview. A typical sequence of events in the employment pro-cess is illustrated in Figure 2.5.

The Application   The initial application is an important document to deter-mine a candidate's competence for the job. All applicants should complete a form that contains, at minimum, the following information: full name, cur-rent address and phone number, date of birth, education, previous employ-ment, military record (if any), physical conditions as they relate to the job, per-sonal references and fingerprints.[2] A consent statement or release form should be signed to allow the right to verify any information on the application.

Administrators must be able to show that all questions are relevant to the position they are seeking applicants for. A **bona fide occupational qualifica-tion (BFOQ)** is one that is reasonably necessary to perform a job. An example of a BFOQ in private security might be that the applicant has normal or correct-able-to-normal hearing and vision or that the person be able to drive a vehicle.

The following subjects are *not* allowed for either an application form or an employment interview: race, religion, national origin, gender, age (you may ask whether the applicant is between the ages of 18 and 70), marital status and physical capabilities. Administrators must be able to show that all questions are relevant to the position they are seeking applicants for.

Tests   Basic skills in math and reading can be assessed using standardized tests. Writing skills are also important to assess. Other job-related tests, psy-chological tests and detection of deception (honesty) tests are sometimes used by employers when they hire security personnel. Where permitted by law, polygraph examinations are sometimes required. Use of such examinations is highly controversial.

Background Investigations   Candidates should undergo a thorough back-ground check. Background checks can prevent many potential problems and save the cost of training an unsuitable employee. The *Preemployment Background Screening Guideline* (2006, p.10) gives the following benefits of making the best hiring decisions through background screening: gaining a competitive advan-tage, reducing turnover, increasing productivity, increasing morale, reducing risk of business disruptions, complying with mandates created by state or fed-

---

[2]Local fingerprint and police checks should be made because national agency checks often over-look important data.

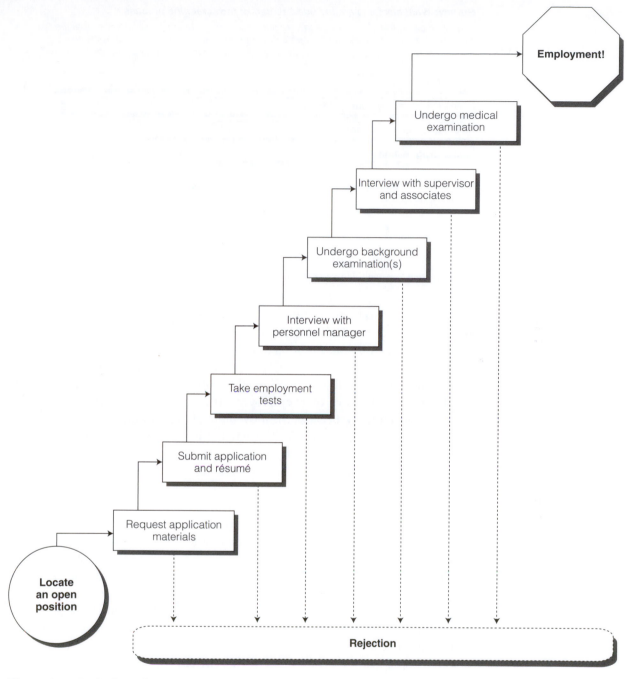

Figure 2.5 Typical Employment Process

SOURCE: J. Scott Harr and Kären M. Hess, *Careers in Criminal Justice and Related Fields: From Internship to Promotion,* 5th ed. (Belmont, CA: Wadsworth Publishing Company, 2006) p.130.

eral government for certain industries (health care, child care and the like) and fulfilling other legal or contractual obligations. A thorough background investigation not only ensures that the most qualified candidates are hired, but also can help avoid damaging legal actions.

The background check includes past employers and references. The person who conducts the background check should contact every reference, employer

Survey: *What elements are included as part of the screening process?*

"I believe background checks are a very necessary tool in hiring personnel. Companies that don't perform these checks leave themselves open to liability if something happens . . ."

—Bill Irwin, security manager, Palms of Pasadena Hospital, St. Petersburg, FL

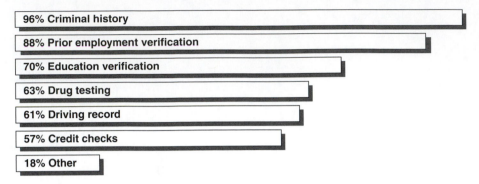

96% Criminal history

88% Prior employment verification

70% Education verification

63% Drug testing

61% Driving record

57% Credit checks

18% Other

Figure 2.6   Elements Included in the Screening Process

SOURCE: From "Newspoll" in *Security Director News*, September 2006, p.31.

and instructor. No final candidates should be selected until reference checks are made. Reference checks should be done from not only those who provided letters of recommendation but others as well. The information on the application should be verified. This is particularly true if the person was formerly employed in a security position. If employers would cooperate in exchanging information on the previous work of their employees, the overall personnel quality would improve substantially. Because the movement of individuals from one employer to another in the security field is extremely high, cooperation among employers helps eliminate unqualified, untrustworthy personnel. Personal references listed by the applicants should be contacted and interviewed.

A *Security Director News* "Newspoll" (2006, p.31) reported that 90 percent of the respondents had a pre-employment screening program for all open positions. The most common elements included in the screening process were verification of education, prior employment and criminal history, as shown in Figure 2.6.

Security directors may also conduct employee security clearances when employees are being considered for promotion to sensitive positions or positions with access to valuable assets. Conducting a background check on a long-time employee is a sensitive but important responsibility that requires tact and diplomacy.

Many organizations who outsource services or use temporary workers mistakenly assume that the staffing firms are screening the workers: "Even where screening is contractually mandated, the lack of depth and thoroughness of those checks may make them meaningless" (Erlam, 2005, p.82). A correctly set-up contract will specify that independent contractors and client companies are independent of each other (Erlam, p.84).

If an applicant passes all of the preceding hurdles, the next (and often final) step in the selection process is usually a personal interview.

The Interview   Personal interviews with the applicant can help clarify any missing or vague information on the application form and can provide an opportunity to observe the applicant's appearance and demeanor. Questions can be geared to probe the applicant's honesty, dependability, judgment and initiative. For example, applicants might be asked why they want the job, what their goals are, why they left their last job, and so on. When permitted by law, information on such items as arrest record, use of drugs and alcohol, credit and interpersonal relations with fellow workers should be obtained. Psychological stress interviews are sometimes used, but their value is controversial.

Following a successful interview, a job offer may be made. Once individuals are hired, it is up to management to assist them in performing well.

Increasing Job Performance

 To increase effective job performance, security directors should provide security personnel with a job description, basic training, a security manual or handbook and the necessary equipment.

Job Descriptions   Because private security is a complex, diverse field, personnel are assigned to many kinds of security functions. Carefully prepared job descriptions help ensure that each function is properly carried out. The job description can also help in the selection process, increase productivity and promotability, and ensure that training programs are job related.

Most job descriptions specify the type of work involved and the type of employee best suited for this work. The description should include a summary of the major functions of the job; a description of the training, experience, skills and equipment needed; physical requirements, if any; a specific listing of the activities performed and the relationship of this job to other jobs in the department. Many job descriptions also include the normal working hours, the pay range and the name of the supervisor.

In addition, new personnel need an orientation to the company—its philosophy, organization, goals and operating procedures and policies. They should also be oriented to the physical work environment, including the location of all stairways and where they lead, all emergency exits, fire alarm boxes, fire fighting equipment, telephones, emergency switches, water sources and the like. They should be taught the operation of any security equipment for which they may be responsible.

Training   As with screening, management is frequently unwilling to devote much time or expense to training security personnel because of the high turnover rate. Untrained security officers are not only a waste of money, but also may be a direct threat to themselves and to the company.

 Both basic preassignment training and ongoing training should be provided.

Preassignment Training   The preassignment training depends on the type of job to be performed and the existing level of training of the applicant. As soon as possible, new employees should receive training in the following areas:

- *Access control*—employee IDs, visitor IDs, contractors, surveillance cameras, sign-in and sign-out logs, after-hours access
- *Alarms*—operation, controls, panels, actions to take for each alarm state

- *Communications*—telephones (directory of critical numbers, professional answering), walkie-talkies, radios, cellular phones, computers
- *Emergency procedures*—bomb threats, weather emergencies, earthquakes
- *Package control*—what to accept, procedures for accepting, what to allow out, procedures for packages leaving premises
- *Parking*—security permits, traffic control
- *Passes*—property passes, camera passes

Each security employee should have a policy and procedures manual and become thoroughly familiar with it. The manual should be kept current.

Ongoing Training   In addition to preassignment training, security directors should provide security personnel with continuous training, the content of which would depend on the specific company and the job. Such ongoing training can keep personnel informed on things such as issues, changes in company policies, updates in criminal and civil law and technological improvements in the system. This ongoing training is not classroom-oriented like the preassignment training, but rather is individualized and job related. Job descriptions are often the basis for ongoing training. These steps are necessary to establish an ongoing, individualized, job-related training program:

1. Analyze job descriptions and identify the specific skills and knowledge needed to perform effectively. Determine the frequency and importance of each skill identified. Establish priorities and a time line.
2. Write objectives to be met and how each will be evaluated.
3. Implement the training. This may be through audiovisual resources, practical exercises, case studies, roll-call sessions, training bulletins and the like.
4. Evaluate the results. Job performance, not test performance, should determine the effectiveness of the training.

Any discussion of on-the-job training should distinguish between pedagogy, or youth learning, and andragogy, or adult learning, a term coined by Malcolm Knowles, nationally recognized expert in adult education. Research and common sense suggest that adults learn differently from children, differences delineated in the concepts of andragogy and pedagogy. Knowles (1980) set forth the idea that **andragogy**, the art and science of helping adults learn, is vastly different and distinct from **pedagogy**, the science of helping children learn. Adults are not grown children; they learn differently. Because of more advanced cognitive abilities, adults should not be given the "right" answer to a given problem but rather encouraged to think through a problem and to develop an appropriate response.

The principles of adult learning should be considered in training programs: Adults differ in terms of motivation, interest, values, attitudes, physical and mental abilities and learning histories. Adult learners have a different self-image, more life experiences, fear of failure, greater expectation of immediately using the learning and some basic physical differences. In addition, they are responsive to the following principles of learning:

- Base training on an identified need.
- Tell officers the learning objective.

- Tell officers why they need to learn the material.
- Make sure officers have the necessary background to master the skill (the **prerequisites**). Provide a way to acquire the prerequisites.
- Present the material using the most appropriate materials and methods available. When possible, use variety.
- Adapt the materials and methods to individual officers' needs.
- Allow officers to be as active and involved as possible.
- Engage as many senses as possible.
- Break complex tasks into simple, easy-to-understand steps.
- Use repetition and practice to enhance remembering.
- Give officers periodic feedback on their performance.
- Whenever possible, present the "big picture." Teach an understandable concept rather than relying on simple memorization.

Familiarity with the basic principles of learning will help trainers express key concepts more effectively and enable trainees to absorb such concepts more fully.

Issuing Equipment

After basic preassignment training is completed, security directors should give security officers the equipment necessary to perform their job. This might include a watch clock, flashlight, pocket pager or two-way radio, nightstick, pen and pad, handcuffs and, in some instances, a weapon. If a weapon is issued, appropriate training must be provided.

Firearms Training   A firearm refers to a pistol, revolver, other handgun, rifle, shotgun or other such weapon capable of firing a missile. The serious consequences for both employers and employees when untrained security officers are assigned to take jobs that require firearms include injury to self because of the mishandling of the weapon; injury to others, often innocent bystanders, due to lack of skill when firing the weapon; and criminal and civil suits against both employers and employees resulting from the above actions. To reduce such consequences, all armed private security personnel, including those presently employed and part-time personnel, should be required to successfully complete a firearms course that includes legal and policy requirements—or submit evidence of competence and proficiency—prior to assignment to a job that requires a firearm. They should also be required to requalify at least once every 12 months with the firearm(s) they carry while performing private security duties (the requalification should cover legal and policy requirements).

Scheduling

Security directors are also responsible for determining where personnel are to be assigned—for example, a fixed post, patrol or reserve. They must also decide whether to change assignments and rotate responsibilities. Such changes can keep personnel from getting too familiar with the people with whom they work, and thereby decrease the possibility of corruption. The downside, however, is the time required to learn and become competent in a new position.

Training armed couriers how to handle their weapons is a vital responsibility of security management.

Scheduling personnel is time consuming yet critical to accomplishing goals and objectives. Scheduling is usually done according to the following priorities:

1. Cover the shift; ensure that competent staff is available and trained to provide an acceptable level of security at each post.
2. Provide this coverage in the most cost-effective way (avoiding overtime when possible).
3. Use personnel effectively and fairly.
4. Train and assign personnel to achieve the best balance of capability and desire.

Efficient scheduling begins with a permanent schedule showing all employees when and where they will be working. In some instances employees might be designated as on "standby" in case of illness or other reasons assigned employees cannot fulfill their assignment.

Effective managers are sensitive to the needs of regular part-time employees who are likely to be working under the demands of another regular part-time commitment such as school or another job. Once part-time employees are trained, retaining them is important. Part-timers allow managers to have additional personnel on hand when the need is there and also make scheduling more flexible.

Security directors may also direct undercover operations within the organization to detect internal thefts and rule violations. Or they may hire honesty shoppers to perform the same functions.

Supervising

In larger organizations and companies, the security director or manager may have several supervisors to directly oversee security personnel. In smaller organizations, the security director may also function as the supervisor. The basic differences between the executive security director or manager and the security supervisor are as follows:

Manager	Supervisor
Goal oriented	Task oriented
Long-term planner	Short-term planner
Mission oriented	Program oriented
Works in future	Works in present
Represents whole	Represents unit
Concept oriented	Data oriented
Establishes policies and procedures	Enforces policies and procedures
Internal and external politics	Internal politics

In either case, supervisors must have a basic knowledge of the facility and of the duties of all personnel under their supervision. They must also know the basic policies and procedures of the security department. One primary responsibility of security supervisors is to conduct inspections.

Conducting Inspections

Random inspections of individual facilities and officers during regular shift assignments might include the following:

- Presence of all required personnel and equipment
- Personal appearance and behavior of security personnel
- Orderly appearance of site
- Operability of equipment
- Assessment of potential problems or hazardous situations
- Preparation of reports of inspections

The objective of such inspections is to ensure that time, equipment and personnel are being used as effectively and efficiently as possible.

Taking Corrective Action

If security personnel are not performing as expected, corrective action must be taken. In most instances, security directors or supervisors use *progressive discipline*, going from the mildest reprimand—a warning—to the most severe—termination. Progressive discipline usually involves the following actions:

1. *Warning*—This may be verbal or written, formal or informal. It should always be given in private and should always be documented.
2. *Reprimand*—This is a formal, written statement of an unacceptable behavior, the time line for correcting it and perhaps an offer of assistance.
3. *Suspension*—This should be preceded by a reprimand in all but the most serious problems. Review and appeal procedures should be available.
4. *Demotion or termination*—This should be a last resort. The reasons and previous corrective actions taken should be carefully documented.

In most instances, managers who are skilled at effectively giving warnings need go no further, for they will accomplish the desired behavior change if they tailor the warning to the individual and the situation. The purpose should be to change behavior, not to embarrass the person.

Evaluating Security Personnel

Security directors evaluate their personnel, provide feedback on how well they are performing and determine what is being done well and what can be improved. They provide nonthreatening evaluation, recognize accomplishments and recommend pay raises and promotions.

Factors managers might use in performance evaluations of security personnel include:

- Quality of work and technical skills
- Quantity of work
- Attendance and punctuality
- Organization
- Cooperation
- Problem-solving ability
- Communication skills
- Initiative
- Attitude

Guidelines for Effective Management

To manage effectively and to obtain the most from a security staff, security directors must:

- Create a good work environment—safe, pleasant.
- Be open to suggestions and input.
- Give credit to others when deserved.
- Keep employees informed—let them know what is expected, when it is or is not accomplished; let them know of changes and so on.
- Be fair and impartial.
- Act when necessary, but know their authority.
- Set a good example.

In addition to administrative and managerial responsibilities, a security director must also be a loss prevention specialist.

Loss Prevention Specialist Responsibilities

The appropriate physical and procedural controls discussed throughout this book are selected by security directors in conjunction with top management. Because no individual security director can be knowledgeable in every aspect of private security, and because the expenditures involved are sometimes large, consultants are often used in such areas as electronic or audio surveillance, protective lighting, protective fencing, alarm systems, locking systems, master keying and key control and security training. As private security becomes more specialized, use of security consultants is likely to increase.

Once the appropriate physical and procedural controls have been established, security directors delegate responsibility for maintaining the controls to each department and maintain liaison with each department to ensure that the controls are properly used. The loss prevention responsibility is the focus of the rest of the text, so will not be expanded on here.

One way to ensure that CSOs have the needed skills to accomplish administrative, managerial and loss prevention responsibilities is through certification.

Certification

More companies are requiring security staff to hold specific certifications (Daniels, 2007, p.1). About 55 percent of security professionals are required to have certifications as part of their employment, but the types of certifications available and sought after vary greatly. Eleven percent of security employers require the Certified Protection Professional (CPP) designated certification, 11 percent use association certifications, and 11 percent ask for the International Association for Healthcare Security & Safety's certification. Almost 27 percent identified other certifications.

Mallery (2004, p.40) suggests: "Security certifications come in all types, and they vary in competency and testing requirements." He notes that one area in which certification is expanding is in computer forensics: "One of the oldest and most esteemed certification is the Computer Forensic Certified Examiner (CFCE). However, this vendor-neutral certification is available only to law enforcement personnel" (p.42). Mallery points out that some certification programs are not worth much and concludes: "It is important to take the time to investigate the true value of a certification" (p.42). He recommends the Certified Protection Professional (CPP) offered by ASIS International: "This certification has been in existence for [more than] 26 years and is highly regarded" (p.44).

The ASIS Certified Protection Professional (CPP)

In 1977 the American Society for Industrial Security (ASIS) organized the Professional Certification Board to grant a designation of **Certified Protection Professional (CPP)** to individuals meeting specific criteria. The CPP program gives special recognition to those security practitioners who have met certain prescribed standards of performance and professional protection knowledge and conduct, and who have demonstrated a high level of competency by improving the practices of security management. It also encourages security professionals to continue to develop professionally by requiring continuing education to renew the certification. The program is administered by a board appointed by the president of the ASIS. Applicants must meet specific experience and education requirements to be eligible to take the written exam.

 A Certified Protection Professional (CPP) has met specific experience and educational requirements and has passed a comprehensive examination.

According to Bernard (2005, p.36): "Nearly 10,000 professionals have earned the designation of CPP™. This group of professionals has demonstrated its competency in the areas of security solutions and best-business practices through an intensive qualification and testing process."

Education and Experience   To be eligible to take the CPP examination, candidates must meet the following basic standards (Mallery, p.44):

- No criminal convictions that would negatively reflect on the security profession, ASIS International or the CPP program; and

- Nine years of security experience, with at least three of those in responsible charge of a security function; or
- A bachelor's degree or higher from an accredited institution of higher education and seven years of security experience, with at least three of those in responsible charge of a security function.

If these basic requirements are met, the person is eligible to take the written examination.

The Written Examination   The CPP exam consists of 200 multiple-choice questions covering tasks, knowledge and skills in eight subjects identified by CPPs as the major areas involved in security management:

Security principles and practices	22.8%
Business principles and practices	10.9%
Personnel security	9.9%
Physical security	24.4%
Information security	5.5%
Emergency practices	8.5%
Investigations	12.4%
Legal aspects	5.3%

(Note: adds up to 97.7%.)

Other Types of ASIS Certification

The ASIS has developed other certification programs as well, as shown in Figure 2.7. The CPP is by far the most popular program and is designed for security managers.

One certification program not shown in the figure is that of the Professional Certified Investigator (PCI), which is described in Chapter 10. The Physical Security Professional (PSP) certification is designed for those in the physical security field. These other types of certifications provide people who already have the CPP something additional in which to specialize or gives those who have already specialized a chance to be certified without having the broad knowledge required for a CPP. Working toward new certification(s) helps keep security professionals current on industry practices. Figure 2.8 shows the median compensation from 2003 through 2007 by professional certification.

Benefits of Certification

The certification of protection professionals benefits the individual practitioner, the profession, the employer and the public. The evidence of competency in security protection furnished by certification will improve the individual, raise the general level of competency in the security profession, promote high standards of professional conduct and provide evidence to management of professional performance capability. Many companies are now requiring applicants for employment to have a CPP, and this trend is likely to continue.

Recertification

The security industry is in a constant state of evolution. To protect the integrity and advance the professionalism of the CPP, PCI and PSP designations, the

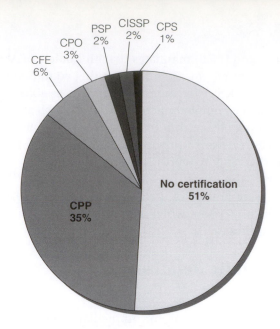

CPP: Certified Protection Professional
CPO: Certified Protection Officer
CISSP: Certified Information Systems
         Security Professional
CFE: Certified Fraud Examiner

CPS: Certified Prevention Specialist
PSP: Physical Security Professional
CISM: Certified Information Security Manager
PCI: Professional Certified Investigator

Figure 2.7 Certifications Held by Top-Level Security Executives

NOTE: Some respondents hold more than one certification.

SOURCE: From 2004 ASIS International U.S. Security Salary Survey. Reprinted with the written permission of ASIS International, Alexandria, VA.

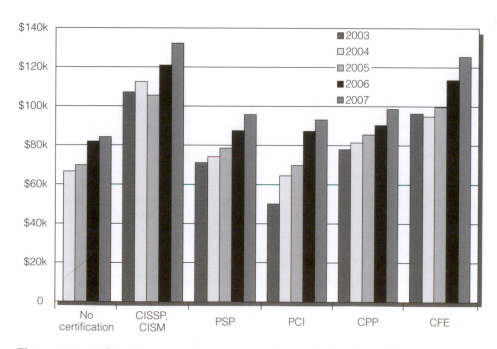

Figure 2.8 Median Compensation 2003–2007 by Professional Certification

SOURCE: From "What Are You Worth?" by Mike Moran. © 2007 ASIS International, 1625 Prince Street, Alexandria, VA 22314. Reprinted by permission from the August 2007 issue of *Security Management* magazine.

Professional Certification Board (PCB) mandates that all holders of ASIS certifications pursue professional development and continuing education to maintain proficiency and credibility. Recertification requirements established by the PCB involve obtaining a specified number of credits in areas such as education, training, teaching and volunteer leadership in security and business management associations. The PCB reviews and revises activities approved for credit as appropriate. Recertification activity reports must be submitted to the Certification Program Office every three years for holders of the CPP and PCI designations and every two years for holders of the PSP designation. Recertification protects the integrity of the profession, which is important to public relations and the image of security professionals.

Beyond Security: Public Relations and Image

When you enter a business establishment and immediately encounter a uniformed security officer, how this officer acts toward you will greatly influence how you feel about the business itself. If the officer smiles, requests that you sign in with the receptionist and indicates exactly where the receptionist is, you are likely to feel welcomed and as though you have been helped. If, in contrast, the security officer bars your way and demands to know your business, you will likely have a completely different reaction. The image projected by security officers is critical to a business's or organization's public relations efforts.

Public relations is a planned program of policies and conduct designed to increase the public's confidence in and understanding of a business or organization. The public may include customers, suppliers, creditors, competitors, employees, stockholders, members of the community, the media, the public police or the government. Public relations includes all activities undertaken to enhance image and create goodwill.

The Role of Security Personnel in Public Relations

Properly attired security officers who look professional and act professionally make a positive impression on those who come into contact with them. Such security officers, in fact, make a statement to employees and the public about how this particular company or organization does business, that is, that it takes itself, its business and it customers seriously.

 Private security officers convey an image of their employer that can either promote or detract from public relations efforts. Promoting good public relations is a vital part of any security officer's job.

In addition to greeting people in a friendly manner and answering their questions politely, security personnel should know their facility so they can guide and direct people as requested. And they should be skilled at handling telephone conversations properly, an important way to build a positive image. When security officers encounter situations where they must intervene in an "enforcing" way, their actions should be objective, unemotional and understandable. For example, if a visitor is in an unauthorized area, the security officer should calmly explain the situation and escort the visitor out of the area.

There is no need to be rude or brusque. A clear explanation and a firm request for action of some sort is generally all that is required.

If security officers are to act professionally, they must fully understand what they are protecting and why it must be secure. They need to understand the company's policies as well as its goals and mission. They must understand what is expected of them and be trained to do it. And they must feel that they are supported by management. Many companies have a firm policy that a direction given to an employee by a security officer carries the same force as a direction given by the employee's supervisor, as long as the security officer is acting within the bounds of his or her authority.

In addition, security personnel may also interact with members of the media and the press. Security managers should balance the public's "right to know" and the reporters' First Amendment right to publish what they know with their employers' needs to withhold certain information and to protect their privacy.

Security officers who look professional and act professionally will have a greater likelihood of preventing crime. Good public relations can also promote the security program and its safety and protection objectives.

The fact is that security is not a nine-to-five job, and it is not for everyone. It takes a special person to be a security officer, to work seven days a week, rotating shifts in some cases, and to work weekends and holidays. There is much more than money at stake when a person decides to enter security as a career.

SUMMARY

- A security director's primary roles are those of administrator, manager and loss prevention specialist.

- As administrators, security directors are responsible for security goals; policies, procedures and daily orders; financial controls and budgets; educational programs and the image of security within the organization.

- The ultimate goal of private security systems is loss prevention, thereby maximizing return on investment.

- Other employees and staff can be educated about the security and safety system through posters, signs, manuals, training sessions, drills and the suggestions and examples of security officers.

- As managers, security directors are responsible for hiring, writing job descriptions, training, issuing equipment, scheduling, supervising, conducting inspections, taking corrective action and evaluating security personnel.

- If the vicious circle leading to high rates of turn over is to be broken, private security personnel

selected for employment should meet minimum employment standards, including being at least 18 years old, having a high-school diploma or equivalent written examination, having no criminal record, passing a written examination to determine the ability to understand and perform the duties assigned and meeting minimum physical standards.

- To increase effective job performance, security directors should provide security personnel with a job description, training, a security manual or handbook and the necessary equipment.

- Both preassignment training and ongoing training should be provided.

- A Certified Protection Professional (CPP) has met specific experience and educational requirements and has passed a comprehensive examination.

- Private security officers convey an image of their employer that can either promote or detract from public relations efforts. Promoting good public relations is a vital part of any security officer's job.

APPLICATIONS

Following is a list of public relations efforts a business or organization might engage in. Check those in which security personnel might play a role and describe how that role might play out.

- Open house
- Reception
- Tour of the establishment
- Newsletter
- Speaking to local schools

DISCUSSION QUESTIONS

1. How can private security directors enhance the image of the private security officer?
2. List the resources one might use to obtain qualified people to hire as security officers.
3. What are three characteristics of a good training program?
4. What are the minimum requirements for an effective security officer?
5. What additional qualifications are required for a security supervisor? A security director?

REFERENCES

ASIS International Security Certifications. Arlington, VA: American Society for Industrial Security, 2007.

Blanchard, Kenneth. "Getting Back to Basics." *Today's Office*, January 1988, pp.14, 19.

Bernard, Ray. "Security Certifications." *Security Technology and Design*, September 2005, pp.36–43.

Chief Security Officer (CSO) Guideline. Arlington, VA: American Society for Industrial Security, 2006.

Daniels, Rhianna. "Certifications: Value Drives Demand for Programs." *Security Director News*, June 2007, pp.1, 10.

Erlam, N. Alexander. "You Mean He Works for Us?" *Security Management*, May 2005, pp.82–88.

Fay, John. "The Emergence of the Chief Security Officer." *Security Technology and Design*, April 2004a, pp.50–56.

Fay, John. "Leadership in Security Management." *Security Technology & Design*, June 2004b, pp.50–54.

Friedrick, Joanne. "Companies Ramp Up Pre-Employment Screening." *Security Director News*, July 2004, p.19.

Harowitz, Sherry L. "The Very Model of a Modern CSO." *Security Management*, April 2005, pp.42–51.

Hersey, Paul and Blanchard, Kenneth H. *Management of Organizational Behavior*, 3rd ed. Englewood Cliffs, NJ: Prentice-Hall, 1977.

Knowles, Malcolm S. *The Modern Practice of Adult Education: From Pedagogy to Andragogy*. Englewood Cliffs, NJ: Prentice-Hall/Cambridge, 1980.

Mallery, John. "Certification Update." *Security Technology & Design*, July 2004, pp.40–44.

"Newspoll." *Security Director News*, September 2006, p.31.

Plante, William and Craft, James. "The CSO/CISO Relationship." *Security Technology & Design*, September 2005a, pp.44–49.

Plante, William and Craft, James. "The CSO/CISO Relationship: Pick Up the Phone." *Security Technology & Design*, September 2005b, pp.52–58.

Preemployment Background Screening Guideline. Arlington, VA: American Society for Industrial Security, 2006.

Rosen, Lester S. "Cost-Effective Safe Hiring Techniques for Large Employers." *Security Technology & Design*, June 2004, pp.36–40.

Rosen, Lester S. "The Good, the Bad, and the Ugly." *Security Technology & Design*, July 2005, pp.26–29.

Telders, Eduard L. "Ready to Rumble: CIOs and CSOs Face Off." *Security Technology & Design*, November 2004, pp.18–22.

CHAPTER 3

The Public/Private Interface

Private security and public police share a common goal of protecting people and property in the community. Today, law enforcement agencies have fewer resources to accomplish their goals. This is a major driving force behind the trend to outsource certain duties to private firms.

© Michael Newman / PhotoEdit

Do You Know . . .

■ How private security officers compare in numbers with public police officers?

■ How much movement occurs between the fields of public and private security?

■ How private security officers and public officers are alike?

■ How private security officers differ from public police officers?

■ What authority private security officers have?

■ What restrictions are placed on private security officers?

■ What advantages private security offers public police and vice versa?

■ In what areas private security officers might share responsibilities with law enforcement officers?

■ What areas in the justice system might be privatized?

■ When the privatization of corrections began and whether it has been increasing or decreasing?

Can You Define?

authority	power	tort law
exclusionary rule	privatization	vetted

Introduction

Many do not stop to realize that private security professionals in business places, at public gathering sites, and in corporate environments are truly first responders to every conceivable calamity from crime to natural disasters. . . . Most people tend to think of public fire, law enforcement and emergency response personnel as first responders, but private security practitioners are often the first responders in their business or corporate environments. They played a key role during the initial moments after the September 11, 2001, terrorist attacks and were instrumental in getting many people safely out of the buildings. They were first responders; they were already on the scene at the time of the attacks, and unfortunately, in some instances, they were also first victims (Cooke and Hahn, 2006, p.16).[1]

In addition to the critical responsibility of staffing and training first responders, security managers must be concerned with their own loss prevention programs and the individuals hired to implement them. And they must know how the private "policing" function differs from that of the public police, how they might contribute to public policing efforts and, in numerous instances, how they might benefit from public policing efforts. They must also be completely familiar with the legal authority they and their employees have and the restrictions on that authority.

This chapter introduces the public-private connection and a look at the friction that has historically existed between public and private officers. Next the complementary roles of private security and the public police are discussed, as is the growth of private security and the need for cooperative efforts. This is followed by a discussion of considerations when implementing a public-private partner-

---

[1]SOURCE: Cooke, Leonard G. and Hahn, Lisa R., "The Missing Link in Homeland Security" in *The Police Chief*, November 2006, p.16.

ship. Then specific areas in which private security might lessen the burden of the public police as well as other areas in the justice system are discussed. The chapter concludes with recommendations on private-public partnerships that might be established and a brief look at examples of successful partnership in action

The Public-Private Connection

Loss prevention, security, privacy—such goals are not the sole domain of private security. They have been of concern since recorded time. Recall from Chapter 1 that the history of public policing and private security is intertwined. According to Shering and Stenning (1987, p.15):

> With contemporary corporations as the modern-day equivalents of feudal lords, reigning supreme over huge feudal estates, the search for a historical parallel leads us back beyond frankpledge to more ancient concepts of private peaces and conflicting private authorities. Indeed, the very distinction between private and public takes on a new significance that blurs, and contradicts, its liberal meanings. This is true not only because private "individuals" are engaged in maintaining public order but also because more and more public today life is conducted on privately owned and controlled property.
>
> Corporate orders are defended on the grounds that corporations, like any other "persons," have the right to a sphere of private authority over which they have undisturbed jurisdiction. Furthermore, this right is sacrosanct, for to encroach upon it would undermine the very freedoms that are definitive of liberal democracy.[2]

This "right to a sphere of private authority" has long been recognized by governments and by the wide variety of policing mechanisms they have established, with public and private policing continuing to coexist:

> Policing has been done under an enormous variety of auspices—national and local governments, revolutionary and non-revolutionary parties, neighborhoods, churches, landowners, workers, peasants, businesses and professional associations. Even more interesting, varieties of policing are complexly mixed. . . . Although the proportions in the mixture vary, similar forms appear again and again. In particular, "public" and "private" policing never wholly supplant one another. Indeed, the distinction itself becomes problematic in many circumstances. Public and private police institutions cooperate, sometimes interpenetrate, and often share modes of operation. . . . Policing is a reciprocating engine in that groups regulate individuals but individuals collectively regulate groups (Bayley, 1987, p.6).[3]

Authority is the legal right to get things done through others by influencing behavior. **Power** is the ability to get things done with or without a legal right. Authority is generally granted by law or an order. Power is the influence of a person or group without benefit of law or order. Authority and power both imply the ability to coerce compliance, that is, to *make* subordinates carry out or-

---

[2]SOURCE: Shearing and Stenning, 1987, p.15.
[3]SOURCE: Bayley, 1987, p.6.

ders. Both are important to managers at all levels. However, authority relies on a law or order, whereas power relies on persuasion. The authority and power of public and private policing differ, as will be discussed shortly.

Historical Friction

Friction has often existed between the police and private security. Police often view private security employees as poorly trained and poorly paid individuals who are "wannabe" cops but cannot make the grade.

Historically, public and private security have seen themselves as being in competition, with private security usually coming out on the "short end of the stick." Youngs (2004) suggests: "While the 1960s characterized a period of indifference toward private security and the 1970s one of changing perceptions and some mistrust of the industry, the 1980s and 1990s most likely will be regarded as the era of collaboration and joint ventures between public law enforcement and private security. Individual and corporate citizens policed by public law enforcement also increasingly are becoming the clients of private security, as illustrated by increases in the use of corporate security and the number of gated communities."

Such gated communities may indicate dissatisfaction with public safety and could result in public-safety "haves" and "have-nots." The concern is that this pattern, over time, could lead to those who are rich and stable enough being able to buy their way out of a city's overall crime problems, leaving less affluent areas to flounder. In addition, affluent residents who personally pay to buy private security for their neighborhoods may resist paying higher city property taxes to improve public safety for the rich and poor alike ("Public or Private?" 2006).

Despite similar interests in protecting our citizens, law enforcement and private security have rarely collaborated. In fact, law enforcement agencies embracing the community policing philosophy have collaborated extensively with almost every group *except* private security. By some estimates, 85 percent of the country's critical infrastructure is protected by private security, a figure highlighting the need for complex coordination and a boosting of the level of partnership between public policing and private security (*Private Security/Public Policing*, 2004, p.1).[4]

Even though the need for cooperation has been nationally recognized, the two groups are often not confident in each other. For example:

■ Some police lament the paucity of preemployment screening, training, standards, certification and regulation of security officers.

■ Some police feel security officers receive insufficient training (particularly those who carry weapons).

■ Some police view security officers as individuals who sought a career in law enforcement but were unable to obtain a position.

■ Some police see private security as a threat to their domain.

■ Police generally have little understanding of the broad range of private security functions, capabilities, expertise and resources and therefore fail to appreciate the role of private security.

---

[4]SOURCE: *Private Security/Public Policing* (Washington, DC: Office of Community Oriented Policing Services, 2004) p.7.

- Some private security practitioners view police as elitists.
- Some private security practitioners feel law enforcement professionals do not care about private security until they are considering a job in that field (*Private Security/Public Policing*, p.7).

Another source of friction may be the growth of private security compared to public policing and the extent that resources are made available to sustain such growth.

The Growth of Private Security

Private security officers outnumber public law enforcement officers by 5 to 1 nationally, with the ratio even greater in some states, such as California where it is 6 to 1. This growth in the number of private security officers compared to public officers was predicted in a study conducted over a decade ago (see Figure 3.1) (Cunningham et al., 1991, p.3).

 Private security officers now outnumber public officers by 5 to 1.

These numbers reflect only private security officers. Thousands of other private security positions exist. Furthermore, some 33,000 security managers oversee these positions. Such figures illustrate the substantial contribution private security officers make to safeguarding Americans and their property. Given the enhanced state of alert within the United States following the 9/11 terrorist attacks, it seems safe to say the demand for security forces will most certainly remain high in the foreseeable future. This is in contrast to the public policing arena, where a shortage of recruits is reaching crisis proportions.

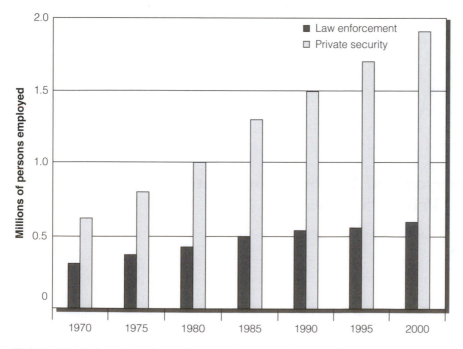

Figure 3.1 Private Security and Law Enforcement Personnel Compared

SOURCE: William C. Cunningham et al. *Private Security: Patterns and Trends.* Washington, DC: National Institute of Justice Research in Brief, August 1991, p.3.

Shortage of Applicants in the Public Sector

Egan (2005) notes: "In a generation's time, the job of an American police officer, previously among the most sought-after by people with little college background, has become one that in many communities now goes begging." He points out that the career has little appeal among many young people and that those who are interested are frequently lured away by aggressive counteroffers from the military or by better pay at entry-level jobs in the private sector. The supply of good police recruits is down throughout the country, with more than half of small agencies and two-thirds of large agencies reporting a lack of qualified applicants (Koper, 2004, p.2).

Stockton (2007, p.10) contends: "The perfect storm of police staffing is upon us. Nearly every agency in this country is having difficulty meetings its most basic staffing needs, and it's going to get much worse before it gets better. From the smallest departments to the massive NYPD, agencies are going short, often by hundreds of officers." Police officials estimate more than 80 percent of the nation's 17,000 law enforcement agencies have vacancies that many cannot fill (Kriel, 2006). For example, Dallas needs another 800 officers; Houston could use up to 1,200 more.

The generational transition currently under way and at the center of the workforce crisis has resulted from the convergence of two trends: the growing number of aging baby boomers and the much smaller cohort of younger people, the generation Xers, who follow behind them (Henchey, 2005, p.108). Members of the 102 million–strong millennial generation (born between 1982 and 2002) have yet to fully impact the law enforcement workplace, but they will be the majority of new police officers and deputies hired in the coming decade: "By the year 2020, most police officers will be members of the millennial generation" (Henchey).

Finding qualified police recruits has become much tougher since the events of 9/11, as the expansion of federal law enforcement has created more options for people interested in the field (Mitchell, 2007). In addition, the wars in Iraq and Afghanistan have "siphoned off public-service minded people to the military" (Woska, 2006, p.54). Yet another contributor to the reduction in qualified applicants may be the negative publicity over high-profile incidents of racial profiling and excessive use of force (Woska). Finally, the lure of higher-paying jobs in security management can drain public policing ranks.

Movement of Personnel between the Public and Private Sectors

 Public and private officers often move from one sector to the other.

An exchange of personnel often occurs, with individuals moving from one field to the other. Some individuals use private security as a stepping stone into public policing. Likewise, some individuals in public policing opt, at some point, to enter private security, whether that move comes after retiring from public policing or as a part-time job to supplement income while working as a public police officer. Many retired law enforcement officials at the federal, state and local levels move to positions in private security. In fact, some agencies straddle the line between public law enforcement and private security. For example, the Amtrak Police department is a private sector police force with over 300 sworn officers. And many college campuses have private sector, sworn police agencies. In addition, many law enforcement officers work as private security officers in their off-hours (*Private Security/Public Policing*, p.6).

Moonlighting—A Legal Issue

The practice of police officers moonlighting is not without its problems. In *Mount Sinai Hospital v. City of Miami Beach* (1988), a Miami Beach police officer was injured while moonlighting at a hospital. The question became, "Under what conditions does a police officer's authority cease and the officer become a private citizen able to obtain injury compensation?"

The Officer, Lehman, was going out the emergency room door to check the parking lot, one of his specific duties, when he slipped and his right knee gave way. The hospital contended that the officer was an agent of the city and that it should not be liable. The compensation commission, however, found the hospital liable, and the hospital appealed. The case hinged on determining if the officer was engaged in his primary responsibility as provided in a Florida statute stating that an injured law enforcement officer "shall be deemed to have been acting within the course of employment" when injured if the officer was discharging his or her "primary responsibility" (that is, preventing or detecting crime and enforcing the law) and "was not engaged in services for which the officer was paid by a private employer."

The hospital based its case on the precedent set in *City of Hialeah v. Weber* (1986). This case involved a moonlighting police officer working as a security guard at a lounge who was injured in apprehending individuals slashing car tires at a business across the street. The court held that the moonlighting officer was an employee of the city police department at the time of the injury and hence the city was responsible for compensating him for his injuries.

In *Mount Sinai Hospital v. City of Miami Beach* (1988), the court described a spectrum along which moonlighting cases should be judged. At one end is a case where a moonlighting officer is "unequivocally" performing a police function, as in the case of a moonlighting lounge employee who acted to stop a crime being committed in his presence and was not performing a task for which he had been hired by his private employer. Therefore, the city was responsible for the compensation. At the other end of the spectrum is the case of a moonlighting officer who is clearly performing a service for which he is paid by the employer, and not performing a police function. In such a case, the employer would be responsible. Although these two situations present opposite ends of the spectrum, the vast majority of cases are not as clear-cut, falling somewhere along the spectrum and posing much more difficulty for the court.

Public and Private Officers Compared

To understand how public and private officers might work together to ensure the safety of our communities, it is important to recognize how these two groups are alike and how they differ.

Similarities between Private and Public Officers

Private and public officers have many things in common, including wearing a uniform and a badge, being trained to compel obedience to their authority and being liable for their actions. Both private and public officers seek to prevent losses from criminal actions and, if such losses occur, to investigate and apprehend the person(s) responsible.

 Private and public police officers wear uniforms and badges, are trained in compelling obedience and liable for their actions. Both also seek to prevent crime and to apprehend criminals.

Both public and private officers may receive respect and cooperation from those they work with or may face hostility and aggression. In addition, both public and private officers have a tremendous influence on the image of those for whom they work. Their every action has an impact on public relations.

Differences between Private and Public Officers

Four basic differences exist between private and public officers: (1) the financial orientation, (2) the employer, (3) the specific functions performed and (4) the statutory power possessed.

Private Security:

- Profit-oriented enterprise
- Serving specific private clients
- To prevent crime, protect assets and reduce losses
- To regulate noncriminal conduct not under the authority of public police

Public Law Enforcement:

- Nonprofit, governmental enterprise
- Serving the general public
- To combat crime and disorder, preserve the public peace, enforce laws and apprehend offenders
- Statutory authority

Other important differences are that training of law enforcement officers is substantially more rigorous than that of most security officers, and standards and certification are also more demanding in law enforcement. However, private security has the resources to develop specializations beyond the capacity of most law enforcement agencies, for example, protecting computer networks, chemical plants, financial institutions, healthcare institutions and retail establishments (*Private Security/Public Policing*, p.6).

One seldom-discussed difference between the public police and private security officers is that of the corporate culture. It is well established that the police have a culture steeped in tradition and pride. They know what their peers expect of them and are usually governed by clear policies and procedures. In contrast, security officers lack strong traditions to sustain pride in their work. They must adapt to the corporate culture which is more focused on the bottom line than on the goals of security. This area will doubtless evolve as the security profession matures.

Other basic differences between private and public officers exist in the authority they have and the restrictions placed on them.

Legal Authority

Law enforcement has legal powers far exceeding those of private security. Because private security officers wear uniforms, often carry weapons and have been placed in a position of authority, they may appear to have more legal authority than private citizens; however, this is not always the case.

 Private security officers usually have no more powers than private citizens. As citizens, they have the power to arrest, to investigate, to carry weapons, to defend themselves and to defend their property or property entrusted to their care.

Often private security officers conduct periodic inspections of personal items such as briefcases, purses and lunchboxes as directed by management and specific policy. Generally, private security officers have no police authority. However, their training and experience make it more likely that they will be able to exercise this authority.

 Private security officers can deny access to unauthorized individuals into their employers' business or company, and they can enforce all rules and regulations established by their employers. They can also search employees and question them without giving the *Miranda* warning in most states.

In *Bowman v. State* (1984), an Indiana court ruled that private security officers, unlike public law enforcement officials, are *not* required to issue *Miranda* warnings. Giving warnings, the court observed, is required only in situations involving action by a government agent, such as the public police.

Weingarten Rights

Although *Miranda* rights do not apply in circumstances where a private security officer is questioning an employee, other rights may come into play. For example, if security personnel are conducting an investigation that involves interviewing or questioning an employee, and that employee reasonably believes the interview may lead to disciplinary action, the employee may request representation by the union at an investigatory interview with his or her supervisor. This employee right to have union representation during investigatory interviews was announced by the U.S. Supreme Court in *NLRB v. J. Weingarten, Inc.* (1975). Since that case involved a clerk being investigated by the Weingarten Company, these rights have become known as Weingarten rights.

Employees have Weingarten rights *only* during investigatory interviews. An investigatory interview occurs when a supervisor questions an employee to obtain information that could be used as a basis for discipline or asks an employee to defend his or her conduct. If an employee has a reasonable belief that discipline or other adverse consequences may result from what he or she says, the employee has a right to request union representation. Investigatory interviews usually relate to subjects such as:

absenteeism	insubordination	lateness
drinking	sabotage	theft
fighting	work performance	violation of work procedures

poor attitude	damage to state property
violation of safety rules	falsification of records
accidents	drugs

Management should have clearly specified policies on such questioning and what type of employee conduct may invoke an investigatory interview.

Weingarten Rules

Under the Supreme Court's *Weingarten* decision, when an investigatory interview occurs, the following rules apply:

Rule 1 – The employee must make a clear request for union representation before or during the interview. The employee cannot be punished for making this request.

Rule 2 – After the employee makes the request, the employer must choose from among three options: (1) grant the request and delay questioning until the union representative arrives and has a chance to consult privately with the employee, (2) deny the request and end the interview immediately or (3) give the employee a choice of (a) having the interview without representation or (b) ending the interview.

Rule 3 – If the supervisor denies the request for union representation and continues to ask questions, he or she commits an unfair labor practice and the employee has the right to refuse to answer. The supervisor cannot discipline the employee for such a refusal.

Other Restrictions on Private Security Officers

Laws governing private security officers' conduct are derived from several sources: tort law, state statues, criminal law, constitutional guarantees and contract law. Because of actions they must perform in fulfilling their responsibilities, private security officers are more open to civil lawsuits than most other citizens, as discussed in the next chapter.

 Private security officers cannot invade another's privacy, electronically eavesdrop, trespass or, in some jurisdictions, wear a uniform or badge that closely resembles that of a public police officer.

Many of the restrictions on private security officers come from the tort law of each state. **Tort law** is civil law. It defines citizens' responsibilities to each other and provides for lawsuits to recover damages for injury caused by failing to carry out these responsibilities. Civil liability is discussed in the next chapter.

State and federal criminal laws prohibit security officers from committing crimes such as assault. Other state and federal laws regulate wiretapping, surveillance, gathering information on individuals, impersonating public police officers, and purchasing and carrying firearms. For example, in *National Labor Relations Board v. St. Vincent's Hospital* (1984), the U.S. Court of Appeals held that the interrogation of hospital employees by their supervisors in connection with several thefts did *not* constitute coercive action. The court did observe, however, that placing hospital employees who were engaged in union activities under surveillance did violate the National Labor Relations Act.

Although it is well known that the U.S. Constitution places the major legal limitations on police powers, such restrictions are applied only to actions of government officials, including law enforcement officers. However, the distinction between government and private activity is not always clear-cut. This is true, for example, when a private security officer is hired by a public institution or when a private security officer is deputized. In such instances, the constitutional restrictions may apply to those private security officers.

Usually private security officers who are deputized or are contracted by a public authority are subject to the same restrictions as public officers. In addition, public police officers who work during off-hours in private security positions are considered to be public law enforcement officers in many states. Consequently, many police departments do not allow their officers to moonlight in private security positions. Some states specifically deny a private security license to anyone vested with police powers.

Clearly, the distinction between public and private police is not always black-and-white but, instead, various shades of gray. In some states shopkeeper statutes and other similar legislation dealing with railroad officers, nuclear facility officers, bank security officers and the like give private security officers greater powers than those of the general public. A few jurisdictions recognize private security officers who have total public police authority based on compliance with certain legal and training requirements.

State laws also regulate the arrest powers of private security officers. In the majority of 31 states surveyed, private security officers can arrest for a misdemeanor. In all 31 states they can arrest for a felony, but in none of the states are they granted police arrest powers. Other restrictions are placed on private security officers by local ordinances and state statues that establish licensing regulations. These restrictions vary greatly from state to state, as discussed in Chapter 2. Finally most security officers are further restricted by the contract they sign to provide their services to an agency or to an employer.

The similarities in goals and objectives of private and public policing and the differences in their legal authority suggest that, in many ways, public and private efforts are complementary.

Complementary Roles of Private and Public Officers

Private and public security forces engage in similar activities and have similar goals, including preventing crime. However, private security officers also perform functions that cannot be performed by public law enforcement officers, which makes their roles complementary.

Private security has become a major player in safeguarding Americans and their property. As our increasing elderly and business populations are likely to continue their inhabitation of high-rise condos and office buildings, their reliance on private security will also increase. The traditional police officer patrolling public roads or a beat officer on foot cannot practically be expected to patrol such structures. Unlike public police officers, private security officers can and do patrol specific buildings, even specific floors or rooms within buildings.

It can be anticipated that the fields of public law enforcement and private security may tend to blend together as society recognizes the need for each and as the professions develop methods of working together—to the benefit of all.

Need for Cooperative Efforts

Promoting cooperative interaction between private and public police officers is of utmost importance. Although public police officers also seek to prevent crime, a large portion of their time is devoted to enforcing laws, investigating crimes and apprehending suspects. Their presence may serve as a deterrent to crime, but they cannot be everywhere at once. The vital role played by private security in preventing crime is clear.

In many jurisdictions, the police are simply overwhelmed. Given the reality that the United States is the most violent industrialized nation in the world, public-private cooperation is essential. Youngs notes: "Today's police departments are under monumental pressure to perform, keep crime rates low and do it all with fewer resources. Agencies can accomplish this seemingly impossible mandate by forming supportive partnerships with private security providers." This is the essence of **privatization**, in which duties traditionally performed by police officers are performed by private security officers. "Fortunately, privatization of certain police department functions has proven a powerful solution to the problem. The steady decline of governments' capital resources and their increasingly urgent search for ways to continue providing the services that citizens demand without raising taxes are driving the privatization trend. Some federal agencies have saved as much as 50 percent by hiring contractors to provide services" (Youngs).

According to Youngs: "Police in today's environment typically spend less than 20 percent of their time on crime-related matters. In California, a police officer may cost $100,000 a year taking into account salary, benefits and such overhead expenses as squad cars. Faced with rising calls for service, this proves expensive for tasks, such as transporting prisoners, providing court security, conducting traffic control and serving summonses. The real trend in the future will be contracting out the functions of public police that do not involve crimes or emergencies."

Today, law enforcement agencies have fewer resources to accomplish their goals. This is a major driving force behind the trend to outsource certain duties to private firms: "Police departments in 18 states currently use, or plan to use, private security guards to fill support roles. One firm provides security for six major public transit systems around the country" (Youngs). Departments can form partnerships with private security firms to save money as well as to free trained police officers to conduct duties that only they should address.

Mutual Advantages
The advantages of the private police using public police are numerous.

 Public police offer private security the power of interrogation, search, arrest and use of electronic surveillance. They may reduce or eliminate their legal liability, and they offer training, experience and backup.

Private police can interrogate without giving the *Miranda* warning and conduct searches and seizures without warrants. Private police are not bound by the **exclusionary rule**, which makes inadmissible any evidence obtained by means of violating a person's constitutional rights.

 Private security offers the public police information, access to private places and extended surveillance and coverage. In addition, private security officers are not bound by the exclusionary rule, so they can question without giving the *Miranda* warning and can search without a warrant.

In fact, employees' obligations to their employers may sometimes allow public police greater freedom in their investigations. In *Unites States v. Dockery* (1984), for example, this was true. A bank employee suspected of embezzlement submitted to questioning by FBI agents under instructions from her employer. Her attorney later argued that her confession should be barred. The U.S. Court of Appeals for the 8th Circuit disagreed. It observed that the statements had been made voluntarily, and the suspect had consented to the interview as part of her obligation to her employer.

Although not as rigidly controlled as public police, private security officers must still respect the rights of others. Failure to do so can and often does result in civil lawsuits, as discussed in the next chapter.

Areas Where Private Security Can Help Public Police

One area that police seem willing to let private security personnel handle is economic crime. Crimes such as shoplifting, employee theft and pilferage, and credit card and check fraud are usually a low priority with public police and are usually well developed by the time the police are notified. In addition, management is usually more interested in the deterrent value of prosecution and in plea bargaining than in a conviction. Private security professionals are well positioned to share some responsibilities of law enforcement. Investigative responsibilities are the focus of Chapter 10.

 Some areas of cooperation are investigating internal theft and economic crimes, responding to burglar alarms, examining evidence from law enforcement in private crime labs, conducting background checks, protecting VIPs and executives, and controlling crowds and traffic at public events.

Responding to Alarms

One area in which private security is providing vital services is in the alarm industry. The false alarm problem is of immense proportions. A survey of law enforcement agencies by Honeywell (*Building a Powerful Partnership*, 2007) found that over half of the respondents contended with 11 or more false alarm calls per week. Other studies report that some jurisdictions experience, on average, a false alarm rate as high as 98 percent. Nonetheless, police do see benefit in properly installed, maintained and used security systems (*Working Hand in Hand*, no date, p.3). In fact, the Honeywell survey found that 96 percent of police value the alarm industry, with 80 percent of respondents expressing a belief that monitored electronic burglar alarms help prevent loss of property and life.

Betten and Mervosh (2005, p.68) assert: "Police response to private burglar alarms isn't the best use of public law enforcement resources, which are already stretched thin." They note that law enforcement agencies around the country are adopting a policy known as *verified response*, whereby criminal activity must first be identified or confirmed by either private security officers or through some type of electronic surveillance before police will dispatch personnel to the scene of an alarm.

Many security systems now incorporate sound-activated listen-in features, which allow the monitoring station to hear sounds from the protected site when an alarm has been received. A listen-in feature can provide valuable information such as if a weapon is being used or a hostage situation has developed. This feature also helps reduce false alarm relays.

Some police departments retain a nonresponse policy regarding security alarms on private property. The security industry is concerned about the "proliferation" of blanket nonresponse policies because they not only reduce the crime deterrent effect of alarm systems but also raise the risk to those at the alarm site: "Beyond the concern over asset losses is the issue of life-safety. The safety of employees is endangered when there is no longer a police response" (Martin, 2005, p.62). Further, private security officers do not have the same authority as law enforcement.

Examining Evidence in Private Labs

Budget cuts and layoffs have led to massive backlogs of evidence at state crime labs, hampering local police departments' ability to solve crimes and get criminals off the street. Hickman and Peterson (2004, p.1) report that the 50 largest publicly funded forensic crime labs entered 2002 with over 93,000 backlogged cases, including about 270,000 requests for forensic services, more than twice the backlog at the beginning of the year. In Michigan, the state police crime labs have eliminated 24 of the 160 scientists who analyze DNA samples, fingerprints, ballistics and other forms of evidence, and there are more layoffs ahead: "With more than 40,000 new felons to process each year and a steady stream of requests from old cases that were originally investigated before DNA evidence could be analyzed, the staff reductions have left laboratories overwhelmed and local police departments frustrated" (Martindale, 2007).

Clearly private forensic laboratories can be of great assistance in this area. In Michigan, for example, state labs outsource over 2,400 DNA cases annually. Such cases, if not outsourced, would languish for more than a year before being tested in the state labs.

Conducting Background Checks

Another area in which private security can help law enforcement is in the completion of employee background checks, which are very time consuming but also very important. Turley (2006, p.7) states: "Conducting background checks is a practice that employers of all sizes should make standard operating procedures for all new hires. The proactive approach provides employers with comfort in knowing risks associated with making bad hiring decisions are limited." Nadell (2004, p.108) points out: "Background checks can protect a company from negligent hiring allegations and promote a safe environment for employees and the public." The liability posed by negligent hiring is examined in more detail in Chapter 4.

Background screening must be conducted with care or the results can cause as many legal problems as hiring the wrong person (Worsinger, 2006, p.90). The benefits of well-conducted background checks include:

- Higher work attendance, low turnover.
- Reduced healthcare and workers' compensation costs.
- Less employee theft.
- Fewer incidents of litigation. Screening reduces the risk of accidents, criminal activity and violence—any of which may result in litigation.
- Better productivity.
- More qualified employees.
- Confirmation that employees are who and what they claim to be (Turley).

As important as background checks are, and as helpful as security professionals can be in conducting such checks, Giles (2004, p.45) contends: "Security professionals and investigators face new and evolving challenges regarding access to criminal and other public records. These include shrinking budgets at records repositories, privacy concerns, logistical obstacles and the conflicting patchwork of public records authorities."

The Fair Credit Reporting Act (FCRA) allows employers to obtain consumer reports for "employment purposes." Federal law requires that subjects of record searches be notified of the employers' intent and asked for authorization. If an employer takes an adverse action, such as not hiring an applicant, it must provide the applicant with notice of the action taken; the name, address and phone number of the credit bureau from which the report was obtained; notice of the applicant's right to obtain a free copy of the credit report within 60 days and notice of the applicant's right to dispute the accuracy of the credit report.

Anderson (2007, p.202) points out that in *Safeco Insurance Company v. Burr* (2007) the Supreme Court ruled that to willfully violate the FCRA a company must commit an illegal act knowingly and recklessly. To be reckless, the Court held, the company's actions must be "objectively unreasonable." This ruling affects observing the FCRA in employment investigations.

A final consideration is whether to outsource the task of conducting background checks, as is often done. Gilbert (2005, p.75) cautions employers who use background screening providers to first thoroughly screen the providers themselves.

Protecting Executives and VIPs

Most law enforcement agencies do not have the personnel to provide protection for high-profile individuals, most of whom travel extensively and do not perceive the risks they face. And the risks are many, including criminals, disgruntled employees, politically motivated groups or individuals and even well-meaning groups such as environmentalists. Security problems involved in providing personal security include the principal's mobility and lack of concern, and the potential for threats, assaults, blackmail, harassment or kidnapping.

Specialized strategies are required to reduce the security threats inherent in personal protection. *Most* depend on the skills of the security professional rather than on equipment. Security problems associated with providing personal protection may be reduced by heightening the principal's awareness of the risk, watching for preincident indicators (any signals that an attack on an individual is being planned or is about to occur) and avoiding routines.

It is also important to check out choke points—locations a person must go through to get to his or her intended destination. Such a choke point is often the location of an ambush. In most instances, someone should go through such choke points in advance of the person being guarded, looking for any signs of an ambush.

Another key component to comprehensive personal protection is advance work—physically preceding the person being protected to check out the situation in its entirety, including means of transportation, lodging, restaurants, meetings and offices to be visited. Before the advance work is undertaken, preadvance work should be completed. One important step is to review the records of previous trips to determine what went well and what went poorly. Newspapers from the area to be visited should be read to determine any potential violence likely to be encountered. Also important for those who provide personal protection is training in how to respond to illnesses, accidents or injuries.

The three essential components of any executive protection (EP) program are threat assessments, advance procedures and protective operations (Gips, 2007, p.54). Risk assessment includes getting all details about a facility where a principal will stay and keep an ongoing file of threats in areas to which the principal travels. Advance planning involves visiting everywhere the principal will go and coordinating all necessary security arrangements for a principal, before, during and after his or her arrival. The EP professional also checks out hotels, restaurants, transportation systems, routes, hospitals and any other site the principal may visit. During protective operations the EP professional is in the field with the principal. These operations include covert countersurveillance, facilitation, defense, rescue and use of cars.

Controlling Crowds at Demonstrations and Special Events

Controlling crowds at protests and demonstrations is usually a joint responsibility of private security and law enforcement: "At the very least, public demonstrations may cause street closures that disrupt business operations. At worst, public demonstrations can deteriorate into civil unrest or violence during which law enforcement agencies will prioritize protection of the citizenry over the protection of personal and commercial property. Companies will fare best if they plan ahead" (Walsh et al., 2004, p.105). It is recommended that companies build rapport and trust with local law enforcement before any events or protests are anticipated (p.106). Companies should then plan to work together, with law enforcement controlling the streets and private security protecting company personnel and assets.

Successful security operation begins with a plan, including event security. Verden (2007, p.6) suggests using subcommittees and a steering committee for the planning, and he stresses having the proper representatives from law enforcement, public safety, fire, medical and the private sector, including the host organization on these subcommittees. O'Connor (2004, p.93) stresses: "Before every special event, security teams should look at the specific venue, including the physical security measures in place and other elements. . . . Even without a terrorist incident that threatens lives, the cost of inadequate event security can be staggering. For example, at many venues—such as high-tech shows or events in which a new line of technology is being introduced—there are hundreds of thousands of dollars worth of equipment placed on site." In addition: "Whether it is a sporting event or a rock concert, medical emergencies can spoil the fun and create liability unless management plans ahead" (Jolly and Martinez, 2004, p.94). Again, handling such emergencies often requires cooperation between not only private security and law enforcement but EMS personnel as well.

Events such as the Kentucky Derby and the Super Bowl require months, even years of advanced planning for security. Elliott (2006, p.82) describes the "unbridled" security at the Kentucky Derby:

> The Kentucky Derby is a wide-open affair where heavy drinking, smoking and betting by more than 150,000 spectators makes for a security challenge much bigger than what can be handled by the Churchill Downs staff. On Derby day, the track's in-house security team is bolstered by more than 1,000 officials representing some 35 federal agencies, including the FBI, CIA, U.S. Postal Service, Bureau of Alcohol, Tobacco and Firearms and Explosives and others.
>
> Among the more prevalent problems facing the security team are unruly patrons who drink to excess; pickpockets; purse-snatchers; ticket scalpers; and those smuggling booze and weapons into Churchill Downs. To cut down on the problems, bag checks are performed and metal detectors are in use at the gates, spotters are placed in various key locations on the grounds, and a ubiquitous closed-circuit television network is monitored by the in-house security staff. For the rowdiest patrons who get arrested, there is an on-site jail where they are kept until a paddy wagon takes them to the downtown Louisville prison. Cameras are trained on the money-counting rooms to watch over the enormous amounts of cash being handled.
>
> Fire is greatly feared; veteran fire department officials constantly make the rounds during the races, particularly in the barn area, where hay, straw and wooden buildings present the matchsticks for a blaze.[5]

Other Candidates for Privatization

The range of police-related roles that are handled in the private sector is expanding rapidly and includes such areas as surveillance, investigation, crowd control, prison escorts, court security, guarding and patrolling, proactive crime prevention, risk management and insurance assessment, weapons training, crime scene examination and forensic evidence gathering (Sarre, 2005). Other services that are other likely candidates for privatization include public building security, parking enforcement, patrolling of public parks, animal control, funeral escorts, public housing development patrol, handling applicant screening and conducting civilian fingerprinting. According to Youngs: "Just as corporations outsource many services to enable them to concentrate on core competencies, the use of private firms by law enforcement agencies frees them to concentrate

[5]SOURCE: Elliott, Robert, "The Derby's Unbridled Security" in *Security Management*, October 2006, p.82.

© AP/ Wide World Photos

As government budgets tighten, many states are turning to private facilities to secure their correctional population. At the Guadalupe County Correctional Facility near Santa Rosa, New Mexico, a private security guard handcuffs a prisoner before removing the inmate from his cell.

their efforts on duties that only trained police officers can, and should, do. Over the past several decades, privatization in law enforcement has grown to such an extent that virtually every function, including security, jails, prisons, and court-related services, is being contracted out somewhere in the United States."

Privatization of Public Justice

The private policing upsurge affects not just the public police, but the other two components of the criminal justice system: courts and corrections, as well as the juvenile justice system. At least 40 states now employ private security to maintain order in their courtrooms (Youngs). Private security officers may also transport defendants to and from the courtroom.

 The trend toward privatization of public justice can be seen in the areas of courts, corrections and juvenile justice.

Transporting Prisoners

Thousands of prisoners being held in jails throughout the country need to be transported to court each day. Counties that use private security personnel to transport these prisoners can realize substantial savings. Youngs provides the following example: "The Fresno, California, Sheriff's Department reaped savings by outsourcing its transport of prisoners. The total cost for the department to transport a prisoner from San Diego to Fresno was $284 using a private firm. The same trip using sheriff's department personnel and equipment would cost three times as much."

Novak and Turner (2005, p.14) note that many counties have numerous separate jurisdictions each operating their own criminal justice system, a situation that creates tremendous duplication of services. Such redundancy typically comes with a high price tag. King County, Washington, for example has 42 separate jurisdictions costing about $670 million each year. Figure 3.2 illustrates a violator's progress through the criminal justice system in King County.

Private Corrections

The privatization of corrections is controversial. Critics fear the quality of inmate care will be compromised as private facilities focus on generating a profit. Opponents also raise concerns about the degree of control the government will have over the nation's criminals if they are housed in privately operated facilities. Nonetheless, the privatization of corrections has been slowly gaining ground since the 1980s.

Segal (2003) notes three-fifths of all U.S. states host private prisons, most of them contracting with private companies to house prisoners. At year-end 2005 privately operated facilities held over 107,447 or 7.0 percent of prisoners, compared to 93,912 prisoners in 2002. Of the 107,447 prisoners, 27.046 (14.4 percent) were federal prisoners, and 73,860 (6.0 percent) were state prisoners (*Sourcebook of Criminal Justice Statistics*, 2005, p.97). Furthermore, privately operated facilities held almost one-third of all juveniles in residential placement, representing more than 30,000 juvenile offenders. Numerous companies are capitalizing on the expanding niche for private corrections, some of the largest companies being the Corrections Corporation of America, Wackenhut Corrections Corporation, Management and Training Corporation and Cornell Corrections, Inc. (*Sourcebook*, p.96).

 The privatization of corrections has been increasing since the 1980s.

Factors to consider in the private sector concern staffing levels and the resultant impact on staff security. Private prisons, concerned about the bottom line, often reduce expenditures by having smaller staffs or paying employees less.

Private Sector Involvement in Juvenile Justice

Some juvenile justice agencies, finding their jurisdictions lack adequate services and expertise, are also contracting with private sector vendors to meet their clients' needs. Scores of residential treatment facilities for youths exist across the country. Common programming options found in these facilities include mental health and psychiatric treatment; substance abuse treatment; sexual offender treatment; therapy for disruptive, aggressive or impulsive behaviors; anger management classes; cognitive-behavioral restructuring therapy; social and life skills development; educational classes to keep kids moving toward completing their high school diploma or general equivalency diploma (GED); vocational training; athletic and intramural programs and extracurricular activities.

The Debate over Privatization of Correctional Facilities

Four key issues surround the debate over the privatization of correctional facilities (Austin and Coventry, 2001, pp.13–20)

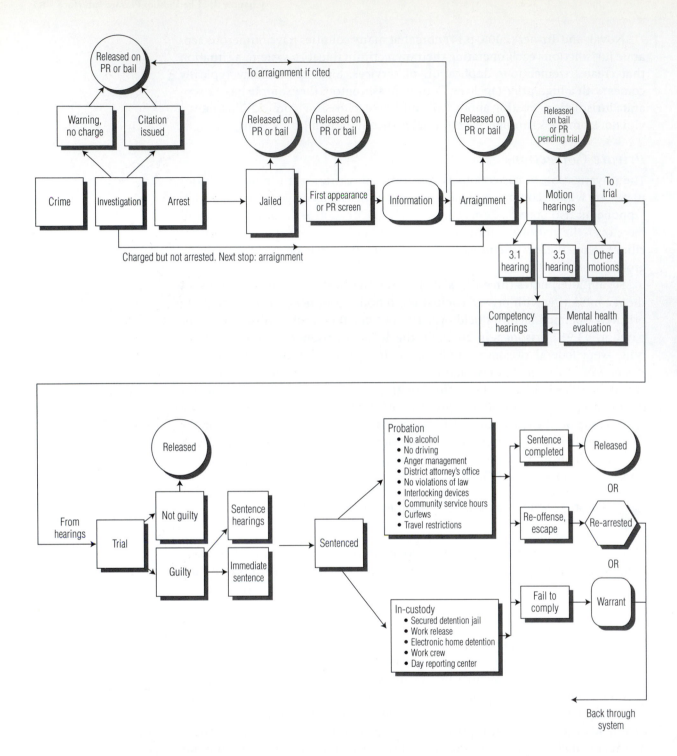

PR: Personal recognizance

Figure 3.2 A Violator's Progress through the Criminal Justice System in King County

SOURCE: Reprinted from Julia D. Novak and Denise Turner, "Finding Resources: Addressing Prisoner Transport Costs in King County, Washington" in *The Police Chief*, January 2005, p.15. Copyright held by the International Association of Chiefs of Police, 515 North Washington Street, Alexandria, VA 22314 USA. Further reproduction without express written permission from IACP is strictly prohibited.

1. *Are they legal?* Yes, the courts have decided that government may privatize basic services such as education, law enforcement and imprisonment, with private prisons being assigned the same management responsibilities as those undertaken by state and local government. However, the government cannot wholly delegate its functions and duties to a private provider. Several recent court rulings have held the government responsible for incidents in private facilities where actions taken by a private provider have either violated an inmate's constitutional rights or put the prison staff, inmates or surrounding community at risk.
2. *Are they more effective?* The research to date is mixed and inconclusive on this issue.
3. *Are they cheaper to operate?* While advocates of privatization like to contend that private contactors, accountable to their investors and, therefore, motivated by the bottom line and the obligations to return a profit, are better able to run a cost-effective operation, the published literature to date reveals little, if any, evidence to support this claim.
4. *Do they produce a better prisoner?* In other words, do private facilities have greater success in turning out offenders who are less likely to recidivate? Again, no studies thus far have documented whether privately incarcerated offenders are more or less likely to reoffend than are their publicly held counterparts.[6]

Bales et al. (2005) studied recidivism of public and private state prison inmates in Florida and found that private prisons were no more effective than public prisons in reducing recidivism. Their sample included a large cohort of prisoners released from 1995 to 2001, including adult males and females, and youthful offenders: "While limited only to Florida, the study provides no empirical justification for the claim that private prisons outperform public facilities in terms of recidivism."

Thus little data exists to form an evidence-based conclusion regarding the superiority of either private or public prisons over the other. Private prisons have no unique management system, innovative architectural design or high-tech innovations. The same people who were wardens in public prisons are now governing the private systems. Although rehabilitative programs exist at varying levels, access to such programs and the rate of participation is relatively low in both types of facilities. Depending upon how they are financed and managed, both private and public prisons can be either well administered or mismanaged.

Critics of Privatization

Private firms with outright police powers have been proliferating, and despite their lack of police authority, many private officers carry weapons, some dress like SWAT team members and some routinely make citizen's arrests. However, civil libertarians, academics, tenants' rights organizations and even a trade group representing the nation's large security firms say some private security officers are inadequately trained or regulated. Ten states do not regulate private

[6]SOURCE: James Austin and Garry Coventry, *Emerging Issues on Privatized Prisons* (Monograph). Washington, DC: U.S. Department of Justice, Bureau of Justice Assistance and National Council on Crime and Delinquency, February 2001. (NCJ181249).

officers at all. Others warn that the constitutional safeguards that cover police questioning and searches do not apply in the private sector.

Schneier (2007, p.A11) contends that abuses of power and brutality are more likely among private security officers than among law enforcement. Schneier, noting that private security officers outnumber "real" police by more than 5 to 1, also observes that private officers are increasingly acting like public ones: "They wear uniforms, carry weapons and drive lighted patrol cars on private properties . . . and public areas like bus stations and national monuments." He argues that the trend to privatization should greatly concern citizens and that law enforcement should be a government function: "Privatizing it puts us all at risk." He notes the most obvious problem is that of mission or agenda. Public police forces are charged with protecting the citizens of their jurisdiction. In contrast, private police officers do not work for the citizens; they work for corporations, focused on the priorities of their employers. They are less concerned with due process, public safety or civil rights. He concludes: "Privately funded police [officers] are not protecting us or working in our best interests."

Despite such criticism, the trend toward privatization is likely to continue, as is the recognition that partnerships between public and private officers is key to safer communities.

Considerations in Using Public-Private Partnerships

Public-private security partnerships exist throughout the country. The following should be considered when forming public-private partnerships (Youngs):

- Services with the potential to be priced should be considered as candidates for private provision or user charges.
- To save money and help police officers become more available to perform the tasks that only they can conduct, agencies should privatize tasks that do not require the full range of skills of police officers.
- Private companies should provide such services as response to burglary alarms, and people with alarm systems should pay for the services that they demand.
- Private security can prove effective in a distinct geographic area; therefore, owners of apartment complexes should consider private policing. Further, agencies should encourage competition between apartment complexes to provide safer environments. Requiring publication of apartments' safety experience helps renters make informed decisions.
- Any relatively low-skill or specialized high-skill services are candidates for transfer to private security.
- State legislatures should be asked to consider whether the current legal status and regulations pertaining to private security are appropriate in view of the expanded role expected from them, such as emergency vehicle status and expanded powers of arrest.[7]

Simeone (2006, p.75) describes the power of Public-Private Partnerships (P3) Networks that allow law enforcement agencies to leverage the vast re-

[7]SOURCE: Al Youngs, "The Future of Public/Private Partnerships" in *FBI Law Enforcement Bulletin*, January 2004.

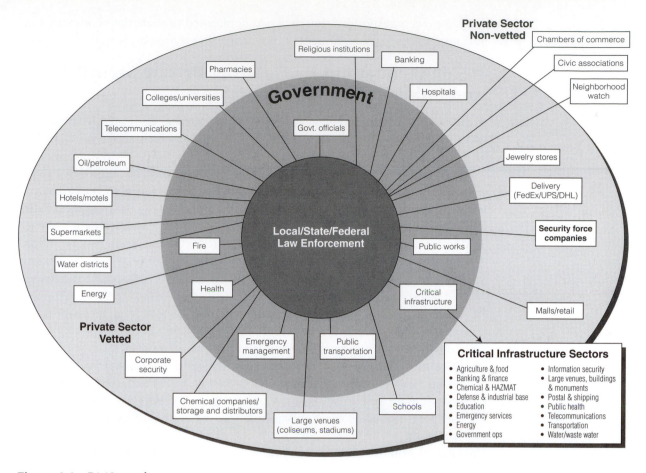

Figure 3.3   P3 Network

SOURCE: Reprinted from Matthew J. Simeone, Jr., "The Power of Public-Private Partnerships P3 Networks in Policing" in *The Police Chief*, May 2006, p.76. Copyright held by the International Association of Chiefs of Police, 515 North Washington Street, Alexandria, VA 22314 USA. Further reproduction without express written permission from IACP is strictly prohibited.

sources of the private security industry, as well as community-based civic organizations to significantly enhance public safety and homeland security: "A P3 network, if integrated into the operations of a police department, can assist not only in preventing crime and apprehending criminals but also in bridging the gap between all that needs to be done and that can be accomplished with limited policing resources." He notes that today's e-mail technology can disseminate important, timely information to keep the private sector informed and connected to the local police department. Among the most important members of the network are private security directors responsible for protecting key assets and critical infrastructures. These individuals should be **vetted**, that is, approved to share information with assuredness that sensitive need-to-know information will be handled appropriately. Figure 3.3 shows all the participants to consider including in a P3 network and whether they should be vetted.

Simeone (p.77) emphasizes replacing the need-to-know culture of information isolation with a need-to-share culture of integration. In fact, a *Security Director News* survey found a "resounding" 97 percent of respondents said they thought the government and the private sector needed to improve cooperation, and 82 percent responded that they had or planned to share their company's information with the government to move the process forward (Gural, 2006, p.8).

Recommendations on Building Private Security and Public Policing Partnerships

Public sector law enforcement appears eager to partner with private security in making America safer. The International Association of Chiefs of Police (IACP), in partnership with the U.S. Department of Justice's Office of Community Oriented Policing Services (COPS), announced the release of "Building Private Security/Public Policing Partnerships to Prevent and Respond to Terrorism and Public Disorder," a report that outlines a national strategy to strengthen existing partnerships between private security and public law enforcement agencies and to assist in the creation of new ones. The report is the product of a national policy summit on the issue that IACP held earlier in the year. Five recommendations are made that are considered crucial to successful partnerships between the private sector and public policing:

1. Leaders of major police organizations and private security organizations should make a formal commitment to cooperation.
2. Research and training on relevant legislation, private security, and law enforcement and private security cooperation should be funded.
3. An advisory council to oversee the day-to-day implementation issues of law enforcement and private security partnerships needs to be created.
4. Key practitioners to move this agenda forward in the future should be convened.
5. Local partnerships should set priorities and address key problems.

Carl Peed, director of the COPS office, declared: "Embracing these partnerships will benefit both parties immensely" ("IACP Issues Policy Recommendations. . .," 2004, pp.16–17).

Many segments of the population, including police chiefs, business managers and government officials, believe that services provided by the private sector are more efficient, more effective and less costly. Because of this, privatization of services and partnerships are likely to continue to expand.

Benefits of Public-Private Cooperation

Law enforcement agencies are under tremendous pressure today to conduct their traditional crime prevention and response activities, plus a large quantum of homeland security work, in a time of limited government funding and budgeting cutbacks. Private security organizations are under similar pressure, performing their traditional activities to protect people, property and information, as well as contributing to the nationwide effort to protect the homeland from external threats, all while minding the profitability of the businesses they serve (*Private Security/Public Policing*,8 pp.14–15). It is in the interests of both parties to work together. For example, law enforcement agencies can:

---

[8]SOURCE: *Private Security/Public Policing* (Washington, DC: Office of Community Oriented Policing Services, 2004) pp.14–15.

- Prepare private security to assist in emergencies (in many cases, security officers are the first responders).
- Coordinate efforts to safeguard the nation's critical infrastructure, the vast majority of which is owned by the private sector or protected by private security.
- Gain additional personnel resources and expertise.
- Obtain free training and services.
- Make use of private sector knowledge specialization (e.g., in cyber crime) and advanced technology.
- Obtain evidence in criminal investigations (e.g., through CCTV recordings of a crime scene).
- Gather better knowledge of incidents (through reporting by security staff).
- Reduce the number of calls for service.

Both large and small law enforcement agencies can benefit. In heavily populated jurisdictions, the law enforcement workload is likely to be too great to be carried solely by the police department. In less populous jurisdictions, security personnel may greatly outnumber law enforcement personnel, who would benefit from tapping security as a resource.

Private sector security also has much to gain from cooperation. This segment can:

- Coordinate its plans with the public sector, in advance, regarding evacuation, transportation, food and other emergency issues.
- Gain information from law enforcement regarding threats, crime trends and other matters.
- Develop relationships so that practitioners know whom to contact when they need help or want to report information.
- Build law enforcement's understanding of corporate needs (such as confidentiality).
- Boost law enforcement's respect for the security field.

Joint benefits include:

- Creative problem solving.
- Increased training opportunities.
- Information, data and intelligence sharing.
- "Force multiplier" opportunities.
- Access to the community through private sector communications technology.
- Reduced recovery time following disasters.

Partnerships in Action

Youngs provides the following example of a public-private partnership:

Lakewood, Colorado, offers an example of the benefits of outsourcing law enforcement tasks to private firms. Lakewood boasts a population of 145,000 within the metropolitan Denver area. Its progressive approach to public-private partnerships in law enforcement is demonstrated by its track record—the city has contracted with outside firms for police department assistance for nearly 10 years. As a result, the Lakewood Police Department considers the public-private partnership beneficial. It helps in terms of deployment, as well as economically. "Paying a private security officer an hourly rate to guard a prisoner or a crime scene frees up police officers. Police don't have to call in an officer on overtime or pull someone off patrol duty." . . .

The Lakewood Police Department contracts with a private security firm to guard prisoners hospitalized in facilities in the Denver metropolitan area and to provide assistance in protecting crime scenes. These private security officers are specially selected for crime-scene detail based on their background and experience, and they often attend Lakewood Police Department roll calls for training (similarly, members of the Lakewood Police Department attend the security roll calls). These private security firm officers know the rules of evidence, and, in fact, many are certified police officers in the state of Colorado. They provide 24-hour assistance and typically respond with officers within 4 hours of the department's request. In addition, for security purposes, background investigations have been completed on each of these officers.

In Lakewood, the cost of an off-duty police agent is $37 per hour, including vehicle. Many crime scenes take an average of 2 days to process. Because 24-hour protection is required, using private security at $29 per hour for this assignment, a savings of nearly 22 percent, makes economic sense. Furthermore, the partnership has strengthened the lines of communication and trust between police and private security personnel. "In this partnership, everyone's a winner. The police department is a winner in that we are providing essential services at a reduced cost. Through the private portion of it, it's good for business; it employs people; it's good for our economy."[9]

Siitari (2005–2006, pp.22–27) describes another public-private partnership, the Twin Cities Security Partnership (TCSP), a public-private partnership dedicated to enhancing security, safety and quality of life in the greater Twin Cities metropolitan area (Minneapolis, St. Paul and surrounding suburbs). Members include top-level community and government leaders; senior law enforcement leaders from local, state and federal agencies; and senior security executives from the state's largest companies and the private security industry.

The private sector security executives in the partnership are some of the best minds in the business, with many coming from law enforcement backgrounds: "With private security personnel in the Twin Cities now outnumbering police by a ratio of 15 to 1, chances are good that if a serious incident should occur—whether from natural causes or human initiative—they're going to be the first ones on the scene and we're going to need their support. Look no further than Hurricane Katrina for proof that the private sector is a critical partner in the face of a catastrophic event" (Siitari, p.23).

---

[9]SOURCE: Al Youngs, "The Future of Public/Private Partnerships" in *FBI Law Enforcement Bulletin*, January 2004.

SUMMARY

- Private security officers now outnumber public police officers 5 to 1.

- Private security officers and public law enforcement officers often move from one field to the other.

- Private security officers and police officers have many similarities. Both may wear uniforms and badges, are trained in compelling obedience and are apt to be sued. Both seek to prevent crime and to apprehend criminals, with private security focusing efforts more on prevention than apprehension.

- Private security officers differ from public officers in that private security officers operate in a profit-oriented enterprise serving specific private clients to prevent crime, to protect assets and reduce losses and to regulate noncriminal conduct not under the authority of law enforcement. They are given their authority by their private employers. Public police officers, in contrast, operate in a nonprofit, governmental enterprise serving the general public to combat crime and disorder, enforce laws and apprehend offenders. They have statutory authority.

- The amount of authority and the restrictions placed on both private and public officers also differ. For example, private security officers usually have no more powers than private citizens. As citizens, they have the power to arrest, to investigate, to carry weapons, to defend themselves and to defend their property or property entrusted to their care. They can deny access to unauthorized individuals into their employers' business or company, and they can enforce all rules and regula-

tions established by their employers. They can also search employees and question them without giving the Miranda warning in most states.

- Private security officers cannot invade another's privacy, electronically eavesdrop, trespass or, in some jurisdictions, wear a uniform or badge that closely resembles that of a public police officer.

- The roles of private and public officers are also complementary. They may work together or may hire or delegate authority to each other. Public police offer private security the power of interrogation, search, arrest and use of electronic surveillance. They may reduce or eliminate their legal liability, and they offer training, experience and backup. Private security officers offer the public police information, access to private places and extended surveillance and coverage. In addition, they are not bound by the exclusionary rule, so they can question without giving the Miranda warning and can search without a warrant.

- Some areas of cooperation are investigating internal theft and economic crimes, responding to burglar alarms, examining evidence from law enforcement in private crime labs, conducting background checks, protecting VIPs and executives, protecting crime scenes, transporting prisoners, moving hazardous materials and controlling crowds and traffic at public events.

- The trend toward privatization of public justice can also be found in the areas of courts, corrections and juvenile justice.

- The privatization of corrections has been increasing since the 1980s.

APPLICATIONS

1. The Metropolitan Transit Commission has decided to hire the Action Security Company to furnish private security officers on their buses because of frequent attacks on their drivers and the armed robbery of some of their riders. They need about 68 security officers to give the transit commission adequate policing. The officers of Action Security Company are reluctant to sign a contract unless it states that they will be sworn in as either city reserve police officers or as deputy sheriffs. What would be the advantages or disadvantages of the Action officers' request were it suitable to take this course of action? Would granting the company's request affect the officers' authority or power?

2. The Quality Private Security Services Company has assigned you to the parking lot of the Interstate

Manufacturing Company to assist in the flow of traffic and parking. At the end of the day, you are somewhat exhausted because of the sheer volume of paperwork and forms you were required to fill out, but also during the tour of duty you had to assist three employees by jump-starting their cars, you assisted in changing two flat tires, you helped another two people who had locked their keys in their cars and you gave another person a ride to the bus stop because his car had a leaky radiator.

You do not think all these services you performed were part of your instructions to keep the flow of traffic and parking orderly. You complain to your supervisor about all this responsibility. What do you think your supervisor would say to you about parking lot management?

DISCUSSION QUESTIONS

1. What are the advantages and disadvantages of private security officers not being restricted by the U.S. Constitution (e.g., not having to give the *Miranda* warning)?

2. How do private security officers assist public police officers in some aspects of handling unruly individuals? Discuss both the positive and the negative aspects of such handling.

3. Should the private police be trained by the public police in some aspects of handling unruly individuals? Discuss both the positive and negative aspects of such training.

4. Do you think police officers should be allowed to moonlight as private security providers? Why or why not?

5. Who do you think has more status, private or public officers? Why? Do you foresee a change in status for either group in the future?

REFERENCES

Anderson, Teresa. "U.S. Judicial Decisions." *Security Management*, September 2007, pp.200–205.

ASIS. www.asisonline.org

Austin, James and Coventry, Garry. *Emerging Issues on Privatized Prisons* (Monograph). Washington, DC: U.S. Department of Justice, Bureau of Justice Assistance and National Council on Crime and Delinquency, February 2001. (NCJ 181249)

Bales, William D.; Bedard, Laura E.; Quinn, Susan T.; Ensley, David T.; and Holley, Glen P. "Recidivism of Public and Private State Prison Inmates in Florida." *Criminology and Public Policy*, Vol. 4, No. 1, February 2005, pp.57–82.

Bayley, David H. "Forward." In *Private Policing* edited by Clifford D. Shearing and Philip C. Stenning. Beverly Hills, CA: Sage Publications, 1987, pp.6–8.

Betten, Micahel and Mervosh, Mitchell. "Should Police Respond to Alarms?" *Security Management*, June 2005, pp.68, 66.

Building a Powerful Partnership. Special Supplement from Bobit Business Media, 2007.

Cooke, Leonard G. and Hahn, Lisa R. "The Missing Link in Homeland Security." *The Police Chief*, November 2006, pp.16–21.

Cunningham, William C.; Strauchs, John J.; and Van Meter, Clifford W. *Private Security: Patterns and Trends*.
Washington, DC: National Institute of Justice Research in Brief, August 1991.

Egan, Timothy. "Police Forces, Their Ranks Thin, Officer Bonuses, Bounties and More." *The New York Times*, December 28, 2005.

Elliott, Robert. "The Derby's Unbridled Security." *Security Management*, October 2006, pp.72–82.

Gilbert, Craig. "Checking the Checkers." *Security Management*, May 2005, pp.75–80.

Giles, Frederick G. "What Trouble Lurks in Record Searches?" *Security Management*, May 2004, pp.44–51.

Gips, Michael A. "My Short Life as an EP Specialist." *Security Management*, March 2007, pp.52–60.

Gural, Andrea. "Private Sector Reports Cooperation." *Security Director News*, July 2006, p.8.

Henchey, James P. "Ready or Not, Here They Come: The Millennial Generation Enters the Workforce." *The Police Chief*, September 2005, pp.108–118.

Hickman, Matthew J. and Peterson, Joseph L. *50 Largest Crime Labs, 2002*. Washington, DC: Bureau of Justice Statistics Fact Sheet, September 2004. (NCJ 205988)

"IACP Issues Policy Recommendations on Building Private Security/Public Policing Partnerships." *NCJA Justice Bulletin*, November 2004, pp.16–17.

Jolly, B. Tilman and Martinez, Ricardo. "Heart-Stopping Action." *Security Management*, April 2004, pp.94–100.

Koper, Christopher S. *Hiring and Keeping Police Officers*. Washington, DC: National Institute of Justice, July 2004. (NCJ 202289)

Kriel, Lomi. "Cities Face Troubles in Hiring Cops." *My San Antonio*, June 28, 2006.

Martin, Stan. "What's Best for Alarm Response Policies?" *Security Management*, March 2005, pp.62, 60.

Martindale, Mike. "Cutbacks Pinch State Crime Labs." *The Detroit News*, April 13, 2007.

Mitchell, Josh. "Police Forces Get Creative to Attract Scarce Recruits." *Maryland News*, January 16, 2007.

Nadell, Barry J. "The Cut of His Jib Doesn't Jibe." *Security Management*, September 2004, pp.108–116.

Novak, Julia and Turner, Denise. "Finding Resources: Addressing Prisoner Transport Costs in King County, Washington." *The Police Chief*, January 2005, pp.14–18.

O'Connor, T. J. "Before the Show Begins." *Security Management*, November 2004, pp.93–98.

Private Security/Public Policing. Washington, DC: Office of Community Oriented Policing Services, 2004.

"Public or Private?" *Charlotte Observer*, April 17, 2006.

Sarre, R. "Researching Private Policing: Challenges and Agendas for Researchers." *Security Journal*, Vol. 18, No. 3, 2005, pp.57–70.

Schneier, Bruce. "Privatizing the Police Puts Us at Greater Risk." (Minneapolis/St.Paul) *Star Tribune*, February 27, 2007, p.A11.

Segal, Geoffrey F. "Private Prisons Save Money, Boost Productivity, Study Finds." *The Heartland Institute*, November 1, 2003. Online: http://www.heartland .org

Shearing, Clifford D. and Stenning, Philip C. "Reframing Policing." In *Private Policing* edited by Clifford

D. Shearing and Philip C. Stenning. Beverly Hills, CA: Sage Publications, 1987, pp.9–18.

Siitari, Mike. "Strength in Unity: Police Partner with Private Industry to Build a Safer Community." *Minnesota Police Chief*, Winter 2005–2006, pp.21–28.

Simeone, Matthew J., Jr. "The Power of Public-Private Partnerships P3 Networks in Policing." *The Police Chief*, May 2006, pp.75–79.

Sourcebook of Criminal Justice Statistics 2005. Online: http://www.albany.edu/sourcebook

Stockton, Dale. "Our Police Staffing Crisis." *Law Officer Magazine*, April 2007, pp.10–12.

Turley, Kristin. "Seven Reasons You Should Be Conducting Background Checks." *Security Director News*, September 2006, p.7.

Verden, G. Michael. "The Ins and Outs of Event Security." *Security Director News*, May 2007, p.6.

Walsh, David; Rice, Robert; Syms, Deirdre; and Davis, Joe. "Preparing for Protests." *Security Management*, October 2004, pp.105–112.

Working Hand in Hand. Security Sales & Integration and *Police*, no date.

Worsinger, Laura P. "Tips for Background Checks." *Security Management*, October 2006, pp.85–91.

Woska, William J. "Police Officer Recruitment: A Public Sector Crisis." *The Police Chief*, October 2006, pp.52–59.

Youngs, Al. "The Future of Public/Private Partnerships." *FBI Law Enforcement Bulletin*, January 2004.

CASES CITED

Bowman v. State, 468 N.E.2d 1064, 1068 (Ind. Ct. App. 1984).

City of Hialeah v. Weber, 491 So. 2d 1204 (Fla. App. 1986).

Mount Sinai Hospital v. City of Miami Beach, 523 So. 2d 722 (Fla. App. 1988).

National Labor Relations Board v. St Vincent's Hosp., 729 F.2d 730 (1984).

NLRB v. J. Weingarten, Inc., 420 U.S. 251 (1975).

Safeco Insurance Company v. Burr, No. 0684 (U.S. Supreme Court, 2007).

United States v. Dockery, 736 F.2d 1232 (1984).

CHAPTER 4

Legal and Ethical Considerations

© AP/Wide World Photos

In our post-9/11 society, the American public has grown more accustomed to being searched in public venues. Here a security guard scans a spectator entering PNC Park for the Futures Game, in Pittsburgh. Preventive measures such as this help private security avoid liability issues should incidents arise.

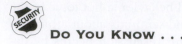

Do You Know . . .

- How laws may be classified?
- How a crime differs from a tort?
- How tort law is categorized?
- What the elements of negligent liability are?
- What a nondelegable duty is and how it compares to vicarious liability?
- For what actions security officers are most frequently sued?
- What Section 1983 of the U.S. Code, Title 43, the Civil Rights Act, establishes and how it might affect private security?
- How civil liability can be reduced?
- What three personal ethics-check questions are?
- What three organizational ethics-check questions are?
- What purpose is served by a code of ethics for security professionals?
- How an ethical organization can be promoted?
- How ethics can relate to problem solving?

Can You Define?

assault	intentional tort	plaintiff	strict liability
battery	interrogatories	punitive damages	substantive damages
crime	libel	respondent superior	tort
defamation	moral	restitution	
ethics	negligence	Section 1983	
excessive force	nondelegable duty	slander	

Introduction

As with many other professions, private security personnel must work within certain legal and ethical guidelines. They must know how to effectively protect themselves against civil lawsuits, as civil liability has become a matter of increasing concern in the private security profession. Reasons for the dramatic increase in lawsuits involving private security include the significant rise in the number of people working in the security field and the variety of jobs performed.

This chapter begins with a discussion of the types of law and liability governing all citizens, including private security personnel. Next categories of civil offenses are presented, followed by the elements of negligent liability and the most commonly encountered lawsuits. This is followed by a discussion of how liability might be reduced, including tightening hiring practices, providing effective training, establishing clear procedures for the use of force and the use of firearms, using clear contracts and carrying adequate insurance. The discussion of legal considerations concludes with some common defenses against charges and a brief discussion of how to survive a lawsuit.

The second part of the chapter looks at ethical behavior, a hot topic in the twenty-first century with numerous workshops and seminars about ethics being conducted throughout corporate America. This discussion begins by defining ethics and what it involves. This is followed by a discussion of how to develop one's own personal ethics and then how to promote ethical behavior throughout an organization. The chapter concludes with a look at ethical (and unethical) practices.

Law and Liability in the United States

English colonists brought with them the common law, which remains the basis of law in the United States. While common law was unwritten, it gradually evolved in this country into written law, with distinctions made between various types of offenses, the parties involved and the source of origination.

 Laws may be classified by:

- Type—written or common law
- Source—constitution, statutory, case
- Parties involved—public, private
- Offense—criminal, civil

Law can be classified by where it originates: constitutional law from the numerous state constitutions and the federal Constitution; statutory law, referring to laws passed by federal or state legislatures; and case law, originating in specific cases that serve as *precedents*, that is, following what was decided in previous cases. The most common distinction, however, is between criminal and civil law.

Criminal versus Civil Law

Criminal law deals with offenses against the public, called *crimes*, and fixes punishments for them. The case is filed by the government, who then becomes the prosecutor in court, and the punishment for those found guilty may include a fine paid to the government, imprisonment or, in extreme cases, execution.

Civil law, in contrast, deals with offenses against individuals, called *torts*, and seeks **restitution** for the victim, that is, payment of some sort. The private party who files the lawsuit becomes the **plaintiff** in court. Defendants who lose in civil court do not face imprisonment or execution but may be ordered to pay substantial monetary damages.

 A criminal offense or **crime** is a wrong against the public that the state prosecutes in seeking punishment. Criminal intent is required. A civil offense or **tort** is a private wrong where an individual sues seeking restitution. Intent is not necessary.

An offense may be both a crime and a tort. For example, if one person strikes another person, the assailant can be charged with the crime of assault and also sued for the tort of assault.

Security officers may be called on to investigate crimes, as discussed in Chapter 10. And while security personnel may also be charged with crimes if they break the law, the focus of this chapter is on the *civil* liability of security officers, their agencies and their employers. A civil suit may be brought against any private security personnel who commits an unlawful action against another person. Often, the officer's employer is sued as well as the officer.

Categories of Civil Offenses

Civil law regulates private legal affairs and deals with a broad array of issues concerning relationships among individuals and organizations, including administrative law, commercial law, contract law, probate law, family law and tort law. This discussion of legal liability as it concerns private security focuses on tort law, as this is where the overwhelming majority of cases occur.

 Tort law is divided into three categories: strict liability, intentional torts and negligence.

Strict liability refers to instances when a person is held liable to an injured party even though the person may not have knowingly done anything wrong. Strict liability, also called liability without fault, usually involves ultrahazardous activities such as using explosives or keeping wild animals as pets. Although this area is seldom a problem for private security, it may become more so as high-tech equipment is used to compel compliance with orders. Any injuries from such high-tech equipment might fall into this category.

An **intentional tort**, as the name implies, is an illegal act committed on purpose. Recall that an illegal act might be both a criminal and a civil offense. Intentional civil wrongs (torts) include assault, battery, defamation of character (both libel and slander), false imprisonment, false arrest, fraud, illegal electronic surveillance, intentional infliction of emotional distress (IIED), invasion of privacy, malicious prosecution and trespass.

Negligence, the third category of tort law, is the most frequently brought civil charge. Basically, negligence is a failure to use due care to prevent foreseeable injury that results in damages. Civil negligence torts include negligence in hiring and selection, training, supervising and retaining; negligence in operating a motor vehicle; failure to protect and use of force.

Elements of Negligent Liability

Although specific statutes regarding negligent liability may vary from state to state, five basic elements are well established.

 The elements of negligent liability include:

- Existence of some duty owed.
- Foreseeable likelihood of the incident occurring.
- Failure to meet a reasonable standard of care.
- Proximate results—the injury resulted from the failure to protect.
- Damages.

Duty to Protect or Duty Owed

Employers have a "duty to protect" their employees and the public. If an employer hires an employee who injures others, the employer and the company may be sued for negligent retention. Solensky (2007, p.80) notes: "The liability of a security company must be established by showing that personnel failed to exercise reasonable care." **Respondent superior** is a concept that implies that premises owners cannot delegate their responsibility. Simply because an employer hires a security officer does not relieve the employer of responsibility.

Nondelegable Duty versus Vicarious Liability   Stua (2005) explains: "Nondelegable duties are duties in which the performance of an activity requires the permission of local, state, or other governmental authority, as by license or franchise. Implied within that permission is the requirement that the activity will be performed with due regard to the protection of the public." For example, a restaurant has a direct duty to sell safe food; a childcare facility has a direct duty to provide a safe environment for children; a public transit bus service has a direct duty to keep its vehicles properly maintained and in safe working order. Closely related to nondelegable duty is the concept of vicarious liability.

Vicarious liability is the legal responsibility for the acts of another person based on some relationship with that person, for example, the liability of an employer for the acts of an employee. Using the authority of vicarious liability, it has become common for individuals to sue not only individual security officers, but their supervisors and the institution for which they work.

 A **nondelegable duty** is one for which authority can be given to another person, but responsibility cannot. Civil liability remains with the person who has the legal duty to act. In contrast, vicarious liability is the responsibility of one person for the acts of another.

Foreseeable Danger

Foreseeable danger refers to knowing a problem is likely to occur. For example, if a number of attacks have taken place in a certain parking lot, it is foreseeable that more attacks might occur there. Steps must be taken to reduce the likelihood, or the owner and security officers responsible for the area may be sued if another incident occurs. In some cases a plaintiff's attorney has won a suit by citing crime statistics about the area in question.

Reasonable Standard of Care and Proximate Result

Reasonable care is that amount of caution a sensible person would use in similar circumstances. This has also been called standard of care. Some say it could be called using simple common sense. In some industries, standards have been established to provide guidance as to what would constitute reasonable care.

Proximate result means the injury must have been the result of the negligence or failure in the duty to protect.

Damages

The person suing (plaintiff) must also prove actual damages suffered, whether physical, emotional or financial, or that he or she incurred medical expenses. It is this area that determines the amount of any settlement made. Damages are of two types: substantive and punitive. **Substantive damages** relate to actual damages a judge or jury feels the plaintiff is entitled to, such as medical expenses incurred as a direct result of the injury. **Punitive damages**, on the other hand, are awards made to punish a defendant deemed to have behaved in such an abhorrent manner that an example must be made to keep others from acting in a similar way. These awards are often astronomical.

For instance, in *Romanski v. Detroit Entertainment* (2005) Stella Romanski and two friends visited the MotorCity Casino in Detroit. Romanski, age 72, played the slot machines and then took a walk around the casino floor. She saw a five-cent token in a slot machine. Seeing no one playing the machine, she picked the token up and put it with her winnings. A male casino employee in uniform approached her and asked her to come to the office with him. She was told casino policy prohibited picking up abandoned tokens, a practice known as slot walking. However, the policy was not posted anywhere in the casino. Romanski was ejected from the casino and escorted to the valet parking area to wait in 90-degree weather for several hours before the bus arrived. She was not allowed to eat lunch, which she had already paid for, nor was she allowed to go to the restroom unescorted. Romanski sued Detroit Entertainment, which owns MotorCity casino, for false arrest and false imprisonment. She also claimed that one of the security officers was a police officer. Under state law security employees of casinos have the same arrest powers as the police. The jury found in favor of Romanski and awarded her $279 in compensatory damages and $875,000 in punitive damages. When Detroit Entertainment appealed the decision, the U.S. District Court for the Eastern District of Michigan upheld the verdict. Detroit Entertainment then appealed the decision to the U.S. Court of Appeals for the Sixth District. The appellate court upheld all aspects of the lower court's ruling except for the amount of punitive damages, which it reduced to $600,000. Nonetheless, the court condoned the large punitive award: "Defendants' conduct was particularly egregious, and a higher award to deter the casino from sanctioning such conduct in the future was appropriate" (Anderson, 2007, pp.72–73). Detroit Entertainment appealed that decision to the U.S. Supreme Court, which refused to hear the case, in effect validating the lower courts' decision.

Security managers and those they employ must be aware of those actions that are most likely to put them at risk of a civil lawsuit or criminal charges.

Common Civil Lawsuits Brought against Private Security

 The most common civil suits brought against private security are for assault, battery, defamation, false imprisonment, intentional infliction of emotional distress (IIED), invasion of privacy, malicious prosecution and negligence.

Assault and Battery

Assault is an intentional act causing reasonable apprehension of physical harm in the mind of another. An example is threatening someone, with or without a weapon, into obeying a demand. **Battery** is the nonconsensual, offensive touching of another person, either directly or indirectly. An example is angrily or rudely touching a person. Use of bodily force should be avoided whenever possible. At times, however, security officers may have to use force to defend themselves or others from serious bodily harm.

Defamation

Defamation is injuring a person's reputation, such as by falsely inferring, by either words or conduct, in front of a third disinterested party, that a person committed a crime. An example is to falsely accuse someone of shoplifting in front of friends or to falsely accuse an employee of pilferage in front of coworkers or visitors. **Libel** generally refers to written defamatory remarks, whereas **slander** typically refers to verbal statements.

False Imprisonment

False imprisonment is unreasonably restraining another person using physical or psychological means to deny that person freedom of movement. An example is requiring someone to remain in a room while the police are being called. If a person *is* detained, there must be reasonable grounds to believe that a crime was committed and that the person being detained actually committed it. *Mere suspicion is not enough.*

Intentional Infliction of Emotional Distress

Intentional infliction of emotional distress (IIED) refers to outrageous or grossly reckless conduct intended to and highly likely to cause a severe emotional reaction. An example is to threaten to have an employee fired because he or she is suspected of stealing.

Invasion of Privacy

Invasion of privacy refers to an unreasonable, unconsented intrusion into the personal affairs or property of a person. An example would be searching an employee's personal property outside of search guidelines established by the employer. In *Cramer v. Consolidated Freightways, Inc.* (2001), the court ruled that the trucking firm who installed audio and video surveillance equipment behind the mirrors in the men's restroom had violated state privacy laws, despite company claims that such measures were necessary to prevent and detect drug use among employees. In *Mark Jackson v. Rohm & Hass Co.* (2001), a Pennsylvania jury awarded a man $150,000 for invasion of privacy after he was interrogated by security at his workplace following a coworker's false accusation of rape.

An emerging area of privacy litigation involves computer use and Internet access. After being found guilty of using his workplace computer to receive child pornography, Brian Ziegler filed an invasion of privacy lawsuit against his employer. The U.S. District Court for the District of Montana held that Ziegler had no expectation of privacy in the files he accessed on the Internet, so those rights could not be violated by the government or his employer (Meklinsky and Bancroft, 2007, p.94). Ziegler appealed the decision, and the U.S. Court of Appeals for the Ninth Circuit ruled that Ziegler's expectations of privacy were not reasonable (*U.S. v. Ziegler*, 2006). The court noted that the company had an employee monitoring program and that employees were informed about it through training and a manual. Employees were specifically told that the computers were owned by the company and were not to be used for personal activities (Meklinsky and Bancroft, p.96). The court stated: "Employee monitoring is largely an assumed practice, and thus we think a disseminated computer use policy is entirely sufficient to defeat any [privacy] expectation that an employee might harbor."

Meklinsky and Bancroft note: "Many organizations have resorted to monitoring their employees' use of e-mail and Internet systems to prevent abuses and to protect themselves and their employees. However, as the *Ziegler* case illustrates, employers must be mindful of employee privacy rights as they implement monitoring programs if they are to steer clear of liability."

By nature of the work, security personnel walk a fine line regarding privacy issues. As Bernard (2004, p.20) explains: "A primary reason people tolerate monitoring is the assertion put forth by the Security Industry Association's President, Richard Chase, who . . . said the main point about surveillance technology is, 'It is designed to watch out for you . . . not to watch you.'"

An authority in CCTV training and design makes this observation about IP-based cameras: "Twenty years ago, you could go about your daily business, to work and back, shopping, and maybe out to a restaurant, and your image might be recorded by a camera once every two or three months. . . . Five years from now, it is projected that you will be recorded from 25 to 50 times per day. And we [security practitioners] are the ones who are doing it. . . . Cameras have their positions, but privacy is the greatest thing we have, and we are giving it up camera by camera by camera" (Bernard, p.24). Bernard (p.24) concludes: "When people allow us as security practitioners to establish the monitoring and recording of their activities and the accumulation of their personal data, they do so trusting that the information will be used solely as intended—to provide them with increased safety and security."

One of the most recent innovations to enter the technology-versus-privacy debate is the radio frequency identification (RFID) tag, which is slowly replacing the barcode as a means of inventorying and tracking assets (Piazza, 2006, p.63). Supporters of the tags argue that the devices help businesses save millions of dollars by making supply chains more efficient and by reducing theft of high-value items. Opponents raise the specter of businesses tracking consumers without their knowledge or consent in a way not possible with barcodes. Piazza (p.68) recommends educating the public about the tags, how they work, what they can and cannot do and how to proactively address privacy concerns. RFID tags are discussed in Chapter 7.

Malicious Prosecution

Malicious prosecution occurs when the person making the accusation does not believe the accused is guilty but makes the charges out of spite, hostility or ill will to obtain an advantage over the person or to force the payment of money. For example, in the case of *Eastman v. Time Saver Stores, Inc.* (1983), a clerk, Alice P. Eastman, brought a malicious prosecution action against her employer, Time Saver Stores, Inc., after she was arrested for theft. Eastman was employed on the 3:00 P.M. to 11:00 P.M. shift, and during this time there were repeated cash shortages. Eastman's supervisor and a member of the Time Saver security department helped another employee climb into an air-conditioning vent above the cash registers where he could observe Eastman. He saw Eastman put a handful of quarters, a $20 bill from the customer and a $20 bill from a special envelope into her pocket. Store employees closed the business and called the police.

In her suit against Time Saver, Eastman explained to the court that she was just holding the money temporarily and fully intended to put the funds in their proper place. The judge, however, ruled that Eastman's testimony regarding why she was in possession of company money at the time of her arrest was unconvincing and did not overcome the other circumstances which led Time Saver to have her arrested. The systematic cash shortages that always coincided with her shift, regardless of whoever else was working at the same time, combined with the testimony of store employees who had observed her acting suspiciously when she pocketed the money was enough for the judge to rule in favor of the defendant, Time Saver Stores, Inc. One alternative that might have saved the company the time and anxiety of a criminal trial would have been to seek civil recovery from the individual accused of theft.

Negligence

Negligence, as previously noted, occurs when a person has a duty to act reasonably but fails to do so and, as a result, someone is injured. An example is failing to correct a dangerous situation on the premises or failing to give assistance to an employee in distress. Negligence suits are common, as illustrated in the following cases. These early cases have been, and in many cases continue to be, significant to the private security profession by providing early indications and direction as to how the courts would perceive private security's expanding role and responsibilities as well as the general standards to which the profession would likely be held and judged. It is too early to know the significance of more recent cases in providing general direction for avoiding liability. More recent cases will be presented, however, throughout the remainder of this text.

- *Taylor v. Centennial Bowl, Inc.* (1966)—The plaintiff was attacked in a bowling alley's parking lot. Earlier in the evening, while she was in a cocktail lounge on the premises, a man had been bothering her, and she had asked the bouncer to keep him away from her. When the business closed for the evening, the bouncer warned her not to go out to her car because the man was in the parking lot. The plaintiff left anyway and was attacked by the man. The court held that the proprietor's knowledge of a threat of harm gave rise to a duty to take positive action to prevent the attack. A warning alone was not sufficient.

- *Kline v. 1500 Massachusetts Avenue Apartment Corp.* (1970)—The plaintiff was assaulted and robbed in the hallway outside her apartment. The premises had been the site of an increasing number of criminal attacks during the years of the plaintiff's residency, but despite this clear trend, the owner/landlord made no effort to maintain or continue the security devices that had been in place when the tenant moved in. The court found the landlord liable for the injuries suffered in the criminal attack.

- *Picco v. Ford's Diner, Inc.* (1971)—The plaintiff in this case presented no evidence of prior criminal acts on the premises. The plaintiff, a customer at the diner, was assaulted in an unlighted parking lot at the diner's rear. The court held that it is common knowledge that lighting an area during nighttime hours deters criminal activity. Therefore, the proprietor was found liable, even though no prior criminal acts had occurred on the premises.

■ *Atamian v. Supermarkets General Corp.* (1976)—Three men raped the plaintiff in a grocery store parking lot. Prior to the rape, five assaults had occurred on the premises, and the store had employed a security guard. However, the court reasoned that where a proprietor has knowledge of previous criminal attacks on its premises, a security guard might not be enough. The proprietor has the duty to ensure adequate lighting and other preventive measures to protect customers from criminal assaults. Trying to give content to the nebulous standard of "reasonable care" is difficult at best and often impossible.

■ *Florence Trentacost v. Brussel, Dr. Nathan T.* (1980)—A tenant was robbed and beaten in the unlocked hallway of her apartment. The court held that the landlord-tenant relationship carries with it an implied warranty that the premises will be safe, even without requiring proof of notice of dangerous neighborhood conditions.

■ *Meyers v. Ramada Inn of Columbus* (1984)—An Ohio court held that hotel owners *can* be held liable for any injuries a guest suffers as a result of a criminal assault. However, the court stated that the guest must first demonstrate that the defendant should have anticipated the assault.

■ *Pittard v. Four Seasons Motor Inn, Inc.* (1984)—A New Mexico court held that a hotel *can* be held liable if one of its employees assaults a guest, provided the injured party can demonstrate that the hotel had notice of similar past conduct by the employee in question.

■ *Kolosky v. Winn Dixie Stores, Inc.* (1985)—A Florida court awarded $80,000 to a woman who was knocked to the floor while at a supermarket and injured by an unruly customer. The court observed that a supermarket has an obligation to take all necessary steps to ensure the security and safety of its customers.

In addition to the types of situations illustrated in these precedents, security officers must be careful not to violate anyone's constitutional rights.

The Civil Rights Act—Section 1983

In 1871, following the Civil War, the United States passed U.S. Code, Title 42, Section 1983, the Civil Rights Act, which states:

> Every person who, under color of any statue, ordinance, regulation, custom or usage, of any State or Territory, subjects or causes to be subjected any citizens of the United States or other person within the jurisdiction thereof to the deprivation of any rights, privileges, or immunities secured by the constitution and laws, shall be liable to the party injured in an action at law, suit in equity, or other proper proceeding for redress.

 Section 1983 of the U.S. Code, Title 42, the Civil Rights Act, says that anyone acting under the authority of local or state law who violates another person's constitutional rights—even though they are upholding a law—can be sued.

Another area often involved in lawsuits is when security officers use force to fulfill their responsibilities.

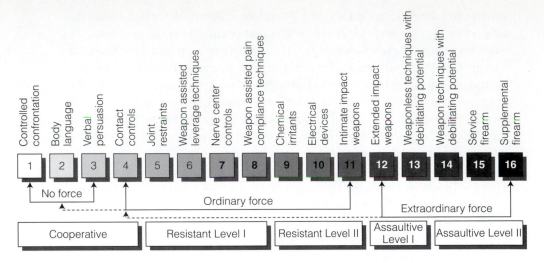

Figure 4.1   Use of Force Continuum

SOURCE: Adapted from G. Connor, "Use of Force Continuum: Phase II" in *Law and Order*, March 1991, p.30. Reprinted by permission.

The Use of Force

Security officers are sometimes required to use force to fulfill their responsibilities—for example, ejecting a disorderly intoxicated person from the premises or detaining a shoplifter and recovering the stolen merchandise. The amount of force allowable is restricted by the amount of resistance encountered and can be envisioned as existing along a continuum, with no force used with a cooperative person to extraordinary force, used with an assaultive person. Figure 4.1 illustrates a use of force continuum.

This use of force continuum helps answer the question as to when handcuffs or more extensive restraints should be used. If a person is not resisting being detained, handcuffs or other restraint devices might be deemed as unreasonable or excessive force by the court. **Excessive force** is force beyond that which is reasonably necessary to achieve a legitimate security objective. The challenge is in knowing where to draw the line: "Reasonable levels of force are guessed by merchants daily, second-guessed by the merchant's policymakers, and sometimes tested in civil lawsuits and criminal prosecutions on a case-by-case basis. Ultimately, however, the question of the reasonableness or excessiveness of the force used is one to be resolved by a jury after hearing all the facts and circumstances" (Aronsohn, 2003, p.26). Following are some tips for security practitioners faced with use of force issues in a variety of scenarios (Aronsohn, pp.26–27):

- Unreasonable Force on a Convicted Shoplifter: "Take into account the person's size, age and gender. Accommodate reasonable requests related to a suspect's medical or physical condition. Process the suspect quickly and according to store policy."
- Reasonable Force Used in Trespass Action: "Be professional and courteous even when the suspect doesn't cooperate."
- Liability to Injured Bystander: "Have at least backup security guard present—particularly when the detention [of a suspected shoplifter] is

made with customers nearby. It is also recommended that there is always one witness (of the same sex as the shoplifter) present. Where possible, don't confront suspects inside the store."

■ Unreasonable Force by Assertion of Authority: "Unreasonable use of force isn't always found in physical touching alone, but also in threats, insults or assertions of authority."

■ Submission to Repeated Threats of Force: "Excessive force can be found in submission to duress of pressure as well. Also, if a mistake in the allegation is later discovered, it is important to back off and apologize for the error."[1]

If a security officer uses force on a subject, the circumstances should be clearly described in a written report.

Liability Associated with Armed Security Personnel

As private officers are being called on to provide services in an increasingly violent society, the question arises as to whether these officers should be armed. Many contract security officer companies refuse to arm their officers because of the financial liability. Other companies limit the number of contracts they will accept requiring armed personnel.

Because of the liability issues surrounding the use of firearms, many agencies are turning to less lethal weapons to enhance security. Such alternatives include mace, CN and CS tear gas, oleoresin capsicum (OC) pepper spray, the Taser, projectile launchers and specialty impact munitions such as beanbags and flexible baton rounds, designed to deliver blunt trauma. Although no statistics are available regarding the use of alternative weapons by private security officers, manufacturers of these options report that thousands of security officers nationwide are using their products, including electronic stunning devices, chemicals and pepper spray. It must be acknowledged, however, that these "lesser force" options may still, in certain circumstances, be lethal.

Trends in Security Liability Lawsuits

In the aftermath of 9/11, the private security industry has gained increased exposure and importance. And in today's litigious society, security has also become a greater target for civil lawsuits. A study of premises security liability cases filed between 1992 and 2001 revealed some noteworthy trends, and security practitioners are encouraged to stay abreast of such developments impacting their field.

According to Anderson (2002, p.44): "Assault and battery cases have increased over the past eight years, with parking lots being the most likely venue for crimes leading to premises security liability lawsuits." Furthermore: "Of the cases studied, assault and battery made up 42 percent; rape/sexual assault, 26 percent; wrongful death, 15 percent; robbery, 9 percent; and false imprisonment, 4 percent. The remaining 4 percent of cases included categories such as burglary, arson, and motor vehicle theft" (Anderson, p.44).

---

[1]SOURCE: Audrey Aronsohn, "Forcing the Issue: When Is the Use of Force Excessive?" in *Loss Prevention and Security Journal*, March 2003, pp.26–27.

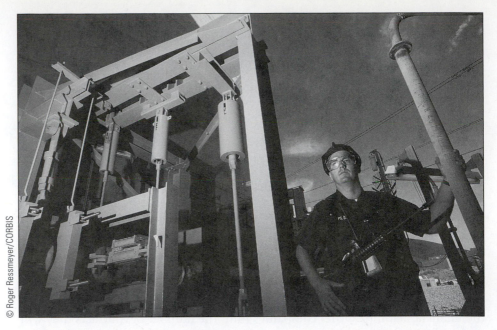

© Roger Ressmeyer/CORBIS

PG&E security officer Dan Phillips stands outside a reactor at the Diablo Canyon Nuclear Power Plant, located along the Pacific Ocean in Avila Beach, California. It has become increasingly common for security personnel at sites such as power plants to be armed with high capacity-issue weapons like the one carried by Phillips, which provide substantial and versatile firepower. But because of liability issues surrounding the use of firearms, many agencies are turning to less lethal weapons to enhance security.

Regarding the specific types of crimes and the categories of premises on which they occurred, the study found that bars topped the list regarding cases involving assault and battery, followed by apartment buildings and condos, restaurants, retail stores and security companies. Robbery cases also involved a diverse range of businesses, but the top five categories of litigants were hotels, retail stores, shopping malls, apartment buildings/condos and restaurants (p.45). In rape and sexual assault lawsuits, the study found apartment buildings and condos were the type of establishments most often sued, followed by health-care facilities, hotels, management companies, security companies and shopping malls (p.46).

Arguments in civil liability cases involving security may be based on one of several legal theories but generally involve either a claim of inadequate security or one of negligent hiring and retention: "According to the study, premises security liability cases predicated on inadequate security are more likely to result in higher awards than those based on the criminal act of an employee. Inadequate security awards averaged $1 million, and settlements averaged $1.5 million. Cases centering on crime by an employee—based on negligent hiring, retention, or supervision—yielded awards of around $775,000 and averaged settlements of $1.4 million" (Anderson, p.48).

Inadequate Premises Security

"Inadequate security is the No. 1 cause for liability-related lawsuits," contends one security expert in the hospitality industry (Friedrick, 2007, p.21). Thousands of premises security cases have passed through the courts, and each presents its own unique details and facts. However, consideration of a few of these cases can help security managers understand the pervasiveness of the challenge to provide adequate security, regardless of the specific type of business involved, and help security professionals better prepare for the variety of situation and circumstances that may lead to a claim of inadequate security.

- *Bond v. BH Acquisition Corp.* (1997)—A waitress was attacked and murdered in the parking lot of the motel where she worked. Her family sued both the motel owner and the management company, claiming inadequate security by noting that only one security officer was on duty to patrol several properties covering 240 acres and that the only light for the motel parking lot had been inoperable for several months before the murder. The case settled for $1.6 million (Anderson, p.50).

- *Simms v. Prime Hospitality Corp.* (1997)—Gaylene Simms was staying at a Wellesley Inn, owned by Prime Hospitality Corp. One evening, Ms. Simms got out of the elevator to return to her room and noticed a clean, neatly dressed man standing in the hallway near her room. He pointed a gun at her and forced her into her room, where he robbed and raped her. Simms sued Prime Hospitality for inadequate security. During the trial, Simms's lawyer presented evidence of 56 crimes, including robberies, having occurred on the premises over the previous three years. The hotel argued that the victim, Simms, was partially liable for the attack because, instead of continuing down the corridor when she saw the man near her room, she should have gotten back on the elevator, returned to the lobby and reported him. The jury, however, disagreed with the defense and awarded Simms $400,000 in damages. A court of appeals upheld the decision (Anderson, p.45).

- *Roe v. Interstate Properties* (1994)—Roe worked as a sales clerk in a mall kiosk shop. One evening after the mall had closed and as Roe was preparing the night deposit, a former mall employee robbed her at gunpoint, took her to the parking lot and drove her to a remote location, where he assaulted her. He then tried to shoot Roe, but she struggled and was able to escape when a passing car distracted the attacker. Roe sued the mall owners and operators for inadequate security. In pretrial depositions, witnesses testified that a night security officer was supposed to be on duty at the mall but was not there the night of the attack. Furthermore, the plaintiff's lawyer discovered that in the previous four years, 170 crimes had been committed against individuals at the mall. The mall's security director testified that he had requested funds to hire four guards to patrol the area but had received approval for only one new hire. The mall settled out of court for $360,000 just before the trial was set to begin (Anderson, pp.48–49).

Anderson (p.51) offers this advice: "Property owners can learn a great deal by studying premises security liability cases: who is most likely to sue, what types of crimes lead to lawsuits, and the legal theories that prevail in such cases. Most important, by looking at these cases, companies can clearly see the high cost of premises security liability—and the true value of putting in adequate security measures before it's too late." Security directors must also pay attention to what their competitors are doing regarding security: "While companies assess their risk and seek ways to mitigate it, they can still leave themselves open to liability claims if they haven't kept up with the standards set by others within their industry" (Friedrick, 2007, p.21).

Crimes Committed by Employees

The second major category of security liability lawsuits involve crimes committed by employees. Such cases are usually tried on the basis of employer negligence, either in hiring, retention or supervision. Although these types of lawsuits are increasing, they are also more difficult to prove than those alleging inadequate security (Anderson).

For example, in *Sparks Regional Medical Center v. Smith* (1998), a hospital patient who was sexually assaulted by an employee assigned to bathe her sued not only the employee, who was convicted of assault, but also the hospital, for negligent hiring and supervision. The plaintiff claimed that the hospital failed to conduct a thorough background check and, thus, hired an individual who had already been discharged from one previous job for harassing a patient and disciplined at another job for engaging in sexual contact with two female patients. The court ruled in favor of the plaintiff, stating that the hospital, through its negligent supervision, was responsible for the criminal acts of its employees. A court of appeals upheld the verdict (Anderson).

As these cases and their concomitant facts demonstrate "Security managers can reduce the chances that the company will lose lawsuits by assessing risk, developing countermeasures, documenting the security plan and implementing awareness programs" (Ahrens and Oglesby, 2006, p.84). Such risk management is the focus of Chapter 5.

Reducing Liability

 Civil liability might be reduced by hiring wisely, setting minimum standards for job performance, establishing clear policies and procedures, providing effective training and supervision, using clear contracts and carrying insurance.

Hiring

One extremely important way to reduce liability is to hire trustworthy, qualified individuals, whether proprietary or contractual. "The hiring process is one of the most challenging chores that any manager faces. How it is handled will affect both the company's prospects for building a good team and the likelihood of future litigation. By working with human resources and legal professionals, security can help ensure that the firm hires talented employees and minimizes its liability risk at the same time" (Nixon, 2005, p.48). Today's courts tend to favor the employee and push the majority of responsibilities on the employer.

Negligent hiring litigation is becoming more common. The majority of these cases involve failure to use an adequate selection process or to check for prior offenses or misconduct. Two-thirds of all negligent hiring trial cases result in jury awards, which average $600,000 in damages (Turley, 2006, p.7). The Workplace Violence Research Institute reports that the average jury award for civil suits on behalf of the injured is $3 million.

One of the best ways to safeguard against lawsuits is to conduct thorough pre-employment screening and eliminate unqualified individuals from the hiring pool as early as possible: "Concerns about factors ranging from the general quality of the hiree to workplace safety to exposure to litigation have spurred the ramp-up in pre-employment background screening" (Friedrick, 2004, p.19). Rosen (2004, p.36) asserts: "American industries . . . know that if they don't take measures to conduct pre-employment screening and exercise due diligence in hiring, it is a statistical certainty they are sitting ducks for expensive litigation, workplace violence, false claims, theft, embezzlement and economic loss. Just one bad hire can cost a firm millions. Studies show that screening reveals criminal records for up to 10 percent of job applicants, and at least one-third of all resumes contain material falsehoods." According to Lamb (2005, pp.34C–34D): "The pre-employment screening industry is most commonly defined as all background investigative work performed on applicants during the hiring process. Arguably, one could include other screening tools like assessment testing or job fit analysis tools. In any case, pre-employment screening is part of the overall hiring process market."

Setting Minimum Standards for Job Performance

Another critical aspect of liability reduction is establishing job performance standards and ensuring employees meet or exceed these standards, lest an employer be held liable for negligent retention. Latzel (2003, p.34) states: "Before reaching the point of making an offer to a prospective employee, the employer must first clearly define the important duties and responsibilities that the incumbent performs and what knowledge, skills and abilities are needed to get the work done." Latzel (p.37) also stresses: "A new hire should be put through a probationary period, during which job performance is closely monitored. . . . Even after successfully passing the probationary period, an employee's performance should be continually observed to make sure the standards of the job are being met."

Establishing Clear Policies and Procedures

Clear policies lay out *what* employees are to do, and procedures describe *how* it should be done. Establishing clear, written policies and procedures helps limit employer liability. In addition, every company should have written plans for evacuations and other contingencies in the event of crises or disasters, reflecting developments related to local, state and federal laws and regulations (Ahrens and Oglesby, p.83).

Training

Once minimum job standards have been set and written policies and procedures established to help personnel meet these standards, employees must be adequately trained on how to perform and fulfill their job responsibilities. "Failure to train" can be defined as "inadequately preparing employees to perform their duties; minimal or too easy academy training; little or no in-service training; no educational tuition reimbursement" (O'Connor, 2004). The potential for "failure to train" lawsuits conceivably becomes greater as the private security profession becomes more complex.

Phelan (2005, p.142) reports: "Cities across the United States are considering bills that would mandate a minimum number of hours for security officer training. There is no discussion of quality, only quantity. That's a mistake. In an age where the range of skills and knowledge that officers must have is growing, it is more critical than ever that the industry move away from measuring training strictly by hours and, instead, begin to emphasize the quality of training that employees are receiving." The ASIS *Private Security Officer (PSO) Selection and Training Guide*[2] (2004, pp.16–17) recommends the following training guidelines:

Training should include the following core topics:

- Nature and role of private security officers including security awareness, legal aspects of security and security officer (ethics, honesty and professional image)
- Observation and incident reporting (observation techniques, note taking, report writing, patrol techniques)
- Principles of communication (interpersonal skills, verbal communication skills, and customer service and public relations)
- Principles of access control (ingress and egress control procedures and electronic security systems)
- Principles of safeguarding information (proprietary and confidential)
- Emergency response procedures (critical incident response to natural disasters, accidents, human-caused events; evacuation processes)
- Life safety awareness (safety hazards, emergency equipment placement, fire prevention skills, hazardous materials, Occupational Safety and Health (OSHA) requirements)
- Job assignment and post orders

Depending on the assignment, the following additional training topics should be considered: substance abuse; workplace violence; conflict resolution; traffic control and parking lot security; crowd control, procedures for first aid, cardiopulmonary resuscitation (CPR) and automatic external defibrillators (AEDs); crisis management; and labor relations (strikes, lockouts and the like).

Finally, each PSO should be required to pass a written or performance exam to demonstrate understanding of the subject matter.

Cottringer (2004, p.33) suggests adding teaching common sense to the preceding subjects: "In security work, common sense means to exercise good judgment and take the same action that any reasonable person would under similar circumstances. Some specific behaviors that make up common sense in security work include asking questions, double-checking the facts, knowing where to refer people for more information, anticipating likely problems and being proactive in suggesting solutions. Other common sense security behaviors include paying close attention to details, predicting likely consequences of certain actions and always following through."

In addition to providing thorough training, these efforts need to be carefully documented. Some employers are reluctant to train their employees because of the high cost of training and the high turnover rate, believing that once

---

[2]SOURCE: *Private Security Officer (PSO) Selection and Training Guide* (Arlington, VA: ASIS International, 2004) pp.16–17.

their officers are well trained they will leave for "greener pastures." But as motivational guru Zig Zigler is fond of saying, "I'd rather train an employee and lose him than not train him and keep him."

Contracts

Most security officers work under some sort of contract. Terms and conditions that might be included are the specific services to be provided and the location, the amount of supervision to be provided, the equipment needed and who will provide it, hours/days to be worked and compensation, including benefits. Some contracts also specify how an employee might be terminated and contain an indemnification clause in which the employee asserts that the employer is not responsible for any civil or criminal offenses committed by the employee. Some contracts specify whether insurance is to be carried, and if so, who pays for it.

Insurance

Insurance is important to any business. Security agencies commonly carry insurance against civil lawsuits, but in many instances coverage may be excluded in certain areas. One frequently excluded area is punitive damages—compensation awarded by a court to a person harmed in an especially malicious or willful way. This is meant to serve as a warning to anyone else thinking of behaving in a similar way. Insurance is discussed further in Chapter 5.

A Recap

Ways that security officers might minimize civil lawsuits include the following (Hess and Wrobleski, 2006, p.468):

- Know and follow the department's guidelines.
- Stay in the scope of assigned duties.
- Always act professionally.
- Know and respect constituents' rights.
- If in doubt, seek advice.
- Carefully document activities.
- Maintain good communication relations.
- Keep current on civil and criminal liability cases.

Laws regarding civil liability vary from state to state. Nonetheless, certain guidelines will usually help reduce civil liability of on-line security personnel. Officers should:

- Consistently and fairly enforce policies and procedures regarding all security matters and employee safety.
- Know and understand the duties and responsibilities.
- Always identify themselves as a security officer before taking any actions involving an employee or visitor.
- Know the limits of their authority and recognize the authority of others. If officers do not have the authority to act they should go to someone who does.
- Ask for help if they are unsure and do not feel confident to handle a problem.
- Maintain a helpful, courteous attitude when assisting employees and visitors.
- Always be aware of and sensitive to an individual's privacy.

- Guide their behavior by the standard of *reasonableness*, making every effort to act objectively and fairly in all situations.
- Maintain high visibility in common areas to deter crime.
- Be alert to and remedy any safety risks or potential safety hazards they observe.
- Remain calm at all times to perform their duties efficiently and safely.
- Cooperate fully in investigations or inquiries.
- Know who to call in emergencies and keep names and telephone numbers easily accessible.
- Consciously observe and promptly record observations in a clear, concise, complete report.
- Following any incident, immediately record all information on an incident report form. Include all facts. Avoid conclusions and opinions.

Security officers should not:
- Cause an employee or visitor to believe he or she is not free to leave, whether it be through physical restraint or words.
- Make physical contact either directly or indirectly with employees, visitors or intruders while questioning them or escorting them to an exit.
- Use unnecessary force.
- Search any person, purse, lunchbox or toolbox unless the search is specifically authorized by management and the search guidelines have been communicated to all employees.
- Search employees or visitors selectively.
- Issue a statement or opinion or discuss any issue associated with their duties with any reporter.
- Question individual employees or visitors in front of others. If they must ask sensitive questions the person should be asked to accompany the officer to a private area.
- Discuss sensitive information with people who do not have a genuine right or need to know.
- Accuse an employee or visitor of committing a crime.
- Deviate from actions authorized by the security manual.

A Liability Checklist
- Have potential liabilities been identified?
- Have ways to reduce these risks been implemented?
- Are there clear policies on:
  - Detaining?
  - Searching?
  - Arresting?
  - Emergencies?
  - Using force?
  - Carrying a weapon?
- Have all employees been trained in these areas?
- Has a record of such training been kept?
- Are there clear, stringent employment standards?
- Are employees evaluated periodically?
- Are supervisors adequately trained?

- Are employees properly supervised?
- Are all incidents having potential civil liability investigated and remedial actions implemented?

Properly reporting all incidents is critical. Lawsuits can be filed several years after an incident. Information from reports can be invaluable in refreshing the memory of those involved or if those involved are no longer employed there.

Common Defenses against Civil Lawsuits

The most common defenses used by security officers and those for whom they work are that:

- They did not intend to deprive a plaintiff of a constitutional right.
- They acted in good faith.
- They acted with what was considered reasonable judgment at the time and with valid authority.

Surviving a Lawsuit

Even with carefully selected and trained security officers, lawsuits may still occur. Should this happen, officers should know what to expect as defendants. Lawsuits often involve **interrogatories**, written lists of questions to which the defendant is asked to respond. Interrogatories may be several pages long and may include questions attempting to obtain information that might be damaging to the defendant—for example, questions about financial or marital difficulties. The defendant need not answer each question, but any question not answered must include an explanation for the omission.

In addition to knowing what is legal and what might result in a lawsuit, security personnel should also consider if an action is ethical.

Ethics Defined

Most people have a general idea of what the term *ethics* refers to. Ethics refers to standards or principles of fair, honest conduct. Other definitions are:

- A system of moral principles or values.
- Rules or standards governing the conduct of a profession.
- Accepted standards of right and wrong.

Ethics deal with questions of right and wrong, of moral and immoral behavior. Ethical behavior refers to actions considered right and moral, such as being honest, being considerate of others and keeping promises. Unethical behavior, in contrast, is behavior that is considered immoral, corrupt and against accepted standards, such as lying, taking advantage of others and reneging on promises. Table 4.1 provides an inventory of ethical issues.

The difficulty with ethical behavior is that it varies from individual to individual, group to group and even country to country. At the heart of ethical behavior is what is considered **moral**—that is, right or virtuous. Questions of morality often involve what people commonly refer to as their "conscience." Moral standards may be:

- Constructed by an individual.
- Set forth by a particular society or culture.
- Laid down by a religious body or doctrine.

Table 4.1   Inventory of Ethical Issues

The Individual and the Organization

Work ethic

Petty theft

Overtime abuse

Gifts and gratuities

Falsifying reports

Misuse of sick days

Personal use of supplies or equipment

Personal demands interfering with work performance

The Organization and Employees

Sexual or racial harassment

Discouraging honest criticism

Unfair decisions

Inadequate compensation

No recognition of good performance

Inadequate training

Unrealistic demands

The Individual and Other Employees

Backstabbing and lack of support

Gossip

Sexual or racial harassment

Lying to cover up blame

Taking credit for another's work

The Individual and the Public

Misuse of authority

Inadequate performance of duty

Sexual, racial, ethnic harassment

Special treatment

Lack of expertise in profession

SOURCE: Joycelyn M. Pollock, *Ethics in Crime and Justice*, 4th ed. (Belmont, CA: Wadsworth Publishing Company, 2004) p.11.

The Ten Commandments are an example of religious doctrine. They would seem to be very clear—for example, "Thou shalt not kill." But this commandment is at the heart of the heated debates involving abortion and capital punishment. Opinions do differ.

Philosophers such as Epicurus and Thomas Hobbes believed that the good of the individual is the ultimate factor in determining ethical behavior. In contrast, such philosophers as Jeremy Bentham and James Mill believed that the ethical criterion is the greatest good for the greatest number. Who decides what is good? The individual? The corporation? The state? A certain group? Again, opinions differ.

Developing Personal and Organizational Ethics

Blanchard and Peale (1988) provide direction for developing personal ethics and place at the heart of their philosophy this simple statement (p.9): "There is no right way to do a wrong thing." They (p.20) suggest three questions that can serve as a personal "ethics check."

Three personal ethics-check questions are:

- Is it legal?
- Is it balanced?
- How does it make me feel about myself?

Obviously individuals entrusted with the safety and security of an establishment's assets and personnel must always act legally. The question of balance deals with whether the decision or action is fair to all parties involved. Does it create a win-win situation or are there losers? The third question is often referred to as a "gut check." To answer it honestly, ask yourself such questions as "Would I feel good if my family knew about this decision or action?" "Would I mind seeing this decision or action as a headline in the local newspaper?"

In addition to developing personal ethics, security professionals also should seek to promote ethics throughout the organization. Three questions can serve as an organizational "ethics check."

Three organizational ethics-check questions are:

- Are we delivering what we promise in terms of quality and customer service?
- Are we selling a product or service that is harmful to society?
- Are we honest in the way we do business?

Cunningham et al. (1990, p.49) stress: "The best security people in the world can't be effective if they have to function in a climate where integrity and honesty are the exception rather than the rule. It's up to management to establish the highest ethical standards for business conduct and to see that those standards are adopted throughout the company." One starting point in developing an ethical organization is with a clear vision statement and goals as to how this vision is to become a reality—a code of ethics.

Code of Ethics

Even without legislative guidance from the state level, private security directors can set their own standards for conduct and service to increase the professionalism of the field. Both those hired and those hiring should adhere to a code of ethics similar to that guiding professionals. In fact, a self-enforcing code of ethics is required to meet the definition of a true profession.

A code of ethics sets forth self-enforcing moral and professional guidelines for behavior in a given field.

Codes of ethics have been developed and adopted by numerous organizations, including the American Society for Industrial Security (ASIS), the Council

Aware that the quality of professional security activity ultimately depends upon the willingness of practitioners to observe special standards of conduct and to manifest good faith in professional relationships, ASIS International (ASIS) adopts the following Code of Ethics and mandates its conscientious observance as a binding condition of membership in or affiliation with the organization:

ARTICLE I

A member shall perform professional duties in accordance with the law and the highest moral principles.

ARTICLE II

A member shall observe the precepts of truthfulness, honesty, and integrity.

ARTICLE III

A member shall be faithful and diligent in discharging professional responsibilities.

ARTICLE IV

A member shall be competent in discharging professional responsibilities.

ARTICLE V

A member shall safeguard confidential information and exercise due care to prevent its improper disclosure.

ARTICLE VI

A member shall not maliciously injure the professional reputation or practice of colleagues, clients, or employers.

Figure 4.2   ASIS Code of Ethics

SOURCE: From *Security Management*, July/August 1995, p.22. Reprinted with the written permission of ASIS International, Alexandria, VA.

of International Investigators, the National Council of Investigation and Security Services, the National Burglar and Fire Alarm Association, Inc., the World Association of Detectives, Inc. and the Law Enforcement/Private Security Relationship Committee of the Private Security Advisory Council. The ASIS has established a code of ethics for its membership (Figure 4.2).

Private security directors may want to obtain copies of additional codes of ethics and draw from them those guidelines that seem most relevant to their particular situations.

 Ethics can be promoted throughout the organization by the security manager serving as a role model, by having a clear vision statement and by having a code of ethics. Prescreening potential employees and ongoing inservice training can help promote ethical behavior as well.

Ethics and Decision Making

 Values and a strong sense of ethics should be the core of the decision-making/ problem-solving process.

Ethical dilemmas occur when an individual is forced to choose between two or more choices of behavior. Pollock (2004, p.21) provides the following example:

George Ryan, the ex-governor of Illinois, declared a moratorium on the use of the death penalty in his state in 2000 when at least five individuals on death row were exonerated through the use of DNA evidence. One of his last acts as he left office at the end of 2002 was to pardon the rest of those on death row and commute their sentences to life without parole. Governor Ryan faced a difficult personnel dilemma because he was in a position to do something about his belief that the death penalty was implemented in a way that could never be just. The fact that there was strong support *and* strong opposition to his action indicates the depth of his dilemma and the serious-ness of the issue. Although most of us do not have the power to commute death sentences, we can do something about our beliefs.[3]

Pollock (pp.21–22) suggests five analytical steps that might be taken to clarify a dilemma:

1. Review all the facts. Make sure that one has all the facts known—not future predictions, not suppositions, not probabilities.
2. Identify all the potential values of each party that might be relevant.
3. Identify all possible moral issues for each party involved. This is to help us see that sometimes one's own moral or ethical dilemma is caused by the ac-tions of others. For example, an officer's ethical dilemma when faced with the wrongdoing of a fellow officer is a direct result of the other officer mak-ing a bad choice. It helps to see all the moral issues involved to address the central issue.
4. Decide what is the most immediate moral or ethical issue facing the indi-vidual. This is always a behavior choice, not an opinion. For example, the moral issue of whether abortion should be legalized is quite different from the moral dilemma of whether a woman who becomes unexpectedly preg-nant should have an abortion. Obviously, one affects the other, but they are conceptually very distinct.
5. Resolve the ethical or moral dilemma.[4]

Summary

- Laws may be classified in several ways: by type (written or common law), by source (constitu-tional, statutory, case), by the parties involved (public, private) or by the offense (criminal, civil).

- A crime is a wrong against the public which the state prosecutes and which seeks punishment. Criminal intent is required. A tort is a private wrong where an individual sues seeking restitu-tion. Intent is not necessary.

- Tort law is divided into three categories: strict li-ability, intentional torts and negligence.

- The elements of negligent liability include (1) the existence of some duty owed, (2) the incident oc-curring was foreseeable, (3) the defendant failed to meet a reasonable standard of care, (4) proxi-mate results, that is, an injury resulted from the failure to protect and (5) damages.

- Laws may apply to individuals who are unaware that they are liable. One instance of this is the non-delegable duty. This is a duty for which authority can be given to another person, but the responsi-bility cannot. Civil liability remains with the person

[3]SOURCE: Joycelyn M. Pollock, *Ethics in Crime and Justice*, 4th ed. (Belmont, CA: Wadsworth Pub-lishing Company, 2004) p.21.
[4]SOURCE: Joycelyn M. Pollock, *Ethics in Crime and Justice*, 4th ed. (Belmont, CA: Wadsworth Pub-lishing Company, 2004) p.21–22.

- who has the legal duty to act. In contrast, vicarious liability is the responsibility of one person for the acts of another.

- The most common civil suits brought against private security are for assault, battery, false imprisonment, defamation, intentional infliction of emotional distress, invasion of privacy and negligence.

- Increasingly, private security is affected by Section 1983 of U.S. Code, Title 42—the Civil Rights Act—which says anyone acting under the authority of local or state law who violates another person's constitutional rights, even though they are upholding a law, can be sued.

- Civil liability might be reduced by hiring wisely, setting minimum standards for job performance, establishing clear policies, providing effective training and supervision, using clear contracts and carrying adequate insurance.

- Ethics deal with questions of right and wrong, of moral and immoral behavior. Three personal ethics-check questions are: (1) Is it legal? (2) Is it balanced? and (3) How does it make me feel about myself?

- In addition to practicing ethical behavior individually, security managers also should promote ethical conduct throughout the organization. Three organizational ethics-check questions are:

  1. Are we delivering what we promise in terms of quality and customer service?
  2. Are we selling a product or service that is harmful to society?
  3. Are we honest in the way we do business?

- A code of ethics sets forth self-enforcing moral and professional guidelines for behavior in a given field.

- Ethics can be promoted throughout the organization by the security manager serving as a role model, by having a clear vision statement and by having a code of ethics. Prescreening potential employees and ongoing in-service training can help promote ethical behavior as well.

- Values and a strong sense of ethics should be the core of the decision-making/problem-solving process.

APPLICATIONS

1. On a Sunday in late November, James Stiles, a supervisor for the Mid-Atlantic Security Company, and Dean Duncan, security officer for the same company, were on duty at the Glass House Office complex. Their primary duty was to check tenants in and out. Both security officers had worked this assignment many times, and both were veterans in the security field.

   About 5:00 P.M. on a Sunday, a female attorney, Estelle Grambling, came into the building to do some work in her office. Noting no one at the sign-in desk, she assumed there was no security officer on duty, although she did see the sign-in book open on the counter. Without signing in, she went to the elevator and up to her office.

   About 7:00 P.M. the security officers were approached by two public police officers who stated they were called by a woman to come to room 918 because she was accosted by an intruder, assaulted and robbed of her purse and credit cards. The two police officers and James Stiles, the supervisor, went up to 918 and found a hysterical victim, Estelle Grambling. After calming down, she stated that a man had struck her in the head while she

   was at her computer and stole her purse containing a considerable amount of money and credit cards. Before he left, he struck her in the face with his fist. Although dazed, she managed to dial 911 and summon the police. She had not tried to contact the front security desk, believing no one was on duty there.

   This incident resulted in Estelle Grambling filing a lawsuit against the Pronto Management Company, which managed the building and hired the Mid-Atlantic Security Company, and the Mid-Atlantic Security Company for negligence of duty. She alleged that the private security officers were negligent in their duty, were careless in performing their patrol throughout the building and were completely oblivious to the fact that she was in the building. She was suing for one hundred thousand dollars in negligent damages and another one hundred thousand dollars in punitive damages.

   a. Did the security officers owe a duty to the plaintiff to protect her while she worked in her office?

   b. Did Grambling create a risk by not signing the log book even though the officers were not present when she entered the building?

c. What is your overall assessment of the situation, and what liability does the security company have, if any?

d. Evaluate the totality of the situation. What would you recommend to settle the damage claim?

2. Johnny Abrams, a supervisor for the Seymour Private Security Agency, was making his inspection of personnel under his supervision. He entered the men's room of the Mainline Corporation and came upon subordinate security officer Hynes and an employee talking. Officer Hynes had come upon George Simon as Simon was snorting cocaine. Simon was crying, begging the security officer not to turn him in to management because he would lose his job. He was desperate economically, and his wife was about to have their third child. Simon said he would do anything to get out of the situation so the company would not fire him. Officer Hynes lectured him and warned him that if it happened again, he would be reported.

Unfortunately, Abrams, a person being paid to supervise and advise subordinates, did not offer Officer Hynes any suggestions as to what he should do. The fact that Officer Hynes let George Simon off with a verbal warning may indicate two things: that the officer had no experience in handling this type of situation or that he did not realize that sending him back to his job under the influence of a drug may have been devastating to other employees, particularly if Simon was working with highly volatile chemicals, machinery or any type of work that could lead to a disaster.

Had the private security officers notified Simon's immediate supervisor at the time of the incident, he could have been placed into a drug rehabilitation program that the company sponsored.

Evaluate how this incident was handled.

a. Was this a fair decision by Officer Hynes?

b. Do you think it was a good decision?

c. Should the supervisor have been more assertive in handling the situation?

d. Should Officer Hynes have called the public police?

e. Four days later Simon was picked up by the public police for possession of cocaine. Do you think the actions of the security officers perpetuated Simon's use of cocaine?

DISCUSSION QUESTIONS

1. There is a continuous ravaging of the Old English common law principle that the master is not responsible for the criminal acts of his servants. Explain what this actually means as far as legal liability is concerned.

2. As a security officer, would you believe in the theory of foreseeable danger?

3. What is your understanding of punitive damages?

4. Security personnel, whether guards, supervisors or managers, frequently are in a position to obtain information that could prove embarrassing to a company that relies on the contractual or the proprietary services to see that the business is creating a good image and that all violators of unethical conduct are handled in a manner conducive to good company business. To uphold this philosophy, as a security supervisor or manager, how would you proceed?

5. Johnny McGuire, a security officer at the Glenview Nursing Home, during the hours of midnight to 8:00 A.M., makes coffee during the course of his shift without the knowledge of the complex managers and periodically has a cup to stay awake. What is your opinion of this unsupervised activity?

REFERENCES

Anderson, Teresa. "Laying Down the Law: A Review of Trends in Liability Lawsuits." *Security Management*, October 2002, pp.43–51.

Anderson, Teresa. "Legal Reporter" *Security Management*, February 2007, pp.72–74.

Ahrens, Sean A. and Oglesby, Marieta B. "Levers against Liability." *Security Management*, February 2006, pp.80–84.

Aronsohn, Audrey J. "Forcing the Issue: When Is the Use of Force Excessive?" *Loss Prevention and Security Journal*, March 2003, pp.26–27.

Bernard, Ray. "We're Watching." *Security Technology and Design*, December 2004, pp.18–24.

Blanchard, Kenneth and Peale, Norman Vincent. *The Power of Ethical Management*. New York: Fawcett Crest, 1988.

Cottringer, William. "Teaching Common Sense." *Security Management*, April 2004, pp.33–34.

Cunningham, William G.; Strauchs, John J.; and Van Meter, Clifford W. *Private Security Trends—1970–2000: The Hallcrest Report II*. Stoneham, MA: Heinemann, 1990.

Friedrick, Joanne. "Companies Ramp Up Pre-Employment Screening." *Security Director News*, July 2004, p.19.

Friedrick, Joanne. "Documentation, Regularly Updated Policies Reduce Risk of Liability." *Security Director News*, September 2007, p.21.

Hess, Kären M. and Wrobleski, Henry M. *Police Operations*, 4th edition. Belmont, CA: Wadsworth Publishing Company, 2006.

Lamb, John. "Ladies and Gentlemen: Start Your Engines!" *Security Products*, February 2005, pp.34C–34E.

Latzel, Greta. "Setting Job Requirements." *Security Products*, October 2003, pp.34–37.

Meklinsky, Ian D. and Bancroft, Anne Ciesla. "Mindful Monitoring." *Security Management*, April 2007, pp.94–102.

Nixon, W. Barry. "How to Avoid Hiring Hazards." *Security Management*, February 2005, pp.43–48.

O'Connor, Thomas R. "Civil Liability for Government Wrongdoing." Online: http://faculty.ncwc.edu/toconnor/205/205lect12.htm. Site updated July 16, 2004; accessed April 11, 2005.

Phelan, Michael. "What's the Value of Training Time?" *Security Management*, April 2005, pp.140, 142.

Piazza, Peter. "A Chip Off the Privacy Block." *Security Management*, July 2006, pp.63–69.

Pollock, Joycelyn M. *Ethics in Crime and Justice*, 4th edition. Belmont, CA: Wadsworth Publishing Company, 2004.

Private Security Officer (PSO) Selection and Training Guide. Arlington, VA: ASIS International, 2004.

Rosen, Lester S. "Cost-Effective Safe Hiring Techniques for Large Employers." *Security Technology and Design*, June 2004, pp.36–40.

Solensky, Edward. "Who's Liable Now?" *Security Management*, March 2007, pp.80–88.

Stua, David. "Independent Contractor versus Employee: Definitions and the Law." Online: http://home.inu.net/davidstua/Ind_con.htm. Accessed February 2, 2005.

Turley, Kristin. "Seven Reasons You Should Be Conducting Background Checks." *Security Director News*, September 2006, p.7.

CASES CITED

Atamian v. Supermarkets General Corp., 369 A.2d 38 (N.J. Super. 1976).

Bond v. BH Acquisition Corp. (Hinds County Circuit Court, Mississippi, 1997).

Cramer v. Consolidated Freightways, Inc., U.S. Court of Appeals for the Ninth Circuit, No. 98–55657 (2001).

Eastman v. Time Saver Stores, Inc. 428 So. 2d 1163 (La. App. 1983).

Florence Trentacost v. Dr. Nathan T. Brussel, 412 A.2d 436 (N.J. 1980).

Kline v. 1500 Massachusetts Ave. Apartment Corp., 439 F.2d 477 (1970).

Kolosky v. Winn Dixie Stores, Inc., 472 So. 2d 891 (Fla. 1985).

Mark Jackson v. Rohm & Hass Co., Court of Common Pleas, Philadelphia, Pennsylvania, No. 990601906 (2001).

Meyers v. Ramada Inn of Columbus, 471 N.E.2d 176 (Ohio 1984).

Picco v. Ford's Diner, Inc., 274 A.2d 301 (N.J. Super. 1971).

Pittard v. Four Seasons Motor Inn, Inc., 688 P.2d 33 (N.M. App. 1984).

Roe v. Interstate Properties (District Court of the Eastern District of Virginia, 1994).

Romanski v. Detroit Entertainment, U.S. Court of Appeals for the Sixth Circuit, No. 04–1354 (2005).

Simms v. Prime Hospitality Corp. (Florida District Court of Appeals, 1997).

Sparks Regional Medical Center v. Smith (Arkansas Court of Appeals, 1998).

Taylor v. Continental Bowl, Inc., 416 P.2d 793 (Cal. 1966).

U.S. v. Ziegler (U.S. Court of Appeals for the Ninth Circuit, 2006).

CHAPTER 5

Risk Management
The Foundation of Private Security

Effective risk management makes an organization's environment secure and reduces the likelihood of loss or crises. Risk managers must consider not only the possible targets of attack and existing security measures as they relate to profits, but also the aesthetic and operational needs of the enterprise.

DO YOU KNOW . . .

- What the two most basic types of risk are?
- What risk management is?
- What the worth of an asset depends on?
- What is included in a systematic approach to preventing loss through risk management?
- What three factors risk analysis considers?
- What alternatives for handling risk exist?
- Whether risk management is a moral or legal responsibility?
- How qualitative and quantitative risk analysis can work together in risk assessment?
- What a security survey includes?
- How the information needed for a security survey is obtained?
- When components of the security system should be evaluated?

CAN YOU DEFINE?

asset	enterprise risk management	pure risk	risk assessment
attack tree	indemnity	qualitative risk assessment	risk management
audit	law of large numbers	quantitative risk assessment	security survey
criticality			subrogation
dynamic risk	probability	risk	vulnerability

Introduction

The concept of risk management lies at the heart of private security and has become a critical element in effecting security for businesses and organizations worldwide. As the nature of business has evolved, the words *disaster*, *crisis* and *risk management* have become increasingly intertwined. Indeed, it often takes a tragedy to bring about necessary upgrades in an organization's overall risk management and security plan. Consider this excerpt of an analysis by noted risk management expert, John O'Connell, on lessons learned from 9/11/01, specifically as applied to the business community:

> "The scope and urgency of security, safety and risk management challenges are increasing rapidly. . . . We've learned that one should never underestimate a crisis. We should anticipate its growth and that the public will become aware."

> [It is] recommended that businesses reconsider concentrating their people and resources in one location, develop alternative communication systems to stay in touch with customers and employees, expand the list of business risks to include a world view, and look more closely at their supply chain and inventory processes ("Risk Management Expert Unveils . . .," 2002).

Risk management is much more than dealing with crisis. In fact, effective risk management should greatly reduce such crises. The purpose of risk management is to make an organization's environment secure, yet consistent with its operations and philosophy. Consequently, risk managers must consider not only the possible targets of attack and existing security measures as they relate to profits, but also the aesthetic and operational needs of the enterprise. Efficiency, convenience, appearance and profit are all important factors as security systems are planned.

This chapter begins by defining the various types of risks and looking at the big picture of risk management. Then the risk management process is discussed, including an explanation of risk assessment and selecting alternatives to handle identified risks. The challenge of balancing security costs with level of protection is examined next, followed by a discussion of quantitative and qualitative risk assessment, the enterprise risk management model and security as a business center. The critical role of the security survey is explained, as is the need for routine, ongoing evaluation of the security plan and system. The chapter concludes with suggested keys to successful risk management.

Risk Defined

The concept of risk is familiar to most people. A risk is a known threat that has unpredictable effects in either timing or extent. The effects can include actual losses, interruption of production cycles, reduction of sales opportunities, injury to persons, liability claims and property damage.

 The two most basic types of risk are pure risk and dynamic risk. **Pure risk** is the potential for injury, damage or loss with no possible benefits. **Dynamic risk**, in contrast, has the potential for both benefits and losses.

Pure risk includes crimes, acts of terrorism and natural disasters, and examples include fire; flood; earthquakes; landslides; avalanches; civil unrest and riots; power outages; accidents; hackers, crackers and industrial espionage; and negligent or disgruntled employees. Pure risks offer no benefit to management—only added cost. Also included within the category of pure risk is the employer's liability to protect employees, customers and visitors. People have a right to be reasonably safe when on the property of businesses or organizations.

In contrast to pure risk, *dynamic risk* results from a management decision and may produce both benefits and losses. For example, management decides to accept checks because doing so stimulates business. At the same time, they recognize that some loss may occur from the pure risk of check fraud. Or, management decides to hire security personnel (benefit) but is then liable for the actions of such personnel (loss). Both pure and dynamic risk must be recognized and dealt with in a systematic approach to private security.

Rejda (2008, p.6) classifies risk into several distinct, yet sometimes overlapping, categories, the first pair of which parallel pure and dynamic risk:

- Pure and speculative risk
- Fundamental and particular risk
- Enterprise risk

As noted, pure risk presents only the possibilities of loss or no loss. This is in contrast to what Rejda calls *speculative risk*, a situation in which either profit or loss is possible, such as when betting or investing. The distinction between pure and speculative risk is important because most private insurers typically insure only pure risks. Insurance is a risk management tool discussed later in the chapter.

Risk may also be classified as fundamental or particular. A *fundamental risk*— for example, rapid inflation, a natural disaster or even war—affects the entire economy or large numbers of people or groups within the economy. In 2005, Hurricane Katrina destroyed much of New Orleans, Louisiana, and caused billions of dollars of property damage in Louisiana, Florida, Mississippi and Texas. Katrina was the largest single catastrophe in the history of the United States (Rejda, p.6). Risk of a large-scale terrorist attack such as that on September 11, 2001, is also a fundamental risk. In contrast, a *particular risk* affects only individuals. This distinction is important because, again, government assistance may be needed to insure fundamental risks, for example, flood insurance subsidized by the federal government may be available to business firms.

The fifth category of risk, *enterprise risk*, encompasses all major risks faced by a business or organization, including pure risk, speculative risk, strategic risk, operational risk and financial risk. *Strategic risk* is the uncertainty regarding an organization's financial goals and objectives, for example, entering a new line of business that may be unprofitable. *Operational risk* refers to procedures that might result in a loss, for example, accepting checks. *Financial risk* is the uncertainty of loss due to adverse changes in commodity prices, interest rates, foreign exchange rates and the value of money (Rejda, p.7). This type of risk is discussed later in this chapter.

Risk should not be confused with the terms *peril* and *hazard* (Rejda, p.5). A peril is the cause of a loss. If a business burns to the ground, the peril is fire. Other common perils include lightning, hail, tornadoes, earthquakes, hurricanes, criminal actions and terrorist attacks. A hazard is a condition that creates or increases the chance of a loss. Four major types of hazards are: (1) physical, (2) moral, (3) morale and (4) legal (Rejda). A *physical hazard* is an observable condition that increases the chance of loss. For example, defective wiring can increase the chance of fire, and an unlocked door can increase the chance of theft. A *moral hazard* is dishonesty or character defects in individuals that increase the frequency or severity of a loss. Employees who steal, who manipulate data and the like can cause tremendous losses to an organization or business, as discussed later. A subtle distinction exists between a moral hazard and a morale hazard. A *morale hazard* is carelessness or indifference to a potential loss, for example, not locking a door. A *legal hazard* is one created by legislation or regulatory requirements such as large adverse jury verdicts or statutes requiring employers provide certain benefits for employees. The distinction among these terms may seem unimportant, but such terms are often used by risk managers and by insurance representatives.

Risk should not be viewed as all negative. Risk in itself is not bad. What is bad is risk that is mismanaged, misunderstood or unintended. Enter *risk management*.

Risk Management: The Big Picture[1]

In a market economy companies must take risks; this situation has always existed. But businesses today face a wider variety of new challenges in their quest to maximize value: Globalization, e-business, mergers and new organizational partnerships, and the increasing speed of business activity are rapidly changing and expanding the risks organizations face. Given our sophisticated technology and the demand for high production, even a minor disturbance can cause a substantial economic setback. Thus, a primary responsibility of the security manager has become anticipating and thwarting any such disturbances or risks, major or minor. Microsoft's *The Security Risk Management Guide* (2006, p.13) defines *risk management* as "the process of determining an acceptable level of risk, assessing the current level of risk, taking steps to reduce risk to the acceptable level and maintaining that level of risk."

 Risk management is anticipating, recognizing and analyzing risks; taking steps to reduce or prevent such risks; and evaluating the results.

To be effective, risk management must protect an organization's important assets by implementing controls to reduce negative risks. Aggleton (2005, p.74) notes: "The classical approach to understanding security needs is first to identify what requires protection—the assets—and then to determine from what the assets need to be protected—the threats." An **asset** is anything of value to a business or organization, including people, equipment, computer hardware and software, manufactured products, formulas, data and other information.

Determining the monetary value of assets is an important part of security risk management. Security managers rely on the value of an asset to guide their decisions in determining how much time and money should be spent securing it. Many organizations keep a list of asset values (AVs). Often this value can be calculated or estimated in direct financial terms. For example, if a business has an e-commerce Web site that runs 24/7, generating an average of $2,000 an hour from orders, the annual value of this site in sales revenue is $17,520,000. The total value of assets is important when assessing the risks posed by natural disasters or fire.

 The worth of an asset depends on three primary factors: the overall value of the asset to the organization, the immediate financial impact of losing the asset and the indirect business impact of losing the asset.

Risk management is sometimes referred to as loss prevention or loss prevention management. To avoid the ambiguity inherent in the term *risk*, Rejda suggests substituting *loss exposure* for risk, as his definition of risk management is "a process that identifies loss exposures faced by an organization and selects the most appropriate techniques for treating such exposures."

Effective risk management provides an integrated, comprehensive approach to a secure environment and, necessarily, involves a wide variety of partici-

---

[1]The following discussion provides an overview of risk management. What is important at this point is the overall security system and how it is developed. Specific risks and alternatives to eliminating or reducing them are the focus of later chapters.

pants. Figure 5.1 illustrates the numerous risks, loss prevention measures and responsibilities for which the security professional may be responsible. The outer area shows a company's risk environment—all the risks that affect a company. These will vary, of course, from business to business. The second circle shows the various components of the protection a company can include. The third circle shows the positions involved in a company's protection plan and each individual's areas of responsibility. At the center of the risk management circle is the coordinator, the person who manages the entire security effort and all its components. An overall security plan should consider all stakeholders in the facility.

A much less complex view of risk management is that used by the U.S. military, which puts the word *operational* in front of it. Their formal Operational Risk Management (ORM) strategy has five steps: (1) identify hazards, (2) assess the hazards, (3) make risk decisions, (4) implement controls and (5) supervise and watch for change. Since the five steps are difficult to remember, signs in all work areas read ORM = IRC, which stands for **i**dentify the risks in your work

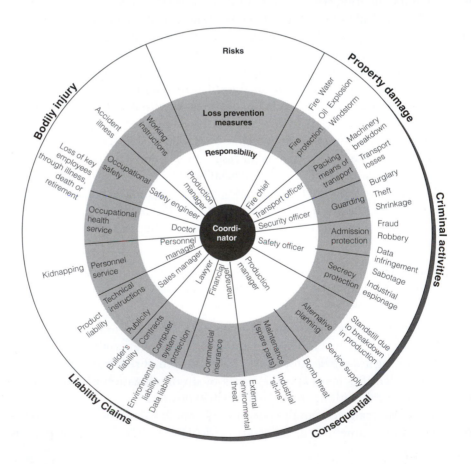

Figure 5.1 The Risk Management Circle

SOURCE: Adapted from Statsforetag AB, Skandia Insurance Co. and Skandia Risk Management Ltd., Stockholm, Sweden. Reprinted by permission.

area, **r**educe those risks as much as reasonably possible and **c**ommunicate the remaining risks to those who could be exposed to them (Hess, 2007).

Bernstein (1998) stresses: "The essence of risk management lies in maximizing the areas where we have some control over the outcome while minimizing the areas where we have absolutely no control over the outcome." In most instances the greatest degree of control over an outcome lies in managing pure risk. In fact, traditional risk management limited itself to pure loss exposures such as property risks, liability risks and personnel risks. In the 1990s, many organizations and businesses began expanding their focus to the other types of risk previously discussed. Another trend in recent years has been a shift to a more proactive philosophy of risk management.

Reactive (Incident Response) versus Proactive (Loss Prevention) Approaches to Risk Management

Change necessitates taking risks. As knowledge proliferates and organizations restructure, security managers must deal with the inevitable uncertainty that results from change. They should not be bound by tradition, but rather be willing to take some risks. Security managers who fail to take risks have a rigid, inflexible approach, perceiving change as a threat. Such security managers tend to seek stable, unchanging environments in which they feel safe, but also in which obsolescence and stagnation are found. These security managers also commonly find themselves in a reactive, incident-response position instead of a proactive, loss prevention position.

Organizations often undertake risk management by responding to a security incident after the fact. For example, an employee's computer becomes infected with a virus, and someone must figure out what to do. Although an in-depth examination into incident response is beyond the scope of this chapter, the following six steps provide a basic guideline to help security managers respond to security incidents quickly and efficiently.

First and foremost, protect human life and safety. This must always be the top priority in responding to any incident. Second, contain the damage. Next assess the extent of the damage and, if possible, determine the cause. Then repair the damage. Finally, thoroughly review the response and make any changes that would make future responses more effective. Microsoft's incident response process is illustrated in Figure 5.2.

Many organizations get frustrated with responding to one incident after another. An alternative to this reactive approach is to reduce the probability of security incidents occurring in the first place—being proactive. Instead of waiting for bad things to happen and then responding, proactive security risk management minimizes the probability of the bad things occurring and reduces the likelihood of a loss being incurred.

Figure 5.2   The Incident Response Process

SOURCE: From "The Security Risk Management Guide" in *Microsoft*, October 15, 2004, updated March 15, 2006, p.5 (Figure 2.1).

The Risk Management Process—An Overview

An efficient, effective security system that is not crisis-oriented does not just happen. Developing such a system involves critical observations and judgments made during a step-by-step process.

 A systematic approach to preventing loss through risk management includes risk analysis, policy formulation, specification of a protection plan and follow-up.

The purpose of the *risk analysis* is to create an awareness within a company of any risks and to determine as far as possible their potential influence on the business, as discussed in detail momentarily. After the risk analysis is completed, *policy* is formulated. The necessary security measures are arranged in order of importance, the cost of such measures is computed and management determines the level of protection the company should choose.

Next a *protection plan* is specified that includes which risks are to be eliminated and how; the degree of need for loss prevention and loss limitation, for protective company healthcare and for training in company protection; risks to be insured; and allocation of responsibility, management and coordination. *Follow-up* should ensure a reasonable balance between the risks with which the company has to live and the protection against these risks. New risks can rapidly materialize (e.g., as a result of a kidnapping threat). Other risks may become less serious.

While risk management is an ongoing cycle, it typically resets at regular intervals and is commonly aligned with an organization's financial accounting cycle. This annual "refresh" interval allows budget requests for new control solutions to be worked into the annual budgeting cycle of the business. Regardless of when the risk management cycle begins, it always starts with risk analysis or assessment.

Risk Assessment

"Whether it's developing the big picture or reacting to a specific event, a risk assessment serves as the foundation upon which an organization builds it physical security plan as well as its policies and procedures" (Friedrick, 2006, p.19). **Risk assessment** is the process of identifying and prioritizing risks to a business. Table 5.1 illustrates the important distinctions between risk management and risk assessment.

Risks facing security managers vary from organization to organization, and numerous surveys and polls indicate the wide variety of perceived risks. An

Table 5.1   Risk Management versus Risk Assessment

	Risk Management	*Risk Assessment*
Goal	Manage risks across business to acceptable level	Identify and prioritize risks
Cycle	Overall program	Single phase of risk management program
Schedule	Ongoing	As needed
Alignment	Aligned with budgeting cycles	N/A

SOURCE: From "The Security Risk Management Guide" in *Microsoft*, October 15, 2004, updated March 15, 2006, p.5 (Table 3.1).

Overseas Security Advisory Council (OSAC) analysis identified increased political radicalism, rising crime and corruption, pirating of intellectual property and military conflict as among the top security challenges U.S. businesses and organizations operating globally faced in 2006 (Daniels, 2007, p.8). A recent survey asked security directors nationwide to rank 18 critical security issues in order of concern (ASIS/Security Management Survey, 2007, p.27). The top three security issues identified were business interruptions, security equipment/resources and workplace violence. A *Security Director News* "Newspoll" (2007, p.23) that asked "What is the top security concern you have identified for your organization in 2007?" revealed that the most common concern was a breach in physical security (34 percent). Of least concern was a terrorist incident (7 percent). Figure 5.3 summarizes the responses to this survey.

The American Society for Industrial Security (ASIS) guideline *General Security Risk Assessment* (2004, p.7) suggests the following sources of information on risks for a given organization: local police crime statistics; Uniform Crime Reports (UCR) or comparable data; internal organization documents (e.g., security incident reports); prior complaints from employees, customers, guests, visitors and the like; prior civil claims for inadequate security; intelligence from local, state or national law enforcement agencies; industry-related information about trends; general economic conditions of the area and presence of a crime magnet (e.g., the proximity of a popular nightclub, continuous presence of vagrants, property in disrepair).

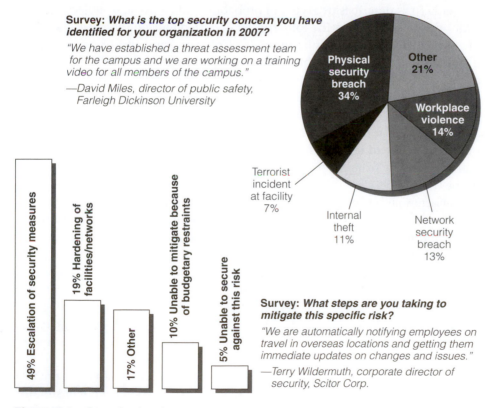

Figure 5.3   Organizations' Top Security Concern in 2007

NOTE: Survey results based on 104 respondents in December.

SOURCE: From "Newspoll" in *Security Director News*, January 2007, p.23.

Three factors to consider in risk analysis are (1) vulnerability, (2) probability and (3) criticality.

Establishing **vulnerability** involves identifying threats. Where could losses occur? How? What types of thefts might occur? What safety hazards exist? Security managers should consider their vulnerability to such risks as accidents, arson, assault, auto theft, bombs, burglary, fraud (including credit-card and check fraud), kidnapping, larceny/theft (both internal and external), robbery, sabotage, sex crimes, shoplifting and vandalism. They should also consider their vulnerability to natural disasters such as earthquakes, fires, floods, tornados and the like, as well as their vulnerability to terrorist attacks. Finally, consideration must be given to existing conditions or procedures that may increase vulnerability, for example, unlocked doors and windows, unprotected access to computers, insufficient fire suppression systems and flammable materials used in construction, poorly designed buildings, old wiring and the like.

Establishing **probability** involves analyzing the factors that favor loss. Probability is difficult to assess and is often determined by educated guesswork (Fay, 2005, p.24). Is the establishment located in a high- or low-crime area? How tight is existing physical security? Records of past losses help establish probability. Where is shrinkage occurring? Is it primarily due to internal or external causes? Where is it most likely to occur? Are OSHA requirements being met? How likely are civil disturbances in the area? Would the establishment be a probable target?

Rejda (p.4) describes two types of probability: objective and subjective: *"Objective probability* refers to the long-run relative frequency of an event based on the assumptions of an infinite number of observations and of no change in the underlying conditions."* For example, the probability of a perfectly balanced coin landing on "heads" is 1 in 2. The probability of rolling a six with a single die is 1 in 6. Objective probabilities can also be calculated by a careful analysis of past experience. Insurance companies and actuaries use objective probabilities in determining rates and premiums. Calculating objective probability involves the **law of large numbers**, which states that the more statistical information available from the past, the better the prediction as to what will happen in the future.

Subjective probability, in contrast, is an individual's personal estimate of the chance of something occurring. Many factors can influence subjective probability, including a person's age, gender, intelligence, education, experiences and the use of drugs or alcohol.

Establishing **criticality** involves deciding whether a loss, if it occurs, would be of minimum or maximum consequence. How serious would it be? Pilferage may appear to be of negligible seriousness, but if it is continuous and engaged in by many employees, it may be more costly than a robbery or burglary. Of course, when considerations such as human life or the national security are involved, cost becomes secondary.

A consideration for many businesses and organizations is whether the risk assessment should be conducted by in-house staff or outsourced. Consultants can bring objectivity to such assessments and provide the necessary level of expertise to those organizations lacking experienced risk management personnel.

© Ed Kashi/CORBIS

Computer server rooms and other places where large volumes of valuable data or other assets are stored receive enhanced security because of their high vulnerability and criticality factors. The probability of loss occurring is lessened through adequate access control, which may be accomplished through traditional lock and key techniques, although biometric measures are becoming increasingly common, as shown by the hand readers located outside this enclosed computer network bank.

Selecting Alternatives to Handle Identified Risks

Once risks are identified, alternatives are selected to reduce vulnerability to them. Inherent in risk management is a logical, systematic approach to deal with the recognized hazards. Usually a combination of alternatives provides the most comprehensive and effective level of risk management.

 Alternatives for risk handling include the following:

- Risk elimination
- Risk reduction
- Risk spreading
- Risk transfer
- Risk acceptance

Risk Elimination

The best alternative, if realistic, is to eliminate the risk entirely. For example, the risk of losses from bad checks or credit-card fraud can be avoided if the business does not accept checks or credit cards. The risk of employees till-tapping is eliminated if they are denied access to the cash register. Dynamic risks can be avoided or eliminated. They exist because of a management decision and can be eliminated by a change in management decision.

Risk Reduction—Establishing Controls

Pure risk will always exist and cannot be completely eliminated, and some dynamic risks cannot be avoided without incurring some other type of loss.

Frequently, the best alternative is to establish procedures and use physical hardware to reduce or minimize the risk. Controls refer to any organizational, procedural or technological means to manage risk. They are sometimes called safeguards or countermeasures. The approach is also referred to as *abatement, mitigation* or *loss prevention* (Brady, 2004, p.32). Figure 5.4 shows a simplified threat assessment and response continuum. Vulnerability exists wherever the security of an organization stops short of the adversary's ability to act. So the greater the security's capability, the smaller that window of opportunity gets for the attacker ("adversary").

For example, establishing and implementing check-cashing policies can reduce the risk of loss from bad checks. Installing locks, security lighting and alarm systems can reduce the risk of loss from burglary by delaying or detecting intruders. If the assets at risk are of high value, such risk-reducing methods should be considered.

Attack Trees An attack tree is one tool used to examine avenues of risk reduction (Almay, 2006). An **attack tree** visually represents the goal of an attack on some asset as the trunk of the tree and the possible and probable ways to accomplish the attack as branches (see Figure 5.5). For example, if someone wanted to gain unauthorized physical access to a building, possible means of attack would be to unlock the door with a key, pick the lock, break a window or follow an authorized person into the building. The branches can be further detailed, for example, unlocking the door with a key might involve stealing a key, borrowing a key or convincing a locksmith to unlock the door. Any measures taken to thwart a specific means of attack lop off the branch.

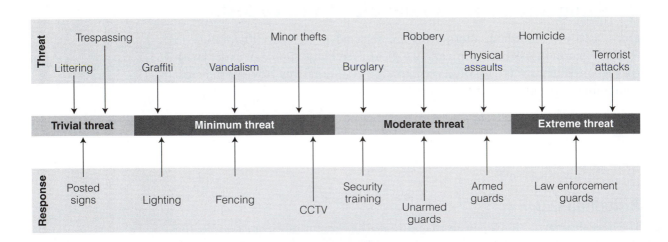

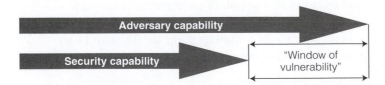

Figure 5.4 Threat Assessment and Response

SOURCE: From "Seeing the Risk Through the Trees" by Ted Almay. © 2006 ASIS International, 1625 Prince Street, Alexandria, VA 22314. Reprinted by permission from the September 2006 issue of *Security Management* magazine.

Risk Spreading

Closely related to risk reduction is the practice of risk spreading. This approach uses methods that ensure the potential loss in any single incident is reduced, for example, splitting up the placement of expensive jewelry into separate display cases so a breach of one display case does not necessarily allow access to all of the high-value items. Such risk spreading further reduces exposure to threats after risk-avoidance and risk-reduction measures have been instituted.

Risk Transfer

If risk elimination, risk reduction and risk spreading do not bring the risk to an acceptable level, the risk may be transferred either by raising prices or obtaining

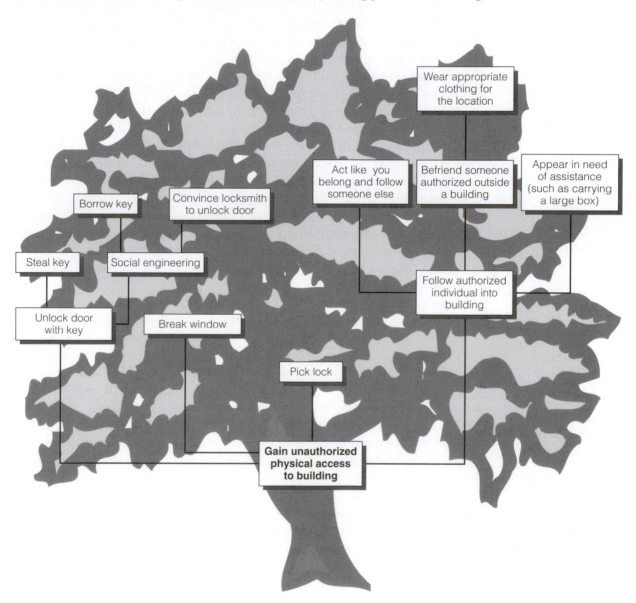

Figure 5.5 Attack Tree Model

SOURCE: From "Seeing the Risk Through the Trees" by Ted Almay. © 2006 ASIS International, 1625 Prince Street, Alexandria, VA 22314. Reprinted by permission from the September 2006 issue of *Security Management* magazine.

insurance. An important principle in insurance is that of **indemnity**, which states that the insurer pays only the actual amount of the loss and no more: "Stated differently, the insured should not profit from a loss" (Rejda, p.175). Most property and casualty insurance contracts are contracts of indemnity. Not all covered losses are always paid in full. Deductibles, dollar limits on the amount paid and other contract provisions may result in the amount paid being less than the actual loss.

The typical way to indemnify the insured is to consider the actual cash value of the damaged property at the time of loss. Three methods used to determine actual cash value are replacement cost less depreciation, fair market value and the broad evidence rule (Rejda, p.176). *Replacement cost less depreciation* considers both inflation and depreciation of property values over time. Replacement cost is the current cost of restoration; depreciation deducts for physical wear and tear and economic obsolescence. *Fair market value* is the price a willing buyer would pay a willing seller in a free market. The *broad evidence rule* says that the determination of actual cash value should include all relevant factors an expert would use to determine the value of the property.

An additional principle, that of subrogation, supports the principle of indemnity: "**Subrogation** means substitution of the insurer in place of the insured for the purpose of claiming indemnity from a third person for a loss covered by insurance. Stated differently, the insurer is entitled to recover from a negligent third party any loss payments made to the insured" (Rejda, p.179). Consider the common occurrence of a car crash: The driver of a red car negligently goes through a stop sign and hits a blue car, causing $2,000 in damage to the blue car. If the blue-car driver has collision insurance, that insurance company will pay the physical damage loss to the blue-car owner (less any deductibles) and then try to collect an equivalent amount from the negligent red-car driver who caused the crash.

Most establishments carry insurance against fires and other types of natural disasters, as well as liability insurance in case an employee or other person is injured on the premises. Bonding employees is another risk transfer alternative.

Rising insurance costs, however, can drastically affect reliance on insurance as a way to guard against unforeseen business losses. In addition, some losses are virtually impossible to insure against, for example, loss of customer confidence, lowered employee morale and loss of reputation. Vassar (2006, p.35) suggests that losses with low frequency and high severity are good targets for insurance: "Pay the little losses that happen all the time and insure those big losses that don't happen so much." Clearly, insurance can never be a substitute for a security program.

Another alternative to effective risk transfer is price raising, which also has obvious drawbacks. Most retail establishments raise prices to cover shoplifting losses. The key element of this method is the absorption of the loss by a third party. In effect, the cost of potential loss is transferred to the consumer.

Risk Acceptance

It is never cost-effective, practical or, indeed, possible to provide 100-percent security for an establishment. Risks can never be entirely eliminated. Some must simply be accepted. If a security survey has been conducted thoroughly and the results analyzed completely, the greatest and most likely risks will be identified and dealt with by the appropriate alternative or combination of alternatives. The remaining risks will be accepted as a part of the "cost of doing business."

Risk Balance: Cost versus Level of Protection

Management makes the preliminary decisions on the degree of security desired or required. Common sense plus the establishment's past history are key ingredients in stating security objectives. Security measures should neither obstruct operations nor be neglected; rather they should be an integrated part of the establishment's operations.

Risk management seeks to establish a cost-efficient protection system. In theory, the higher the protection costs, the lower the costs for loss and damage. But as can be seen in Figure 5.6, there is a point in the protection cost curve that should not be passed, that is, the point where the lowest total cost is obtained. In addition, the protection must be organized so that the requirements prescribed in state law are fulfilled. It is not always possible to calculate the cost of these requirements.

A well-functioning company protection system means that few disturbances will arise and, thus, company operations can carry on according to plan. Consequently, management can devote more time to proper working tasks. Investment in such protection is profitable.

Numerous tools and formulas have been developed to help security managers objectively assess the cost of various levels of protection.

Formulas Used in Risk Management
Among the formulas used in risk management are the following:
- Single Loss Expectancy (SLE)—the total amount of revenue lost from a single occurrence of the risk. It is calculated by multiplying the asset value by the exposure factor (EF). The exposure factor is the percentage of loss a

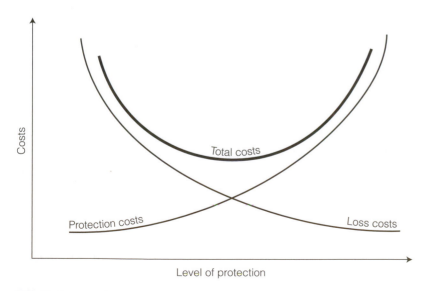

Figure 5.6   Cost versus Level of Protection

SOURCE: Adapted from Statsforetag AB, Skandia Insurance Co. and Skandia Risk Management Ltd., Stockholm, Sweden. Reprinted by permission.

realized threat could have on an asset. For example a fire might result in an estimated 25 percent loss of value. If an asset is valued at $150,000, the SLE in this case would be about $37,500.

- Annual Rate of Occurrence (ARO)—the number of times a risk is reasonably expected to occur during one year. This estimate is difficult to make and is similar to the probability of a risk occurring, ranging on a scale of 0 (never) to 100 percent (always). A risk such as fire that is anticipated to occur only once in 10 years would be given the value of 0.1.

- Annual Loss Expectancy (ALE)—the total amount of money an organization will lose in one year if nothing is done to eliminate or reduce the risk. This value is calculated by multiplying the SLE by the ARO. This is similar to the relative rank in qualitative risk assessment. In the example, if a fire results in $37,500 in damages and the probability (ARO) of a fire occurring is 0.1 (once in 10 years), the ALE value would be $3,750. An organization can work with this value to budget an amount that will establish controls to prevent this type of damage and provide adequate protection.

- Cost-Benefit Analysis—an estimate and comparison of the relative value and cost associated with each proposed control so the most effective are selected.

- Return on Security Investment (ROSI)—sometimes called simply return on investment (ROI). The total amount of money an organization expects to save in one year by implementing a given security control. This is calculated using the following equation:

(ALE before control) − (ALE after control) − annual cost of control = ROSI

One security director notes that describing the ROI is difficult because security's success is measured by the absence of loss, an intangible that is difficult to quantify: "One way to approach this is to look at three primary effects from a breach in security. First is the tangible cost, such as replacing stolen merchandise or damaged property. The second effect is the reputational cost, including bad press or lost customer confidence. Third are the indirect costs, such as increased insurance premiums and increased security patrols. Such costs are rarely included in loss assessments after a breach in security" (Roberts, 2005, p.69).

Risk Perception

In many instances, risk assessment needs to go beyond evaluating the likelihood and consequences of risks. Another factor to consider is risk perception, which deals with the psychological and emotional aspects of risk ("Taking Risk Assessment to Extremes," 2005, p.14). Do employees and visitors feel safe? Do they perceive that their security concerns are important to management?

 Risk management is both a moral and a legal responsibility.

The moral responsibility is obvious. People expect that the places they work or visit will be safe. The legal responsibility was the focus of Chapter 4. The legal liability and inherent cost of *not* providing adequate security can have significant negative consequences for businesses.

Quantitative and Qualitative Risk Assessment

Many organizations make the distinction between quantitative and qualitative risk assessment. In **quantitative risk assessment**, the goal is to calculate objective numeric values for each component gathered during the risk assessment and cost-benefit analysis (Microsoft). For example, to estimate the true value of each business asset in terms of what it would cost to replace it, what it would cost in terms of lost productivity, what it would cost in terms of brand reputation, and other direct and indirect business values. The same objectivity is used when computing asset exposure, cost of controls, and all the other values identified during the risk management process. Quantitative risk assessments have several weaknesses, including their reliance on estimates, their cost and the amount of time and staff required.

Qualitative risk assessment, in contrast, assigns relative values to assets, risks, controls and effects. What differentiates qualitative risk assessment from quantitative risk assessment is that the latter tries to assign hard financial values to assets, expected losses and cost of controls, whereas the former assigns relative values. The basic process for qualitative assessments is very similar to the quantitative approach. The difference is in the details. Comparisons between the value of one asset and another are relative, and participants do not invest a lot of time trying to calculate precise financial numbers for asset valuation. The same is true for calculating the possible impact from a risk being realized and the cost of implementing controls.

The benefits of a qualitative approach are that it overcomes the challenge of calculating accurate figures for asset value, cost of control and so on, and the process is much less demanding on staff. Qualitative risk assessment can typically start to show significant results within a few weeks, whereas most organizations that choose a quantitative approach see little benefit for months, and sometimes even years, of effort. The drawback of a qualitative approach is that the resulting figures are vague.

 Qualitative risk assessment identifies the most important risks quickly. Quantitative risk assessment then analyzes the most important risks with precision to balance cost and effectiveness.

Microsoft suggests "[c]ombining the simplicity and elegance of the qualitative approach with some of the rigor of the quantitative approach. A qualitative approach is used to quickly triage the entire list of security risks. The most serious risks identified during this triage are then examined in more detail using a quantitative approach. The result is a relatively short list of the most important risks that must be examined in detail" (*Security Risk Management Guide*).

ASIS Guidelines for a Qualitative Approach to Risk Management

The ASIS has developed a seven-step approach to qualitative risk management, as illustrated in Figure 5.7.

1. Understand the Organization and Identify the People and Assets at Risk　Considerations include hours of operation; staffing levels during each shift; type of labor (labor union, unskilled, use of temporary workers, immigrants, etc.);

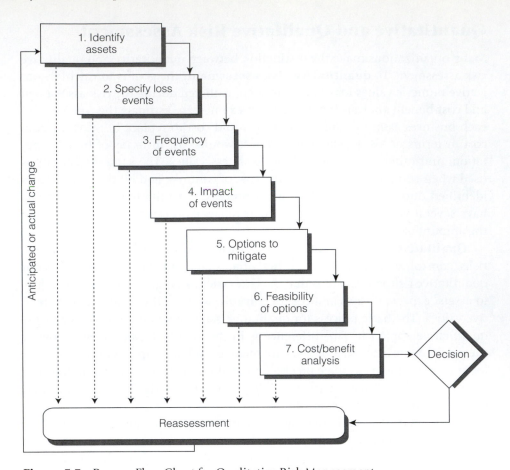

Figure 5.7 Process Flow Chart for Qualitative Risk Management

SOURCE: From "The Security Risk Management Guide" in *Microsoft*, October 15, 2004, updated March 15, 2006, Chapter 3, p.7.

types of clients served; nature of the business activity; types of services provided or products produced, manufactured, stored or otherwise supplied; the competitive nature of the industry; the sensitivity of information; the corporate culture; the perception of risk tolerance and the like.

2. Identify the People and Assets at Risk and Loss Events *People* includes employees, customers, visitors, vendors, contract employees and any one else lawfully present on the property. Trespassers may also be at risk for open, obvious hazards or where an attractive nuisance exists (abandoned warehouse, vacant building or shortcut). In most states, trespassers need only be warned by signs identifying the hazard. *Assets* include property and information. Property includes real estate, land and buildings, facilities; tangible property such as cash, precious metals and stones; high-theft items such as drugs, securities and cash; as well as almost anything that can be stolen, damaged or otherwise adversely affected by a risk event. Information includes proprietary data such as trade secrets, marketing plans, business expansion plans, plant closings, confidential personal information about employees, customer lists and other data that, if stolen, altered or destroyed, could harm the organization.

Loss events fall into three categories: crimes, noncriminal events such as human-made or natural disasters, and consequential events caused by an enterprise's relationship with another organization when the latter organization's poor or negative reputation adversely affects the enterprise.

3. Establish the Probability of Loss Risk and Frequency This is not based on mathematical certainty but on a consideration of the likelihood that a loss risk event may occur based on historical data at the site, the history of like events at similar enterprises, the nature of the neighborhood, immediate vicinity, overall geographical location, political and social conditions, and changes in the economy. For example, an enterprise located in a flood zone or coastal area may have a higher probability for flooding and hurricanes than an enterprise located inland and away from water.

4. Determine the Impact of the Event All potential costs should be considered—direct and indirect, financial, psychological and hidden or less obvious. *Direct costs* may include financial losses associated with the event, such as the value of goods lost or stolen; increased insurance premiums for several years after a major loss; deductible expenses on insurance coverage; lost business from an immediate post-risk event, for example, shortage of stock due to theft; labor expenses incurred as a result of the event; management time dealing with the disaster or event and punitive damages awards not covered by ordinary insurance.

Indirect costs may include negative media coverage; long-term negative consumer perception; additional public relations costs to overcome poor image problems; lack of insurance coverage due to a higher risk category; higher wages needed to attract future employees; shareholder derivative suits for mismanagement; poor employee morale leading to work stoppages, higher turnover and the like.

5. Develop Options to Mitigate Risks A range of options are theoretically available to address the risk events and losses an enterprise may face. "Theoretically" alludes to the fact that some options are not feasible or are too costly to implement. Options include security equipment and hardware; policies, procedures and post orders and management practices; and staff as previously discussed. Post orders should be carefully drafted, detailed and in writing, to ensure security officers do not go beyond their contracts and create an unintended duty (Solensky, 2007, p.88). Employees should be instructed to refrain from assuming duties or making decisions beyond the written post orders. Other options include transferring financial risk through insurance coverage or contract terms such as indemnifications clauses in security services contracts or simply accepting the risk as a cost of doing business.

6. Study the Feasibility of Implementing the Options While financial cost is usually a factor, a common consideration is whether the strategy will interfere with the enterprise's operation. An example would be an enterprise open to the public that increases access control so severely it creates a negative environment, discouraging people coming to the facility. A balance must be maintained between sound security and the enterprise's operational needs as well as the psychological impact on the people affected by the security program.

7. Perform a Cost-Benefit Analysis The cost of implementing the selected alternatives should be weighed against the potential loss, financially or otherwise. It would make no sense to spend more money protecting an asset than the asset is worth, as already discussed.

ASIS Quantitative Approach

As in Microsoft's quantitative approach, the ASIS approach uses formulations to assess risk. The first step is to calculate the probability and criticality of an event. In this calculation, the loss event must produce an actual, measurable loss, and the loss should not be the result of a speculative risk in which non-occurrence of the event would not result in a gain.

One formula for probability or frequency of occurrence is to determine the number of ways a particular event can result from a large number of circumstances that could produce that event, divided by the actual number of those occurrences:

$$P = f/n$$

where:

P = the probability that a given event will occur

f = the number of actual occurrences of that event

n = the total number of circumstances that could cause that event

For example, the probability of shoplifting at a given location during a given year is determined as: p (probability) equals the number of days on which actual shoplifting events occurred during the year divided by 365. However, the result may not be realistic, as some events will occur more than once and others only once, and the reaction will change the environment in an effort to prevent future occurrences. As a general consideration, the more ways a particular event can occur in given circumstances, the greater the probability it will occur.

Rather than relying on simplistic formulas, the ASIS recommends that probability ratings be used to allow priority scheduling in countermeasures. It may be enough to be able to say one event is more probable than another. Five categories of probability, coded alphabetically, can help make this distinction:

A. Virtually certain—given no changes, the event will occur, for example, a closed intake valve on a sprinkler riser will prevent water flow in the event of fire.
B. Highly probable—the likelihood of occurrence is much greater than that of nonoccurrence, for example, unprotected money lying visible on a counter is very likely to be taken.
C. Moderately probable—the event is more likely to occur than not to occur.
D. Less probable—the event is less likely to occur than not to occur, but it is not impossible.
E. Probability unknown—insufficient data are available for an evaluation.

Once the probability of an event has been determined, the criticality of the event must be established. Criticality can be measured in several ways, with the most common being financial loss. Another cost is effect on employee morale.

Some losses, such as loss of human life, loss of national infrastructure elements or loss of community goodwill, cannot be analyzed. Cost-of-loss formulas are complex and beyond the scope of this discussion. Again, the ASIS recommends using criticality ratings, this time coded numerically, rather than mathematical formulas:

1. Fatal—the loss would result in total recapitalization or abandonment or long-term discontinuance of the enterprise.
2. Very serious—the loss would require a major change in investment policy and would have a major impact on the balance sheet assets.
3. Moderately serious—the loss would have a noticeable impact on earnings and would require senior executive management attention.
4. Relatively unimportant—the loss would be charged to normal operating expenses for the period in which it was sustained.
5. Seriousness unknown—before priorities are established, this provisional rating is to be replaced by a rating from one of the first four classes.

A risk identified as A1 would require much more attention than one coded C4.

Conducting qualitative and quantitative risk assessments can give security managers a fairly comprehensive picture of an organization's security needs. Consider next an emerging trend that takes a holistic approach to an organization's security needs: the enterprise risk management model.

The Enterprise Risk Management Model

Longmore-Etheridge (2006, p.92) describes the enterprise risk management model as the "creeping *force majeure* facing security professionals." She suggests that the enterprise risk management model requires the convergence of traditional and information technology (IT) security to better define security risks and interdependencies between business functions and processes within an enterprise.

Enterprise Risk Management: An Emerging Model for Building Shareholder Value (no date) states: "Enterprise risk management (ERM) has emerged as an important new business trend. ERM is a structured and disciplined approach aligning strategy, processes, people, technology and knowledge with the purpose of evaluating and managing the uncertainties the enterprise faces." ERM removes the traditional functional, divisional, departmental and cultural barriers and takes a truly holistic, integrated and future-focused approach to security.

Enterprise Risk Management—Integrated Framework (2004, p.2) states: "**Enterprise risk management** is a process, affected by an entity's board of directors, management and other personnel, applied in strategy setting and across the enterprise, designed to identify potential events that may affect the entity, and manage risk to be within its risk appetite to provide reasonable assurance regarding the achievement of entity objectives" [boldface added]. Fundamental concepts reflected in this definition are that enterprise risk management is:

- An ongoing process flowing through an entity.
- Affected by people at every level of an organization.
- Applied in strategy setting.
- Applied across the enterprise, at every level and unit.

- Designed to identify potential events that, if they occur, will affect the entity and to manage risk within its risk appetite.
- Able to provide reasonable assurance to an entity's management and board of directors.

Fay (p.25) describes a step-by-step process that can be used to conduct a vulnerability assessment (VA) using the enterprise risk management approach: identify critical assets, identify potential threat elements, estimate the probability of threat occurrences, estimate the severity of threat occurrences, identify the enterprise's current capability to mitigate and counter threat occurrences, identify the absence of measures needed to mitigate and counter threat occurrences, and formulate a scheme for integrating the acquired countermeasures with existing countermeasures. This should sound quite familiar, as it nearly parallels ASIS's process flow chart for qualitative risk management (refer back to Figure 5.7). Enterprise management steps in when the VA is completed and a final report submitted (Fay).

It must be noted that enterprise risk management will not apply to all organizations and businesses. In addition, to fully understand enterprise risk management, security managers must understand the various components within the system. Organizations that do not have a comprehensive risk management program in place leave themselves open to disgruntled employees and customers as well as to potential civil liability discussed in Chapter 4.

The enterprise risk management model is not the only model being used in organizations. Some models view security as a business center.

Security as a Business Center

Historically, security has been viewed as an overhead function—a necessary evil where security expenditures are justified by citing risk mitigation and management, loss prevention and loss reduction (Telders, 2005, p.44). This is the *commodity model*, viewing security operations purely as overhead. As little time, effort and money as possible is expended to accomplish security. The benefits of the commodity model are low cost and low labor; the obvious drawbacks are the potential for low-quality security. Telders contends that the commodity model limits the scope of security and that, instead, security should be seen as a dynamic, challenging function within the organization that directly affects the bottom line. He presents several alternative models of security's function in an organization that can contribute to the bottom line in different ways.

The *business partner model* focuses on the needs of the individual business, not of the business sector in general. In this model security professionals are trusted advisors who suggest solutions on a variety of issues, as is frequently the case in larger organizations with a set of products and services. This model works well when a close working relationship is required between security and other departments. The benefits of this model include specific controls and strong internal relationships. Drawbacks include lack of research on the model and variable controls at multiple locations.

The *quality model*, as the name suggests, focuses on the quality of the products and services an organization provides: "When the focus becomes doing the job right, especially on the first try, the approach taken to provide security needs to reflect quality" (Telders). This can be done by using products and services provided by companies that have high quality standards. In this model officers are given substantially more training when hired and usually have regular training updates and continuing education that are site-specific. The benefits of the quality model include higher security and high quality. Drawbacks include increased cost and increased management.

The *business enabler model* is often appropriate if a business is attempting to expand by broadening its range of products and services. New territory often comes with additional security challenges and risks. This presents an opportunity for security professionals, working closely with the IT department, to create a remote access security architecture that provides secure, safe connectivity. If security can show the benefits of creating such an architecture and work proactively, the security department becomes a business enabler. The benefits of this model are improved image and support, and the company benefits. Drawbacks include increase project risk and more effort to obtain funding.

The *visionary model* focuses on creating something unique. Telders (p.47) provides as an example the merger of companies and the security director being charged with consolidating security controls and reducing costs. This model requires close working relationships with other departments. The benefits of this model include better security and industry leadership. Drawbacks include project risks and research and development expenses.

Most organizations will not fit neatly into only one model. Some operations may have elements of all the models. Telders (p.47) recommends that security professionals not be trapped in a single approach. Sometimes the commodity approach is the best answer because the solution is well defined and requires only standard treatment. Other times groundbreaking methods may be required: "The bottom line is to be flexible and aware of the best approach to deal with each challenge." A key to determining the best approach is often found by conducting a security survey or audit.

The Security Survey or Audit

A **security survey** or **audit** is an objective but critical on-site examination and analysis of a business, industrial plant, public or private institution or home. Its purpose is to determine existing security, to identify deficiencies, to determine the protection needed and to recommend improvements to enhance overall security. Brady (p.32) explains the technical difference between a survey and an audit: "A security survey consists essentially of mapping existing systems or programs. . . . A security audit is a means of measuring or testing existing programs against client documentation or expectation." In actuality, the security managers often use the two terms interchangeably.

Silverman (2004, p.54) contends: "A good security audit or survey entails a combination of common sense, experience and a keen eye." The actual survey can be in the form of a checklist, prepared with adequate space between entries for detailed notes. Often aerial maps or diagrams of the facility are included with the security survey. The amount of detail in the survey will vary depending on the general area, as well as all roads and streets leading to the facility; the perimeter, including fencing, warning signs and no-parking signs; the buildings, including construction and possible points of unauthorized entry, entrances and exits, entry control, locks and keys, alarm systems and lighting; identification of restricted areas, including computer rooms; procedures to control theft or pilferage of property or information; employee safety, including fire protection and emergency plans; security personnel required, including needed training and responsibilities; and security indoctrination of all employees.

All potential targets of attack should be identified and the means for eliminating or reducing the risk to these targets specified. Pure risks should also be identified. For example, is the facility susceptible to accidents, arson, auto theft, bombs, burglary, fraud, kidnapping, larceny, sabotage, theft or vandalism? For each pure risk identified, appropriate security measures should be recommended.

 The security survey (audit) is a critical, objective and on-site analysis of the total security system.

The survey lists the components of the security system to be observed and evaluated. Many such surveys exist. Figure 5.8 illustrates a basic security survey.

Skorka (2004, p.40) suggests that everything need not be surveyed or audited at the same time: "One of the most beneficial actions a building manager can take is authorizing a top-to-bottom security audit on the effective use of electronic access control (EAC). . . . Such an assessment can identify potential threats or 'soft targets' that might not otherwise be recognized and recommend the best, most cost-efficient methods and technologies to harden these targets and protect the facility and its people."

A security audit often surveys employees and customers to see if they are satisfied with security's services and, if so, why (McCoy, 2006, p.44). Such a survey can foster positive feelings toward the security department as well as security awareness throughout an organization. For example, a security survey in one company revealed that many managers resented the delays that background screening caused in bringing in new workers. This finding led security to explain the importance of background screening and also to shorten the delay from several weeks to only three days.

Businesses and industries that work for the federal government *must* meet certain security standards and complete self-audits.

Conducting the Security Survey

After the survey is developed, someone should physically walk through the establishment, observing and talking to personnel to obtain the required information. Usually the survey is conducted by the security director, but it may also be conducted by an outside consulting firm.

 The information needed for a security survey is obtained by observing and by talking to personnel.

Evaluation may be inherently threatening to employees. No one wants to be found responsible for a breach in security. But employees must be honest in their responses if the results of the survey are to be valid. Therefore, the correct climate must be established so that employees will cooperate and answer questions honestly. Of utmost importance is explaining the purpose of the survey to

J&B Innovative Enterprises, Inc.
123 South Street, Anywhere, U.S.A.
Holiday/Weekend Security Checklist

Instructions: Check all items, ensure each area has been inspected for general safety, see General Safety checklist.** **DO NOT leave this facility unattended if ANY of the *Bold* items on this checklist cannot be checked**. Refer to the emergency personnel list at the receptionist desk, contact one of the persons on the list for further instructions. Minor problems that can be resolved the next working day should be logged under comments. This checklist must be submitted to the plant manager the next working day.

**GENERAL SAFETY (check each area)
- ☐ *All cigarettes extinguished*
- ☐ *All roof access doors locked*
- ☐ *All water faucets closed*
- ☐ *Flammable spills which may ignite*
- ☐ *Obvious frayed/defective wiring*
- ☐ *All fire doors secured*
- ☐ Floors' condition okay
- ☐ Aisles clear
- ☐ Stairways clear
- ☐ Lights (no burned-out bulbs)
- ☐ First aid kits visible & stocked
- ☐ Fire extinguishers visible & charged

PRODUCTION AREA (Do not power down any equipment, unless specified)
- ☐ *Windows secured*
- ☐ *Compressor off, relief valve open*
- ☐ *Fans & machinery off*
- ☐ Compressor room locked
- ☐ Air hose service lines bled
- ☐ Rest rooms empty
- ☐ Lights off/night lights on

SHIPPING & RECEIVING AREA
- ☐ *Fans & machinery off*
- ☐ *Garage doors secure*
- ☐ *Battery chargers turned off*
- ☐ Rest rooms empty
- ☐ Forklift secure
- ☐ Windows secure
- ☐ Lights off/night lights on

STOCK/CRIB ROOM
- ☐ *Stock room locked*
- ☐ *Crib window locked*
- ☐ Rest room empty
- ☐ Lights off/night lights on

OFFICE AREA (Do not power down any equipment including computers)
- ☐ *Safe locked*
- ☐ *File cabinets locked*
- ☐ All office doors closed
- ☐ Lights off/night lights on

BUILDING EXTERIOR
- ☐ *All external doors & windows locked*
- ☐ Outside lights timer set
- ☐ Parking lot empty
- ☐ Gates in parking area locked

COMPUTER ROOM (Do not power down any equipment)
- ☐ *Doors locked, alarm set*

CHECKLIST COMPLETED (minor problems logged under comments)
- ☐ *Plant secured*
- ☐ *Security alarm tested & armed*

I understand and have completed the preceding checklist. It will be submitted to the plant manager the next working day.

Name _____

Time _____ Date _____

Comments: _____
_____

Figure 5.8 Basic Security Survey
SOURCE: Courtesy of J&B Innovative Enterprises, Inc.

those from whom information is requested. Without such an explanation, the people interviewed may feel they are "under suspicion" for their actions.

Koverman (2004, p.52) points out: "A professional review of the security program can and should be a worthwhile experience for a facility. If the review is conducted professionally and the report written objectively, it will evolve into a partnership that provides a proactive management tool for identifying and dealing with risks and vulnerabilities."

How Vulnerable Is Your Business?

- Are you and your employees careful and alert when opeining and closing your place of business?
- Do you keep a record of equipment and merchandise serial numbers?
- Are your employees thoroughly screened before hiring?
- Do you keep more than a minimum amount of money on hand?
- Is your alarm system checked regularly?
- Do you have a key control system?
- Are locks re-keyed after an employee leaves your employment?
- Is your safe combination changed periodically?
- Are any company vehicles parked where they block the view of doors and windows, or can be used for climbing onto the roof?
- Do you vary your route and schedule of banking?
- Are your employees trained in procedures for a robbery, burglary, shoplifter, short change check and credit card artist?
- Have you participated in Operation Identification?

Figure 5.9   Sample Security Survey

NOTE: Operation Identification is a burglary prevention program for private citizens and businesses in which property is permanently marked with an identifying number (typically a driver's license number or business name) as a way to discourage burglary and theft, as marked property is difficult for a thief to dispose of or resell.

SOURCE: Mecklenburg County Police Department, Charlotte, NC.

Many of the interviewing techniques discussed in Chapter 1 are applicable when conducting a security survey. The Mecklenburg County Police Department has developed a list of questions to ask when assessing vulnerability during a security audit (Figure 5.9). These questions can be modified and adapted to suit a variety of establishments and organizations.

Reporting the Results

Once the survey is conducted, the risk analysis is completed and the alternatives for handling the risks are selected, the information must be communicated to individuals who can act on the findings. The information should be written into a comprehensive report that includes, at minimum, the following sections:

1. Introduction—a brief summary of the purpose of the survey, the anticipated risks and the identified needs and objectives of the total security system; also, a description of the survey developed and conducted to assess the system (a copy of the survey should be included in an appendix at the end of the report)
2. A discussion of the risk analysis
3. Strengths of the system—what is working well
4. Weaknesses of the system—areas of vulnerability and potential risk, arranged in order of priority
5. Recommendations for alternatives for managing the risks, including the estimated cost and savings and who should be responsible for making the changes

The professional security manager must devote as much time to quantifying and qualifying security initiatives as any other department within an organization to justify resource allocations and expenditures. The complete security survey, the security report and any copies of these documents should be treated as *confidential* documents.

Kovacich and Halibozek (2004, p.28) stress: "Managers must market security programs like any product, selling top management and staff on the seriousness of threats and the importance of their roles." Vaughn (2006, p.44) offers the following advice: "Any business presentation requires careful thought and a plan for success. The decision maker may be an individual manager or a group, such as an executive committee. In either case, the fundamentals are the same. For a proposal to succeed, it must have broad grassroots support, substantive content, good design and a credible presenter."

Grassroots support means involving not only decision makers but also those who will be affected by the program. This includes anyone who might oppose the program, perhaps out of fear of change. *Content* should strike a medium between being too sketchy or too detailed and should include the "M resources," as listed by Vaughn, that will get the attention of senior managers: What money, materials, methods, minutes, machinery, maintenance, management, markets or manpower are involved? *Design* will depend on the level of formality. Presenters should understand the corporate culture and what practices are generally followed for similar proposals from other business units within the organization. *Credibility* is very subjective, but it is wise to "scope out the audience and play to their preferences. Vaughn (p.48) recommends letting decision makers know when a project accomplishes what was promised to build long-term credibility and support for the next proposal. In summary, an effective security proposal presentation will include the following (Vaughn, pp.44–48):

- A clear statement of what the proposal is and why it is needed
- The problem or opportunity that led to the proposal and its background
- The need for the proposal tied to dollars and time
- The implementation plan
- Support for the plan based on credible references
- A recap of main points and an opportunity for questions

Implementing the Recommendations

Implementing the recommended changes is management's responsibility. Changes might include modifying procedures, improving or upgrading security equipment or adding security equipment personnel. Consider the example illustrated in Figure 5.10 of recommended security measures identified through a security survey to prevent burglary at a generic, hypothetical facility.

Ahrens and Oglesby (2006, p.82) note that most companies do not have the money to implement everything at once, so they should consider making security improvements over several years in a staged, documented approach, allowing the company to defer extremely large expenses while showing it is taking steps to improve security.

Budgeting is always an important consideration in implementing any recommended changes. Budgeting efforts may be facilitated by dividing costs into specific categories, as illustrated in Table 5.2. Budget requirements may limit somewhat the extent of implementation. Some changes may not be made for weeks or months, but a schedule should be established so that high-priority changes are made first.

Implementing the recommendations also frequently requires tact and diplomacy. Security managers must recognize their establishment's overall plan,

Prevention can be best achieved by:
1. Recognition of security risks.
2. Initiation of corrective action to remove them.

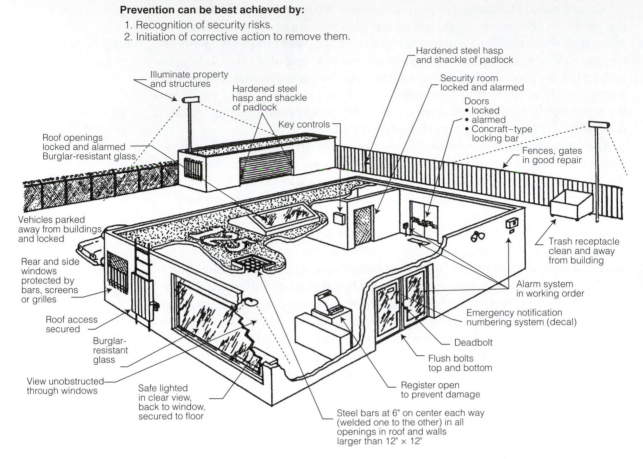

Figure 5.10   Illustrated Checklist of Security Measures

SOURCE: Courtesy of the Mecklenburg County Police Department, Charlotte, NC.

goal and needs. The security system does not operate in a vacuum but relies on the understanding and support of all persons involved in the business or industry. Consequently, security managers must build acceptance and trust, and they must act as professionals who understand and respect the needs and wants of others.

Evaluating the Security System

Evaluation, or auditing, of security should be ongoing. As management guru Peter Drucker has said: "What gets measured, gets managed." The effects of any changes made as a result of the security survey should be studied. For example, if a need for personnel training is identified and a program instituted, the effectiveness of that training should be assessed. Periodic, unannounced audits should be conducted of security procedures, such as cash handling or check cashing. Some aspects of the security system, such as closing procedures, are checked daily. Other components should have a regular schedule of inspection.

 Each component of the security system should be periodically evaluated (audited) and changes made as needed.

Table 5.2 Example of a Budget for Security

	Investment		Operating Cost		
	Prevention	**Loss Limitation**	**Prevention**	**Loss Limitation**	**Insurance**
Work Protection					
Common equipment	X		X		
Individual equipment	X		X		
Surveillance					
Identity card			X		
Personnel			X		
Technical	X		X		
Fencing, locks	X				
Fire Service					
Prevention	X		X		
Extinguishing		X	X		
Company Health Care					
Sick care	X	X	X	X	
Insurance					
Company insurance					X
Personal insurance					X
Product liability					X
Labor market no-fault					X
Liability insurance					
Reserve Equipment				X	
Training and Information in Company Protection Questions			X	X	
Total Sum					

SOURCE: From Statsforetag AB, Skandia Insurance Co. and Skandia Risk Management Ltd., Stockholm, Sweden. Reprinted by permission.

The needs and objectives of the entire security system should be reevaluated annually. Security needs change as an establishment grows or as the neighborhood changes. If the city installs street lights or provides routine patrol by local police, the establishment may need less of its own external security. However, if the neighborhood deteriorates and vandalism and crime increase, it may need more security. Figure 5.11 illustrates a typical audit process.

Keys to Success

Whenever an organization undertakes a major new initiative, various foundational elements must be in place if the effort is to be successful. Microsoft has

An effective audit of a risk management program includes four steps:

- Have they identified risks and requirements?

- Have they prepared risk control program?

- Have they implemented risk control program?

- Have they maintained and overseen program?

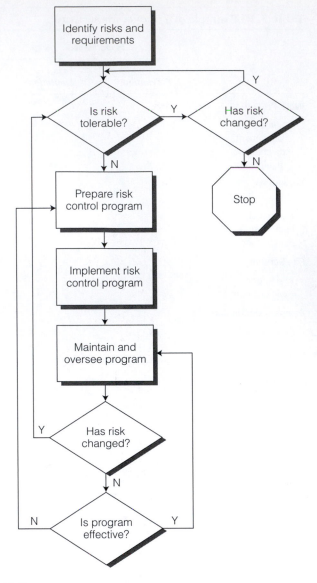

Figure 5.11 The Security Audit Process

SOURCE: From Arthur D. Little, Inc., "Put Security to the Test". © 1994 ASIS International, 1625 Prince Street, Alexandria, VA 22314. Reprinted by permission from the December 1994 issue of *Security Management* magazine.

identified components that must be in place before implementing a security risk management process and that must remain in place once it is underway. They are:

- Executive sponsorship.
- A well-defined list of risk management stakeholders.
- A clear definition of roles and responsibilities.
- An atmosphere of open communication.
- A spirit of teamwork.
- A holistic view of the organization.
- Authority throughout the process.

Microsoft (p.3) has stressed: "Security risk management will fail without executive support and commitment. When security risk management is led from the top, organizations can articulate security in terms of value to the business."

SUMMARY

- Private security managers must recognize and deal with both pure risk—risks with the potential for injury, damage or loss with no possible benefits—and dynamic risks—risks that have potential for both benefits and losses.

- Risk management involves anticipating, recognizing and analyzing risks; taking steps to reduce or prevent such risks and evaluating the results.

- The worth of an asset depends on three primary factors: the overall value of the asset to the organization, the immediate financial impact of losing the asset and the indirect business impact of losing the asset.

- A systematic approach to preventing loss through risk management includes risk analysis, policy formulation, specification of a protection plan and follow-up.

- Risk analysis focuses on three factors: vulnerability, probability and criticality.

- Once risks are identified, alternatives to handle these risks must be selected. Alternatives for risk handling include risk elimination, risk reduction, risk spreading, risk transfer and risk acceptance.

- Risk management is both a moral and a legal responsibility.

- Qualitative risk assessment identifies the most important risks quickly. Quantitative risk assessment then analyzes the most important risks with precision to balance cost and effectiveness.

- A key tool in risk analysis is the security survey, a critical, objective, on-site analysis of the total security system.

- The information needed for a security survey is obtained by observing and by talking to personnel.

- In addition to the comprehensive security survey that may be conducted yearly or at even more lengthy time intervals, periodic audits should be made of each component of the security system, and changes should be made as needed.

APPLICATIONS

1. List the pure and dynamic risks in your own daily life. Then indicate whether you have taken steps to reduce these risks and, if so, list the actions you have taken.

2. As the security manager for a local hotel, list the dynamic and pure risks that could affect the operation and rank them in order of priority.

3. As security manager in charge of organizing company protection, list the statutes in your state that affect a cost-effective security program (e.g., licensing, bonding, training requirements and the like).

DISCUSSION QUESTIONS

1. What types of programs would you implement to eliminate pure risks in a company?

2. How much responsibility and authority should be placed at the security supervisory level to cope with dynamic risks?

3. What could cause the needs and objectives of a security system to change? Elaborate.

4. In developing a security survey, what areas should receive a high priority?

5. Is it better for security managers to develop their own security survey or to use one developed by someone else?

REFERENCES

Aggleton, David G. "Designing Your Security Video System." *Security Technology & Design*, March 2005, pp.74–80.

Ahrens, Sean A. and Oglesby, Marieta B. "Levers against Liability." *Security Management*, February 2006, pp.80–84.

Almay, Ted. "Seeing the Risk through the Trees." *Security Management*, September 2006, pp.101–112.

ASIS/Security Management Survey of Security Directors. "Security Market Trends." *Security Management*, November 2007, p.27.

Bernstein, Peter L. *Against the Gods: The Remarkable Story of Risk*. New York: John Wiley and Sons, 1998.

Brady, Michael. "So You Want a Security Survey." *Security Technology & Design*, October 2004, pp.32–34.

Daniels, Rhianna. "Report Names Top Challenges." *Security Director News*, February 2007, p.8.

Enterprise Risk Management: An Emerging Model for Building Shareholder Value. KPMG (Klynveld, Peat, Marwick and Goerdeler), no date.

Enterprise Risk Management—Integrated Framework: Executive Summary. COSO (Committee of Sponsoring Organizations of the Treadway) Commission, September 2004.

Fay, John. "Security's Role in Enterprise Risk Management." *Security Technology & Design*, July 2005, pp.22–25.

Friedrick, Joanne. "Risk Assessment Is Foundation of a Strong Security Plan." *Security Director News*, December 2006, p.19.

General Security Risk Assessment. Arlington, VA: American Society for Industrial Security International, 2004.

Hess, Timothy S. "ORM=IRC." U.S. Kunsan Air Force Base, South Korea, Personal Correspondence, February 21, 2007.

Kovacich, Gerald L. and Halibozek, Edward P. "Make Security a Hot Product." *Security Management*, January 2004, pp.28–30.

Koverman, Robert. "Security Vulnerability Study: Requirements & Expectations." *Security Technology & Design*, January 2004, pp.34–37, 52.

Longmore-Etheridge, Ann. "Converging Goals." *Security Management*, January 2006, pp.92–96.

McCoy, R. Scott. "Better Service through Surveys." *Security Management*, May 2006, pp.44–46.

"Newspoll." *Security Director News*, January 2007, p.23.

Rejda, George E. *Principles of Risk Management and Insurance*, 10th ed. Boston, MA: Pearson Education, Inc., 2008.

"Risk Management Expert Unveils 'Lessons Learned' from 9/11/01." *PRNewsWire*, July 8, 2002. http://www.prnewswire.com/cgi-bin/stories.pl?ACCT=104&STORY=/www/story/07-08-2002/0001759844&EDATE=. Accessed January 8, 2008.

Roberts, Marta. "From Back Burner to Business Imperative." *Security Management*, August 2005, pp.67–72.

The Security Risk Management Guide. Microsoft, October 15, 2004, updated March 15, 2006.

Silverman, Lionel. "Security System Audits and Surveys." *Security Technology & Design*, May 2004, pp.54–58.

Skorka, Donald. "Updating the Facility Security Process." *Security Technology & Design*, May 2004, pp.40–42.

Solensky, Edward, Jr. "Who's Liable Now?" *Security Management*, March 2007, pp.80–88.

"Taking Risk Assessments to Extremes." *Security Management*, February 2005, p.14.

Telders, Eduard L. "Security as a Business Center." *Security Technology & Design*, February 2005, pp.44–47.

Vassar, Rick. *HIDE! Here Comes the Insurance Guy: A Practical Guide to Understanding Insurance and Risk Management*. Lincoln, NE: iUniversity Inc., 2006.

Vaughn, Robert H. "Presentation Prowess." *Security Management*, March 2006, pp.44–48.

CHAPTER 6

Enhancing Security through Physical Controls

Physical controls are a critical element in a facility's security. Fencing, lights, surveillance cameras and observation towers are integrated components in this nuclear plant's security plan.

Do You Know . . .

■ What CPTED is and how it applies to physical security?

■ What four purposes are served by physical controls?

■ What three lines of defense are important in physical security?

■ What basic security equipment consists of?

■ What functions are performed by lighting?

■ Where alarms may be received?

■ What the generic name for a variety of surveillance systems is?

■ How the perimeter of a building can be made more secure? The building exterior? The interior?

■ What factors must be balanced in selecting physical controls?

■ What the human element of security consists of?

Can You Define?

access control

activity support

biometrics

commissioning

concentric zone theory

crash bar

crime prevention
through
environmental
design (CPTED)

defensible space

envelope (building)

exculpatory clauses

meta-analysis

natural surveillance

panic bar

physical security
footprint

territoriality

watch clock

Introduction

Throughout time, people have used physical controls to protect themselves and their property. Among other things, they have built their dwellings on poles, constructed high fences, rolled boulders in front of doors, buried money, tied gaggles of geese where an intruder would startle them, stationed lookouts and built fires to frighten away wild animals. Although modern physical security controls are usually much more sophisticated, the intent is the same: to prevent any outsider from harming the owner or the owner's property.

The American Society for Industrial Security (ASIS) has a certification program for the physical security professional (PSP). The program culminates with an exam covering three areas (*Physical Security Professional (PSP) Examination Structure and Content,* 2007):

■ Physical security assessment (41 percent of the test questions)—includes identifying assets, assessing the nature of the threats, conducting a physical security survey and performing a risk analysis

■ Selecting integrated physical security measures (24 percent of the test questions)

■ Implementing physical security measures (35 percent of the test questions)

The first exam area, physical security assessment, was the focus of Chapter 5. The second and third areas of the PSP exam are the focus of this chapter, which begins with a brief introduction to the concept of crime prevention through environmental design (CPTED) and a discussion of basic physical controls, including the three fundamental lines of defense: the perimeter, the building exterior or shell and the interior. This is followed by an examination of basic security equipment: locks, lights and alarms. Next is a discussion of surveillance systems, other types of security devices and how all the preceding can come together into an integrated physical security system.

Note that the following discussion presents general procedures that might apply in most facilities. Additional procedures frequently required in industrial, retail, commercial, institutional and other specific types of establishments are discussed in later chapters.

Crime Prevention through Environmental Design (CPTED)

An important concept in security planning is **crime prevention through environmental design**, most commonly referred to as **CPTED**. According to the International CPTED Association (ICA): "CPTED has as its basic premise that the proper design and effective use of the physical environment can lead to a reduction in the incidence and fear of crime, thereby improving the quality of life."

The concept of CPTED as an approach to security design began evolving in the early 1960s, when Jane Jacobs explored the relationships between urban decay, social interactions and crime in *The Death and Life of Great American Cities*. Building on Jacobs's work, Angel (1968) proposed the idea that community residents could play a more active part in crime prevention by recognizing the environmental conditions that make certain areas more attractive as targets to criminals. In 1969, architect Oscar Newman was commissioned by the National Institute of Justice (then called the National Institute of Law Enforcement and Criminal Justice, or NILECJ) to study the relationship between the physical environment and risk for criminal victimization, with the results of his research published in 1972 as *Defensible Space: Crime Prevention through Urban Design*. Newman defined **defensible space** as "the range of mechanisms that combine to bring an environment under the control of its residents."

At the same time Newman was setting forth his defensible space theory, C. Ray Jeffery was working on *Crime Prevention through Environmental Design* (1971) and is, thus, credited with coining the term that has since grown into a basic premise of contemporary security (Robinson, 1998). In fact, CPTED is now a staple course offered at ASIS conferences, seminars and professional development programs every year; it has been a featured topic at the National Association of Convenience Food Stores conventions and it was one of the sessions offered at the American Institute of Architects (AIA) Design Technology Expo 2008.

 Crime prevention through environmental design (CPTED) is a fundamental concept in security design. It is based on the premise that effective use and manipulation of the physical environment can affect criminal behavior in a way that will reduce the incidence and fear of crime and improve the quality of life.

CPTED builds on the four key strategies of territoriality, natural surveillance, activity support and access control (National Crime Prevention Council, 2004):

- **Territoriality:** People protect territory that they feel is their own and have a certain respect for the territory of others. Fences, pavement treatments, art, signs, good maintenance and landscaping are some physical ways to express ownership. Identifying intruders is much easier in a well-defined space.

- **Natural surveillance:** Criminals do not want to be seen. Placing physical features, activities and people in ways that maximize the ability to see what is going on discourages crime. Barriers, such as bushes, sheds or shadows, make it difficult to observe activity. Landscaping and lighting can be planned to promote natural surveillance from inside a home or building and from the outside by neighbors or people passing by. Maximizing the natural surveillance capability of such "gatekeepers" as parking lot attendants and hotel desk clerks is also important.
- **Activity support:** Encouraging legitimate activity in public spaces helps discourage crime. A basketball court in a public park or community center will provide recreation for youths, while making strangers more obvious and increasing active natural surveillance and the feeling of ownership. Any activity that gets people out and working together—a clean-up day, a block party, a Neighborhood Watch group, a civic meeting—helps prevent crime.
- **Access control:** Properly located entrances, exits, fencing, landscaping and lighting can direct both foot and automobile traffic in ways that discourage crime. Access control can be as simple as a neighbor on the front porch or a receptionist in a front office. Other strategies include closing streets to through traffic or introducing neighborhood-based parking stickers.[1]

These principles are blended in the planning or remodeling of public areas that range from parks and streets to office buildings and housing developments. Some jurisdictions have incorporated these principles into more comprehensive approaches.

Newman's theory of defensible space posited that four situations in the built environment must be addressed to deter criminal activity: massive buildings, multitude of exits, location in crime areas and the "Broken Window Syndrome" (Barnard, 2006, p.118). Massive buildings and multiple entrances and exits pose significant security challenges. If an establishment's location is already in a high-crime area, many of the measures implicit in CPTED might reduce crime. Finally, implications of the Broken Window Syndrome must be considered, as this syndrome holds that if broken windows go unrepaired, soon more broken windows will appear. "Broken windows" refers to any obvious signs of "incivilities" such as trash in yards, unmown lawns, peeling paint, persistent structural disrepairs and the like—indications that people do not care about their neighborhood or what goes on there. Community residents might be enlisted to clean up the neighborhood and make it aesthetically pleasing.

Barnard suggests three choices for situational crime prevention: (1) increase the difficulty to commit the crime by frequent patrols or environmental design or other security measures, (2) increase the risk of getting caught, either by surveillance, patrols, proactive and aggressive neighborhood involvement and (3) remove rewards, such as instituting a graffiti management program.

The proactive approach inherent in CPTED can decrease costs related to security breaches and can reduce insurance premiums, business downtime and

---

[1]SOURCE: National Crime Prevention Council, 2004. http://www.ncpc.org.

the cost of repairing or replacing assets (Macdonald and Kitteringham, 2004, p.129). Additional intangible benefits may also result. For example, in the decade since Calgary (Canada) began conducting CPTED training for police and private security, the city has realized not only the material benefits of decreased security-related costs, but has also seen the ties between public law enforcement, private security, city planners and area builders strengthened. Included in Calgary's efforts to improve the built environment is the requirement that a CPTED audit be part of the permitting process for all new construction of liquor stores, schools, parking garages and strip malls.

Macdonald and Kitteringham (p.132) give as an example a downtown property with a 1950s-era six-story "parkade" that had fallen prey to car thefts, vandalism and property damage. CPTED students used the site for practice and repeatedly recommended that lighting be improved to encourage natural surveillance. Initially, the parking facility owners did not adopt the recommendations, but as incidents increased and evening business dwindled, the owners implemented the audit recommendations, installing brilliant white light fixtures and painting the walls with reflective white paint. The new lights radiated into areas where illegitimate users had previously concealed themselves. The stairwell doors were removed to make the stairwells less attractive for criminal activities. The lighting and increased natural surveillance made the parkade uncomfortable for thieves, muggers, graffiti artists and other troublemakers. Evening business increased as criminal activity decreased.

McKay (2004, p.146) notes: "Crime prevention through environmental design (CPTED) has been effectively used for more than 40 years to reduce crime and improve a community's quality of life." However, he suggests it may be time to consider its limitations and how it could be improved. One way might be to expand its traditional approach and introduce a new proactive methodology, behavioral-based design (BBD). Behavioral-based design looks at the predictable ways people interact with an environment and then factors that interaction into the design when developing the most appropriate physical settings for inducing desired behavior. For example, the thirst to be noticed and perhaps famous drove the first generation of graffitists and taggers to leave their marks on walls in the late 1960s. Given that they seek out highly visible locations, a standard CPTED response, such as adding lighting, can actually aggravate the problem.

Interestingly, this "new" methodology is not as innovative as many today would think, for when Jeffery first developed his CPTED model, it included both the external environment of the place *and* the internal environment of the person who commits the crime. However, since that time the "internal" part of the formula has been largely ignored: "[F]or, as CPTED exists in government, architecture, academia, and corporate business, little if any consideration is given to the internal, physical environment of the offender. Rather, attention is given only to the external physical environment of the place. In academia particularly, CPTED has been developed only with regard to the external environment. . . . This is a serious limitation of the current body of CPTED literature" (Robinson).

Use of CPTED in specific applications is discussed in later chapters. For now, take a closer look at the following basic physical controls.

An Overview of Physical Controls

Physical controls are often the first things that come to mind when one thinks of *security*. And, as emphasized in the previous discussion on CPTED, controlling the physical environment is crucial in achieving effective security.

 Physical controls serve to reduce risk of loss by:

- Denying unauthorized access.
- Deterring or discouraging attempts to gain unauthorized access.
- Delaying those who attempt to gain unauthorized access.
- Detecting threats, both criminal and noncriminal.

The **concentric zone theory** of asset protection, illustrated in Figure 6.1, is based on the premise that the more valuable an asset is, the more layers of protection it needs. Such circles of protection create a defensible space. A business or organization's defensible space is often separated into three distinct zones, each of which offers a line of physical security.

 The three basic lines of physical defense are the perimeter of a facility, the building exterior and the interior.

Sometimes all three lines of defense are available, as with, for example, a manufacturing firm situated on its own acreage. Other times only one line of defense is available, for example, the interior office space of a small company occupying a single room in a large business complex. Although the office man-

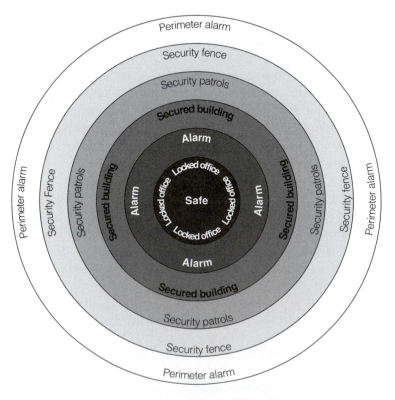

Figure 6.1   Concentric Layers of Physical Security

ager can bring pressure to bear on the office complex manager to ensure security, the individual office manager has very limited control.

These three distinct layers or zones of physical security will be discussed shortly. First, consider the equipment commonly used throughout the various areas of an organization's overall security system.

Basic Security Equipment

At all three lines of defense—perimeter, exterior and interior—certain basic equipment can add considerable security. The degree of physical security required will determine which of the basic components is used. In some instances, locks may be all that are required. In other instances, lights, alarms and surveillance systems may also be needed.

 Basic physical security equipment consists of locks, lights, alarms and surveillance cameras.

Locks

Locks were used in Egypt more than 4,000 years ago, and they have been important security devices ever since. Locks are, in fact, one of the oldest, most commonly used, cost-effective means to physically control access to an area, a building, a room or a container.

The primary function of a lock is to deter or deny access into a protected area. Although any lock can be opened by a determined, skilled person, locks are valuable because they increase the amount of time an intruder must spend gaining access, thereby increasing the probability of being detected. Additionally, locks frequently provide evidence of forced entrance, evidence that may be required to collect insurance. Available types of locks include key-operated, combination, card-activated and electronically operated. Kozoil (2005, p.22) contends that moving from mechanical locks to an electronic locking system is the first step toward integrated access control. The next step involves computer-managed (CM) locking systems, which use stand-alone, programmable, battery-powered locks that provide audit-trail capability and time-based scheduling for restricting access.

Key-operated locks are most frequently used and are simple to operate. *Combination locks* are often used on padlocks as well as on safe and vault doors. Some combination locks are operated by *pushbuttons* rather than dials. One or more buttons are pushed, either in sequence or simultaneously. Such locks are often used on individual rooms or on entrances to semiprivate rooms in large buildings. Many *keypads* rely on microchip technology and have great flexibility.

Card-operated locks are inserted into a card reader installed near a restricted door or passageway. When an authorized card is inserted into the slot, a minicomputer activates the locking device, thereby opening the door, traffic control arm, gate or turnstile. Some card-operated locks are also equipped so that the identification of the person operating the lock and the time it was operated are automatically recorded.

Freeman (2004, p.12) reports: "Proximity cards have been king of the hill for some time now, and they continue to dominate pass-card technology." In fact, a survey of security users across the county revealed 84 percent use proximity (prox) cards, which operate on a radio frequency, for access control. What was once the industry standard, the magstripe card, has lost ground to prox cards. Magstripe cards are capable of storing data by modifying the magnetism of tiny iron-based magnetic particles on a band of magnetic material on the card.

Smart cards have also gained in popularity. A smart card, chip card or integrated circuit card is a pocket-sized card with embedded microprocessors that can dynamically process information (Piazza, 2005, p.42). In August 2004, President Bush signed Homeland Security Presidential Directive 12 (HSPD 12) calling for a mandatory governmentwide issuance of a common form of identification, in effect endorsing smart card technology (Anderson, 2005a, p.27). The directive set a new federal standard for issuing personal identify verification (PIV) cards and covers all federal employees and on-site contractors, entailing as many as 50 million credentials (Anderson, p.30). The smart card's computational capabilities offer other benefits: "The same card that allows an employee to enter the building can be used to purchase food at the company cafeteria, while at the same time tracking access into highly secured company area" (Feeser, 2005, p.60).

Biometrics   *Biometrics* is serving an increasingly important function in access control, replacing the traditional "key" or access card, which is relatively easy to duplicate or steal, with a uniquely identifying personal attribute or trait held only by the individual seeking access. **Biometrics**, from the Greek root words *bios* meaning *life* and *metron* meaning *measure*, is the science of using individual physiological features or behavioral characteristics to positively identify a person and verify the person's identity. Some biometric technologies, such as those systems that scan fingerprints or palm prints, voices, retinas, irises, facial features, hand geometry or signatures, are relatively well established and used extensively in industrial, commercial, financial and banking, governmental, military, educational, medical and scientific and research-oriented facilities worldwide. Other emerging biometric technologies are using odor, gait (how someone walks), DNA, ear recognition and vascular recognition (the unique vein patterns in the human finger or hand) to positively identify individuals. Table 6.1 provides a comparison of various biometric technologies.

Ryan (2004, p.17) describes the two primary biometric functions—identification and verification—and notes an important distinction between them. Identification seeks to answer "Who are you?" by comparing a presented characteristic to all pre-enrolled individuals in a database. Identification biometric systems can be used without the subject's knowledge or consent, for example, facial recognition at a sporting event or mass transit hub. Verification, on the other hand, asks "Are you who you say you are?" and authenticates the identity of an individual by comparing a presented characteristic to a pre-enrolled (stored in a database) characteristic of that same individual.

If there is no pre-existing databank, and biometrics are used simply to verify an individual's identity in situations where such verification is permissible, identification biometrics present no conflicts with current U.S. federal law. When there is a databank, biometrics may be legally used to identify a person in circumstances where the public has a justifiable need to know who that person is and whether that person poses a threat (Ryan).

Table 6.1 Comparison of Various Biometric Technologies, According to A. K. Jain

(H=High, M=Medium, L=Low)*

Biometrics:	Universality	Uniqueness	Permanence	Collectability	Performance	Acceptability	Circumvention
Face	H	L	M	H	L	H	L
Fingerprint	M	H	H	M	H	M	H
Hand geometry	M	M	M	H	M	M	M
Keystrokes	L	L	L	M	L	M	M
Hand veins	M	M	M	M	M	M	H
Iris	H	H	H	M	H	L	H
Retinal scan	H	H	M	L	H	L	H
Signature	L	L	L	H	L	H	L
Voice	M	L	L	M	L	H	L
Facial thermograph	H	H	L	H	M	H	H
Odor	H	H	H	L	L	M	L
DNA	H	H	H	L	H	L	L
Gait	M	L	L	H	L	H	M
Ear recognition	M	M	H	M	M	H	M

*A.K. Jain ranks each biometric based on the categories as being either low, medium, or high. A low ranking indicates poor performance in the evaluation criterion whereas a high ranking indicates a very good performance.

SOURCE: From Jain, A.K. (April 28–30, 2004) "Biometric recognition: How do I know who you are?", *Signal Processing and Communications Applications Conference, 2004. Proceedings of the IEEE*, 12th: 3–5.

Despite periodic resistance from civil liberties groups, most people who use biometrics to clock in at work or log onto computers know their biometric information cannot be easily duplicated and that the government is not secretly collecting biometric data to add to a mammoth Orwellian database (Zunkel, 2005, p.46). As biometrics is increasingly used in private business, the International Biometrics Industry Association has developed privacy principles that call for safeguards on biometric data, strict user control over biometrics in private sector applications and laws that compartmentalize and carefully regulate use of biometrics in the private sector. Several states have also passed their own legislation on gathering and distributing biometric data.

Harowitz (2007, p.48) cautions tests of various biometric systems in recent years have shown that they are not foolproof. She notes that fingerprint authentication systems could be fooled by dusting a latent print with graphite powder, placing adhesive film over it and applying pressure. Iris recognitions systems have been "spoofed" with high-resolution photographs with an eyehole cut for the pupil and custom contact lenses with high-resolution iris patterns printed on them.

Despite the privacy infringement concerns and possible loopholes in the application of the technology, Ryan (p.20) observes: "Biometrics are here to stay. While the technology and applications are still in their infancy, technology advancements are improving performance, lowering cost and expanding

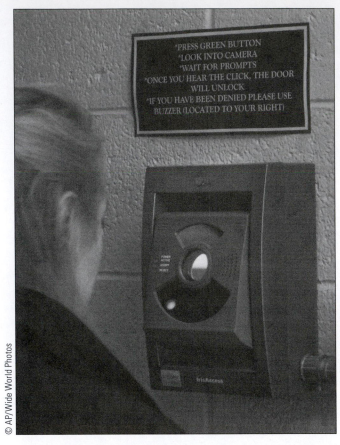

A parent looks in an iris-recognition scanner to gain entrance to her child's elementary school in New Jersey. Iris recognition systems use a video camera to record the colored ring around the eye's pupil. More accurate than fingerprints and other biometric markers, iris technology is considered a nearly foolproof way of identifying people because markings in the iris are unique to each person and do not change as people age. The district also has the system in place in its middle and high schools.

to broader applications." Echoing the enormous security potential afforded through biometrics, Kalocsai and Imparato (2006, p.34) note that a host of technological advances have accelerated improvement in face recognition accuracy. Equally important, public attitudes are becoming less negative. Policy efforts, such as developing rigorous standards, also underscore the likelihood that face recognition has gained the traction needed to become an enduring security tool. Ryan (2005, p.50) concludes: "Biometric technology is capable of defending the United States and its citizens from terrorists, criminals, identity thieves, computer hackers and other villains. As this technology readies itself to soar, it must wait for the slow and deliberate legal machinery and social acceptance to catch up."

Combined Measures—Integrating Biometrics and Smart Cards As a way to further enhance security, organizations can now develop smart cards embedded with a variety of biometric technologies (Piazza, 2005, p.48). An example of an integrated access control approach might involve scanning a person's fingerprints and taking the person's photo, and then embedding a smart card with this data. The issued card can be used in both contact and contactless environments, enabling the user to gain access to areas with both technologies.

In addition to controlling access to certain areas and information, adequate lighting also enhances security.

Security Lighting

Intruders prefer the cover of darkness to conceal their actions. The majority of nonresidential burglaries occur at night. In fact, three out of four commercial burglaries are committed within buildings with little or no light. A total lighting system includes four types of lighting:

- *Continuous*, on a regular schedule, for secure areas
- *Standby*, for occasions when more light is needed
- *Moveable*, for when light is needed in areas not usually lit
- *Emergency*, to be used as an alternate power source when the regular power source fails

 Adequate light inside as well as outside a building enhances safety, deters would-be intruders and makes detection of actual intruders more probable.

The effectiveness of various crime prevention programs and policies can be assessed using **meta-analysis**, a quantitative tool to evaluate several separate but similar experiments by combining the results and testing the pooled data for statistical significance. Researchers found 13 studies where improved street lighting was the main intervention being tested and an experimental area was compared to a control area. A meta-analysis concluded that improved street lighting reduced crime 20 percent (Sherman and Schlossman, 2006). Of interest was that nighttime crimes did not decrease more than daytime crime, appearing to support the community pride theory of situational crime prevention, which argues that improved street lighting signals community investment and leads to greater community cohesiveness and informal social control. The researchers concluded that street lighting "appears to be a feasible, effective and inexpensive method of reducing crime."

Lighting and locks are often supported by alarms for additional security.

Alarms

Alarm systems date back to at least 390 B.C., when squawking geese alerted the Romans to surprise attacks by the Gauls. Centuries later, geese were used to protect the perimeter of the Ballantine Scotch distillery in Scotland. Many homeowners depend on their dog's senses of smell and hearing to detect intruders and to then warn them by barking. Alarms have always been an effective supplement to locks, especially if the locks do not stop a persistent intruder.

Many federally insured institutions, such as banks, are required by law to install alarm systems. Additionally, many insurance companies offer lower premiums to businesses protected by alarm systems. Alarms are used not only to detect intruders, but also to detect fires. In some instances, alarms monitor physical conditions such as temperature, humidity, water flow, electrical power usage and machinery malfunction.

Trade magazines can provide current information on specific alarm systems' characteristics and capabilities. When selecting an alarm system, security managers should pay careful attention to the contract and whether it contains a limitation of liability clause. **Exculpatory clauses**, clauses that limit liability, are reasonable in that alarm systems are not designed to guarantee that no loss will occur.

Alarm Respondents An important decision facing a security manager who selects an alarm as one means of reducing risk is where the alarm should be received.

 Alarm systems may be local, proprietary, central station or police connected.

Local alarms sound on the premises and require that someone hears the alarm and calls the police. Such alarms are the least expensive but are also the least effective because no one may hear them; they may be heard but ignored and they are easily disconnected by a knowledgeable intruder. In addition, they are extremely annoying to others in the area.

Proprietary alarms use a constantly manned alarm panel that may receive visible and/or audible signals to indicate exactly where the security break has occurred. Such systems are owned and operated by the property owner. Taylor (2006, p.8) recommends that when a critical alarm is received at a monitoring station, a highly distinctive visual and audio cue should annunciate, alerting of the critical event. A critical alarm must always have priority on the monitoring screen. The entire alarm system configuration should be designed to assist the operator at the console in accurately assessing the alarm.

Central station alarms are similar to the proprietary system, except that observation of the control panel is external to the alarm's location and is usually under contract with an alarm agency. The central station can receive alarms from hundreds of different businesses.

Police-connected alarm systems direct the alarm via telephone wires to the nearest police department.

False Alarms Although alarm systems are important means of physical control, they also pose a very serious problem: false alarms. More than 90 percent of all intrusion-alarm signals are false alarms, resulting in needless expense, inappropriate responses and negative attitudes toward alarm systems, as discussed in Chapter 3.

Because of the high percentage of false alarms, many cities prohibit alarms directly connected to the police department. Even with such restrictions, however, local law enforcement officers are usually called to alarms received by central stations or proprietary centers. Department policy usually dictates that a burglary or robbery-in-progress call be treated as an emergency and that officers respond as rapidly as possible, presenting possible danger to the responding officers and any individuals along the route to the scene. Many departments throughout the country have instituted fines to alleviate the problem.

The false alarm problem has been addressed in many organizations by connecting the alarm to a surveillance system.

Surveillance Systems

Many companies use surveillance systems in place of or to supplement security officers. These systems may be used at any of the three lines of defense: the perimeter, the entrances and exits to a building or specific locations within the building. According to Feeser (p.58): "Surveillance cameras have begun to take center stage over access control in security system design."

Many forms of surveillance are available including analog and digital video cameras, Internet video systems and night cameras that use infrared or thermal imaging technology. Surveillance systems can operate continually or on demand and can be monitored or unmonitored. The most common form of surveillance is closed circuit television (CCTV).

Closed Circuit Television (CCTV)   Closed circuit television (CCTV) is "a system in which a number of video cameras are connected in a closed circuit or loop, with the images produced being sent to a central television monitor or recorded" (Ratcliffe, 2006, p.3). The term *closed circuit television* was originally used to differentiate between public television broadcasts and private camera-monitor networks.

 Currently CCTV is used as a generic term for a variety of video surveillance technologies.

Although some systems are extremely sophisticated, employing bulletproof casing, night-vision capability, motion detection and advanced zoom and automatic tracking capacities, many existing systems are more rudimentary. More common CCTV installations include a number of cameras connected to a control room where human operators watch a bank of television screens. Often an operator can pan, tilt and zoom the cameras. As the technology has developed, cameras with a full range of movement and control facilities have become the norm, and it is likely there will be continual improvements in optical and digital zoom, color and pixel resolution, all of which will enhance image quality.

Surveillance cameras may be overt, semi-covert or covert. In *overt* systems the cameras are exposed and readily visible to the public and are often accompanied by signs indicating that the area is under CCTV surveillance. Overt systems have a strong crime prevention rationale but are more vulnerable to tampering and vandalism. *Semi-covert* systems still place the cameras in public view but enclose them behind a one-way transparent casing. Familiar designs include the black sphere suspended near the ceiling or the black, covered dome protruding from the ceiling. This surveillance method retains most of the preventative rationale of the overt system but provides some protection for the cameras. It also prevents the public from determining who is under surveillance and the exact number of cameras in a system. In *covert* systems the aim is to hide camera locations. These systems are particularly well suited to crime detection; however, without public signage or a publicity campaign, they have little crime prevention function until word spreads within the offender community (Ratcliffe, p.22).

A main benefit of CCTV is its purported ability to deter crime. People who know they are being monitored are much less likely to engage in criminal behavior. A meta-analysis of 19 separate evaluations of CCTV aimed to evaluate the effectiveness of CCTV on reducing crime (Sherman and Schlossman). To be included in the review, CCTV had to be the focus of the intervention and the studies had to compare an experimental area with a control area. Some studies indicated that CCTV reduced crime, but others showed no clear effect or that crime actually increased in CCTV areas. But among the 19 studies included in the meta-analysis, the overall effect was that CCTV reduced crime by 8 percent in experimental areas compared to control areas. CCTV also was more effective when used in parking lots to prevent auto theft than it was in city centers or on public transportation systems. It was most effective used in combination with improved lighting. A number of other benefits, beyond crime reduction, may be accrued from a CCTV system, including reduced fear of crime, assistance in investigations and information gathering.

Analog versus Digital Cameras   Analog CCTV systems became popular in the 1970s, but as security challenges increased and technology advanced, analog systems proved ineffective and inefficient for all but the smallest security environments (Gorovici, 2004, p.40). When digital video recorder (DVR) technology emerged in the mid-1990s, it offered a high-performance, cost-effective alternative to the VCR. The advantages of DVR over analog recording include image superiority, increased storage space, near-instant access to key information, reduced maintenance time and costs, and flexible recording control. But DVR is not the last stop for surveillance technology. A survey of dealers and surveillance integrators revealed a common belief that while DVR will still be "the king of the road" in 2009, networked video systems (NVS) will follow close behind (Freeman, 2005b, p.14). The research shows little doubt that the video network business is moving away from analog. Perhaps both analog and digital systems will grow in parallel as some users decide to simply upgrade their analogs while other go completely digital.

An analog-digital hybrid is available to "connects the dots" between presently installed analog and new digital equipment and between traditional security and IT-based solutions (Apple, 2005, p.68). This hybrid provides an upgrade path that is forward-compatible with evolving digital architectures but does not require users to throw away perfectly good analog equipment. A hybrid solution supports today's cost-effective analog systems while providing a cabling infrastructure ready for Internet protocol (IP) video systems once full IP-switchover occurs.

Internet Protocol (IP) Video Systems   The increased use of corporate networks marks one of the biggest turning points the security industry has ever witnessed (Anderson, 2005b, p.31). Surveillance technology has evolved to where video can be sent across a company's data network, allowing the video feed to be accessed from wherever the company so chooses (Piazza, 2006, p.92). The camera becomes like any other network device, given an IP address and plugged into the network. IP video can use a local area network (LAN), a wide area network (WAN), a wireless network or the Internet. However: "The security of the video information being sent via the network—both internal and external—is an important consideration" (Piazza, p.94). In addition: "High-resolution IP-based systems increase quality but also greatly raise the amount of data on a company's network, causing bandwidth and storage concerns. Companies must carefully balance the need for high-quality video against what it will cost them to capture, transmit, and store the necessary data" (Spadanuta, 2007, p.80).

Freeman (2005a, p.16) suggests: "IP video may be the last missing link in the relationship between an enterprise's security department and its IT department. The transition from analog cameras and DVRs to IP cameras and NVRs is critical to the security department of any protected enterprise, because it is the last step in the complete digitization of video surveillance systems."

Intelligent Video   Intelligent video is science-based, computer vision-based software that constantly analyzes scenes based on core indicators (Daniels, 2007b, p.1). The capabilities of video equipment, especially digital video equipment, are advancing faster and with more impact than any other security technology. Spadanuta (p.80) states: "Intelligent video options like video motion detection, facial recognition, and left-object detection are some of the applications that are growing more common in the CCTV world and promising to change the way video surveillance is done."

Intelligent video systems can now tell if something has been added permanently to a scene, if a fixed item has been removed from the scene, if an object is moving fast or slow and the direction of the motion, if a moving object is large or small and the estimated distance to an object (Aggleton, 2005, p.78). Algorithms can detect, classify and track objects and generate alerts when user-defined rules are violated, for example, a vehicle traveling at 50 mph in a 30 mph zone.

Voice Over Internet Protocol (VoIP)   "VoIP is a compelling technology that offers great promise but is still bumpy in its implementation" states Feeser (p.61). This technology takes surveillance one step further by allowing security personnel to hear what is happening at a remote site and also be heard at the site. The two-way conversation travels completely over the Internet. Allowing voice and data communications to share networks increases efficiency, reliability and cost savings (*Voice Over Internet Protocol*, 2007, p.1).

Night Cameras   Davis (2007, p.59) notes that since humans mastered fire, they have used it to shine light on the darkness and keep the wolves at bay. Even though our ancestors faced different threats, contemporary security is still concerned with "things that go bump in the night." The most popular and common night vision is based on *image intensification* technology that amplifies available visible and near infrared light to achieve better vision (Clemens, 2007, p.28). In contrast to image intensification, *thermal imaging* operates on the principle that all objects emit infrared energy as a function of their temperature. This type of "night vision" uses a thermal imager to collect the infrared radiation from objects in a scene and create an electronic image. Thermal imagers are entirely independent of the ambient light level and can also penetrate obscuranats such as smoke, fog and haze (Vallese, 2007, p.51).

Another advancement in surveillance cameras is *smart night vision*, which employs a device designed specifically to address the needs of users in an urban environment. Smart night vision is used everywhere from shopping mall parking lots to the proverbial dark alley—any environment where the varying degrees of shadows and light and dark areas present significant nocturnal visual challenges (Hopkins, 2007, p.89). This technology provides a "smart" device that can discriminate light from dark, bumping up the pixels from the inky blackness around a dumpster in the shadowy fringe of an industrial center while simultaneously harmonizing the sudden glare of a car's headlight turning into view.

The following section discusses some concerns related to security surveillance systems.

Security, Surveillance and Privacy Concerns

In the United States, privacy issues related to the use of CCTV surveillance are first and foremost in regard to the Fourth Amendment of the U.S. Constitution, which protects a citizen from unreasonable searches and seizures by government agencies. The courts, however, have thus far held that the constitutional emphasis is on protecting people, not places. As a result, at least in terms of clearly public places, citizens cannot have a reasonable expectation of privacy. While reasonable expectations of privacy tend to be subjective, where the simple video (not audio) surveillance of individuals in public space is occurring, the use of CCTV would appear to be constitutionally acceptable.

Gips (2007, p.18) notes a trend toward local jurisdictions legislating CCTV use. For example, in Chicago and Milwaukee, bars and nightclubs are required to post surveillance cameras on their premises. Baltimore County has required all shopping centers to install CCTV. In El Cerrito, California, an ordinance has been proposed that would require 73 local businesses, including liquor stores, convenience stores, takeout restaurants, banks, shopping centers, check cashing establishments, pawnshops and second-hand brokers and firearms dealers to install surveillance cameras at all structural entrances and exits, loading dock areas, customer and employee parking areas, and entrances and exits to parking areas (Daniels, 2007a, p.1). Local law enforcement believes these establishments will benefit most from surveillance technology because of their history as locations where serious crimes have previously occurred.

However such ordinances may infringe on both privacy rights and the right to free expression. Concern exists among security professionals that in some of these settings, CCTV is not a good use of resources and may actually create liability, particularly where an ordinance requires surveillance recording but not concurrent monitoring (Gips). Even if a business has posted signs informing the public that surveillance is not monitored, a person may have a viable claim for damages if they are injured within the view of a camera.

New technology using laser-based monitoring addresses privacy concerns.

Laser-Based Surveillance

The Department of Energy's Oak Ridge National Laboratory has developed a Laser-Based Item Monitoring System (LBIMS) that balances the need for high-resolution monitoring and personal safety with respect for confidentiality and personal privacy: "[The] system is specifically designed to address surveillance requirements in places where video would be unacceptable because of the presence of proprietary information or other privacy concerns" ("Laser-Based

Device Offers Alternative," 2007). LBIMS uses low-cost reflective tags placed on objects to map the precise location of high-value items. The laser can scan many points per second and can detect small changes—less than a centimeter—in the reflected signal, enabling the immediate detection of tampering.

Consider next how basic security equipment can be used at all three lines of defense, beginning with the perimeter.

The Perimeter

The location of a facility influences its security needs, and site selection for new construction requires carefully consideration. Is the site in a high-crime area? Is there ample public lighting? Do local law enforcement officers patrol there? If a facility has grounds around it, security measures can be used to protect this perimeter. Perimeter barriers, any obstacles that physically limit a controlled area and impede or restrict entry into the area, are the first line of defense against intrusion.

 The perimeter can be physically controlled by fences, gates and locks; alarms; lighting; surveillance systems; vehicle barriers; dogs and security personnel; and signs. Parking lots, garages and ramps require additional security planning. The perimeter's physical layout and neatness are important factors.

Fences

Some facilities are protected by a natural barrier, such as the water surrounding Alcatraz. Usually, however, a barrier must be constructed as a physical and psychological deterrent to intruders.

Two basic fence types are ornamental and chain link. Ornamental fencing is both functional and aesthetic. It can be made of materials ranging from powder-coated steel and aluminum to wrought iron. Not only do ornamental fences offer curb appeal, but they are very rigid and durable and require less maintenance than fences constructed with wood. In addition, if these fences are equipped with sensors, they are less likely than other fencing types to produce false alarms (Traxler, 2005, p.88).

If aesthetics is not a major consideration, chain-link fences are useful and cost-effective. They can be enhanced by adding security features such as razor or barbed wire. Many companies and facilities take the practical approach of using a combination of fencing types, placing ornamental fences in areas most visible to visitors or the public and chain-link around all other areas (Traxler, p.90). For example, a business serving as both an industrial and tourist site placed attractive ornamental fencing around the areas frequented by tourists, including the visitor's center, and used a chain-link fence to enclose the industrial areas. In addition to saving money, by using this combination, the chain-link fence helped differentiate between public and private areas (Traxler).

Issues to consider in fence placement include proximity to facilities, climbing aids, disruptive landscaping, character of the neighboring areas and placement of entryways (Traxler, p.88). As a general rule, the fence should be placed as far away as possible from the structure it is protecting to allow optimum warning time and should be at least 10 feet away from any climbing aids such as telephone poles, light poles and large trees.

For maximum security, *all* perimeter openings must be secured, including not only gates, but also air-intake pipes, chutes, culverts, drain pipes, exhaust conduits, sewers, sidewalk elevators and utility tunnels. Perimeter openings that cannot be permanently sealed because they serve a function should be barred or screened if they are larger than 96 square inches. If a gate exists along the fence line, additional attention must be given to securing the gate with appropriate locks and, perhaps, supplementary surveillance at this entrance or exit point.

Alarms

Often the fence, the gates and all perimeter openings are connected to an alarm system. Such sensored fencing acts as both a physical barrier and a detection device if properly installed and maintained (Traxler, p.87). As noted, ornamental fencing is better suited to such sensors. According to Reddick (2005, p.42): "Modern technological advances and years of real-world experience have produced reliable, affordable outdoor sensors that are easy to install and to use." Sensored fences must be calibrated to accommodate the normal weather conditions and need to be tested periodically to avoid false alarms.

Perimeter Lighting

Adequate lighting on the perimeter is another prime consideration. An unobstructed view is of little consequence in complete darkness. Four types of lights are commonly used:

- *Floodlights* form a beam of concentrated light for boundaries, fences and area buildings and, positioned correctly, produce a desired glare in the eyes of anyone attempting to see in.
- *Streetlights* can cast a diffused, low-intensity light evenly over an area and are often used in parking lots and storage areas.
- *Fresnal units* provide a long, narrow, horizontal beam of light ideally suited for lighting boundaries without glare.
- *Searchlights*, both portable and fixed, provide a highly focused light beam that can be aimed in any direction and are ideal for emergencies requiring additional light in a specific area.

Boundary lighting is often provided by floodlights that create a barrier of light, allowing those inside to see out, but preventing anyone on the outside from seeing in (see Figure 6.2). Although the glare may deter intruders, it can also pose a traffic hazard or annoy neighbors; therefore, the technique is not always possible to use.

Surveillance Cameras

Perimeter surveillance systems commonly go hand-in-hand with perimeter fencing and lighting. For industrial plants and other facilities where the outside grounds and peripheral property area is vast, such surveillance systems, monitored by a central security station, can offer far more comprehensive security coverage than can a roaming patrol or stand-alone security device, such as fencing.

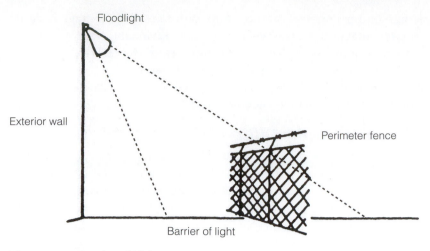

Figure 6.2   Barrier of Light

Vehicle Barriers

"Vehicle barriers are for today's businesses what city walls were millennia ago. They represent a first line of defense against potentially devastating car-bomb attacks, which remain one of the most common and lethal weapons of choice for terrorists" (Kessinger, 2004, p.57). Perimeter fencing is *not* an obstacle to vehicle penetration and should not be considered adequate protection (Kessinger, p.64). Several types of barriers might be used if risk assessment reveals that a facility might be the target of a car-bomb attack. These barriers may be active or passive, fixed or movable and categorized by their form (Kessinger, pp.60–64).

Active barriers require some action either by people or equipment to be raised and lowered or moved aside to allow vehicles to enter and exit. These include barricades, bollards, beams and gates operated manually, pneumatically or hydraulically. Bollards are metal posts embedded in a concrete foundation at a depth of four feet. These are the most versatile type of barrier and can be fixed or movable.

Passive barriers have no moving parts and include bollards, guardrails, ditches, large reinforced concrete planters, hardened trashcans, benches, water fountains, walls, raised planting beds, earth beams, boulders and Jersey barriers. Wedge barriers are rectangular steel plants rising from 24 to 38 inches from the road surface at a 45-degree angle. Jersey barriers are passive barriers originally designed as highway dividers to stop vehicles approaching at a maximum angle of 30 degrees. They were not designed to be a high-speed vehicle-arrest system. Their usefulness is limited "at best" (Kessinger).

In addition to selecting the most appropriate type of barrier, placement must be considered. Because force from an explosion decreases rapidly with distance, the most effective protection from an explosive-vehicle threat results with a maximized setback zone (Kessinger, p.58). The setback zone, also called the "standoff distance," is the distance between the target building and an accessible location from which a terrorist could park or drive a bomb-laden vehicle. Vehicle barriers should be placed as far from the building as possible to ensure the maximum standoff distance. Although maximum footage is desirable, this is rarely practical in areas where real estate is valuable. Kessinger notes that in urban environments, 12 feet—the distance from the curb to the facility entrance—may be the maximum practical standoff distance.

A final consideration if vehicle barriers are used is that the barrier must not impede pedestrian traffic or emergency vehicles.

Patrols: Dogs and Security Officers

The perimeter may also be patrolled by dogs or security personnel. Security dogs may be classified as *patrol dogs* or *guard dogs. Sentry* or *patrol dogs* are usually leashed and make rounds with a security officer, providing companionship and protection. Because of their keen senses of smell and hearing, they can easily detect intruders. Sentry dogs, frequently German Shepherds or Doberman Pinschers, are the most expensive security dogs.

Guard dogs roam alone inside a perimeter or building to deter intruders. They may be alarm dogs whose growl and bark are intended to frighten intruders away, or they may be attack dogs, trained to physically restrain any intruders. Guard dogs are frequently used by the military, by some contract security firms, by car dealers, by junk dealers, by warehouse operators and in large stores. Often the dogs are leased from a security dog contractor. Such dogs usually respond to only one handler and therefore pose a potential risk, especially for police officers or fire fighters who might be called to the premises in an emergency. Although security dogs are expensive and do present a potential risk for lawsuits, and although they can be shot, hit, anaesthetized or poisoned, they remain a viable alternative for many establishments.

Some establishments have security officers patrol the perimeter, either on foot or in a vehicle. Patrols on foot offer a better stealth factor, but if the grounds are expansive, this option may not be feasible. Security patrol officers may be armed or unarmed.

Signs

Signs are a simple security tool and can be used to provide instructions and warnings; for example, "Restricted Area," "No Unauthorized Personnel Beyond This Point," "No Admittance," "One Way," "Premised Patrolled by Guard Dog." Such written notices can effectively improve safety and discourage crime. In most jurisdictions signs are a legal requirement for trespassing prosecutions.

Parking Lots, Garages and Ramps

Often the perimeter area of a business is where the parking lot for employees, customers, clients, vendors and other visiting individuals is located. Some larger organizations and institutions, such as hospitals, government agencies, large corporations, airports, hotels and casinos, have parking garages or ramps attached or adjacent to the physical structure as a place for employees and the public to park. In some cases, a private company operates the parking facility. Regardless of who owns or operates the parking area, the security considerations are the same. Establishments that own or lease parking lots have a responsibility to protect those who park there or face costly litigation.

Most of the security problems encountered in parking lots are apparent. Patrons are exposed to assault, robbery, theft, kidnapping and vandalism of their vehicles.

Parking Lots   Tokaji and Youngston (2004, p.51) contend: "Parking lots can be dangerous places. Many are plagued by poor lighting, blind corners and floor plans that do nothing to prevent cars from speeding." They assert that with attention to traffic patterns, barriers, guard posts, access controls, lighting, CCTV systems, pedestrian safety, vehicle speed and call stations, parking lots can be both convenient and safe.

Ideally, privately owned vehicles should be parked outside the perimeter in a parking lot with its own fence, gate and lights. Employees or visitors who park adjacent to a loading dock or warehouse doors present a security risk. Many thefts are committed by friends or family waiting in the parking area for an employee to get out of work. Some security managers believe that if employees and visitors must walk a long distance to their vehicles, the chances of theft are reduced. Others argue that a lengthy walk to a vehicle needlessly exposes people to the possibility of being the victim of an assault, robbery or rape.

When possible, all privately owned vehicles should be parked in a common parking lot on only one side of the building, thus reducing the number of common entrances to the building. Parking lots should have proper drainage and lighting, as well as appropriate marking and signing, including pedestrian crosswalks, if needed. Sometimes stickers or parking permits are used to identify vehicles with legitimate access to parking areas.

Parking Garages and Ramps   Rich (2005, p.56) reports: "There are thousands of parking structures throughout the United States that pose serious safety hazards because they weren't designed with safety in mind." He contends the two primary safety threats in a parking structure are crime and vehicles hitting pedestrians, and that improved visibility helps reduce both threats (p.60). For example, stairwells and lobbies leading to elevators should include as much glass as possible. Hiding places can be avoided through good lighting and attention to landscaping. In addition, access control, CCTV and sound monitoring can be incorporated to enhance safety.

Additional safety and security recommendations including limiting entrance and exit points to no more than two to allow better monitoring of traffic, using vandal-resistant convex mirrors to help patrons see around blind corners, having emergency call boxes and voice-activated two-way speaker phones, and having security officers patrol the structure (Jones, 2006, p.74).

Physical Layout and Appearance

A clear zone of at least 20 feet on either side of the perimeter should be maintained when possible. Neatness is important not only for appearance, but also for security. Ladders and piles of debris or merchandise close to fences or buildings could easily be used to an intruder's advantage. Bushes and hedges should be no more than two feet tall and should be kept away from the boundary and buildings. Weeds should be cut, hedges and bushes trimmed and all discarded material or merchandise properly disposed of. Trash and boxes strewn around the premises not only are a safety hazard, but also can provide hiding places for intruders.

Buildings can be connected by tunnels or walkways, reducing the number of main entrances to be made secure. Tunnels, however, pose other security risks and should be used only after careful consideration. If tunnels are used, adequate lighting, surveillance cameras and perhaps patrol should be used to increase safety.

The Building Exterior

The first line of defense for some facilities is the building exterior, also called the building **envelope** or shell by some architects and security planners. In the majority of break-ins, entrance is gained through windows. The next most common method of entrance is through doors, followed by roof hatches, skylights, vents and transoms. A few break-ins have involved chopping or cutting holes through walls, floors and ceilings.

 Strong, locked doors and windows, limited entrances, secured openings (if larger than 96 square inches), alarms, surveillance and lighting help establish the physical security of a building's exterior.

The number of doors and their placement is extremely important to physical security. The number of personnel entrances should be limited to control access and to reduce thefts while the building is open. In some instances security officers or receptionists are stationed at the entrance. All doors not required for efficient operation should be locked. If a door is required as an emergency exit, it can be equipped with an emergency exit locking device called a **panic bar** or **crash bar**. The exterior of the door has no hardware; it can be opened only from the inside. Many emergency exit locking devices are equipped with an alarm that sounds if the door is opened. Some also have a lock so that if a key is used, the alarm does not sound.

About 50 percent of all criminal intrusions are achieved by breaking window glass. Any opening larger than 96 square inches and less than 18 feet from the ground should be protected. If the window is not needed for ventilation, the panes can be replaced with glass block.

Any accessible openings larger than 96 square inches should be protected the same way as windows. Utility tunnels, elevator shafts, ventilation openings, skylights and the like should all have protective screens or metal bars to prevent access to the building's interior. Such openings can also be connected to the alarm system.

Lights should be mounted on the sides and corners of buildings, with the illumination cone directed downward and away from the structure to prevent shadows and glare. The alley, the rear of the building and all entry points should be lit. The lights can be turned on by an automatic timer if desired.

The Building Interior

Because no perimeter or building exterior can be 100 percent secure, internal physical controls are usually required as well. The physical layout of a building's interior directly affects its security. Secure areas should be separate from non-secure areas and should be located deep within the interior so no windows, exterior doors or walls are in common with another building. Cashier offices, research laboratories, storage rooms and rooms containing classified documents or valuable property often require extra security.

 Interior physical controls begin with the physical layout and construction of the building. Other interior security measures include locked doors, desks and files; safes and vaults; internal alarms and detectors; lock-down devices for equipment; lighting; mirrors; document shredders; communications systems; surveillance systems; signs; and dogs and security personnel. Points of ingress and egress may be equipped with metal detectors, backscatter low-level x-ray devices and antishoplifting devices.

The interior construction of the building is also important. The ceiling in many modern buildings is simply acoustical tile laid in place with a crawl space above it that provides access to any room on that floor. Older buildings are better constructed from this perspective, but they often have door transoms and inferior glass and locks.

Card-operated locks are often used to secure areas restricted to the general public but accessible to large numbers of employees. In fact, a single card can be used to control access to parking, turnstiles, elevators, files, computer rooms, copy machines, fuel pumps, restrooms and executive offices. The same card could provide time and attendance reporting information. Card-operated systems can be easily programmed to reject cards that are no longer valid, such as in the case of terminated employees. Electronic access control cards provide a vast array of potential uses for employers and security professionals, including time and attendance, purchases, inventory and after-hours entry records. Electronic locks are frequently used in apartment buildings and in offices where strict physical security is required.

Businesses and organizations commonly hold assets requiring additional security, such as cash, stocks, inventory and records. Sometimes the assets are kept in a vault, a completely fire-resistive enclosure to be used exclusively for storage. Because vaults are primarily for fire protection, many vaults also contain a burglar-resistant safe. Most safes are *either* fire resistant or burglar resistant, but *not* both. Alarms and time locks are often additional security precautions in safes. Although some controversy exists over whether a safe should be hidden or in clear view, most experts feel that hiding a safe just helps the burglar. It is better to have a safe located where it is plainly visible from the outside and clearly lit at all times. It should always be locked and the combination secured.

At industrial businesses, factories and other companies where large and expensive manufacturing equipment is housed inside, and where it is impractical to secure such equipment inside a vault or locked safe, a common security practice is to bolt down or otherwise permanently attach this property to a fixed surface inside the structure, such as the floor or a concrete wall. Lock-down devices may also be installed on office machines and other valuable equipment such as microscopes.

Adequate light inside a structure is critical to security for the same reasons as provided in the discussion of perimeter and building exterior security. Lighting is one of the simplest and most prevalent security measures available. Another simple and commonly used security tool is the convex mirror, which allows clerks to see areas not observable from a checkout station. Mirrors also enable employees and customers to see around corners in hallways for potential threats. Document shredders, used to make certain no classified information is improperly discarded, are yet another relatively inexpensive and easy-to-implement security tool.

Numerous types of communications system are available, including telephones and cell phones, public address or loudspeaker systems, intercoms, radios or walkie-talkies, pagers, tape recorders and teletypes. Although means of communication are often taken for granted, they are vital in situations such as emergencies or natural disasters. Some businesses opt to install a computerized telephone system that not only automatically routes outgoing calls over the least expensive lines but can also detect and control long-distance phoning abuses and the like.

Surveillance systems have become one of the most common security measures used. As noted, surveillance systems can operate continually or on demand. They can be monitored or unmonitored. If video surveillance is used without employees' knowledge, employers must be careful they do not violate their employees' privacy rights. Security managers are cautioned to remember the restriction on surveillance and appropriate legal and privacy issues that might arise.

© Alvis Upitis/Brand X Pictures/Photolibrary

Many types of businesses use surveillance cameras to monitor activities occurring both inside and outside of the facility. Some organizations take a reactive or passive approach with these surveillance systems, using unmonitored cameras that send CCTV feeds directly to a recording device which is accessed only after an incident is reported. Other companies use a proactive approach by stationing a security officer in a central monitoring room to actively observe the screens and, thus, be better able to respond to a developing threat or other potentially negative situation.

As with perimeter security, signs can be used inside a facility to provide instructions and warnings and enhance overall security; for example, "This area under video surveillance," "All shoplifters will be prosecuted to the full extent of the law," "Restricted Area," "No Unauthorized Personnel Beyond This Point," "No Admittance," "This Area Protected by an Alarm," "No Smoking" and so on.

Many establishments also depend on the presence of a uniformed security officer, perhaps armed, perhaps accompanied by a guard dog, as a deterrent to most would-be offenders. In addition, security officers can perform the numerous functions discussed in Chapter 1, and they can ensure the effectiveness of security equipment. Some security officers patrol the facility interior and may carry a **watch clock**, a seven-day timepiece, on their rounds. Keys are located at various stations throughout a facility, and the security officer simply inserts the key into the watch clock at each station, thereby making a record of the time the location was checked. Any stations not visited at the appropriate time can be monitored.

Some facilities have sophisticated automatic officer-monitoring systems that transmit a message to a central security office if an officer does not arrive at a predetermined station at the appointed time. The central security office is thus alerted to any illness, accident or crime-related problems. One disadvantage of this system, however, is that an established patrol pattern can be learned by unauthorized people and used to their advantage.

Devices to scan people entering or exiting a building and detect concealed objects are becoming increasingly common. Most people are familiar with the metal detectors used in airports, but such detectors are used in a wide variety of other settings, including emergency rooms, sporting events, government buildings, art exhibitions and educational institutions. Backscatter low-level x-ray imaging is a technology that provides the potential to see through clothing and detect weapons and other prohibited materials (Ratcliffe). However, equipment that uses x-ray technology to examine inside and under clothing may potentially fall foul of Fourth Amendment protections. Detection devices are also placed by exits to alert security of unauthorized or illegal attempts to remove property from the premises, such as in cases of shoplifting. Of course, consumer items or company property susceptible to theft must first be marked with tamper-resistant electronic tags capable of setting off the alarm.

Many businesses and organizations coordinate their perimeter, exterior and interior security efforts through a central command center located inside the facility.

The Command Center

Ideally, the communication center should be linked to the security control center and should be in a controlled area. The communication center area might receive any alarm signals and might be the control for the switchboard, a closed-circuit television monitoring system and a public address system. The command center, sometimes referred to as the central station, can also monitor access control and, if needed, provide access to patrons based on lists or passwords. If appropriate training has been provided, staff in the central station can also deal with computer network issues involving patches, viruses and operating system updates, although this is often beyond the scope of many security generalists.

Other Means to Enhance Security through Physical Controls

In addition to the well-established physical controls of locks, lights, alarms and surveillance systems, new security devices and alternatives are continuously being produced and marketed. Magazines such as *Security Management*, *Security Technology & Design* and *Security World* can help security managers keep abreast of new developments in security equipment, from the most basic to the most sophisticated items. For example, the bulletproof vest—a standard piece of equipment issued to security personnel—is periodically improved through research and design modification; thus, a security manager may wish to reevaluate a company's stock supply of such equipment if significant improvements have been made over the span of several generations of product. At the other extreme, the security needs of some organizations may require use of more sophisticated items, such as bug detection systems that protect privacy during personal conversations in offices, hotels and at home; a bionic briefcase that contains a bomb and bug detector and is wired to prevent theft; or an electronic handkerchief that allows a person to disguise his or her voice over the telephone.

The Physical Security System

All too often, managers concentrate on appearance, efficiency and convenience of operations to the neglect of security and safety. The key factors in any physical security program are to identify risks and then to alleviate them when possible.

A security survey allows managers to assess the vulnerability of assets as well as the criticality of their loss and then to select physical controls to meet the needs of their particular facility. Providing either more or less physical security than is needed is never desirable, as discussed in Chapter 5. The security checklist in Figure 6.3 summarizes the key physical controls used to provide security.

 Aesthetic, operational, safety and security needs must be balanced.

Working with Vendors

Vendors tend to know their own product's features, but often do not know how products can be integrated into an existing system (Jung et al., 2006, p.61). The security director is responsible to ensure that real-world installation issues are addressed. Vendors must be able to install a system correctly, troubleshoot any problems, provide hardware in a timely manner and respond promptly to service calls. To ensure that all expectations have been met, the security director should inspect and test the installation, called commissioning.

The **commissioning** process is a chance for the vendor to prove the equipment works. It entails having all the parties involved—the electrical contractor, the security vendor, the general contractors and so on—test every door, panel, camera and other component. If the test results are acceptable, the vendor turns

Portland Police Bureau Commercial Security Survey

Business name _____   File no. _____

Address _____   Date _____

Name of person contacted _____   Position _____

Type of premise _____   Phone no. _____

Key: STND = Standard   REC = Recommendation   COMM = Comments

1. Building front

	STND	REC	COMM
Doors	_____	_____	_____
Locks	_____	_____	_____
Windows	_____	_____	_____
Lights	_____	_____	_____
Vents	_____	_____	_____
Misc.	_____	_____	_____

4. Building left side

	STND	REC	COMM
Doors	_____	_____	_____
Locks	_____	_____	_____
Windows	_____	_____	_____
Lights	_____	_____	_____
Vents	_____	_____	_____
Misc.	_____	_____	_____

7. Alarms

	STND	REC	COMM
Audible	_____	_____	_____
Silent	_____	_____	_____
Other	_____	_____	_____

Alarm permit # _____

2. Building right side

	STND	REC	COMM
Doors	_____	_____	_____
Locks	_____	_____	_____
Windows	_____	_____	_____
Lights	_____	_____	_____
Vents	_____	_____	_____
Misc.	_____	_____	_____

5. Building roof

	STND	REC	COMM
Roof access	_____	_____	_____
Roof skylight	_____	_____	_____
Roof vents	_____	_____	_____
Misc.	_____	_____	_____

8. Safes

	STND	REC	COMM
Anchored	_____	_____	_____
Shielded dial	_____	_____	_____
Visible	_____	_____	_____
Lighted	_____	_____	_____
Money chest	_____	_____	_____
File	_____	_____	_____

3. Building rear

	STND	REC	COMM
Doors	_____	_____	_____
Locks	_____	_____	_____
Windows	_____	_____	_____
Lights	_____	_____	_____
Vents	_____	_____	_____
Misc.	_____	_____	_____

6. Loading doors

	STND	REC	COMM
Overhead	_____	_____	_____
Sliding	_____	_____	_____
Sidewalk elevator	_____	_____	_____
Roller	_____	_____	_____

9. Miscellaneous

	STND	REC	COMM
Key control	_____	_____	_____
Fencing	_____	_____	_____
Lighting	_____	_____	_____
Landscaping	_____	_____	_____
Office equipment engraved	_____	_____	_____

Comments: _____
_____
_____
_____
_____
_____
_____
_____
_____
_____
_____
_____

This report is advisory only and does not purport to list all hazards or the adequacy of present hazard controls.

Officer:	No.	Pred/Div:	District:

Precinct _____

Figure 6.3   Security Checklist

SOURCE: Courtesy of the City of Portland Police Bureau.

responsibility for the system over to the owner and product warranties come into effect (Jung et al.).

Braden (2004, p.127) takes a somewhat different approach, using the analogy of an orchestra playing a symphony. The difference between a good and a great performance is how well the individual players and their instruments work together to produce the desired effect. That is the conductor's role. The security director carries the conductor's baton in a physical security program, tasked with bringing multiple applications and measures together into a coherent security framework. To do so, the director must address both the technological and the human factor. Many security professionals focus on physical security equipment and electronic security systems when "orchestrating" their physical security program but ignore the human and psychological aspects of the security program; the result is discordance (Braden, p.128).

 The human element of security—physical security users—consists of the people who own the property being protected, the people who work at or visit the protected area and the security forces.

Braden contends that the human factor is the most critical component of the security program and is also the most neglected: "If people do not properly use the systems or ignore the alarms these systems produce, the security system will fail." He notes that in countless cases, high-tech security systems have turned out to be worthless because the users did not know how to operate them, became frustrated and ended up ignoring or circumventing the systems. In some cases systems are imposed on users who do not recognize the threat. Because these systems inconvenience users who see no reason for them, the users find a way to bypass the inconvenience.

In addition to physical security equipment, electronic security systems and physical security system users, the physical security footprint is important as a security multiplier. The **physical security footprint** is the mark left during or after a security action. It is what the public sees and what lets them know security is present: "It can be obvious and threatening or subtle and aesthetically pleasing. But in all cases, the footprint must be seen by the public and be clearly related to security" (Braden, p.128). The key to an effective footprint is perception by an adversary or by the public: "Everything that makes a protected asset appear to be hardened acts as an effective security multiplier" (Braden).

SUMMARY

- Crime prevention through environmental design (CPTED) is a fundamental concept in security design. It is based on the premise that effective use and manipulation of the physical environment can affect criminal behavior in a way that will reduce the incidence and fear of crime and improve the quality of life.

- Physical controls serve to reduce risk of loss by denying unauthorized access, deterring or dis-

couraging attempts to gain unauthorized access, delaying those who attempt to gain unauthorized access and detecting threats, both criminal and noncriminal.

- The three basic lines of physical defense are the perimeter of a facility, the building exterior and the interior.

- Basic security equipment at any of the three lines of defense includes locks, lights and alarms.

- Adequate light inside as well as outside a building enhances safety, deters would-be intruders and makes detection of actual intruders more probable.

- Alarm systems may be local, proprietary, central station or police connected.

- Currently CCTV is used as a generic term for a variety of video surveillance technologies.

- The perimeter can be physically controlled by fences, gates and locks; alarms; lighting; surveillance systems; vehicle barriers; dogs and security personnel; and signs. Parking lots, garages and ramps require additional security planning. The perimeter's physical layout and neatness are important factors.

- The physical security of a building's exterior can be established by strong, locked doors and windows, limited entrances, secured openings (if larger than 96 square inches), alarms, surveillance and lighting.

- Interior physical controls begin with the physical layout and construction of the building. Other interior security measures include locked doors, desks and files; safes and vaults; internal alarms and detectors; lock-down devices for equipment; lighting; mirrors; document shredders; communications systems; surveillance systems; signs; and dogs and security personnel. Points of ingress and egress may be equipped with metal detectors, backscatter low-level x-ray devices and antishoplifting devices.

- When selecting physical controls to reduce losses from recognized risks, security managers must balance aesthetic, operational, safety and security needs.

- The human element of security—physical security users—consists of the people who own the property being protected, the people who work at or visit the protected area and the security forces.

APPLICATION

Obtain from several police departments statistics data regarding responses to false alarms in the community. Also obtain a copy of the community's false-alarm ordinance, if available, and bring it to class for a discussion and analysis of the ordinance's effectiveness in bringing the consumer, the law enforcement agency and the alarm company together to curb the false-alarm problem.

DISCUSSION QUESTIONS

1. Most adults have several keys in their possession. How many keys are in your possession? What types of locks do they fit? Compare the different types of keys that others have with your own.

2. Local communities frequently pass ordinances to curtail false-alarm responses by the public police. From the alaram system user's standpoint, is this an advantage or a disadvantage?

3. Despite the numerous advantages offered by a reliable surveillance system, what disadvantages might be expected?

4. Security managers frequently overcompensate in protecting areas with fencing. List some guidelines you would consider before recommending any type of outside security fencing.

5. Do you agree that the human factor is the most critical component of the physical security program?

REFERENCES

Aggleton, David G. "Designing Your Security Video System." *Security Technology & Design*, March 2005, pp.74–80.

Anderson, Rich. "FIPS 201: The New Smart Card Standard for Federal IDs." *Security Technology & Design*, April 2005a, pp.26–30.

Anderson, Rich. "IP Access on the Way." *Security Technology & Design*, January 2005b, pp.30–34.

Angel, Schlomo. *Discouraging Crime through City Planning*. University of California, Berkeley, 1968.

Apple, Guy. "Analog/Digital Hybrid." *Security Technology & Design*, September 2005, p.68.

Barnard, L. "Crime Prevention through Environmental Design." *Law and Order*, May 2006, pp.118–119.

Braden, Timothy J. "Orchestrating an Integrated Performance." *Security Management*, July 2004, pp.127–131.

Clemens, Candace. "From Star Light to Street Light." *Law Enforcement Technology*, May 2007, pp.26–35.

Daniels, Rhianna. "Inside the City Limits?" *Security Director News*, October 2007a, pp.1, 9.

Daniels, Rhianna. "What Defines Intelligence?" *Security Director News*, June 2007b, pp.1, 21.

Davis, Kevin R. "Winning at Night." *Police*, June 2007, pp.56–59.

Feeser, Bill. "Welcome to the New World." *Security Technology & Design*, June 2005, pp.58–61.

Freeman, J. P. "Is Card Technology Getting Smarter?" *Security Technology & Design*, April 2004, p.12.

Freeman, J. P. "The IP Boom." *Security Technology & Design*, January 2005a, p.16.

Freeman, J. P. "Video Networks in 2009." *Security Technology & Design*, February 2005b, p.14.

Gips, Michael A. "CCTV Ordinances on the Rise." *Security Management*, January 2007, pp.18–26.

Gorovici, Eli. "A New Era Is upon Us." *Security Technology & Design*, September 2004, pp.40–42.

Harowitz, Sherry. "Faking Fingerprints and Eying Solutions." *Security Management*, March 2007, pp.48–50.

Hopkins, Cameron. "The Digital Solution for Urban Policing." *Law and Order*, May 2007, pp.88–91.

International CPTED Association. Online: http://www.cpted.net

Jacobs, Jane. *The Death and Life of Great American Cities*. New York: Random House, 1961.

Jeffery, C. Ray. *Crime Prevention through Environmental Design*. Beverly Hills, CA: Sage, 1971.

Jones, Steve. "Parking Aligns with Protection." *Security Management*, December 2006, pp.69–74.

Jung, Geoffrey; Morris, Ronald J.; and Hogan, Mary Alice. "Putting Vendors to the Test." *Security Management*, April 2006, pp.61–67.

Kalocsai, Peter and Imparato, Nick. "Snapshots for Our Times: Face Recognition in 2005." *Security Technology & Design*, June 2006, pp.28–34.

Kessinger, Richard. "From Jerico to Jersey Barrier." *Security Management*, August 2004, pp.57–66.

Kozoil, Jeff. "Moving Beyond Mechanical Locks." *Security Products*, January 2005, pp.22–23.

"Laser-Based Device Offers Alternative to Video Surveillance." *Space Daily*, May 23, 2007.

Macdonald, Kathy and Kitteringham, Glen. "A Case of Rogue Gatherings (and Other CPTED Tales)." *Security Management*, June 2004, pp.129–134.

McKay, Tom. "How Are Behavior, Crime and Design Related?" *Security Management*, May 2004, pp.146–144.

National Crime Prevention Council. 2004. Online: http://www.ncpc.org

Newman, Oscar. *Defensible Space: Crime Prevention through Urban Design*. New York: MacMillan, 1972.

Physical Security Professional (PSP) Examination Structure and Content. Arlington, VA: American Society for Industrial Security, 2007.

Piazza, Peter. "The Smart Cards Are Coming . . . Really." *Security Management*, January 2005, pp.41–55.

Piazza, Peter. "Sizing Up IP Video Systems." *Security Management*, October 2006, pp.92–98.

Ratcliffe, Jerry. *Video Surveillance in Public Places*. Washington, DC: Office of Problem-Oriented Policing: Problem-Oriented Guides for Police Response series, Guide No. 4, February 2006.

Reddick, Ron. "What You Should Know about Protecting a Perimeter." *Security Products*, April 2005, pp.36–42.

Rich, Richard C. "Ramping Up: Garage Design." *Security Management*, December 2005, pp.56–62.

Robinson, Matthew B. "The Theoretical Development of Crime Prevention through Environmental Design (CPTED)." In William Laufer and Freda Adler (Eds.), *The Criminology of Criminal Law, Advances in Criminological Theory*, Volume 8, 1998.

Ryan, Russ. "The Path of the Biometrics Industry." *Security Technology & Design*, June 2004, pp.17–22.

Ryan, Russ. "Biometrics and the Law." *Security Technology & Design*, June 2005, p.50.

Sherman, Lawrence W. and Schlossman, Michael B. *The Campbell Crime and Justice Group Expedited Review Project, Final Report*, 2006.

Spadanuta, Laura. "Decoding the Digital Picture." *Security Management*, October 2007, pp.71–81.

Taylor, Brian. "Effective Alarm Management Allows Firms to Maximize Performance." *Security Director News*, May 2006, p.8.

Tokaji, John E. and Youngston, James P. "Illuminating Parking Protection." *Security Management*, December 2004, pp.51–57.

Traxler, Roddy. "Fence and Sensibility." *Security Management*, January 2005, pp.87–90.

Vallese, Frank. "Sight after Sundown." *Law Enforcement Technology*, February 2007, pp.46–56.

Voice Over Internet Protocol. Washington, DC: National Institute of Justice, May 2007. (NCJ 217864)

Zunkel, Dick. "Protecting Information with Biometrics." *Security Technology & Design*, June 2005, pp.46–53.

CHAPTER 7

Enhancing Security through Procedural Controls

Procedural controls, such as consistently applied check-in processes, are as important as physical controls in achieving organization-wide security.

DO YOU KNOW . . .

- What hiring procedures can help reduce shrinkage and negligence lawsuits?
- What educational measures can help promote security?
- What specific procedures can be used to control access to an area?
- What characterizes an effective employee badge or pass?
- What constitutes effective key control?
- When opening and closing should be a two-person operation?
- What effective closing procedures include?
- What areas are particularly vulnerable to theft?
- What accounting procedures can help prevent shrinkage?
- When searches or inspections of people, packages, lockers and vehicles are usually acceptable?
- What procedures can help detect theft or pilferage?
- What procedures to use when transporting valuables?
- What additional protection against financial loss is available to owners and managers?

CAN YOU DEFINE?

blind receiving	liability without fault	RFID	surety bond
fidelity bonds	perpetual inventory	shrinkage	

Introduction

The BuildMore Construction Company has installed a sophisticated alarm system, the most modern security lighting and the best locks available. Management is confident that the facility is secure. It is unaware, however, that Employee A is taking small tools home in his lunch pail almost daily; Employee B is placing several lengthy personal long-distance calls a month; Employee C is loading extra lumber on his truck and using it to build his own garage; Employee D is falsifying her time card regularly; and Employee F is submitting false invoices to be paid to his wife under her maiden name. In addition, the service technician who just carried out a computer is not really a technician but a thief.

The physical controls described in the last chapter would be of little use in the preceding scenario. Numerous books on private security differentiate between the "enemy from without"—the robber and burglar—and the "enemy from within"—the dishonest employee who systematically depletes a company's assets and causes **shrinkage**, the polite term for employee theft. Losses may be incurred due to employees actually stealing or because they are not doing the job as they should be. Internal theft may account for up to 70 percent of all shrinkage. Such thefts may be of cash, merchandise, industrial tools and supplies, office supplies, time and vital information. Assets also are lost because of employees who are absent or late, and frequently as the result of drug and alcohol abuse.

This chapter begins by examining the importance of the hiring process and employment practices in helping to reduce shrinkage, including employee education and supervision procedures. This is followed by a discussion of access control, property control and restriction of camera use—all critical procedural considerations for security management. Next the focus turns to how accounting and receiving procedures can help prevent or reduce shrinkage. The chapter concludes with a look at some other procedures, such as inspecting, inventorying and insuring assets, which can help enhance a company's safety and security. Note that the chapter discussion presents *general* procedures that might apply in most facilities. Additional procedures frequently required in industrial, retail, commercial and other *specific* types of establishments are discussed later in the text.

The First Line of Defense—Hiring Well

One way to reduce shrinkage and avoid negligence suits is to improve the quality of personnel hired, as discussed in Chapter 2.

 Hiring well is the first line of defense against shrinkage and negligence lawsuits. Preemployment screening should include an application and résumé, intellectual and psychological tests, a thorough background check including references and a personal interview. It may include drug testing.

Integrity tests are valuable tools. Paper-and-pencil tests are often very reliable, and psychological tests are also valuable. A wide range of other tests are available for preemployment screening, including tests that measure job aptitude, job abilities, emotional stability and mental health. A test should be *valid*, that is, it should measure attitudes or skills that are directly related to the position.

Interviews can also help employers select the best candidates. According to Bolles (2004, p.248), employers should ask five key questions:

- Why are you here? (Why did you pick us?)
- What can you do for us?
- What kind of person are you?
- What distinguishes you from nineteen other people who can do the same tasks that you can?
- Can I afford you?

Harr and Hess (2006, p.256) observe: "The primary purposes of the personal interview are for the employer to get a look at you, listen to you, see how you perform under stress, observe how you analyze problems, test your people skills and test your knowledge." All questions asked must be job related and nondiscriminatory.

Occasionally those who make the best impression during a job interview are actually those who are the most skilled in lying. Despite careful screening and checking of job applicants, some dishonest people are likely to be hired.

The Second Line of Defense—Education and Supervision

Hire good people and then maintain the climate that will keep them honest. For example, an organization of fast-food restaurants was noted for its good employee relations. Management treated people fairly and displayed faith in their integrity and ability, but also provided uniforms without pockets. When the opportunity to steal is removed, half the battle is won. Nothing can substitute for rigid, well-implemented preventive measures.

Owners and managers should have a continuing program of investigation and training on ways to eliminate stock shortages and shrinkage. For example, one small retailer trained his employees to record each item, such as floor cleaner, taken out of stock for use in the store. Unless recorded, it was an inventory loss, even though it was a legitimate store expense. Management must let employees know that is it always aware and always cares. Employees should be accountable for all assets entrusted to them.

 Education and supervision can help prevent losses. All employees should know their responsibilities and restrictions, and reasonable rules should be established and enforced.

Policies must not be stated as suggestions but rather as rules that are enforced. In addition, posters might be strategically placed emphasizing "Zero Shrinkage." A more negative but possibly effective poster might illustrate frequently pilfered items, a price tag attached to each and a caption reading, "Is your future worth more than this?"

The Third Line of Defense—Access Control

Most *physical* controls are aimed at limiting access to restricted areas, particularly "after hours" or during the time when an establishment is not conducting business. During business hours, however, access cannot be completely limited or the company could not function. Therefore, *procedural* controls are used to limit access during "open" business hours to specific areas by unauthorized personnel. Access control includes identifying, directing and limiting the movement of vehicles, employees, contractors, vendors and visitors. The purpose of access control is to facilitate authorized entry and to prevent the unauthorized entry of those who might steal material or information, or might bring harmful devices onto the premises.

Many facilities require strict access control. In such cases they may require that all employees (including security), contractors and visitors sign in and out and may in addition require them to have identification badges. The only exceptions may be emergency service personnel such as fire and police officers and ambulance EMTs responding to a call for assistance.

Sometimes it is necessary to limit access to nonemployees only. Other times, however, even employees are denied access to certain areas of a facility. From a security standpoint, it is best to limit the number of people having access to cash, important documents, valuable merchandise and areas where these assets are stored. The importance and variety of identification cards was discussed in Chapter 6.

 Procedural controls to limit access to specified areas include stationing security officers; restricting vehicle traffic; requiring registration and sign out; requiring display of IDs, badges or passes; ensuring key control; using effective opening, closing and after-hour procedures; and controlling access to vulnerable areas and equipment.

Even in retail establishments where traffic flow is encouraged, certain areas are usually off-limits to nonemployees and perhaps even to some employees.

Restricted areas and boundaries should be clearly specified and the restrictions unconditionally enforced.

Vehicle Control

Vehicle traffic can be restricted in several ways. The simplest way is to have only one gate, with a card-key system or a guard to check identities and allow or refuse admittance to drivers seeking entrance to the premises. Sometimes stickers on the bumper or windshield constitute the necessary identification for admittance.

Another method is to have two parking lots, both equipped with traffic control arms. Employees can gain entrance to their parking lot by use of a card-key. Visitors can gain entrance to their parking lot simply by driving in, but they cannot exit without a token obtained from the receptionist.

Check-In/Check-Out Register

A check-in/check-out register can be used with employees as well as with vendors, contractors and visitors. This system requires the person seeking entrance to sign in with a receptionist or security guard, present identification, state the purpose of the visit and sign out before leaving. The date, time of entrance and

© Tim Rue/Corbis

A security guard checks the manifest of a produce truck entering a Ready Pac Foods facility in Irwindale, CA. The purpose of access control is to facilitate authorized entry and to prevent the unauthorized entry of those who might steal material or information, or who might bring harmful devices onto the premises.

Date	Name	Employees	Visitors & Vendors		Temporary badge # issued	Time IN	Time OUT
		ID #	License plate #	Purpose of visit & company you represent			

ABC Company
Registration Log

Figure 7.1   Sign-In/Sign-Out Log

time of departure are recorded. Figure 7.1 shows an example of a generic sign-in/ sign-out log for all persons entering and exiting an establishment. Columns can be added or deleted, depending on specific needs. After signing in, the person may then be directed to the desired location, may be given a badge or pass or may be met in the reception area by the person he or she is visiting.

Badges and Passes

Sometimes supervisory personnel and security officers know all of the employees, at least by sight, and the areas they are authorized to enter. Often, however, in large businesses and organizations, employees are required to wear badges or to carry passes that identify them. Some badges are simply name plates and serve little security function: "The security badge indicates a great deal about the security department. It reflects the quality of the security program and the level of support the security department receives from upper management" (Pearson, 2005, p.48). A poorly designed badge implies that it is more an "instrument of necessity" than part of a well-developed security program (Pearson). An inferior-quality badge is not only easier to counterfeit but may also make the company a more suitable target for criminals. An effective badge often presents a combination of text and colors to mark years of service, security clearance, interim clearance, escort privileges, employee number, special program access, building access, the badge-issuing site and any personal information deemed necessary (Pearson).

 At minimum, effective employee badges and passes display the employee's name, employment number, signature and photograph as well as an authorized signature. They are sturdy, tamper-proof and changed periodically.

The security procedures should specify where, when, how and to whom identification is displayed, what is to be done if the identification is lost or damaged and the process to follow if an employee is terminated. Temporary badges may be provided to employees who lose or forget their regular issued badge, but such passes should be valid for only one day and should be turned in at the end of the day.

Procedures for canceling or reissuing identification passes or badges must be clearly established. For example, in cases of lost, stolen or damaged company IDs, employees should be instructed to report the loss immediately to their supervisor, complete a form authorizing the issue of a new badge and have that form approved. A replacement fee may also be assessed.

Security officers should be given a "hot sheet" of lost or stolen badges or passes, as well as those of terminated employees who have retained theirs. Security officers should also compare the photographs, signatures and descriptions with those of the wearer. They should *not* assume the pass or badge is valid but should periodically check their "hot sheet."

Visitor Management Systems   Visitor management, or lack of it, has the potential for serious security consequences. A Harris poll entitled "A Study about Workplace Security" found that nearly 50 percent of respondents said their workplaces do not have a visitor registration system in place (Scott, 2004, p.33). An additional 30 percent said their building security officers used handwritten log books to track visitors.

If visitors are required to sign in and are issued a pass or badge, the number should be recorded in a "badge number" column added to the check-in/checkout register. The visitor should return the pass or badge when signing out. If the visitor retains the pass, a potentially serious security breach is created. Visitor badges or passes should be distinct from employee badges. If both employees and nonemployees are required to have a badge or pass, supervisors and security personnel can immediately ascertain whether a specific person is authorized to be in a specific location.

One fairly progressive ID system generates a photo ID with a barcode to log visitors in and out (Roberts, 2005, p.24). Under this system, entering guests must stop at the guard desk whether they are preregistered or not, say who they are visiting and show a photo ID. The guest's picture is taken, and a badge is printed on a self-adhesive label, with a color-coded stripe to denote the day of the week. The badge-issuing process takes fewer than three minutes. When the visitor leaves, the barcode is scanned and the user is logged out of the system. Visitor management systems such as this can store data for recurring guests and vendors, thus decreasing the check-in time for people who visit frequently. Furthermore, these systems are capable of generating reports on which tenants have the most visitors and who they are (Sanchez, 2005, p.88).

Another visitor management system uses optical portal turnstiles placed in the lobbies of buildings. The customized turnstiles are matched to the exact décor of each lobby. Each turnstile includes an entry proximity reader for tenant access cards and an entry barcode reader for access cards given to visitors. Both card readers control pedestrian traffic within each building (Grant and Lawn, 2005, p.42).

The importance of visitor management cannot be overstated. "Five Reasons to Consider a Visitor Management System" (2004, p.54) lists as the first reason the fact that facility entrances that are not secure leave companies more vulnerable to workplace violence, industrial espionage, terrorism and, consequently, liability. For example, in 1994 an armed suspect walked into a Washington, DC, police headquarters and shot and killed three people, including two FBI agents. A jury awarded $1.7 million to the husband of one of the slain agents after determining the facility should have had a better visitor sign-in system and other safeguards in place. The same article noted that Timothy McVeigh, the Oklahoma City Federal Building bomber, reportedly conducted preliminary walkthroughs of the Murrah Building's ground floor before his attack.

Second, the lobby is the first line of defense, perhaps the most important security point in any building. According to "Five Reasons," visitor management systems must be capable of

- Accurately and quickly capturing visitors' pictures, signatures, business cards and driver's license information.
- Authenticating their ID or credentials.
- Performing discrete security checks using watch lists.
- Creating one-time-use visitor badges that feature the visitor's photo, name, affiliation, host name and authorized areas of access, as well as the expiration time.
- Allowing employees to register visitors online ahead of time and be notified electronically or by phone when a visitor arrives.

Third, digital is preferable to paper for security. Handwritten information in a log book can be illegible or false. The record of visitors may be inaccurate and provide no warning that visitors are not who they say they are. Fourth, visitor management has already proven successful in many facilities. And finally, the system offers benefits beyond security, including improved productivity, enhanced image, improved visitor service, control of resources and enhanced emergency response.

If employees wish to have guests (relatives, children, friends) visit, some facilities require prior approval, using a form such as that shown in Figure 7.2.

Nonbusiness Visitor Access Request

Requests for any visit to the facility by individuals not conducting company business must be approved by your supervisor before the visit.

Visitors are not allowed in any restricted or hazardous area.

The host employee must maintain control of and responsibility for visitors and their actions.

Employee name _____ Phone extension _____

Employee number _____

Date of visit _____

Guests' names _____   _____

_____   _____

_____   _____

_____   _____

Approximate time _____

Manager's approval _____
Signature

Figure 7.2 Nonbusiness Visitor Access Request

Tour groups may present a special security problem in that a would-be thief, terrorist or industrial spy may join the group with the intention of slipping away and gaining access to a restricted area. Passes or badges can help prevent such illegal activity. Ideally, every member of a tour group should sign in with the receptionist or security guard and be issued a pass or badge that is clearly marked "Tour Group." The members should be required to stay together and be accompanied by a uniformed guard. When the tour is over, a head count should be done, all badges collected and all members signed out. Even though the tour will not likely be going into restricted areas, these measures will deter anyone from leaving the group to gain access to restricted areas or will detect such illicit activity early.

Contractors and vendors are frequently treated like visitors; that is, they sign in and receive a temporary badge or pass that identifies them as nonemployees and indicates the areas to which they have access. When registering, contractors and vendors should be required to give their name, company, purpose, vehicle license number and badge number, and to sign in. The date, time in and time out should always be recorded. Employees using contracted services often must arrange for access ahead of time and request a badge to be issued to any individual who will be providing service (see Figure 7.3). Some regular contractors and vendors may be issued long-term passes, but caution should be exercised in using such passes. Holders of permanent passes should be required to use only one entry-exit, and the security guard should have a list of those with permanent passes, along with their signatures, to compare when they sign in. Such permanent passes should be reissued periodically, just like those of employees.

Key Control

Another procedure important in controlling access to restricted areas is adequate key control. A lock is only as secure as the key or combination that operates it.

Having a key is often a status symbol. In small businesses, it is common for every employee to have a key, but from a security standpoint, this is unsound. The only valid reason for holding a key should be *job necessity*. The greater the number of people having keys, the greater the security risk. A written record, such as the one shown in Figure 7.4, should be kept of all keys in use.

 A key-control system limits the number of persons having keys, establishes a master list of all existing keys and to whom they are assigned, keeps all duplicate keys secure and requires a physical audit periodically.

To eliminate the inconvenience of a person having to carry several keys, perhaps even hundreds, a *master keying system* is sometimes used. Under this system, a *change key* opens only one specific door. A *sub-master key* opens the locks in a specified area. A *master key* opens the locks in the entire building. Sometimes the system extends even further if multiple buildings are concerned, with a *grand master key* opening all locks in two or more buildings. Typically custodial staff hold grand master keys, as do property managers of multiple-dwelling residential facilities.

Contract Employee Access Request

Complete this form if you want a contract employee to be issued a badge. Allow three days for processing.

A contracted badge will be issued for the requested individual each day at the gate designated. They will sign in on the Visitor Register at that time. The badge must be returned at the end of the day.

Contract company _____

Contract company telephone number _____

Contract employee(s) name(s) _____

Dates of contract employment   From _____ To _____

Type of employment _____

☐ Overload/temporary help
☐ Service/maintenance
☐ Construction work/mover

Facility required _____   Gates required _____

Supervised by _____

Telephone extension _____   Mail station _____

Restrictions (if any) _____

Department manager authorization _____

Contractor badges are generally issued only during working hours unless other arrangements are made with the security office.

Contractor Badge Sign In/Out

Date _____

Name	Badge no.	Representing (company)	Calling on	Time in	Time out

Figure 7.3 Contract Employee Access Request

Name/Department	Exterior	Office	Store Room	Supply Room
H. King/Accounting		Aug. 2005		
S. Lewis/Administration	Sept. 2007	Sept. 2005		
B. Jones/Purchasing		May 2004	May 2004	Aug. 2004
T. Hall/Administration	Jan. 2003	Jan. 2003		

Figure 7.4 Sample Record of Keys in Use

Although master keying offers advantages to the user, it also is much less secure. If the master key falls into the wrong hands or is duplicated, the system poses a much greater security risk than a single key system. It is also much more costly to rekey an entire building should a risk be discovered. A checklist such as that illustrated in Figure 7.5 can help ensure effective key control. The same principles apply if a card-key system is used.

Items with locks	Number of locks	Items with locks	Number of locks	Items with locks	Number of locks
Access space		Dispensers		Mail boxes	
Air conditioning		Sanitary napkin		Money bags	
Alarms		Soap			
Athletic supplies		Towel			
Automotive				Penthouse	
		Doors (exterior)		Plan case	
		Entrance			
Book cases		Exit			
Bulletin boards		Doors (interior)		Refrigerators	
		Cafeteria		Rolling grills	
		Classroom		Roof vents	
Cabinets		Closet			
Electric		Connecting			
Filing		Elevator		Safe compartments	
Instrument		Fan room		Safe deposit boxes	
Key		Fire		Screens	
Medicine		Garage		Slop sink closet	
Storage		Office		Switch key	
Supply					
Wardrobe					
		Drawers		Tabernacle	
		Bench		Tanks (oil & gas)	
		Cash		Thermostat	
		Drafting room		Trailers	
		Lab. table		Trap doors	
Camera cases		Safe		Trucks	
Cash boxes		Tool		Trunks	
Cash registers					
Chute doors		Gasoline pump			
Clock		Gates		Valves	
				Vaults	
		Lockers			
		Gym			
Dark rooms		Paint		Watchman's box	
Desks		Student			
Display cases		Teachers		X–ray	

Figure 7.5   Key-Control Checklist

SOURCE: Courtesy of TelKee Inc., Subsidiary of Sunroc Corporation, Glen Riddle, PA 19037.

All keys, but especially master keys, should be stamped "Do Not Duplicate." This does not, however, guarantee that duplication is prevented. Some security experts recommend scratching off the serial numbers on keys and padlocks because locksmiths can make duplicates if given the make and number. Though marking keys "Do Not Duplicate" may seem futile, it will have some effect. The best way to hamper key copying, however, is to purchase locks that use restricted keys. These are particularly secure because lockmakers limit the distribution of restricted key blanks, even among reputable locksmiths.

When any employee having a master key leaves or is terminated, the locks should be changed, as should combinations of safes and vaults if the terminated individual knew them. It is also a good security practice to periodically change locks, even if no employee having a key has been terminated.

Periodic key audits should be conducted to ensure that those to whom keys have been issued still have the keys in their possession. Auditing key inventories requires physical verification that each assigned key is actually in the possession of the specified person. If it is discovered that a key to a critical area has been lost, the door should be immediately rekeyed.

Keys to internal areas of the building should be controlled in the same way as external keys. Only those who really need the keys should have them.

Opening, Closing and After-Hours Procedures

Controlling access after hours is a critical part of any security system. Usually physical controls are heavily relied on, but certain procedures are required to ensure that these physical controls are effective.

 In an establishment where the risk of burglary is high and no security personnel are on night duty, opening and closing should be, at minimum, a two-person operation.

Opening and closing procedures with specific assigned responsibilities should be written out. Before someone opens an establishment, it is prudent to drive by the entrance at least once before parking. If anything looks suspicious, call the police. If everything looks normal, one person should unlock the exterior door that is most exposed to public view and traffic, enter, check the alarm and premises to ensure that everything is as it should be and then signal the person waiting some distance away from the premises. The time this takes is preestablished. The person outside waits until the "all clear" is given. If it is not given on schedule, the outside person notifies the police.

The closing procedure is similar to the opening procedure, with one person waiting some distance away while another person makes a routine check of the premises, paying particular attention to areas where someone might hide, such as washrooms, perimeter stock areas, fitting rooms and the maintenance department. This person then checks and activates all security measures and joins the person waiting outside to lock up.

 Effective closing procedures include checking all restrooms and areas where someone might be concealed, turning off all unnecessary lights and machinery, opening cash registers and placing money in the safe, locking the safe as well as all windows and interior doors, turning on security lighting, activating the alarm and securing all exterior doors.

Opinions vary on whether blinds or shades should be drawn during closing procedures. Drawn blinds or shades do prevent intruders from seeing available "targets" inside, but they also give privacy to a successful intruder.

Procedures for admittance after hours should also be established and strictly enforced. The security officer should have a list of individuals authorized to be in the building after hours, whether they stay late, arrive early or return after the building is closed. Employees who consistently arrive early or stay late with no good reason may be doing so to steal or to use company equipment without authorization. If an authorized person is in the building after hours, a record should be made of the reason for the person's being there, the time in and the time out. A sign-in/sign-out log such as that shown in Figure 7.1 can be used.

Controlling Access to Vulnerable Areas and Equipment

 Particularly vulnerable to theft or employee pilferage are storage areas; areas where cash, valuables, records and forms are kept; mail rooms; supply rooms; duplicating rooms; and computer rooms.

All these areas should have limited access and should be kept locked or have an authorized person in attendance at all times to monitor the activities of others present.

Warehouses and *stockrooms* are particularly vulnerable to theft and, as such, are locations where physical and procedural controls are especially important. Such areas should be locked or have an attendant on duty. In addition, high-value rooms or cages should be used for small valuable items vulnerable to theft. Temporary help should work with a regular, full-time employee to prevent the temptation to steal.

Forklifts should be kept locked when not in use. In one warehouse burglary, the burglar gained access through the roof, but was unable to exit the same way. Alertly, he used the forklift that had been left with the key in the ignition to pry open the warehouse door. He then used the forklift to transport large quantities of merchandise to his pickup truck parked outside.

Access to important *documents* as well as to *business forms* such as purchase orders, checks, vouchers and receipts should also be limited. Such forms, in the wrong hands, can cost a business thousands of dollars. Important papers and records that are no longer needed should not be discarded in the trash but incinerated or shredded.

Mail rooms should have one person in charge to handle all incoming and outgoing mail. A postage meter eliminates the possibility of stamps being stolen. This meter should be kept locked when not in use. The practice of having routine outgoing mail unsealed, so that contents can be checked to ensure that the letter is indeed business related, can eliminate personal use of company postage. Of course, confidential or sensitive correspondence should be sealed and marked as such. Periodic checks should be made of unsealed letters and packages before they are sealed, stamped and sent.

Some mailrooms have a separate mailbox for the personal letters and packages of employees. Although the employees pay for their postage, they see this as a service provided by their employer.

Supply rooms are very susceptible to pilferage and, therefore, should be restricted to authorized personnel. As with the mail room, one individual should be in charge of the supply room. Employees should obtain supplies by completing a requisition form, not by simply going to the supply room and helping themselves or asking for the supplies. An inventory should be taken regularly.

Copy machines may be a source of shrinkage if employees use them for making personal copies. Given that a single copy usually costs from three to ten cents depending on the system used, excessive personal use of copiers can cost an establishment hundreds, even thousands, of dollars a year. Some establishments have attempted to alleviate the problem by having the copy machine locked and issuing keys to only a few authorized individuals. Others have machines installed that have an element bearing a coded number that must be inserted into the machine before it will run, or use a card-key system for access. In either case, the code and number of copies made are automatically recorded. Other companies have only one person authorized to run the copy machine and require that a work order or copy requisition be completed before copies can be made by the authorized person (see Figure 7.6).

Some companies recognize that being able to make copies of documents for personal use is appreciated by employees and, consequently, allow their employees to use the copy machine and pay for their copies. Such a practice is good public relations, but it can easily be abused if individuals are placed on the honor system, as is frequently the case.

Computers can also be a source of shrinkage if employees use them for personal benefit, at substantial cost to the company. In some instances, employees have been discovered to have established their own sideline computer business, using the company's computer after hours and on weekends. One such

---

Reproduction Work Order

Name _____

Cost center code _____   Assembled _____

Date & hour received _____   Back-to-back ☐ Not back-to-back ☐

Date & hour due _____   Total number of originals _____

Number of copies _____   Other _____

Color of paper/card stock _____   _____

Special instructions:

- -

Return to _____   Will pick up in duplicating _____

Secretary _____

Figure 7.6   Sample Reproduction Work Order

employee rationalized the use by saying, "It [the computer] was just sitting there, going to waste. I wasn't hurting anyone." Computer security is discussed in Chapter 11.

Property Control

Property control is of concern in most security systems. One means of controlling property loss is radio frequency identification or **RFID**: "In its most basic form, asset tracking with RFID can let security know if company assets are walking out the door" (Blades, 2005, p.36). All assets to be protected are equipped with either passive or active RFID tags that communicate with readers built into door frames. Passive tags hold a limited amount of information and have a limited "read" range, requiring a strong signal to power its response. Passive tag readers have difficulty tracking several items going through a door at one time. Active tags hold much more information and power themselves through an internal battery. Therefore they read quickly and at a longer range. In addition active tags can recognize who is leaving with what. For example if an employee tries to leave a facility with a laptop or a company PDA that belongs to another employee, the system can recognize that the asset is leaving with the wrong individual and generate an alarm.

The technology, while used extensively, is not foolproof and does, occasionally, have problems reading tags, which leads to generation of false positive or false negative alerts. If, for example, someone rolls a cart through a door with 20 things on it and 19 of them are allowed out, but 1 isn't, the software may have difficulty reading the cart. Another obstacle to implementing an effective RFID system is cost: Passive tags often do not give the degree of protection desired, but active tags are expensive: "The real question is, what are your assets, and how valuable are they? If your facility houses a significant number of high-value physical assets that can be moved, perhaps this is the best solution. But for protection of mobile workstations like laptops and PDAs, RFID is generally cost prohibitive" (Blades, p.38). Use of RFID in its various applications is discussed in greater detail in later chapters.

Control may be exercised over the employer's property as well as the property of individual employees, vendors, contractors and visitors.

Employer Property

Any property of the employer that is to be taken from the facility may require a pass such as that illustrated in Figure 7.7. Property passes play a major role in property control. A log such as that shown in Figure 7.8 should be kept of all property signed out.

Nonemployer Property

If employees, contractors, vendors, visitors or others bring personal property into a secure facility, they might be required to register it so that when they leave there is no question as to their legitimate right to remove the property. A form such as that shown in Figure 7.9 might be used for this purpose. Such passes are not usually necessary for briefcases, laptops, purses or lunchboxes.

Property Pass

_____

| Manager name |
| Telephone ext. |

Property passes are returned to the approving manager for verification of items removed from the building.

Description of items to be taken from the building (include model, serial and tag number)	To be returned		Date to be returned
	Yes	No	

From (building)	To (building or home)	Checked employee name against badge or I.D. ☐
Employee (print or type) and signature	Employee number	Receptionist or guard	Date out
Manager signature		Receptionist or guard	Date in

Follow-up

☐ Equipment returned

☐ Equipment not returned

Comments

_____

Signature   Date

Figure 7.7 Property Pass

Property Sign-Out/In Log

Please print

Name	Property	Pass number	Date removed	Date returned

Figure 7.8 Property Sign-Out/Sign-In Log

Personal Property Registration		
Complete this form if you wish to bring personal property into the building.		

Quantity	Description of material	

Please print

Name	Representing	Department or person visited

I understand that items are to be removed from the plant only at the gate of entry, unless other arrangements are made at the gate of entry. This is not a property pass and applies only to people, vendors or employees who have a reason to bring in material.

Signature	Guard signature	Time entered	Date

Figure 7.9   Personal Property Registration

Restricting Use of Cameras and Video Equipment on Site

Many facilities do not allow cameras or video equipment to be brought into the facility without prior approval. This restriction may apply to all employees, contractors, visitors and even security personnel. A form such as that shown in Figure 7.10 might be used for this purpose. After the form is approved, the person authorized to take pictures or videos might be issued a pass such as that illustrated in Figure 7.11. This potential security problem has intensified with the popularity of photo cell phones.

Accounting and Receiving Procedures to Prevent or Reduce Shrinkage

Security managers are not expected to be accountants, but they should be aware of where potential security problems exist within the accounting system and the receiving department. Temptation to steal can be reduced by following some basic procedures.

 Accounting procedures to prevent or reduce shrinkage include the following:

- Keep limited cash on hand.
- Establish strict procedures for obtaining petty cash.
- Keep purchasing, receiving and paying functions separate.
- Use prenumbered purchase orders in sequence.

The limited amount of cash that is kept should be secured in a safe at closing. People requesting petty cash should have an authorization and a signed

Request for Authorization to Take Pictures

Date and time equipment will be used

Date(s) _____   Time(s) _____

_____   _____

Purpose of pictures _____

_____

_____

_____

_____

Location/area pictures will be taken _____

_____

_____

_____

Person(s) taking pictures

Name	Company name	Employee #
_____	_____	_____
_____	_____	_____
_____	_____	_____

Requested by _____

Approved by _____

Figure 7.10   Request for Authorization to Take Pictures

Camera Pass

_____ is authorized to take

pictures of _____

on _____ , in _____

        (date)   (plant)

_____

                    (area)

Company represented _____

Escort _____

Purpose _____

Dept. manager _____

Security officer _____

Figure 7.11   Camera Pass

voucher or request form before being given the cash. Strict records should account for every cent disbursed, including receipts provided by the person receiving the petty cash.

Whenever possible, purchasing, receiving and paying functions should be kept separate. Purchasing should be centralized, not only to minimize opportunity for unauthorized purchases, but also because buying in bulk is usually less expensive. Purchase orders should be prenumbered and used in sequence. If more than one department does purchasing, each should be issued a purchase order book and made accountable for every number contained in the book before another is issued. Any purchase orders that are ruined should be marked void, *not* simply discarded. Copies of the purchase orders should be sent to the receiving and the paying departments.

The receiving department should check the orders received against the purchase orders on file. Any missing or damaged items or extra items should be promptly reported. The supplier should be notified if a shipment is not received within a reasonable time; it may have been stolen or misrouted. It is usually best to have one central receiving area.

Merchandise should be received in a protected area such as a sheltered inside dock. Only suppliers' vehicles and company cars should be allowed in the receiving area. The receiving area should be physically separated from the shipping area. If a great security risk exists, the hours for receiving should be limited and a security guard assigned during this period. The doors should be kept closed and locked when not in use. A buzzer or bell can be used to alert personnel when a delivery is being attempted.

Suppliers should never leave merchandise unattended on the dock. If they do, the receiver is not legally responsible. Any supplier whose delivery agents simply unload merchandise on the dock and leave should be promptly notified of this break in security.

Train boxcars and truck trailers may use a numbered metal seal bar. In such cases, receivers should check the seal number with the bill of lading. If it appears to have been tampered with, the delivery should not be accepted.

Once a delivery is accepted, it should be unloaded and properly stored as soon as possible. If this cannot be done, the doors on the boxcar or truck trailer should be padlocked or nailed shut.

Receivers should not go by the packing slip (called **blind receiving**), but should actually count the items delivered. Some purchasing departments omit the quantity on the copy of the purchase order sent to receiving, forcing the receiver to do a careful count. A hazard inherent in this procedure is that an incomplete shipment may be accepted. If a shipment is ordered by weight, the merchandise should be weighed when received. The accuracy of the scales should be checked periodically.

The paying department should issue checks for only those orders for which they have an authorized purchase order and authorized verification from the receiving department that the shipment has arrived as specified on the purchase order.

Although many organizations have all their accounting and receiving functions computerized, the same principles apply. Keeping purchasing, receiving and paying functions separate will thwart such dishonest practices as writing purchase orders for nonexistent materials, writing double purchase orders and making payments for materials that were never ordered. Bill padding can be thwarted by insisting that competitive bids be obtained for any major purchases. Acceptance of gifts or gratuities from suppliers should be strictly forbidden, as this may foster doing special "favors" for each other.

Other Procedures to Enhance Security

In addition to effective hiring and employment practices and controlling access to restricted or vulnerable areas and financial assets, other procedures can also help ensure company safety and security, including drug testing, making rounds, conducting routine searches and inspections, keeping an accurate inventory and performing periodic audits, taking precautions when transporting valuables and further protecting through insurance and bonding.

Drug Testing in the Workplace

Gips (2006, p.50) observes: "Drug dealers and users are more savvy in workplaces today. Businesses need policies and training to counter these trends." According to the U.S. Department of Justice's Web site (2002), tests for illegal use of drugs are not medical examinations under the ADA and are not subject to the restrictions of such examinations. The ADA does not encourage, prohibit or authorize drug tests. Therefore, employers may conduct such testing of applicants or employees and make employment decisions based on the results. An employer can discipline, discharge or deny employment to an alcoholic whose use of alcohol adversely affects job performance or conduct. An employer also may prohibit the use of alcohol in the workplace and can require that employees not be under the influence of alcohol.

Drug testing is often used in pre-employment screening. According to Gips (p.54) all employees in safety-sensitive positions are already subject to mandatory drug testing, including airline pilots and mechanics, bus and truck drivers and workers in nuclear power plants. In the past decade, three-quarters of all drug tests performed by companies on the general workforce were for pre-employment screening; random drug testing occurred infrequently (Gips). However this is slowly changing, as are the methods used for testing.

Testing of urine remains the most commonly used procedure because the specimens are easy to handle and collect and the standard is already established. However, an entire industry of products to adulterate or substitute for urine specimens has cropped up, making alternative types of testing, such as hair analysis, more appealing to some companies. Table 7.1 summarizes the pros and cons of drug testing methods.

Workers have challenged the employer's right to require drug tests, but the courts have usually upheld the right to test if the employer has instituted a fair drug-testing program. In the Michigan case, *Baggs v. Eagle-Picher Industries* (1992), employees for an automobile trim manufacturing plant sued their employer for wrongful discharge after they had refused to submit to or failed a drug test. The Sixth District Court ruled in favor of the employer, and the decision was upheld on appeal.

In *Hazlett v. Martin Chevrolet, Inc.* (1986), the Ohio supreme court ruled held that alcoholism and drug addiction are handicaps and that the firing of an alco-

Table 7.1   Pros and Cons of Drug Testing Methods

SPECIMEN	BEST FOR	WORST FOR	COMMENTS
Urine	Preemployment After an accident Random	Alcohol detection	Widely accepted Often adulterated
Hair	Preemployment Reasonable suspicion Historic use	After an accident	Trouble detecting marijuana Expensive
Oral Fluids	After an accident Reasonable suspicion	Preemployment	Short detection window Hard to adulterate
Blood	After an accident Law enforcement Extreme cases Subjects on dialysis	Other uses	Highly invasive Drugs must still be in system Expensive Medical waste issues
Pupillometry	N/A	N/A	Still experimental

SOURCE: From "High on the Job" by Michael A. Gips. © 2006 ASIS International, 1625 Prince Street, Alexandria, VA 22314. Reprinted by permission from the February 2006 issue of *Security Management* magazine.

holic employee who was also addicted to cocaine was unlawful discrimination under state law. But in *Glide Lumber Products Company v. Employment Division* (1987), an Oregon court of appeals ruled that a positive drug test, by itself, was not sufficient grounds to fire an employee. The employer must also show that the drug use negatively affected the employee's job performance.

In *National Treasury Employees Union v. Von Raab* (1989), the Court ruled that an employer, the U.S. Customs Service, could require job applicants applying for sensitive positions to undergo drug and alcohol testing and that such testing did not violate an employee's Fourth Amendment privacy rights.

An Alternative Method of Drug Testing   The Old Town Trolley in San Diego tests strictly for impairment using a 30-second computer examination that checks hand-eye coordination and psychomotor responses. The test detects motor impairment whether it is caused by drugs, alcohol, stress or fatigue. It is the impairment, not the cause, which is important. Every employee completes the test every morning.

The hazards of drug abuse on the job and security measures to counteract them are discussed in Chapter 12.

Making Rounds

Often security personnel are responsible for *making rounds*, that is, for conducting a visual check of the facility to observe conditions. Security officers should be alert to hazards that might lead to an accident, such as water or grease on the floor, materials stacked too high, faulty railings and stairs, loose carpeting or rugs and inadequate lighting in walkways. They should also be alert to hazardous weather-related conditions such as slick sidewalks or ice or snow falling from the roof or window ledges. In addition, they should recognize and intervene in any employee behavior that might pose a safety hazard such as "goofing off," working without safety glasses and hard hats where designated, fighting, running or reckless driving in parking lots.

Being alert to fire hazards is also important. Security officers should note blocked aisles, stairway exits or fire doors. They should also note uncovered containers of solvent, oily rags, roof leaks, unusual odors or defective electrical wiring, as well as the operability of fire extinguishers and hoses.

Being alert to opportunities for theft is yet another responsibility of security officers as they make their rounds. They should check for evidence of illegal entry such as broken windows and locks, check that all doors that are to be locked have been and that certain safes and vaults are locked. They should also check to be sure that sensitive information is not being left out on desks or discarded in the trash.

Another function security officers often fulfill while making their rounds is that of energy and resource conservation. They should be authorized to and responsible for turning off water left running and unneeded lights or equipment left on after hours, including copy machines, desk lights and space heaters. Security officers should *not* turn off any computers or test equipment.

Yet another important function of security personnel making rounds is to ensure access control. They should question suspicious individuals. Suspicious behavior includes a person being in an unlighted area, being in a secured area without authorization, being at someone else's desk or going through someone else's desk drawers or file cabinets, going through wastebaskets and loitering near a trash container or card-controlled entry. When security officers observe suspicious behavior, they should request identification from the individual, determine his or her purpose for being there and take appropriate action.

While making rounds, security officers are also usually responsible for checking monitoring devices for climate control and responding to any alarms. Last, but of utmost importance, security officers should be helpful and friendly to employees and all others they encounter while conducting their rounds.

If any risk-producing factors are encountered during rounds, security officers should promptly report them to the appropriate person and also make a written report. They should follow up to ensure that the risk has been eliminated.

Conducting Routine Searches and Inspections

Although most employees and visitors are honest, security requires that periodic inspections be made to ensure that theft is not occurring. Individual facilities may adopt policies and procedures to allow searches of work areas, including lockers, desks and files, and items being brought into or removed from the facility, including packages, briefcases, purses and boxes. Inspections may also be made of lunchboxes, vehicle interiors and trunks, and individuals, unless expressly prohibited in the labor contract. Notices such as those in Figure 7.12 might be used to inform employees and visitors of a search policy.

Searches are extremely sensitive. Security personnel must be courteous and nonthreatening. Each inspection should be entered in the officer's daily log, including the person's name and time of the inspection. Employees should not feel they are under suspicion or not trusted when a personal inspection is made. The chances of this are lessened if everyone is inspected or a systematic inspection is made (e.g., every tenth person is inspected) and if everyone has been in-

---

Work Area Search Notice
to All Employees

Effective _____ we are establishing work area search procedures to improve security.
(date)

Work areas will be subject to search at our discretion. We will post the following notice in conspicuous places informing people of this policy.

> WE RESERVE THE RIGHT TO INSPECT AND SEARCH EMPLOYEE LOCKERS, DESKS, FILES, BOXES, PACKAGES, BRIEFCASES, LUNCHBOXES, PURSES OR BAGS WITHIN THE WORK AREA.

Because this program will increase our work and work area security, we expect and appreciate your full cooperation. Failure to cooperate with this procedure will result in disciplinary action.

THE MANAGEMENT

Entrance and Exit Search Notice
to All Employees/Visitors

Effective _____ we are establishing new entry and exit procedures to improve security.
(date)

People entering and leaving this facililty may be subject to questions at our discretion. Packages, handbags, purses, briefcases, lunchboxes and other possessions may be subject to search.

The following notice will be posted in conspicuous places informing people of this policy.

> WE RESERVE THE RIGHT TO QUESTION PEOPLE ENTERING OR LEAVING THE PROPERTY AND TO INSPECT ANY PACKAGE, HANDBAG, PURSE, BRIEFCASE, LUNCHBOX, OR OTHER POSSESSION CARRIED INTO OR OUT OF THE COMPANY PROPERTY.

Because this program will increase our work and work area security, we expect and appreciate your full cooperation. Failure to cooperate with this procedure will result in disciplinary action.

Figure 7.12   Sample Search Notification

formed *prior* to employment that periodic personal inspections are part of the established security system. Likewise, visitors and customers should not be annoyed when their packages are inspected if a sign obviously displayed clearly states: "We reserve the right to inspect all packages."

Packages brought into or taken from the premises are routinely subject to inspection. Frequently people are required to check all packages before entering an area. College bookstores, for example, often require all books and backpacks to be left in a rack before entering the store. Discount and department stores often require that all packages brought into the store be checked. Some stores even require women to check their purses until they are ready to make their purchases. Such requirements may anger customers and visitors, but if the procedure is adequately explained, public relations need not suffer. If people are allowed to take packages, briefcases or other containers into restricted areas, a reception or security guard frequently inspects the contents, lists what is being taken in and then reinspects the package or briefcase when the person leaves.

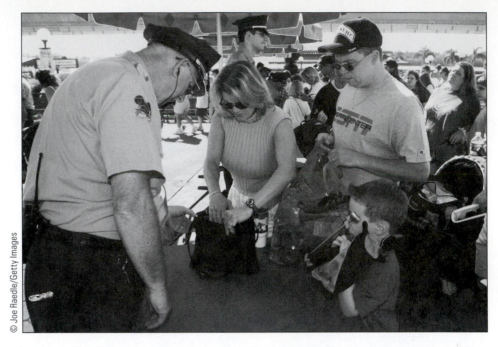

Security officials check bags as people enter Walt Disney World's Magic Kingdom in Orlando, Florida.

If a visitor, employee or repair worker takes a package or item from a secure area, effective security procedure should require them to present a completed property pass authorizing the removal. The employee who authorizes the removal should sign a removal pass, in ink, with their full name, since initials can be easily forged. All uncompleted lines on the form should then be crossed out so the person receiving the authorization cannot add additional items to the pass. Because thieves may pose as repair workers and simply walk out of an establishment with expensive electronic equipment or office machines, the person authorizing the removal must first check the service person's credentials before signing the pass and should require the service person to sign a receipt for the items to be removed. This removal pass system should also be used if it is company policy to lend tools and office machines to employees for personal use after hours or on weekends.

If security officers find during an exit search that a person has property that belongs to the facility and no pass has been issued, one should be completed on the spot, or the person attempting to take the property should write out an explanation as to why they are removing those items. Likewise, if security officers find unauthorized property such as alcohol or illegal drugs during a routine search of a work area, such employees might be asked to submit to their manager a written explanation of why the property was in their possession.

If the person refuses to comply with any of the proceeding package inspection procedures, policies should be in place as to whether the security officer confiscates the package, calls a supervisor or simply records the person's name and employee number or company represented and allows the person to leave. Security officers should not argue or forcefully attempt to conduct a search.

Providing employees with *lockers* is a sound security practice because it helps employees keep their personal possessions safe. On the other hand, lockers are also a security risk because employees can conceal stolen property or goods in their lockers until such time that they have an opportunity to remove them undetected from the premises. Employee lockers should be considered a privilege, not a right. They are not the employees' private property. Employees should not be allowed to use their own locks. They should be informed when they are given a locker that the locker is provided by the company as a convenience to the employee and that the company retains the right to inspect the locker at any time. Periodic inspections can and should then be made without fear of legal entanglements.

 Searches of people, packages, lockers and vehicles are usually acceptable if:

- All employees and visitors are notified about the program before it is implemented.
- The inspection procedure is clearly explained.
- The program itself is courteous, fair and nondiscriminatory, that is, it includes all employees or visitors.

Trash containers and trash removal procedures should also be checked periodically. Dishonest employees can hide stolen items in the trash and later retrieve them, or items may be accidentally discarded. In some cases, employee/thieves have worked with trash collectors to steal vast quantities of merchandise.

Given that 70 percent of losses are caused by employees, probabilities are good that some dishonest employees will be caught stealing from the company. Usually an employee caught stealing from the company should be fired and prosecuted. Frequently, however, such is not the case. Employees are given second, third and even fourth chances. Or, if they are dismissed, the reasons for the dismissal are kept secret. When the discharged person seeks employment elsewhere and the new potential employer makes a background check, the reason for the dismissal may be hidden. Such practices only encourage internal theft and should be discontinued.

Because there are degrees of seriousness of crimes and there may be mitigating circumstances, policies should exist setting forth actions to be taken for varying types of criminality, dollar amounts, safety considerations and the like, with punitive actions ranging from verbal reprimands to criminal prosecution.

Firing dishonest *security* personnel is a must. If the security profession is to grow and build respect, dishonest security personnel must be weeded out.

Inventorying and Auditing

Accurate records help management discover when and where shrinkage is occurring.

 Some thefts can be detected by using a perpetual inventory and periodic internal and external audits.

A **perpetual inventory** is ongoing, reflecting all additions and deletions from specific assets. Although keeping a perpetual inventory requires time and effort, the benefits are worth it because the owner or manager has real-time data on existing supplies and stock and therefore is immediately alerted to inventory shrinkage. A perpetual inventory also serves as a psychological deterrent to theft. This is in contrast to the annual inventory system in which an employee may be stealing shortly after completion of the inventory, knowing that the shortage will not be discovered until almost a year later. Computerized inventories make this security procedure much easier.

When inventories are taken, do not assume closed cartons or containers contain what they are supposed to contain. Spot checks should be made to ensure that the merchandise is actually there. In one filling station, an attendant pocketed any cash received for oil sold in cans and put the empty cans in the storeroom at the back of the shelf. A cursory visual count of the cans would not reveal the shrinkage; only the physical manipulation of the inventory itself would detect this loss.

Careful, periodic internal and external audits also help detect shrinkage. An internal audit of accounting procedures can be conducted by intentionally introducing errors. For example, what does the purchasing department do if a purchase order is submitted without an authorized signature? What does the receiving department do if it is sent a shipment containing extra items? Is the error reported, do the extra items simply disappear or does the error go unnoticed? What does the paying department do with a bill for which there is no purchase order? Prompt reporting of shortages, losses and errors should be encouraged and positively enforced. Periodic external audits are also important to security.

Transporting Valuables

Procedures for transporting valuable goods and cash should be established and strictly adhered to. All employees entrusted with transporting valuables should be thoroughly checked and perhaps bonded, as discussed shortly. Large shipments might be divided into two or three smaller, separate shipments. All vehicles used to transport valuables should be in good mechanical condition.

 Secrecy should be maintained when transporting valuables. Times, routes, personnel and vehicles used should be varied.

Many businesses prefer to use commercial firms for transporting valuable merchandise and cash. When armed courier services are used, employees should be instructed to always check the couriers' credentials carefully before handing over the cash or items to be transported.

Insurance and Bonding

One means to deal with risk is to *transfer* it, as discussed in Chapter 5. If the risk is still unacceptable after all measures to eliminate or reduce it are completed, insurance and bonding are viable alternatives. One important source of information on insurance, rates and the like is the Insurance Services Office (ISO).

 Insurance and bonding of specific employees may help reduce losses.

Most managers carry insurance on their buildings and on expensive equipment. If the risk is great that, despite effective physical and procedural controls, large value losses might be sustained by employee dishonesty, external crime or a natural disaster, many security managers recommend that the company take out insurance and have individuals in key positions bonded.

Commercial property insurance commonly includes buildings, named insured's business personal property and personal property of others in the care, custody or control of the insured (Rejda, 2008, p.569). Additional coverage might provide for debris removal, preservation of property, fire department service, pollutant cleanup and removal, increased cost of construction and electronic data (pp.570–571). Such policies frequently have deductibles.

The causes-of-loss basic form typically provides coverage for the following causes of loss to covered property: fire, lightning, explosions, windstorm or hail, smoke, aircraft or vehicles, riot or civil commotion, vandalism, sprinkler leakage, sinkhole collapse and volcanic action. Additions to the basic form may include coverage against falling objects; weight of snow, ice or sleet; and water damage (p.572).

Business income insurance is also available: "Business firms often experience an indirect loss as the result of a direct physical damage loss to covered property, such as the loss of profits, rents or extra expenses during the period of restoration. Business income insurance (formerly called *business interruption insurance*) is designed to cover the loss of business income, expenses that continue during the shutdown period and extra expenses because of loss from a covered peril" (Rejda, pp.574–575).

Transportation insurance is a common option, as businesses ship billions of dollars of goods each year that are exposed to damage or loss from numerous transportation hazards. These goods can be protected by ocean marine and inland marine contracts. Such contracts contain three implied warranties: seaworthy vessel, no deviation from planned course and a legal purpose (Rejda, pp.580–581).

Commercial liability insurance is another alternative to manage risks: "The litigious nature of American society is a risk that can impact a company's bottom line. Liability insurance is a key tool for managing this risk" (p.592). The important general liability loss exposures include premises and operations liability, products liability, completed operations liability, contractual liability and contingent liability (p.593). Such insurance usually covers bodily injury and property damage liability, personal and advertising injury liability, medical payments and certain supplementary payments, as well as attorney fees. Bodily injury and property damage are self-explanatory. Personal and advertising injury liability includes false arrest, detention or imprisonment; malicious prosecution; wrongful eviction or entry; oral or written publication that slanders or libels; oral or written publication that violates a person's right to privacy; use of another's advertising idea in your advertisement and infringing on another copyright, slogan or trade dress. These areas of civil liability were introduced in Chapter 4. Most such policies have limits of insurance stating the maximum amount the insurer will pay regardless of the number of insured, claims made or suits brought.

Employment-related practices liability insurance protects against employers being sued by employees and potential employees based on wrongful termination, discrimination, sexual harassment, failure to promote, failure to hire and other employment-related practices such as retaliatory action against employees, coercing an employee to commit an unlawful act or omission (Rejda, pp.600–601).

Another important form of insurance is *workers' compensation insurance*. All states have laws providing benefits to workers with a job-related injury or occupational disease. This insurance provides medical care, cash benefits, survivor benefits and rehabilitation services. These benefits are paid based on the principle of **liability without fault**, meaning the employer is held absolutely liable for job-related accidents and disease regardless of fault.

Table 7.2 Comparison of Insurance and Surety Bonds

Insurance

1. There are two parties to an insurance contract.
2. The insurer expects to pay losses. The premium reflects expected loss costs.
3. The insurer normally does not have the right to recover a loss payment from the insured.
4. Insurance is designed to cover unintentional losses that ideally are outside of the insured's control.

Surety Bonds

1. There are three parties to a surety bond.
2. The surety theoretically expects no losses to occur. The premium is viewed as a service fee, by which the surety's credit is substituted for that of the principal.
3. The surety has the legal right to recover a loss payment from the defaulting principal.
4. The surety guarantees the principal's character, honesty, integrity and ability to perform. These qualities are within the principal's control.

SOURCE: From Rejda/McNamara, *Principles of Risk Management & Insurance*, 10th edition, p.627, © 2008, 2005, 2003, 2001 Pearson Education, Inc. Reproduced by permission of Pearson Education, Inc. All rights reserved.

In addition to insurance, many security directors recommend that employees in sensitive positions be bonded. **Fidelity bonds** protect a company from losses that result directly from dishonest or fraudulent acts of employees acting alone or in collusion with others with the active and conscious purpose of causing the insured to sustain a loss (Rejda, p.625). Most insurance companies require that all reasonable preventive measures be instituted before they will bond employees against crime. When such security devices and procedures exist, significant savings in insurance premiums often result—sometimes as high as a 70-percent reduction.

A **surety bond**, in contrast, usually provides monetary compensation if the bonded party fails to perform certain promised acts, for example, when an overextended contractor is unable to complete a construction project (Rejda, p.626). Surety bonds are similar to insurance contracts because both provide protection against specific losses. However, important differences exist, as shown in Table 7.2.

SUMMARY

- An important first step toward establishing security and reducing shrinkage and negligence lawsuits is to hire well. Pre-employment screening should include an application and résumé, intellectual and psychological tests and a thorough background check including references.

- Education and supervision can also help prevent losses. All employees should be educated as to their responsibilities and restrictions. Reasonable rules should be established and enforced.

- Most procedural controls seek to prevent loss or shrinkage by limiting access to specific areas by unauthorized personnel. Procedural controls to limit access to specified areas include stationing guards; restricting vehicle traffic; requiring registration and sign-outs; requiring display of badges or passes; ensuring key control; using effective opening, closing and after-hours procedures; and controlling access to vulnerable areas and equipment.

- At minimum, effective employee badges and passes display the employee's name, employment

- number, signature and photograph as well as an authorized signature. They are sturdy, tamper-proof and changed periodically.

- A key-control system limits the number of persons having keys, establishes a master list of all existing keys and to whom they are assigned, keeps all duplicate keys secure and requires a physical audit periodically.

- In an establishment where the risk of burglary is high and no security personnel are on night duty, opening and closing should be, at minimum, a two-person operation.

- Effective closing procedures include checking all restrooms and areas where someone might be concealed, turning off all unnecessary lights and machinery, opening cash registers and placing money in the safe, locking the safe as well as all windows and interior doors, turning on security lighting, activating the alarm and securing all exterior doors.

- Particularly vulnerable to theft or employee pilferage are storage areas; areas where cash, valuables, records and forms are kept; mail rooms; supply rooms; duplicating rooms and computer rooms.

- In addition to procedures for controlling access to certain areas, accounting and receiving procedures can help control shrinkage. A limited amount of cash should be kept on hand. Strict procedures for obtaining petty cash should be established. Purchasing, receiving and paying functions should be kept separate. Prenumbered purchase orders should be used in sequence.

- Searches of people, packages, lockers and vehicles are usually acceptable if all employees and visitors are notified about the program before it is implemented; the inspection procedure is clearly explained; and the program itself is courteous, fair and nondiscriminatory, that is, it includes all employees and visitors.

- Some thefts can be detected by using a perpetual inventory and periodic internal and external audits.

- When valuables are being transported, secrecy should be maintained and the times, routes, personnel and vehicles used should be varied.

- Insurance and/or bonding of specific employees may also help reduce financial losses.

APPLICATION

Company rules are important in setting up a strong loss-prevention program. Following are some rules from *Preventing Employee Pilferage* by S. D. Astor (1977, pp.4–5) to help ensure against employee theft:

- Make a dependable second check of incoming materials to rule out the possibility of collusive theft between drivers and employees who handle the receiving.
- No truck shall approach the loading platform until it is ready to load or unload.
- Drivers will not be allowed behind the receiving fence.
- At the loading platform, drivers will not be permitted to load their own trucks, especially by taking goods from stock.
- Every lunchbox, toolbox, bag, or package must be checked by a supervisor or security officer as employees leave the plant.
- All padlocks must be snapped shut on hasps when not in use to prevent the switching of locks.
- Keys to padlocks must be controlled to prevent duplicates from being made.

- Trash must not be allowed to accumulate in, or be picked up from, an area near storage sites of valuable materials or finished goods.
- Trash pickups must be supervised.
- Rotate security officers to discourage fraternization with other employees who may be dishonest and to prevent monotony from reducing officer alertness.
- Never assign two or more members of the same family to work in the same area. (You can expect blood to be thicker than company loyalty.)
- Control receiving reports and shipping orders (preferably by numbers in sequence) to prevent duplicate or fraudulent payment of invoices and the padding or destruction of shipping orders.
- Employees caught stealing will be prosecuted. (Settling for restitution and an apology is inviting theft to continue.)

Green and Farber (1978, pp.146–147) describe several types of employee dishonesty that account for 7 to 10 percent of business failures annually. Read the list, keeping in mind Astor's rules to thwart pilferage:[1]

[1]Reprinted with permission of the publisher from Green and Farber, *Introduction to Security,* revised edition (Woburn, MA: Butterworth Publishers, Inc.). Copyright © Elsevier 1978.

- Payroll and personnel employees collaborating to falsify records by the use of nonexistent employees or by retaining terminated employees on the payroll.
- Padding overtime reports, part of which extra unearned pay is kicked back to the authorizing supervisor.
- Maintenance personnel and contract servicemen in collusion to steal and sell office equipment.
- Receiving clerks and truck drivers in collusion to falsify merchandise count. Extra unaccounted merchandise is fenced.
- Purchasing agent in collusion with vendor to pay inflated price and split profit.

- Mailroom and supply personnel packing and mailing merchandise to themselves for resale.
- Accounts payable personnel paying fictitious bills to an account set up for their own use.
- Taking incoming cash without crediting the customer's account.
- Appropriating checks made out to cash.
- Removal of equipment or merchandise with trash.
- Invoicing goods below regular price and getting a kickback from the purchaser
- Under-ringing on a cash register.

Which rules in the first selection might thwart specific dishonest practices in the second selection? What other rules might be required?

DISCUSSION QUESTIONS

1. Why is curbing pilferage so important to a security manager?
2. What factual information should be obtained to make the decision to employ or to not employ an applicant?
3. What procedures can be used regarding employee coats, purses and packages to deter internal theft?
4. What are some rationales frequently given by employees for stealing from their employers?
5. What employee actions might lead security personnel to suspect dishonesty?

REFERENCES

Astor, S. D. *Preventing Employee Pilferage*. Small Business Administration. Management Aids No. 209. Washington, DC: U.S. Government Printing Office, 1977.

Blades, Marleah. "Welcome to Shangri-La: The Integrated RFID Asset Management Conundrum." *Security Technology & Design*, February 2005, pp.34–38.

Bolles, Richard Nelson. *What Color Is Your Parachute? A Practical Manual for Job-Hunters & Career-Changers*. Berkeley, CA: Ten Speed Press, 2004.

"Five Reasons to Consider a Visitor Management System." *Security Technology & Design*, October 2004, p.54.

Gips, Michael A. "High on the Job." *Security Management*, February 2006, pp.50–58.

Grant, Stephanie and Lawn, Michael. "Integration of Access Control, Visitor Management Systems Part of Elite Properties." *Security Products*, January 2005, p.42.

Harr, J. Scott and Hess, Kären M. *Careers in Criminal Justice and Related Fields: From Internship to Promotion*, 5th edition. Belmont, CA; Wadsworth Publishing Co., 2006.

Pearson, Robert. "Well-Designed Badges Help Prevent Loss." *Security Technology & Design*, July 2005, pp.48–66.

Rejda, George E. *Principles of Risk Management and Insurance*, 10th edition. Boston, MA: Pearson/Addison-Wesley, 2008.

Roberts, Marta. "Problems Passe in Passaic Valley." *Security Management*, February 2005, pp.24–25.

Sanchez, Karina. "The Demise of the Visitor Logbook." *Security Products*, January 2005, p.88.

Scott, Kathy. "Case in Point: Manhattan." *Security Technology & Design*, December 2004, p.33.

U.S. Department of Justice. "Americans with Disabilities Act: Questions and Answers." Updated August 23, 2002. Online: http://www.usdoj.gov/crt/ada/q%26aeng02.htm

CASES CITED

Baggs v. Eagle-Picher Industries, 750 F. Supp. 264, 957 F.2d 268 (1992).

Glide Lumber Products Company v. Employment Division, 741 P.2d 907 (Or. App. 1987).

Hazlett v. Martin Chevrolet, Inc., 25 Ohio St. 3d 279, 496 N.E.2d 478 (Ohio 1986).

National Treasury Employees Union v. Von Raab, 489 U.S. 656, 109 S. Ct. 1384 (1989).

Preventing Losses from Accidents, Emergencies and Natural Disasters

© AP/ Wide World Photos

Natural disasters present formidable security challenges for entire communities. Here a man pushes his bicycle through flood waters near the Superdome in New Orleans, August 31, 2005, after Hurricane Katrina left much of the city under water.

DO YOU KNOW . . .

■ Why accident prevention is often a security responsibility?

■ What causes the vast majority of accidents?

■ How accidents can be prevented or reduced?

■ What the 3 Rs of emergency management are?

■ What security's role during civil disturbances or demonstrations, riots and strikes is?

■ What the primary defenses against bombs are?

■ How a bomb threat can be prepared for? Received?

■ What three elements are required for a fire to occur?

■ How fires are classified?

■ How fires can be prevented?

■ What personnel and equipment can help protect lives and assets from fire?

■ What procedures should be followed in the event of a fire?

■ What the four phases of a natural disaster usually are?

■ What postemergency "killers" usually are?

CAN YOU DEFINE?

FEMA	Occupational Safety and Health Act (OSH Act)	Occupational Safety and Health Administration (OSHA)	pandemic
fire triangle			universal precautions
fire-loading			

Introduction

Preventing losses from accidents, emergencies and natural disasters is a critical responsibility of security managers. Despite the best efforts to reduce the possibility of accidents, emergencies or natural disasters occurring, they will happen. Security managers and personnel must be prepared to deal effectively with them. The simple fact that an accident, emergency or natural disaster happened might be the basis for a lawsuit if an organization is not prepared. How the incident is handled might also be cause for civil action against security personnel and the employers.

While the goals of security and loss prevention teams are similar to those of environment, health and safety (EHS) groups—to prevent loss of life and protect assets—their approaches might be in conflict (Crosby, 2004). For example, security might be concentrating on access control that might be counterproductive to EHS evacuation plans. Various obstacles make integration of safety and EHS a challenge: "Collaboration threatens either department, with each fearing that it will be subsumed by the other. In addition, the corporate culture might have created a divide and perhaps a rivalry between the departments" (Gips, 2005b, p.90). Despite obstacles, safety and security are natural allies.

Not only is it common sense to protect against accidents, it is also federally mandated that such protection be provided. This chapter begins by discussing the Occupational Safety and Health Act (OSH Act), which regulates many of the safety standards in business and industry. This is followed by a discussion of accident prevention. Next, general guidelines for dealing with emergencies are presented, followed by a look at handling specific incidents such as medical emergencies; hazardous materials incidents; civil disturbances, riots and strikes; and bombs and bomb threats. The chapter concludes with a discussion of preventing and protecting against loss by fire and natural disasters.

The Occupational Safety and Health Act

Traditionally, security has focused on preventing and minimizing losses from internal and external crime. However, since the passage of the Occupational Safety and Health Act in 1970, the security function has gradually expanded to include specific safety responsibilities. Security managers involved in these safety programs often have titles such as Director of Loss Prevention, Director of Security and Prevention or Director of Safety and Security, reflecting these dual functions.

Prompted by a disturbing pattern of increasing occupational injuries, Congress enacted Public Law 91–596, the **Occupational Safety and Health Act**, the stated purpose of which is "to assure so far as possible every working man and woman in the nation safe and healthful working conditions and to preserve our human resources." The **Occupational Safety and Health Administration (OSHA)**, a federal agency within the Department of Labor, was established to administer this act.

The OSH Act applies to every employer engaged in interstate commerce or whose business affects interstate commerce and who has at least one employee. The vast majority of employers in the nation are, therefore, under the jurisdiction of OSHA. The act excludes employees of federal, state and local governments and those protected under federal occupational safety and health laws, such as the Atomic Energy Act of 1954 or the Federal Coal Mine Safety and Health Act.

Complying with OSHA Requirements

The Occupational Safety and Health Act requires employers to post a notice informing employees of their protection under the act. In addition, all employees must have access to OSHA regulations and standards. Employees can request an OSHA inspection of their workplace, and they can request medical tests to determine if they are being exposed to unhealthy conditions at work.

OSHA requires employers covered by the act to keep a log of all occupational injuries, accidents and illnesses, as well as an annual summary of the log's information. The annual summary must be compiled and posted within one month after the close of the year and left up for 30 days. The act also requires employers to keep the detailed safety and health records for five years, subject to OSHA review at any time.

Inspections

To ensure that its requirements are fulfilled, the OSH Act stipulates that OSHA inspectors can investigate any facility subject to OSHA standards to assess compliance. Inspectors can appear at any reasonable hour to inspect the facility. If they request an employee to accompany them, this request should be honored.

In 1975, small businessman Ferrol G. Barlow refused to allow an OSHA inspector onto the premises of his plumbing and electrical installation business without a warrant, contesting the surprise inspection. This refusal set off a three-year legal battle that led to the Supreme Court, which ruled five-to-three that government agents checking for safety and health hazards cannot make spot checks without a warrant (*Marshall v. Barlow's Inc.*, 1978). Such inspections, the Court contended, did amount to a violation of the Fourth Amendment, which protects not only private homes but commercial premises as well. Certain establishments were held exempt from the warrant requirement, including those engaged in producing liquor and firearms. Unlike other search warrants, a warrant to check for safety and health hazards does *not* have to be based on the probable cause that unsafe conditions exist. Therefore, the surprise nature of the inspections, a necessary feature to avoid cosmetic changes, remains intact. Representatives from management, employees or both have the right to accompany an OSHA inspector and to see the results of that inspection.

The U.S. Department of Labor is responsible for enforcing OSHA standards and imposing penalties on violators. The penalties apply *only* to the employer. Although the OSH Act requires employee compliance with all safety and health standards and regulations, the employer is responsible to see that the employees comply. For example, if a worker is seen without a hard hat in an area where such safety equipment is required, it is the employer, not the employee, who gets the citation. Additional information on OSHA and specific standards for a given type of facility can be obtained from the state labor department or online from the U.S. Labor Department.

In addition to OSHA inspectors, premises are often subject to safety and fire inspections by insurance underwriters and city and state inspectors.

Accident Prevention

OSHA reports that thousands of workplace accidents occur throughout the United States every day. The failure of people, equipment, supplies or surroundings to behave or react as expected causes most of these accidents. Although no specific OSHA standards address accidents, Section 5(a)(1) of the OSH Act, the general duty clause, requires employers to "furnish to each employee employment and a place of employment which are free from recognized hazards that are causing or are likely to cause death or serious physical harm to employees."

 Security managers are often responsible for accident prevention programs as one means to prevent losses and protect assets.

Often safety hazards such as toxic chemicals and hydraulic presses, saws, grinders and punches are very apparent. Although accidents are commonly associated with heavy industry, the National Safety Council reports that more accidents occur in wholesale and retail businesses than in heavy industry. Accidents take an enormous human and economic toll each year.

 The National Safety Council states: "Ninety-five percent of all accidents (on or off the job) are caused by human error, especially lack of safety consciousness."

The vast majority of accidents result from carelessness, failure to have or follow safety rules and regulations and engaging in horseplay. The remaining 5 percent result from mechanical failures or natural disasters.

Chapter 8: Preventing Losses from Accidents, Emergencies and Natural Disasters   **215**

 Accidents can be prevented by removing hazards, using protective equipment, making employees aware of hazards that cannot be removed, following good housekeeping practices and making employees safety conscious.

Accidents are more apt to occur in cluttered areas, so good housekeeping practices are essential. Trash and rubbish accumulations not only are unsightly, but also can block fire exits, extinguishers and alarm boxes. Neatness provides a safer working environment and usually increases efficiency as well.

When accidents or injuries do occur, they should be reported, recorded and investigated. An effective accident investigation determines why and how the accident happened and includes the date of the accident, the name and occupation of the person injured, details of the accident, identification of the hazard or cause and the corrective actions taken.

Many managers use safety incentive plans such as cash or merchandise awards to employees with the best safety record. Trucking companies often provide awards for drivers who reach designated mileage checkpoints without an accident or ticket.

Despite a company's best efforts to prevent accidents, some may still occur, and a response must be prepared in advance. In addition, security managers must anticipate that emergencies and natural disasters are unavoidable and must, therefore, also be planned for.

General Guidelines for Dealing with Emergencies

Security managers and their staff may be faced with a variety of emergencies including medical emergencies; hazardous material incidents; civil disturbances, riots and strikes; bombs and bomb threats; fire and natural disasters. Every emergency presents a unique security challenge. Before looking at specific responses to the various types of emergencies a company may encounter, consider some general guidelines that can help ensure the most effective response possible.

 The 3 Rs of emergency management are readiness, response and recovery.

The American Society for Industrial Security has developed guidelines for a business continuity plan (BCP) following an emergency, crisis or natural disaster, depicted in Figure 8.1. In this approach, readiness might prevent an emergency, crisis or disaster or at least lessen the effect. At the heart of the plan is training and evaluation.

Before the Emergency—Readiness

The first step to preventing losses from accidents, emergencies and natural disasters is to anticipate them and be ready for them. The general guidelines in this stage include:

- Be prepared. Be proactive. Anticipate the emergencies and the personnel needed to deal with them.
- Have written plans in place. Specify *in writing* who does what, how and when. The more common elements there are among the plans for different

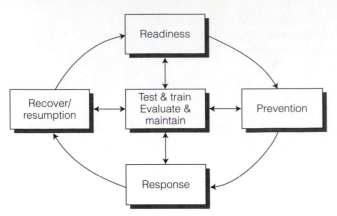

Readiness

Objective
Address the preparatory steps required to provide a strong foundation on which to build a BCP.

Tasks
1. Assign accountability
2. Perform risk assessment
3. Conduct business impact analysis
4. Agree on strategic plans
5. Crisis management and response team development

Figure 8.1 The Business Continuity Plan

SOURCE: From *Business Continuity Guideline: A Practical Approach for Emergency Preparedness, Crisis Management, and Disaster Recovery* (Alexandria, VA: American Society for Industrial Security, 2005) p.10. Reprinted with the written permission of ASIS International, Alexandria, VA.

types of emergencies, the better. This should include posting evacuation routes and emergency phone numbers for different types of emergencies. It should also include determining who will communicate with the media and what kind of information will be communicated.

- Identify the equipment and resources required and make certain they are either available or immediately accessible.
- Know how to use the emergency equipment: fire protection systems, first-aid equipment, hazardous material control equipment, communications systems.
- Inspect emergency equipment at least monthly. Check batteries in flashlights.
- Practice when possible.

Practicing the emergency response is a critical part of readiness. In a true emergency, valuable time will be wasted if employees must first track down the plan and then read what is written while trying to carry out their response. Phelps (2007, p.55) asserts: "Cities and companies that take emergency planning and business continuity seriously know better. They conduct exercises regularly, usually rotating between simple tabletop simulations and full-blown exercises, culminating with interactive exercises that involve other agencies." However, a survey of security directors found that only 56 percent of respondents practiced and tested their crisis management plan regularly (*Security Director News's* "Newspoll," 2007, p.23).

To be most effective, emergency response training should occur at least once every three months and should include all employees, including upper management: "Senior management needs to be aware of its responsibilities in an emergency. Human resources, legal, IT, and finance directors as well as the CEO will all have different roles to play" (Phelps, p.56). Finally, the major areas that need to be practiced and tested involve internal communications, external communications, resources, systems, safety, coordination, record keeping and legal issues (p.60).

To better prepare for emergencies, security managers may perform a risk analysis considering specific threats, the likelihood of them happening and the impact such an event would have on the business. Table 8.1 shows the incidents that might be considered and how to weigh their relative significance.

Additional variables to consider in assessing risks include onset speed (1=slow, 2=fast), forewarning (1=sufficient, 2=insufficient), duration (1=short, 2=long) and intensity (1=low, 2=high).

Once likely loss scenarios have been identified, response plans written out and simulated emergencies practiced, the company should be in a much better position to respond if and when an actual emergency occurs.

Table 8.1 Risk Assessment

The sample matrix below illustrates threat examples and demonstrates how risks can be categorized and quantified. Note: This list is not exhaustive and should be tailored to reflect the organization's operating environment.

Additional variables such as onset speed (1 = slow, 2 = fast), forewarning (1 = sufficient, 2 = insufficient), duration (1 = short, 2 = long) and intensity (1 = low, 2 = high) can also be added as additional columns and entered in the formula: e.g., likelihood × (onset speed + forewarning + duration + intensity) × impact = relative weight.

Threat or Trigger	Likelihood (Rate 1–5)	×	Impact (Rate 1–5)	=	Relative Weight
	1 = Very low 2 = Low 3 = Medium 4 = High 5 = Very high		1 = Negligible 2 = Some 3 = Moderate 4 = Significant 5 = Severe		
Earthquake		×		=	
Power failure		×		=	
Fire		×		=	
Hurricane		×		=	
Flood		×		=	
Bombing		×		=	
NBC* attack at site		×		=	
NBC* attack within 50 miles		×		=	
Cyber attack		×		=	
Kidnapping		×		=	
Sabotage		×		=	
Hazmat accident		×		=	
Product recall		×		=	
Public health		×		=	
Work stoppage		×		=	

*Nuclear, Biological and Chemical

SOURCE: From *Business Continuity Guideline: A Practical Approach for Emergency Preparedness, Crisis Management, and Disaster Recovery* (Alexandria, VA: American Society for Industrial Security, 2005) p.12. Reprinted with the written permission of ASIS International, Alexandria, VA.

During the Emergency—Response

Emergency procedures are designed to save lives; minimize injury, loss or damage and get back to normal as rapidly and safely as possible. In most instances, the primary responsibility of security personnel is to respond rapidly and appropriately and to maintain control of the situation until support professionals such as police, firefighters or medical specialists arrive. The *Business Continuity Guidelines* (2005, p.19) suggest that the response should address the following goals, in order of priority:

- Save lives and reduce chances of further injuries.
- Protect assets.
- Restore critical business processes and systems.
- Reduce the length of the interruption of business.
- Protect reputation damage.
- Control media coverage (e.g., local, regional, national).
- Maintain customer relations.

The following general guidelines apply to the actual response during an emergency:

- Take time to assess the situation. Do not make the situation worse by acting without thinking.
- Keep the channels of communication open and the information flowing as required to those who need it.
- Keep as many options open as possible. Avoid "either/or" thinking.
- Do not get sidetracked by personal, individual requests for help, but rather focus on the "big picture," routing individual requests to the appropriate source of assistance.
- Involve key personnel as rapidly as possible. Do not hesitate to call for help from the police, fire department, medical centers and any other assistance that might be needed. When calling for help:
  - Speak slowly and clearly.
  - Give your name, position, company name, address and location of the emergency.
  - Answer any questions.
  - Do *not* hang up until directed to do so.
- Accept the fact that security cannot do everything. The security manager must prioritize and delegate responsibilities quickly. Mistakes probably will happen.
- Keep top executives fully informed of progress and problems.
- Ensure that someone is tending to "normal" security needs during the emergency.
- Maintain control of the media. Follow established procedures.

Communication   Scott (2006, p.20) states: "Ask any public safety professional what the most critical technology to use in the aftermath of a natural disaster is and the answer invariably comes back 'communication.' " Pogar (2007, p.98) stresses: "Despite the clear lessons of 9–11 and Hurricane Katrina about the criticality of communications, many organizations remain unprepared to provide key employees with reliable communications. . . . Often these organizations already have a key element of their infrastructure in place to provide business continuity—in the form of Internet protocol (IP) functionality—they just fail to take advantage of it." Included in this technology are Voice over IP (VoIP), call center numbers, voice mail, e-mail and collaborative online environments for virtual meetings.

Several audiences need to be kept informed. *Internal audiences* include employees and their families, business owners and partners, boards of directors and onsite contractors and vendors. *External audiences* include customers and clients, present and potential; contractors, vendors and the media; government and regulatory agencies; local law enforcement; emergency responders; investors and shareholders and surrounding communities (*Business Guidelines*, p.20).

The following considerations are important when communicating with the various audiences. Communications should be timely and honest, providing objective and subjective assessments. Give bad news all at once. All employees should be informed at about the same time. To the extent possible, an audience should hear news from the organization first. Provide the opportunity for questions if possible. Provide regular updates, and let people know when the next update will be given (*Business Guidelines*, p.20).

Evacuation   If evacuation is required, an announcement such as the following should be made over the public address system:

> Attention. Please turn off all equipment and machines and leave the building through the nearest exit immediately. Move 200 feet away from the building. Stay there. Do not leave the premises unless directed to do so.

This message should be repeated at least three times. People should be instructed to not leave the area so that a check can be made of all personnel to determine if anyone is still inside the building.

Once the crisis has passed, the emergency plan enters the recovery stage.

After the Emergency—Recovery

The general guidelines to follow after the emergency has ended include:

- Get back to normal as soon as possible.
- *Document* everything that happened and was done. Accurate records are critical. (Expect that lawyers will get involved at some point.)
- Evaluate the response after the situation has returned to normal. Look at "mistakes" as the "least effective alternatives" as well as learning opportunities.
- Modify any identified risks remaining and modify emergency-preparedness plans as needed based on what was learned.

Following a crisis, it is not unusual for some employees to suffer emotional problems that affect their job performance (McKee and Guthridge, 2007, p.102). It is management's responsibility to be aware of disaster-related performance problems and to help employees through the trauma caused by the disaster. Among the behavioral warning signals are absenteeism, difficulty concentrating, inflexibility and poor personal relationships on the job (McKee and Guthridge).

Having looked at the general guidelines for handling crises, the discussion now turns to various types of emergencies and the incident-specific responses required for effective loss prevention.

Medical Emergencies

If the security personnel responding to a medical emergency have the necessary training, such as first aid or CPR, they should render aid. If they do not have such training, they should wait for trained personnel to arrive. Responding security personnel *must not* do more than they are trained to do. Any injured or seriously ill person should *not* be moved unless to leave them would put them in greater danger than if they were not moved (such as with a fire). Improper moving could cause further injury or death and could easily result in a civil lawsuit. Facilities should have a wheelchair, stretcher and basic first-aid equipment readily available.

Pandemics

A **pandemic** is a disease occurring over a wide geographic area and affecting an exceptionally high proportion of the population. The last three influenza pandemics in 1918, 1957 and 1968 killed about 40 million, 2 million and 1 million people worldwide respectively. History and science suggest we will face one or more pandemics in the twenty-first century. A pandemic or worldwide outbreak of a new influenza virus could potentially result in hundreds of thousands of deaths, millions of hospitalizations and hundreds of billions of dollars in direct and indirect costs (*A Quick Reference Guide*, 2006).

Of concern to many businesses today is avian flu. Ninety-three percent of respondents to a new survey consider avian flu a risk to the worldwide business community, and 80 percent report they consider the possible pandemic to be a threat to their specific organization (Daniels, 2006, p.2). Figure 8.2 shows the measures businesses are taking to prepare for such an emergency.

Protecting against AIDS and Hepatitis B

Care must be exercised by security personnel who deal with accident victims. Blood is frequently present, often in great quantity. Security personnel should take precautions because blood can transmit not only the potentially deadly human immunodeficiency virus (HIV) but also hepatitis B virus (HBV) and tuberculosis (TB). The concept of **universal precautions** applies to infection control techniques and states that all blood and infectious materials other than blood must be treated as if infected, meaning persons responding to accidents or other incidents where blood and body fluids are present should *always* wear protective equipment such as nonporous gloves.

HIV, the virus that can lead to AIDS, can survive at least 15 days at room temperature in dried and liquid blood. Those responsible for cleaning up any blood at an accident scene should be cautioned about the potential hazard and provided with appropriate protection such as latex gloves.

Hepatitis B viral infection affects the liver and poses a much greater risk than HIV. It can progress to chronic liver disease or liver cancer and death. Symptoms range from fever, aching muscles and loss of appetite to prolonged

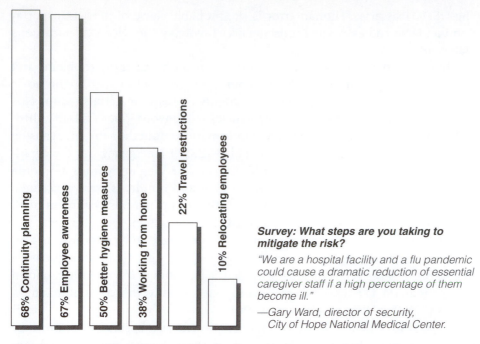

Survey: What steps are you taking to mitigate the risk?

"We are a hospital facility and a flu pandemic could cause a dramatic reduction of essential caregiver staff if a high percentage of them become ill."

—Gary Ward, director of security, City of Hope National Medical Center.

Figure 8.2   Measures Taken to Mitigate the Risk of an Avian Flu Pandemic

SOURCE: From: "Newspoll." *Security Director News*, May 2005, p.23. Reprinted by permission.

nausea and vomiting as well as yellowing of the skin (jaundice). A vaccine is available that provides protection for approximately nine years. If an employee in a particular line of work is likely to be exposed to HBV, OSHA has required that the employer offer the vaccine at no cost to the employee.

Carbon Monoxide Poisoning

Another hazard in the workplace is carbon monoxide (CO), often called the silent killer because it is difficult to detect (colorless, odorless) and, over time, can build to deadly levels. Areas with insufficient ventilation in which appliances, heaters, word-burning stoves or fireplaces, internal-combustion engines or propane-fueled equipment are operating are susceptible to deadly CO buildup. Other possible sources of CO are forklifts, ice resurfacers (Zambonis) and tools such as floor buffers, concrete saws and welders. Consequently, any people working with such equipment in enclosed spaces may suffer CO poisoning.

Accidents and medical emergencies are not the only situations to which security personnel might need to respond. Several other types of emergency situations and other security problems may also present hazards.

Hazardous Materials Incidents

Hazardous materials (H/M or HAZMAT) incidents are an increasing concern, considering that the number of HAZMAT shipments occurring each day in the United States exceeds 800,000, a traffic rate that translates into more than 3.1 billion tons of hazardous materials being transported annually throughout our country. In 2000 the USDOT received reports of 17,514 HAZMAT incidents resulting in 13 deaths, 246 injuries and more than $72 million in damages.

The USDOT asserts: "Human error is the probable cause of most transportation incidents and associated consequences involving the release of hazardous materials."

HAZMAT incidents can cause serious, even life-threatening problems and must be dealt with immediately and appropriately. Contact with highly toxic chemical liquids, solids or gases or with highly corrosive materials requires extreme care. Hazardous materials emergencies may involve poor visibility, difficult breathing, fire, hysteria and lack of information about the substance causing the problem. An example of an accidental HAZMAT emergency was the derailment in North Dakota of a train with four cars carrying anhydrous ammonia leaking following the crash. One person died and hundreds were evacuated, with many requiring hospitalization. HAZMAT events may also be intentional, such as the dispersal of anthrax using the U.S. mail system.

OSHA mandates training for all employees engaged in hazardous waste activities and developing an emergency response plan. Agencies that might assist in a hazardous materials incident include the state fire marshal's office, a local EMS system, the U.S. Coast Guard, a shipping company, the material manufacturer and CHEMTREC (1–800-424–9300).

If hazardous materials are commonly present at a specific location, they should be clearly labeled as such. In addition, the security manager should consider having an H/M control team trained to respond to those materials that might cause a problem. In some instances special equipment such as chemical suits, gloves, boots and air packs should be available for emergency use.

When hazardous cargo is being transferred, federal law requires the hauler to carry a manifest specifically detailing what they are carrying, how much and the shipment destination. Many manifests also provide an MSDS, or material safety data sheet, with information on handling, containing and neutralizing the hazardous materials or dangerous goods in the event of a spill, leak or other inadvertent release. Haulers are also required to display a colored placard and symbol identifying the hazardous nature of their shipment. The most familiar warnings are the colored placards on the sides and back of the trailer or shipping container, generally more visible from a greater distance than a symbol, thereby allowing first responders to tailor their approach accordingly. The standard placard colors and what they represent are:

- Flammable – red
- Corrosive – black and white
- Explosive – orange
- Poison – black and white
- Nonflammable gas – green
- Oxidizer – yellow

Short of any specialized training, officers should know some basic guidelines if responding to HAZMAT emergencies. If the hazard occurs indoors, it should be isolated and sealed off by closing doors and shutting down the area's ventilation system. If the HAZMAT incident is outside, stay upwind from the incident and assess the situation from as great a distance as possible before moving in. Officers should have binoculars in their vehicles so they can read placards and markings on trucks or railroad cars involved in accidents. Robinson (2004, p.64) suggests: "If the fire department has a ladder truck, [officers] might be able to set up at a distance, raise the ladder and use binoculars to read the placard on the side of an overturned tanker." Because the danger of explosion, fire or toxic fumes is always present, responders should stay as far away as possible but also try to identify what the truck or railroad car was transporting.

New York City's Center for Emergency Medical Services (CEMS) has as key aspects of its operations an operations center and communication network, advanced detection equipment and intensively trained staff (Roberts, 2005a, p.131). The center is located away from the hospitals it services and is equipped with police and fire scanners and several TVs displaying local weather, local traffic, and local and national news. Emergency medical technicians (EMTs) and paramedics trained in emergency medical dispatch procedures staff the center around the clock. According to Roberts: "The chemical library is so specific that it can differentiate between Gold Bond Medicated Power and Dr. Scholl's." The center also serves as an early-warning monitoring system for the hospitals it serves.

Crowds and Civil Disturbances, Demonstrations, Riots and Strikes

Crowds might be classified into four general categories:

- Casual—at a shopping mall, concert, and so on
- Specific purpose—there for one purpose (e.g., accident, fight, fire, etc.)
- Expressive—there for a religious, political or other cause
- Aggressive—highly emotional, out to accomplish something

Any of these types of crowds, especially if an emergency occurs, can turn into a mob—acting without reason, emotionally, sometimes hysterically. Any group gathering in or near an establishment should be reported to the appropriate people and then observed. If the situation warrants, outside doors might be locked. Any violent disturbance, especially if weapons are involved, is usually the responsibility of law enforcement. It is security's responsibility to protect people and property and to support the police responding to the scene.

 In the event of civil disturbances or demonstrations, riots or strikes, the security manager is responsible for maintaining order and protecting lives and assets.

Certain security challenges exist with specific types of crowds, particularly those gathered for demonstrations, riots and strikes. In any of these instances use of force might be required: "The public, media and judicial system, it has been shown, will readily support the proper application of force under such circumstances. However, . . . when inappropriately used, such [less-lethal] options have, at best, led to severe criticism and, at worst, to loss of life and injury" (Narr et al., 2006, p.59). Use of less-lethal options must be balanced against the threat faced by the officers and the goal of maintaining order. Use of force was discussed in Chapter 4.

Civil Disturbances or Demonstrations

A demonstration is a "public display of feeling toward a person or cause" and applies to a wide array of occasions in which large numbers of people come together for a common purpose (e.g., a political convention, a labor dispute or even a major sporting or social event) (Narr et al., p.3). Protests, demonstrations, sit-ins, picket lines, blockades and confrontations can threaten the safety of employees and assets. The challenge in managing civil disturbances or mass demonstrations is balancing the competing goals of maintaining order and protecting the freedoms of speech and assembly. According to Narr et al. (p.7): "The key to effectively managing mass demonstrations and other major events is planning and preparation" or, as Colin Powell is quoted as saying: "There are no secrets to success. It is the result of preparation, hard work and learning from failure."

Officer safety is important in any mass demonstration, especially if disorder is anticipated (Narr et al., p.58). Demonstrators often use abusive language and attempt to provoke security officers. When selecting gear, flexibility of movement must be balanced against level of protection. Use of basic equipment such as straight- or side-handle batons, handheld pepper spray and conducted energy devices (tasers, stunguns, etc.) might be appropriate.

Although nonviolent demonstrations are usually legal, a company may protect its rights, its personnel and its property. If demonstrators act illegally (e.g., by destroying property), they should be arrested and charged. Often the assistance of the public police is requested in civil disturbances.

Riots

Some civil disturbances erupt into full-blown riots, causing tremendous destruction, as vividly demonstrated during the Watts riots of 1965, when 36 people were killed, 700 were injured and property losses estimated at half a billion dollars were incurred.

In April 1992, riots broke out in Los Angeles after jurors acquitted four white police officers charged with beating black motorist Rodney King. At least 37 people were killed, 1,419 were injured, nearly 4,400 were arrested and damage was assessed at $550 million. Retail stores are usually hit the hardest during riots, but wholesalers, manufacturers and institutions such as hospitals and colleges may also be involved.

Access control is critical in a riot situation. It is best to lock up and sit tight. Protecting personnel and assets becomes a proprietary responsibility because police and firefighters are usually busy and cannot respond to private calls for assistance.

Management may seek to hire supplemental security forces, but often such forces are unavailable during a riot. Some establishments have paid a retainer to private contract security forces to ensure their availability in an emergency situation. Others have their own "auxiliary" security force.

If it is safe to do so, employees should be evacuated. The lights should be left on, and store windows and entrances should be barricaded. Some establishments keep rolls of concertina wire on hand for use during riots.

Strikes

Although strikes are unpleasant even when nonviolent, they pose an especially difficult situation for security officers who belong to a union themselves. The situation can become next to impossible when labor contracts for employees and security personnel are not separate. As management's representatives, security officers are hired to protect the premises even though the employees are out on strike; they may have to cross picket lines.

Security officers must remain neutral and do the job they were hired to do. Picketing is legal as long as it remains nonviolent and there is no restraining order against the strike. Those who wish to cross the picket line to enter a picketed building must be allowed to do so. Any assaultive action should be prosecuted. As in any other potentially high-risk situation, management should have a preestablished strike plan, including what the consequences will be for security officers who honor the picket line.

Bombs and Bomb Threats

The bombing of the World Trade Center on February 26, 1993, killed six people, injured 1,000 and caused $500 million in damage to the Twin Towers complex. The bombing of the Alfred P. Murrah Federal Building in Oklahoma City on April 19, 1995, again reminded Americans of their vulnerability. However, the attacks of September 11, 2001, made an impression that changed the face of America forever, elevating security to a resource to be recognized and appreciated.

Terrorists are not the only groups using bombs. Hard-core criminals may use explosives to gain access to buildings or to sterilize a crime scene. Explosives are often associated with drug deals. Interestingly, the most common motive for bombings is vandalism, followed by revenge.

© AP/Wide World Photos

Rescue workers stand in front of the Alfred P. Murrah Federal Building in downtown Oklahoma City after a truck bomb exploded outside the structure on April 19, 1995. The explosion killed 168 people and injured more than 800.

The north side of rebuilt Oklahoma City Federal Building. The new building design includes a defined setback perimeter as well as posts and other security devices to prevent cars from stopping too close to the building; a reinforced building structure enveloped in blast-resistant laminated glass, which does not fragment in case of a blast; and blast-resistant stone walls.

Bomb threats are a major security concern and are also a federal offense. Common victims of bombings and bomb threats are airlines, banks, hospitals, industrial complexes, utilities, educational institutions, government buildings and office buildings, although any business, industry or institution can be the victim of a bomb threat or an actual bombing.

Most bomb threats are received by telephone, and 98 percent of these phoned-in threats are hoaxes. The caller may simply want the day off if he or she is an employee, or the caller may want to disrupt the business. Few actual bombings are preceded by a warning. When such a warning is given, it is almost always to save lives. Most bombings occur at night for the same reason—to lessen the chance of killing someone. Despite the fact that the vast majority of telephoned bomb threats are hoaxes, such a threat is disruptive and disquieting. In addition, the response to the threat may be costly, emotionally charged and even dangerous.

Several underground publications provide detailed instructions on making bombs. One common type of homemade bomb consists of a lead pipe filled with black powder, caps screwed on either end and a fuse. Another common type of bomb is made with sticks of dynamite taped together and set off by a timer or a trip wire. Incendiary bombs can consist of a container such as a glass bottle filled with a highly flammable substance, usually gasoline. The wick can be lit and the bomb thrown, or it can be attached to a timing device. Such bombs are frequently referred to as "Molotov cocktails."

Hanson (2004, p.66) describes the variety of other chemicals that may be used to make improvised explosive devices (IED) including ammonium nitrate (fertilizer), sodium azide, magnesium azide, methenamine, potassium nitrate, anhydrous hydrazing (boiler cleaner, rocket fuel component), liquid nitromethane (racing fuel), sulphuric and nitric acid and the like. Vehicle-borne improvised explosive devices (VBIED) are a separate group of bombs distinguished from pipe bombs, individual suicide bombers and other land devices (p.65). IEDs and VBIEDs are discussed in detail in Chapter 13.

Preventing Bombings

Orderliness, keeping things in their proper places, will make it easier to detect unfamiliar objects that might be bombs. Employees should be instructed to be alert for any suspicious items they come across in their work area. Trash should be stored in metal containers outside the facility. Shipments of merchandise should be checked as soon as possible and then moved promptly to their appropriate locations. Fire doors should be kept shut at all times except for emergency use.

 Access control, orderliness and regular inspections are the primary defenses against bombs.

Some establishments are especially susceptible to explosives through the mail, including those that engage in animal testing, nuclear waste, abortion and the like. If an envelope or package is suspicious, security should contact the local law enforcement agency for assistance. The envelope or package should not be submerged in water or put into an enclosed area.

Responding to a Bomb Threat

A bomb threat is a frightening experience fraught with potential danger, and therefore a response plan must exist *before* such a call is received. Decisions made under the pressure of the moment should be based on previously established guidelines, so being prepared is vital.

 To be prepared for a bomb threat, security managers should teach personnel how to talk to a person making such a threat and whom to notify. Security should determine who makes the decision on whether to evacuate and, if an evacuation is necessary, how personnel are to be informed and what they are to do. Security should also have a plan that specifies how to search for the bomb and what to do if one is found.

All personnel who answer the telephone should be taught to respond appropriately to a telephoned bomb threat. Some phones have tape recorders that can be activated to record the conversation. Others have phone traps that keep the line open until the *receiver* of the call hangs up, allowing the telephone company to trace the call. (Such traps do not work for long-distance calls.) Many organizations have a report form kept by the switchboard to record information on bomb threats (see Figure 8.3).

 The receiver of a bomb threat should:

- Keep the caller talking as long as possible.
- Try to learn as much as possible about the bomb, especially when it will go off and where it is located.
- Try to determine the caller's sex, age, accent and speech pattern, and whether he or she is drunk or drugged.
- Listen for any background noises.
- Immediately notify the appropriate person of the call.

**General Services Administration
Region 8
Bomb threat information**

Date _____
Received   Ended

Time
call _____

Exact words of caller

_____
_____
(Continue on reverse)

Questions to ask

1. **When** is bomb going to explode?

_____

2. **Where** is bomb right now?

_____

3. **What** kind of bomb is it?

_____

4. **What** does it look like?

_____

5. **Why** did you place the bomb?

_____

Description of caller's voice   Tone of voice

☐ Male   ☐ Female   _____

☐ Young   ☐ Middle-aged   ☐ Old

Accent   Background noise
_____   _____

Is voice familiar?   If yes, who did it sound like?

☐ Yes   ☐ No   _____

Additional comments

_____

_____

Name of person receiving call   Organization & location
_____   _____

Home address   Office phone
_____   _____

                                      Home phone
                                      _____

Figure 8.3 Sample Bomb Threat Report Form

SOURCE: Reprinted with permission of the publisher from Green and Farber, *Introduction to Security*, revised edition (Woburn, MA: Butterworth Publishers, Inc.). Copyright © Elsevier 1978.

After the bomb threat is reported to the appropriate person, usually the chief administrator or manager, this individual decides who else is to be notified as well as whether the call is to be taken seriously. Evaluating the legitimacy of the bomb threat is important. Laughter in the background may indicate it is a practical joke. Even if the decision is made that the call is a hoax, the police should be notified.

Because any bomb threat may be the real thing, many experts recommend that all such threats be treated as real. Assuming this, the decision must be made as to whether to evacuate. This decision is usually made by management, often in conjunction with the police. Although evacuation may seem the safest approach, this is not always true. Moving large groups of people may expose them to greater danger than not moving them. Evacuating may be exactly what the caller wanted and may prompt further calls. In addition, unnecessary evacuation can be extremely costly.

Sometimes the best alternative is to evacuate either the area where the bomb is suspected or the entire building. Total evacuation may cause panic and may expose more people to danger, especially if the bomber knows the evacuation plan. Sometimes it is thought that evacuation encourages or excites the caller. Planning carefully in advance should result in a safe, orderly evacuation.

Ideally, personnel are informed of a bomb threat over a central public address system rather than by an alarm. If an alarm is used, it should be different from that used for fire because the procedures to be followed are somewhat different. In a fire, windows and doors are closed; in a bomb threat situation, windows and doors are opened to vent any explosion. In both fire and bomb threat evacuations, personnel should *walk* out of and away from the building until they are a block away and then wait until they are informed it is safe to return to the building.

The Bomb Search

Whether employees are evacuated or not, a search must be conducted if the threat is assumed to be real. A bomb search is an ultrahazardous task. It will be more effectively conducted by those familiar with the facility, so employees are often asked to search their own area before they evacuate.

Areas that are usually unlocked and unwatched are the most common sites for bombs, for example, restrooms, lobbies, lunch rooms, elevators and stairwells. Bombs can be hidden in lunch pails, briefcases, shopping bags, candy boxes and any number of other types of containers. The key is to look for anything out of place or foreign to the area, for example, a briefcase in the restroom.

A command post should be established as soon as the decision is made to treat the threat as legitimate. The entire building should then be diagrammed and areas crossed off as they are searched. Some security managers have the searchers mark the doors of areas after they have been searched. If enough security officers are available, they should be positioned around the perimeter of the area in which a bomb may be planted to keep curious onlookers from endangering themselves.

A system of communicating among searchers must be established, but it must not involve the use of portable radios, as they may detonate the bomb. All searchers should be cautioned not to turn on lights, as this might also detonate the bomb. Searchers should move slowly and carefully, listening for any ticking sounds and watching for a trip wire. Sometimes metal detectors or dogs are used to assist in the search.

Searchers should not touch or move any suspicious object found during a bomb search. They should provide a clear zone of at least 300 feet around the device and then call the nearest bomb disposal specialist or the police. In addition, doors and windows should be opened to reduce shock waves, all fire extinguishers should be readied and highly flammable materials should be removed as should valuable documents, files and papers if time permits.

Bomb detection technologies continue to improve and are being used in increasingly effective ways. The two broad categories of detection technology are trace detection and x-ray technology, which are often used in tandem (Cohen, 2004, p.48). *Trace detectors* use ion mobility spectrometry to pick up the unique electrical properties of explosive substances, which contain molecules that ionize. When they do so, the trace detector recognizes the explosive particles. *X-ray systems* can show the shapes of items inside luggage; however, explosive materials can be molded into shapes resembling common travel items, so many airports have started using bomb screening machines based on computed tomography (CT), similar to the CAT scan x-ray technology used in medicine.

Dogs and pigs have also been used to detect bombs. Pigs are supposedly easier than dogs to train. However: "The sniffer dog is an incredible bomb detection machine, provided the dog is properly rewarded, not overworked and its handler is properly trained" (Cohen, p.48).

An explosives detection technology being developed places sensors inside cell phones to detect the presence of nuclear, biological or chemical traces in the atmosphere (Cohen, pp.53–54). Equipped with such technology, the phone would alert a command center and at the same time warn the user to seek medical help: "Scientists are hopeful that the sensors could detect anything from anthrax to sarin gas and could cut casualty rates by up to 70 percent" (Cohen).

All procedures for dealing with bomb threats should be practiced, if possible. The operator may be called with a fake bomb threat to see the response. A suspicious container capable of concealing a bomb may be planted and a practice bomb search conducted. The evacuation plan may be practiced as well.

Preventing and Protecting against Loss by Fire

Fire is probably the single greatest threat security must deal with. Many businesses struck by serious fires never open again. In 2005, U.S. fire departments responded to an estimated 1,602,000 fires resulting in 3,675 civilian fire fatalities, 17,925 civilian fire injuries and an estimated $10,672,000,000 in direct property loss (Karter, 2006, p.11). Security personnel should be continuously alert to the potential for fire. Eliminating fire hazards is a prime responsibility of all security personnel and, indeed, of all personnel within a business, company or organization.

Access control is the primary area of conflict between security and life-safety professionals (Minieri, 2005, p.95). Although locking outside doors to prevent people from entering a building is permissible, under all the published fire-code requirements, inhibiting free egress is not. According to the National Fire Protection Association's (NFPA) Life Safety Code 101, every person within the building must be able to exit all doors in their path to the outside without using a key, a tool or special knowledge or effort for operation from the egress side. Many security managers opt to install panic bars on these doors, which allow employees and other building occupants to push the door open for escape but also trigger an alarm that the door has been opened. These panic bars may be mechanical or electrical.

Security managers can better prevent and protect against fire loss by understanding how fires occur, what frequently causes them and what equipment and procedures can help minimize losses. Knowing how fires burn helps one understand potential fire hazards and how to control them.

 The **fire triangle** consists of three elements necessary for burning: *heat*, *fuel* and *oxygen*.

Because oxygen and fuel are always present in business and industry, the potential for fire always exists. When a flammable substance is heated to a specific temperature, called its ignition temperature, it will ignite and burn as long as oxygen is present. If any of the three elements is eliminated, however, the fire is extinguished. Oxygen is removed by smothering, fuel by isolating and heat by cooling.

 The National Fire Protection Association has established four classifications of fires:

- Class A fires involve ordinary combustible materials such as paper, packing boxes, wood and cloth.
- Class B fires involve flammable liquids such as gasoline and oil.
- Class C fires involve energized electrical installations, appliances and wiring.
- Class D fires involve combustible metals such as magnesium, sodium and potassium. (Class D fires are sometimes called "exotic metals fires.")

Destruction and death are caused not only by flames, but by smoke, heat, gas and panic. Smoke can blind and choke. Carbon dioxide and carbon monoxide, by-products of burning, can poison and cause buildings to explode. Intense heat can explode gases, ignite materials and expand air. Expanded air can exert tremendous pressure, shattering doors and windows. Because smoke, gas, heat and expanded air all rise, it is possible to determine safe and unsafe areas and to control the direction of a fire if building construction and preplanning are adequate.

Causes of Fires

The major sources of ignition in industrial fires are electrical circuits, overheating, sparking, friction, chemical reaction, flames and heat transfer. Materials that present a fire hazard include acids, oil, paint, solvents, explosives, flammable or combustible liquids, flammable gases and materials subject to spontaneous ignition.

Often fires result from carelessness or poor housekeeping practices, such as improperly storing or using flammable liquids; replacing electric fuses with ones that have too high amperage or with coins, wires or nails; placing combustibles within three feet of an electrical access box; overloading electric circuits; carelessly discarding cigarette butts and matches; leaving hot plates, coffee pots and space heaters on and unattended; and allowing oily rags, rubbish or other materials to accumulate, resulting in spontaneous combustion. Fires have also been caused by faulty wiring and connections, use of long or wrong-size extension cords, ignition sparks from static electricity, lightning and arson.

An effective fire safety program has two parts: (2) preventing fires and (2) protecting against losses caused by fires that do occur.

Preventing Fire

Most fires can be prevented. The greatest single precipitant is human error and carelessness. Although many modern buildings are built to be fire-resistive, a fireproof building does not exist. Despite the facts that an exterior of steel and concrete does not burn, the interior contains numerous flammable substances that can burn, causing the building to become like a furnace. Given sufficient heat, the structure can collapse.

 Fires can be prevented by reducing fire-loading, properly storing and handling flammable materials, enforcing no-smoking regulations, using proper wiring and following good housekeeping practices. Access controls can lessen the chance of arson.

Fire-loading refers to the amount of flammable material within an area, including flammable rugs, curtains, paper and liquids such as paints and solvents. To the extent possible, reduce fire-loading by using flame-resistant curtains and furniture.

When highly combustible chemicals, glues and the like are used, make sure ventilation is adequate. The main supply of such materials should be kept in protective containers stored in properly ventilated areas. Packing boxes containing excelsior and paper materials should be metal and should preferably be equipped with a lead link that causes the lid to drop into place if heat is generated in the metal box, reducing the oxygen supply and smothering a potential fire. Fire-preventive waste receptacles designed to smother a fire are also available. Oily rags and other flammable materials should never be allowed to accumulate.

Protecting against Losses from Fire

In spite of all efforts, the potential for fire is always present. The best protection against loss from fire is to *be prepared*.

 Protection from fire losses is provided by fire wardens, detectors and alarms; properly marked and sufficient exits, fire doors and fire escapes; fire-resistive safes and vaults; and fire extinguishers, sprinkler systems and an adequate, accessible water supply.

Fire Wardens   Protecting lives is always top priority. Organizations should recognize the importance of training personnel to serve as fire wardens. These people should be volunteers from among the ranks of company employees, not security personnel, who are trained in the critical task of helping to ensure that all staff members are safely evacuated from a building during an emergency (Hewitt, 2005, p.100). It is up to the fire wardens to ensure that the evacuation plan is carried out. A ratio of 1 warden to 50 employees is usually sufficient.

Fire Extinguishers   The importance of protection against fire cannot be overstated. One of the easiest steps to take is to place fire extinguishers strategically throughout a facility and ensure they are kept secure yet accessible and in proper working condition: "Fire extinguishers are among the safety devices

© Image Source/Corbis

Fire extinguishers must be readily available and easily accessible throughout a facility, especially in areas where flammable chemicals or other combustible materials are located.

most likely to be moved, vandalized or accidentally set off. Sometimes people thoughtlessly use them as door props or for other nonsafety purposes" (Elliott, 2006a, p.40).

Using the proper type of extinguishing is a crucial part of an effective fire response plan. For example, water or a Class A extinguisher should never be used on energized electric equipment (Class C fires), because the electric charge can follow the water stream to the holder, causing instant electrocution. Similarly, water or a Class A extinguisher should not be used in a Class B fire because it can splatter the burning oil or gasoline, spreading the fire to a larger area instead of extinguishing it. Multipurpose extinguishers eliminate some of the confusion and risk that accompanies deciding which type of extinguisher to use on the various classes of fires. Table 8.2 summarizes how to extinguish specific types of fires.

Computer Rooms   Computer rooms present special fire hazards and require special fire precautions. They often are equipped with an ionization detector or a thermal rate of rise detector. They should *not* be equipped with a sprinkler system because steam and water can damage the computer and because water should not be used on Class C fires, the type most commonly occurring in computer rooms.

Procedures for Protecting against Fire Loss

In addition to obtaining and maintaining equipment to help prevent fires, an effective fire safety program establishes specific procedures for protecting life and assets should a fire occur.

Table 8.2 How to Extinguish Specific Types of Fires

Class	What Is Burning	How to Extinguish
A	Ordinary combustibles, e.g., wood, paper	Quench or cool with water or water fog. Use soda acid, pump tank (water) or foam. (Smothering is ineffective.)
B	Flammable liquids, e.g., gasoline kerosene	Blanket or smother. Use carbon dioxide (CO_2, dry chemicals or foam.)
C	Electrical	Use dry chemicals, carbon dioxide (CO_2) or vaporizing liquid extinguishers.
D	Metals, e.g., magnesium, titanium	Use Class D extinguisher.

 Security should always call for help before attempting to extinguish a fire. Employees should be taught what to do in case of fire. Other procedures for protecting against fire loss include having and practicing a plan for evacuation, shutting doors and windows and using stairs rather than elevators.

The Security Manager's Responsibility in Case of Fire

All security personnel should know the location of fire extinguishers, fire-alarm boxes, sprinkler valve controls, escalator and elevator shutoffs, light control panels, emergency lights, wheelchairs, stretchers and first-aid equipment. Security managers should have a plan, take charge, stay calm and take immediate action to protect lives first, assets second.

Although some security managers dread fire inspections, in actuality they should be thoroughly prepared for and welcomed.

Natural Disasters

Natural disasters are a fact of life, but their effects can be minimized through proper preparation. Unfortunately: "Despite another year filled with hard lessons learned from tornadoes, floods and fires, there has been no increase in the percentage of U.S. companies with business continuity plans" (*2007 AT&T Business Continuity Study*). Thirty percent of companies said business continuity was not a priority, indicating that they may have a false sense of security. And of businesses hit by a disaster, only 41 percent took action when the government issued an alert. Security managers should recognize the four phases of most natural disasters.

 Most natural disasters happen in four phases: (1) the *warning* period, (2) the *impact* period, (3) the *immediate reaction* after impact and (4) the period of *delayed response.*

Usually as much *warning* as possible is desirable. Two monitoring systems can assist security personnel by alerting them to impending hazardous weather conditions:

- A weather alert radio tuned exclusively to the weather bureau's frequency, left on continuously and activated by the weather bureau when conditions warrant
- An AM radio for weather information

The difference between a *watch* and a *warning* is important. A *watch* means that the weather conditions are right for a specific event to occur, for example, a tornado, blizzard or severe thunderstorm. A *warning* means such a condition has developed and will probably pose a problem for the area. Precautions should be implemented immediately, including a "take-cover" announcement such as the following if the emergency is a tornado or destructive winds warning:

> Attention. A tornado warning has been issued for our area. Turn off all equipment, extinguish all flames, and take cover immediately under your desk, a heavy table or in our designated shelter areas. Do NOT go near windows, glass doors or outside. Stay under cover until the all clear is given.

This message should be repeated at least three times. First-aid equipment should be made readily available, and emergency telephone numbers for ambulances, fire departments, police and other available assistance should be posted.

Sometimes, however, warnings are impossible, as is the case, for example, with earthquakes. In addition, advance warning might have an adverse effect on some individuals, who may panic and become totally helpless, as though the emergency had already occurred. Their panic may spread to others. For example, this reaction sometimes occurs following the posting of a hurricane warning when the eye of the storm is projected to make landfall over a heavily populated area.

During the *impact period,* when the emergency is actually happening, different people will react differently. For many it will be stunned inactivity, a paralysis of sorts, with people unable to act effectively. Others, fueled by adrenaline, may act with determination, purpose and strength. Some report going "on automatic pilot." The period *immediately following the disaster* is the most crucial from the standpoint of rescue operations. Effective performance can save lives and property. A *delayed response* may occur once the immediate danger is past. Those who were functioning effectively may cease to do so, and vice versa.

Types of Natural Disasters

As a first step security managers should identify natural disasters that might occur in their geographical location. Natural disasters necessitating a contingency plan might include floods, tornadoes, hurricanes and earthquakes.

Floods   A flood, although damaging and usually predictable, demands a coordinated response and implementation of a previously thought-out plan. Normally, police will assist residents and merchants in the affected areas to evacuate their homes and their businesses. As soon as a police department receives notice of an impending flood, the regular and reserve officers are usually called to duty. In some instances, they may be put on alert or on standby in case they are needed.

During an evacuation and while the emergency is in progress, the police must seal off the affected area to prevent looting and vandalism. Special passes can be issued to residents who have legitimate business in the area. All others not living or having business in the flood area should be excluded.

Cyclones: Hurricanes and Tornadoes   In strict meteorological terminology, a cyclone is an area of low atmospheric pressure surrounded by a wind system blowing, in the Northern Hemisphere, in a counterclockwise direction. When this weather system develops over water, it is called a *hurricane* or, in the western Pacific, a *typhoon*. Cyclones occurring on land are t*ornadoes*. Many of the emergencies already discussed may also occur during a hurricane or tornado, including flooding, fires and explosions, accompanied by looting and vandalism. A hurricane is a very strong tropical cyclone involving heavy rains and sustained winds over 74 mph. It may also be accompanied by strong storms with large waves causing extensive damage to coastal property and nearby structures.

In addition to the tragic loss of life and damage to property, those responding to the disaster may face communication and mobility problems. Regular phone lines may be down, two-way radio communications may be unavailable due to damaged repeaters and cellular communications networks may be overwhelmed by ongoing use. Getting around may be difficult because road signs and their landmarks may be gone, street lights may be out and many roads may be blocked by such obstacles as fallen trees, live utility wire and other debris. Some areas may be flooded and impassable. Highways and other main travel arteries may become gridlocked during the evacuation efforts, and debris scattered across roadways may cause numerous flat tires and other traffic mishaps, involving not only citizens but first responders as well.

The destruction and chaos resulting from Hurricane Katrina and Hurricane Rita are vivid examples of the destructive force of hurricanes. Over two dozen 911 call centers went down, more than a thousand cell sites were knocked out of service, and in excess of 20 million phone calls did not go through (Piazza, 2005, p.70). In addition, different radio frequencies hampered intercity emergency communications (p.72).

Eventually, things will come under control, but time, and perhaps lives, may be saved if a predisaster plan is in place. Citizens should be educated on the steps to take, such as evacuating if advised to do so, boarding up windows or closing shutters if not evacuating and having ample potable water and flashlights or candles available.

Other parts of the country are threatened by tornados—dark, funnel-shaped clouds containing violently rotating air that twists, rises and falls, and where it reaches the earth causes great destruction. A tornado's diameter can range from a few feet to over a mile, with winds circulating between 200 and 300 mph. The length of a tornado's path on the ground varies from under a mile to several hundred miles. In an average year in the United States, some 800 tornadoes injure more than a thousand people. Again, preparedness is the key to limiting the amount of destruction. Tornado warning systems are an integral part of preparedness, as is public education as to steps to take, where to seek shelter and the like.

Earthquakes   While floods and hurricanes usually can be predicted, earthquakes strike with no warning. Areas in which earthquakes are likely to occur must have preestablished plans to deal with such emergencies. Included within these plans should be measures to deal with collapsed buildings and bridges, downed power lines, fires, explosions, injuries and deaths. As in other kinds of emergencies, traffic problems, vandalism and looting must also be anticipated.

Predisaster Plans

A plan to protect lives and assets in the event of a natural disaster should be developed, written out, distributed and practiced periodically. A good plan is logical and uncomplicated, yet comprehensive. It stipulates who does what and when, who is to be notified and what assistance is available. It should also include where a radio is available to be tuned to emergency frequencies.

The Federal Emergency Management Agency (FEMA)   The Federal Emergency Management Agency, or **FEMA**, is an independent federal agency founded in 1979, the mission of which is to reduce loss of life and property and protect our nation's critical infrastructure from all types of hazards through a comprehensive, risk-based, emergency management program of mitigation, preparedness, response and recovery. FEMA is staffed by more than 2,600 full-time employees and nearly 4,000 standby disaster assistance employees available to help after disasters. On March 1, 2003, FEMA became part of the Department of Homeland Security (DHS). FEMA has three strategic goals:

1. Protect lives and prevent the loss of property from natural and technological hazards
2. Reduce human suffering and enhance the recovery of communities after disaster strikes
3. Ensure that the public is served in a timely and efficient manner

FEMA recommends communities address the following functions in disaster plans: (1) communication, (2) transportation, (3) public works, (4) firefighting, (5) intelligence efforts to assess damage, (6) mass care for those people displaced from their homes, (7) resource support (contracting for the labor needed to assist in a disaster), (8) health and medication, (9) search and rescue, (10) hazardous materials, (11) food or feeding and (12) energy. Communications should be the number one priority. FEMA came under intense criticism for their ineffective response to conditions resulting from Hurricanes Katrina and Rita. Consequently, the agency is undergoing extensive modification.

Other Aspects of the Emergency Plan   The emergency plan should also identify the levels of emergencies that might occur. As many elements as possible should be the same in plans for responding to emergencies and to different natural disasters. For example, procedures for evacuating in the event of a fire might be the same used in evacuating during a flood. In both instances elevators should *never* be used. In some situations, evacuation is not the proper procedure, as in a tornado alert. In such cases, the alarm should be different from that used for fires. Employees should be directed to a clearly marked shelter within the facility, usually on the lowest level, in the center of the building, away from glass. The Civil Defense Department (called Emergency Service and Disaster Agency in many areas) can help security managers determine the most appropriate "safe zone" locations and develop effective plans for such disasters. According to Civil Defense authorities, the safest areas in the workplace during some natural disasters such as tornadoes are under office desks, under heavy tables or in specific shelter areas.

After the Disaster Has Passed

In the aftermath of a natural disaster, many departments find their most significant problem is not, as might be expected, the cleanup but rather the quick depletion of their yearly overtime budgets and completion of the massive amount of paperwork required for the jurisdiction to be reimbursed for expenses resulting from the disaster.

 Postemergency "killers" may be overruns in overtime and excessive paperwork.

Other Emergencies

Plans are needed for all other potential emergencies, such as plane crashes, power failures, water main or gas line breaks and toxic chemical leaks or explosions. The best emergency plans are simple. They specify *in writing* who does what, how and when. The more common elements there are among the plans for different types of emergencies, the better.

Lessons Learned from Hurricane Katrina

Harowitz (2005, p.60), commenting on Hurricane Katrina, contends: "Neither the multiple governments involved nor most of the many private companies affected had adequate plans in place to deal with the disaster—but once the magnitude of the crisis became clear, private industry was much more nimble in reacting to the situation, both in helping employees and in dealing with asset protection and business continuity." Among security service providers, the story was similar, as providers struggled to meet the needs of not only their own employees but also their clients in the impacted areas.

Following are observations of what should be learned from this disaster:

- A company must be prepared to fend for itself in the early days of a severe crisis. They should be able to handle evacuation, asset protection and recovery efforts with little or no help from the government (Harowitz, p.61).
- First and foremost, companies must ensure that their people are safe, for example, by hiring buses to evacuate employees, creating centers to help displaced persons and continuing to pay salaries (Harowitz).
- Before disaster hits, companies should cross-train security personnel in other specialties (Straw, 2007, p.32).
- Emergency generators should not be located in basements that might become flooded (Harowitz, p.65).
- Displaced persons need to be treated with dignity and respect (Gips, 2005a, p.66).

- Evacuees should be processed on the buses as they are being moved rather than when they arrive at their destination and should be enlisted to help with their care and housing (Gips).
- Aggressive lane reversals should be instituted (Gips).
- Traffic cameras and embedded strips in highway pavement can allow officials to assess vehicle flow and suggest alternative routes in real time (Gips).
- Separate shelters should be available to serve people with special needs such as the poor, disabled and infirm (Gips).
- Trailers should be used to serve as temporary housing (Gips).
- Shelter-in-place (SIP) plans can help protect employees during various emergencies. To prepare, managers must analyze needs, designate safe shelter areas, stock supplies and prepare employees (Lee, 2007, p.59).
- Resources should focus on achieving interoperability among first responders (Piazza, p.72).
- On the healthcare front, hospitals and community responders need to plan extensively for emergencies, to build redundancy into their plans and to drill (Roberts, 2005b).
- The financial sector has to deal with evacuees who have left their identification and all their financial records behind. It showed its resiliency by relying on Internet transactions, sharing locations among various banks and relaxing red tape such as easing restrictions on check cashing (Elliott, 2005).
- Adequate disaster plans should include provisions for when critical resources fail—build in redundancy (Piazza, p.76).
- First responders and those from outside the area responding to the call for assistance should bring the basics with them so when they are in place, they are setting up and not trying to do procurement in a disaster area (Piazza, p.73).
- Clients should be called ahead of impending disasters to warn them of necessary precautions (Elliott, 2006b, p.90).

Educating the Public

Families should be educated as to how to prepare for a disaster. They should develop their own disaster plan, including what the family would do if a disaster struck and where they might go to evacuate—a shelter, hotel, family, friends. They should design a family communication plan, identifying a family member or friend in another city or state to serve as a contact point in case the family members are separated. They should also put together a disaster kit containing at least a three-day supply of food and bottled water, a manual can opener, a battery-powered radio and flashlights with extra batteries, a first-aid kit, all family members' medications, hygiene and personal care items, an emergency contact list and phone numbers and, if needed, pet supplies (Scott, p.23).

Risk Analysis for Extreme Events

Extreme events involve considerable ambiguity and uncertainty of their likelihood of occurrence as well as their potential impacts, for example, the September 11, 2001, attacks on the United States (Kunreuther et al., 2004, p.1). Such events often exhibit certain interdependencies, for example, if a homeowner has not strapped the water heater, an earthquake can cause it to topple over and start a fire. The following questions must be addressed to develop effective strategies to deal with extreme events (Kunreuther et al.):

■ What are the interdependencies associated with these risks and what impact do they have on individual decisions to invest in protective measures?

■ How can risk assessment and knowledge of risk perception develop risk management options likely to be successfully implemented?

■ What economic incentives can encourage investment in cost-effective mitigation measures and how can these incentives link with other tools such as insurance, regulation and building codes?

Figure 8.4 provides a conceptual framework for examining these questions. Kunreuther et al. (p.2) note that the figure does not reflect the considerable interdependencies, that is, the fact that if a particular event strikes one unit, it may increase the risk that another unit experiences the same event. In addition, the figure does not reflect the need for cooperation between the public and private sectors.

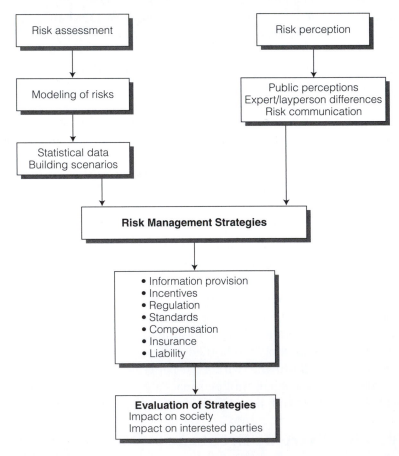

Figure 8.4   Conceptual Framework for Assessing and Managing Extreme Events

SOURCE: Howard Kunreuther, Robert Meyer, and Christopher Van den Bulte, *Risk Analysis for Extreme Events: Economic Incentives for Reducing Future Losses* (Washington, DC: National Institute of Standards and Technology, 2004).

Empirical data shows that relatively few individuals in hazard-prone areas adopt protective measures even if the costs are low (Kunreuther et al., p.35). Two primary reasons are underestimation of the probability of a disaster and high discount rates coupled with short-term horizons. The conclusion is that people are more likely to view protection as attractive if probabilities using concrete comparisons are presented in a form that they are sufficiently large so they will be taken seriously (Kunreuther et al.).

SUMMARY

- Security managers are often responsible for accident prevention programs as one means to prevent losses and protect assets.

- Ninety-five percent of all accidents (on or off the job) are caused by human error, especially lack of safety consciousness.

- Accidents can be prevented by removing hazards, using protective equipment, making employees aware of hazards that cannot be removed, following good housekeeping practices and making employees safety conscious.

- The 3 Rs of emergency management are readiness, response and recovery.

- In the event of civil disturbances or demonstrations, riots or strikes, the security manager is responsible for maintaining order and protecting lives and assets.

- Access control, orderliness and regular inspections are the primary defenses against bombs.

- To be prepared for a bomb threat, security managers should teach personnel how to talk to a person making such a threat and whom to notify. They should determine who makes the decision on whether to evacuate and, if an evacuation is necessary, how personnel are to be informed and what they are to do. They should also have a plan that specifies how to search for the bomb and what to do if one is found.

- The receiver of a bomb threat should keep the caller talking as long as possible; try to learn as much as possible about the bomb, especially when it will go off and where it is located; try to determine the caller's sex, age, accent and speech pattern, and whether he or she is drunk or drugged; listen for any background noise and immediately notify the appropriate person of the call.

- The fire triangle consists of three elements necessary for burning: *heat*, *fuel* and *oxygen*.

- The National Fire Protection Association has established four classifications of fires: Class A fires involve ordinary combustible materials such as paper, packing boxes, wood and cloth; Class B fires involve flammable liquids such as gasoline and oil; Class C fires involve energized electrical installations, appliances and wiring; and Class D fires involve combustible metals such as magnesium, sodium and potassium. (Class D fires are sometimes called "exotic metals fires.")

- Fires can be prevented by reducing fire-loading, properly storing and handling flammable materials, enforcing no-smoking regulations, using proper wiring and following good housekeeping practices.

- Protection from fire losses is provided by fire wardens, detectors and alarms; properly marked and sufficient exits, fire doors and fire escapes; fire-resistive safes and vaults; and fire extinguishers, sprinkler systems and an adequate, accessible water supply.

- Security should always call for help before attempting to extinguish a fire. Employees should be taught what to do in case of fire. Other procedures for protecting against fire loss include having and practicing a plan for evacuation, shutting doors and windows and using stairs rather than elevators.

- Most natural disasters happen in four phases: (1) the *warning* period, (2) the *impact* period, (3) the *immediate reaction* after impact and (4) the period of *delayed response*.

- Postemergency "killers" may be overruns in overtime and excessive paperwork.

APPLICATION

Read the following emergency procedures established for a college faculty and evaluate their effectiveness.

EMERGENCY PROCEDURES FOR STAFF MEMBERS

Separate procedures have been developed for administrators, switchboard operators and buildings and grounds workers.[1]

Fire Alarm

1. All alarms should be treated as a real fire.
2. If a fire is spotted, the individual should find the nearest pull station and turn in the alarm.
3. Next, notify the switchboard operator as to the location of the fire.
4. Instructors should direct their students to leave quickly through the nearest safe exit in a safe and orderly manner, to a position at least 250 feet away from the buildings.
5. Instructors should be the last persons to leave their classrooms or other assigned space and should see that the lights are off, the lab gas is shut off and hazardous chemicals secured where possible. All doors should be shut.
6. No one should enter their car to leave the campus. This will affect the ability of fire fighting equipment to reach the scene of the fire.

Power Failure

1. The switchboard operator should be notified so that Northern States Power can be contacted.
2. Call Northern States Power [phone #] when switchboard is closed.
3. All students and staff should remain in offices and classrooms unless told otherwise.
4. The maintenance staff will check each building to see if anyone needs assistance. They will also check the elevators.

Tornado Alert

1. The switchboard operator will immediately call the administrator on duty and tune to WCCO when the Civil Defense alarm sounds.
2. If the decision is made to take cover, the administrator in charge will make the appropriate announcement over the PA system. **Tornado announcement**: We are having a tornado emergency. Please go to the Commons lower level, LRC tunnel or the Activities tunnel. Please stay inside and away from all windows. Wait for the all clear to be given.
3. Once the alarm is sounded, all staff and students should take cover. No one should be in the following areas: gym, theater, auditorium, LRC reading room and all areas with outside windows.

Water Main Break

Day—switchboard open
1. Call switchboard—explain location and nature of break.
   a. Move anything which could be damaged by water flow.

Night—switchboard closed
1. Call police emergency (911) and explain location and nature of break.
2. Meet emergency crew and direct them to area of break.
3. Notify [the administrator on duty].

Gas Line Break

Day—switchboard open
1. Clear immediate area.
2. Call switchboard operator with location and extent of break.
3. If necessary, evacuate the area by pulling the fire alarm.

Night—switchboard closed
1. Call the fire department at [phone #]. Give location and extent of break.
2. Clear immediate area.
3. Notify [the administrator on duty].

Medical Emergency

1. The switchboard operator should be notified and given as much information as possible. The exact location of the individual needing assistance should be given and an individual sent to the closest main entrance to meet the emergency vehicle.
2. The switchboard operator will then notify the police.
3. When switchboard is closed, call the police at 911 and give them as much information as possible. One individual should stay with the person in need and another should meet the emergency vehicles at the nearest door.

Student Disturbances

1. The individual witnessing a major disturbance or disorder should notify the Dean of Students or the administrator on duty and

---

[1]SOURCE: From *Staff Handbook of Policies and Procedures* (Bloomington, MN: Normandale Community College). Reprinted by permission.

give him/her all the important details. It will then be up to the administrator to decide what action is to be taken.

2. At times when an administrator is not present, a staff member should use his/her best judgment. Police can be reached at [phone #]. The incident should be reported to the Dean of Students on the next class day.

Bomb Threats

1. Keep caller on the telephone as long as possible.
2. Try to get as much information as possible regarding the bomb. That is, the bomb's location, type of device, time of detonation

and anything else that might be pertinent to the safety of the college and individuals inside.

3. Try to remember everything about the call, voice, accent, background noises. These items or anything else you might think of might help identify the caller.
4. Report the incident to the president or the administrator on duty.
5. The president or administrator on duty will make the final decision on what action is to be taken.
6. If the switchboard is closed, call the police at 911 and evacuate the buildings. If necessary, pull the fire alarm.

DISCUSSION QUESTIONS

1. What alternatives are available to security managers in handling personnel conflicts? Are they the responsibility of the security manager?
2. What natural disasters are likely to occur in your geographical area, and how should a security manager prepare an adequate response to them?
3. What resources would you contact to counter a series of bomb threats against your facility?
4. When a strike is certain to occur, what contingency plans should a security manager be concerned about?
5. If a security director notices OSHA violations and reports them to top management, and top management chooses to ignore the violations, what should the security director do?

REFERENCES

Business Continuity Guidelines: A Practical Approach for Emergency Preparedness for Crisis Management and Disaster Recovery. Arlington, VA: American Society for Industrial Security, 2005.

Cohen, Lawrence Mark. "Bombs Away." *Security Management*, August 2004, pp.47–54.

Crosby, Peter A. "Are Health and Safety in Sync?" *Security Management*, March 2004, pp.158–156.

Daniels, Rhianna. "Survey: Avian Flu Poses a Major Risk to the Business Community." *Security Director News*, May 2006, pp.2–4.

Elliott, Robert. "Banking on Recovery Plans." *Security Management*, November 2005, pp.78–81.

Elliott, Robert. "Extinguishing Fire Safety Problems." *Security Management*, May 2006a, pp.40–42.

Elliott, Robert. "Masters of Disasters." *Security Management*, January 2006b, pp.87–91.

Gips, Michael A. "Evacuation Procedures." *Security Management*, November 2005a, pp.66–69.

Gips, Michael A. "Safe and Secure." *Security Management*, February 2005b, pp.83–90.

Hanson, Doug. "Bomb Attack in Your Town." *Police and Security News*, November/December 2004, pp.65–68.

Harowitz, Sherry L. "Engulfed by Disaster." *Security Management*, November 2005, pp.60–65.

Hewitt, John. "Preparing Fire Wardens." *Security Management*, July 2005, pp.100–101.

Karter, Michael J., Jr. *Fire Loss in the United States during 2005: Full Report.* Quincy, MA: National Fire Protection Association, September 2006.

Kunreuther, Howard; Meyer, Robert; and Van den Bulte, Christopher. *Risk Analysis for Extreme Events: Economic Incentives for Reducing Future Losses.* Washington, DC: National Institute of Standards and Technology, 2004.

Lee, James D. "Gimme Shelter." *Security Management*, January 2007, pp.52–59.

McKee, Kathryn and Guthridge, Liz. "Working through Emotional Turmoil." *Security Management*, February 2007, p.102.

Minieri, Michael. "Don't Lock in Fire Code Violations." *Security Management*, July 2005, pp.95–98.

Narr, Tony; Toliver, Jessica; Murphy, Jerry; McFarland, Malcolm; and Ederheimer, Joshua. *Police Management of Mass Demonstrations: Identifying Issues and Successful Approaches.* Washington, DC: Police Executive Research Forum, 2006.

"Newspoll." *Security Director News*, May 2007, p.23.

Occupational Safety and Health Administration (OSHA), www.osha.gov

Phelps, E. Floyd. "No Lights, No Camera, Just Action." *Security Management*, November 2007, pp.55–61.

Piazza, Peter. "Communication Breakdown." *Security Management*, November 2005, pp.70–72.

Pogar, Joel A. "Keep Communications in a Crisis." *Security Management*, June 2007, pp.98–107.

A Quick Reference Guide for Handling Disasters, Emergencies and Pandemics. Insert in *Security Management*, August 2006.

Roberts, Marta. "A Dash of Danger." *Security Management*, June 2005a, pp.129–133.

Roberts, Marta. "Emergency Medical Services." *Security Management*, November 2005b, pp.74–76.

Robinson, Patricia A. "The Leaking Tanker." *The Law Enforcement Trainer*, March 2004, pp.59, 64.

Scott, Mike. "Preparing for Disasters." *Police and Security News*, July/August 2006, pp.20–25.

Straw, Joseph. "Disaster Management Done Right." *Security Management*, July 2007, pp.30–36.

2007 AT&T Business Continuity Study. Online: http://www.att.com/gen/press-room?pid=7922

CASE CITED

Marshall v. Barlow's Inc., 436 U.S. 307 (1978).

CHAPTER 9

Preventing Losses from Criminal Actions

Criminal actions, including vandalism and burglary, affect companies not only in terms of property loss and cost to repair damaged structures but also by driving away customers, who may either consciously or subconsciously choose to distance themselves from targets of criminal activity.

DO YOU KNOW . . .

- What rights private security officers may be called on to enforce?
- What crimes are of major importance to private security?
- How the risks of these crimes can be reduced?
- How to differentiate among theft, burglary and robbery?
- What circumstances can indicate arson?
- What the most common types of white-collar crime are?
- What the most common computer crimes are?
- What three key characteristics of computer-related crime are?
- When and how private security officers can make an arrest?
- When force or deadly force may be justified?
- When and how searches of suspects can be conducted?

CAN YOU DEFINE?

check kiting	felony	phishing	vetting
citizen's arrest	hacker	spam	white-collar crime
cybercrime	identity theft	trailers	
cyberspace	igniter	Uniform Crime	
dark figure of crime	misdemeanor	Reports (UCRs)	

Introduction

"The world is experiencing a crime pandemic" (Naim, 2007). Criminal activity in business and industry takes many forms, ranging from simple property loss through shoplifting or pilfering to property loss by physical violence, as in armed robbery. The impact of burglary and robbery on the business community is substantial.

Consider the annual cost of crime in the United States: $78 billion for the criminal justice system, $64 billion for private protection, $202 billion in loss of life and work, $120 billion in crimes against business, $60 billion in stolen goods and fraud, $40 billion from drug abuse and $110 billion in drunken driving incidents, for a staggering total of $675 billion (K. Anderson, 2007). Various studies estimate Americans pay between $1.7 trillion and $2 trillion each year on direct and indirect crime-related expenses ("Senate Judiciary Committee Explores the True Cost of Crime on Society," 2006, p.4; D. Anderson, 2007).

Preventing losses from criminal actions is a critical responsibility of security managers. Despite the best efforts to reduce the possibility of crimes occurring, they will happen. Security managers and personnel must be prepared to deal effectively with them. This chapter begins by introducing the proprietary rights security officers may be called upon to enforce. It then introduces losses from criminal actions and those crimes of most concern to private security. Next, actions that might be required in expelling, detaining and arresting; using force; and searching suspects are explained. This section then presents an in-depth discussion of computer crime, the seriousness of the problem and the specific types of threats existing. Next, legislation related to computer crimes and security measures for computer systems are discussed. The chapter concludes with a brief discussion on investigating computer crime and prosecuting perpetrators of such crimes.

Civil and Criminal Offenses in Review

Chapter 4 discussed the differences between civil and criminal offenses. Unlike public police, private security officers must concern themselves with both.

Civil Offenses

Civil offenses, or torts, are offenses against individuals for which the individual may be sued. If any such offenses occur on private property, the involved parties will expect a complete report of the incident from security. In addition to being alert to civil offenses, security officers are often called upon to enforce their employers' proprietary rights.

Enforcing Proprietary Rights

Not all crimes will be prevented. When they are not, security responsibilities change. It is often not possible to simply leave the matter up to local authorities, however. Security managers are expected to *act* to protect the assets of their employers.

 Security managers may be called on to enforce the following rights:

- Prevent trespassing
- Control conduct of persons legally on premises
- Defend self, others and property
- Prevent the commission of a crime

How these rights are enforced varies from establishment to establishment. Standards and procedures for arresting, searching and questioning persons should be clearly defined, because mistakes in these areas can result in either criminal or civil lawsuits, or both. Security managers should be thoroughly familiar with their state laws regarding the enforcement activities of private security. As in other areas of private security, common sense and reasonable actions are critical.

Criminal Offenses

Crimes range in seriousness from pick-pocketing to murder and are classified as misdemeanors or felonies according to their seriousness. A **misdemeanor** is a minor crime such as shoplifting or petty theft that is punishable by a fine or a relatively short jail sentence, or both. In contrast, a **felony** is a serious crime, such as murder, robbery or rape, which is punishable by death or by imprisonment in the state prison or penitentiary.

In the United States, state and federal statutes define each crime, the elements involved and the penalty attached to each. The elements of the crime are the specific conditions and actions proscribed by law that must exist to constitute a specific crime. These elements vary from state to state.

The Seriousness of the Problem A major source of information on crimes is the **Uniform Crime Reports (UCR)**.[1] These reports are compiled annually by the FBI, which serves as the national clearinghouse for crime-related statistical information. The UCR program provides a yearly, nationwide summary of crime based on the cooperative submission of data by nearly 17,000 law enforcement agencies throughout the country. Figures from the 2005 UCR indicate the seriousness of the crime problem in this country:

- One violent crime every 22.7 seconds
- One murder every 31.5 minutes
- One forcible rape every 5.6 minutes
- One robbery every 1.3 minutes
- One aggravated assault every 36.5 seconds
- One property crime reported every 3.1 minutes
- One burglary every 14.6 seconds
- One larceny-theft every 4.7 seconds
- One motor vehicle theft every 25.5 seconds

It must be noted that these statistics are based only on those crimes reported to law enforcement. Experts estimate that *less than half* of all crimes committed are actually reported to the police. Thus the true number of crimes, called the **dark figure of crime**, remains unknown.

According to Eggen (2006, p.A01): "A surge in violent crime that began [in 2005] accelerated in the first half of 2006, providing the clearest signal yet that the historic drop in the U.S. crime rate has ended and is being reversed." Violent crime increased by nearly 4 percent, the largest increase in 15 years, suggesting that the 2005 increase was not an anomaly but rather the "first significant uptick in violent crime since the early 1990s."

Crimes of Concern to Private Security

Security managers should carefully analyze the potential for crime in their establishments. What type of crime is likely to occur? At what rate? When? What method of attack is likely to be used? What is it likely to cost? If the risk is high, appropriate security measures should be taken to reduce, spread or shift the risks.

When considering foreseeability of crime, the best indicator is the occurrence of past crimes in this particular location. Often cases are divided into no prior crime, one to a few prior crimes and several prior crimes. Even one prior crime, however, should lead to a careful examination of underlying causes and whether any changes in security are called for. Although this chapter emphasizes the security officer's role in dealing with potential and actual crimes, the majority of the security manager's time is spent dealing with noncriminal matters.

The data contained in UCR reports can be used by private security managers in making administrative, operational and management decisions. In addition to the UCR, security managers should be familiar with their state statutes for the crimes they are most likely to deal with. They should be familiar with

---

[1]These reports are entitled *Crime in the United States* (CIUS) and are published yearly.

the elements that must be proven if they are to assist in prosecuting perpetrators of crime.

 The crimes of most concern to private security are larceny/theft, burglary, robbery, trespassing, vandalism, assault, arson and white-collar crime, including embezzlement.

Definitions in the following discussions of specific crimes are based on those used in the Uniform Crime Reports.

Larceny/Theft[2]

Larceny/theft is (1) the unlawful taking (2) of the personal goods or property of another (3) valued above (grand larceny) or below (petty larceny) a specified amount, (4) with the intent to permanently deprive the owner of the property or goods. This crime includes shoplifting, to be discussed in Chapter 15, and employee pilferage, previously discussed in Chapter 7. It also includes such crimes as pick-pocketing, purse-snatching, thefts from motor vehicles, thefts of motor vehicle parts and accessories and other thefts, where *no* use of force or violence occurs. The person simply takes something that does not belong to him or her. Figure 9.1 shows the percent distribution of larceny-theft offenses in 2006.

The value of the property is usually determined by the actual value at the time of the theft or the cost of replacing it in a reasonable time. The value determines if the offense is grand or petty larceny. State statutes establish the dollar amount above which a theft is considered grand larceny, a felony, and below which a theft is considered petty larceny, a misdemeanor.

 To prevent or reduce losses from larceny/theft, limit access to assets and use basic security equipment and procedures to deter employee pilferage as well as theft by nonemployees.

Fidelity bonds are one of the strongest protections against internal theft. These bonds are a form of insurance protecting employers from losses suffered from dishonest employees. Businesses often investigate their own internal losses, and when they find someone to be guilty, they simply fire them. The police and the media often are not called.

One of the country's fastest-growing crimes is **identity theft**, a crime involving misappropriation of names, Social Security numbers, credit card numbers or other pieces of personal information for fraudulent purposes (Fleck, 2004, p.3). Identity theft became a federal crime in the United States in 1998 with passage of the Identity Theft Assumption and Deterrence Act. The National Crime Victimization Survey (NCVS) defines identity theft as including three behaviors (Baum, 2006, p.1):

1. Unauthorized use or attempted use of existing credit cards
2. Unauthorized use or attempted use of other existing accounts such as checking accounts
3. Misuse of personal information to obtain new accounts or loans, or to commit other crimes

---

[2]Larceny/theft is used here because the two terms are interchangeable. Some state statutes refer to larceny, others to theft. The Uniform Crime Reports use larceny-theft.

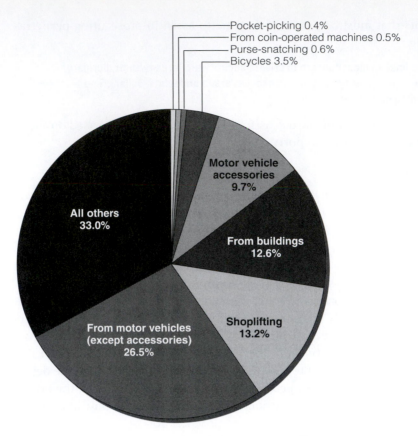

Figure 9.1   Percent Distribution of Larceny-Theft Offenses, 2006

NOTE: *Due to rounding, the percentages may not add up to 100.0.*

SOURCE: www.fbi.gov/ucr.

The Federal Trade Commission (FTC) reports that nearly 10 million people a year are victims of identity theft. The results are nearly $48 billion in losses to businesses, nearly $5 billion in losses to individual victims and nearly 300 million victim hours spent trying to resolve the situation (Majoras, 2005, p.14). The FTC also reports that of the fraud-related complaints filed with them in 2007, for the eighth year in a row identity theft topped the list of complaints (*Consumer Fraud and Identity Theft Complaint Data*, 2008).

The FBI ("Corporate Takeover: A New Twist on Identity Theft," 2007) states that identity theft went to a whole new level when one company tried to steal $23 million by pretending to be another company. The scam was made possible by a remarkable coincidence: two private security companies with nearly identical names. One, based in Michigan, was named Executive Outcome Inc. The other, in South Africa, was named Executive Outcomes Inc. The crime began in late 2001 when a British debt collector called the Michigan-based Executive Outcome asking if they wanted help collecting $23 million owed by the government of Sierra Leone for military equipment, security and training. But the debt was actually owed to the other firm, Executive Outcomes, half a world away. Expectedly, a legal skirmish followed, and the conflict turned malicious. A representative of the South African company called the police and a special

Despite efforts to educate the public on how to avoid becoming victims of identity theft, the crime continues to spread. To effectively thwart identity thieves, businesses and private citizens alike must be vigilant in shredding or otherwise permanently disposing of any document containing sensitive personal or corporate data.

FBI agent assigned as a Legal Attaché in London took over the case. With a search warrant, they searched the American company and found evidence of forged documents. The perpetrators both pled guilty to conspiracy, wire fraud and other charges and received prison time and paid $51,000 to the South African representative they threatened.

Specific types of employee pilferage and nonemployee theft in various businesses are discussed in later chapters.

Burglary

Burglary is (1) entering a structure without the owner's consent (2) with the intent to commit a crime. Usually the intended crime is theft, but it may be another offense, such as rape or assault. Commercial burglaries are often committed in service stations, stores, schools, warehouses, office buildings, manufacturing plants and the like. Often burglars specialize in one type of facility.

In 2005, 2,154,126 burglaries were reported, a 0.5 percent increase from 2004, accounting for 21.2 percent of the property crimes. The average dollar loss was $1,725. Of all burglaries, 65.8 percent were of residences, and most (62.4 percent) took place during the day, between 6 A.M. and 6 P.M. Among nonresidential structures when time of occurrence was known, 58.0 percent occurred at night.

Entrance to commit burglary can be made in any number of ways, but the most common method is prying open a door or window—the jimmy method. Entrance can also be made by simply walking through an unlocked door, an open window, a tunnel or a ventilation shaft, or by remaining in a building after closing time. The smash-and-grab burglar breaks a display window and grabs whatever merchandise is available.

In many states, if a person is found in a structure and the person has no legal right to be there at that time, it is *presumed* the person intends to commit a crime, unless the suspect can prove otherwise. Some states require an actual *breaking* into the structure—that is, a forced entry. Other states require that the structure be a *dwelling* or that the crime occur during the *nighttime*. Provisions such as these make it necessary for security managers to be familiar with the statutes of their own state to deal effectively with crimes that are attempted or actually committed. The security checklist in Figure 9.2 might be used in assessing a facility's protection against crime.

 These steps can prevent or reduce the risk of loss from burglary:

- Install and use good locks, adequate indoor and outdoor lighting and an alarm system. This may be supplemented with security patrols.
- Keep valuables in a burglar-resistant safe or vault.
- Keep a minimum amount of cash on hand.
- Leave cash registers open and empty at closing time.
- Be sure all security equipment is functional before leaving.

Robbery

Robbery is (1) the unlawful taking of personal property (2) from the person or in the person's presence, (3) against the person's will by force or threat of force. The person from whom the property is taken need not be the owner of the property, but can be someone to whom the property has been entrusted. Usually "from the person or in the person's presence" means the victim actually sees the robber take the property, but this is not always the case. The robber may lock the victim in a room and then commit the robbery. This does not remove the crime "from the presence of the person" if the separation from the property is the direct result of force or threats of force used by the robber.

Nationwide in 2006, an estimated 447,403 robberies were committed, an increase of 7.2 percent over 2005 figures. The average dollar value of property stolen per robbery was $1,268. Bank robbery had the highest average dollar value, $4,330 per robbery. Figure 9.3 summarizes robbery locations in 2006.

Most robberies are committed with a weapon or by indicating that a weapon is present and by a command suggesting that if the robber's demands are not met the victim will be harmed. The demands may be given orally or in a note; the threat may be against the victim, the victim's family or another person with the victim. In 2006, firearms were used in 42.2 percent of reported robberies. The possibility of violence or a hostage situation must always be considered if a robbery occurs.

 These steps can prevent or reduce losses from robbery:

- Train employees how to react if a robbery occurs.
- Do not build up cash. Used armed couriers to transport cash.
- Establish strict opening and closing procedures, and use extreme caution if someone seeks entrance to the facility after hours.

All employees in positions where they might become involved in a robbery should be informed on how to react in such a situation. It should be stressed

Name _____ **Phone** _____
Address _____
Person interviewed _____

☐ Owner   ☐ Other

Construction   ☐ Wood   ☐ Metal   ☐ Concrete   ☐ Masonry   ☐ Other _____

Condition   ☐ Excellent   ☐ Good   ☐ Fair

Doors	Adequate	Wood	Metal	Glass	Combination	Nonremovable hinge pins
Front	☐ Yes ☐ No	☐	☐	☐	☐	☐ Yes ☐ No
Rear	☐ Yes ☐ No	☐	☐	☐	☐	☐ Yes ☐ No
Side	☐ Yes ☐ No	☐	☐	☐	☐	☐ Yes ☐ No
Side	☐ Yes ☐ No	☐	☐	☐	☐	☐ Yes ☐ No

Locks	Adequate	Dead bolt	Drop bolt	Key in knob	Padlock	Slide bolt	Other
Front	☐ Yes ☐ No	☐	☐	☐	☐	☐	☐
Rear	☐ Yes ☐ No	☐	☐	☐	☐	☐	☐
Side	☐ Yes ☐ No	☐	☐	☐	☐	☐	☐
Side	☐ Yes ☐ No	☐	☐	☐	☐	☐	☐

Lights	Adequate	Weak	None	Left on	Location
Interior	☐ Yes ☐ No	☐	☐	☐ Yes ☐ No	☐ Good ☐ Bad
Exterior	☐ Yes ☐ No	☐	☐	☐ Yes ☐ No	☐ Good ☐ Bad
Front	☐ Yes ☐ No	☐	☐	☐ Yes ☐ No	☐ Good ☐ Bad
Side	☐ Yes ☐ No	☐	☐	☐ Yes ☐ No	☐ Good ☐ Bad
Side	☐ Yes ☐ No	☐	☐	☐ Yes ☐ No	☐ Good ☐ Bad
Rear	☐ Yes ☐ No	☐	☐	☐ Yes ☐ No	☐ Good ☐ Bad

Windows	Adequate	Bars	Gate	Mesh	Locks
Front	☐ Yes ☐ No	☐	☐	☐	☐ Yes ☐ No
Rear	☐ Yes ☐ No	☐	☐	☐	☐ Yes ☐ No
Side	☐ Yes ☐ No	☐	☐	☐	☐ Yes ☐ No
Side	☐ Yes ☐ No	☐	☐	☐	☐ Yes ☐ No

Remarks:

Alarms	Doors			Windows			Ceiling			Walls		
	Adequate	Weak	None	Adequate	Weak	None	Adequate	Weak	None	Adequate	Weak	None
Local	☐	☐	☐	☐	☐	☐	☐	☐	☐	☐	☐	☐
Central	☐	☐	☐	☐	☐	☐	☐	☐	☐	☐	☐	☐
Telephone	☐	☐	☐	☐	☐	☐	☐	☐	☐	☐	☐	☐

Safe
Visible from street   ☐ Yes ☐ No   Anchored   ☐ Yes ☐ No
Lighted   ☐ Yes ☐ No   Adequate   ☐ Yes ☐ No

Cash register
Visible from street   ☐ Yes ☐ No   Anchored   ☐ Yes ☐ No
Lighted   ☐ Yes ☐ No   Adequate   ☐ Yes ☐ No

Overall evaluation: ☐ **Excellent**   ☐ **Good**   ☐ **Fair**   ☐ **Inadequate**

To the storekeeper:
This is part of a program being conducted by your Police Department to help you protect yourself against burglars.
If you follow the recommendations in this report, you will make it more difficult for a burglar to enter your business.

Investigating officer _____   Telephone number _____
Burglary Prevention Team

Recommendations: _____   Compliance date _____

Figure 9.2   Security Checklist
SOURCE: Fargo (North Dakota) Police Department.

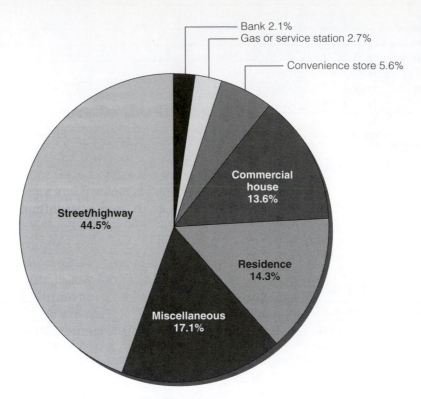

Figure 9.3 Robbery Locations, 2006

NOTE: Due to rounding, the percentages may not add up to 100.0.

SOURCE: www.fbi.gov/ucr.

that heroics are *not* expected and, in fact, could be a deadly mistake. Robbers are completely unpredictable, but employees should be taught to follow these guidelines to reduce the risks involved should a robbery occur:

- Stay calm.
- Do exactly as you are told.
- Assure the robber that you will cooperate totally, but do not volunteer to do anything.
- Treat any firearm displayed as though it is real and loaded.
- Activate alarms only if you can do so undetected.
- Try to alert others if possible.

To assist in investigating the robbery, employees should mentally note the robber's appearance, clothing, voice and unique characteristics—anything distinctive. Some employers place a reference point on a wall or door frame to give employees who might face robbers something to use to estimate the robber's height.

Correctly Classifying "Unlawful Taking"

The preceding discussions illustrate several types of "unlawful taking" security managers may encounter. It is important to keep the basic distinctions among these types of stealing separate.

Larceny/theft is the unlawful taking of the property of another without unlawful entrance or confrontation. *Burglary* includes unlawful taking *and* unlawful entry. *Robbery* includes unlawful taking *and* confrontation.

Private security is most often concerned with larceny/theft. However, the amount of losses sustained in a burglary or robbery may be significant if proper precautions are not followed. In addition, robbery carries with it the potential for violence.

Trespassing and Vandalism

Two frequently encountered problems of private security managers are trespassing and vandalism. *Trespassing* refers to the unlawful presence of a person on the property or inside the premises of someone else. The trespasser may mean no harm; in fact, the trespass may be unintentional if boundaries are not clearly marked and signs are not posted. Often, however, trespassers may smoke where it may be hazardous, or they may intend to steal or damage property. "No Trespassing" signs can eliminate the excuse that the intruder's presence was accidental.

Vandalism refers to the malicious or intentional damaging or destroying of property. It is also called criminal damage to property or malicious destruction of property. The gravity of this crime depends on the extent of property damage. In one sense, destruction of property is more serious than theft because it eliminates the possibility of recovering the property. Intent is always a factor in vandalism. School buildings, factories, warehouses, vehicles and homes are all vulnerable targets for the vandal. How much vandalism occurs internally in business and industry is not documented; however, it is likely to be a great amount. In some instances, vandalism may actually be sabotage. For example, assembly workers who become dissatisfied with their jobs may cause machinery breakdowns (to be discussed in Chapter 11).

 Trespassing and vandalism can be prevented or reduced by strict access controls, security lighting, signs and patrols.

Assault

Some private security managers must face the risks to their employees from verbal or physical assault, including sexual assault. *Assault* refers to an attack on a person.[3] It may be committed to cause bodily injury or may result while committing another crime, such as robbery or rape. Establishments having night shifts and those employing large numbers of women are especially susceptible to this risk.

The UCR defines aggravated assault as an unlawful attack by one person upon another for the purpose of inflicting severe or aggravated bodily injury. This type of assault is usually accompanied by a weapon or by other means likely to produce death or great bodily harm. When aggravated assault and larceny-theft occur together, the offense falls into the category of robbery. Nationwide, an estimated 862,947 aggravated assaults were reported in 2005, a 1.8 percent increase over 2004.

[3]Some states distinguish between assault (threat) and battery (actual physical contact), but the UCR combines them into a single crime termed *assault*.

Adequate lighting, patrols and communication systems are means to reduce the risk of assaults. Escort services may also be used.

The distance to parking lots is a key factor in employees' susceptibility to assault. When practical, this distance should be minimal. Parking areas should be well lit and fenced, as discussed in Chapter 6.

Arson

Arson is any willful or malicious burning or attempting to burn, with or without intent to defraud, a dwelling house, public building, motor vehicle or aircraft, personal property of another and the like. Nationally 67,504 arsons were reported in 2005, a decline of 2.7 percent from 2004. Arsons involving structures (residential, storage, public, etc.) accounted for 43.6 percent of the reported arson offenses. The average value loss per arson offense was $14,910. Arsons of industrial and manufacturing structures resulted in the highest average dollar losses ($356,324 per arson).

Arson can be committed for financial gain, to hide other crimes such as burglary or embezzlement, for revenge or as a form of terrorism. Common sites for setting fires include the basement; stockrooms; duplicating, file and mail rooms and utility closets. Access control to such areas is critical to preventing arson. Fahim (2006) notes that arson is one of the hardest crimes to investigate. Usually a fire marshal is called in to help with the investigation.

Security managers might suspect arson in a fire where one of the three elements of the fire triangle is present in abnormal amounts. Greater than normal *oxygen* can come from opened windows, doors, pried-open vents or holes knocked in walls. Piled-up newspapers, excelsior or other combustible materials present at or brought to the scene can provide abnormal amounts of *fuel*. Excessive *heat* can be caused by accelerants, including gasoline (the most commonly used), kerosene, turpentine or paint remover.

Another indicator of arson is an **igniter**, including matches, candles, cigars, cigarettes, cigarette lighters, explosives and electrical, mechanical and chemical devices. Time fuses, shorted light switches, electrical devices left in the "on" position, kerosene-soaked papers in wastepaper baskets, magnifying glasses, matches tied around a lighted cigarette and numerous other igniters have been used to commit arson.

Yet another indication of arson is the presence of **trailers**, paths of paper or accelerants used to spread the fire from one location to another. Arsonists may also set multiple fires to ensure complete destruction, and they may disable the firefighting apparatus. Any of the preceding would be strong evidence of arson.

 Security managers should suspect arson in fires that:

- Have more than one point of origin.
- Deviate from normal burning patterns.
- Show evidence of trailers.
- Show evidence of having been accelerated.
- Indicate an abnormal amount of air, fuel or heat present.
- Reveal evidence of incendiary igniters at the point of origin.
- Produce odors or smoke of a color associated with substances not normally present at the scene.

Other suspicious circumstances include goods being removed from the premises shortly before a fire occurs, over-insurance, economic difficulties of the owner, surplus out-of-date or damaged inventory or needed repair—perhaps to comply with violations discovered by an OSHA inspector.

Every fire, no matter how small, should be investigated and the cause determined so corrective steps can be taken to prevent a recurrence.

White-Collar or Economic Crime

White-collar crime, sometimes referred to as *economic crime*, is business-related crime. The U.S. Chamber of Commerce has described *white-collar crimes* as "illegal acts characterized by guile, deceit, and concealment . . . not dependent upon the application of physical force or violence or threats thereof." White-collar crimes may be committed by individuals acting independently or by those who are part of a well-planned conspiracy. The objective may be to obtain money, property or services; to avoid the payment or loss of money, property or services; or to secure business or personal advantage. Often computers are involved in white-collar crimes, as discussed shortly.

Corporate crime is a type of white-collar crime whose distinctive feature is that the offense is committed primarily for the benefit of an ongoing legitimate business enterprise, rather than for the individual who carries out the offense. Such crimes include consumer fraud, securities fraud, insurance and tax fraud, environmental offenses, illegal payment and unfair trade practices. Some notorious white-collar criminals have been in the headlines in recent years, including executives from Tyco International, Health South, Adelphia Communications, Enron, WorldCom and even Martha Stewart.

 White-collar crime includes (1) credit card and check fraud, including identity theft; (2) securities theft and fraud; (3) insurance fraud; (4) consumer fraud, illegal competition and deceptive practices; (5) bankruptcy fraud; (6) embezzlement and pilferage; (7) bribes, kickbacks and payoffs; and (8) receiving stolen property.

The FBI's Financial Crimes Section (FCS) investigates matters related to theft or embezzlement occurring within or against the national or international financial community. It concentrates on such crimes as corporate fraud, health-care fraud, mortgage fraud, identity theft, insurance fraud and money laundering (*Financial Crimes: Report to the Public*, 2005, p.1). Corporate fraud is currently the highest priority of the FCS.

Fraud   Wetzel (2007) describes how the rebuilding of lower Manhattan will present numerous opportunities for fraud. Over the next five years, a total of more than $22 billion in construction work will be carried out by an estimated 10,000 construction workers. The Lower Manhattan Construction Command Center has developed a fraud prevention program. Its key components are a hotline for anonymously reporting fraudulent practices, awareness training, contractor **vetting** (being evaluated for security approval or acceptance), employee screening and access controls, and oversight by integrity monitors. The program includes fraud prevention training for contractors to remind them what conduct is prohibited and what the consequences are for breaking the law. It all begins with close coordination among the agencies and their inspectors general.

Identity Theft   Although not new, identity theft has evolved into a serious and pervasive threat to consumers and the financial services industry alike, costing billions of dollars each year. Discussed previously in the section on larceny/theft, identity theft is also included in the FBI's economic crime priorities, illustrating the overlap in many offenses and the difficulty in cleanly classifying some offenses: "Fraud in the form of identity theft has risen to the top [of white-collar crime]. It's out of control" (Mills-Senn, 2005, p.16). Figure 9.4 shows the complaint categories reported to the FTC during 2007, with identity theft heading the list.

Other Crimes

Several other crimes, such as shoplifting, bad-check writing, espionage and sabotage are discussed in following chapters, as they relate more specifically to cer-

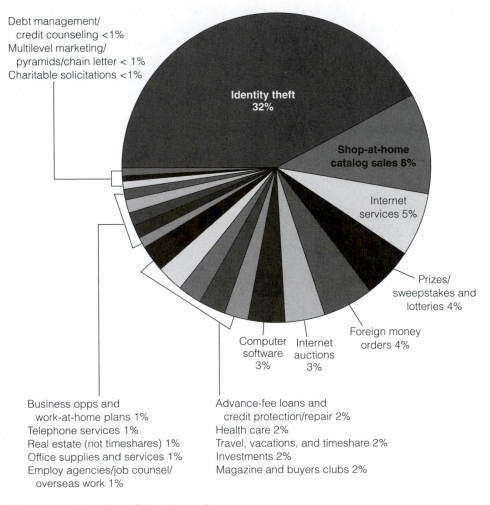

Figure 9.4   Top Complaint Categories

NOTE: Percentages are based on the total number of Sentinel complaints (635,173) received between January 1 and December 31, 2007.

SOURCE: *National and State Trends in Fraud & Identity Theft, January–December 2004* (Washington, DC: Federal Trade Commission, February 1, 2005).

tain types of establishments. The last category of crime to be discussed here—computer crime—is of such concern that it merits its own section.

Computer Crime

In the nineteenth century, Thomas Carlyle observed: "Man is an animal who uses tools. Without tools, he is nothing; with tools he is all." Computers might be thought of as the ultimate tool—they process, transmit, print and store information at lightning speed. Likewise, computers can be used to commit crimes—crimes that are simple to commit and extremely difficult to detect. Adequate security requires not only physical security but at least a basic knowledge of how the computer works and how it can be used to commit crime. Because computer crimes exist, computer security becomes mandatory for businesses and corporations.

The definitions of computer crime, sometimes referred to as **cybercrime**, are varied. Computer crime includes accessing a computer's database without authorization or exceeding authorization for the purpose of sabotage or fraud. It includes theft or destruction of software and hardware as well. (Note: A comprehensive discussion of IT security is provided in Chapter 11; the following section merely provides a brief overview of computer crime.)

The Seriousness of the Problem

For most businesses, computers are at the heart of their operations and their communications. Therefore, computer crime is a serious security challenge and a rapidly increasing threat to American businesses and consumers, costing hundreds of millions of dollars annually. Financial losses to corporations from computer crime have been estimated to be as high as $10 billion annually but even the experts are unsure of the true amount lost (Whitlock, 2004, p.11).

Many organizations rely extensively on electronic data processing (EDP) and could not function effectively for long without their computers. In fact computer crime or database failure can destroy a business. Robert Huber, computer security expert with National Cash Register Company, suggests that a business that relies on computers will close its doors in three to five days if the computers fail. Yet computers are neither infallible nor invulnerable. Therefore, establishments that rely on computers cannot ignore the inherent risks involved in their use.

Types of Threats to Computer Security

Most big corporations have been victims of cybercrime, from employees' snooping through confidential files to criminals stealing trade secrets. But even small businesses and organizations may fall victim to computer crime. Respondents to a CSO [Corporate Security Officer] survey reported 20 percent of electronic crimes were caused by insiders; 80 percent by outsiders (*2005 E-Crime Watch Survey*, p.18).

At a very basic level, computer-related crimes can involve the input data, the output data, the program itself or computer time. *Input data* can be altered; for example, a fictitious supplier can be entered into the billing system or figures can be changed or removed, leaving absolutely no trace. Some schools have experienced difficulties with student grades being illegally changed. *Output data* may be obtained by unauthorized people through wiretapping, electromagnetic pickup or theft of data sheets or punch cards. The *computer program* itself might be tampered with to add costs to purchased items or to create double payments for particular accounts. *Computer time* also is sometimes used for personal use and/or profit.

A survey conducted by the Data Processing Management Association (DPMA) questioned one thousand data processing executives in *Fortune 1000* companies and found that the majority of computer abuses were rather mundane. Nearly half of all incidents reported involved misuse of computer services, such as game-playing or using the computer for personal work, to divert funds or to alter records. The next most prevalent area was program abuse, that is, copying or changing programs. Third was data abuse—diverting information to unauthorized individuals. Fourth was hardware abuse, that is, damaging or stealing computer equipment.

 The most common types of crimes are employee use of computers for personal reasons, unauthorized access to confidential files and unlawful copying of copyrighted or licensed software. Other security threats to computer centers are theft by fraud or embezzlement (credit card fraud, telecommunications fraud), hackers, sabotage (viruses/malware, spyware, phishing and spam), employee carelessness or error, and fire.

Theft by Fraud or Embezzlement   Funds may be stolen by an outsider using a telephone and the necessary passwords from a remote terminal to make an unauthorized transfer of millions of dollars to a designated account. Instances of such fraud include the Equity Funding Fraud of the late 1970s that resulted in losses of more than $100 million.

Computerized banks are frequently the victims of **check kiting**, where a person makes simultaneous deposits and withdrawals using two or more banks to obtain credit before enough time has elapsed to clear the checks. Before the use of computers, bank personnel examined such transactions when they were made. Now, however, kiting can be detected only by using a special computer program to monitor unusually large transactions and continuous activity involving accounts with small running balances. Funds can also be stolen by insiders, for example, employees who falsify claims in an insurance company, or the computer programmers with their fictitious supply company cited previously.

It is not always money that is stolen; sometimes the theft involves information or data. Computer databanks contain information worth billions of dollars, such as lists of customers, bank records, consumer records, trade secrets, business plans and the like. In addition, secrets regarding the manufacturing of computers are also sometimes the target of computer thieves.

The thefts need not involve huge sums of money or information. Theft of services is also a problem. Employees may use company computers to play games, run their own programs or, as in a few documented cases, even run their own businesses with their employers' computers and on their employers' time.

Hackers   Another serious threat to computer security is the **hacker**—the computer enthusiast who engages in electronic snooping, software piracy and other types of high-tech illegal activities. Sometimes the activities of such hackers are relatively harmless. Other times, they cause great damage and chaos for companies. Hacking is relatively easy to do, and the tools are readily available (Albrecht, 2005).

In addition to accessing computers without authorization, hackers also frequently engage in software piracy, costing computer companies millions of dollars in lost sales. Selling software is big business. Companies have tried many ways to stop such pirates. One video-game maker hired full-time lawyers to sue the pirates, while other companies have used special codes to prevent copying.

Sabotage   Another risk to protect against is sabotage. Competitors, activists or dissatisfied employees might make the computer their target. Activists may see the computer room as the "vulnerable heart" of a business and make it the target of their attack. For example, one disgruntled programmer who thought he might be fired programmed the computer to destroy its database if it did not create a salary check for him when payroll was done. Poor employee morale can greatly enhance the likelihood of computer sabotage.

Sabotage may be done by a computer virus, which is a "bug" entered into a computer program that can cause serious memory problems, destroying files or even entire programs. It can also spread from computer to computer. A virus can lay dormant for weeks or months until activated by someone with access to the computer. The CSO survey (*2005 E-Crime Watch Survey*) reported that 82 percent of respondents (N=554) cited viruses or other malicious code (malware) as the most prevalent type of electronic crime followed by spyware (61 percent), phishing (57 percent) and illegal generation of spam e-mail (48 percent).

Malware and spyware are discussed in Chapter 11. **Phishing** is a general term for criminals' creation of fraudulent e-mails and Web sites, designed to look like e-mails and Web sites of well-known, legitimate businesses, financial institutions and government agencies, used to deceive Internet users into disclosing their bank and financial account information or other personal data such as usernames and passwords. The phisher then uses the information for criminal purposes such as identity theft and fraud (*Special Report on "Phishing,"* no date). Phishing is illegal.

Spam, electronic junk mail, is technically termed unsolicited commercial e-mails (UCEs). E-mailboxes can be overloaded with hundreds of these UCEs, and some Internet service providers (ISPs) estimate spam accounts for two-thirds to three-quarters of the 20.7 billion e-mail messages received weekly in the United States (Donofrio, 2004, p.86). Of concern is that one of the most common types of spam is adult pornography ads. Sending spam is also illegal, and some states have passed antispam legislation.

Other Threats   Employee carelessness and errors are also significant risks. Improperly stored computer tapes and disks can be damaged beyond use. Excessive heat or humidity can destroy data. A magnet closer than 12 cm might erase a computer disk.

Another problem is the controlled environment required for the computer to function correctly. Fluctuations in power can cause inaccuracies, so a continuous supply of unvarying power must be available. Air conditioning must be maintained, or the computer can malfunction. Computers must also be protected against moisture; therefore, the location of water mains, air-conditioning pipes, sewer pipes and the like should be checked to ensure that they do not pose a threat to the computer should they break. If such pipes do exist, a drain should be installed in the computer room's floor. The computer and disks should be covered if construction or sandblasting is going on outside because the fine powder resulting from such activities can ruin a computer.

The threat of fire is another serious risk. The large number of electric wires and connections involved in computer installations, often located under a raised floor, and the fact that computer rooms are fire-loaded with large quantities of combustible materials make the risk of fire great. Even if a fire is detected early, the steam and humidity from extinguishing it may ruin computer tapes, drives or other data.

No matter what type of computer crime is involved, some common characteristics are usually found.

 Characteristics of computer-related crime include:

- Computer crimes are relatively easy to commit.
- Computer crimes are often difficult to detect.
- Most computer crimes are not prosecuted.

Detecting and Reporting Computer Crime

As mentioned, only a small number of all computer crimes are detected. Of these only 12 percent are reported to the authorities and only 3 percent of offenders go to jail. The chance of a computer criminal being caught and going to jail is approximately one in twenty-seven thousand.

One resource developed to aid in the detection of computer crime is the Cyber Incident Detection Data Analysis Center (CIDDAC), a nonprofit, private sector cyber threat reporting system that centralizes information from participating organizations. The "catalyst" for the CIDDAC was the 9/11 attack on the United States (Moore, 2005, p.86). CIDDAC connects participants' computer networks to "Real-Time Cyber Attack Detection Sensors" or RCADSs. If the networks are attacked, the sensors instantly send valuable forensic data to the CIDDAC operations center for analysis. CIDDAC personnel monitor the situation, analyze the data and immediately send information to their cyber investigators and to the Department of Homeland Security.

The importance of this new organization is that it recognizes that cyber villains can, and have, attacked major infrastructures—hospitals, water systems, power grids, banks, 911 services, universities, transportation systems and the like (*Sharing Information Real-Time*, 2005). Eighty-five percent of these infrastructures are owned by private industry (Moore, p.88). It is critical to have real-time attack data from these agencies and organizations.

Another effort aimed at improving the detection of cybercrime is the National Crime Prevention Council's "Take a Bite Out of Cyber Crime" campaign. McGruff, the well-known Crime Dog, will be "Guarding the Home Net," training thousands of Junior Cyber Guards to spot and report cyber crime in homes and businesses across America (*"Take a Bite Out of Cyber Crime" Campaign*, 2006).

If a computer crime is detected, it must be reported and investigated. However, surveys indicate that most computer crime is not reported. The reasons for not reporting computer crimes are varied. The suspect may be an employee with a long record of trusted service; the employer may fear a tie-up of the computer system; management may fear that others will see how easy it is to access the system; or the organization may fear criticism by stockholders.

Several sites and services allow computer-crime victims themselves to get more directly involved and report suspected cases of cybercrime. One example is the Internet Fraud Complaint Center (IFCC), created by the FBI and the National White Collar Crime Center (NW3C). Such agencies staff a variety of cyber-sleuths who are proficient in investigating a range of computer-related crimes.

Investigating Computer Crime

Factors to consider in investigating computer crime include the investigator's knowledge and whether outside expertise is required, the likelihood of the victim or an employee being involved and the difficulty in detecting such crimes. The typical computer "criminal" is a young, middle-class technical person, highly educated, with no prior criminal record, employed by the firm reporting the crime. Therefore, when investigating computer crimes, it is logical to start with a careful check of all employees having access to and knowledge of the computer and its programs. (Note: Investigation as a general responsibility of security officers is discussed in Chapter 10; this discussion focuses only on the investigation of computer crimes because the investigative requirements and skills tend to be somewhat more unique.)

It will be necessary to know exactly how the security system was breached and what type of crime has been committed (altering of data, theft of data, etc.). Often it is necessary to know specifically what information was stolen to obtain a search warrant.

Also, investigation of computer crimes often crosses several jurisdictional boundaries, including international borders: "The global world network, which united millions of computers located in different countries and opened broad opportunities to obtain and exchange information, is used with criminal purposes more and more often" (Golubev, 2005). The anonymity afforded in **cyberspace**, a term used to refer to the artificial world created online and between computer systems, and the lack of physical boundaries makes the Internet an efficient and powerful weapon for criminals: "Investigation and prevention of computer crimes turns into a 'headache.' In the virtual space criminals usually act from sites in other countries. In such cases it is necessary to cooperate with foreign law enforcement agencies" (Golubev). Consequently, security personnel usually do not handle investigation of such crimes alone. Often public law enforcement agencies become involved. The U.S. Secret Service may be of great assistance in apprehending hackers.

"Hacker Hunters" (2005) describes how an elite force took on a tightly organized cybercrime gang known as the ShadowCrew. Like the Mafia, hacker groups have virtual godfathers to map strategy, capos to issue orders and soldiers to do the "dirty work." Their vow of silence is made easier by the anonymity of the Web. And like legitimate businesses, they have gone global. The ShadowCrew had more than 4,000 members operating worldwide, including Americans, Brazilians, Britons, Russians and Spaniards. The hacker-hunting task force used some of the same tactics used to crush organized crime in the

1980s—informants and the cyberworld equivalent of wiretaps. The bust of the ShadowCrew yielded a treasure trove of evidence. The Secret Service uncovered 1.7 million credit-card numbers, access data to more than 18 million e-mail accounts and identity data for thousands of people. The bust yielded evidence against more than 4,000 suspects.

Prosecuting Perpetrators of Computer Crimes

Even when computer crimes are reported and investigated, the majority are not prosecuted. According to *CSO Magazine* (*2005 E-Crime Watch Survey*), 59 percent of 554 respondents reporting electronic crimes or intrusions were not referred for legal action because of insufficient damage levels. One half (50 percent) cited lack of evidence or information to prosecute. Prosecution is also made difficult because of lack of precedents and clear definitions. Frequently what has been stolen is information, which is intangible property and difficult to place a value on.

Legislation Related to Computer Crime

As computer crime has grown, states have passed legislation to deal with it. The laws aim at plugging loopholes in the criminal code, which prohibits traditional theft but does not include stealing electronic impulses from a computer. For example, in a 1976 case, *United States v. John DiGilio et al.*, DiGilio copied investigative records during office time, using a government machine and printing them on government paper, and then sold the records to individuals who were the subjects of the investigation. The Third Circuit Court ruled that not only were government time and equipment illegally used, but also the contents of the documents themselves had been stolen.

Likewise, in *United States v. Paul A. Lambert* (1978), the defendant was convicted of stealing computer-stored information listing names of informants and the status of government drug investigations.

California has enacted a model computer-crime code that includes the following specific violations:

- Publishing access codes through the use of a computer
- Theft of computer data
- Unauthorized interruption of computer service
- Computer tampering
- Unauthorized access to a computer system

The Electronic Communications Privacy Act of 1986   On November 6, 1986, President Ronald Reagan signed into law the Electronic Communications Privacy Act, which makes it illegal to intentionally access, without authorization, a facility providing electronic communication services, or to intentionally exceed the authorization of access to such a facility. The bill is intended to protect the privacy of high-tech communications such as electronic mail, video conference calls, conversations on cellular car phones and computer-to-computer transmissions.

The bill addresses the growing problem of unauthorized persons deliberately gaining access to, and often tampering with, electronic or wire communications that were intended to be private. If such access is for the purpose of commercial advantage, malicious destruction or damage or private commercial gain, the penalties are much more severe than for "other" types of access, which would include that of hackers. Although hackers may feel their actions are harmless, hacking is now illegal. In the view of most computer experts, it has always been unethical.

Schools often fail to include the moral responsibilities of the computer user in their courses on computer programming. Such "ethical education" should be an integral part of a computer literacy program.

Recommendations for a Computer Security Program to Prevent Computer Crime

As with other aspects of physical security, computer security requires strict attention to access control. Access control is a key to preventing the wide range of crimes that can be committed through use of a computer.

Viruses have become a major concern in computer security. Effective software management can protect against viruses. Not borrowing software and always purchasing from reliable vendors are important steps. All new disks should be checked. And educating employees on how viruses can infect a computer and how to avoid this is of utmost importance.

The National Institute of Standards and Technology (NIST) maintains a Computer Security Resource Center (CSRC) through its Computer Security Division. This agency is a valuable resource for any security manager looking to enhance a company's computer security program. Dozens of documents are available online (go to http://csrc.nist.gov) to help businesses of any size address their computer security concerns. One particularly useful NIST report, *Computer Security Incident Handling Guide*, offers recommended practices for security networks, systems and applications, including patch management, host security, network security, malicious code prevention and user awareness and training (Scarfone et al., 2008, p.3–4). Additional steps to take in implementing a layered computer system defense strategy include authentication and authorization guidelines for password policies and physical security measures to restrict access to critical resources (p.6–2).

Individuals who deal with computer software should be familiar with the following guidelines:

- Avoid contact with recording surfaces of computer disks.
- Never use paper clips or rubber bands around computer disks.
- Store computer disks vertically at approximately 70 degrees Fahrenheit.
- Keep computer disks away from strong light, dust and magnetic fields.
- Do not store computer disks in plastic bags.

Preventing Losses by Fire   Although fire is a potential danger for any business, the hazard is greater for computer centers than for most other areas because of the higher probability of fire, the limitations on how such fires can be extinguished and the tremendous losses of hardware, software and data that could result.

Most computer centers have incorporated means to prevent fires—for example, not allowing smoking, using fire-resistant electric wiring and connectors and removing printout sheets (frequently tons of them) as soon as practical. Other common causes are careless cigarette smoking and faulty electrical wiring. However, many managers fail to recognize that the greatest threat is that of a fire that begins outside the computer center. Therefore, an important preventive measure is to decrease fire-loading of all adjacent areas, including not only the rooms that have common walls with the computer center, but those above and below it as well.

The fire detection systems in computer rooms are most frequently ionization-type detectors installed inside each computer or console cabinet, under the floor, in the ceiling and in the storage cabinets. Some detectors are also designed to shut off the electric power and all air-conditioning units. Many are connected to a visual display panel that shows the exact location of the fire.

Although experts disagree on which type of extinguishing system is best for computer rooms, they oppose the water system because of the danger of electrocution and the damage caused by water and steam, and they oppose the carbon dioxide system because of the lethal gas it produces. Nonetheless, many insurance companies require a water sprinkler system in computer centers before they will issue fire coverage.

In addition to some type of automatic extinguishing system, computer rooms should also have portable carbon dioxide extinguishers located throughout the area and floor pullers (handles with rubber suction cups on each end), which should be easily accessible to remove floor tiles should a fire originate under a floor housing the electrical wiring for the hardware.

Establishing a Backup System   Because establishments using EDP are so reliant upon computers, a backup system is usually mandatory. This includes backup power and air conditioning, backup records and access to backup hardware. Some companies keep duplicate tapes or disks of almost every file, whereas others make duplicates of only very important files. The criticality of the information and budgetary considerations will help determine which data should be copied. The copies should be kept in a secure location away from the facility that houses the computer center.

It is usually not economically feasible to have an "extra" computer in the center to serve as a backup. The common practice is for two establishments to enter into a "mutual aid" agreement whereby one company can use the other's computer during a breakdown. Sensible preplanning can greatly reduce losses. The contingency plan must ensure that adequate time will be available for the computer runs critical to the company's operation. For example, if a company's computer breaks down just before it is to run payroll, it is important that the payroll be issued. If a fire should damage the computer to such an extent that it must be replaced, it is important that the payroll be able to be run on a different computer. For such a "mutual aid" system to work, each must be sure that the computers' programs are compatible. This can most effectively be established through a trial run. Each should keep the other posted on any changes in hardware and scheduling requirements that occur. The initial trial run for compatibility should be periodically retested.

Computer centers should also be fully insured. The hardware and software represent a substantial investment and should be insured accordingly against all risks that may be present.

Additional measures to enhance IT security are the focus of Chapter 11.

When a crime has been committed and detected, be it a computer crime or any of the more "traditional" types of crime, *public* law enforcement officers have a duty to arrest the suspects, by force if necessary. When the person who detects a crime is a *private* security officer, however, the authority to arrest, or to even expel or detain, is sometimes less clear.

Expelling, Detaining and Arresting

To prevent trespassing or to control the conduct of persons legally on the premises, private security personnel may be used in retail establishments as plainclothes personnel to detect shoplifters; in industrial complexes as patrols to deter burglars; in offices as access control personnel or at sporting and entertainment events to expel gate-crashers and control or expel unruly spectators. Officers can use reasonable force to do so, if needed. Frequently, however, the person being expelled will consent to leave. In such cases, no force is justified.

 In many states, private security personnel can do the following:

- Detain persons suspected of shoplifting.
- Make a citizen's arrest of persons who commit a misdemeanor in their presence.
- Make a citizen's arrest of persons who commit a felony if they have probable cause.

Every citizen has the right to arrest a person who is committing or has committed a crime and to turn that person over to the local police. This is called a **citizen's arrest**. However, the extent and power of citizen's arrest authority varies from state to state. Arrest power often depends on whether the offense is a felony or a misdemeanor. In most states, citizens can make an arrest for a misdemeanor only if they actually see the crime committed. They can make an arrest for a felony if they know a felony has been committed and they are reasonably sure the person they arrest committed it.

A citizen's arrest is valid only if the person making the arrest intends to turn the suspect over to local law enforcement officers as soon as possible. The arrested person cannot be detained for questioning or to obtain a confession. Security officers can be sued for an unreasonable delay in turning a suspect over to the police.

In many states, exceptions to the preceding restrictions on arrests are made for instances involving shoplifting. Because most cases of shoplifting are misdemeanors and are not always witnessed by security officers, and because many cases of shoplifting are not prosecuted, several states stipulate that a person suspected of shoplifting can be *detained* for questioning and sometimes for searching. Detention differs from formal arrest in that arrest requires the suspect to be turned over to the authorities.

If an arrest is made, the arrested person must be told the reason for the arrest. Often a citizen's arrest certificate is completed by the arresting citizen (see Figure 9.5). A Mississippi appeals court ruled in *Coleman v. Smith* (2005) that

---

Certificate and Declaration of Arrest by Private Person and Delivery of Person so Arrested to Peace Officer

Date _____

Time _____

Place _____

I, _____ , hereby declare and certify that I have arrested

(Name) _____

(Address) _____

for the following reasons _____
_____
_____
_____
_____
_____

and do hereby request and demand that you, _____ , a peace officer, take and conduct this person whom I have arrested to the nearest magistrate, to be dealt with according to law; and if no magistrate can be contacted before tomorrow morning, then to conduct this person to jail for safe keeping until the required appearance can be arranged before such magistrate, at which time I shall be present, and will then and there sign, under oath, the appropriate complaint against this person for the offense which this person has committed, and for which I made this arrest; and I will then and there, or thereafter as soon as this criminal action or cause can be heard, testify under oath of and concerning the facts and circumstances involved herein. I will save said officer harmless from any and all claim for damage of any kind, nature and description arising out of his or her acts at my direction.

Name of private person making this arrest

_____

Address _____

Peace officer witnesses to this statement

_____
_____
_____

Figure 9.5 Sample Citizen's Arrest Form
SOURCE: U.S. Government Printing Office.

because a casino security officer used proper investigative techniques when arresting a casino employee for theft, the employee's claim of false arrest failed.

Use of Force

Reasonable force was introduced in Chapter 4. Policy and training demands for the minimum or least force possible are *not* mandated by federal constitutional law (Means, 2007, p.12). The fact that an officer could have made better choices or decisions in the events preceding the use of force do not render the officer's force response unconstitutional.

 Force can be used only when and to the extent it is necessary. Deadly force can be used only to protect human life.

What is "reasonable" force depends on the nature of the interest being protected, the kind of act being resisted and the specific facts in a given situation.

Additionally, the amount of force allowed often depends on what right is being defended. If property rights are involved, a request for voluntary cooperation should precede any use of force. If only property is involved, the use of deadly force, a gun, for instance, is *not* permitted.

Use of deadly force to prevent a crime is usually allowed only if the crime threatens life and no other means can prevent the crime. However, some jurisdictions do allow use of deadly force to prevent some felonies. The question of use of deadly force most frequently arises in instances when security officers have used a gun to fulfill their responsibilities. Security officers who are required to carry a gun should be thoroughly trained in its use.

Force in *self-defense* is limited to that which is necessary to protect against a threatened injury. It is not reasonable to use force calculated to inflict death or serious bodily harm unless a person believes he or she is in similar danger and there is no other safe means of defense.

Searching

The law clearly establishes the right of an arresting officer to search a person legally taken into custody to determine if the arrested person has a weapon that could cause harm to the officer or others. Any person who has been apprehended for committing a serious crime (a felony) should be searched. Some agencies advise their security officers to treat persons arrested for a felony as though they would kill the officer if given the chance.

 Security officers usually have the authority to search a suspect's person and anything the person is carrying if the officers have a legitimate reason for detaining or arresting the suspect.

Most security searches do not involve arrests, however. They are conducted based on an established policy such as those discussed in Chapter 7 and involve cars, lunchboxes, lockers, purses, bags and boxes. Even without an arrest, the common-law privilege of reclaiming stolen property would tend to support searching people suspected of stealing. It is preferable if consent for the search can be obtained.

 Any search must be conducted reasonably with the least possible use of force, intimidation or embarrassment.

Searches should be conducted in private, except in emergencies. It is best to have the person conducting the search be of the same sex as the suspect, or, if this is not possible, to have a person of the same sex as the suspect be a witness to the search. Any weapons or evidence found during the search should be turned over to the local authorities if the person is arrested by security personnel. Stolen property found during such a search may be reclaimed by the rightful owner if no prosecution is to be undertaken.

In *United States v. Tartaglia* (1989), the court ruled that a railroad investigator and Drug Enforcement Administration (DEA) agents did not violate the defendant's Fourth Amendment rights when they acted on a tip about drugs being transported on an Amtrak train. The investigator and DEA agents located drugs in the defendant's suitcase with the help of narcotics-detecting dogs.

SUMMARY

- Security managers may be called on to enforce such rights as preventing trespassing, controlling the conduct of persons legally on the premises, defending lives or property or preventing the commission of a crime.

- Security managers are also responsible for preventing or reducing losses caused by criminal or civil offenses. The crimes of most concern to private security are larceny/theft, burglary, robbery, trespassing, vandalism, assault, arson and white-collar crime, including embezzlement.

- Losses from larceny/theft might be prevented or reduced by using the basic security equipment and procedures to deter employee pilferage and theft by nonemployees.

- Loss from burglary might be prevented or reduced by installing and using good locks, adequate indoor and outdoor lighting and an alarm system, possibly supplemented with security patrols; keeping valuables in a burglar-resistant safe or vault; keeping a minimum amount of cash on hand; leaving cash registers open and empty at closing time and being sure that all security equipment is functional before leaving.

- Losses from robbery might be prevented or reduced by training employees how to react if a robbery occurs; by not building up cash; by using armed couriers to transport cash; by establishing strict opening and closing procedures and by using extreme caution if someone seeks entrance to the facility after hours.

- Larceny/theft, burglary and robbery are often confused. Larceny/theft is the unlawful taking of the property of another without unlawful entrance or confrontation. Burglary includes unlawful taking and unlawful entry. Robbery includes unlawful taking and confrontation, that is, force or the threat of force.

- Trespassing and vandalism can be prevented or reduced by strict access controls, security lighting, signs and patrols.

- Assaults might be reduced by adequate lighting, patrols, communications systems and escort services.

- Security managers should suspect arson in fires that have more than one point of origin; deviate from normal burning patterns; show evidence of trailers; show evidence of having been accelerated; indicate an abnormal amount of air, fuel or heat present; reveal evidence of incendiary igniters at the point of origin or produce odors or smoke of a color associated with substances not normally present at the scene.

- White-collar crime includes (1) credit-card and check fraud including identity theft; (2) securities theft and fraud; (3) insurance fraud; (4) consumer fraud, illegal competition and deceptive practices; (5) bankruptcy fraud; (6) embezzlement and pilferage; (7) bribes, kickbacks and payoffs; and (8) receiving stolen property.

- The most common types of crimes are employee use of computers for personal reasons, unauthorized access to confidential files and unlawful copying of copyrighted or licensed software. Other security threats to computer centers are theft by fraud or embezzlement (credit-card fraud, telecommunications fraud), hackers, sabotage (viruses/malware, spyware, phishing and spam), employee carelessness or error, and fire.

- Characteristics of computer-related crime include the fact that they are relatively easy to commit, are difficult to detect and most are not prosecuted.

- If criminal activity is suspected or, in fact, observed, in many states, private security personnel can detain persons suspected of shoplifting and make a citizen's arrest.

- Force can be used when and to an extent that is reasonable and necessary. Deadly force can be used only to protect human life.

- Security officers also usually have the authority to search a suspect's person and anything the person is carrying if the officers have a legitimate reason for detaining or arresting the suspect. Any search must be conducted reasonably and with the least possible use of force, intimidation or embarrassment to the suspect.

APPLICATIONS

1. While on patrol for the Smithtown Security Services, Kathy Ross pulls into the yard of a large warehouse where many semitrailer trucks are parked. As she patrols, her vehicle headlights shine on two juveniles hiding behind one of the tractor wheels. She also notices the tire is going flat. As she orders the two juveniles to come out, she sees one of them throw an instrument away. She has them retrieve it and, on inspection, sees it is an ice pick. Further investigation reveals that two tires are flat, both having been punctured by what appears to be an ice pick. Officer Ross arrests the juveniles and takes them to the police station. The youngsters, ages 12 and 13, have had extensive past contacts with police, all as the result of acts of vandalism. As manager of the Smithtown Security Services, how would you evaluate Officer Ross's actions?

2. The office manager of the Downtown Manufacturing Company states to the security manager that she has just apprehended Joe Myers, an employee, carrying an office computer out the side door of the building, and she is detaining him. The office manager demands that the security manager call the police and have Myers charged with robbery. If you were the security manager, how would you respond to this demand?

3. You are the security director called by the president of the Uptown Department Store to investigate the open, empty safe the president discovered when he went into his office. How would you begin the investigation? What information would you need to obtain?

4. As a member of the Housing Authority Security Police, you are confronted with numerous investigations concerning a rash of arson fires. You are requested to prepare a presentation about what the statistics of the current FBI Uniform Crime Report reveal about the patterns, arrests and types of arson most frequently committed. Go online to find the latest FBI Uniform Crime Report and give a presentation to the class as if you were talking to the residents of a public housing complex.

DISCUSSION QUESTIONS

1. Private security officers are sometimes asked to arrest people. As a security director, what policies or guidelines would you adopt to cover these situations?

2. Discuss the advantages and disadvantages of private security officers carrying firearms.

3. How do the arrest powers of private security officers compare with those of public police officers in your state?

4. Have there been recent computer crimes in your area? If so, what did they involve?

5. How reliant is your local bank on a computer system?

REFERENCES

Albrecht, Trenton. *Combating Computer Crime*. Computer Crime Research Center, January 10, 2005.

Anderson, David A. "New Crime Study Pegs Cost at $1.7 Trillion Annually." *Davidson News and Events*, 2007.

Anderson, Kerby. "Cost of Crime in America." Probe Ministeries, 2007.

Baum, Katrina. *Identity Theft, 2004*. (Estimates from the National Crime Victimization Survey). Washington, DC: Bureau of Justice Statistics Bulletin, April 2006. (NCJ 2122113)

"Corporate Takeover: A New Twist on Identity Theft." Washington, DC: Federal Bureau of Investigation Headline Archives, June 18, 2007.

Data Processing Management Association (DPMA). Park Ridge, Illinois.

Donofrio, Andrew. "What Can Be Done about Spam?" *Law Enforcement Technology*, May 2004, pp.86–91.

Eggen, Dan. "Violent Crime Is Up for 2nd Straight Year: Biggest Cities Showed Largest Increase." *Washington Post*, December 19, 2006, p.A01.

Fahim, Kareem. "In the Hottest of Crimes, Trails Are Often Cold." *The New York Times*, May 4, 2006.

Financial Crimes: Report to the Public. Washington, DC: Federal Bureau of Investigation, May 2005.

Fleck, Carole. "Stealing Your Life." *AARP Bulletin*, February 2004, pp.3–4.

Golubev, Vladimir. *International Cooperation in Fighting Cybercrime*. Computer Crime Research Center, April 16, 2005.

"Hacker Hunters." *Business Week*, May 30, 2005.

Majoras, Deborah Platt. "Combating Identity Theft: Partnerships Are Powerful." *The Police Chief*, February 2005, pp.14–15.

Means, Randy. "Least Force? Or Reasonable Force?" *Law and Order*, June 2007, pp.12–14.

Mills-Senn, Pamela. "Swindles, Cons and Rip-Offs." *Law Enforcement Technology*, October 2005, pp.16–26.

Moore, Carole. "Protecting Your Backdoor." *Law Enforcement Technology*, June 2005, pp.80–89.

Naim, Moises. "The Crime Pandemic." *Los Angeles Times*, June 17, 2007.

Scarfone, Karen; Grance, Tim; and Masone, Kelly. *Computer Security Incident Handling Guide*. Gaithersburg, MD: U.S. Department of Commerce, National Institute of Standards and Training, March 2008. (NIST SP800–61-Rev1)

"Senate Judiciary Committee Explores the True Cost of Crime on Society." *NCJA Justice Bulletin*, September 2006, p.4.

Sharing Information Real-Time. Washington, DC: Federal Bureau of Investigation, June 13, 2005.

Special Report on "Phishing." Washington, DC: Department of Justice Criminal Division, no date.

"Take a Bite Out of Cyber Crime" Campaign. Washington, DC: National Crime Prevention Council, 2006.

2005 E-Crime Watch Survey: Summary of Findings. Conducted and printed by *CSO Magazine* in cooperation with the U.S. Secret Service and CERT© Coordination Center. May 3, 2005. http://www.cert.org/archive/pdf/ecrimesummary05.pdf. Accessed August 10, 2005.

Wetzel, Deborah. "Towers of Integrity: Rebuilding Fraud Free." *Security Management*, July 2007, pp.77–82.

Whitlock, Chuck. "The Con Artist of the Future." *The Law Enforcement Trainer*, March/April 2004, pp.11–15.

CASES CITED

Coleman v. Smith, Mississippi Court of Appeals, No. 2004-CA-01918-COA (2005).

United States v. John DiGilio et al., 538 F.2d 972 (1976).

United States v. Paul A. Lambert, 446 F. Supp. 890 (1978).

United States v. Tartaglia, 864 F.2d 837 (1989).

CHAPTER 10

When Prevention Fails
Investigating, Reporting and Testifying

Despite security's best efforts, losses do sometimes occur. When that happens, security must investigate the incident, present their findings in a written report and, if necessary, testify in court should a suspect be arrested and prosecuted.

Do You Know . . .

■ What the primary responsibilities of an investigator are?

■ What the single most important factor in the successful disposition of an incident is?

■ What crimes security personnel are likely to be asked to investigate?

■ How interviewing differs from interrogating?

■ What nonverbal communication includes?

■ What the characteristics of effective notes are?

■ What the characteristics of a well-written report are?

■ What the usual sequence in a trial is?

■ What kinds of statements are inadmissible in court?

■ How to testify most effectively?

■ What strategies can make testifying in court more effective?

■ What defense attorney tactics to anticipate?

Can You Define?

bench trial

chain of custody/ evidence

conclusionary language

connotative words

cross-examination

denotative words

deposition

direct examination

empathy

hot spot

impeaching

interrogatories

jargon

nonverbal communication

predication

the well (in a courtroom)

Introduction

The preceding chapters looked at ways to prevent losses and to ensure a safe, productive workplace. Despite security's best efforts, however, prevention does not always work. When accidents occur or crimes are committed, it is the responsibility of security to investigate, sometimes singly, sometimes in cooperation with government officials or the public police. A key to effective investigation is good communication skills, both verbal (to obtain the needed information) and written (to complete professional reports that convey this information to others). In addition, security officers and managers may be called on to testify in civil or criminal matters in which their employers become involved.

This chapter begins with a brief discussion of the Professional Certified Investigator (PCI) and the characteristics of an effective investigator as well as the responsibilities involved. Next the communication process is described. This is followed by information on investigating accidents, fires and sexual harassment allegations. Then the importance of writing effective reports is described after which an overview of testifying in court is presented. This is followed by examining what happens before the trial and then an in-depth examination of the trial itself. Next, tips for excelling in the courtroom are presented, followed by a discussion of how security personnel might qualify themselves as expert witnesses.

The Professional Certified Investigator (PCI)

To better meet employers' growing demand for effective security investigations, ASIS International has designed a program for the Professional Certified Investigator (PCI) to help ensure that those placed in investigative positions possess the knowledge and skills needed to perform quality work. The examination to become a PCI has three mains sections: (1) case management (about 40 percent of test questions), (2) evidence collection (about 40 percent of test questions with the majority on physical and electronic surveillance) and (3) case presentation (about 20 percent of the test) covering preparing reports and presenting testimony in court (*PCI™ Examination Structure and Content*, 2007).

Responsibilities of Investigators

Investigators have several responsibilities that will vary depending on the focus of the investigation. Sometimes investigators use surveillance to ascertain if safety violations or crimes are occurring. A caution when using video surveillance: Do not violate an employee's privacy rights (recall Chapter 4 on legal liability).

 In most investigations, the primary responsibilities of investigators are to provide emergency assistance, secure the area of an incident, gather evidence and information, record information in photographs, notes and reports and testify about civil and criminal incidents in court.

Investigators may also use the polygraph during the course of an investigation. The Employee Polygraph Protection Act stipulates that a lie detector can be used in the context of an ongoing investigation if the following conditions are met:

- The employer's business suffers the loss or injury, and the wrongdoing was intentional.
- The employee must have had access to the property.
- There must be reasonable suspicion the employee was involved.
- The employee must be given a statement explaining these facts before the test.

 The single most important factor in determining the successful disposition of an incident is the information gathered by the security officer at the time of the initial report.

Specific Investigations

The most frequent investigations conducted by the security department, as shown in Figure 10.1, are employee/internal theft, workplace violence and fraud (*Security Director's News* "Newspoll," 2006, p.31). Because it is such a significant problem, employee/internal theft is discussed in later chapters as it relates to specific organizations. Workplace violence is the focus of Chapter 12. Fraud and background checks have been discussed in previous chapters. This section will examine some of the other common types of incidents security may be called on to investigate: accidents, fires, complaints of sexual harassment, losses, fraud and crimes.

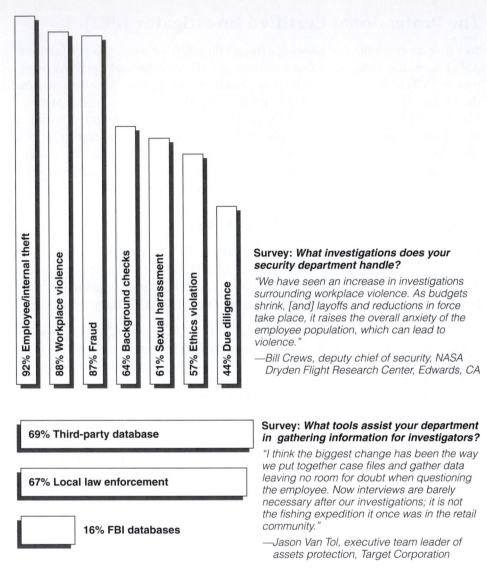

Figure 10.1   Investigations Handled by Security Departments

NOTE: Survey results based on 61 respondents in January.

SOURCE: From "Newspoll" in *Security Director News*, 2006, p.31. Reprinted by permission.

Investigating Accidents

According to OSHA, an accident is any unplanned event that results in personal injury or property damage. When an accident happens, two reasons are often given: the money has not been budgeted for safety equipment or the task had to be done quickly. In reality, however, accidents may not be so simple, and several events can be causes. Three cause levels are found in most accidents: basic, indirect and direct (see Figure 10.2).

It is easy to say the "cause" of an accident was that the employee was careless and did not follow safety precautions. But this will not eliminate future accidents of a similar nature. Accident investigations determine how and why

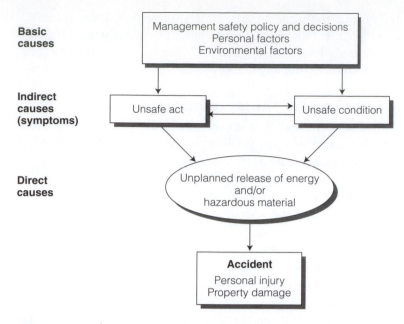

Basic causes

Management safety policy and decisions
Personal factors
Environmental factors

Indirect causes (symptoms)

Unsafe act ⟷ Unsafe condition

Direct causes

Unplanned release of energy
and/or
hazardous material

Accident
Personal injury
Property damage

Figure 10.2 Three Cause Levels of Accidents

SOURCE: U.S. Department of Labor, Mine Safety and Health Administration Safety Manual No. 10, *Accident Investigation*, Revised 1990.

people, equipment, supplies or surroundings fail to behave or react as expected. Careful investigation may prevent similar, or even more disastrous, accidents.

The investigator in charge defines the scope of the investigation; selects the investigators and assigns specific tasks to each (preferably in writing); visits the accident site to get updated information; inspects the accident site; secures the area without disturbing the scene unless a hazard exists; prepares the necessary sketches and photographs, labels each carefully and keeps accurate records; and interviews each victim and witness as well as those present before the accident and those who arrived shortly after the accident.

Investigators must determine what was not normal before the accident, where the abnormality occurred, when it was first noticed and how it occurred. After analyzing the preceding, investigators must determine why the accident occurred, a likely sequence of events and probable causes (direct, indirect, basic), alternative sequences, the most likely sequence of events and the most probable causes.

Next investigators should conduct a postinvestigation briefing and prepare a summary report, including a description of the accident, with damage estimates; normal operating procedures; maps (local and general); location of the accident site; list of witnesses and events that preceded the accident and recommended actions to prevent a recurrence.

Investigating Fires

The role of security should a fire occur is vital. Unconfined smoke and flames must be dealt with immediately. The first step is to call the fire department. After the fire is contained investigators should cordon off the area, record names of persons at and around the scene and the time(s) these people are observed, take photos and videotape, talk to witnesses, determine what started the fire, assess the damage caused, determine what can be done to prevent further damage and notify the insurance company if appropriate.

Investigating Complaints of Sexual Harassment

Several high-profile incidents of alleged sexual harassment have focused attention on this issue. Sexual harassment is illegal based on Title VII of the Civil Rights Act of 1964 and amendments in 1972 and 1991, as well as state and local laws. The Equal Employment Opportunity Commission (EEOC) defines sexual harassment as unwelcome sexual advances, requests for sexual favors, and other verbal or physical contact of a sexual nature made implicitly or explicitly as a condition of employment.

Sexual harassment has two conditions. First, it must occur in the workplace or an extension of the workplace. Second, it must be of a sexual nature that is nonconsensual and does not include romance. Sexual harassment includes sex-oriented comments or humor, subtle or overt pressure for sexual activity, physical contact such as patting or brushing against another person's body, demands for sexual favors that affect an individual's position or salary, posting sexually graphic materials and having different expectations for men and women.

Managers, including security managers, must be knowledgeable of circumstances and conditions comprising sexual harassment and have policies in place to deal with it should it occur. All employees should have copies of the policy and should know the procedure to file a complaint. Managers must also know how to avoid harassment in their own behavior.

Most sexual harassment complaints involve one person's word against another's. Therefore, the investigator's role is to determine who is being truthful. Suggestions for investigating a sexual harassment complaint include the following:

- Determine the relationship of the victim and the suspect.
- Determine the exact nature of the harassment; was it verbal, physical, or both?
- Determine how long the harassment has been occurring.
- Determine if there have been witnesses to the harassment.
- Determine if other complaints of harassment have been made against the suspect.
- Obtain the suspect's version of the harassment.
- Call the personnel officer if company policy requires.
- Refer the incident to the appropriate person or agency.

Interviewers should avoid asking questions that directly address the allegations, focusing instead on the general interaction. Recommendations should be made to avoid future charges. In *Austin v. Norfold Southern Corp.* (2005), a federal appeals court ruled that an employee could not prevail on a harassment claim against her employer because the company took immediate and effective action to respond to her complaints. In this case a female employee complained that she was subjected to offensive graffiti and inappropriate comments from co-workers. After the complaint, company representatives met with the employee, posted notices explaining their harassment policy, interviewed the alleged harassers, inspected the grounds for graffiti and included harassment training in all safety training programs.

Investigating Losses

Any losses that occur should be thoroughly investigated. This sometimes involves cooperation with local authorities, with police and fire departments, and with representatives of the Occupational Safety and Health Administration (OSHA). Careful records of losses should be kept so problems can be more easily identified. Security files should be well organized and current. Internal data on losses can be used to develop, improve and evaluate the security system.

Investigating Crimes

Private security plays an important role in investigating both civil and criminal complaints. Criminal investigations conducted by security officers are usually quite different from those conducted by public police. Investigations by security personnel should be based on adequate **predication,** that is, the total set of circumstances that would lead a reasonable, prudent and professionally trained person to believe an offense has occurred, is occurring or will occur. Predication is not as strong as the probable cause required for public police officers to arrest someone, but it must be more than mere suspicion.

Effective investigators are knowledgeable, creative, patient and persistent (Bennett and Hess, 2007, p.9). They remain open-minded, objective and logical while gathering information, and they are skilled in interacting across gender, ethnic, generational, social and political group lines (p.9).

 Among the most common crimes security personnel will be asked to investigate are assault, breach of peace/disturbing the peace/disorderly conduct, burglary/ unlawful entry/breaking and entering, theft, fraud, trespassing and vandalism.

Investigating fraud is an issue for every company, but insurance companies face a dual challenge as they must be concerned not only with typical employee fraud but also with fraud by customers (Magno, 2005, p.91). In many insurance organizations the special investigation unit (SIU) concentrates on fraudulent claims made by customers, and the internal investigative group focuses on fraudulent acts committed by employees. It is often in the best interests of the company to encourage the SIU and the internal investigative group to cooperate rather than to compete, trying to best each other to show their importance to the company (Magno).

Obtaining Evidence

Processing physical evidence includes discovering or recognizing it; collecting, recording and identifying it; packing, conveying and storing it; examining it; exhibiting it in court; and disposing of it when the case is closed. Evidence must be properly packaged and stored securely to retain its integrity and keep it in substantially the same condition in which it was found. Custody of the evidence must be documented at every stage of the investigation. This is called the **chain of custody** or **chain of evidence.**

Crime scene photographs have typically been admitted into evidence, but this is changing with the advent of digital images, which raise concerns because the images can be readily manipulated. The chain of custody is critical in digital photographs or surveillance tapes: "Some methods for ensuring the authenticity of digital images, such as watermarking, are starting to appear, but these methods are proprietary and, thus, nonstandard" (Davison, 2005, p.140).

Communication Skills: Obtaining Information

Security professionals are also in the communications business. Of all the skills needed to be an effective manager, skill in communicating is the most vital. In addition, a large part of security work at all levels involves some form of communication. Security managers and on-line officers routinely communicate in every facet of their jobs, not only in their interactions with those for whom they work and their employees, but also in their interactions with the public and with professionals in other fields.

Effective communication can produce several positive outcomes. It can be used to inform, guide, reassure, persuade, motivate, negotiate or diffuse. In contrast, ineffective communication can result in confusion, false expectations, wrong conclusions, negative stereotypes, frustrations, anger, hostility, aggression and even physical confrontations.

Interviewing and Interrogating

Security personnel may be called on to interview witnesses and interrogate suspects.

 An *interview* is a controlled conversation with witnesses to or victims of a crime. An *interrogation* is a controlled conversation with persons suspected of direct or indirect involvement in a crime.

Interviewing witnesses and interrogating suspects require often overlapping, but sometimes markedly different, approaches (McDonough, 2005, p.88):

Investigators commonly conduct both conventional interviewing and the more challenging intensive interrogation, often called "adversarial interviewing." These functions are part of a single process, but they use distinct approaches and serve different objectives.

Interviews generally gather basic information, facts and background to further an investigation. They should involve all eye-witnesses and other people who have information bearing on the case. Another reason for conducting an interview is to obtain background information about procedures and processes.

For example, in a case of missing funds from a company's main cash vault, it may be important to determine the standard process used to transfer cash to the vault if that appears to be the process that was exploited. In this way, the investigator can later determine, when questioning the vault staff, whether everyone followed the procedures and if anyone was being deceptive about the normal process.

Effective interviews are conducted in a friendly but businesslike tone, and are not adversarial—at least not at the start. It is simply a matter of asking questions from willing subjects to gather information. In addition, interviews commonly identify other people to question and help determine which subjects show signs of hiding or misrepresenting information. These people are candidates for interrogation.

Theoretically, at least, no one is considered a suspect at the beginning of a case, although many investigators believe they know who is guilty even before conducting the first interview.

An interrogation, unlike an interview, is designed to elicit information from a subject who is either the prime suspect or someone who might want to shield the guilty party and thus does not wish to disclose information. It is the uncooperative nature of the subject that distinguishes interrogations from interviews. They do not all involve suspects, but they do all involve someone with something to hide.[1]

McDonough (p.86) suggests: "An investigator should never begin either an interview or an interrogation without a strategy. Elements include deciding on an approach, studying the facts of the case, establishing timing, finding an apt setting, and knowing what you hope to gain from witnesses and the specific sequence of questions you will ask."

Possible Restrictions on Interrogations   Public law enforcement officers are required to inform suspects of their constitutional rights *before* any interrogation occurs. The well-known Miranda decision *(Miranda v. State of Arizona,* 1966) has specifically protected these rights for more than four decades.

Some states have ruled that Miranda warnings do not apply to private security interviews because they are not done under the coercive threat of arrest by the police. In a California case *(In re Deborah C.,* 1981), a store detective placed a suspect under arrest without advising the suspect of her Miranda rights. The California Supreme Court held that Miranda warnings are not required because private security officers "don't enjoy the psychological advantage of official authority, which is a major tool of coercion." Employers, however, can use other forms of coercion, most notably the threat of terminating employment. On the other hand, businesses exist to make a profit and are not obligated to put the welfare of an employee above that of the company. A correlation often exists between the level of position, amount of power and socioeconomic standing of the employee in the company, and the subsequent amount of disciplinary action received. The higher a person's position in a company, the less disciplinary action is likely to be applied.

Despite the lack of an official ruling, many courts and judges require security officers to notify a suspect of their rights on the basis that they are, in reality, attempting to enforce the law, and in doing so must abide by public law enforcement standards. For example, in *People v. Haydel* (1973), the court ruled, in effect, that private store detectives used state law as authority and, therefore, were acting as agents of the state in the same manner as public police officers:

---

[1]SOURCE: From "Asking the Hard Questions" by Edward McDonough. © 2005 ASIS International, 1625 Prince Street, Alexandria, VA 22314. Reprinted by permission from the July 2005 issue of *Security Management* magazine.

The exclusionary rule is designed to deter illegal conduct by public officials, hence it is inoperative when the evidence is gained by a private citizen not acting as a public agent. The California Supreme Court has recognized, nevertheless, that the well trained and well financed private security forces of business establishments are heavily involved in law enforcement, that state laws such as Penal Code, Section 837, the citizen's arrest statute, blur the line between public and private law enforcement.

Nonverbal Communication

A security manager's physical appearance—a suit and tie or a business-like dress—conveys a message of professionalism. Likewise, security officers' physical appearance—the uniform and badge, sometimes a gun—conveys a message of authority even before they ever say a word. This "image" can be intimidating to many people. A harsh look can add to the intimidation; a smile can weaken or even dispel it. Security officers should be aware of the nonverbal messages they send and use them to their advantage.

 Nonverbal communication includes eye movements, facial expressions, posture, gestures, clothing, tone of voice, proximity and touch.

Listening

Too often people simply hear, but they do not listen. The following guidelines can improve listening:

- Be interested in the person and the message. Be empathetic. Show you care.
- Be less self-centered.
- Resist distractions.
- Do not let personal biases turn you off.
- Prepare to listen. Clear your mind of other things.

A key to effective communication is to have empathy for the person with whom you are communicating. This is not the same as sympathy. **Empathy** means you understand where the other person is coming from, whether you agree with it or not.

Other Sources of Information

Investigators may access several other sources of information beyond those they have identified as having direct knowledge about the case. A survey of security directors showed 69 percent of investigators used a third-party database, 67 percent received information from local law enforcement and 16 percent turned to the FBI databases for assistance in their investigations (*Security Director News* "Newspoll," 2006, p.31).

Security professionals with investigative skills can team up with information technology (IT) experts to enhance the power and success level of their investigation through a process called *data mining*: "Digital data helps detectives go well beyond physical evidence at the scene, such as fingerprints and clothing fibers, to less obvious relational information that can reveal the guilty party through telling patterns of behavior" (Harold, 2006, p.66). While investigators in the past often found success by burning a lot of shoe leather and knocking on a lot of doors, today's effective investigators know how to make the most of technology and are able to mine data for the leads and facts needed to solve cases (Harold, p.72).

Mapping is another useful tool for solving crimes. Although usually used in geographic areas, mapping can also be used by large companies with numerous locations. Mapping is one way to identify crime hot spots. While no common definition of *hot spot of crime* exists, it is commonly understood that "a **hot spot** is an area that has a greater than average number of criminal or disorder events, or an area where people have a higher than average risk of victimization" (Eck et al., 2005, p.2).

Communication Skills: Providing Information

External communications may occur with the general public, with the media or with the courts. It includes all interactions with agencies and individuals outside the employing agency. These communications are critical to effectively conducting business as well as to a sound public relations program.

Most security managers have a policy that front-line officers are not to issue statements or opinions about any activities or conditions related to their duties to any member of the media. Such requests are to be referred to the security manager who, in turn, may refer them to the business's public relations department.

All incidents are to be reported in writing. Some facilities use an incident report log such as that shown in Figure 10.3. This log contains a detailed, chronological description of everything the security officer saw and did during the shift—for example, opening or locking doors, observing minor water leaks or mechanical malfunctions, receiving special requests, escorting individuals to specific locations and noting any significant incidents that occurred.

In addition, officers may complete incident reports for any potential, suspected or actual security risks (see Figure 10.4). Most such reports will deal with a situation that requires a corrective action to be taken. When the corrective action has been taken, a follow-up report is written on a form such as the one shown in Figure 10.5. If no follow-up or report is needed, that should be stated in the incident report.

The content of such reports should be kept confidential, and the reports themselves should be protected from access by unauthorized people. Before looking at how to write effective reports, consider the basis for most reports—effective notes.

Taking Notes

Notes are a permanent aid to memory. As soon as anything of an emergency nature is attended to, all relevant information should be recorded legibly, in ink, in a notebook. Good notes help security personnel remember conditions or incidents they observed, actions they took and actions others took. They form the basis for official reports and may be of great assistance should a court appearance be required.

The ABCs of effective notes are accuracy, brevity, clarity and completeness. Accuracy is ensured by repeating information back, spelling names and verifying numbers. Brevity means conciseness and is accomplished by omitting the articles, *a, an* and *the*; by omitting all other unnecessary words; and by using common abbreviations. Commonly used abbreviations in security notes are summarized in Table 10.1 on page 287.

\multicolumn{3}{c}{**Security Services Daily Activity Log**}			

Officer			Badge #	Shift Time	Date
Assigned Area					

Time	Detailed Activities

Be sure all information is detailed and accurate

This report has been read and approved by _____ Date _____

Figure 10.3   Incident Report Log

Clarity in notes means recording specific, concrete facts; using diagrams or sketches if the scene or incident being described is complex; and writing legibly so the notes can be understood later when converting them into a written report. Completeness means the investigator has received answers to the questions Who? What? Where? When? How? and Why?

 Effective notes are accurate, brief, clear and complete.

Corporate Incident Report

File # _____

Today's date _____ Date incident occurred _____

Incident summary _____
_____
_____

Complete details of event (date, time, individuals, places, situations)
_____
_____
_____
_____
_____
_____
_____
_____

(continue on extra sheet of paper if required)

External involvement (describe location, individual statements, contacts, include law
enforcement contacts, etc.) _____
_____
_____
_____

Estimated loss _____ Estimated recovery _____
            (dollars, assets, etc.)

Planned action to resolve incident _____
_____
_____

Individual responsible for follow-up _____
Reported by_____ Phone (____)_____
Name(s) of managers notified _____

Describe and attach any additional explanations and supporting documents.

Incident information should be protected and held in strict confidence.

Figure 10.4   Incident Report Form

Good notes should also be objective and limited primarily to facts, with minimal reference to speculation or personal opinion. The importance of good notes cannot be overstated—they are the foundation for a good report.

Writing Reports

Most people enter private security for the activity and excitement. They often do not realize the amount of paperwork involved. For almost every action private security officers take, they must write a report. Security managers, too, write much.

Corporate Incident Report Follow-up

Original Incident Report File # _____

Today's date _____ Date of original report _____

This incident was reported and investigated by (include dates) _____

_____

_____

_____

Have or will any disciplinary actions take(n) place as a result of this incident? _____

Explain: _____

_____

_____

_____

Describe any involvement by external organization/law enforcement agencies

_____

_____

_____

What resources, assets, or revenues were lost/recovered? _____

_____

_____

Describe any personal injury, actual or threatened, relating to this incident _____

_____

_____

What lessons have been learned/or recommendations made as a result of this incident?

_____

_____

List any other actions that have been or will be taken as a result of this incident _____

_____

_____

Comments: _____

_____

_____

Attach copies of investigations, supporting documentation, or other information pertinent to this incident.

Figure 10.5   Incident Report Follow-Up Form

Two major types of reports are administrative and operational. *Administrative reports* deal with the routine functioning of the security department and include such items as policies and procedures, reports on proper uniform, reporting procedures, security surveys, evaluation reports and performance reports. *Operational reports* deal with the actions taken by security officers during specific events or incidents. Most agencies have their own forms and procedures for completing operational reports, but many of the forms have common elements. For example, a typical format places at the top of the report form a series of boxes to be completed by the officer (see Figure 10.6).

If the department uses report forms that include boxes and blanks to be filled in, they should *all be filled in*, even if it means writing "N/A" for not applicable or "Unknown" if the information is unknown. After the basic information is recorded, the officer must write a narrative account of the incident in the space following the boxes.

Table 10.1   Common Abbreviations Used in the Security Profession

A&A	Assisted and advised	Off.	Officer
AKA	Also known as (alias)	Rec'd.	Received
Asst.	Assistant	R/F	Right front
Att.	Attempt	R/O	Reporting officer
Dept.	Department	R/R	Right rear
Dist.	District	S/B	Southbound
DOB	Date of birth	Subj.	Subject
DOT	Direction of travel	Sup.	Supervisor
E/B	Eastbound	Susp.	Suspect
GOA	Gone on arrival	S/W	Stationwagon
Hdqtrs.	Headquarters	UNK	Unknown
Hwy.	Highway	UTL	Unable to locate
I.D.	Identification	V.	Victim
L/F	Left front	Viol.	Violation
Lic.	License	W/B	Westbound
L/R	Left rear	Wit.	Witness
Memo	Memorandum	WFA*	White female adult
N/A	Not applicable	WFJ	White female juvenile
N/B	Northbound	WMA*	White male adult
NFD	No further description	WMJ	White male juvenile
NMN	No middle name		

*The "W" indicates the race. It is appropriate to substitute "B" for black, "A" for Asian, "H" for Hispanic and "NA" for Native American.

A report is a permanent written record that communicates important facts to be used in the future. Security officers' reports are *used,* not simply filed away. Swobodzinski (2007, p.48) stresses the importance of a well-written report with the recommendation: "It's a good rule of thumb to write your report as if it will end up before the U.S. Supreme Court one day."

Investigative reports tell the reader about the writer: "Juries and even district attorneys equate sloppy writing with sloppy thinking and careless investigative methods" (Sievert, 2004, p.35). More importantly: "You can do the greatest investigation and collar a criminal. But if can't write a good report that says what you did, and be accurate, clear and concise, you're not going to get a conviction" (Kanable, 2005, p.168).

Characteristics of a Well-Written Report

Because reports are so important in the security profession, it is vital that private security officers develop skill in writing effective reports. Such reports will not only communicate information better, but also reflect positively on the officer's education, competence and professionalism.

 A well-written report is factual, accurate, objective, complete, concise, clear, correct, in simple standard English, legible and on time (Hess and Orthmann, 2008, pp.38, 52).

Canterbury Downs
Security Report

Date	
ICR #	

Classification—Type of Crime or Incident	Officer's Name

Time of Incident	Person Reporting	Address	Phone #	Time Reported

Subject

Name—Last–First–Middle (AKA)	M.R.C. # Year

Sex	Race	D.O.B.	Age	Height	Weight	Hair	Eyes	Social Security #

Employer	Barn # & Tack Room	Occupation	Res. Phone	Bus. Phone

Residence Address—City–State–Zip

Name & Address of Suspect(s)

Suspects (1) _____

(2) _____

Name & Address of Witnesses

Witnesses (1) _____

(2) _____

Details: _____

_____

_____

_____

_____

_____

_____

_____

_____

_____

Page _____ of _____

Officer's Signature

Badge Number

Figure 10.6   Canterbury Downs Operational Report Form

SOURCE: Canterbury Downs Race Track, Shakopee, MN.

Factual   The basic purpose of any operational report is to record the facts. A *fact* is a statement that can be proven. (It may be proven false, but the statement is still classified as a fact.) For example, the man is wearing a black leather jacket that has a bulge in the pocket. Facts need to be distinguished from two other types of statements: inferences and opinions. *Inferences* (sometimes called *judgments*) are statements about the unknown based on the known—they use logic. For example, the bulge in the man's pocket is a gun. Notice that this inference will become a fact *if* the matter is pursued, that is, if the person wearing the black leather jacket is frisked and a gun is, in fact, discovered—or not. Any inferences in official reports should be clearly identified as such.

An *opinion* is a statement of personal belief. For example, people who wear black leather jackets are hoodlums. Opinions have no place in official reports. *A well-written report is factual. It contains no opinions.*

Incident reports must not contain assumptions or **conclusionary language**. Among the most common problems here are making statements about what someone can or cannot do. For example, it is a conclusion to write in an incident report, "The man *could not* answer my questions." The factual report would instead say, "The man *did not* answer my questions." Even clearer, however, would be to say, "The man shrugged and said nothing."

Another common problem is the phrase "signed by" as in, "The camera pass authorization was signed by John Doe." Unless the report writer actually saw John Doe sign the authorization, the report should read, "The camera pass authorization was signed John Doe." The little word *by* can get an officer into a lot of trouble on the witness stand.

Other problems arise when officers write about someone's state of mind, for example, saying a person is *nervous, frightened, uncooperative, belligerent.* These are all conclusions on the officer's part. The report should contain facts that lead to the conclusions. For example, rather than saying a person is *nervous*, describe the person's appearance and actions: "The man began to tremble, he began to perspire heavily and his voice wavered. He repeatedly glanced over his shoulder at the door."

Accurate   An effective report accurately records the correct time and date, correct names of all persons involved, correct phone numbers and addresses and exact descriptions of property, vehicles and suspects. To be accurate, a writer must be specific. For example, it is more accurate to describe a suspect as "approximately 5 feet tall" than as "short."

Objective   Reports must be not only factual and accurate, but also objective. It is possible to include only factual statements in a report and still not be objective. Objective means fair and impartial. Lack of objectivity can result from two things: poor word choice and omission of specific facts.

Objectivity is attained by keeping to the facts, using words with nonemotional overtones and including both sides of the account. Word choice is extremely important in objective writing. A reader would react to the following three sentences very differently:

The man cried.   The man wept.   The man blubbered.

Words that have little emotional effect, for example, *cried*, are called **denotative words.** The denotative meaning of a word is its objective meaning. In contrast, words that have an emotional effect are called **connotative words,** for example, *wept* and *blubbered*. The connotative meaning of a word includes its positive or negative overtones.

Complete   An effective incident report contains answers to at least six basic questions: who, what, when, where, why and how. Even if included in the blanks and boxes at the top of a report form, all relevant details should also be included in the narrative portion of the report. Being thorough in the report is crucial, as what officers write stays with them forever: "The words on the paper cannot be changed, and an omission of critical details cannot later be added to a report without calling the report's veracity into doubt" (Scarry, 2007, p.68). What officers fail to report could have extremely negative consequences in a lawsuit (Scarry).

A subelement of completeness is being reader friendly, meaning the "stock" information entered into the boxes or blanks at the top of the form is also included in the narrative of the report. It is inconsiderate of the reader for the writer to begin a narrative: "On the above date, at the above-specified time, the above-named suspect. . . ." The narrative should be able to stand alone. For example, the same narrative might begin like this: "On December 12, 2008, at 2200 hours, the suspect, Jack Jones, was. . . ."

Concise   To be concise is to make every word count. Reports will be effective if they include *all* relevant information in as few words as possible. This does not mean, however, omitting important details, or leaving out words such as *a*, *an* and *the*, as is acceptable in notes. Wordiness can be reduced in two basic ways: (1) leaving out unnecessary information and (2) using as few words as possible, omitting "empty words." For example, in the phrase "blue in color" the words "in color" are empty—blue *is* a color. Following are some wordy phrases and their more concise counterparts:

made note of the fact that = noted

in view of the fact that = because

square in shape = square

month of April = April

Clear   Statements in a report should have only one interpretation. For example, "The man was tall" is open to interpretation, but the statement "The man was 6'11"" is not. Or consider this statement: "The security officer saw the intruder on the elevator and he fired." *Who* fired—the officer or the intruder? The sentence is not clear.

Sometimes unclear writing produces unintentional humor. Consider the following examples:

- Three cars were reported stolen by ABC Security yesterday.
- Here are some suggestions for handling obscene phone calls from the security manager.
- As the unauthorized person came toward me in the dark hallway, I hit him with my flashlight.
- Guilt, vengeance and bitterness can be emotionally destructive to line staff. You must get rid of them.

To write clearly, keep descriptive words and phrases close to the words they describe. For example, lack of clarity is seen in this statement: "He placed the gun into the holster which he had just fired." It was not the holster he had just fired, it was the gun. It would be clearer to say, "He placed the gun which he had just fired into the holster."

Yet another way to achieve clarity in writing is to use short sentences, organized into short paragraphs. Sentences that are too long are difficult to read. Likewise, paragraphs should be relatively short, usually five to ten sentences. The reports should be logically organized. Most reports commonly begin with "when" and "where," and then tell "who" and "what." The "what" should be in chronological order, that is, going from the beginning to the end without skipping back and forth. Each question to be answered in the report should be contained in its own paragraph. It is also reader friendly to skip a line between paragraphs.

Mechanically Correct   A well-written report is mechanically correct. Specific rules of English must be followed when notes (or the spoken word) are transferred into a written report. These include rules for spelling, capitalization and punctuation. Arp (2007, p.101) asserts spelling is the most important part of writing. He recommends that if you cannot spell a word, do not use it.

In Plain, Standard English   Every profession has its own **jargon**, or specialized language, which is fine for short, quick communication. But it has no place in reports that will be read by people with little or no knowledge of that jargon. Likewise, many writers tend to use big words thinking that will impress the reader. Moore (2004, p.266) gives the example of an officer who wrote that the suspect had been "acting erotically" when what he really meant "acting erratically." The officer should have used a word he understood. A good writer writes to *express*, not to *impress*.

In addition, just as there are rules for spelling, capitalization and punctuation, there are rules for what words are used when. For example, it is "standard" to say *he doesn't* rather than *he don't*, or *I saw it* rather than *I seen it*.

Legible and on Time   A well-written report is legible. It must also be on time. It does little good to learn to write well if no one can read it or if the report is turned in after the need for it is gone.

Evaluating Reports

A checklist such as that in Figure 10.7 might be used to evaluate reports. If a security director determines that the writing level of the staff needs improvement, enlisting a consultant to conduct a report writing workshop or other writing course is highly advised.

In addition to writing effective reports, security professionals may be required to testify in court.

Testifying in Court

The importance of effective investigations and professional-quality reports is never greater than when an incident ends up in court. The case may be a civil matter with the employer and possibly security personnel as defendants. Or it may be a criminal trial where security personnel testify on the side of the prosecution. In either event, it is critical that security personnel be well prepared, appear

Evaluation Checklist for Reports

- Is the report:
  - factual?
  - accurate?
  - objective?
  - complete?
  - concise?
  - clear
  - legible?

- Does the report use:
  - first person?
  - active voice?
  - correct modification?
  - correct pronoun reference?
  - parallel sentence structure?

- Are the sentences effective with:
  - no fragments?
  - no run-on sentences?
  - similar ideas combined into single sentences?

- Are the sentences mechanically correct in terms of:
  - spelling?
  - use of apostrophes?
  - abbreviations?
  - numbers?
  - capitalization?
  - punctuation?

- Are the sentences grammatically correct in terms of:
  - use of pronouns?
  - agreement of subject and verb?
  - use of adjectives and adverbs?
  - use of negation?
  - use of articles?

- Does the report allow the reader to visualize what happened?

Figure 10.7 Evaluation Checklist for Reports

SOURCE: From Kären M. Hess and Christine H. Orthmann, *For the Record: Report Writing in Law Enforcement*, 6th edition (Innovative Systems Publishers, Inc., 2008) p.208. Reprinted by permission.

professional and act professionally. Ideally, all security personnel should attend a few court trials in which they are *not* involved to get a feel for what happens.

Before a trial, interrogatories and/or depositions may be used. **Interrogatories** are a series of questions to which a defendant is asked to respond. A **deposition** is like a mini-trial where the defendant's statements are recorded verbatim. Nyberg (2006, p.20) stresses: "Do yourself and the prosecutor a favor by making sure to review the deposition so you don't make any unintentional missteps during the trial." Preparation plays the biggest part in an officer's success on the witness stand (Nyberg, p.22). The more prepared the officer is, the more confident he or she will appear—and be—in front of a jury and the less likely to fall victim to the many tricks the defense has planned.

Thorough *preparation* should begin with a review of all notes and reports related to the case. If possible, discuss the case with the prosecutor beforehand and anticipate any problems that might arise with the testimony.

Appearance is also very important. In most instances security managers appear at trials in business clothes, whereas officers appear in their uniforms. *Behavior and attitude* are critical in effective testimony. Security personnel should not appear to "know it all" or take the process personally. They should speak clearly and loudly enough so everyone in the courtroom can hear the testimony. They should address individuals by the appropriate title, for example, "Your honor" and "sir."

The defense attorney will make every effort to discredit security's testimony. Discrediting testimony is technically known as "**impeaching** the witness." It is not quite so difficult when the security officer is on the side of the prosecution, having important information about a crime that has been committed. It is much more difficult if the security manager or officer is the defendant, being sued for some action.

The Trial [2]

The main participants in the trial are the judge, jury members, attorneys, the defendant and witnesses. The *judge* presides over the trial, rules on the admissibility of evidence and procedures, keeps order, interprets the law for the jurors and passes sentence if the defendant is found guilty.

The *jurors* hear and weigh the testimony of all witnesses. Jurors consider many factors other than the words spoken. The attitude and behavior of witnesses, suspects and attorneys are constantly under the jury's scrutiny. Jurors notice how witnesses respond to questions and their attitudes toward the prosecution and the defense. They reach their verdict based on what they see, hear and feel during the trial. Typical jurors will have had limited or no experience with the criminal justice system outside of what they have read in the newspaper and seen on television.

Legal counsel presents the prosecution and defense evidence before the court and jury. Lawyers act as checks against each other and present the case as required by court procedure and the rulings of the presiding judge.

Defendants may or may not take the witness stand. If they do so, they must answer all questions put to them. They may not use the Fifth Amendment as a reason for not answering. *Witnesses* present the facts personally known to them. Figure 10.8 shows the relationships among the participants in a trial.

Sequence of a Criminal Trial

If the trial is before a judge *without a jury*, called a **bench trial**, the prosecution and the defense make their opening statements directly to the court. The opening statements are brief summaries of what the prosecution plans to prove against the defendant and what the defense plans to do to challenge the prosecution's allegations. In a *jury trial*, the jury is selected and then the opening statements are made by both counsels before the judge and jury.

 The sequence in a criminal trial is as follows:

- Jury selection.
- Opening statements by the prosecution and the defense.
- Presentation of the prosecution's case.
- Presentation of the defense's case.
- Closing statements by the prosecution and the defense.
- Instructions to the jury.
- Jury deliberation to reach a verdict.
- Reading of the verdict.
- Acquittal or passing of sentence.

The prosecution presents its case first. Witnesses for the prosecution are sworn in by the court, and the testimony of each is taken by direct examination through questions asked by the prosecuting attorney. **Direct examination**

---

[2]The description of the trial is adapted from *Criminal Investigation*, 8th edition, pp.619–629, by Wayne W. Bennett and Kären M. Hess. Belmont, CA: Thomson Wadsworth, 2007. Reprinted by permission.

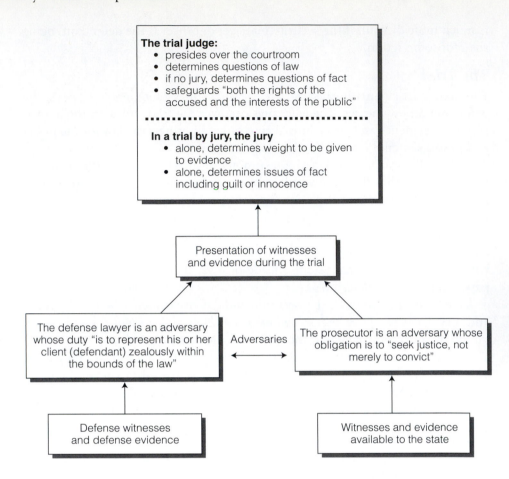

The trial judge:
- presides over the courtroom
- determines questions of law
- if no jury, determines questions of fact
- safeguards "both the rights of the accused and the interests of the public"

In a trial by jury, the jury
- alone, determines weight to be given to evidence
- alone, determines issues of fact including guilt or innocence

Presentation of witnesses and evidence during the trial

The defense lawyer is an adversary whose duty "is to represent his or her client (defendant) zealously within the bounds of the law"

Adversaries

The prosecutor is an adversary whose obligation is to "seek justice, not merely to convict"

Defense witnesses and defense evidence

Witnesses and evidence available to the state

In most civil and criminal jury trials, the names and addresses of jurors are available from public records for people with the interest and knowledge of how to go about obtaining them. It does not occur to most people sitting on juror panels that this could be a problem. However, jurors sitting on criminal cases where defendants are potentially dangerous or retaliatory should have some concerns for their families and themselves.

Trial courts can restrict the disclosure of juror information if the court determines that jurors are in need of protection. Courts have held that factors that could justify restricting jury information include ". . . but are not limited to: (1) the defendant's involvement in organized crime; (2) the defendant's participation in a group with the capacity to harm jurors; (3) the defendant's past attempts to interfere with the judicial process; and (4) extensive publicity that could enhance the possibility that jurors' names would become public and expose them to intimidation or harassment." *United States v. Darden*, 70 F.3d 1507, 1532 (8th Cir. 1995); *United States v. Ross*, 33 F.3d at 1520.

Figure 10.8 Relationships among Participants in a Trial

SOURCE: Thomas J. Gardner and Terry M. Anderson, *Criminal Evidence: Principles and Cases*, 5th ed. (Belmont, CA: Wadsworth Publishing, 2004) p.22.

is the initial questioning of a witness or defendant by the lawyer who is using the person's testimony to further his or her case. At the conclusion of each witness's testimony, the defense attorney may cross-examine the witness. **Cross-examination** is questioning by the opposing side for the purpose of assessing the validity of the testimony. After the cross-examination, the prosecuting attorney may re-direct examine, and the defense attorney may re-cross-examine.

After the prosecutor has completed direct examination of all prosecution witnesses, the defense presents its case. After the direct examination of each

© AP/Wide World Photos

Lois Fraley testifies under cross-examination. Fraley, a prison guard, was held captive, beaten and sexually assaulted for 15 days in 2004 by two inmates during the longest prison hostage siege in U.S. history. She now travels across the country, providing survival training to employees of organizations that are at high risk of becoming hostages, including people working in banks, department stores, restaurants, correctional institutions and government agencies.

defense witness, the prosecutor may cross-examine, the defense counsel may redirect examine, and the prosecutor may re-cross-examine.

After each side has presented its regular witnesses, both sides may present *rebuttal* and *surrebuttal* witnesses. When the entire case has been presented, prosecution and defense counsel present their closing arguments to the jury. In these arguments, the lawyers review the trial evidence of both sides and then tell the jury why the defendant should be convicted or acquitted. Sometimes the lawyers also make recommendations for penalty.

The judge instructs the jurors on the laws applicable to the case and on how they are to arrive at a decision. The jury then retires to the jury room to deliberate and arrive at a verdict. When the verdict is reached, court is reconvened and the verdict is read. If the verdict is for acquittal, the defendant is released. If the verdict is guilty, the judge passes sentence or sets a time and date for sentencing.

Testifying under Direct Examination

You are on trial, too—your credibility, your professionalism, your knowledge, your competence, your judgment, your conduct in the field, your use of force, your adherence to official policies, your observance of the defendant's rights—they're all on trial.

—Devallis Rutledge (2000, p.12)

First impressions are critical. Security personnel must know what they are doing when they enter the courtroom. They should go to the courtroom ahead of time and familiarize themselves with the layout of the room. When their name is called, they should answer "Here" or "Present" and move directly to the front of the courtroom. They should not go between the prosecutor and the judge, but rather go behind the attorneys. The area between the lawyers and the judge is called the **well** and is intended for the judge's protection. No one is allowed there unless invited by the judge.

The prosecutor will ask for the person's name and position. As they respond to questions, they should keep in mind the types of statements that are not admissible.

 Inadmissible statements include:

- Opinion (unless the witness is qualified as an expert)
- Hearsay
- Privileged communication
- Statements about character and reputation, including the defendant's past criminal record

Proper preparation is the key to being a good witness.

 Guidelines for effective testimony:

- Speak clearly, firmly and with expression.
- Answer questions directly. Do not volunteer information.
- Pause briefly before answering.
- Refer to your notes if you do not recall exact details.
- Admit calmly when you do not know an answer.
- Admit any mistakes you make in testifying.
- Avoid jargon, sarcasm and humor.
- Tell the complete truth as you know it.

Although officers are expected to be well prepared, they are not expected to be "omniscient." A response of "I don't know," as long as it is the truth, is always an acceptable answer. Moore (2005, p.84) recommends that officers stop talking once a question is answered: "Never volunteer information beyond the scope of the question." She also suggests that if an officer is asked if he discussed the case with the prosecution, the officer should admit it as a normal part of preparing a case.

Officers can be human on the stand—cry and admit mistakes—but they must never lie or give the appearance of lying (Navarro, 2004, p.29). Officers should not argue or use sarcasm, witticism or smart answers. They should be direct, firm and positive in their answers and be courteous whether the question is from the prosecutor, the defense attorney or the judge. They should not hesitate to give information favorable to the defendant. Their primary responsibility is to state what they know about the case.

Strategies for Excelling as a Witness

Rutledge (2000), a former police officer, presently a prosecutor, offers several strategies for testifying in court.

Strategies for effectively testifying include (1) set yourself up, (2) provoke the defense into giving you a chance to explain, (3) be unconditional and (4) do not stall.

- The rules of court severely restrict you in answering questions. No defense attorney in his right mind is ever going to give you a chance to explain anything. So, if you're ever going to get the chance to explain yourself before the jury's impression of you gets set in their heads, you've got to know how to provoke the defense attorney into giving you a chance to explain. Some of these provokers are: *definitely; certainly; certainly not; naturally; naturally not;* and one that always does the trick: *Yes, and no.* (pp.24–27)[3]

- Be unconditional. Some cops seem to like the sound of the conditional word *would.* When I'm prosecuting a case, I cringe at the sound of it. It's too indefinite.

  Example:
  Q: Who was your partner?
  A: That would be Officer Hill. (p.72)

- Don't stall. Don't repeat the question back to the attorney.

  Example:
  Q: Were you holding a flashlight?
  A: Was I holding a flashlight? Yes, I was. (p.75)

Testifying under Cross-Examination

Cross-examination is usually the most difficult part of testifying. The defense attorney will attempt to cast doubt on a security professional's direct testimony in an effort to win an acquittal for the defendant. The defense attorney's most important task is to destroy an officer's credibility by making the officer look like they're either incompetent, lying or both (Rutledge, p.118). The defense achieves this by attacking, tricking, outsmarting, confusing, frustrating, annoying and probing for an officer's most vulnerable characteristics. Table 10.2 summarizes the common tactics used during cross-examination.

 During cross-examination the defense attorney might:

- Be disarmingly friendly or intimidatingly rude.
- Attack a witness's credibility and impartiality.
- Attack a witness's investigative skill.
- Attempt to force contradictions or inconsistencies.
- Ask leading questions or deliberately misquote the witness.
- Ask for a simple answer to a complex question.
- Use rapid-fire questioning.
- Use the silent treatment.

The best testimony is accurate, truthful and in accordance with the facts. Every word an officer says is recorded and may be played back or used by the defense.

---

[3]SOURCE: Devallis Rutledge, *Courtroom Survival: The Officer's Guide to Better Testimony* (Belmont, CA: Wadsworth Publishing, 2000) p.24–27, 72, 75.

Table 10.2 Brief Review of Common Tactics of Cross-Examination

Counsel's Tactic	Example	Purpose	Officer's Response
Rapid-fire questions	One question after another with little time to answer.	To confuse you; an attempt to force inconsistent answers.	Take time to consider the question; be deliberate in answering; ask to have the question repeated; remain calm.
Condescending counsel	Benevolent in approach, oversympathetic in questions to the point of ridicule.	To give the impression that you are inept, lack confidence or may not be a reliable witness.	Firm decisive answers, asking for the question to be repeated if improperly phrased.
Friendly counsel	Very courteous, polite; questions tend to take you into his confidence.	To lull you into a false sense of security, where you will give answers in favor of the defense.	Stay alert; bear in mind that purpose of defense is to discredit or diminish the effect of your testimony.
Badgering, belligerent	Counsel staring you right in the face, shouts, "That is so, isn't it, officer?"	To make you angry, so that you lose the sense of logic and calmness. Generally, rapid questions will also be included in this approach.	Stay calm, speak in a deliberate voice, giving prosecutor time to make appropriate objections.
Mispronouncing officer's name; using wrong rank	Your name is Jansen; counsel calls you Johnson.	To draw your attention to the error in pronunciation rather than enabling you to concentrate on the question asked, so that you will make inadvertent errors in testimony.	Ignore the mispronunciation and concentrate on the questions counsel is asking.
Suggestive question (tends to be a leading question allowable on cross-examination)	"Was the color of the car blue?"	To suggest an answer to his or her question in an attempt to confuse or to lead you.	Concentrate carefully on the facts, disregard the suggestion. Answer the question.
Demanding a yes or no answer to a question that needs explanation	"Did you strike the defendant with your club?"	To prevent all pertinent and mitigating details from being considered by the jury.	Explain the answer to the question; if stopped by counsel demanding a yes or no answer, pause until the court instructs you to answer in your own words.
Reversing witness's words	You answer, "The accident occurred 27 feet from the intersection." Counsel says, "You say the accident occurred 72 feet from the intersection?"	To confuse you and demonstrate a lack of confidence in you.	Listen intently whenever counsel repeats back something you have said. If counsel makes an error, correct him or her.
Repetitious questions	The same question asked several times slightly rephrased.	To obtain inconsistent or conflicting answers from you.	Listen carefully to the question and state, "I have just answered that question."
Conflicting answers	"But, Officer Smith, Detective Brown just said…"	To show inconsistency in the investigation. This tactic is normally used on measurements, times and so forth.	Remain calm. Conflicting statements have a tendency to make a witness extremely nervous. Be guarded in your answers on measurements, times and so forth. Unless you have exact knowledge, use the term "approximately." Refer to your notes.
Staring	After you have answered, counsel stares as though there were more to come.	To have a long pause that one normally feels must be filled, thus saying more than necessary. To provoke you into offering more than the question called for.	Wait for the next question.

Of equal or greater importance, however, are the results of research conducted over 25 years ago by Dr. Albert Morabian and the oft-cited UCLA study, which found that communication typically occurs via three very unequal avenues:

- 7 percent is communicated through *what* we say—the actual words used.
- 38 percent is conveyed in *how* we say it—tone of voice, pitch, modulation, and so on.
- 55 percent of communication occurs via *nonverbal* avenues—body language, gestures, demeanor.

The results of this research carry tremendous implications for those testifying in court. Van Brocklin (2005, p.48) lists the following behaviors that weaken an officer's credibility on the stand: using a defensive or evasive tone of voice, appearing ill at ease or nervous, using indirect eye contract, crossing the arms defensively across the chest, quibbling over common terms, sitting stiffly, looking to the attorney for assistance during cross-examination, cracking jokes inappropriately and using lots of "ah"s or "uh"s.

Handling Objections

Rutledge (p.97) gives the following suggestions for handling objections: "There are at least 44 standard trial objections in most states. We're only going to talk about the 2 that account for upwards of 90% of the problems a testifying officer will have: that your answer is a *conclusion*, or that it is *non-responsive*."

- One way [to avoid conclusions] is to listen to the form of the question. You know the attorney is asking you to speculate when he starts his questions with these loaded phrases: *Would you assume. . .? Do you suppose. . .? Don't you think that. . .? Couldn't it be that. . .? Do you imagine. . .? Wouldn't it be fair to presume. . .? Isn't it strange that. . .?* And the one you're likely to hear most often: *Isn't it possible?*" (pp.98–99)
- Another major area of conclusionary testimony is what I call mindreading. You can't get inside someone else's brain. That means you don't know for a fact—so you can't testify—as to what someone else *sees, hears, feels, thinks* or *wants*; and you don't know for a fact what somebody is *trying* to do, or is *able* to do, or whether he is *nervous, excited, angry, scared, happy, upset, disturbed,* or in any of the other emotional states that can only be labeled with a conclusion. (pp.102–103) [4]

Expert Testimony

Officers who qualify as experts in an area are allowed to give opinions and conclusions, but the prosecution must qualify the officer as an expert on the stand. It must be established that the person has special knowledge that persons of moderate education or experience in the same field do not possess. To qualify as an expert witness, one must have:

- Present or prior employment in the specific field.
- Active membership in a professional group in the field.

---

[4]SOURCE: Devallis Rutledge, *Courtroom Survival: The Officer's Guide to Better Testimony* (Belmont, CA: Wadsworth Publishing, 2000) p.97–115.

- Research work in the field.
- An educational degree directly related to the field.
- Direct experience with the subject if not employed in the field.
- Papers, treatises or books published on the subject or teaching experience in it.

When security personnel qualified as experts take the witness stand, they might expect three types of questions: (1) those based on their personal knowledge, (2) those based on the facts of the case and (3) those based on hypothetical questions. All hypothetical questions must be based on facts already admitted into testimony or likely to be admitted. Finally, the ASIS suggests that security personnel should not be embarrassed about getting paid to testify if such is the case. They should simply state the facts.

SUMMARY

- Primary responsibilities of investigators are to provide emergency assistance, secure the area of an incident, gather evidence and information, record information in notes and reports and testify in court about civil and criminal incidents.

- The single most important factor in determining the successful disposition of an incident is the information gathered by the security officer at the time of the initial report.

- Among the most common crimes security personnel will be asked to investigate are assault, breach of peace/disturbing the peace/disorderly conduct, burglary/unlawful entry/breaking and entering, theft, trespassing and vandalism.

- An *interview* is a controlled conversation with witnesses to or victims of a crime. An *interrogation* is a controlled conversation with persons suspected of direct or indirect involvement in a crime.

- Nonverbal communication includes eye movements, facial expressions, posture, gestures, clothing, tone of voice, proximity and touch.

- Effective notes are accurate, brief, clear and complete.

- A well-written report is factual, accurate, objective, complete, concise, clear, mechanically correct, written in standard English, legible and on time.

- The sequence in a criminal trial is jury selection, opening statements by the prosecution and the defense, presentation of the prosecution's case, presentation of the defense's case, closing statements by the prosecution and the defense, instructions to the jury, jury deliberation to reach a verdict, reading of the verdict and acquittal or passing of sentence.

- When testifying, security personnel must avoid making inadmissable statements, including opinion (unless the witness is qualified as an expert), hearsay, privileged communication and statements about character and reputation, including the defendant's past criminal record.

- Guidelines for effective testimony include the following:
  - Speak clearly, firmly and with expression.
  - Answer questions directly. Do not volunteer information.
  - Pause briefly before answering.
  - Refer to your notes if you do not recall exact details.
  - Admit calmly when you do not know an answer.
  - Admit any mistakes you make in testifying.
  - Avoid jargon, sarcasm and humor.
  - Tell the truth as you know it.

- Strategies for testifying in court include (1) setting yourself up, (2) provoking the defense into giving you a chance to explain, (3) being unconditional and (4) not stalling.

■ Anticipate the tactics commonly used by defense attorneys during cross-examination. They may be disarmingly friendly or intimidatingly rude, attack credibility and impartiality, attack investigative skill, attempt to force contradictions or inconsistencies, ask leading questions or deliberately misquote, request a "yes" or "no" answer to complex questions, use rapid-fire questioning or use the "silent treatment."

APPLICATIONS

1. Bart Gibson, a security officer for the M.C. Auto Parts distribution center, has been told that the latest inventory indicates that many boxes of spark plugs have been unaccounted for and the losses are mounting. It is his job to find out what is happening and how these losses can be curtailed.

   After considerable investigation and interviewing of personnel in the distribution center, Gibson is told that some employees throw parts out the window at lunchtime into the bushes that surround the complex. After completing their shifts for the day, they then retrieve the stolen items and leave the premises. He also has heard rumors that a garage in the vicinity is purchasing these stolen spark plugs at a very reduced price.

   On Gibson's first surveillance of the window that abuts the shrubbery, where, according to his sources, some of the items are leaving the plant, he notices that several branches are moving as if someone has thrown something into the bushes. After the lunch hour, he makes a cursory search of the area where he observed the branch movement and finds one box of spark plugs, a water pump and a box of PCV valves.

   He stakes out the site, and at 4:30 P.M., at the end of the shift, he notices Gary Schmitz go into the shrubbery area and come out with the described items. He lets Schmitz get into his car and drive off. He then stops Schmitz five blocks from the distribution center, confiscates the stolen items and brings Schmitz back to the plant security officer. There he notifies the security chief and begins to interview Schmitz about his activities.

Schmitz is somewhat cooperative but reluctant to tell the security officers about the thefts. The officers continue to verbally pressure Schmitz and threaten to prosecute him to the fullest extent of the law and to recommend jail time if he is convicted. Schmitz consents to tell all if the security officers will make a deal. He wants no prosecution because he would lose his job. However, he knows just about everything that is going on as far as parts thefts are concerned, and he knows who else is doing it.

This poses a problem for the security officers because they would like to show their bosses they have done a good job and have broken up a theft ring within the plant. You are the decision maker.

■ Under the circumstances, how far are you willing to concede to Schmitz's demands in order to stop further thefts?

■ Should you deal with him at all?

■ Do you think you can trust him?

■ Will he lead you to the purchaser of the stolen parts?

■ Is it ethical to make a deal with him?

■ What will be the effect on the other employees?

It's your decision. What are you going to recommend?

2. You are a supervisor with the Allen Security Company, and one of your security officers approaches you about an upcoming court appearance in a civil case. Security Officer McDuff has never testified in court and asks you to suggest how he can present a professional image. What suggestions would you make to Officer McDuff?

DISCUSSION QUESTIONS

1. How would you go about obtaining the basic skills needed to become an effective investigator?

2. What do you feel is the most important factor in determining the successful disposition of an incident you investigate?

3. What is your understanding of the word *predication* as it applies to private security?

4. How can you improve your skills in note taking? In report writing?

5. How should a security officer on the witness stand deal with an attorney who is trying to confuse him or her with rapid-fire questioning so that the answers the officer gives might be inconsistent?

REFERENCES

Arp, Don, Jr. "Effective Written Reports." *Law and Order*, April 2007, pp.100–102.

Bennett, Wayne W. and Hess, Kären M. *Criminal Investigation*, 8th edition. Belmont, CA: Thomson Wadsworth, 2007.

Davison, Dean P. "The Verdict on Digital Evidence." *Security Management*, May 2005, pp.142–139.

Eck, John E.; Chainey, Spencer; Gameron, James G.; Leitner, Michael; and Wilson, Ronald E. *Mapping Crime: Understanding Hot Spots*. Washington, DC: National Institute of Justice, August 2005.

Harold, Charles A. "The Detective and the Database." *Security Management*, March 2006, pp.66–72.

Hess, Kären M. and Orthmann, Christine H. *For the Record: Report Writing in Law Enforcement*, 6th edition. Bloomington, MN: Innovative Systems – Publishers, 2008.

Kanable, Rebecca. "Getting It Right." *Law Enforcement Technology*, September 2005, pp.160–168.

Magno, Cynthia. "Where Crimes Converge Investigations Merge." *Security Management*, April 2005, pp.91–96.

McDonough, Edward. "Asking the Hard Questions." *Security Management*, July 2005, pp.85–93.

Moore, Carole. "Plain English." *Law Enforcement Technology*, December 2004, p.266.

Moore, Carole. "Taking the Stand." *Law Enforcement Technology*, July 2005, pp.76–84.

Navarro, Joe. "Testifying in the Theater of the Courtroom." *FBI Law Enforcement Bulletin*, September 2004, pp.26–30.

"Newspoll." *Security Director News*, March 2006, p.31.

Nyberg, Ramesh. "How to Testify in Court." *Police*, April 2006, pp.18–22.

Occupational Safety & Health Administration. Online http://www.osha.gov

PCI™ Examination Structure and Content. Arlington, VA: American Society of Industrial Security, 2007.

Rutledge, Devallis. *Courtroom Survival: The Officer's Guide to Better Testimony*. Belmont, CA: Wadsworth Publishing, 2000.

Scarry, Laura L. "Report Writing." *Law Officer Magazine*, February 2007, pp.68–71.

Sievert, Gordon. "The Essence of Quality: Writing Successful Reports." *The Law Enforcement Trainer*, Fourth Quarter 2004, pp.35–39.

Swobodzinski, Kimberle. "The Crime Scene Report." *Law Officer Magazine*, February 2007, pp.47–49.

Van Brocklin, Valeria. "Winning Courtroom Confrontations." *The Law Enforcement Trainer*, April/May/June 2005, pp.44–49.

A helpful pocket-sized reference for taking notes and writing reports for private security is *An Outline Guide for Private Security* by Floyd Stokes, Kären Hess and Henry Wrobleski. Available online from www.innsyspub.com.

CASES CITED

Austin v. Norfolk Southern Corp., U.S. Court of Appeals for the Third Circuit, No. 04–1568 (2005).

In re Deborah C., 635 P.2d 446 (Cal. 1981).

Miranda v. State of Arizona, 384 U.S. 436, 86 S. Ct. 1602 (1966).

People v. Haydel, 109 Cal. Rept. 222 (Cal. 1973).

Information Technology (IT) Security

Information technology (IT) security has become a critical piece of overall organizational security. Here, students at the Norwich University computer security training program in Northfield, Vermont, watch a simulated computer attack unfold. During this training, students learn to look for signs of an attack in scrolling numbers on a computer screen and how to tell when an adversary is probing a computer network looking for a way in.

Do You Know . . .

■ What the buzz words of twenty-first century security are?

■ What the three integral components of a holistic physical security process are?

■ How IT projects can effect change in an organization?

■ What newer technologies security directors should become familiar with?

■ What common equipment can pose security threats?

■ What computer attacks commonly focus on?

■ What proprietary information includes?

■ What potential threats to proprietary information exist?

■ What one of the most cost-effective measures to protect corporate information assets is?

■ What factors in conducting an investigation are critical?

■ What security measures can be taken to reduce losses from IT threats?

Can You Define?

bot	intellectual property	nondisclosure	secrecy agreements
competitive	rights	agreements	technology escrow
intelligence	malware	patent	telecommunications
contextual integrity	mesh network	proprietary	trademark
copyright	noncompete	information	Trojan horse
encryption	agreements	Sarbanes-Oxley	
exculpatory evidence		legislation	

Introduction

Your [security] career is over as you know it. The change that will befall the security industry in the next few years will create a time of significant turbulence and consolidation.

The fact that the protection of information is of growing value within an organization—more than 85 percent of a company's value lies in proprietary information—is in direct contrast to the past, when companies used to be concerned with physical assets. This is a huge difference from where it was two decades ago.

The value of information has propelled the security market into a new era. The transition from guns, guards and gates to information, intelligence and integration is technology centric, not people centric (Daniels, 2007b, pp.8, 10).[1]

These words from Kevin Coleman, as he addressed an audience at the International Association of Professional Security Consultants annual conference in May 2007, indicate a striking sea change in the landscape of modern security

---

[1]SOURCE: From "Practitioners Face Change in Industry" by Rhianna Daniels in *Security Director News*, June 2007, p.8, 10. Reprinted by permission.

provision. There is no way to avoid it—information technology (IT) security has become a critical part of an organization's overall security program.

This chapter begins with a brief overview of information technology (IT) and a discussion of convergence, integration, unification and holistic security. This is followed by a look at newer technologies security professionals should be aware of as well as commonly used equipment that can pose a security threat. Next targets of attack and potential threats to proprietary information are described. Then the role of competitive intelligence and the issue of privacy protection are explained. This is followed by a discussion of some basic principles of protecting information assets and security measures that might be undertaken against IT threats. The chapter concludes with recommendations for an IT security program, a look at the issue of IT security and lawsuits, and a caution that security professionals must look beyond technology to the human factor as they plan for and implement IT security measures.

Information Technology: An Overview

Many security practitioners find the topic of information technology (IT) fairly daunting. Complicating the situation is the fact that the definition of just what constitutes *information technology* continues to change as the technology itself evolves: "For the last several decades our conception of IT has been synonymous with computers and cables, wires and components that link computers with one another through Local Area Networks (LANS), Wide Area Networks (WANS) and the Internet. Today, however, the IT arena incorporates a wide array of technologies far beyond simple computers and wired networks, making it difficult even for IT professionals to fully comprehend all of the vast components and systems that compose the field" (Cowper, 2005, pp.113–114).

Indeed: "Implementing a new technology, whether for purposes of automation, information sharing or more effective communication is always difficult" (Wexler, 2005, p.v). It can be risky, time consuming and a drain on budgets and other resources. But the benefits, long-term efficiencies and opportunities for reform can far outweigh the costs (Wexler). The good news is: Most security professionals are already using IT in some form and have become comfortable with many facets of it.

Boyd (2005, p.1) notes: "In today's rapidly changing technology landscape, keeping pace with IT innovations has become an essential part of the [security director's] job." As a starting point, security directors need to consider their basic philosophy about IT: Do they see it as a tool to make existing processes more efficient or to change existing processes—or perhaps both? Stephens (2005, p.17) offers the following guiding principles:

- Management of our existing investments in technology will be our first priority.
- New investments in technology will be tied to clear, measurable improvements and efficiency gains in day-to-day services.
- Investment decisions will be made through strategic collaborative processes.
- The [organization] will actively pursue solutions that foster achievement of current strategic plan initiatives and the business goals they represent.

The FBI Example

FBI Chief Information Officer (CIO) Zai Azmi says that overhauling the FBI's technology infrastructure has been compared to changing a tire on a speeding car—it's a challenge, but slowing down or stopping for repairs simply isn't an option. Add to that someone looking over your shoulder to make sure everything is humming along smoothly and you have an apt description for what CIO Azmi is overseeing as he moves the Bureau into an entirely new way to manage information.

Traditionally, agents, analysts and others using the FBI's central repository for case files and other sensitive data had to search through several "green screens" to manage basic information. The Bureau's mainframe technology predated even use of a computer mouse, with users having to wade through a series of keyboard prompts and commands to simply view case information. But all that came to an end in June of 2007 when the Bureau deployed to 30,000 FBI users the first phase of Sentinel, an intuitive Web-based information management system that makes it easier to keep tabs on cases and to share and access information.

Azmi's vision for the FBI is to model its IT infrastructure on the standards and best practices used in private industry. This first major Web-based application is the foundation for the entire enterprise. The four-phase project with contractor Lockheed Martin should be finished in 2011 at a total cost of about $423 million.

Convergence, Integration, Unification and Holistic Security

An examination of the multitude of IT opportunities and projects available to security is beyond the scope of this discussion. The most common undertakings in adopting IT focus on the merging of physical security and information security, as introduced in Chapter 2: "The security industry is at an intersection of change—driven by evolving threats and the looming convergence of IT and physical security" (Daniels, 2007b, p.8).

 Convergence, integration, unification, holistic security—these are the buzzwords of twenty-first century security.

No longer is security viewed as an isolated function with easily identified responsibilities. Total security now requires an integrated and unified approach that links together previously separate aspects of the business or organization. In fact: "Convergence is one of the hottest topics in the security world" (Lasky, 2005, p.6). The gap generated between physical and IT security makes organizations vulnerable to attack: "The importance of bridging the physical and IT security chasm presents the security industry with an opportunity to learn and adopt integrated practices that will grow business and add value to their customer base" (Piccolomini, 2005, p.8).

A *Security Director News* "Newspoll" (2007, p.22) asked security directors about the benefits of merging IT and physical security departments. The most frequently mentioned benefit was a broader view of risks (20 percent) followed by more efficient technology installs (15 percent). Results of the poll are shown in Figure 11.1.

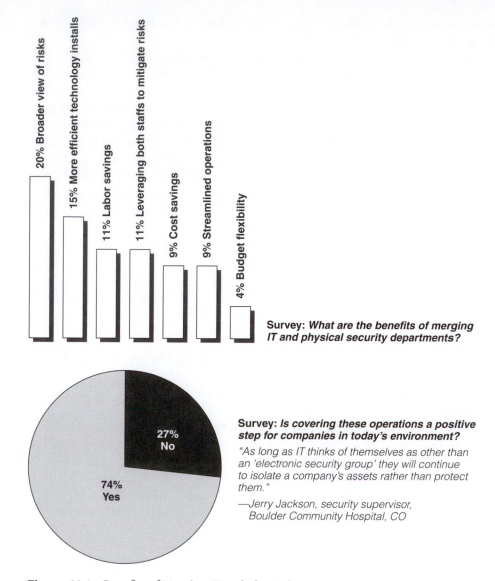

Survey: *What are the benefits of merging IT and physical security departments?*

Survey: *Is covering these operations a positive step for companies in today's environment?*

"As long as IT thinks of themselves as other than an 'electronic security group' they will continue to isolate a company's assets rather than protect them."

—Jerry Jackson, security supervisor, Boulder Community Hospital, CO

Figure 11.1 Benefits of Merging IT and Physical Security Departments

SOURCE: From "Newspoll" in *Security Director News*, April 2007, p.22. Reprinted by permission.

Hamilton (2004, p.14) observes: "The rise of the C-level [chief security officer] security position marks a dynamic change in the structure of security, which has historically been an under-managed and fragmented function in many organizations. It is evidence of a powerful trend toward a holistic approach to security through which various elements such as information security, building systems and physical security are integrated into a single function." For example, the U.S. General Accounting Office has applied holistic security to federal buildings, implementing three integral concepts of a holistic security process (Hamilton).

 The three integral components of a holistic physical security process are protection, detection and reaction.

Protection provides countermeasures to defend against attacks on assets being secured. Detection monitors breakdowns in these protection controls.

Reaction requires human response to detected breaches to thwart attacks before damage can be done.

Harowitz (2005, p.75) goes a bit further in looking at where the security system fits within an organization, noting how advances in connectivity among markets, companies and systems are reshaping security operations: "Advances in connectivity—sometimes wired and sometimes wireless—continue to play a strong role in every business sector." Suppliers are responding to competition by specializing in vertical markets, focusing on core strengths and partnering: "Partnering has definitely taken hold as a new paradigm" (Harowitz, p.77).

Despite the many benefits to integration, challenges exist. Straw (2007, p.48) notes: "A lack of manufacturer standards for ensuring that products can talk to each other is just one barrier to the illusive goal of interoperable communications."

Whether an organization is implementing IT systems to accomplish integration of existing systems or is undertaking a new IT project, security directors should be aware of the changes that might be anticipated as well as the realities they may face.

How IT Projects Can Effect Change

Information technology (IT) projects can effect changes in four substantive categories (Kolpack, 2005, p.79):

1. Automate tasks that are too expensive or too time consuming for staff to complete.
2. Send appropriate information up the chain of command to aid in effective management.
3. Send appropriate information down the chain of command to empower employees in performing their jobs.
4. Transform components of the organization's work, either through increased efficiency or through the creation of a new process that positively alters how the organization functions.

 Information technology (IT) projects can effect change by automating tasks, sending appropriate information up and down the chain of command, and making work more efficient.

Why Some IT Projects Fail

Stephens (p.8) asserts that "the landscape is littered with failed IT projects." He reports on research in the private sector by the Standish Group showing: 52.7 percent of projects will cost 189 percent of their original estimates; 31.1 percent of projects will be canceled before completion; only 42 percent of the project's original features are in the end product; and 16 percent of the large-scale projects are completed on time and within budget.

An evaluation of IT projects by Integrated Computer Engineering, Inc., using their database of more than 800 indicators of successful projects, has identified several common characteristics of failed projects (Kolpack, p.80):

- Failure to apply essential project management
- Unwarranted optimism and unrealistic expectations by management
- Failure to implement effective software processes

- Premature victory declarations
- Lack of leadership in program management
- Untimely decision making
- Lack of productive risk management

As noted, many IT projects seek to integrate existing technologies into a holistic security system, often incorporating some of the new technologies.

New Technologies

The quote at the beginning of this chapter spoke of technology-centric security. A more apt description might be net-centric security. Emerging IT systems will provide security with unprecedented opportunities to collect, analyze and disseminate a wide range of information in real-time to every member of an organization: "When real-time information is delivered to all the right people in an entire networked organization, there are benefits far beyond the sum of the individual members' accomplishments" (Cowper, p.121). Advancements in IT can result in tremendously improved efficiency and effectiveness.

 New technologies that security directors need to become familiar with include IP video surveillance systems, VoIP, USB technology, mesh networks and computer telephony interface (CTI).

IP Video Surveillance Systems

IP video surveillance systems were described in Chapter 6 as one effective means of physical control. Since many businesses already have a network in place, an IP-based system is a relatively simple and cost-effective application to add, as it reduces the need for costly coaxial cabling with all its associated installation difficulties and allows users to view live and recorded images from any networked PC (Goy, 2005, p.94). The latest IP surveillance products are paving the way toward fully integrated solution, for example, allowing a company's existing IT infrastructure to integrate not only CCTV but also a plethora of building management functions, including access control, fire systems and intruder alarms (Goy).

This technology can also be beneficial to departments other than security, such as risk management, operations, legal, training and IT departments (Longmore-Etheridge, 2006, p.42). For example, a risk management department can use surveillance feeds in identifying false workers' compensation claims as well as bolstering genuine claims sent to insurers. The training department may use the video in creating new safety manuals and training program, such as clips of actual safety violations to illustrate what not to do. Legal departments can use the video in determining the validity of—or defending against—lawsuits and insurance claims filed by customers.

The world market for IP video surveillance products increased by 41.9 percent in 2006 and is forecasted to continue growing strongly in the future: "The emergence—and increasingly growing demand—of IP-based security technology affects the industry in various ways, but probably most significantly, it increases the numbers of stakeholders in an organization's security program and adds to the growing level of information needing to be managed" (Daniels, 2007c, p.7).

Not only is IP-based security technology helping security directors achieve better video quality, but the new techniques also help security directors be more proactive in security (Edwards, 2007, p.20). For example, video analysis can play an important role in stopping a threat or an event before it appears, in contrast to simply helping investigators analyze the crime after the fact.

Voice Over Internet Protocol (VoIP)

Voice Over Internet Protocol (VoIP) was introduced in Chapter 6 as an advance in surveillance technology. Former FCC Chairman, Power, calls VoIP "the most significant paradigm shift in the history of modern communications since the invention of the telephone" (Wilkins, 2007, p.21). Every month 35,000 customers are switching their phone service over to VoIP providers. Equipment providers sold about $2.4 billion worth of dedicated VoIP infrastructure products in 2005, a number that is predicted to grow to $4.7 billion by 2010.

Despite the fact that VoIP represents the wave of the future, few have even tried to integrate this increasingly popular platform into their existing telecommunications, IT infrastructure and voice-recording operations (Swette, 2007, p.37).

Universal Serial Bus (USB) Technology

Universal serial bus (USB) flash drives were once regarded as trade show giveaways to transfer files and folders from a company laptop to a home computer, but USB drives have evolved into something more useful—and potentially dangerous (Piazza, 2007, p.48). For example, one evolving threat comes from programs which, when installed on a computer, will suck data off any connected USB drive without any visible sign (Piazza). Widespread use of USB drives has given attackers a new way to socially engineer their way into corporate systems. USB technology allows hardware to be plugged in and automatically recognized (Plug and Play) by the computer while the computer is running, unlike conventional serial and parallel ports. USB also eliminates many other hassles that come with serial and parallel ports, like IRQ (device) conflicts and limited expandability.

Mesh Networks

A **mesh network,** in its simplest form, is a wireless communications technology that allows each radio to function as a router, meaning data can be sent to or through any other radio in the network to reach the intended destination (Canning, 2007, p.96). In effect, this provides radio communication on a peer-to-peer level and resulting "in adaptive, flexible connections among users that would not be possible with traditional communication technologies" (Canning). According to Cowper (p.121): "The greatest advantage to a mesh network is its ability to reconfigure, independent of the land-based communication infrastructure, to provide increased coverage without having to build additional towers."

Computer Telephony Interface (CTI)

Computer telephony interface (CTI) is technology that allows interactions on a telephone and a PC to be integrated or coordinated (Scott, 2007, p.32). As contact channels expanded from voice to include e-mail, Web and fax, the definition of CTI expanded to include the integration of all customer contact channels (voice, e-mail, Web, fax, etc.) with computer systems. CTI applications are used by businesses and organizations not only to manage and route phone calls, but also to provide quick and comprehensive information to the organization.

A CTI application can recognize a caller's number and provide, through the receiver's PC, a wealth of useful information to the person taking the call, such as the caller's address, their emergency contact info, the location of the nearest public service officer, caller history, incident history, billing history and countless other types of data that could be used for making informed decisions. A security director who has a well-designed CTI application in place has the opportunity to reduce the time and effort needed to confidently take action and make decisions in situations that start with telephony-based communication.

Dangers in Implementing New Technologies

Johnston and Warner (2005, p.114) caution: "High-tech devices have an important role to play when it comes to security, but there is a real danger in implementing the newest technologies and assuming that they are unbreakable. In fact, many commonly used high-tech devices and systems can be broken by the simplest means. This is due in part to users not understanding how the systems work." Technology vendors may downplay potential weaknesses in the systems or try to sell a product for a use other than that for which is was designed. For example, some devices being promoted as security tools are really meant for inventory control applications (Johnston and Warner).

The relative ease with which some products can be counterfeited—radio-frequency identification (RFID) tags, contact memory buttons, tamper-indicating seals and other types of security tags—actually reduces, rather than increases, security, as companies who rely too heavily on such products to lower risk of loss are operating under a false sense of security (Johnston and Warner). In addition, some very low-tech methods have been used to defeat relatively high-tech applications. For example, an attacker who is able to gain access to the physical location from which encrypted communications are sent can very easily thwart the encryption software. Similarly, global positioning system (GPS) devices can be jammed with a piece of aluminum foil (Johnston and Warner).

These potential technology pitfalls are pointed out not to discourage use of high-technology products, which can offer important security improvements while saving time, money, personnel and resources, but to emphasize the need for security personnel to be realistic and recognize technology's limitations and vulnerabilities: "We must not engage in wishful thinking or automatically believe every unsubstantiated claim for high technology" (Johnston and Warner, p.121). Security directors are urged to be mindful of this quote from noted cryptologist Schneider: "If you think technology can solve your security problems, then you don't understand the problems and you don't understand the technology" (Johnston and Warner).

While security managers strive to keep abreast of IT innovations, they should not overlook commonly used technologies that might pose a security risk.

Common Equipment That Can Pose Security Threats

 Common equipment that can pose security threats includes laptops, cell phones and PDAs.

To illustrate the pervasiveness of security threats associated with laptops, consider the instance in which insecure laptop computers were found at the Federal Emergency Management Agency (FEMA) by the Inspector General of the Department of Homeland Security (DHS). FEMA has more than 32,000 laptop computers, allowing employees to work more efficiently. However, this mobility allows for increased risk of theft, unauthorized data disclosure and virus infection. In 2006, DHS reported 16 security incidents related to the FEMA laptop computers. Further, the Government Accountability Office discovered FEMA had more than 100 missing and presumed stolen laptop computers, at a cost of $300,000.

Telecommunications is the science of communicating by the transmission of electronic impulses (e.g., telegraph, telephone, fax, etc.). Telecommunications security includes information communicated by voice, fax and computer using wirelines, microwave links, satellite systems and fiber optic lines. Unsecured telephone communications, including wireless phones, intercoms and cellular phones, pose a security risk in that others may intentionally or unintentionally hear transmitted messages.

Unsecured fax machines are common in most businesses, as they make communication rapid and convenient. But they also present a security risk in the form of faxpionage—unauthorized access to facsimile transmissions. Satellite transmissions also are at risk, such as those used in teleconferencing.

Information Asset Protection (2007, p.26)[2] offers the following recommendations regarding portable equipment that might threaten IT security:

- As a condition of issuing any portable equipment capable of generating or storing information (e.g., notebook computers, blackberries, etc.), employees should sign a release acknowledging that the equipment and any information produced or stored on it are the employer's property.
- Use of mobile devices with embedded cameras (e.g., cell phones) should be controlled and discouraged, particularly around sensitive materials or in restricted areas.
- Avoid storing sensitive information such as social security numbers, credit card numbers and passwords on any wireless device.
- Be careful about posting cell phone numbers and e-mail addresses. Attackers often use software that browse Web sites for e-mail addresses, which then become targets for attacks.
- Do not follow links in an e-mail or text message. Be suspicious of URLs sent in unsolicited e-mail or text messages. While the links may appear to be legitimate, they may actually direct you to a malicious Web site.
- Consider locking your phone when not using it or creating a password for phone access.

---

[2]SOURCE: From *Information Asset Protection Guideline, DRAFT* (Alexandria, VA: American Society for Industrial Security, 2007) p.26. Reprinted with the written permission of ASIS International, Alexandria, VA.

- Consider installing software that allows you to remotely lock the phone or erase the data if the phone is lost or stolen.
- Asset tag or engrave the laptop. Permanently marking or engraving the outer case of the laptop with the organization's name, address and phone number may greatly increase the odds of getting the laptop returned.
- Use a nondescript carrying case.
- Be careful when logging online in a wireless hot spot, such as a hotel, cafe or airport lounge, as you may not be logging on to a valid wireless network. You may log on to someone nearby with a wireless computer attempting to steal your identity.

Other IT Security Threats

Chapter 9 discussed the problem of computer crime. This is just one of many challenges facing security as it moves to capitalize on the advantages offered by information technology. "The new conventional wisdom has it that losses from computer-related crimes top those from traditional crimes" (Gips, 2006a, p.24). It is difficult to nail down precise figures because losses across sectors and types of crime are based on extrapolation and guesswork: "What numbers there are show that the toll of physical crime in the United States still easily outpaces the cost of cyber crime" (Gips). For example, FBI estimates put the annual cost of cybercrime at about $400 billion annually while occupational fraud alone, not involving the Internet, is estimated at $660 billion per year.

A study by Trend Micro, Inc. found that Web threats increased 540 percent from 2005 to 2007 ("Study: Web Threats Increase 540 Percent in Two Years," 2007). According to "Cyberspace Protection Tips" (2007): "You can never have enough protection when surfing the Web, as online criminals increasingly turn to malware to attack systems and unearth sensitive information such as passwords and account information."

Security researchers have labeled 2005 as the year of the capitalist crooks, with cyber attackers turning from wanting bragging rights to wanting financial gain (Piazza, 2006d, p.49). Many of the threats involve **malware,** *malicious software* designed to infiltrate or damage a computer system. A Panda Software study indicates that new malware appears every day, with PandaLabs detecting as much new malware in the single year 2006 as in the previous 15 years combined. Currently antivirus laboratories cannot process all the new threats that appear daily, so many computers are infected without users' knowledge ("Panda Software Study," 2007).

Criminal malware has surged ahead as the virus threat fades, with Trojans now outweighing viruses and worms by four to one (Jaques, 2006). In 2005, the threat landscape included 27 percent Trojan horses (including rootkits), 25 percent viruses or worms, 18 percent adware, 11 percent spyware and 10 percent bots.

Trojan Horses

A **Trojan horse** installs malicious software while under the guise of doing something else. For example, it may claim to be a free rainbow screen saver, but instead the software opens computer ports allowing hackers remote access to the computer. A Trojan horse differs from a virus in that a Trojan horse does not insert its code into other computer files and appears harmless until executed. The term is derived from the classical myth of the Trojan horse, where a Greek army compromised Trojan security by hiding inside a giant wooden horse and, thus, were allowed to pass undetected through the gates of Troy.

An important facet of Trojan horse programs is that they cannot operate autonomously, unlike viruses or worms. A Trojan horse depends on some action taken by the victim, such as clicking on a link or downloading a file, to activate the program's malicious code.

Viruses and Worms

According to Piazza (2004, p.67): "As traditional antivirus protection has been outpaced by new types of malicious code, companies are challenged to find more effective solutions." A survey conducted by the FBI and the Computer Security Institute found that virus contamination remained the costliest type of incidents in 2003 for the third straight year at $15.7 million per year. The survey also found no fewer than 99 percent of the 530 respondents were using antivirus solutions and 98 percent of respondents were using firewalls. Yet the same survey indicated that 82 percent of organizations had nevertheless been infected by a virus (Piazza, p.76).

Spyware

Spyware is a dangerous, prolific code that logs a user's activity and collects personal information, then sends that information to a third party (Honen, 2005, p.64). Spyware can create several problems. First, it can take over system resources and slow Internet response time. It can also delete or alter files to hide its presence. And it can open a backdoor to communicate with other networks, one way it secretly sends personal or proprietary data to a third party. Spyware can also easily download and install malicious code (Honen).

The most common way a user's computer can get infected with spyware is a user looking to get a free program. Many types of spyware are bundled with applications such as photo editors and file sharing software. Some malicious applications infect computers using a "drive-by download," where infection (installation of the spyware program) occurs when a user visits a Web page that has been maliciously configured to exploit a vulnerability in a Web browser.

One option to block spyware is an antispyware solution that runs at the organization's Internet gateway—the place where the network ends and the Internet begins. This solution blocks the ability of spyware to install files and prevents any spyware that may already be on the network from going through the gateway. The layers of protection around the network overlap. Gateway antispyware solutions may also stop the occasional piece of malware that has skirted the firewall and IPS, which those products help filter out (Honen, p.70).

Adware

Adware, a relative of spyware, is typically found with free software. It displays an advertisement when the program is running. The advertisements help software creators recover the cost of programming and maintaining the software. However, recently many adware vendors have been implementing spyware components into their software, making it an active program that can monitor user activity and report that activity back to a third party.

Bots

New computer worms are carrying software agents called bots that can use a company's network to send spam, launch attacks and infect other computers (Piazza, 2006b, p.71). A **bot** is a type of malware that allows an attacker to gain complete control over the affected computer (Bradley, 2007). Computers infected with a bot are often referred to as "zombies." Attackers are able to access lists of zombie PCs and activate them to execute DoS (denial-of-service) attacks against Web sites, host phishing attacks or send out thousands of spam e-mail messages: "SophosLabs estimates more than 60 percent of all spam today originates from zombie computers" ("Zombie Computers . . .," 2006). Should anyone trace the attack back to its source (the zombie PC), they will find an unwitting victim rather than the true attacker. There are tens of thousands of computers on the Internet infected with some type of bot and the users are unaware of this infection.

An example of one international case where zombie PCs were used for a distributed denial-of-service (DDoS) attack involved an online Russian blackmail gang that allegedly extorted more than $4 million from several British companies, primarily online casinos and betting Web sites ("Online Russian Blackmail Gang . . .," 2006). One victim of the online blackmail gang, Canbet Sports Bookmakers, refused to pay the $10,000 ransom demand and had their Web site knocked offline by the hackers during the Breeders' Cup Races, which cost Canbet more than $200,000 in lost business for every day their site was down. Prosecutors contend the gang made more than 50 such blackmail attacks in 30 different countries during their six months of activity.

While the perpetrators in this online gang were caught and convicted, and each was sentenced to 8 years in prison and a $3,700 fine, many computer criminals continue to operate with impunity. According to a senior technology consultant at Sophos Security: "Malicious DDoS attacks on commercial websites can cause serious financial damage to the businesses affected and are a major nuisance to internet users. . . . These sentences should send a strong message to other internet hackers considering online blackmail that they can expect stiff sentences if caught. However, many gangs may believe that the relative anonymity of the internet gives them carte blanche to carry on. All computer users should ensure that they have secure defenses in place to protect against abuse like this."

One particularly dangerous trend is targeted attacks, where bots are sent on a limited basis, evading the attention of programs designed to detect the usual volume of traffic a bot attack generates (Elliott, 2007, p.52). Further, botnets (groups of computers hijacked and controlled by bots) are using HTTP traffic or peer-to-peer communication channels, making them appear innocuous and harder to track.

One of the best defenses against threats like these is to run antivirus and antispyware software on a computer. It is important to update the software frequently and use a firewall program to shield the computer from unauthorized access.

However, the most frequent method of infection is from an employee taking a laptop home, hooking it up to a cable modem, getting the laptop infected, and then bringing it back to work and connecting to the corporate network, bypassing firewalls and antivirus scans. Forward-thinking companies preach proactively about the dangers of connecting outside the office and avoid trouble by having an employee's laptop always running antivirus programs and having the employee connect back to the corporate network through a virtual private network (VPN).

Targets of Attack

A *Security Director News* "Newspoll" (2007, p.23) that asked "What information assets does your company deem to be of highest value?" found 76 percent of respondents considered proprietary information the asset of highest value, 10 percent responded patents and 3 percent responded trade secrets and copyrights respectively. Seventy-two percent of the respondents said their company had a strategy to protect intellectual property and other intangible assets.

 Computer attacks commonly focus on proprietary information.

Proprietary information is defined by the Federal Acquisition Regulation (48 CFR 27.402 Policy) as a property right or other valid economic interest in data resulting from private investment. Protection of such data from unauthorized use and disclosure is necessary to prevent the compromise of such property right or economic interest.

 Proprietary information includes intellectual property, trade secrets, patented material and copyrighted material.

Intellectual Property

Information Asset Protection (p.7) defines **intellectual property rights (IPR)** as: "A category of intangible rights protecting commercially valuable products of the human intellect. The category comprises primarily trademark, copyright and patent rights, but also includes trade secret rights, publicity rights, moral rights and rights against unfair competition." (Note: Some areas of the world differ significantly in their recognition and enforcement of patents, trademarks, copyrights and other IPR. It is important to understand the IPR climate and the ability of the legal safeguards that are applicable in each jurisdiction where there is a necessity to support your business requirements.)

An organizations' competitive edge often results from the creativity and innovation of its employees. Loss of such assets could negatively affect a company's investment in personnel, time, finances, products and property (Daniels, 2007a, p.2). Security directors can no longer take a silo approach to risks like trade secrets, focusing only on a certain "self-contained" aspect, such as espionage (Daniels). All types of proprietary information face risks, including trade secrets, trademarks and copyrights. The issues become even more important when businesses expand to operate globally.

In *International Airport Centers v. Citrin* (2006) a U.S. Court of Appeals for the Seventh Circuit ruled that an employee violated federal law when he destroyed information on his employer's laptop computer. The employee erased confidential company files and documents, indicating he was planning to steal the data and start his own competing company.

Technology Escrow   **Technology escrow** is like an insurance policy for intellectual property. Technology escrow is required when two or more parties negotiate a license for technology, such as mission-critical software or other proprietary information (Johnson, 2005, p.68). If the licensee-company of the technology is concerned it may not be able to operate its mission-critical software because the developer—the only source of the technology—may no longer be able to provide support in the future, the licensee should request that the technology (typically software source code) be placed into an escrow account. In such an arrangement, a technology escrow agent acts as a neutral third party to set up the contract spelling out the conditions under which the code held in escrow would be released to the licensee-company. The cost of the escrow and verification typically runs just under 5 percent of the cost of the code being protected (Johnson, p.68).

Trade Secrets

A trade secret can be defined as: "All forms and types of financial, business, scientific, technical, economic or engineering information, including patterns, plans, compilations, program devices, formulas, designs, prototypes, methods, techniques, processes, procedures, programs or codes, whether tangible or intangible, and whether or how stored, compiled, or memorialized physically, electronically, graphically, photographically or in writing if (a) the owner thereof has taken reasonable measures to keep such information secret; and (b) the information derives independent economic value, actual or potential, from not being generally known to, and not being readily ascertainable through proper means by, the public" (*Information Asset Protection*, p.8). The Economic Espionage Act of 1996 created the first criminal statutes specifically aimed at the theft of trade secrets.

Often the products of such secrets are also protected by a **trademark**, which is defined as: "A word, phrase, logo or other graphic symbol used by a manufacturer or seller to distinguish its product or products from those of others" (*Information Asset Protection*, p.8). The Lanham Act of 1946 codified civil law into a national system of trademark protections. The Trademark Counterfeiting Act of 1984 made trafficking in goods and services using a counterfeit trademark a felony.

Need-to-know criteria should be established to ensure individuals have access to only the specific information they need to do their jobs. In addition, effective information warning notifications should be initiated to ensure individuals are aware of exactly what needs to be protected.

To prove a trade secret case in court, it is important to document identification and valuation of the asset, its role in establishing competitive advantage in the industry, and the full scope of protection measures instituted to protect it. Security managers should ensure that reasonable and prudent traditional and cyber security measures are in place to prevent unauthorized access to trade secrets. Periodic, random security audits should be conducted to ensure compliance.

Patented Information

A **patent** is: "Information that has the government grant of a right, privilege or authority to exclude others from making, using, marketing, selling, offering for sale or importing an invention for a specified period (20 years from the date of filing) granted to the inventor if the device or process is novel, useful and non-obvious. Follow trade secret guidelines for all newly discovered processes/products until a patent has been issued. Establish a patent strategy to ensure that patent protection is acquired in all appropriate jurisdictions" (*Information Asset Protection*, p.7).

Copyrighted Material

A **copyright** is: "A property right in an original work of authorship (including literary, musical, dramatic, choreographic, pictorial, graphic, sculptural and architectural work; motion pictures and other audiovisual works; and sound recordings) fixed in any tangible medium of expression, giving the holder exclusive right to reproduce, adapt, distribute, perform and display the work" (*Information Asset Protection*, p.7). "The Internet's freewheeling environment can lead to lax attitudes about stealing copyrighted materials" (Gips, 2006c, p.22). Adding to the problem is that many Internet users do not know they are violating copyright laws: "Copying on the Internet is rampant, including among security companies and security professionals. . . . A lot of people think that just because it's on the Internet it's free" (Gips). The Copyright Act of 1976 provides the basic framework for today's copyright laws. The Copyright Felony Act of 1992 targeted the mass reproduction of computer software and made copyright infringement involving 10 or more copies a felony.

To protect against copyright infringement, attorneys recommend putting copyright notices at the bottom of every Web page and registering copyrights for the site quarterly with the U.S. Copyright Office. Candidates for copyright include mission statements, business plans and any policies, standards or guides in which companies have invested time and resources. Generally copyright law covers expression of an idea, not the idea itself, so for a copyright infringement to occur, the person stealing the material must use the exact words of the original—usually at least 35 words.

Copyrighting material provides the presumption of ownership and bolsters a claim should a company end up challenging someone's use of their material in court. But more importantly, it allows plaintiffs to obtain statutory damages authorized by the Copyright Act up to $30,000 for each work infringed or up to $150,000 per work if the infringement was willful. If the infringer is based outside the United States, often there is little the copyright holder can do.

Piracy Twenty-three billion dollars was lost in 2004 as a result of criminals swiping copyright-protected digital copies of music, movies, software and games and distributing them through Web sites, chat rooms, mass e-mail, file transfer protocol (FTP) and peer-to-peer networks ("Pirates in Cyberspace," 2004). Online piracy rings, known as "warez" (pronounced *wares*), function as underground cyberspace co-ops, in which members swap the latest copyrighted material. Warez groups are difficult to penetrate as many are based overseas

Randy Saaf is president and CEO of MediaDefender Inc. in Los Angeles, a company that uses decoys and "interdiction" (tying up download queues with fake requests from his computers) to thwart file-sharing and other means of Internet piracy. Businesses like MediaDefender Inc. act as agents for copyright holders, creating technical defenses behind the scenes.

and users are tech-savvy, communicating in encrypted messages and requiring codes and passwords ("FBI Piracy Bust," 2005).

In 2005 the Justice Department seized hundreds of computers and arrested four people in an international crackdown on Internet pirates illegally distributing copyrighted video games, software and movies. Agents executed 90 search warrants in the United States and 10 other countries as part of Operation Site Down. The raids shut down at least eight major online distributors and seized pirated works worth more than $50 million. Criminal complaints charged the four with copyright infringement and conspiracy to commit criminal copyright infringement ("FBI Piracy Bust").

According to a study by the Motion Picture Association of America ("FBI Breaks Worldwide Piracy Ring," 2006), the major motion picture studios lost $6.1 billion to piracy in 2005. In 2006, FBI agents arrested 13 members of an organized network of movie thieves in the New York area, culminating a three-year investigation conducted by the FBI and the U.S. Attorney's Office for the Southern District of New York. Camcorders supply 90 percent of newly released movies that end up on the Internet and the streets. The recordings are duplicated and sold on the black market and loaded onto the Internet, resulting in millions of illegal downloads.

Digital Rights Management (DRM) Digital Rights Management (DRM) is antipiracy technology used by digital copyright owners, such as software programmers, musicians and movie artists, to control who has access to their work.

DRM allows the copyright holder some ability to remotely control how people can install, listen to, view and duplicate digital files. Access control is achieved through use of a digital padlock, called "licensed encryption key," placed on the files to keep unauthorized users from accessing or copying the file. Authorization is effectively granted when someone pays for a code to unlock the encryption key.

Watermark Technology   The concept of watermarking, such as that traditionally used on currency, has evolved into digital forms as the need to protect digital data has increased. Various companies have developed digital watermarks to help copyright holders protect their assets. For example, Fraunhofer Integrated Publication and Information Systems Institute (Fraunhofer IPSI) has developed digital image watermark technology to help companies with popular brand name logos embed watermarks in pictures of their products in an effort to protect those images from being stolen by groups trying to promote cheap imitations. Fraunhofer has also developed a Web search system to hunt down trademark violators on the Internet. The watermark technology makes slight changes in the color, contrast or brightness of a picture. The changes, made in tiny areas across the picture, are invisible to the human eye (Blau, 2006).

Potential Threats to Proprietary Information

 Potential threats to the security of proprietary information include employees, vendors, visitors and discarded information.

Employees

Although most managers would agree that people are an organization's most important asset, they can also be their greatest liability. Consider the example of a member of an IT security department who was fired for poor performance. He went home angry and frustrated, had a drink or two and decided to see if he still had access to his former employer's network. He did. He had access to every system and every file on every system. He poured himself another drink and felt entitled to revenge, so he deleted every file and every application management program needed to perform their jobs: spreadsheets, memos, letters, network accounts, everything. He knew this would really hurt the company because he was the one responsible for doing the backups on these systems, and he had not done a complete backup for weeks. When he sobered up, he realized he forgot to delete the log files that revealed his activity and he was arrested. However, the company had to spend thousands of dollars to manually recreate their data (Mallery, 2005, p.54).

Most cases of employee security risks are not so dramatic, but they can still be devastating. Other actions disgruntled employees have engaged in include entering the accounting department and stealing company checks, disseminating proprietary information to competitors, modifying the company Web site to advertise a business specializing in the taxidermy of family members, changing passwords and the like (Mallery, p.56).

Other times employees can be a security threat unintentionally. Employees should be instructed not to use cell phones to discuss sensitive information, as such calls can be intercepted. Employees might also be asked to sign nondisclosure, noncompete and/or trade secrecy agreements. **Nondisclosure agreements** are usually requested of high-level executives, research-and-development personnel and other employees who have access to sensitive information. The agreements prohibit employees from disclosing sensitive information to outsiders. **Noncompete agreements** are designed to prevent employees from quitting and going to work for a competitor. **Secrecy agreements** are directed at individuals who come into contact with vital trade secrets of a business—for example, technicians called in to repair a vital piece of machinery. Such individuals may be asked to sign an agreement to keep such information confidential.

Kresevich (2007, p.47) contends: "Any store can make itself an incubator for disgruntled employees primed for crime, or it can recognize the problem and instead proactively create the environment in which employees thrive and business prospers." Interviews with hundreds of employees caught stealing revealed that no matter what policies and procedures corporations established, employees react to how they are treated and to the prevailing culture (Kresevich). A training program has been created that teaches employees to communicate with one another effectively, comply with ethics policies, address specific situations and build a foundation of integrity (Kresevich, p.50). Part of this culture might include an employee hotline.

Well-managed hotlines supported by robust investigations can help uncover fraud and other unethical activities that might ultimately hurt an organization (Mohr and Slovin, 2005, p.51). Tipsters must, however, be free to report abuses without fear of retaliation. For example, when the CFO of Cardinal Bankshares, David Welch, became suspicious of potential accounting misconduct by other insiders and reported these concerns his supervisors, he was fired shortly thereafter. Welch sued Cardinal Bankshares for unlawful termination and retaliation under the whistleblower's act. While the bank testified that Welch was terminated based on his failure to cooperate with the company's investigation of the alleged financial irregularities, the court found that the evidence did not support the bank's claim and ruled that Cardinal Bankshares was, in fact, guilty of retaliating against Welch for his whistleblower activities (Mohr and Slovin).

This case is significant because it is one of the first instances of whistleblower retaliation brought to court based on the **Sarbanes-Oxley legislation**, which requires as one of its corporate governance provisions that companies give employees a way to report financial irregularities anonymously: "A hotline must offer around the clock service, because 40 percent of all calls happen outside of traditional business hours" (Mohr and Slovin, p.53).

Vendors

Suppliers and distributors should also be included in the information security link. Those with access to what could be considered valuable information should be asked to sign nondisclosure agreements.

Visitors

Procedures to ensure that visitors do not obtain proprietary information were discussed in Chapter 7, including sign-in and sign-out procedures, wearing badges, being escorted and being restricted to certain areas of a facility.

Discarded Information

"One man's trash is another man's treasure." This saying has never been truer than as it applies to discarded company documents, ripe with personal identification data. Businesses must be exceedingly careful about disposing of any papers that might contain information which, in the wrong hands, could be used for great harm. The *Minnesota Daily*, an independent, student-produced newspaper on the Twin Cities campus of the University of Minnesota, reported that school employees left thousands of documents, including medical records, social security numbers and credit card numbers, outside in open trash containers for more than a week (Longmore-Etheridge, 2004, p.59). In another case a healthcare company in St. Louis discarded sensitive records, including those of patients treated for psychological problems, drug and alcohol addictions and sexually transmitted diseases, in an open dumpster (Longmore-Etheridge). These incidents illustrate the public relations and potential legal perils of poor document destruction policies: "Companies that discard sensitive documents should not plan for a peaceful burial but rather utter annihilation" (Longmore-Etheridge).

Too often, sensitive or secret information is discarded in trash cans and then collected in plastic bags and put into a dumpster. Most dumpsters are in areas where the public has access to them. Anyone seeking information about a given company or employee need simply sort through the bags until they come across one with envelopes or documents pertaining to their target.

Some companies have instituted a "shred everything" policy and have placed secured bins at copy machines and in other locations. Employees are educated that if it's paper, put it in the bin. For most large companies, however, it is usually not possible or cost effective to handle their own document destruction. The job is commonly outsourced. To make due diligence easier, security directors should look for a shredding company certified by the National Association for Information Destruction, Inc. (NAIDI) (Longmore-Etheridge, p.60).

Document destruction policies must avoid violating any federal or state laws or regulations. For example, Sarbanes-Oxley makes it a criminal offense to destroy corporate documents because of a possible or pending federal investigation. Companies that have a set policy of routinely destroying documents after a set period of time may protect a company from charges that it destroyed documents to avoid liability.

Security directors should recognize that what may appear to be illegally obtained information is, in actuality, not illegal at all but is open to the public if they are intelligent enough to find the information.

Competitive Intelligence

Competitive intelligence (CI) is a fact of life in the business world. Those engaged in CI have even formed a professional association, the Society of Competitive Intelligence Professionals, complete with a code of ethics. It is imperative that security directors recognize the difference between theft of intellectual property, infringement of copyright laws and competitive intelligence.

Competitive intelligence (CI) consists of two overall facts: "First is the use of public sources to develop data (raw facts) on competitors and the market environment. Second is the transformation, by analysis, of that data into information (usable results)" (McGonagle and Vella, 2007, p.64). In this context, the term *public* means all information that can be legally and ethically identified, located and accessed by someone who knows what to look for. McGonagle and Vella (p.66) caution that in many cases, what is called theft is actually the result of effective CI against a company by a competitor. They provide an example of "burger wars" between Big Rick's and Little Joe's:

> Every time Big Rick's Burgers launched a new product, its executives were distressed to see a major competitor, Little Joe's, launch a similar product shortly before and for a few cents less. After this happened three times in a row, Big Rick's executives became convinced that these occurrences were not coincidental and that a very serious breach of corporate security needed to be identified and stopped. At this point, no one knew whether it was a disloyal employee or a security hole in the computer system.
>
> Senior management called in corporate security personnel to investigate. At the CIO's suggestion, the competitive intelligence unit was also called in to run a parallel investigation. As it turned out, a loophole in the franchise agreements allowed an unethical franchisee to play for both sides, legally.
>
> CI found these key facts to explain what was happening. New product announcements were sent to all franchisees. The announcements were not marked "confidential" because everyone assumed this was implicit and thus unnecessary. Franchise rules contained a blanket prohibition on owning competing franchises, but a handful of "legacy" franchisees from the company's early days were not subject to this prohibition. Among the holders of these legacy franchises, research disclosed that two also held Little Joe's franchises.
>
> When one of Big Rick's CI analysts called some of the legacy franchises, she learned that one was sharing the information with Little Joe's because he felt loyalty to both sides and stood to benefit from transmitting the information.[3]

Other measures that should be taken are to have new hires sign a nondisclosure agreement (NDA), which is: "A legal contract between at least two parties that outlines confidential materials or knowledge the parties wish to share with one another for certain purposes, but wish to restrict from generalized use" (*Information Asset Protection*, p.8). In other words, it is a contract through which the parties agree not to disclose information covered by the agreement.

Common targets of CI are research-and-development (R&D) departments, marketing, manufacturing and production, and human resources. Information may be obtained from employees, facility tours, corporate publications, business associates, distributors, suppliers, maintenance workers—in fact, anyone associated with the business. The preceding are all instances of active CI. Companies may also engage in defensive CI.

Defensive CI protects a company's information assets from legal collection efforts. It consists of monitoring and analyzing a company's own business activities as their competitors would see them and then working to cloak company data from CI efforts (McGonagle and Vella, p.68). Cloaking involves three

---

[3]SOURCE: From "I Spy Your Company Secrets" by John J. McGonagle, Jr. and Carolyn M. Vella. © 2007 ASIS International, 1625 Prince Street, Alexandria, VA 22314. Reprinted by permission from the February 2007 issue of *Security Management* magazine.

basic concepts: (1) the company must understand the channels through which a competitor could gather company data; (2) it should seek to control what goes into these channels; and (3) it should consider how competitors might analyze collected data, which will help assess the kind of data competitors need to conduct their analysis (McGonagle and Vella, p.68).

Privacy Protection

Almost all organizations handle some form of "privacy" information about their employees, management, relationships, customers or others. The ASIS *Guidelines* (*Information Asset Protection*, 2007) stress that to maintain the necessary level of trust and to meet legal and regulatory requirements, distinct controls on privacy information such as the following should be implemented:

- Establish specific privacy policies and designate an employee responsible for implementing and managing the privacy program.
- Evaluate privacy information relating to employees, partners, vendors, customers, and others and determine legal and regulatory requirements.
- Ensure systems are in place to make certain employee privacy is not compromised.
- Review applicable federal, state and international guidelines to ensure adequate internal controls are in place to protect employees' privacy.
- Clearly mark privacy information properly released to indicate (1) how the information will be used and made available to others, (2) proper notifications and actions if a compromise should occur and (3) destruction or disposition instructions when the information is no longer needed.
- Conduct program audits to ensure privacy policies are practiced effectively.[4]

Privacy policies should also mandate that employees not carry any files, documents or data on their laptops they do not need, minimizing the chance that loss of a laptop might expose sensitive customer or employee information. Losing such data could not only hurt a company's reputation, it could put it in violation of more than 20 federal and state privacy disclosure laws.

Research is being done at Stanford University on **contextual integrity**, which defines privacy using complex social principles expressed in algorithms written into software to monitor data use (Barth et al., 2007, p.56). The goal of this application is to help companies comply with privacy laws and their own privacy policies. The model relies on four variables: behavioral norms that apply to transmitting personal information, the appropriateness of the information involved, the roles of the individuals sending and receiving the information, and the principles of transmission. The last variable focuses on the constraints regulating the information flow from one entity to another. For example, someone might receive information because the person deserves to know it, because someone chooses to share it or because the person receiving it promises to keep it confidential.

---

[4]SOURCE: From *Information Asset Protection Guideline, DRAFT* (Alexandria, VA: American Society for Industrial Security, 2007) pp.13–14. Reprinted with the written permission of ASIS International, Alexandria, VA.

Notifying Customers of Electronic Security Breaches

Many states have passed laws requiring companies to notify consumers if an electronic security breach occurs. The laws provide exceptions when such notification would be extremely costly, though the figures differ by state (Anderson, 2007, p.90). For example, in Vermont notification is required if the amount is $5,000 or greater, but in Washington state, the notification threshold is $250,000. In addition, most state laws do not require disclosure if misuse of the data is unlikely to occur. Three states have created the specific crime of phishing, as first discussed in Chapter 9. For example, an Oklahoma law makes phishing illegal and allows Internet service providers (ISPs) to bring civil actions, including being able to recover actual damages of up to $100,000 for each violation.

Compliance

Companies that comply with regulations requiring data security should, in theory, be moving toward having more secure networks, but studies show compliance achievement may actually be having the opposite effect (Piazza, 2006c, p.50). Compliance is not a one-time, "we've done this so now we can relax" type of security measure. It is ongoing and ever changing. Although more time is being spent on compliance than ever before, corporate leadership may be lulled into a false sense of security if they are compliant. For instance, an organization can be International Standardization Organization (ISO) compliant, Sarbanes-Oxley compliant and the like and still not necessarily have a secure infrastructure. A better way to ensure a sound security program is to base it on established principles of asset protection.

Basic Principles of Information Asset Protection

The ASIS's *Information Asset Protection Guidelines* (p.6) state that asset protection, whether in electronic, verbal, written or any other format, involves five basic principles:
1. Classifying and labeling information
2. Handling protocols to specify use, distribution, storage, security expectations, declassification, return and destruction/disposal methodology
3. Training
4. Incident reporting and investigation
5. Audit/compliance processes and special needs (disaster recovery)

Classifying and Labeling Information

ASIS recommends that all information be classified into one of four categories: unrestricted, internal use, restricted and highly restricted. Table 11.1 summarizes its recommendations for classifying proprietary information.

Protocols for Distribution

ASIS also provides guidance on protocols for distributing proprietary information. Table 11.2 suggests issues to consider when determining the sensitivity of the materials. Table 11.3 summarizes their recommendations for protecting proprietary information at the various levels.

Table 11.1 Classifications of Proprietary Information

Categories of information assets may include:

- Proprietary information (customer lists, marketing plans, pricing strategies, test results, etc.)

- Trade secrets

- Patent information

- Copyright information

- Physical products (prototypes, models, molds, dyes and manufacturing equipment, etc.)

- Trade marks and service marks

- Privacy information (personal data, evaluations, credit info, etc.)

- Regulation information (health information such as protected information under HIPAA, financial data, classified government information etc.)

SOURCE: From *Information Asset Protection Guideline, DRAFT* (Alexandria, VA: American Society for Industrial Security, 2007) p.10. Reprinted with the written permission of ASIS International, Alexandria, VA.

Table 11.2 Determining the Classification of Material

Unrestricted	Internal Use	Restricted	Highly Restricted
This information can be shared within the organization and outside the organization.	1. Read access is unrestricted within the company. Version control and updates are managed by the content owner. 2. Sharing externally without a nondisclosure requires a clear understanding between the parties that the information is to be treated as confidential. 3. This information is not to be shared with the public.	1. Content owners manage access lists and authorize sharing. 2. Access is limited to certain organizations, groups or people in certain roles (i.e., legal, engineering, marketing, etc.). 3. Breadth and type (e.g., create, read only, update or delete) of information access is limited and is based on role and fraud control requirements. 4. A signed NDA and an established "need to know" policy are required to share this information with the extended enterprise.*	1. Content owners manage access lists for type of access and authorized sharing. 2. Access is restricted to specifically named individuals with an established "need to know." 3. Authorizing a fellow employee requires verification of employee status and a clear understanding of intended use. 4. In authorizing sharing information with an individual from the extended enterprise, verify that a signed NDA and an appropriate contractual agreement are in place. 5. Quarterly review of continued access.

* "Extended enterprise" consists of both individuals and entities with access to the organization's information assets, people and facilities.

SOURCE: From *Information Asset Protection Guideline, DRAFT* (Alexandria, VA: American Society for Industrial Security, 2007) p.37. Reprinted with the written permission of ASIS International, Alexandria, VA.

Table 11.3 Protection Requirements for Sharing Information

	Internal Use (Green)	Restricted (Yellow)	Highly Restricted (Red)
Marking			
Documents (paper and electronic)	Only items with broad corporate circulation are marked "Internal Use" and these are shared in noneditable form.	Mark "Restricted" on the *first* page or mark at Application/Web site entry.	Mark "Highly Restricted" on *every* page and every screen that displays or provides access to Highly Restricted data.
Mailing/Shipping			
Within the company	Routing envelope with no special markings.	Use double sealed envelopes. Mark inner envelope "Restricted: to be opened by addressee only." No security marks on outer envelope.	Use double sealed envelopes. Mark inner envelope "Highly Restricted: to be opened by addressee only." No security marks on outer envelope.
Facsimile (FAX)			
Within the company	No special requirements.	Confirm fax number and ask if machine is physically secured. Ask recipient to be present while fax is received.	Avoid faxing across international borders, if possible. If sent, neutralize or sanitize contents to degree practical.
Over outside lines	Notify recipient and confirm the fax number.	Ask that recipient be present while fax is received.	Fax if other more secure methods of transference are unavailable. 1. Neutralize/sanitize contents to degree practical. 2. Request recipient to be present during receipt. 3. Do not draw attention to sensitivity by marking cover sheet.
E-mail/Electronic Transfer			
Within the company (intranet, encrypted links, dedicated lines)	No special requirements.	Encryption is recommended but not required for internal electronic communications.	1. Encrypt e-mail messages or files, if possible. 2. Use encryption technology, if possible. 3. Validate business need and identity of the receiver.
Through outside networks (Internet)	1. Address to specific individuals. 2. Do not post on bulletin boards or send to public forums.	1. Use encryption technology, if possible. 2. Validate business need and identity of the receiver.	
Storage			
Within the company	Use password enabled screen saver with timeout less than 15 minutes.	1. Encrypt electronic documents and control access. 2. Maintain personal control or use locked storage.	
Off company and premises	1. Keep information under your control. 2. Use password enabled screen saver with timeout less than 15 minutes.		
Destruction/Disposal			
Within the company and offsite	1. Where appropriate, adhere to the organization's retention limits. 2. Shred hard copy or use locked recycle bins. 3. Delete electronic information. 4. Destroy removable media (e.g., diskettes, CDs, tape cartridges, zip disks, etc.) before disposal.		

SOURCE: From *Information Asset Protection Guideline, DRAFT* (Alexandria, VA: American Society for Industrial Security, 2007) p.39. Reprinted with the written permission of ASIS International, Alexandria, VA.

Security Awareness Training

Protection of information, generally more so than any other asset, is best achieved through routine business practices that permeate every element of an organization. Therefore, where each individual entrusted with sensitive information takes prudent measures and personal responsibility for protecting those assets, a robust security environment should occur naturally.

 Almost invariably, security awareness and training is one of the most cost-effective measures to protect corporate information assets.

The ASIS *Guidelines* (*Information Asset Protection*, p.13) recommend the following:

- Determine the need for and scope of an Information Security Awareness Training program within the organization based on a comprehensive risk assessment and the nature of the business.
- Consider developing and delivering tailored security awareness training for all individuals in a trusted relationship.
- Include nonemployees such as part-time personnel, temporary employees, consultants, subcontractors and on-site vendors in such training.
- Deliver recurring awareness training via multiple modes to effectively reach all appropriate personnel.
- Whenever possible, document information security awareness and training.[5]

Incident Reporting and Investigating

Six factors are critical to conducting a good investigation (Albrecht et al., 2004, p.78):

 The critical factors to conducting an effective investigation are keeping management informed, being objective, exercising discretion in discussing investigations, independently corroborating the facts, using the right investigative tools and avoiding ineffective, unproven or illegal investigative techniques.

Albrecht et al. (p.78) stress: "Early management involvement ensures accountability for the investigation, thus helping the investigator gain credibility and protection from allegations." Objectivity is also critical. The investigator's approach and demeanor are important to the successful outcome of the case. Failure to corroborate evidence is a common mistake of inexperienced investigators. Reports and other documents related to the investigation should include not only information pointing to guilt, but also information that may exonerate a suspect—**exculpatory evidence**. Effective investigators let the facts speak for themselves, ensuring the general tone of their reports is objective.

Investigators must look beyond company records which may have been altered (Albrecht et al.). In addition, data analysis tools can help investigators cull evidence from corporate databases and servers.

A survey by the U.S. Secret Service and Carnegie Mellon's Computer Emergency Response Team (CERT) found that insiders are often careless (as in the example opening this discussion), and it may be possible to catch them by

---

[5]SOURCE: From *Information Asset Protection Guideline, DRAFT* (Alexandria, VA: American Society for Industrial Security, 2007) p.13. Reprinted with the written permission of ASIS International, Alexandria, VA.

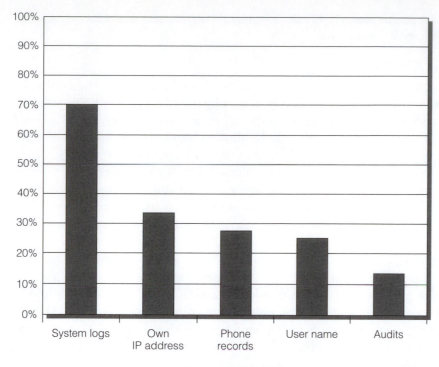

Method of detection

Figure 11.2   Detecting Insider Attacks

SOURCE: Portions of *Insider Threat Study: Computer System Sabotage in Critical Infrastructure Sectors* by Michelle Kenney, Eileen Kowalski, Dawn Cappelli, Andrew Moore, Timothy Shimeall and Stephanie Rodgers, © 2005 by Carnegie Mellon University, are reproduced with special permission from the Software Engineering Institute.

tracing illicit activity back to their own computer (IP) address, phone or user name (Keeney et al., 2005). Figure 11.2 shows how insider attacks were detected in 2005.

Audits

Gips (2006b, p.18) reports: "Leading-edge companies are expanding their codes of conduct and asking audit committees to focus on fraud." He notes that even the best antifraud controls are ineffective if top management can override them, as is the case in between 60 to 80 percent of all controls. The result: "Deference to management and reluctance (or inability) on the part of a board of directors or audit committee to look behind the override of internal controls have resulted in huge fraud losses" (Gips).

The American Institute of Certified Public Accountants (AICPA) recommends that internal audit committees brush up on their understanding of the company's business, maintain a constant skepticism, brainstorm to identify fraud risks, cultivate a "vigorous" whistleblower program and adopt other measures (Gips, 2006b, p.18).

Security Measures against IT Threats

Protecting computers and the information they contain is a vital function of security personnel.

Security measures for IT include logical controls, physical access controls and administrative controls.

Logical Controls

Logical controls are special programs written into the software. The most common are those that restrict access by requiring use of a password. The software might also determine what types of specific information a given user is allowed to access. Specific employees might be allowed into only certain parts of a file. Or they might be allowed to only read the data, but not make any changes in it.

Remote terminals must also be protected. When companies share time on a computer, care must be exercised to ensure that time-sharing customers are limited to their own database. Three ways to identify users wanting access to a computer by phone or terminal are a password (usually a word or phrase), a key or card and physical characteristics.

Use of a password is most common, but because passwords can be overheard or given to unauthorized persons, they should be changed often. Use of generic passwords should be eliminated and, instead, employees should be assigned passwords that are randomly generated using an online tool (Elliott, 2006, p.32). Such passwords are alphanumeric but pronounceable so they can be easily remembered, and they avoid using common dictionary terms that can be cracked by simple hacking tools.

Key- or card-controlled systems must, of course, be protected by rigid key/card control procedures, as described in an earlier chapter. The safest system of authorization and user identification is one that relies on physical characteristics (biometrics). However, such identification systems are expensive, and if voice identification is used, the system may deny access to authorized individuals whose voice characteristics have changed temporarily because of a cold or other illness.

Multilevel access capability makes a computer more flexible. Some access systems allow different operators to obtain different types of information, but only a limited number to have access to the total program.

One of the most effective types of logical controls is *data encryption*, in which an **encryption** device is placed between the host computer and a modem. The device puts the data into a code before it enters the transmission line. It is then decoded at the receiving end. The military uses sophisticated encryption systems that scramble messages to protect national security data. Many encryption tools are free but require that the user know how to apply and manage them. Proper use of encryption can prevent the most powerful supercomputers from breaking a code for 20 years. However, even with logical controls, no system is 100 percent safe. If hackers can break into a cancer hospital for a lark, what might serious criminals or terrorists do?

Programs can be built into the computer that will detect fraud and embezzlement. Currently, however, most computer crimes are discovered by chance, not by audit, because there is no visible evidence of tampering—no erasures or doctored numbers. The crimes are committed by removals and changes that are done in seconds and leave no trace.

Physical Controls

Physical controls restrict access to computer terminals and other equipment and software. Physical access control is critical to computer security. The practice of including computer centers in company tours to enhance public image has been discontinued by most establishments. Most computer centers are now in restricted areas with locked doors, alarm systems and supervisory personnel on duty whenever the computer is operating. Potential for access through air vents, windows and doors must be assessed. In computer centers where rigid access control is required, there is a single entrance/exit—ideally a riot door—then a corridor and a second (riot) door, both electronically controlled and guarded. Entrance may be obtained through use of an employee ID badge system, keys, key-cards or identification systems using biometric characteristics such as fingerprints, palm prints or voice characteristics. In addition, various devices are available that lock computers to desktops.

The computer printouts should also be safeguarded. When they are no longer needed, they should be run through a shredder. Company secrets can be obtained more easily through carelessly discarded printouts than through "bugging." Nonetheless, "bugging" must also be guarded against. Equipment is available that can indicate when a "bug" is in operation.

Removable PC media, which includes all types of discs, optical media, USB drives, memory cards and other devices that store data, need to be securely stored in locked files. The removable PC media library should be protected against unauthorized access and should make use of a rigidly enforced sign-out/sign-in procedure.

To minimize the threat of employee fraud or embezzlement and collusion, the functions of computer technicians, operators and programmers should be clearly separated. Programmers should not operate the computers except to try out new programs, and then only under supervision. Typically, developers are given a test environment where they can do anything they want without affecting production systems or data. A programmer should not be in the computer room or have access to production systems unsupervised. And only authorized people should be allowed to change programs. Sometimes such separation is not practical, but where it can be accomplished, it should be. *Content management* and *release management* are terms commonly used to define who handles and is responsible for data as it is processed at the various distinct stages. It is also a good policy to rotate personnel working on various programs.

Administrative Controls

Administrative controls include making careful background checks on all employees and assuming responsibility for security, including stressing security during management meetings: "Strong checks, including criminal background, education, and employment are particularly important for IT staff because of their high-level access to systems and data. . . . 'Professionally, they really do have the keys to the modern-day kingdom,' says [the] vice president of operations at . . . an employment background screening firm" (Wagley, 2007, p.76). Other administrative security measures to protect against theft are periodic external audits as well as involving auditors in designing computer programs.

Administrative controls can also be used to reduce employee carelessness and ignorance, which can result in tremendous losses for companies that rely on computers. All computer operators should be well qualified and should then be further trained on the specific hardware and software they will be using. Checklists and written instructions should be affixed to each machine and should delineate the procedures to be followed and any cautions to be taken. Detailed daily logs should be completed by each operator. Even the most skilled operators can make mistakes, however. Reporting employee mistakes must be encouraged so the mistakes can be corrected rather than covered up, thereby creating even more serious problems than the original mistake may have caused. A system of error analysis should be established to reduce further errors. Clearly established rules and procedures as well as regular reviews and inspections will help reduce losses that result from employee carelessness or ignorance.

Recommendations for an IT Security Program

Chapter 9 outlined the Bureau of Justice Statistics recommendations for a computer security program. *The Trend of Threats Today* (2005) offers the following additional recommendations to avoid cyber attacks:

- Deploy HTTP (hypertext transfer protocol) scanning methods. HTTP is a communication protocol to transfer information on the Web. It is highly recommended to implement a Web virus scanning system, much in the same way administrators started deploying e-mail scanning long ago. Detecting and stopping threats before any infected file can reach the end user adds a new layer of protection in the corporate network infrastructure. Spyware protection in the network layer is a bonus because these threats use HTTP exclusively to enter the corporate environment.
- Block unnecessary protocols from entering the corporate network. The most dangerous are 1M P2P communication protocols and IRC (chat). These two are part of the bot arsenal of weapons to propagate and communicate with their botmaster and should be disallowed in the corporate firewall.
- Deploy vulnerability scanning software in the network. Being constantly up-to-date can minimize the impact of any new network vulnerability and diminish the risk of being infected by this kind of worm.
- Do not give administrator privileges to all users. The most dangerous of all privileges is "load and unload device drivers." This is the most recommended measure to prevent being affected by rootkits. Usually rootkits are implemented as device drivers to have access to all operating system internals. Redesigning the user policy to limit users in this fashion can be one of the most useful ways to secure a network. If the administrator deprives users of admin rights there is an added bonus: Aggressive malware will not be able to kill antivirus processes in the system.
- Deploy corporate antispyware scanning. As spyware is becoming a prevalent threat for corporate businesses, administrators need to deploy specific software to detect and stop this threat.
- Educate users; enforce a strict security policy within the network. Not only do software and defense systems help fight against malware, most users needs to take some kind of action to infect the machine. Be it a Web page that installs spyware or an infected e-mail, the user needs to know in advance the ways new malware attacks users. User awareness is the key to a clean network, and administrators should conduct ongoing education

initiatives to keep users informed and protected with updated malware technology.[6]

Following recommendations such as these will not only help protect information assets, but can also help protect against lawsuits.

IT and Lawsuits

New rules regarding discovery of electronic evidence are likely to save companies time and money if they have to provide evidence in litigation: "These rules—part of the Federal Rules of Civil Procedure (FRCP)—affect the ways companies must preserve and make available any email, Word documents, Excel spreadsheets, PowerPoint presentations and other electronic information in the case of civil litigation" (Piazza, 2006a, p.44).

The new rules specify that responding parties need only provide electronically stored information that is "reasonably accessible." The rules also mandate that lawyers conduct "meet and confer" conferences early on to discuss what is being requested and how it should be provided.

Who Owns the Net?

One key question to address before leaving the discussion of IT security is: Who owns the net? And the answer, according to Piazza (2006e, p.50), is that nobody knows. He suggests a possible candidate is the National Cyber Response Coordination Group (NCRCG) within the Department of Homeland Security, a forum of 13 agencies that coordinate intragovernmental and public-private preparedness operations to respond to and recover from large-scale cyber attacks. However, according to this group, three gaps impede the nation's ability to reconstitute the Internet should a major disruption occur.

First is a lack of "trip wires" that would indicate immediately that an attack or emergency was underway. Second, too many institutions have responsibility for managing internal reconstitution of their Internet connections. Third, limited resources have been allotted to reconstitution of the Internet's infrastructure.

Recommendations to address these gaps include having the private sector "undertake most of the responsibility for fixing weaknesses in key Internet assets" (Piazza, 2006e, p.50). This might be accomplished by "establishing single points of contact and consolidating early warning and response organizations; having the federal government define key terms, designate responsible parties and communicate a policy for Internet reconstruction; and ensuring that the public and private sectors work together to improve the ability to warn globally of and quickly respond to Internet attacks."

Beyond Technology

Although this chapter focuses on technology, without the appropriate human element, all the technology in the world will not protect an organization: "You

---

[6]SOURCE: From *The Trend of Threats Today: 2005 Annual Roundup and 2006 Forecast* published by Internet Security Systems, Inc.

may have employed the best technology throughout your firm, but it can be defeated by careless or uninformed workers who fail to perform their roles in keeping the network secure. . . . In the final analysis, protecting a firm's cyberspace is much like achieving security generally. It's not only a matter of goals and tools; it's also a matter of culture and commitment" (Imparato, 2005, p.62). Some examples of the human element include employees being tricked into giving up their passwords or being careless in protecting their access codes. At an airport, coffee shop or any other public place, a "stranger" might engage someone in lighthearted conversation, with the hopes of prolonging the interaction long enough to observe that person logging onto an application or Web site and "capturing" the password as it is typed. Another very simple human error that breaches security includes allowing physical access to the company by holding an otherwise locked door open for someone to come in.

In addition to careful and informed workers, the importance of leadership from top management is essential, as Wexler (p.v) stresses: "The need for effectively addressing strong executive leadership is the cornerstone to IT planning and implementation."

SUMMARY

- *Convergence, integration, unification, holistic security*—these are the buzzwords of twenty-first century security.

- The three integral components of a holistic physical security process are protection, detection and reaction.

- IT projects can effect change by automating tasks, sending appropriate information up and down the chain of command, and making work more efficient.

- New technologies that security directors need to become familiar with include IP video surveillance systems, VoIP, USB technology, mesh networks and computer telephony interface (CTI).

- Common equipment that can pose security threats includes cell phones, laptops and PDAs.

- Computer attacks commonly focus on proprietary information.

- Proprietary information includes intellectual property, trade secrets, patented material and copyrighted material.

- Potential threats to the security of proprietary information include employees, vendors, visitors and discarded information.

- Almost invariably, security awareness and training is one of the most cost-effective measures to protect corporate information assets.

- The critical factors to conducting an effective investigation are keeping management informed, being objective, exercising discretion in discussing investigations, independently corroborating the facts, using the right investigative tools and avoiding ineffective, unproven or illegal investigative techniques.

- Security measures for IT include logical controls, physical access controls and administrative controls.

APPLICATIONS

1. In the movie *War Games,* David, a bright young high-school student, is an adept hacker. Computers are his entire life, except for his girlfriend. Outwardly shy, he's totally different when he's with his computer. At first his hacking involves tapping into his school's computer and changing grades. Later,

however, he accidently plugs into a secret Defense Department computer and is faced with the ultimate computer game—diverting thermonuclear war.

   a. How likely is it that David could actually break into his school's computer and change his grades? What crime would be involved?

---

b. How likely is it that he could break into the Defense Department's secret computer? What crime would be involved?

2. A man named George Nickolson (spelled with a "k"), former sales manager of a Honda distributor, used his position to tap into the credit records and social security number of George Nicholson (spelled with an "h"), a schoolteacher. Using the information obtained from the illegitimate inquiry, Nickolson obtained a $5,000 loan from a local bank, obtained a $7,500 loan from another local bank and charged purchases to American Express for more than $6,750.

Shortly thereafter, the banks began hounding Nicholson for payment on the debts which he obviously knew nothing about. He and his wife then went through three years described as a nightmare, being hounded by creditors. Ultimately, Nickolson was arrested and charged with incurring $26,750 in debts over the previous three years.

a. What would the formal charge probably be?

b. How would investigators probably locate the suspect? What evidence would be required?

c. Could Nicholson sue Nickolson for the nightmarish three years?

DISCUSSION QUESTIONS

1. Do you know any computer hackers (or are you one yourself)? What types of activities are they most interested in? Do they perceive anything illegal about their activities?

2. What are the advantages of merging physical and IT security? The disadvantages?

3. How can security professionals keep abreast of IT advances and available programs?

4. Which of the malware described in this chapter poses the greatest threat to information security?

5. What do you think characterizes an effective password to access a computer?

REFERENCES

Albrecht, W. Steve; Albrecht, Conan; Albrecht, Chad; and Williams, Timothy L. "Guilt by Investigation and Other Pitfalls." *Security Management*, November 2004, pp.77–85.

Anderson, Teresa. "State Legislature Wrap-Up." *Security Management*, January 2007, pp.88–93.

Barth, Adam; Datta, Anupam; Mitchell, John; and Nissenbaum, Helen. "A New Perspective on Protecting Personal Data." *Security Management*, May 2007, pp.54–56.

Blau, John. "Digital Image Watermarks Could Combat Trademark Theft." *ComputerWorld*, IDG News Service, August 16, 2006. Online: http://www.computerworld.com/action/article.do?command=viewArticleBasic&articleId=9002500

Boyd, David. "Introduction." In *Issues in IT*. Washington, DC: Police Executive Research Forum, 2005, pp.1–6.

Bradley, Tony. "What Is a Bot?" About.com: Internet/Network Security, 2007.

Canning, Ryan. "All Mesh Networking Is Not Created Equal." *Law Enforcement Technology*, June 2007, pp.96–105.

Cowper, Tom. "Emerging Technology." In *Issues in IT*. Washington, DC: Police Executive Research Forum, 2005, pp.113–125.

"Cyberspace Protection Tips." *Security Products Online*, July 5, 2007. Online: http://www.secprodonline.com/print.aspx?aid=48988. Accessed July 13, 2007.

Daniels, Rhianna. "ASIS Seeks to Protect Intellectual Property." *Security Director News*, February 2007a, pp.2, 4.

Daniels, Rhianna. "Practitioners Face Change in Industry." *Security Director News*, June 2007b, pp.8, 10.

Daniels, Rhianna. "Security Directors Look for Methods to Manage the Information from Sensors." *Security Director News*, Supplement on IP Security Technology, 2007c, p.7.

Edwards, Al. "IP Gives Security Directors Strong Weapon to Mitigate Today's Risks." *Security Director News*, Supplement on IP Security Technology, 2007, p.20.

Elliott, Robert. "Healthy Approach to Data Protection." *Security Management*, February 2006, pp.32–34.

Elliott, Robert. "Malware's Evolving Threat." *Security Management*, June 2007, p.52.

"FBI Breaks Worldwide Piracy Ring." Motion Picture Association of America Press Release, June 28, 2006.

"FBI Piracy Bust." Federal Bureau of Investigation Press Release, July 1, 2005.

Gips, A. Michael. "Has Cybercrime Surpassed Physical Crime?" *Security Management*, July 2006a, p.24.

Gips, Michael A. "Tips for Tightening Fraud Control." *Security Management*, 2006b, pp.18–19.

Gips, Michael A. "Where Copyright Meets the Internet." *Security Management*, October 2006c, pp.22–24.

Goy, John. "Tapping In on IT." *Security Products*, April 2005, pp.94–95.

Hamilton, Caroline R. "The Future Is Holistic Security." *Security Technology & Design*, April 2004, pp.14–18.

Harowitz, Sherry L. "Unification Theory." *Security Management*, January 2005, pp.75–80.

Honen, Tomer. "Don't Be Spooked by Spyware." *Security Management*, December 2005, pp.64–70.

Imparato, Nicholas. "Foxes in the Coop." *Security Technology & Design*, February 2005, pp.60–62.

Information Asset Protection Guidelines, DRAFT, Arlington, VA: American Society for Industrial Security, 2007.

Jaques, Robert. "Criminal Malware Surges as Virus Threat Fades." *Computing*, July 5, 2006.

Johnson, Jeffrey. "With IT, You Get Escrow." *Security Management*, July 2005, pp.67–74.

Johnston, Roger G. and Warner, Jon S. "The Dr. Who Conundrum." *Security Management*, September 2005, pp.112–121.

Kenney, Michelle; Kowalski, Eileen; Cappelli, Dawn; Moore, Andrew; Shimeall, Timothy; and Rogers, Stephanie. *Insider Threat Study: Computer System Sabotage in Critical Infrastructure Sectors.* Washington, DC: U.S. Secret Service, and Pittsburgh, PA: Carnegie Mellon University CERT Program, May 2005.

Kolpack, Bryce. "What the Police Chief Needs to Know about IT Management." In *Issues in IT.* Washington, DC: Police Executive Research Forum, 2005, pp.79–90.

Kresevich, Millie. "Using Culture to Cure Theft." *Security Management*, February 2007, pp.47–51.

Lasky, Steven. "Convergence: Catch the Fever." *Security Technology & Design*, February 2005, p.6.

Longmore-Etheridge, Ann. "On the Eve of Destruction." *Security Management*, December 2004, pp.59–62.

Longmore-Etheridge, Ann. "Olden Days, New Technology." *Security Technology*, September 2006, pp.42–44.

Mallery, John. "You're Fired!" *Security Technology & Design*, March 2005, pp.54–60.

McGonagle, John J., Jr. and Vella, Carolyn M. "I Spy Your Company Secrets." *Security Management*, February 2007, pp.64–70.

Mohr, Timothy L. and Slovin, Dave. "Making Tough Calls Easy." *Security Management*, March 2005, pp.51–56.

"Newspoll." *Security Director News*, March 2007, p.23.

"Newspoll." *Security Director News*, April 2007, p.22.

"Online Russian Blackmail Gang Jailed for Extorting $4M from Gambling Websites." Sophos Online, October 5, 2006: www.sophos.com/pressoffice/news/articles/2006/10/extort-ddos-blackmail.html

"Panda Software Study Evaluates Criminal Activity on the Internet." Panda Software, as indicated by a *PRNewswire* Press Release, May 31, 2007. Online: http://www.prnewswire.com/cgi-bin/stories.pl ?ACCT=109&STORY=/www/story/05–31-2007/0004599087&EDATE=

Piazza, Peter. "Defenses Morph as Viruses Mutate." *Security Management*, March 2004, pp.67–72.

Piazza, Peter. "Discovery Rules of the Digital Age." *Security Management*, December 2006a, pp.44–48.

Piazza, Peter. "I, Bot." *Security Management*, February 2006b, pp.71–78.

Piazza, Peter. "More Compliance, Less Security?" *Security Management*, June 2006c, pp.50–52.

Piazza, Peter. "When Cybercriminals Turn Pro." *Security Management*, May 2006d, pp.48–49.

Piazza, Peter. "Who Owns the Net?" *Security Management*, October 2006e, p.50.

Piazza, Peter. "The ABCs of USB." *Security Management*, January 2007, pp.48–50.

Piccolomini, Paul J. "Developing a United Front." *Security Products*, January 2005, p.8.

"Pirates in Cyberspace." Federal Bureau of Investigation Press Release, February 19, 2004.

Scott, Mike. "CTI and VoIP: IP-Based Trends in Computer Telephony Interface." *9–1-1-Magazine*, June 2007, pp.32–35, 52.

Stephens, Darrel W. "IT Changes in Law Enforcement." In *Issues in IT.* Washington, DC: Police Executive Research Forum, 2005, pp.7–28.

Straw, Joseph. "The Barriers to Interoperability." *Security Management*, July 2007, pp.48–49.

"Study: Web Threats Increase 540 Percent in Two Years." *Security Products Online*, July 9, 2007. Online: http://www.secprodonline.com/articles/49038/. Accessed July 13, 2007.

Swette, Robert. "Meeting the Challenges of the VoIP Revolution." *9–1-1-Magazine*, June 2007, pp.36–37, 53.

The Trend of Threats Today: 2005 Annual Roundup and 2006 Forecast. Internet Security.

Wagley, John. "Checking IT Backgrounds." *Security Management*, September 2007, p.76.

Wexler, Chuck. "Foreword." In *Issues in IT.* Washington, DC: Police Executive Research Forum, 2005, pp.v–vi.

Wilkins, Elisabeth. "The VoIP Revolution." *Security Director News, Supplement on IP Security Technology*, 2007, p.21.

"Zombie Computers—Are Your PCs under Someone Else's Control?" Sophos Online, October 5, 2006: www.sophos.com/pressoffice/news/articles/2006/10/extort-ddos-blackmail.html

CASE CITED

International Airport Centers v. Citrin, U.S. Court of Appeals for the Seventh Circuit, No. 05–1522 (2006).

CHAPTER 12

Drugs and Violence in the Workplace

Violence can erupt in nearly any workplace, including educational institutions. Here, students and employees watch from the doorway of McBryde Hall on the Virginia Tech campus in Blacksburg, Virginia, as police infiltrate the area where a shooting took place, April 16, 2007. Gunman Seung-Hui Cho opened fire in a Virginia Tech dorm and then, two hours later, in a building across campus, killing a total of 32 people and wounding many more before turning the gun on himself.

© AP Photo/The Roanoke Times, Matt Gentry

Do You Know . . .

- What act made it illegal to sell or use certain narcotics and dangerous drugs?
- What drugs are commonly abused in the workplace?
- What the most commonly observed drugs on the street and in possession of users are?
- What the most available and most abused illegal drug in the United States is?
- What common effects of the various narcotics and other dangerous drugs are?
- What potential causes of violence are?
- How many people are victims of violent crime at work each year?
- What common motivations behind workplace violence are?
- What characteristics of the typical perpetrator of workplace violence are?
- What might indicate the potential for workplace violence?
- What most violent people do before they commit acts of violence?
- How threats might be classified?
- What the FBI's four-pronged threat assessment consists of?
- What characteristics are common to workplace violence and school violence?

Can You Define?

amphetamines

barbiturates

conditional threat

deliriants

direct threat

gateway theory

hallucinogens

indirect threat

leakage

methamphetamine

narcotics

nystagmus

psychosocial

sinsemilla

stepping stone theory

toxic work
   environment

veiled threat

zero tolerance

Introduction

> Research has long shown that the abuse of alcohol, tobacco, and illicit drugs is the single most serious health problem in the United States, straining the health care system, burdening the economy, and contributing to the health problems and death of millions of Americans every year. Today, substance abuse causes more deaths, illnesses and disabilities than any other preventable health condition.
>
> —Nels Ericson

In addition, the correlation between drugs and crime is well established. Approximately three-fourths of prison inmates and more than half of those in jails or on probation are substance abusers. Drug users often commit crimes to support their habit. Of the 500,000 inmates serving time on federal, state and local drug charges of all kinds, most were not jailed for possession alone (Katel, 2006).

Crime and drugs are clearly linked, but the relationship between illicit drugs and crime is complex. Some acts involve offenses in which the *effect* of the drug or the *need* for the drug is a contributing factor. These are called drug-related offenses, examples of which might include a user high on PCP who becomes violent and commits an assault because of the drug's pharmacologic effects, or an addict stealing to get money to buy drugs. Such violence can spill over into the workplace, creating another security challenge.

This chapter begins by looking at the threat of drugs and the extent of the problem of drugs in the workplace. Next is a discussion of narcotics, marijuana and other dangerous drugs as well as abuse of prescription drugs. This is followed by an explanation of how to recognize individuals high on drugs. Then the national war on drugs and the role of security is discussed. The portion of the chapter dealing with drugs in the workplace concludes with a look at the challenge of alcohol in the workplace.

The second major discussion in the chapter deals with violence in the workplace and the various forms it can take. It begins with a general discussion of violence in the United States, its increase and some of its causes. Next is a comprehensive definition of workplace violence and various ways to classify the forms it might take. This is followed by a discussion of possible causes, the extent of the workplace violence problem and recognizing the potential for workplace violence, including possible warning signs of impending violence and who is vulnerable. Then preventing violence and responding to it should it occur are examined. The chapter concludes with a discussion of the impact of domestic violence on workplace violence, violence in our schools and some legal issues related to workplace violence.

The Threat of Drugs

American history is filled with drug use, including alcohol and tobacco. As the early settlers moved west, one of the first buildings in each frontier town was a saloon. Cocaine use was also common by the 1880s. At the beginning of the twentieth century, cocaine was the drug of choice, said to cure everything from indigestion to toothaches. However, in 1909 a presidential commission reported to President Theodore Roosevelt that cocaine was a hazard, leading to loss of livelihoods and lives. As the public became increasingly aware of the hazards posed by cocaine and other drugs, it pressed for legislation against use of such drugs.

 In 1914 the federal government passed the Harrison Narcotics Act, which made the sale or use of certain drugs illegal.

In 1920 every state required its students to learn about narcotics' effects. In 1937 under President Franklin Delano Roosevelt, marijuana became the last drug to be banned. For a quarter of a century, the drug problem lay dormant.

Then came the 1960s, a time of youthful rebellion, of Haight Ashbury and the flower children, a time to protest the Vietnam War. A whole culture had as its theme: tune in, turn on and drop out—often through marijuana and LSD. By the 1970s marijuana had been tried by an estimated 40 percent of 18- to 21-year-olds and was being used by many soldiers fighting in Vietnam. Many other soldiers turned to heroin. At the same time, an estimated half million Americans began using heroin back in the States.

The United States became the most drug-pervaded nation in the world, with marijuana leading the way. The 1980s saw a turnaround in drug use, with celebrities advocating, "It's not cool to do drugs," and "Just say no to drugs." At the same time, however, other advertisements suggested that alcohol and smoking were where the "fun is."

The economic cost of drug abuse in 2002 was estimated at $180.9 billion, representing both use of resources to address health and crime consequences as well as the loss of potential productivity from disability, death and withdrawal from the workforce. The costs of drug abuse have increased an average of 5.3 percent per year from 1992 through 2002, making it one of the most costly health problems in the country (*The Economic Costs of Drug Abuse in the United States, 1992–2002*, 2006, p.xiii). Table 12.1 presents a different, more comprehensive perspective on the cost of drug abuse.

Large or small, urban or rural, communities throughout America confront many of the same threats, one of the biggest threats being illegal drug abuse. Drugs destroy lives and spoil the quality of life for entire communities. Government programs alone cannot stop the flow of drugs or keep people from using them. Real progress requires the active support and participation of key leaders, professionals and concerned citizens at the local level (Walters, 2005, p.1).

Table 12.1   Costs of Illegal Drug Use

Criminal Justice Expenditures on Drug-Related Crime	*Health Care Costs*	*Lost Productivity Costs*	*Other Costs to Society*
■ Investigating robberies, burglaries and thefts for drug money and adjudicating and punishing the offenders ■ Investigating assaults and homicides in the drug business by drug users who have lost control and adjudicating and punishing the offenders	■ Injuries resulting from drug-related child abuse/neglect ■ Injuries from drug-related accidents ■ Injuries from drug-related crime ■ Other medical care for illegal drug users, including volunteer services and outpatient services, such as emergency room visits ■ Resources used in nonhospital settings	■ Of victims of drug-related accidents ■ Of victims of drug-related crime ■ Time away from work and homemaking to care for drug users and their dependents ■ Drug-related educational problems and school dropouts ■ Offenders incarcerated for drug-related or drug-defined crimes	■ Loss of property value due to drug-related neighborhood crime ■ Property damaged or destroyed in fires, and in workplace and vehicular accidents ■ Agricultural resources devoted to illegal drug cultivation/production ■ Toxins introduced into public air and water supplies by drug production ■ Workplace prevention programs such as drug testing and employee assistance programs ■ Averting behavior by potential victims of drug-related crime ■ Pain and suffering costs to illegal drug users and their families and friends

SOURCE: *Drugs, Crime and the Justice System: A National Report from the Bureau of Justice Statistics* (Washington, DC: Bureau of Justice Statistics, December 1992) p.127.

The Problem of Drugs in the Workplace

Although some drug users report that drugs such as cocaine increase their concentration and improve their performance on a variety of tasks, no concrete evidence supports such statements. Most drugs are short-acting, with the effects wearing off within an hour, leaving the user tired and depressed. In addition, users may steal to support their habit.

 Drugs commonly abused in the workplace include alcohol, marijuana and cocaine—snorted or smoked as freebase or crack.

In *Largo Corp. v. Crespin* (1986), a Colorado Supreme Court ruled that an employer or proprietor could be held liable for the conduct of an intoxicated employee or patron if the drinking occurred at work or at the place of business. Drinking on the job is discussed later in the chapter.

Studies on Current Drug Use

Although drug use in general is declining, it is still a significant problem. An estimated 19.1 million Americans age 12 years and older currently use illicit drugs, with an estimated 8 percent of the country's population having used some kind of illegal drug in the past 30 days (*Cities without Drugs*, 2005, p.3). There are continued high rates of nonmedical use of prescription medications, especially opioid painkillers including Vicodin and OxyContin. Long-term trends show a significant increase in the abuse of OxyContin. Figure 12.1 illustrates the relative difficulty, or ease, in obtaining various illicit drugs.

Two national studies of drug use in the United States shed light on the current threat of drugs: the *National Drug Threat Assessment 2007* and *Pulse Check: Trends in Drug Abuse*.

National Drug Threat Assessment 2007   The Justice Department's National Drug Intelligence Center (NDIC) provides an annual report describing the availability and distribution of common drugs. According to the *National Drug Threat Assessment 2007* (2007, p.1):

> The trafficking of illicit drugs such as cocaine, heroin, marijuana, methamphetamine and MDMA [Ecstasy] (the leading drug threats to the United States) is undergoing strategic shifts in response to sustained and effective international and domestic counterdrug efforts. These changes—shifting cocaine and methamphetamine production trends, the increasing influence of Mexican and Asian criminal groups in domestic drug distribution, rising availability of more potent forms of methamphetamine and marijuana, and the substitution of illicit drugs for prescription narcotics—represent great challenges.

Other *Assessment* findings include:

- Domestic methamphetamine production has been greatly reduced.
- Marijuana potency has increased sharply.
- MDMA trafficking has increased significantly since 2004.
- Rates of pharmaceutical drug abuse exceed that of all other drugs except marijuana, resulting in a high number of pharmaceutical overdose deaths annually.

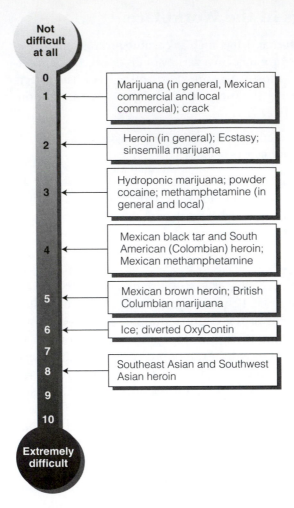

Figure 12.1 Difficulty in Buying Illicit Drugs

SOURCE: *National Drug Threat Assessment, 2007* (Washington, DC: National Drug Intelligence Center, October 2007) p.1.

Pulse Check: Trends in Drug Abuse (2004) The Justice Department's Office of National Drug Control Policy (ONDCP) follows drug trends in 25 large cities.[1] Of the agencies surveyed, 77 percent believe the drug problem is "very serious" while the rest label it as "somewhat serious." The majority (66 percent) perceive the drug problem has not changed much. Key findings of this report include the following (*Pulse Check*, 2004, p.5):

■ Marijuana remains the country's most widely abused illicit drug.

■ Crack remains a serious problem in 18 cities. It is considered the most commonly used drug by 16 sources in 12 cities.

■ Methamphetamine is reported as an emerging or intensifying problem in 15 cities.

■ MDMA, or Ecstasy, continues to emerge or intensify as a problem in 16 cities.

---

[1]The 25 cities are Atlanta, Baltimore, Boston, Chicago, Cincinnati, Cleveland, Dallas, Denver, Detroit, Houston, Los Angeles, Miami, Minneapolis/St. Paul, New York City, Phoenix, Philadelphia, Pittsburgh, Portland, Sacramento, San Diego, San Francisco, Seattle, St. Louis, Tampa/St. Petersburg and Washington, DC.

- Heroin is the drug associated with the most serious consequences—such as overdose deaths and involvement in emergency department episodes.
- Illicit drug prices generally remained stable between the spring and fall of 2002.[2]

 The most commonly observed drugs on the street or in possession of users are heroin, opium, morphine, codeine, cocaine, crack and marijuana.

Narcotics, Marijuana and Other Dangerous Drugs

The Controlled Substances Act (CSA) of 1984 placed all federally regulated substances into one of five schedules based on each substance's effects, medical use, potential for abuse and safety or dependence liability. Drugs in Schedule I have the highest potential for abuse, unpredictable effects and no generally accepted medical use. Schedule I drugs include heroin, LSD, GHB and marijuana. At the other end of the scale, Schedule V drugs have the lowest potential for abuse, may lead to limited physical or psychological dependence and have many accepted medical uses. Drugs in this category include Lomotil, Robitussin A-C and over-the-counter (OTC) or prescription drugs containing codeine. Drugs falling between these two extremes include the Schedule II substances of morphine, PCP, cocaine and methamphetamine; Schedule III substances such as anabolic steroids, codeine and some barbiturates; and Schedule IV substances including Valium, Xanax and Rohypnol. In most states narcotics and other dangerous drugs may not be used or sold without a prescription. Federal law prohibits sale or distribution not covered by prescription.

Narcotics

Narcotics are drugs that produce sleep, lethargy or relief of pain and include heroin, cocaine and crack. *Heroin*, a commonly abused narcotic, is synthesized from morphine and is up to 10 times more potent. Heroin is physically addictive and expensive. It causes an easing of fears, followed by euphoria and finally stupor. While this drug can be smoked, snorted or eaten, injecting is the most common route of heroin administration.

Cocaine is a white crystalline powder extracted from the South American coca plant. Until recently, most users "snorted" cocaine; that is, they inhaled the powdered mixture. Another form of cocaine is *freebase*, which is made by chemically converting the street drug into a basic form that can be smoked. This is an extremely dangerous, yet popular, practice. Whether inhaled or injected cocaine produces euphoria, excitation, anxiety, a sense of increased muscular strength, talkativeness and reduced feelings of fatigue. The pupils often become dilated, and the heart rate and blood pressure usually increase. Psychological dependence can be extreme.

The most pressing concern in recent times has been the use of *crack*, the street name given to freebase cocaine that has been processed from cocaine hydrochloride to a base, using ammonia or baking soda and water and heating it to remove the hydrochloride. It resembles hard shavings like slivers of soap and is sold in small vials, folding papers or heavy aluminum foil. Like freebase, it is

---

[2]SOURCE: *Pulse Check: Trends in Drug Abuse, 2004* (Washington, DC: Office of National Drug Control Police, January 2004) p.5. (NCJ 201398).

smoked in a pipe or sprinkled on a marijuana or tobacco cigarette and smoked. Crack produces the same intense rush and euphoria that cocaine does but at a greatly reduced cost. One or two doses of crack can be obtained for five to ten dollars, making it available to almost everyone. In fact, it has been called the "poor-man's coke" and the "equal opportunity drug."

Marijuana

Marijuana is almost certainly the most socially accepted illegal drug as evidenced by the frequent proposal for legislation lessening penalties for its use. Although it has been known for nearly 5,000 years, it is one of the least understood, yet most versatile, of all natural drugs.

 Marijuana is the most available and abused illegal drug in the United States.

Derived from the cannabis plant, marijuana is a hardy weed adaptable to most climates. It still grows wild in many parts of the United States. It grows at a phenomenal rate from a seedling to a 20-foot plant in one year. Many domestic marijuana growers are switching from outdoor to indoor cultivation. A highly potent form of marijuana obtained from unpollinated female plants is called **sinsemilla**.

Marijuana is most commonly rolled into a cigarette (joint) and smoked, producing a distinctive odor. When smoked, marijuana enters the bloodstream quickly, causing rapid onset of symptoms. The drug's effects on the user's mood and thinking vary widely depending on the marijuana's strength and the amount used, as well as the social setting and the anticipated effects. The effects usually occur in about fifteen minutes and last two to four hours.

Major Challenges Posed by Abuse of Marijuana   Federal drug policy continues to focus on marijuana use because it is seen as a "gateway" or "stepping stone" to harder drugs (Katel). However, some have questioned the **gateway** or **stepping stone theory**: "The evidence is not by itself sufficient to support a causal relationship between marijuana and other drug use" (Caulkins et al., 2005, p.11). These researchers contend (p.9): "The single most important factor promoting drug use is whether family or friends engage in it." They further observe that most drug users begin using drugs in their teens or young adult years and suggest that most people who try any drug, even heroin, use it only experimentally or continue use moderately and without ill effects: "The problem (among others) is not that [marijuana] *will* inevitably lead to addiction, but that it *can* lead to addiction" (Caulkins et al., p.11). According to Bennett and Hess (2007, p.518): "Whether marijuana abusers progress to hard narcotics or other controlled substances has not been totally researched. The vast majority of hard-narcotics users once used marijuana, but how many marijuana users proceed to hard drugs is unknown."

Other Dangerous Drugs

Other dangerous drugs include depressants, stimulants, hallucinogens and deliriants. Although the various narcotics and other dangerous drugs produce different effects, they have certain common effects.

Common effects of the various narcotics and other dangerous drugs include: (1) they are mind altering, (2) they may become addicting—either physically or psychologically and (3) overdosage may result in convulsions and death.

Depressants (Barbiturates) Depressants, or **barbiturates**, are sedatives taken orally as a small tablet or capsule to induce sleep or to relieve tension. Small amounts of barbiturates make the user relaxed, sociable and good-humored. Heavy doses cause sluggishness, depression, deep sleep or coma. A barbiturate addict often shows symptoms of drunkenness: speech becomes slurred and indistinct, physical coordination is impaired, and mental and emotional instability occurs. Overdoses are common and frequently cause intentional or accidental death.

Stimulants (Amphetamines) Stimulants, or **amphetamines**, are taken orally as a tablet or capsule, or intravenously, to reduce appetite and/or relieve mental depression. Normal doses produce wakefulness, increased alertness and initiative, and hyperactivity. Large doses produce exaggerated feelings of confidence, power and well-being.

Heavy users may exhibit restlessness, nervousness, hand tremors, pupil dilation, mouth dryness and excessive perspiration. They may be talkative and experience delusions and hallucinations. Handling this deviant behavior has always been a source of concern and danger for security officers.

Methamphetamine One stimulant posing a major problem for employers is **methamphetamine**, or "meth," also known as *speed*, *ice* and *crystal*. Like cocaine, meth is a potent central nervous system stimulant that the Drug Enforcement Administration (DEA) calls dangerous, unpredictable and sometimes lethal (DEA Web site). "Methamphetamine is an insidious and dangerous drug that causes severe addictive behavior and physical and psychological damage to its victims" (Wuestewald, 2005, p.34). Meth is typically a white, odorless, bitter-tasting powder that easily dissolves in water. It is made in clandestine laboratories using common household chemicals and over-the-counter cold remedies. It can be smoked, snorted, injected or taken orally. Methamphetamine use frequently results in violent and erratic behavior. According to Irvin and Me Hoang (2007): "For much of the country, researchers say it appears the latest meth epidemic reached its peak in 2004 and 2005." While the meth problem has spread throughout all areas of the country, it nevertheless remains regionally concentrated: "The number of meth users as measured by positive workplace drug tests . . . was highest in the West" (*National Drug Control Strategy*, 2007, p.6).

Hallucinogens **Hallucinogens** may produce distortion, intensify sensory perception and lessen the ability to discriminate between fact and fantasy. The unpredictable mental effects include illusions, panic, psychotic or antisocial behavior and impulses toward violence and self-destruction. Although hallucinogens are usually taken orally as a tablet or capsule, their physical characteristics allow them to be disguised as various commonly used powders or liquids. Probably the best-known hallucinogen is LSD (lysergic acid diethylamide).

Another hallucinogen, PCP (phencyclidine), was developed as an anesthetic and is still used as such by veterinarians. It appeared in San Francisco in the 1960s and was called the "Peace Pill." As its use spread across the country, it was called by various other names, including angel dust. Symptoms of PCP intoxication vary greatly from person to person, depending on the dosage, previous use and how it was ingested. A symptom almost always present in PCP intoxication is **nystagmus**, an uncontrolled bouncing or jerking of the eyeball when the intoxicated person looks to the extreme right or left, and up or down. Much of the concern over the widespread use of PCP is the drug's ability to produce bizarre, sometimes tragic, *aggressive, violent behavior*. Users often have hallucinations and disturbed thought patterns that may produce panic, which triggers aberrant or aggressive behavior. Security officers have been injured attempting to subdue a person under the influence of PCP. Overwhelming evidence shows that some users "freaked out" on PCP exhibit *superhuman strength* while showing aggression. One explanation is that users believe their hallucinations are real. The adrenalin flows, and they fight desperately for survival using any method to escape the terror. The superhuman strength is also directly related to the drug's analgesic qualities under which users feel little or no pain.

Deliriants   **Deliriants** are volatile chemicals found in more than 1,000 common household products, such as glues, hair spray, air fresheners, lighter fluid and paint products. Deliriants are inhaled and generally produce a "high" and loss of inhibition similar to that produced by alcohol. The inhalant high is usually followed by depression. Users may also experience headaches, wheezing, nausea, slurred speech, diminished motor coordination and distortion in perceptions of time and space. A characteristic redness or irritation called "glue sniffer's rash" commonly occurs around the nostrils and lips. Inhalant abuse is common among children and adolescents.

Abuse of Prescription Drugs

In 2005 the DEA initiated 100 new Internet investigations involving the online sales of pharmaceutical controlled substances, resulting in the seizure of $44 million in cash, property, computers and bank accounts (Garrett, 2006, pp.79–80). Burke (2004, p.21) suggests: "Although prescription drug abuse is not commonly associated with street violence, the deaths and destruction that surround pharmaceutical diversion often exceed that of illicit substances. The abuse and diversion of prescription drugs remains a very healthy criminal enterprise." Security professionals must become more aggressive and proactive in their response to these offenses.

Recognizing Individuals Using Illegal Drugs

Employers must be able to recognize when a person is probably under the influence of drugs and must also be aware of the dangers the person might present. Table 12.2 summarizes the primary physical symptoms, what to look for and the dangers involved in the most commonly used drugs, including alcohol.

Drug addicts frequently become unfit for employment as their mental, emotional and physical condition deteriorates. The following are possible symptoms of drug abuse:

Table 12.2 Common Symptoms, Signs and Dangers of Commonly Abused Drugs

Drug Used	Physical Symptoms	Look for	Dangers
Alcohol (beer, wine, liquor)	Intoxication, slurred speech, unsteady walk, relaxation, relaxed inhibitions, impaired coordination, slowed reflexes	Smell of alcohol on clothes or breath, intoxicated behavior, hangover, glazed eyes	Addiction, accidents as a result of impaired ability and judgment, overdose when mixed with other depressants, heart and liver damage
Cocaine (coke, rock, crack, base)	Brief, intense euphoria, elevated blood pressure and heart rate, restlessness, excitement, feeling of well-being followed by depression	Glass vials, glass pipe, white crystalline powder, razor blades, syringes, needle marks	Addiction, heart attack, seizures, lung damage, severe depression, paranoia (see Stimulants)
Marijuana (pot, dope, grass, weed, herb, hash, joint)	Altered perceptions, red eyes, dry mouth, reduced concentration and coordination, euphoria, laughing, hunger	Rolling papers, pipes, dried plant material, odor of burnt hemp rope, roach clips	Panic reaction, impaired short-term memory, addiction
Hallucinogens (acid, LSD, PCP, MDMA/Ecstasy, psilocybin mushrooms, peyote)	Altered mood and perceptions, focus on detail, anxiety, panic, nausea, synaesthesia (e.g., smell colors, see sounds)	Capsules, tablets, "microdots," blotter squares	Unpredictable behavior, emotional instability, violent behavior (with PCP)
Inhalants (gas, aerosols, glue, nitrites, Rush, White Out)	Nausea, dizziness headaches, lack of coordination and control	Odor of substance on clothing and breath, intoxication, drowsiness, poor muscular control	Unconsciousness, suffocation, nausea and vomiting, damage to brain and central nervous system, sudden death
Narcotics: heroin (junk, dope, Black tar, China white); Demerol, Dilaudid D'sl; morphine, codeine	Euphoria, drowsiness, insensitivity to pain, nausea, vomiting, watery eyes, runny nose (see Depressants)	Needle marks on arms; needles; syringes; spoons; pinpoint pupils; cold, moist skin	Addiction, lethargy, weight loss, contamination from unsterile needles (hepatitis, AIDS), accidental overdose
Stimulants (speed, uppers, crank, bam, black beauties, crystal, dexies, caffeine, nicotine, cocaine, amphetamines)	Alertness, talkativeness, wakefulness, increased blood pressure, loss of appetite, mood elevation	Pills and capsules, loss of sleep and appetite, irritability or anxiety, weight loss, hyperactivity	Fatigue leading to exhaustion, addiction, paranoia, depression, confusion, possibly hallucinations
Depressants: barbiturates, sedatives, tranquilizers (downers, tranks, ludes, reds, Valium, yellow jackets, alcohol)	Depressed breathing and heartbeat, intoxication, drowsiness, uncoordinated movements	Capsules and pills, confused behavior, longer periods of sleep, slurred speech	Possible overdose, especially in combination with alcohol; muscle rigidity, addiction, withdrawal, and overdose require medical treatment

SOURCE: ©1991 *Drug Education Guide*, The Positive Line #79830, Positive Promotions, 222 Ashland Place, Brooklyn, NY 11207.

- Sudden and dramatic changes in discipline and job performance
- Unusual degrees of activity or inactivity
- Sudden and irrational flareups
- Significant change in personal appearance for the worse
- Dilated pupils or wearing sunglasses at inappropriate times or places
- Needle marks or razor cuts, or long sleeves constantly worn to hide such marks
- Sudden attempts to borrow money or to steal
- Frequent association with known drug abusers or pushers

The addict is generally unkempt, appears drowsy, does not feel well, has copious quantities of tears or mucous in eyes and nose and suffers from alternate chills and fever. Needle marks resembling tattoos may be present in the curve of the arm at the elbow or, after prolonged drug use, in other areas of the body.

The "War on Drugs" and the National Drug Control Strategy

In 1973 President Nixon declared "war" on drugs. Since that time federal spending on this war against drug smugglers, users and sellers has increased 30-fold—from $420 million in 1973 to $12.7 billion (Katel). Drug arrests have nearly tripled since 1980, when the federal drug policy shifted to arresting and incarcerating users. Approximately 1.7 million people were arrested on drug charges in 2004, about 700,000 of them for marijuana use (Katel).

The key to reducing drug abuse is prevention coupled with treatment. When President George W. Bush took office in 2001 he endorsed a three-pronged approach, repeated in the *National Drug Control Strategy 2008*:

1. *Stop drug use before it starts: education and community action.* In homes, schools, places of worship, *the workplace*, and civic and social organizations, Americans must set norms that reaffirm the values of responsibility and good citizenship while dismissing the notion that drug use is consistent with individual freedom. The National Drug Control Strategy ties national leadership with community-level action to help recreate the formula that helped America succeed against drugs in the past.

2. *Heal America's drug users: getting treatment resources where they are needed.* Getting people into treatment will require the creation of a new climate of "compassionate coercion," which begins with family, friends, *employers* and the community. Compassionate coercion also uses the criminal justice system to get people into treatment.

3. *Disrupt the market: attacking the economic basis of the drug trade.* Domestically, attacking the economic basis of the drug trade involves the cooperative, combined efforts of federal, state and local law enforcement.[3]

Security can help in two core components of the national drug control strategy: (1) stopping drug use before it starts—prevention, and (2) healing America's drug users—seeing that employees get treatment. An important part of addressing the drug problem is addressing the challenge posed by alcohol.

Alcohol Abuse

Many do not think of it as such, but alcohol is a drug. Although drinking alcohol is legal, laws have been established that regulate the age at which it becomes legal to drink, as well as the amount a person can drink and then operate a vehicle. The widespread abuse of alcohol is partly due to its legality but also to its social acceptance. Researchers have found that children of alcoholics are 70 percent more likely than children of nonalcoholics to abuse drugs and alcohol at some point in their lives.

---

[3]SOURCE: *National Drug Threat Assessment, 2007* (Washington, DC: National Drug Intelligence Center, October 2007).

The Institute of Alcohol Studies reports that, globally, 3 to 5 percent of the average workforce are alcohol dependent, and up to 25 percent drink heavily enough to be at risk of alcohol dependence (*Alcohol and the Workplace*, 2007, p.3). This publication contends that alcohol can impair work performance in three main ways:

1. A raised blood alcohol level can jeopardize both efficiency and safety, for example, increased likelihood of mistakes, errors of judgment and increased accident proneness.
2. The after-effects of drinking (hangovers) can impair both work attendance and performance.
3. Persistent heavy drinking can lead to a range of social, psychological and medical problems, including dependence, and is associated with impaired work performance and attendance.

Drinking alcohol on the job can threaten public safety, affect job performance and result in costly medical, social and other problems affecting employees and employers alike. Although drinking rates vary among occupations, alcohol-related problems are not characteristic of any single social segment, industry or occupation. According to *Alcohol Alert*, a variety of factors contribute to problem drinking in the workplace: Drinking is associated with the workplace culture and acceptance of drinking, workplace alienation, the availability of alcohol, and the existence and enforcement of workplace alcohol policies.

The *workplace culture* may either accept and encourage drinking or discourage and inhibit drinking, partly influenced by the gender mix of its workers. Studies of male-dominated occupations have described heavy drinking cultures in which workers use drinking to build solidarity and show conformity to the group. Boring, stressful or isolating work can also contribute to employees' drinking. Employee drinking has been associated with low job autonomy, lack of job complexity, lack of control over work conditions and products, boredom, sexual harassment, verbal and physical aggression, and disrespectful behavior. The availability and accessibility of alcohol may be an additional influence on employee drinking. More than two-thirds of the workers surveyed at a large manufacturing plant said it was "easy" or "very easy" to bring alcohol into the workplace, to drink at work stations and to drink during breaks. This is frequently the result of limited supervision, often a problem on evening shifts. Alcohol policies, employees' awareness of them, and their enforcement also vary widely and affect whether employees drink on the job.

Alcohol-related job performance problems are caused not only by on-the-job drinking but also by heavy drinking outside of work, with a positive relationship between the frequency of being "hungover" at work and the frequency of feeling sick at work, sleeping on the job and having problems with job tasks or coworkers.

Preventing Alcohol Problems in the Workplace

Health promotion programs offered in the workplace may reduce employees' alcohol-related problems. Employee assistance programs (EAPs) may also identify and intervene in employees' alcohol problems. To address alcohol and drug problems, treatment services should (1) be based on formal theories of drug dependence and abuse, (2) use the best therapeutic tools available and (3) give participants opportunities to build cognitive skills.

Alcohol and drug use may also be contributing factors in workplace violence. But because violence in the workplace is a subset of violence in general, the discussion turns first to an overview of violent behavior in the United States before looking more specifically at workplace violence.

Violence in the United States

Our nation was born in the violence of the Revolutionary War, and the union remained intact after a bloody Civil War that pitted brother against brother. Since then America has been willing to fight for freedom. It also cherishes the peace and freedom at home, however, that others fought to secure. But violence continues to exist. In its most extreme form, violence turns fatal. Newspaper headlines and national television news reports of deadly shooting sprees by disgruntled employees have created a national awareness of workplace violence. Although the great majority of workplace violence does not end in death, violence in any form can be destructive to the morale of all employees of an establishment. According to the Federal Bureau of Investigation's (FBI's) Uniform Crime Reports:

- An estimated 1.4 million violent crimes occurred nationwide in 2006.
- During 2006 there were an estimated 473.5 violent crimes per 100,000 inhabitants.
- From 2005 to 2006, the estimated volume of violent crime increased 1.3 percent.

The most current data on criminal victimization rates from the NCVS (National Crime Victimization Survey), the FBI and other sources are available on the Bureau of Justice Statistics (BJS) Web site at www.ojp.usdoj/gov/bjs.

The National Association of Safety Professionals (NASP) reports: "Violence in America is epidemic with over 15,000 homicides reported annually, but when adjusted for estimated unreported incidents the estimate may double that. Assaults reported equal 7,560,000 but adjusted for estimated unreported incidents total 37,800,000. Sexual assaults reported are over 500,000, but when adjusted for estimated unreported incidents the total exceeds 5,000,000. The American crime clock ticks off one murder every 23.9 minutes, one assault every .83 seconds and one sexual assault every 6 seconds" (*Violence: Prevention, Management and Survival* (VPS)).

An Increase in Violent Crime

FBI data for the first six months of 2006 shows an increase of 3.7 percent in violent crime in the United States (Ryan, 2006). According to Eggen (2006, p.A01): "A surge in violent crime that began last year accelerated in the first half of 2006, providing the clearest signal yet that the historic drop in the U.S. crime rate has ended and is being reversed." These findings, the "first significant uptick in violent crime since the early 1990s," signal the end of a 15-year decline in violent crime. Headlines highlight this trend: "Startling New Stats Show Cross-Country Crime Spike" (Thomas et al., 2006) and "Spike in Violent Crime Creates Fears for Future" (Cormier, 2007).

Wexler (2006a, p.ii), executive director of the Police Executive Research Forum (PERF), notes that in 2005 the United States had more than 16,000 homicides while the United Kingdom had just more than 1,000 and Canada reported only 658. Over the past 5 years, the United States has had more than 80,000 murders, 2 million robberies and 4 million aggravated assaults.

The increasing rate of violent crime is occurring irrespective of region, population or environment—that is, urban or suburban (Wexler, 2006b, p.2). Acknowledging that no single definitive explanation can be given for these increases, Wexler reports that police chiefs from across the country have suggested several plausible reasons: significant increases in gang activity; the movement of former gang members from New Orleans to other cities; release of offenders who were incarcerated at high rates during the 1990s; displacement of crime from cities where some crime-infested public housing was dismantled; the changing nature of the drug market; and petty fights that escalate into major violent crimes.

Causes of Violence: An Overview

The causes of violence are as difficult to pinpoint as the causes of crime. Many suggest that the ready availability and lethal nature of guns, especially handguns, is a major factor. But in the colonial days every household had guns— survival depended on it. Yet children did not shoot each other in their one-room schoolhouses. Nonetheless, the gun factor must be considered.

Another major cause of violence is desensitization to violence. Violence permeates our television programs and movies, our video games and DVDs. Violence on our streets is graphically portrayed by the media.

 Causes of violence may include ready availability of guns, drugs and alcohol; a desensitization to violence; disintegration of the family and community; social and economic deprivation; and increased numbers of children growing up in violent families.

Table 12.3 presents risk factors for violent behavior in a matrix illustrating the complexity of social and individual factors that may cause violence. Notice the presence of weapons in both the *macrosocial* (big picture) and *microsocial* (smaller picture) situations. The macrosocial environment includes the amount of social capital available as well as existing diversity, including economic diversity. The microsocial environment focuses on smaller units such as the family. **Psychosocial** factors refer to individual psychological characteristics such as temperament and self-identity.

Having looked at violence in general, consider now the challenge faced by security professionals regarding violence in the workplace.

Violence in the Workplace

The Occupational Safety and Health Act as well as state statutes stipulate that employers owe a "general duty" to protect employees against "recognized hazards" likely to cause serious injury or death. Both federal and state OSHA agencies have identified workplace violence as one such hazard. Workplace violence can range from threats and verbal abuse to physical assaults and homicide, one of the leading causes of job-related deaths. However it manifests itself, workplace violence is a growing concern for employers and employees nationwide

Table 12.3   Matrix for Organizing Risk Factors for Violent Behavior

Units of Observation and Explanation	Predisposing	Situational	Activating
SOCIAL			
Macrosocial	Concentration of poverty	Physical structures	Catalytic social event
	Opportunity structures	Routine activities	
	Decline of social capital	Access: weapons, emergency medical services	
	Oppositional cultures		
	Sex role socialization		
Microsocial	Community organizations	Proximity of responsible monitors	Participants' communication exchange
	Illegal markets	Participants' social relationships	
	Gangs	Bystanders' activities	
	Family disorganization	Temporary communication impairments	
	Pre-existing structures	Weapons: carrying, displaying	
INDIVIDUAL			
Psychosocial	Temperament	Accumulated emotion	Impulse
	Learned social responses	Alcohol/drug consumption	Opportunity recognition
	Perceptions of rewards/penalties for violence	Sexual arousal	
	Violent deviant sexual preferences	Premeditation	
	Social, communication skills		
	Self-identification in social hierarchy		
Biological	Neurobehavioral* traits	Transient neurobehavioral states*	Sensory signal processing errors
	Genetically mediated traits	Acute effects of psychoactive substances	
	Chronic use of psychoactive substances or exposure to neurotoxins		

*Includes neuroanatomical, neurophysiological, neurochemical, and neuroendocrine, "Traits" describe capacity as determined by status at birth, trauma, and aging processes such as puberty. "States" describe temporary condititions associated with emotions, external stressors, etc. Adapted from Albert J. Reiss, Jr. and Jeffrey A.Roth, eds. *Understanding and Preventing Violence*, Washington, DC: National Academy Press, 1993, p.297.

SOURCE: Jeffrey A. Roth, *Understanding and Preventing Violence* (Washington, DC: National Institute of Justice Research in Brief, 1993) p.7.

(*OSHA Fact Sheet*). A newspoll of security directors that asked "What is your biggest security fear for your organization in 2006?" found workplace violence topped the list, with 23 percent of respondents expressing it as their top security concern ("Newspoll: What Is Your Biggest Security Fear for Your Organization in 2006?," 2005, p.23).

Workplace Violence Defined

According to the American Society of Industrial Security (ASIS), any definition of workplace violence must encompass the full range of behaviors that can cause injury, damage property, impede the normal course of work or make workers, managers and customers fear for their safety. The ASIS *Workplace Violence Prevention and Response Guidelines* (2005, p.6) defines workplace violence as follows:

Workplace violence refers to a broad range of behaviors falling along a spectrum that, due to their nature and/or severity, significantly affect the workplace, generate a concern for personal safety, or result in physical injury or death.

At the low end of the workplace violence spectrum lie disruptive, aggressive, hostile or emotionally abusive behaviors that generate anxiety or create a climate of distrust, and that adversely affect productivity and morale. These behaviors of concern could—but will not necessarily—escalate into more severe behavior falling further along the workplace violence spectrum; however, independent of the question of possible escalation, these behaviors are in themselves harmful and for that reason alone warrant attention and effective intervention.

Further along the spectrum are words or other actions that are reasonably perceived to be intimidating, frightening or threatening to employees and that generate a justifiable concern for personal safety. These behaviors include, among others, direct, conditional or veiled threats, stalking, and aggressive harassment.

At the high end of the spectrum are acts of overt violence causing physical injury. These acts include non-fatal physical assaults with or without weapons—including pushing, shoving, hitting, kicking or biting—and, in the worst cases, lethal violence inflicted by shooting, stabbing, bombing or any other deadly means.[4]

Classification of Workplace Violence

The National Association of Safety Professionals divides violence into three levels paralleling this definition: Level I is disruptive behavior including intimidation/bullying, obscene language, obscene gestures, shouting, false statements, threats of nonphysical acts and minimal harassment. Level II is aggressive/threatening behavior, including physical trauma, suicide threats, threats of assault, obscene calls, stalking and serious harassment. Level III is physical assault, including throwing objects, pushing, grabbing, striking, stabbing, sexual assault and shooting.

Rudewicz (2004, p.42) also views workplace violence on a continuum called the HARM model: harassment, aggression, rage and mayhem. *Harassment* is irritating behavior or actions that may or may not cause discomfort to someone else, but is considered inappropriate conduct for the workplace such as acting condescendingly, slamming doors, glaring at others, playing practical jokes or telling lies about a coworker. *Aggression* is hostile behavior that causes harm to or discomfort for a coworker. The next stage, *rage*, is intense behavior that causes fear in others and may result in physical and emotional harm to people or damage to property. *Mayhem*, the final stage, is physical violence aimed at people or property. Figure 12.2 shows this continuum of workplace violence.

The FBI and OSHA both categorize workplace violence into four broad categories based on the relationship between the perpetrator of the violent act and

---

[4]SOURCE: From *Workplace Violence Prevention and Response Guidelines* (Alexandria, VA: American Society for Industrial Security, 2005) p.6. Reprinted with the written permission of ASIS International, Alexandria, VA.

| Behaviors of concern | Threatening behavior | Physical injury | Death |

Figure 12.2 Continuum of Workplace Violence

SOURCE: From *Workplace Violence Prevention and Response Guidelines* (Alexandria, VA: American Society for Industrial Security, 2005). Reprinted with the written permission of ASIS International, Alexandria, VA.

the victim (Table 12.4). The majority of incidents employers deal with daily are lesser cases of assaults, domestic violence, stalking, threats, harassment (including sexual harassment) and physical and emotional abuse that make no headlines (Rugala and Isaacs, p.12).

Extent and Impact of Workplace Violence

Workplace violence has been called "epidemic" with estimates ranging from one million to two million workers experiencing violent victimization every year.

 Annually more than 2 million people become victims of violent crime at work, according to the U.S. Bureau of Justice Statistics.

While workplace homicides continue trending downward in private sector jobs, the overall picture of violence at work is mixed. Worksite homicides declined 14 percent in 2004, nearly four times the 4 percent drop in killings

Table 12.4 Categories of Workplace Violence

FBI Category	OSHA Category	Perpetrator/Victim Relationship	Example of Violence
Type 1 Violence	Type I	No relationship	Perpetrator enters a business to commit robbery or other crime. A terrorist attack directed at a workplace is viewed by OSHA as a subcategory of Type I violence.
Type 2 Violence	Type II	Customer, client, patient, student, inmate, or any other to whom the business or organization provides services	A psychiatric patient assaults a physician, or a disgruntled client or customer threatens a company or one of its employees.
Type 3 Violence	Type III	Worker-on-worker; against coworker, supervisor or management by a present or former employee (or independent contractor)	A recently terminated employee returns to the workplace and guns down her former supervisor and anyone else she can find. Often ends in the attacker committing suicide.
Type 4 Violence	Type IV	Committed in the workplace by someone who doesn't work there but who has a personal relationship with an employee—abusive spouse or domestic partner, etc.	A battered wife has sought an order for protection (OFP) or restraining order against the husband she is divorcing. He waits for her in the parking lot after work and then stabs or shoots her as she goes to her car.

SOURCE: Eugene A. Rugala and Arnold R. Isaacs, *Workplace Violence: Issues in Response* (Washington, DC: Federal Trade Commission) p.113.

for the nation as a whole (Ceniceros, 2006). *Violence in the Workplace—An Updated Analysis* (2006) reports that for some occupations, declines in homicide rates have been especially dramatic—for example, a five-fold decline in homicide rates among taxi drivers between 1992 and 2002. However, in contrast to consistent declines for the simple assault rate in the country as a whole, the incidence rate of lost work-time (LWT) assaults has been trending higher since 1999. Other key findings include the following:

- Robberies are by far the major cause of workplace *homicides,* accounting for roughly 75 percent of homicides where the cause has been identified.
- In contrast, some 60 percent of workplace *assaults* are concentrated in health services, social assistance and personal care occupations.
- A distressingly high fatality rate of 3 percent in workers' compensation claims involves "an act of crime" incidents as compared with claims from other causes.

The National Association of Safety Professionals notes that estimates of the economic impact of workplace violence range from $70 million to $200 million annually. Workplace violence results in 1,175,100 lost work days annually, $55 million in lost wages annually, lost productivity, legal expenses, property damage, diminished public image and increased security costs. So while estimates of costs, from lost work time and wages, reduced productivity, medical costs, workers' compensation payments, and legal and security expenses are not exact, the financial impact of workplace violence clearly runs into many billions of dollars a year (Rugala and Isaacs, p.12).

Motivations for Workplace Violence

Most study results and experts identify the driving forces behind workplace violence as being (1) an economic system that fails to support full employment (downsizing) and leads to widespread layoffs, (2) a legal system that fails to protect citizens and releases criminals from prison early because of overcrowding, (3) a cultural system that glamorizes violence in the media and serves to desensitize individuals to violence and its consequences and (4) the universal availability of weapons.

Workplace violence is likely to occur in a **toxic work environment**, one characterized by a highly authoritarian management style invasive of privacy, supervision patterns that change and are unpredictable, and a work climate cloaked by extreme secrecy. Job frustrations can increase employee aggression to the point of extreme violence. Cumulative frustration may grow over a long time span, where an employee experiences repeated failures in their career, such as failing to get the expected raise, promotion or recognition the person feels he or she deserves, often after many years of service to a company.

 Among the commonly cited causes or motivators of workplace violence are job loss due to downsizing of companies; uncaring working environment; the availability of guns; personality conflicts, resentment, anger from feelings of mistreatment and high levels of stress on the job; substance abuse; and mental problems.

Recognizing the Risk

Security professionals need to recognize who the typical perpetrator is, what warning signs might indicate the potential for violence and who might be vulnerable.

The Typical Perpetrator

The typical perpetrator is a 25- to 50-year-old white male who tends to be a loner, has a history of violence and conflict with others and may exhibit signs of depression. This profile fits Michael McDermott, a shooting suspect who, in December 2000, reportedly upset by an IRS request to garnish his wages, killed seven coworkers in Wakefield, Massachusetts. McDermott is white, is age 42 and had an angry outburst in the accounting department the week before over the prospect of losing some of his wages. McDermott surrendered to police without a struggle.

 The typical perpetrator of workplace violence is a disgruntled, middle-aged white male who is a loner, who either has been or is about to be fired and who is a gun enthusiast.

Often the perpetrator is distraught over a perceived inability to capture the American Dream. He feels entitled to a financially secure future and is deeply resentful if it is threatened. He may be resentful of others who still have jobs or of those who have passed him by in promotions. He may view a gun as the "great equalizer" and use it to get his revenge.

Warning Signs

Many employees provide clues that they may become violent. Warning signs include unusual fascination with weapons, a display of unwarranted anger, irrational beliefs and ideas, feelings of victimization, talk of hurting self and others, substance abuse, inability to take criticism, constant complaining, attendance and productivity problems and past threats or acts of intimidation. Other warning signs of impending violence include frequent aggressive outbursts or excessive displays of temper, verbal abuse of coworkers and customers, harassment through phone calls or e-mails, holding grudges, habitually making excuses and blaming others (*Workplace Violence Prevention and Response Guidelines*, pp.18–19).

Supervisors should be trained to recognize relevant behavioral changes in employees, including increased absenteeism, abrupt departures from work, erratic work patterns, progressive disciplinary problems, dramatic changes in personal appearance, unwarranted anger or difficulty accepting criticism: "The challenge is to know which changes in behavior are worth noting and to train supervisors to identify the warning signs" (Rudewicz, p.42). When companies are able to develop methods for detecting these early signs of impending violence, they are better able to take preemptive measures (p.46).

 Indicators of impending violent behavior may include "leakage" of violent thoughts, depression, paranoia, erratic behavior, fixation on a coworker and threats.

Leakage occurs when a person intentionally or unintentionally reveals clues to feelings, thoughts, fantasies, attitudes or intentions that may signal an impending violent act. These clues can take the forms of subtle threats, boasts, innuendos, predictions or ultimatums. They may be spoken or conveyed in stories, diary entries, essays, poems, letters, songs, drawings, doodles, tattoos or videos. Leakage can be a cry for help, a sign of inner conflict or boasts that may look empty but actually express a serious threat. Leakage is considered to be one of the most important clues that may precede a person's violent act.

 Most violent people "leak" their feelings and intentions in the weeks and months before committing the violent act. Such messages should never be ignored.

Contrary to popular belief, most violent workers do not simply snap. They coldly and methodically plan and carry out their attacks. Their actions are deliberate rather than spontaneous in most instances. Workplace killers may be depressed, despondent, disillusioned or high on drugs, and they generally are not deranged.

Threats The majority of those who commit violent acts against coworkers or management have made threats beforehand. A good example is Paul Calden who vowed he would be back when he was fired from his job at Fireman's Fund Insurance Company in Tampa, Florida. Eight months later he did return, approached three of his former supervisors having lunch in the company cafeteria and announced while taking aim: "This is what you get for firing me." He not only killed the three former managers, but he also wounded two other employees. Then he turned the gun on himself.

A study by the FBI's National Center for the Analysis of Violent Crime (NCAVC) declares: "All threats are not created equal" (O'Toole, p.5). This study (p.7) describes four categories of threats equally applicable to the workplace.

 Threats may be classified as direct, indirect, veiled and conditional.

This is a **direct threat**: "I am going to place a bomb in the break room." It identifies a specific act against a specific target and is delivered in a straightforward, clear and explicit manner. An **indirect threat**, in contrast, is more ambiguous in identifying the specific plan, the intended victim(s) or the motivation behind the violence: "If I wanted to, I could kill everyone at this factory."

A **veiled threat**, such as "This place would be much better off without her around as supervisor," strongly implies the potential for violence but does not explicitly threaten an act. A **conditional threat** is the type often made in extortion cases, warning that violence will occur if certain demands are not met: "If you don't promote me, I will make you regret it."

Who Is Vulnerable?

Workplace violence can strike anywhere; no one is immune. However, some workers are at increased risk, including workers who exchange money with the public; deliver passengers, goods or services; or work alone or in small groups, during late night or early morning hours, in high-crime areas or in community settings and homes where they have extensive contact with the public. This group includes healthcare and social service workers such as visiting nurses, psychiatric evaluators, community workers such as gas and water utility employees, phone and cable TV installers, and letter carriers; retail workers; and taxi drivers (*OSHA Fact Sheet*).

Preventing Workplace Violence

Preventive measures include preemployment screening, drug testing, employee education, a "zero tolerance" for any type of violence, a nontoxic workplace, open communication and humane termination procedures.

Planning

Like most other risks, preventing workplace violence begins with planning. Rugala and Isaacs (p.19) offer the following suggestions:

- A concern for workplace violence must start at the very top of any organization or institution. If a company's senior executives are not truly committed to a preventive program, it is unlikely to be effectively implemented.
- There is no one-size-fits-all strategy. Good plans are tailored to the needs, resources and circumstances of the employer and the workforce.
- The plan should be proactive, not reactive.

Drug testing and "zero tolerance" policies toward drug use are tools employers are using to reduce the problem of workplace violence and accidents.

- The plan should take into account the workplace culture, work atmosphere, relationships, management styles and the like. Any elements contributing to a toxic climate, including tolerance of bullying or intimidation, lack of trust among workers, between workers and management; high levels of stress, frustration and anger; poor communication; inconsistent discipline; and erratic enforcement of company policies should receive remedial action.
- Managers should take an active role in communicating the workplace violence policy to employees and be alert to warning signs.
- The plan should be practiced. Training exercises must include senior executives who will be making decisions in a real or potential incident.
- Reevaluate, rethink and revise. Be open to changing policies and practices as personnel, work environments and business conditions change.

Clear "No Threats, No Violence" Policies

A "No Threats, No Violence" policy should be clearly communicated to all employees and should state the employer's commitment to provide a safe workplace. It should also set forth a code of employee conduct clearly defining unacceptable behavior and prohibiting all violence and threats on-site and during work-related off-site activities. The policy should also require employees to promptly report any suspected violation of the antiviolence policy or other disturbing circumstances that may raise a safety concern. In addition, the policy should clearly advise employees that violations will result in discipline, up to and including termination. If the term *zero tolerance* is used, ideally it should not mean uniform, automatic penalties; instead, it should mean that the organization will not tolerate violent or threatening conduct and will impose penalties appropriate to the nature and severity of the violation (*Workplace Violence Prevention and Response Guidelines*, p.20).

Zero tolerance according to Hershkowitz (2004, p.86) is sometimes viewed in such a way that any behavior in a prohibited category, regardless of mitigating circumstances, results in the same usually harsh punishment such as termination of employment. This one-size-fits-all approach can result in complaints as well as lawsuits. Each case needs to be treated individually, with mitigating factors taken into consideration, if employees are to view the policy as fair. In *Jones v. Potter* (2007), the U.S. Court of Appeals for the Sixth Circuit upheld a lower court's decision regarding the firing of a U.S. Postal Service (USPS) employee who slapped another employee, a clear violation of the company's zero tolerance policy for workplace violence.

Training

One way to promote a safer working environment is through employee training in such areas as stress management, conflict resolution, handling confrontations and drug and alcohol abuse awareness: "Companies can reduce the risk of workplace violence by training staff to recognize warning signs and having procedures for prevention and response" (Gane, 2007, p.140). New York's Public Employee Safety and Security Act mandates that every new employee of a company or business receive workplace violence prevention tips in new hire orientations and then receive refreshers annually (Edwards, 2007, p.4). Managers also need specialized training in such areas as perpetrator profiles, employee risk factors, warning signs and indicators, the sequence of violence, workplace dynamics, sexual harassment and fair treatment of others.

One of the most effective ways to deal with rising emotions or existing frustrations is to use preemptive communications programs such as anonymous hotlines that give employees a way to vent their frustrations or an employee assistance program (EAP) program that provides counseling or stress management (Payson and Piazza, 2007, p.95). Other programs may include some type of mediation or arbitration, such as peer review.

Peer Review

Many peer review programs begin by gauging employees' interest in participating by putting up posters and distributing information in company cafeterias or other locations (Payson and Piazza, p.95). Those interested in participating are trained by human resources in effective listening and questioning and remaining neutral and objective. When employees feel wronged for whatever reason, they can call a panel by drawing a number of names from the peer review pool and select several to be on the panel. After hearing the evidence in a case, the panel has a group discussion and then takes a confidential vote. Its decision is final.

Payson and Piazza (p.81) give as an example a security officer working outside a grocery store who left his post to help a woman with several small children and a shopping cart trying to get into the store. When he returned to his post where he was responsible for checking to be sure that items carried below the shopping cart had a sticker, his supervisor was waiting for him, angry that he had left his post without getting someone to watch it while he was gone. Rather than getting thanked for a good job, the officer received a written warning. The officer could have lost his enthusiasm for his job or become angry or just put in his time without helping customers so as to not risk another warning. Several negative scenarios might have resulted from this incident. But instead, the officer took advantage of the store's peer review program. A panel of five employees—three hourly workers and two managers selected by the officer from the pool of specially trained employees—modified the written warning to a verbal warning. The officer was satisfied with the binding decision, his anger and frustration dissipated, and he remained a satisfied employee.

Peer review programs are not appropriate for every situation, however, such as claims of sexual harassment or discrimination because peer-review panels cannot change policies, work rules, benefits, performance appraisal ratings, pay rates or promotion selections (Payson and Piazza, p.95).

Other Approaches to Preventing Workplace Violence

One important area likely to directly affect the probability of violent retaliation is the termination process. Employees who do not understand why they are being terminated, who are surprised by the termination and who are offered no support may be resentful and act accordingly. If a terminated individual has shown unstable emotional or mental behavior in the past or during the exit interview and is believed to pose a threat, the security force should be alerted and warning notices posted at building entrances.

Preemployment screening is advocated by most security experts when discussing ways to prevent workplace violence. Among the tools available are some recently developed tests designed to identify predictors of violence in the work-place. Screening does have limits, however: "Individuals with a clean and stable background may subsequently deal with problems of divorce, gambling, alcohol, or drug abuse. Any of these could contribute to mental stress and could cause violent tendencies to surface in a person who had no prior history of such behavior" (Harne, 2008, p.102).

As obvious as it may seem, companies should also have written policies prohibiting employees from bring weapons onto company property. A poll of security directors ("Newspoll: Does Your Company Prohibit Employees from Bringing Weapons to Work?," 2007, p.22) that asked "Does your company prohibit employees from bringing weapons to work?" showed that 19 percent of respondents did not have such a prohibition.

The physical security measures discussed in Chapter 6 can help secure the workplace. Where appropriate to the business, video surveillance, extra lighting and alarm systems can be installed and access minimized through identification badges, electronic keys and guards. Organizations might also provide drop safes to limit the amount of cash on hand and keep a minimal amount of cash in registers during evenings and late-night hours.

In addition to reducing the risk of violence occurring on the job, having a proactive approach to avoiding such violence sends a strong message to the workforce that management cares about its people and considers them its most valuable resource.

What Does Not Work

Several practices that do not help prevent violence in most organizations are: one-size-fits-all approaches; rigidity and inflexibility; denial of problems; lack of communication with key parties; lack of collaboration; ignoring respect; no documentation of warning signs; lack of awareness of cultural and diversity issues; passing around "bad apples"; and lack of an organizationwide commitment to safety (Rugala and Isaacs, pp.33–34). Each of these practices should be discontinued and replaced with an opposite approach.

Dealing with Violence That Occurs

Employers should establish a workplace violence response program or incorporate the information into an existing accident response program, employee handbook or procedure manual. All employees must know the policy and that all claims of workplace violence will be promptly investigated and remedied (*OSHA Fact Sheet*). When dealing with threats to an employee made by a co-worker, management must maintain a balance between the accused's rights and the employer's duty. In addition, employers can:

- Provide safety education for employees on what to do if they witness or are subjected to workplace violence and how to protect themselves.
- Equip field staff with cellular phones and hand-held alarms or noise devices, and require them to prepare a daily work plan and keep a contact person informed of their location throughout the day.
- Keep employer-provided vehicles properly maintained.
- Instruct employees not to enter any location where they feel unsafe.

■ Introduce a "buddy system" or provide an escort service or police assistance in potentially dangerous situations or at night (*OSHA Fact Sheet*).

Security professionals may want to have a threat and incident management team trained in how to deal with violence on the job. The team should include at least three elements: security, human resources and legal counsel. Among the responsibilities of this team would be treating injured employees and traumatized observers and providing employee counseling.

If violence should occur, advance preparation should include having specific tasks identified. Communication with employees and clients should be kept open. A record should detail exactly what happened, the possible reasons investigated and corrective steps taken if needed. Figure 12.3 presents the ASIS Incident Management Process suggested in their guidelines.

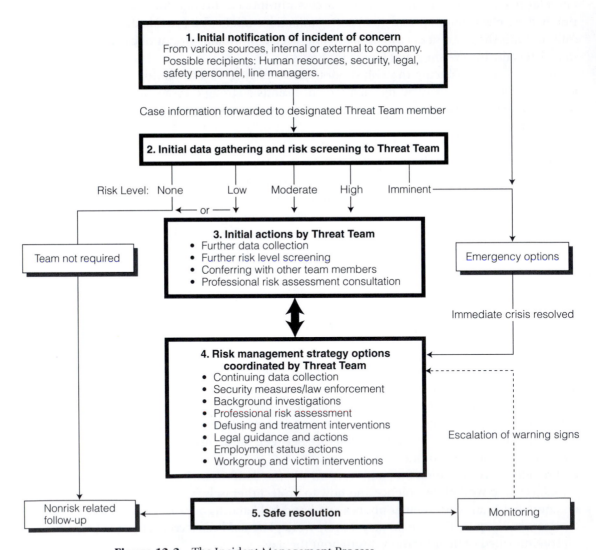

Figure 12.3   The Incident Management Process

SOURCE: From *Workplace Violence Prevention and Response Guidelines* (Alexandria, VA: American Society for Industrial Security, 2005) p.27. Reprinted with the written permission of ASIS International, Alexandria, VA.

Impact of Domestic Violence on Workplace Safety

Most executives and managers in the corporate sector have given little or no thought to the impact of partner abuse on the health and safety of their employees. Potential barriers to understanding and helping employees who are victims of partner abuse include lack of awareness; denial; embarrassment; privacy and confidentiality concerns; victim blaming; expectations of self-identification by abused women; fear of advocating for change; and concern that outreach to abused women may alienate male employees, damage the company image or be too expensive.

A survey of employee assistance professionals (EAPs) found that a large majority of EAP providers had been faced with cases of partner abuse, including restraining order violations and stalking in the workplace. General policies on workplace violence exist, but few specifically address domestic violence. Among larger corporations, EAP staff use a range of practices to assist employees affected by abuse, including use of leaves of absence, medical leaves and short-term disability.

Sometimes it is harassing phone calls to an employee or an angry spouse bursting into the workplace threatening violence or actually assaulting the partner, and it may include homicide. Corporations are increasingly raising their awareness of battered women and encouraging individuals, businesses and communities to take action to prevent domestic violence. Yet another workplace violence area of concern is violence in our nation's schools.

Violence in Schools

Pearl, Mississippi; West Paducah, Kentucky; Jonesboro, Arkansas; Fayetteville, Tennessee; Springfield, Oregon; Richmond, Virginia; Littleton, Colorado; Conyers, Georgia; Santee, California; Red Lake, Minnesota; Barts Township, Pennsylvania—these cities house schools that come to mind when school violence is mentioned. They were shocking instances of violence in our country's schools. Most recently, the shootings at Virginia Tech have highlighted the problem. But these are just the tip of the iceberg. An estimated 100,000 to 250,000 guns are carried to schools every day in this country.

Indicators of School Crime and Safety: 2007 reports that from July 1, 2005 through June 30, 2006, 35 youths ages 5 to 18 were victims of school-associated violent deaths. In addition, in 2005, about 6 percent of students ages 12 to 18 reported they were afraid of attack or harm at school. Black and Hispanic students were more likely than whites to fear for their safety.

Early Warning Signs of Impending Violent Behavior

Early warning signs of impending violent behavior include being a victim of violence, having feelings of being picked on and persecuted, having low interest and poor school performance, feeling uncontrolled anger, having a history of discipline problems, and using drug and alcohol (adapted from *Early Warning, Timely Response*, 1998, pp.8–10). This same publication (p.11) describes signs of imminent violent behavior: serious physical fighting with peers or family

364 Section III: Challenges Facing Security

members, severe destruction of property, severe rage for seemingly minor reasons, detailed threats of lethal violence, possession or use of firearms and other weapons, other self-injurious behaviors and threats of suicide. Among the school-associated violent deaths that receive the most publicity are those involving school shootings.

School Shooters

O'Toole (p.10) describes an innovative model designed to assess someone who has made a threat and evaluate the likelihood that the threat will actually be carried out.

 The FBI's four-pronged threat assessment evaluates four major areas making up the "totality of the circumstances": (1) personality of the person threatening, (2) family dynamics, (3) job (or school) dynamics and the person's role in those dynamics and (4) social dynamics.

Personality Traits and Behaviors   The first behavior listed being associated with violence was *leakage*, discussed earlier. People who commit violent acts typically do not have a moment at which they "snap" from nonviolence into violence, but rather evolve gradually toward violence, with signposts along the way (O'Toole). The task for security personnel, employers and, in the case of schools, teachers, is to learn to interpret the leakage and accurately assess whether an individual poses a true threat to others or is merely having a bad day or blowing off steam.

In addition to leakage, other personality traits or behaviors that may be observed include low tolerance for frustration, poor coping skills, lack of resiliency, failed love relationship, "injustice collector," signs of depression, narcissism (self-centered), alienation, dehumanizing of others, lack of empathy, exaggerated sense of entitlement, attitude of superiority, exaggerated or pathological need for attention, externalizing blame, masking low self-esteem, anger management problems, intolerance, inappropriate humor, manipulative, distrustful, closed social group, change of behavior, rigid and opinionated, unusual interest in sensational violence, fascination with violence-filled entertainment, negative role models, or any other type of behavior that appears relevant to carrying out a threat (O'Toole, pp.17–21). This list is not intended to be used as a checklist to predict future violent behavior, but rather it should be considered only *after* someone has made a threat and an assessment has been made: "No one or two traits or characteristics should be considered in isolation or given more weight than the others. . . . Behavior expresses personality, but one bad day may not reflect a person's real personality or usual behavior patterns" (O'Toole, p.15).

Family Dynamics   Factors associated with the family and violent behavior include a turbulent family relationship, acceptance of pathological behavior, access to weapons and lack of intimacy.

Job Dynamics   According to O'Toole (p.22): "If an act of violence occurs at work, it becomes the crime scene. Factors to consider include the person's attachment to workplace, tolerance for disrespectful behavior, inequitable discipline, inflexible culture and pecking order among employees." In the case of school violence, the school setting is held to the same status as a job setting.

Social Dynamics   "Social dynamics," according to O'Toole (p.13), "are patterns of behavior, thinking, beliefs, customs, traditions, and roles that exist in the larger community where [employees] live." Factors to consider include peer groups, drugs and alcohol, and outside interests.

School Violence as Workplace Violence

School violence shares many characteristics with workplace violence in general and is, in fact, a form of workplace violence for school staff. Although sometimes not recognized as a "workplace," thousands of teachers, administrators, security personnel and others work in our nation's schools.

 Characteristics common to workplace violence and school violence include the profiles of the perpetrators, the targets, the warnings, the means and the pathways to violence.

Effective School Security

A four-pronged approach is needed for effective school security: (1) school/law enforcement/security partnerships, (2) clear policies on accepted behavior with consequences for nonconformity, (3) security procedures and technology and (4) crisis planning. The first two prongs are self-evident.

Security Procedures and Technology   Technologies available to make schools safer include remote surveillance, global positioning system, intelligent surveillance, virtual tours, cellular telephones, biometrics and advanced weapons detection systems.

New Jersey schools are using an iris recognition program to enhance security. The system, nicknamed T-PASS (Teacher-Parent Authorization Security System), links eye-scanning cameras with computers to identify people who have been preauthorized to enter the schools and, once their identity is confirmed, lets them in by unlocking the door (Cohn, 2006). Of the more than 9,400 times someone has attempted to enter the school using the iris scanner, there were no known false positives or other misidentifications. It is important to note that the system made staff members feel safer in the school. A significant loophole in the system occurs, however, when someone who is authorized to enter, having passed the eye-scan check, holds the door open for others, who are then able to access the school without being scanned and authenticated.

Crisis Planning   Another aspect of proactively making schools safer includes having a contingency plan should a crisis occur, including violence by insiders or outsiders. The plan should be carefully thought out based on the unique characteristics of the specific school. It should be made known to and practiced by staff and students.

Preparing for a Terrorist School Takeover

"Someday in the near future, an American community—probably far from an urban center—will find that one of its schools has been taken over by Muslim terrorists who are holding the students hostage. The time for security officers to think about this possibility and train how to respond to it is now, before it has happened" (Giduck, 2006, p.29). Giduck recommends gathering drawings, blueprints, schematics, floor plans and walk-through videotapes of all schools in the community so as to know the target. He notes that assaulting a school full of heavily armed terrorists holding hundreds of terrified hostages is not within most officers' experience. To train for this, officers have to treat it as what it is: war—war in very cramped quarters with a lot of innocents in the way. Campus security is discussed in greater detail in Chapter 15.

Legal Issues

Several legal issues relate to workplace violence. The law puts conflicting pressures on employers and others concerned with preventing or mitigating workplace violence (Rugala and Isaacs, p.47).[5] On one hand, businesses are under a variety of legal obligations to safeguard their employees' well-being and security. Occupational safety laws impose a general requirement to maintain a safe workplace, which embraces safety from violence. As noted at the beginning of this chapter, the "General Duty Clause" of the Occupational Safety and Health Act requires employers to have a workplace that is "free from recognized hazards." Workers' compensation laws also make employers responsible for job-related injuries. Civil rights laws require employers to protect employees against various forms of harassment, including threats and violence.

Employers also may face civil liability after a workplace violence incident on a number of grounds: if there was negligence in hiring or retaining a dangerous person, for example, or a failure to provide proper supervision, training or physical safety measures.

Simultaneously, the law requires employers to safeguard due process and other employee rights. Privacy, antidefamation and antidiscrimination laws may limit an employer's ability to find out about a present or prospective employee's background. The possibility of a wrongful termination lawsuit can make an organization reluctant to fire someone even when there is evidence the person may be dangerous, and can make the process a long, difficult struggle if the company decides to terminate. Employee rights and workplace safety concerns can also collide over such issues as whether and when workers can be compelled to get counseling or treatment as a condition of keeping a job.

Even the Americans with Disabilities Act can sometimes pose obstacles in dealing with potentially violent employees. For example, in *Gambini v. Total Renal Care, Inc.* (2007), a federal appeals court ruled that an employer improperly fired a worker for her violent behavior because that behavior was caused by a disability, bipolar disorder. This ruling contradicts previous cases, which have held that violent behavior in the workplace need not be tolerated by employers, even from workers with disabilities (Anderson, 2007, p.86).

One especially difficult issue is restrictions on disseminating information about employees with records of past violence or other troubling behavior on the job. Those restrictions can significantly limit employers' ability either to screen

---

[5]SOURCE: Eugene A. Rugala and Arnold R. Isaacs, *Workplace Violence: Issues in Response* (Washington, DC: Federal Trade Commission).

out dangerous people before hiring or to obtain highly relevant information in a threat assessment when an incident has occurred. For example, though rules vary somewhat from one jurisdiction to another, agencies are ordinarily not allowed to disclose criminal records or inform employers if a worker or job applicant has been convicted of a violent crime—even though the conviction was a matter of public record. Similarly, strict confidentiality rules shield medical and mental health records that can also have direct relevance to assessing potential threats.

These dilemmas mirror the inherent tension in a legal system with dual objectives: protecting the general good while also protecting individual rights. As in every other legal field, workplace safety law has to strike a balance between those two purposes. Few would question the principles of respecting due process and workers' rights or the need to balance safety precautions and anti-violence policies against appropriate privacy protection. The issue is where the boundary should be drawn.

SUMMARY

- In 1914 the federal government passed the Harrison Narcotics Act, which made the sale or use of certain drugs illegal, including narcotics and other dangerous drugs.

- Drugs commonly abused in the workplace include alcohol, marijuana and cocaine—snorted or smoked as freebase or crack.

- The most commonly observed drugs on the street, in possession of users and seized in drug raids are heroin, opium, morphine, codeine, cocaine, crack and marijuana.

- Marijuana is the most available and abused illegal drug in the United States.

- Common effects of the various narcotics and other dangerous drugs include: (1) they are mind altering, (2) they may become addicting—either physically or psychologically, and (3) overdosage may result in convulsions and death.

- Causes of violence may include ready availability of guns, drugs and alcohol, a desensitization to violence, disintegration of the family and community, social and economic deprivation, and increased numbers of children growing up in violent families.

- Annually more than 2 million people become victims of violent crime at work, according to the U.S. Bureau of Justice Statistics.

- Among the commonly cited causes or motivators of workplace violence are job loss due to downsizing of companies; uncaring working environment;

the availability of guns; personality conflicts, resentment, anger from feelings of mistreatment and high levels of stress on the job; substance abuse; and mental problems.

- The typical perpetrator of workplace violence is a disgruntled, middle-aged white male who is a loner, who either has been or is about to be fired and who is a gun enthusiast.

- Indicators of impending violent behavior may include "leakage" of violent thoughts, depression, paranoia, erratic behavior, fixation on a coworker and threats.

- Most violent people "leak" their feelings and intentions in the weeks and months before committing the violent act. Such messages should never be ignored.

- Threats may be classified as direct, indirect, veiled and conditional.

- The FBI's four-pronged threat assessment evaluates four major areas making up the "totality of the circumstances": (1) personality of the person threatening, (2) family dynamics, (3) job dynamics and the person's role in those dynamics and (4) social dynamics.

- Characteristics common to workplace violence and school violence include the profiles of the perpetrators, the targets, the warnings, the means and the pathways to violence.

APPLICATION

As a security officer for the Gopher Security Company, you have been instructed by your supervisor to admit into the manufacturing plant only individuals who have proper photo identification and presumably are employees.

Keith Wilson comes through your station, presents credentials that appear valid and enters the plant. As he places the identification back into his pocket, you notice he is carrying a concealed gun. No one else notices this, and you are somewhat traumatized by the observation. You are in a dilemma and feel you have to take some kind of action. You have a number of alternatives. Which do you feel is appropriate for this particular incident?

1. Confront Keith Wilson and make him give up his gun.
2. Call the public police and have them seize the weapon.
3. Do nothing because you were never trained or instructed in what to do in this type of situation.
4. Notify your supervisor.
5. Notify the company management.

DISCUSSION QUESTIONS

1. Do you think that security officers working in highly emotionally charged areas should undertake preventive measures in the interest of employee safety? What should their role be?
2. Recently a University of Iowa doctoral student who had lost a cherished dissertation prize stated just before killing five people that the gun was a "great equalizer." What comments do you have about a person who takes such forceful measures to show his feelings?
3. Was violence a problem in the high school you attended? If yes, what was the major problem?
4. Do you believe the gateway or stepping stone theory related to drugs is credible?
5. Have any instances of workplace violence occurred in your city? Your state?

REFERENCES

Alcohol Alert Newsletter. Online, 2007.

Alcohol and the Workplace. IAS Factsheet. Institute of Alcohol Studies, Cambs, England, July 15, 2007.

Anderson, Teresa. "U.S. Judicial Decisions." *Security Management,* July 2007, 86–87.

Bennett, Wayne W. and Hess, Kären M. *Criminal Investigation,* 8th edition. Belmont, CA: Wadsworth Publishing Company, 2007.

Burke, John. "Prescription Drug Diversion." *Law Enforcement Technology,* May 2004, pp.16–21.

Caulkins, Jonathan P.; Reuter, Peter; Iguchi, Martin Y.; and Chiesa, James. *How Goes the "War on Drugs"? An Assessment of U.S. Drug Problems and Policy.* The Rand Corporation, 2005.

Ceniceros, Roberto. "Trends in Workplace Violence Mixed." *Business Insurance,* October 4, 2006.

Cities without Drugs. The "Major Cities" Guide to Reducing Substance Abuse in Your Community. Washington, DC: Office of National Drug Control Policy, November 2005.

Jeffrey P. "Keeping an Eye on School Security: ...is Recognition Project in New Jersey." *NIJ Jour-... ...*2006.

...y. "Spike in Violent Crime Creates ..." *Herald Tribune* (Southwest Flor-... ...07.

DEA Web site, www.dea.gov.

Early Warning, Timely Response: A Guide to Safe Schools. Washington, DC: U.S. Department of Education, April 1998.

The Economic Costs of Drug Abuse in the United States, 1992–2002. Washington, DC: Office of National Drug Control Policy, 2006.

Edwards, Al. "New Video Highlights Workplace Violence Prevention." *Security Director News,* June 2007, p.4.

Eggen, Dan. "Violent Crime Is Up for 2nd Straight Year: Biggest Cities Showed Largest Increase." *Washington Post,* December 19, 2006, p.A01.

Federal Bureau of Investigation, 2006. www.fbi.gov.

Gane, Scott R. "Avoiding Violent Outcomes." *Security Management,* June 2007, pp.140–138.

Garrett, Ronnie. "Part I: Pill Pushers on the 'Net.'" *Law Enforcement Technology,* August 2006, pp.72–81.

Giduck, John. "Responding to School Sieges." *Police,* September 2006, pp.28–34.

Harne, Eric. "Terminations and Violence." *Security Management,* February 2008, p.102.

Hershkowitz, Ronald M. "Zero Tolerance Equals Trouble." *Security Management,* 2004, pp.83–88.

Indicators of School Crime and Safety: 2006. Washington DC: National Center for Education Statistics, 2007, pp.12–17.

Irvin, Martha and Me Hoang, Francis Q. "Preplanning for School Violence." *Law and Order,* December 2007, pp.107–109.

Katel, Peter. "War on Drugs." *CQ Researcher Online,* June 2, 2006.

National Drug Control Strategy 2008. Washington, DC: The White House, February 2008.

National Drug Threat Assessment 2007. Washington, DC: National Drug Intelligence Center, October 2007. http://www .usdoj.gov/ndic/products.htm

"Newspoll: Does Your Company Prohibit Employees from Bringing Weapons to Work?" *Security Director News,* December 2007, p.22.

"Newspoll: What Is Your Biggest Security Fear for Your Organization in 2006?" *Security Director News,* December 2005, p.23.

OSHA Fact Sheet. Washington, DC: Occupational Safety and Health Administration.

O'Toole, Mary Ellen. *The School Shooter: A Threat Assessment Perspective.* Washington, DC: Federal Bureau of Investigation, no date.

Payson, Martin F. and Piazza, Peter. "Peer Reviews Yield Results." *Security Management,* May 2007, pp.81–96.

Pulse Check: Trends in Drug Abuse. Washington, DC: Office of National Drug Control Policy, January 2004. (NCJ 201398)

Rudewicz, Frank E. "The Road to Rage." *Security Management,* 2004, pp.41–49.

Rugala, Eugene A. and Isaacs, Arnold R. *Workplace Violence: Issues in Response.* Washington, DC: Federal Bureau of Investigation, no date.

Ryan, Jason. "FBI Stats Show Spike in Violent Crime." *ABC News,* December 18, 2006.

Thomas, Pierre; Date, Jack; and Ryan, Jason. "Startling New Stats Show Cross-Country Crime Spike." *ABC News,* October 12, 2006.

Violence in the Workplace—An Updated Analysis. National Council on Compensation Insurance, September 2006.

Violence: Prevention, Management and Survival (VPS). National Association of Safety Professionals, 2007.

Walters, John P. "Foreword." *Cities without Drugs. The "Major Cities" Guide to Reducing Substance Abuse in Your Community.* Washington, DC: Office of National Drug Control Policy, November 2005.

Wexler, Chuck. "Foreword." *Chief Concerns: A Gathering Storm—Violent Crime in America.* Washington, DC: Police Executive Research Forum, 2006a, pp.i–ii.

Wexler, Chuck. "Violent Crime Up Nationwide." *Subject to Debate,* March 2006b, p.2.

Workplace Violence Prevention and Response Guidelines. Alexandria, VA: American Society for Industrial Security, 2005.

Wuestewald, Todd. "Enlisting Community Help in the Investigation of Methamphetamine Laboratories." *The Police Chief,* March 2005, pp.34–37.

CASES CITED

Gambini v. Total Renal Care, Inc., U.S. Court of Appeals for the Ninth Circuit, No. 05–35209 (2007).

Jones v. Potter, U.S. Court of Appeals for the Sixth Circuit, No. 06–3845 (2007).

Largo Corp. v. Crespin, 727 P.2d 1098 (Colo. 1986).

CHAPTER 13

Terrorism and Homeland Security Responsibilities

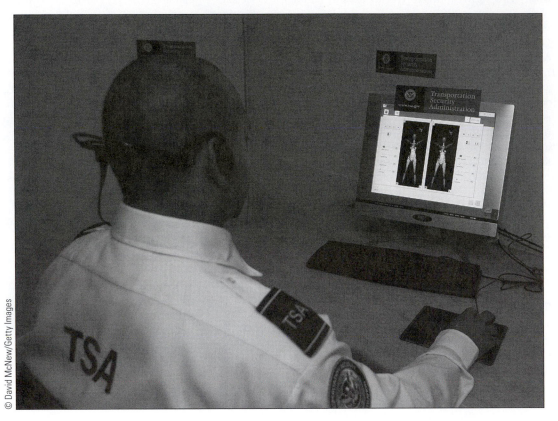

© David McNew/Getty Images

A Transportation Security Administration (TSA) officer checks the body scan of a fully-clothed employee during a demonstration of the ProVision whole-body imaging machine at Los Angeles International Airport (LAX) in April 2008. TSA officers will use the imaging machine to screen for weapons and explosives, despite complaints from privacy advocates that the technology reveals too much of one's anatomy to strangers. Travelers at LAX will be continuously and randomly selected to go through the machine. While signs will inform travelers of a pat-down option, screeners will not announce that choice.

Do You Know?

- What security professionals' responsibilities are in relation to homeland security?
- What most definitions of terrorism include?
- What three elements are common in terrorism?
- What federal office was established as a result of 9/11?
- What the lead federal agencies in combating terrorism are?
- How the FBI classifies terrorist acts?
- What domestic terrorist groups exist in the United States?
- What the three-tiered model of al Qaeda terrorist attacks consists of?
- What motivates most terrorist attacks?
- What methods terrorists may use?
- What two forms militarized terrorist attacks may take?
- What two concerns are associated with the current "war on terrorism"?

Can You Define?

asymmetric war	estimative language	interoperability	sleeper cell
bioterrorism	fusion center	*jihad*	terrorism

Introduction

"Terrorism is one of the oldest forms of human conflict. While the means and ends have changed over time, the strategy of fear, panic, violence and disruption has not changed" (Sanow, 2002, p.5). The United States has not been immune from attacks from within and without: the Ku Klux Klan, the Unabomber, the 1993 attack on the World Trade Center, the 1995 bombing of the Alfred P. Murrah Building in Oklahoma and, of course, the multiple attacks that occurred on September 11, 2001.

Both the FBI and the U.S. Customs Service have made terrorism their top priority. But they cannot fight this war alone: "Since the attacks of September 11, 2001, law enforcement–private security partnerships have been viewed as critical to preventing terrorism and terror-related acts. Because the private sector owns and protects 85 percent of the nation's infrastructure, while local law enforcement often possess threat information regarding infrastructure, law enforcement–private security partnerships can put vital information into the hands of the people who need it. Thus, to effectively protect the nation's infrastructure, law enforcement and private security must work collaboratively because neither possesses the necessary resources to do so alone" (Morabito and Greenberg, 2005, p.vii).

The ASIS *Threat Advisory System Response (TASR) Guideline* (2004) stresses: "Private business and industry, as the primary provider of goods and services and the owner of approximately 85 percent of the national infrastructure, play a significant role in helping to mitigate the physical effects and economic costs of domestic incidents. The public-private sector partnership is a crucial component of the national strategy and infrastructure for combating terrorism." The criticality of such partnerships was the focus of Chapter 3.

The importance of homeland security is attested to by the emergence of a homeland security major at the undergraduate level. In 2006 Virginia Commonwealth University (VCU) in Richmond granted the country's first four bachelor's degrees in homeland security and emergency preparedness (Straw, 2007c, p.34). Graduate degree study in this area is also springing up at other schools around the country. Private security has, indeed, become a major player in our country's security.

 Security professionals' responsibilities related to homeland security include:

- Knowing the enemy, what to look for and being vigilant.
- Taking all possible steps to prevent a terrorist attack.
- Preparing themselves and their agencies/organizations for an attack, should one occur, through education and training.
- Responding to an attack.
- Investigating the attack.

Note: While "homeland security" has come to encompass protecting against both natural and man-made disasters, this chapter will focus on the latter threat, specifically that posed by terrorism. (The private security response to natural disasters was discussed in Chapter 8.)

It is vital that security professionals understand the enemy—the terrorist; therefore, much of this chapter is devoted to explaining who the terrorists are, what motivates them and how they operate. The chapter begins by defining terrorism and presenting a brief chronology of terrorism from the first century up through September 11, 2001. It then explains the new kind of war presented by the terrorists—an asymmetric war—and how likely the threat of terrorism is. This is followed by a discussion of the classification of terrorism as domestic or international and the dual threat presented. Next the importance of knowing the enemy is described, including the differences between the street criminal and the terrorist as well as the training most al Qaeda terrorists receive. This is followed by an explanation of the various motivations for terrorism and the methods commonly used by terrorists. Then efforts to prevent terrorism are described, followed by discussions of responding to and investigating terrorist attacks. The chapter concludes with a brief look at two major concerns related to the war on terrorism: the erosion of civil liberties and retaliation against people of Middle Eastern descent.

Terrorism Defined

No single definition of terrorism is universally accepted because, as The Terrorism Research Center notes: "One man's terrorist is another's freedom fighter." The Center defines **terrorism** as "the use of force or violence against persons or property in violation of the criminal laws of the United States for purposes of intimidation, coercion or ransom." This is similar to the FBI's definition: "Terrorism is the unlawful use of force or violence against persons or property to intimidate or coerce a government, the civilian population, or any segment thereof, in furtherance of political or social objectives." The U.S. Code Title 22 defines terrorism as the "premeditated, politically motivated violence perpetrated against non-combatant targets by subnational groups or clandestine agents, usually intended to influence an audience." A more graphic definition is provided by James Poland: "Terrorism is the premeditated, deliberate, systematic murder, mayhem, and threatening of the innocent to create fear and intimidation in order to gain a political or tactical advantage."

 Most definitions of terrorism include the systematic use of physical violence, either actual or threatened, against noncombatants to create a climate of fear to cause some religious, political or social change.

A Brief Chronology of Terrorism

Terrorism dates back to at least the first century when the Zealots, a Jewish sect, fought against Roman occupation of what is now Israel. Through the eighteenth century most terrorist movements were based on religious beliefs. The word *terrorism* first appeared during the French Revolution (1789–1799) when revolutionaries who seized power in France used violence against their enemies. Their period of rule was called the Reign of Terror.

During the nineteenth century, and into the twentieth, terrorist movements continued to be politically based. In the 1930s Germany's Adolf Hitler, Italy's Benito Mussolini and the Soviet Union's Joseph Stalin all used terrorism to discourage opposition to their governments. In 1945 conflict between Arab nations and Israel resulted in waves of terrorism throughout the Middle East. Since 1960 Palestinian groups have carried out acts of terrorism to establish an independent Palestinian state: "The modern era of terrorism—that is, terrorism as we know it today—began in the late 1960s. . . . Worldwide there were 14,000 terrorist attacks from 1968 through 1999, and they resulted in more than 10,000 deaths" (Van Etten, 2004, p.31).

 Three elements of terrorism are: (1) it is criminal in nature, (2) targets are typically symbolic and (3) the terrorist actions are always aggressive and often violent.

In the United States, during the late 1800s and 1900s, the Ku Klux Klan advocated violence to terrorize blacks and their sympathizers. From 1978 to 1995, the anarchist and terrorist known as the Unabomber, using homemade bombs either mailed or planted, killed 3 people and wounded 23 others. Arrested in 1996, Theodore Kaczynski claimed allegiance to radical environmentalists and those opposed to the effects of industrialization and technology, targeting university professors, computer professionals and corporate executives.

The United States' support of Israel resulted in several acts of terrorism against Americans by Palestinian radicals or supporters, including the 1983 attack by Shiite Muslim suicide bombers on the U.S. embassy in Beirut, Lebanon, and on the U.S. Marine barracks in Beirut, killing nearly 300, mostly Americans. In 1988 a bomb destroyed Pan American Flight 103 over Scotland, killing 259, including 189 Americans, and two Libyan terrorists were later charged with the act. One was found guilty of murdering the 259 passengers and crew. The court concluded it had insufficient evidence against the second suspect.

In the late 1980s the Animal Liberation Front (ALF) used arson to terrorize in Davis, California; Tucson, Arizona; and Lubbock, Texas, and in 1990 the Popular Liberation Party used arson and bombs in Puerto Rico. Islamic radicals used a crude bomb made with agricultural fertilizer in a 1993 attack on the World Trade Center in New York that killed 6, injured nearly 1,000 and caused an estimated $600 million in damage. This blatant, foreign-sponsored act of terrorism was viewed with alarm and disbelief, yet because the towers of the World Trade Center still stood, Americans went on with life with a suppressed sense of invulnerability, and the fear of terrorism faded rapidly.

Then in 1995 a 4,800-pound truck bomb exploded in front of the Alfred P. Murrah Federal Building in Oklahoma City, killing 168 and injuring 500. Not only was this the deadliest terrorist attack the United States had ever endured up to that day, it was carried out by two Americans, Timothy McVeigh and Terry Nichols, both espousing the beliefs of a right-wing militia. The United States now faced the threat of both domestic and international terrorism. That same year the derailment of an Amtrak train in an Arizona desert was linked to terrorists.

In 1996 another truck bomb destroyed a barracks housing American military personnel in Dhahran, Saudi Arabia, killing 19 servicemen. Also in 1996, Osama bin Laden officially declared war on the United States.

In 1998 two U.S. embassies in East Africa were bombed, killing more than 200 people, including 12 Americans. Twenty-two people were charged with the crime. At the end of 2000, one had pled guilty to conspiring in the attacks, five were in custody in New York awaiting trial, three were in England awaiting extradition to the United States, and thirteen were fugitives, including Osama bin Laden. Bin Laden was put on the FBI's 10 Most Wanted List wanted in connection with the August 7, 1998, bombings of U.S. Embassies in Dar Es Salaam, Tanzania, and Nairobi, Kenya.

In 1999 the FBI Director Louis Freeh announced: "Our No. 1 priority is the prevention of terrorism." The FBI added a new Counterterrorism Division with four subunits: the International Terrorism Section, the Domestic Terrorism Section, the National Infrastructure Protection Center and the National Domestic Preparedness Office.

Terrorism continued into the twenty-first century, and on October 12, 2000, 17 sailors died when two suicide bombers attacked the USS Cole while it was refueling in the Yemeni port of Aden. Then came September 11, 2001, the worst terrorist attack in the history of the United States, when terrorists hijacked four commercial airliners shortly after their take-offs, while they still carried great amounts of fuel. Two of the planes were crashed into the twin towers of the World Trade Center in New York, leaving 4,815 people missing and 417 confirmed dead, including the 157 passengers aboard Flight 11 and Flight 175. An hour later Flight 77 crashed into the Pentagon, leaving 189 believed dead, including everyone on board. Soon after that, another hijacked airliner presumed to be en route to either the White House or U.S. Capitol building crashed into a rural area in Pennsylvania, killing 44 aboard Flight 93. Among those missing or confirmed dead were 311 firefighters and 65 police officers.

September 11, 2001

The Terrorism Research Center declared: "The attack of September 11 will be the precipitating moment of a new kind of war that will define a new century. This war will be fought in shadows, and the adversary will continue to target the innocent and defenseless." The Center outlined the effects of this attack:

This threat has not achieved its objectives of fear. Rather, it has galvanized the United States into action. The U.S. now sees a national security threat raised to an unprecedented level. However, the U.S. also sees an opportunity to solidify international support and national unity to combat this threat. . . .

This threat is not directed solely against the United States—it is a threat directed against all countries that seek freedom, peace and stability. The world's response to terrorism will change not only international efforts with respect to terrorism; it will change geopolitics as countries take sides and see mutual interests where few were apparent before.[1]

Indeed, the horrific events of September 11 pulled together and unified the American people in a way most had never seen. Patriotism was suddenly popular—Wal-Mart alone sold 88,000 American flags on September 12. Thousands of volunteers helped search for victims and donated blood and money.

Why did the tragic events of September 11 happen? For one thing, terrorists took advantage of the U.S. aviation security system's permissiveness in allowing knives with less than four-inch blades and small cutting instruments on board planes. In addition, those doing the screening are usually undertrained, underpaid and tired, many having to work two jobs to support themselves. To maintain the steady flow of hurried travelers trying to make their flights, screeners are instructed to spend only three to six seconds on each item passing through x-ray. Any distractions make this task more difficult.

In addition, U.S. immigration policies make it relatively easy for terrorists to enter the country and move freely within it. In fact, several people with connections to Osama bin Laden's al Qaeda group received pilot training in the United States. Michael Chertoff, U.S. Homeland Security Secretary, has stated that without better ways to track immigration: "I guarantee you we will lose the race with the terrorists" (Jackson, 2007).

The U.S. Response to September 11th   In addition to an intense investigation, the United States initiated military action against Afghanistan after the Taliban government refused to turn over Osama Bin Laden. Also, security was heightened at airports and throughout the country.

 As a result of 9/11 the Office of Homeland Security (later renamed the Department of Homeland Security) was established, reorganizing the departments of the federal government.

The mission of the Department of Homeland Security (DHS) is "to develop and coordinate the implementation of a comprehensive national strategy to secure the United States from terrorist threats or attacks." The DHS serves in a broad capacity, facilitating collaboration between local and federal law enforcement to develop a national strategy to detect, prepare for, prevent, protect against, respond to and recover from terrorist attacks within the United States.

 At the federal level, the FBI is the lead agency for responding to acts of domestic terrorism. The Federal Emergency Management Agency (FEMA) is the lead agency for consequence management (after an attack).

Another effort to enhance national security was passage of the USA PATRIOT Act.

---

[1]SOURCE: The Terrorism Research Center, http://www.terrorism.com/index.html.

The USA PATRIOT Act   On October 26, 2001, President Bush signed into law the Uniting and Strengthening America by Providing Appropriate Tools Required to Intercept and Obstruct Terrorism (USA PATRIOT) Act, giving police unprecedented ability to search, seize, detain or eavesdrop in their pursuit of possible terrorists, saying: "This government will enforce this law with all the urgency of a nation at war." Bush asserted that the nation had little choice but to update surveillance procedures "written in the era of rotary telephones" to combat today's sophisticated terrorists. The law expands the FBI's wiretapping and electronic surveillance authority and allows nationwide jurisdiction for search warrants and electronic surveillance devices, including legal expansion of those devices to e-mail and the Internet. These resources can be invaluable to security professionals' efforts to assist in the war on terrorism. The USA PATRIOT Act also establishes new punishments for possessing biological weapons.

A New Kind of Fight—An Asymmetric War

An **asymmetric war** is one in which a much weaker opponent takes on a stronger opponent by refusing to confront the stronger opponent head on. The weaker opponent selects battles where the enemy does not expect to be hit, and the attack causes a huge psychological shock. It creates power for the weaker adversary and renders the stronger adversary unable to use its conventional resources. In this asymmetric war, the police are the most frequent target, followed by government agencies and institutions, as shown in Table 13.1.

These worldwide targets are also vulnerable in the United States and have been for some time. According to Griffith (2006a, p.10):

> We've been officially under attack by Muslim terrorists for five years. Actually, they've been trying to kill us for a lot longer; it's just we decided to take notice when they hit us really hard five years ago.
>
> We took notice. And then we went back to doing what we do. Squabbling with each other over politics, spending more money than we have, enjoying the good life, and denying that we're in danger.

Table 13.1   Worldwide Terrorism by Target

	Incidents			Fatalities			Injuries		
	2005	**2006**	**2007***	**2005**	**2006**	**2007***	**2005**	**2006**	**2007***
Business	248	264	141	323	379	249	1,134	1,188	955
Educational institutions	188	220	139	64	120	233	103	148	454
Government	1,177	1,010	533	1,207	1,147	725	2,201	1,615	1,417
Police	1,166	2,013	1,245	2,714	3,309	2,476	4,701	6,091	4,720
Private citizens and property	909	1,274	519	1,872	4,682	3,334	3,489	8,184	7,590
Religious figures/institutions	178	462	180	494	561	452	1,035	1,141	870
Other	1,130	1,417	722	1,520	1,873	1,294	2,606	2,624	2,688
Total	**4,996**	**6,660**	**3,479**	**8,194**	**12,071**	**8,763**	**15,269**	**20,991**	**18,694**

* 2007 numbers only through the third quarter. Target, Region, and Tactic data on terrorist incidents will be reported in sequential months. Reprinted by permission.

SOURCE: From *MIPT Terrorism Knowledge Base*. Used by permission of the Memorial Institute for the Prevention of Terrorism.

The majority of Americans don't take this war seriously. Part of the problem is that we can't say who we're fighting. In World War II we fought the Germans, Japanese, Italians and a number of lesser players aligned with the Axis powers. In Korea, we fought the North Koreans and the Chinese. Even in Vietnam we could say who we were fighting.

But now we're fighting the Global War on Terrorism.[2]

Griffith (2006b, p.12) concludes: "Many Americans have failed to learn the real message of that day. We were not attacked by a small band of zealots with box cutters but by an ideology that still thrives in the world and must be defeated before there can be peace."

The Threat and Reality of Terrorism

The events of September 11, 2001, turned the threat of terrorism into a reality for U.S. citizens. However, surveys of private security directors show that the vast majority do not consider terrorism as a major threat compared to such issues as workplace violence. Nonetheless, the threat is very real as reported in *National Intelligence Estimate: The Terrorist Threat to the US Homeland* (2007). This report uses **estimative language**, that is, language based on analytical assessments and judgments rather than on facts or hard evidence. The report uses terms such as *we assess* and *we judge* synonymously. Among the key judgments of the report are the following:

> We judge the US Homeland will face a persistent and evolving terrorist threat over the next three years. The main threat comes from Islamic terrorist groups and cells, especially al-Qa'ida, driven by their undiminished intent to attack the Homeland and a continued effort by these terrorist groups to adapt and improve their capabilities.
>
> We assess that greatly increased worldwide counterterrorism efforts over the past five years have constrained the ability of al-Qa'ida to attack the US Homeland again and have led terrorist groups to perceive the Homeland as a harder target to strike than on 9/11. These measures have helped disrupt known plots against the United States since 9/11. We are concerned, however, that this level of international cooperation may wane as 9/11 becomes a more distant memory and perceptions of the threat diverge.
>
> Al-Qa'ida is and will remain the most serious terrorist threat to the Homeland, as its central leadership continues to plan high-impact plots, while pushing others in extremist Sunni communities to mimic its efforts and to supplement its capabilities. We judge that the United States currently is in a heightened threat environment.
>
> We assess that al-Qa'ida will continue to enhance its capabilities to attack the Homeland through greater cooperation with regional terrorist groups. Of note, we assess that al-Qa'ida will probably seek to leverage the contacts and capabilities of al-Qa'ida in Iraq (AQI), its most visible and capable affiliate and the only one known to have expressed a desire to attack

---

[2]SOURCE: Reprinted from "Eyes Wide Shut" by David Griffith in *The Police Chief*, June 2006a, p.10. Copyright held by the International Association of Chiefs of Police, 515 North Washington Street, Alexandria, VA 22314 USA. Further reproduction without express written permission from IACP is strictly prohibited.

the Homeland. In addition, we assess that its association with AQI helps al-Qa'ida to energize the broader Sunni extremist community, raise resources, and to recruit and indoctrinate operatives, including for Homeland attacks.

We assess that al-Qa'ida's Homeland plotting is likely to continue to focus on prominent political, economic and infrastructure targets with the goal of producing mass casualties, visually dramatic destruction, significant economic aftershocks, and/or fear among the US population. The group is proficient with conventional small arms and improvised explosive devices, and is innovative in creating new capabilities and overcoming security obstacles.

We assess that al-Qa'ida will continue to try to acquire and employ chemical, biological, radiological or nuclear material in attacks and would not hesitate to use them if it develops what it deems is sufficient capability.

We assess that other, non-Muslim terrorist groups—often referred to as "single-issue" groups by the FBI—probably will conduct attacks over the next three years given their violent histories, but we assess this violence is likely to be on a small scale.[3]

The next terrorist assault on the United States is likely to consist of relatively unsophisticated, near simultaneous attacks similar to those attempted in Britain in June 2007, intended to cause widespread fear and panic rather than to cause major losses (DeYoung, 2007, p.A01). Counterterrorism officials say the attacks in England and Scotland coincide with U.S. intelligence indicating increased movement of money and people from al Qaeda camps in the ungoverned tribal areas of Pakistan near the Afghan border (DeYoung).

Classification of Terrorist Acts

 The FBI classifies terrorism in the United States as domestic or international terrorism.

Domestic Terrorism

The 1995 bombing of the Alfred P. Murrah Federal Building in Oklahoma City and the pipe bomb explosions in Centennial Olympic Park during the 1996 Summer Olympic Games highlight the threat of domestic terrorists. They represent extreme right- or left-wing and special interest beliefs. Many are antigovernment, antitaxation and engage in survivalist training to perpetuate a white, Christian nation. The right-wing militia or patriot movement is a security concern because of the potential for violence and criminal behavior. Some states have passed legislation limiting militias, including types of training they can undergo.

 Domestic terrorist groups include white supremacists, black supremacists, militia groups, other right-wing extremists, left-wing extremists, pro-life extremists, animal rights activists and environmental extremists.

Animal Rights Activists A very active domestic terrorist groups is the Animal Liberation Front (ALF), which has claimed credit for attacks on meat packing plants, furriers and research labs. ALF has caused millions of dollars in damages and medical research setback through vandalism, arson and freeing laboratory animals.

[3]SOURCE: *National Intelligence Estimate: The Terrorist Threat to the U.S. Homeland* (2007).

Environmental Extremists   Environmental extremists are often referred to as eco-terrorists, with *eco* being derived from *ecology*—the study of the inter-relationships of organisms and their environment. Eco-terrorism seeks to economically damage those who profit from destruction of the environment. One such group is the Earth Liberation Front (ELF), often working with the Animal Liberation Front (ALF).

Arson is a favorite weapon of eco-terrorists, responsible for tens of millions of dollars of property damage, including a U.S. Department of Agriculture building, a U.S. Forest Service ranger station and a Colorado ski resort. ELF claims responsibility for releasing 5,000 mink from a Michigan fur farm, 600 wild horses from an Oregon corral and burning the Michigan State University's genetic engineering research offices. Criminal acts of eco-terrorists include equipment vandalism, package bombs or pipe bombs, destruction of research data, arson of buildings, obliteration of experimental plants and animals and the like.

International Terrorism

International terrorism is foreign-based or directed by countries or groups outside the United States against the United States. The FBI divides international terrorism into three categories. The first threat is foreign state sponsors of international terrorism using terrorism as a tool of foreign policy, for example Iraq, Libya and Afghanistan.

The second threat is formalized terrorist groups such as Lebanese Hezballah, Egyptian Al-Gamm's Al-Islamiyya, Palestinian HAMAS and Osama bin Laden's al Qaeda: "Al-Qaida remains a very real threat, and is still the backbone of the international terrorist movement, although mergers with other groups have made it less centralized" ("FBI: Suicide Bombs a Big Concern," 2007).

Whitelaw (2007, p.32) asserts that al Qaeda's leadership, once on the run, has regrouped and that bin Laden, having found a safe haven in Pakistan, may be stronger than ever: "Al Qaeda retains the ability to organize complex, mass-casualty attacks and inspire others" (p.33). However, a "perverse 'competition' is now in evidence between the Arabic-dominated al Qaeda terrorists and the Iranian-controlled Hezbollah terrorist group" (Jones, 2007a, p.36). These two groups compete for funding as well as recruits.

The third type of threat comes from loosely affiliated international radical extremists who have a variety of identities and travel freely in the United States, unknown to law enforcement or the government.

The Dual Threat

In the war against terrorism, it is important that all security officers keep as close an eye on domestic terrorists as they do on the international variety. It is also important that security professionals learn as much as possible about the enemy they are charged with protecting against.

Indicators of Terrorism: Knowing the Enemy

The importance of knowing one's enemy and maintaining constant vigilance cannot be overemphasized. As mentioned, although time passes and the memory of 9/11 tends to fade, those charged with protecting our nation's citizens and institutions must not allow their eyes and ears to become any less focused on potential threats: "A major problem in the current war on terrorism is how to ensure individual officers remain vigilant" (Dowle, 2006b, p.22). The following list of indicators applies to both domestic and foreign terrorists (Savelli, 2004, pp.18–19):

- Possession of fake or altered identification
- IDs from different states
- Multiple identification in different names
- Possession of IDs or passports in which the person looks dramatically different in each photo
- Possession of anti-American, anti-Jewish, antiminority or anti-Israel material such as an upside down American flag or inflammatory literature
- Possession or use of disrespectful writing or graffiti regarding America, Jews, minorities or Israel
- Residence in several states in the past few years
- Taken multiple trips out of the country or state of residence in the past few years
- Possession of videos, photos or diagrams of public buildings, airports, subways, malls, and so on
- Conducting surveillance of government employees and government sites
- Taken flying lessons or use of flight simulators
- Extreme interest in martial arts and aggressive fighting techniques
- Use of Internet cafes, library Internet access and computer stores with Internet capabilities to avoid tracing
- Use of payphones and phone cards rather than own phone
- Possession of large amounts of money or evidence of an overseas transfer of money (money transactions of under $10,000 are done to avoid filing)
- Receiving large amounts of money from overseas
- Renting first-floor apartments to facilitate an easy escape
- Extended use of inexpensive motels, since there are not usually any surveillance cameras
- Never allowing maids to clean the room alone or always being in attendance while maids are working
- No apparent means of legitimate income
- Member of a radical organization
- Display of terrorist or extremist symbols
- Recent shaving of head and body hair [4]

Any single indicator, or even several indicators, does not constitute proof that an individual is a terrorist, but if more than several of these indicators are present, security officers should be vigilant.

Another aspect of knowing the enemy comes from understanding how terrorists differ from traditional criminals.

Terrorists versus Traditional Criminals

Polisar (2004, p.8) observes: "Suddenly agencies and officers who have been trained and equipped to deal with more traditional crimes are now focused on

---

[4]SOURCE: From *A Proactive Law Enforcement Guide for the War on Terrorism* by Lou Savelli (Flushing, NY: LooseLeaf Law Publications, Inc., 2004) pp.18–19.

3381

13.2Differences in the Street Criminal and the Terrorist

Typical Criminal	Terrorist
Crimes of opportunity	Fighting for political objective
Uncommitted	Motivated by ideology or religion
Self-centered	Group-focused—even berserkers or lone wolves
No cause	Consumed with purpose
Untrained	Trained or motivated for the mission
Escape-oriented	On the attack

SOURCE: Adapted from "Law Enforcement's New Challenge to Investigate, Interdict, and Prevent Terrorism" by D. Douglas Bodrero in *The Police Chief*, February 2002, p.44. Copyright held by the International Association of Chiefs of Police, 515 North Washington Street, Alexandria, VA 22314 USA. Further reproduction without express written permission from IACP is strictly prohibited.

apprehending individuals operating with different motivations, who have different objectives and who use much deadlier weapons than traditional criminals." Table13.2 summarizes the most basic differences between criminals and terrorists.

Miller (2006, p.20) suggests that terrorists and criminals are more different than they are alike: "Criminals have an attitude of indifference, and their stress levels are lower—even while engaged in a crime—because they have accumulated experience. Most terrorists . . . show very high stress levels." Most terrorists are first-timers. In addition, terrorists seek wide-scale damage whereas criminals seek gain. Another striking distinction: "The difference is not just one of semantics; it is a matter of life and death. When fighting terrorists, it's kill or be killed, not capture and convict. The fight against terrorism has blurred the line between crime and war" (Linett, 2005, p.59).

Lessons Learned from the Al Qaeda Manual

Numerous terrorist lessons are taught in the al Qaeda Manual, a copy of which was seized by the Manchester Constabulary in the United Kingdom (White, 2004, pp.99–101). The *first lesson* is a general introduction beginning with a lamentation on the state of the world and ending with a call to holy war (**jihad**). The *second lesson* focuses on the qualities of individual al Qaeda members. The *third lesson* teaches forgery. The *fourth lesson* focuses on safe houses and other hiding places, including instructions for establishing a clandestine terrorist network. The *fifth lesson* concentrates on secret transportation and communication. Contacts are to be quick and to the point, and only commanders are authorized to initiate communication.

The *sixth lesson* discusses training and security during training. The *seventh lesson* covers weapons, one of the keys to terrorism, including building an arsenal and safely storing explosives. The *eighth lesson* discusses secrecy and member safety. It emphasizes the need to maintain family and neighborhood ties in the operational area. The *ninth lesson* is a lengthy discussion of security, emphasizing planning and operations. Secrecy is stressed time and again. The *tenth* and *eleventh lessons* focus on reconnaissance, including methods for clandestine spying and capturing prisoners.

The *twelfth lesson* continues the discussion of intelligence gathering, but focuses specifically on covert methods. It also provides information on counterintelligence. *Intermediate sections* between lessons twelve and eighteen give tips on handling recruited agents and dealing with countermeasures. Operatives are taught to watch for booby traps and when to assassinate potential enemies. The *eighteenth lesson* provides instructions about behavior when arrested. Al Qaeda appears to have a working knowledge of the rights of prisoners in Western justice systems.

White (2004, p.98) also describes the three-tiered model of al Qaeda terrorist attacks using sleeper cells. A **sleeper cell** is a group of terrorists who blend into a community.

 The three-tiered model of al Qaeda terrorist attacks consists of sleeper cells attacking in conjunction with the group's leaders in Afghanistan, sleeper cells attacking on their own apart from centralized command and individuals supported by small cells.

Another approach to understanding and, thus, perhaps being able to prevent acts of terrorism is to examine the motivations that produce it.

Motivations for Terrorism

Religious motives are seen in Islamic extremism. Political motives include such elements as the Red Army Faction. Social motives are seen in single-issue groups such as antiabortion groups, animal rights groups and environmentalists.

 Most terrorist acts result from dissatisfaction with a religious, political or social system or policy and frustration resulting from an inability to change it through acceptable, nonviolent means.

Figure 13.1 describes how hate can develop and result in terrorist acts. In the first stage an undesirable event or condition exists causing an individual or group to think: "It's not right." Next this undesirable condition is seen as an injustice: "It's not fair." This injustice is seen as the result of some wrongful be-

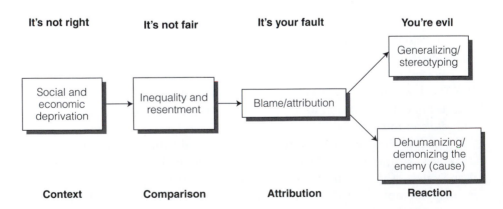

Figure 13.1 The Process of Ideological Development

SOURCE: From Randy Borum, "Understanding the Terrorist Mind-Set" in *FBI Law Enforcement Bulletin*, July 2003, p.9. Reprinted by permission.

havior: "It's your fault." The final step in the process is to perceive the person or group responsible for the injustice as "bad": "You're evil."

From 1978 to 1996 Theodore Kaczynski terrorized the country as the Unabomber, through a string of 16 mail bombings that killed three people apparently in a protest against technology. Ramzi Ahmed Yousef, found guilty of masterminding the first World Trade Center bombing in 1993, declared that he was proud to be a terrorist and that terrorism was the only viable response to what he saw as a Jewish lobby in Washington. The car bomb used to shatter the Alfred P. Murrah Federal Building in 1995 was Timothy McVeigh's way to protest the government and the raid on the Branch Davidians at Waco. In 2002 Lucas Helder terrorized the Midwest with 18 pipe bombs in mailboxes in five states, leaving antigovernment letters with the pipe bombs. Six exploded, injuring four letter carriers and two residents. And the most horrific act of terrorism against the United States occurred on September 11, 2001, when two airplanes were used as missiles to explode the World Trade Center and another plane was used as a missile to attack the Pentagon.

Yet another way to "know the enemy" is to understand the methods they commonly use and how to respond to each.

Methods Used by Terrorists

 Terrorists may use arson, explosives and bombs, weapons of mass destruction (biological, chemical or nuclear agents) and technology.

Some experts suggest that bioterrorism is the third most likely terrorist act to occur. Incendiary devices and explosives are most likely to be used because they are easy to make. Chemical devices are next in likelihood because the raw materials are easy to get and easy to use. Figure 13.2 presents the most likely to least likely terrorist threats; Figure 13.3 illustrates the level of impact by the weapon used. Table 13.3 summarizes worldwide terrorism by the tactic used.

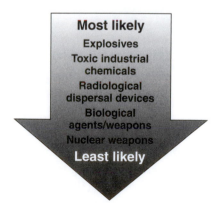

Figure 13.2   Terrorist Threats from Most Likely to Least Likely

SOURCE: From Melissa Reuland and Heather J. Davies, *Protecting Your Community from Terrorism: Strategies for Local Law Enforcement, Volume 3: Preparing for and Responding to Bioterrorism* (Washington, DC: Community Oriented Policing Services Office and the Police Executive Research Forum, September 2004) p.7. Reprinted by permission of the Police Executive Research Forum.

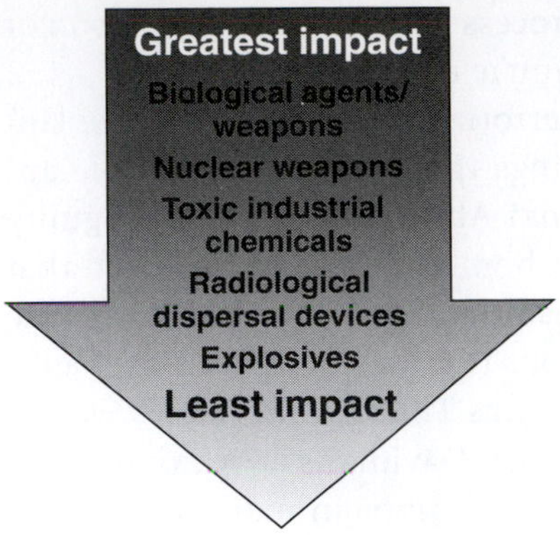

Greatest impact

Biological agents/
weapons

Nuclear weapons

Toxic industrial
chemicals

Radiological
dispersal devices

Explosives

Least impact

Figure 13.3 Level of Impact by Weapon Used

SOURCE: From Melissa Reuland and Heather J. Davies, *Protecting Your Community from Terrorism: Strategies for Local Law Enforcement, Volume 3: Preparing for and Responding to Bioterrorism* (Washington, DC: Community Oriented Policing Services Office and the Police Executive Research Forum, September 2004) p.8. Reprinted by permission of the Police Executive Research Forum.

Table 13.3 Worldwide Terrorism by Tactic

	Incidents			Fatalities			Injuries		
	Full Year 2006	January–May 2006	2007	Full Year 2006	January–May 2006	2007	Full Year 2006	January–May 2006	2007
Armed attack	2,620	1,208	478	5,025	2,105	678	2,446	1,020	340
Arson	140	66	10	4	2	0	10	5	0
Assassination	90	9	15	152	20	34	264	15	85
Barricade/hostage	5	5	0	6	6	0	4	4	0
Bombing	3,346	1,460	900	6,229	2,193	3,086	18,132	6,265	7,485
Kidnapping	358	127	103	487	205	86	57	18	3
Other/unknown	94	23	52	162	23	95	56	12	596
TOTAL	**6,653**	**2,898**	**1,558**	**12,065**	**4,554**	**3,979**	**20,969**	**7,339**	**8,509**

SOURCE: From *MIPT Terrorism Knowledge Base*. Used by permission of the Memorial Institute for the Prevention of Terrorism.

The use of arson has been discussed. Bombs are by far the most commonly used and most deadly tactic.

Explosives and Bombs

The examples of terrorists just discussed, both domestic and international, illustrate how bombs have been used against U.S. citizens. According to Haber (2004, p.14): "Pipe bombs and other improvised explosive devices (IEDs) pose a serious threat to federal, state and local government facilities, considering how easily and inexpensively they can be put together. Schools, shopping malls, stadiums and other public places people can freely walk around and through are also potential targets for terrorist attacks." Directions for making pipe bombs and other incendiary devices can be found on the Internet. Dowle (2006a, p.17)

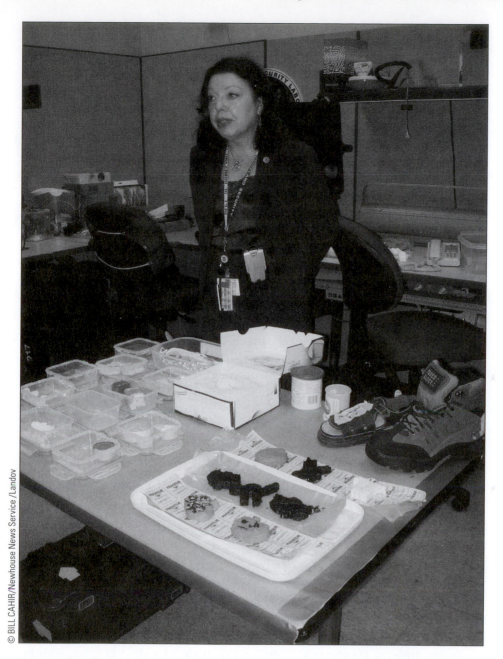

Susan Hallowell, science and technology director of the Transportation Security Laboratory in Atlantic City, New Jersey, displays samples of explosives that terrorists might attempt to sneak onto civilian aircraft, including shoe bombs, a cake with explosive icing, a hot dog with explosive mustard and Halloween cookies made of plastic explosive. "The machines would find these. But they look an awful lot like cookies, don't they?" Hallowell said.

reports that the prevalence of homemade explosives (HMEs) in terrorist IEDs is increasing, citing the example of a Google search for homemade explosives that returned 34.5 million hits.

A terrorist bombing tactic to be aware of is having a second device explode after a first one is set off. This tactic was used in Bali, Indonesia, in October

2003 when a hand grenade was tossed into a nightclub, causing patrons to flee to the streets where they encountered a Jeep bomb. The attack, which killed almost 200 people, was attributed to Muslim extremists in Indonesia with links to al Qaeda.

One way to prevent a bomb attack is to have strict policies and procedures for all employees as to what to do if they observe a suspicious package.

Suspicious Packages   Security officers dispatched to a suspicious package, unattended bag or other such item must be cautious. If an officer suspects that the call involves an actual bomb, the officer should (1) move to an area not in direct line of sight of the device, (2) move away from glass and parked vehicles, (3) move away from secondary hazards such as electricity and gas, (4) move behind hard cover and (5) set cordons at 100 yards for items carried by hand, 200 yards for suspect cars and small vans and 400 to 800 yards for suspect large vehicles (Dowle, 2006c, p.13).

Suicide Bombers   Morgenstern (2006, p.32) asserts: "The suicide terror attack is clearly alive and well—and could easily be carried out on American soil." He (p.36) suggests that the notion of a suicide terrorist as a young male, fundamentalist fanatic is wrong. Potential suicide terrorists may come from different backgrounds, different age groups, be male or female, educated or uneducated, an upstanding citizen or a deviant. Most suicide terrorists consider the act one of martyrdom, assuring them a place in their version of heaven. Their families are usually held in reverence and taken care of. Suicide bombers try to kill as many people as possible.

Although suicide bombers have not yet hit the United States, they remain a "constant concern" because of their determination to die for their causes ("FBI: Suicide Bombs a Big Concern"). However, as Wexler (2007, p.i) suggests: "The 9/11 hijackers were the ultimate suicide bombers. They used commercial aircraft as bombs rather than devices that fit inside a backpack. But at their core, their motivations were the same—they believed that political or religious ideology justified murdering innocent bystanders and killing themselves in the process." Wexler reports that when experts were asked which two types of terrorist attacks are most likely, the most common response was "suicide bombing attacks" closely followed by "attack on major infrastructure."

Agencies are strongly encouraged to develop suicide bomb response protocols, with principles consistent with the agency's use-of-force policies, procedures and training (Spahr et al., 2007, p.13). Table 13.4 depicts recommendations for use of force in various scenarios.

A suggested tactic for first responders facing a potential suicide bomber is to issue the unambiguous verbal command: "Do not move." Any movement is a violation and might trigger the explosives (Chudwin, 2007, pp.62–63). Live-fire shooters should stand ready to make a head shot, preferably with a long gun with a high-velocity round or 12-gauge slug. Officers should not let their guard down with "presumed compliance." Officers should establish a perimeter around the suspected bomber, considering that the blast radius for explosive devices attached to the body can easily cover 100 yards.

Another consideration in thwarting suicide bombers is use of K-9s. Dogs can detect 19,000 types of explosives, making them more effective at catching

Table 13.4   Graduated Force Option Protocol

Threat Assessment	Suicide bomb Incident Scenario	Graduated Force Intervention Level
Low	Person acting suspiciously and: a. No device seen b. No intelligence other than call c. Possibly some behavioral anomalies	Citizen contact: Conventional stop and/or frisk without firearms drawn
Medium	Person acting suspiciously and: a. No device seen b. Suspicion from intelligence information or behavioral anomaly	Armed felony stop including less lethal options—not including conducted energy device (CED; e.g., Taser)
High	Suicide bomb device observed or probable cause that device is present.	Armed Intervention *Graduated Force Option Sequence* 1. When feasible, warning 2. Critical shot to incapacitate
Detonation		

SOURCE: Lisa L. Spahr, Joshua Ederheimer and David Bilson, *Patrol-Level Response to a Suicide Bomb Threat: Guidelines for Consideration* (Washington, DC: Police Executive Research Forum, 2007).

potential suicide bombers than security cameras or random suspect searches (Horwitz, 2005, p.A01).

Weapons of Mass Destruction (WMD)

Nuclear, biological or chemical agents are also referred to as NBC agents. Weather data, such as wind direction and speed, barometric pressure, relative humidity, and so on, is critical to responders at NBC scenes. Robotic detection and identification technology can warn responders of NBC agents' presence and strength. Global positioning systems (GPS) can be applied to determine the coordinates of an NBC release relative to the position of responders, residential or other civilian centers or other critical location information. GPS can also track vehicles charged with transporting NBC materials to and from the site.

Biological Agents   Bioterrorism involves such biological WMDs as anthrax, botulism, salmonella and smallpox. The Central Intelligence Agency reports that at least 10 countries are believed to have or be conducting research on biological agents to be used as WMDs: "The potential for a bioterrorist attack in the United States has become an unfortunate reality following the events of 9/11 and the anthrax scares" (Hanson, 2004, p.18).

In October 2001, a photo editor in Florida died from inhaling anthrax. Several weeks later, anthrax-laced letters were delivered to several major media networks and numerous government offices around Washington, DC. Environmental sampling also indicated massive amounts of anthrax spores at several post offices and mailroom facilities. While no cases of anthrax have been linked to the September 11 terrorist attacks or the al Qaeda network considered responsible for them, the incidents were regarded as terrorism, perhaps domestic in origin, and were investigated as crimes.

Especially susceptible to bioterrorism are the nation's food and water supply, which are also vulnerable to attack through use of chemical agents.

Chemical Agents   The Aum Shinrikyo terrorist attack in the Tokyo subway in 1995 confirmed what had long been feared—a nonstate entity could manufacture a viable chemical agent—in this case, the poisonous gas sarin—and deliver it in a public location—a crowded subway station. Anyone with access to the Internet can obtain the chemical formula for sarin in less than 40 minutes through a Web search and can produce it inexpensively.

One chemical agent receiving increased attention in security periodicals is chlorine gas. Although a chlorine gas attack requires perfect conditions and a poor emergency response to cause heavy casualties, "if properly released in a well-populated area, chlorine gas has the potential to cause tens of thousands of casualties" (Harwood, 2007, p.18).

The four common types of chemical weapons are nerve agents, blood agents, choking agents and blistering agents. "Emergency Procedures for Acts of Terrorism" (2006, p.4) suggests the following signs of a chemical release: difficulty breathing; eye irritation; loss of coordination; nausea; burning sensation in nose, throat and lungs; and the presence of dead insects or birds. This source recommends that, should a chemical attack occur, doors and windows should be closed and all ventilation turned off, including furnaces, air conditioners, vents and fans. The room should be sealed with duct tape and plastic sheeting. After a chemical attack, decontamination is needed within minutes of exposure to minimize health consequences.

The DHS has released interim rules to streamline federal security regulations for high-risk chemical facilities nationwide (Edwards, 2007, p.1). The DHS will screen more than 15,000 chemical facilities and require that those with certain quantities of specified chemicals complete an assessment to determine a risk level. A company found to pose greater risk will be required to conduct vulnerability assessment and submit site security plans that meet DHS performance standards (Daniels, 2007, p.8). Failure to comply could result in penalties up to $25,000 a day and an order to cease operations.

The DHS has developed and implemented the Rapidly Deployable Chemical Detection System (RDCDS), capable of detecting dozens of chemical agents accurately and quickly at fairly low density levels (R. Elliott, 2006, p.40). The goal of RDCDS is to provide chemical detection and protection at public venues large enough to present attractive targets to terrorists.

Nuclear Terrorism   Page (2005, p.124) reports: "Radioactive sources are plentiful, and building a radiological dispersal device (RDD), or dirty bomb, is not hard." The U.S. Nuclear Regulatory Commission (NRC) contends that, on average, approximately 375 devices of all kinds containing radioactive material are reported lost or stolen each year: "Where terror is the goal, a dirty bomb is a good weapon of choice" (Page). However: "The primary destruction and disruption from a dirty bomb detonation will be caused by public panic, not radiation" (Hughes, 2004, p.32).

A new technology uses detectors able to decipher between deadly radiation in nuclear weapons and harmless radiation carried by patients involved in recent medical tests (Faherty, 2007). The technology is currently in its final testing phase and will become part of the $30 million Securing the Cities Initiation, the goal of which is to ban nuclear weapons from New York by creating a 50-mile protective perimeter.

Technological Terrorism

White (2006, p.273) notes: "Technological terrorism is one of the more frightening scenarios one can imagine. Modern societies are susceptible to two methods of technological terror. The first is the employment of mass destruction weapons or the conversion of an industrial site—for example, a chemical plant—into a massively lethal instrument through sabotage. The other method is to attack a source that supplies technology or energy. The results of either type of attack could be catastrophic. Technology looms as a potentially sinister partner in the evolution of terrorism." The irony, of course, is that the United States' status as the most technologically advanced superpower in the world also makes it the most attractive and vulnerable target with respect to attacks on and by technology.

Because of this vulnerability, the federal government has taken a key role in preparing for and responding to terrorism: "Securing American cyberspace has become a national priority" (Keeney et al., 2005, p.1). The President's Critical Infrastructure Protection Board stresses the importance of public-private partnerships in securing the nation's critical infrastructures and improving national cyber security. Likewise, the Department of Homeland Security emphasizes enhancing protection for critical infrastructure and networks by promoting working relationships between the government and private industry because, as repeatedly stressed, most of the United States' critical infrastructure is privately held.

Keeney et al. note: "The nation's dependence on interconnected networks and communications systems significantly increases the risk of harm that could result from the activities of insiders. In addition, the actions of a single insider can cause extensive financial damage or irreparable damage to an organization's data, systems, business operations or reputation." They recommend examining insider activity across critical infrastructures, the motives of insiders, their methodologies and identifying the behaviors and activities to prevent insider incidents and improve cyber security.

The key findings of a study by the Secret Service provides insight into identifying the potential for insider sabotage across critical infrastructure (Keeney et al., p.2):

- A negative work-related event triggered most insiders' actions.
- Most of the insiders had displayed behavior in the workplace that caused others to be concerned.
- The majority of insiders planned their activities in advance.
- When hired, the majority of insiders were granted system administrator or privileged access, but less than half of all insiders had authorized access at the time of the incident.

- Insiders used unsophisticated methods for exploiting systemic vulnerabilities in applications, processes, and procedures, but relatively sophisticated attack tools were also employed.
- The majority of insiders compromised computer accounts, created unauthorized backdoor accounts or used shared accounts in their attacks.
- Remote access was used to carry out the majority of the attacks.
- The majority of insider attacks were only detected once there was a noticeable irregularity in the information system or a system became unavailable.
- Insider activities caused organizations financial losses, negative impacts to their business operations and damage to their reputations.[5]

Given the seriousness of the threat to our nation posed by terrorism, the federal government is actively involved in efforts to prevent it.

Preventing Terrorism

Security professionals should accept all the basic responsibilities of their position as discussed in earlier chapters of this text. They need to conduct risk assessments, establish a risk management plan, establish physical and procedural controls, particularly those dealing with access control and have contingency plans for before, during and after a terrorist attack similar to those required in a natural disaster. Such responsibilities will not be repeated here.

Security officers should stay alert for routine crimes or activities serving as red flags to possible terrorist planning, including any of the following products being produced, stored or sold in large quantities: bleaching products, chlorine products and cleaning solutions, crowd/riot control sprays, disinfectants, drain cleaners, dyes, fertilizers, fumigation products, fungicides, galvanizing solutions, herbicides, insecticides, metal polishes, organic chemicals, pesticides, pharmaceuticals, photographic solutions, plastics/polymers, solvents and weed killers (Buhrmaster, 2005, p.43). Other things for officers to consider are prowling reports, burglaries, thefts, missing inventory and suspicious new applicants for employment (Buhrmaster).

Several federal initiatives are aimed at preventing terrorist attacks or at least mitigating their effects.

The National Infrastructure Protection Plan (NIPP)

Michael Chertoff, Secretary of the Department of Homeland Security (DHS), asserts: "The ability to protect the critical infrastructure and key resources (CI/KR) of the United States is vital to our national security, public health and safety, economic vitality, and way of life" (*National Infrastructure Protection Plan*, 2006, p.i). Because of the importance placed on our nation's infrastructure, the DHS has implemented the National Infrastructure Protection Plan (NIPP) and 17 supporting Sector-Specific Plans (SSPs) in an effort to provide a collaborative, coordinated approach to CI/KR protection roles and responsibilities involving the private sector and federal, state, local and tribal governments (p.iii).

---

[5]SOURCE: Portions of *Insider Threat Study: Computer System Sabotage in Critical Infrastructure Sectors* by Michelle Kenney, Eileen Kowalski, Dawn Cappelli, Andrew Moore, Timothy Shimeall and Stephanie Rodgers, © 2005 by Carnegie Mellon University, are reproduced with special permission from the Software Engineering Institute.

The specific sectors included in the plan include agriculture and food; banking and finance; chemical; commercial facilities; communications; dams; defense industrial base; drinking water and water treatment systems; emergency services; energy; government facilities; information technology; national monuments and icons; nuclear reactors, materials and waste; postal and shipping; public health and healthcare; and transportation.

The NIPP sets national priorities, goals and requirements to ensure the effective distribution of funding and resources to areas where they have the greatest potential to mitigate risk and lower vulnerabilities, deter threats and minimize the consequences of terrorist attacks and other disasters (*National Infrastructure Protection Plan*, 2006). The cornerstone of the NIPP is its risk management framework (see Figure 13.4), which establishes the process for combining consequence, vulnerability and threat information to produce a comprehensive, systematic and rational assessment of national or sector-specific risk that drives CI/KR protection activities. The NIPP is also based on strong public-private partnerships to facilitate coordination, communication and cooperation within and across sectors.

Although an in-depth review of the NIPP and its relevance to private security directors is beyond the scope of this discussion, readers are strongly encouraged to refer to the NIPP (download available online at http://www.dhs.gov/xlibrary/assets/NIPP_Plan.pdf) for invaluable information regarding considerations for protecting various critical infrastructure and key resources. (*Note:* Appendix 5B of the NIPP is called "Recommended Homeland Security Practices for Use by the Private Sector.")

Goals of the DHS

Michael Chertoff, U.S. Secretary of Homeland Security, describes five goals he sees as priorities for the DHS ("An Interview," 2007, pp.16–18):

1. Increase our ability to keep bad people out of the country.
2. Keep bad things out of the country, increasing port security.
3. Protect our infrastructure better.
4. Continue to build a response capability with modern computer tools.
5. Promote intelligence sharing, not only horizontally across the federal government but vertically with the local government as well.

Fusion Centers   An initiative aimed at the fifth goal is development of fusion centers throughout the country. "Fusion refers to the overreaching process

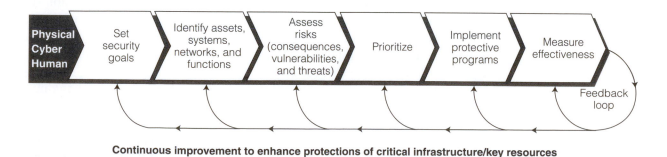

Continuous improvement to enhance protections of critical infrastructure/key resources

Figure 13.4   NIPP Risk Management Framework

SOURCE: National Infrastructure Protection Plan (Washington, DC: Department of Homeland Security, 2006) p.4.

of managing the flow of information and intelligence across all levels and sectors of government and private industry. The fusion process turns information and intelligence into actionable knowledge. . . . A **fusion center** is an effective and efficient mechanism to exchange information and intelligence, maximize resources, streamline operations and improve the ability to fight crime and terrorism by merging data from a variety of sources" (*Fusion Center Guidelines*, 2006, p.3).

Forty-two fusion centers have been established in 37 states and, according to Hall (2007), are making some important connections. However, Hall's general assessment of the centers is that they are a costly but largely ineffective weapon against terrorism. Homeland Security has given states $380 million to set up the centers, but they tend to gravitate to an "all-crimes and even broader all-hazards approach" rather than focusing on recognizing suspicious activity, patterns and people and using the information to prevent terrorist attacks.

Intelligence Gathering and Sharing

Many of the day-to-day-duties of security officers bring them into potential sources of information about terrorism. Such information needs to be shared. Heinecke (2004, p.80) describes what she calls "another layer to the security blanket"—Behavior Pattern Recognition (BPR): "BPR is a security methodology based on two components: observation of irregular behaviors for the environment and targeted conversations with suspects. . . . BPR is an extension of trained observation. Officers, whether they are in an airport, sports arena or convention center, need to look for behaviors that are irregular for that location." Figure 13.5 illustrates a model to help local police implement their new antiterrorism responsibilities.

The most challenging technological issue in any national antiterrorism intelligence effort is **interoperability** (the ability to exchange information seamlessly). Homeland security directors at the state level ranked a communications infrastructure that is interoperable among first responders at the top of a list of priorities for the second year in a row (Gural, 2006, p.2). The directors advocated implementing state fusion centers to collect and analyze data. The directors also felt the DHS focused more on homeland security issues such as antiterrorism measures at the expense of emergency management.

Straw (2007a, p.28) reports: "Despite the clear need for interoperable communications standards, a decade of study has yielded only two of eight critical elements." Project 25, or P25, is the public-private initiative charged with developing technical standards that manufacturers can use to ensure interoperability of communications devices used by first responders in emergencies. Launched in 1989, two of the most crucial elements are close to being finalized: standards for handheld radios and standards for connecting separate radio systems operating on different frequencies (Straw).

The Justice and Public Safety (JPS) software market is rapidly changing, driven by the clear and urgent mandate to "connect the dots" through information sharing. An integrated information-sharing system needs to consider four key components: (1) infrastructure standardization to ensure reliability, scalability and security; (2) data and how it will be distributed, centralized and analyzed; (3) business processes; and (4) the experience of the individuals on the system—how they are identified and ease of use (Richey, 2007, p.34). A stan-

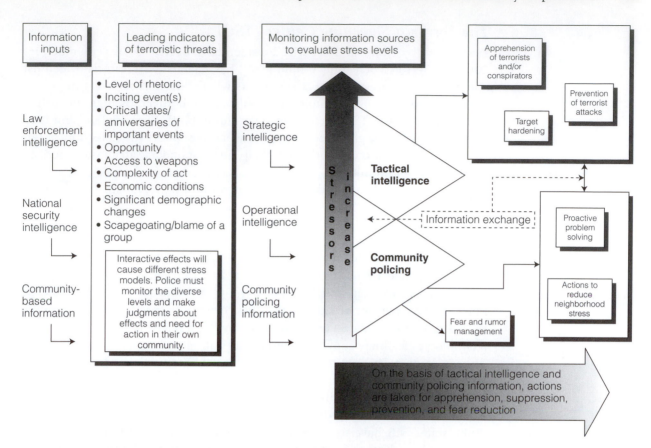

Figure 13.5 Implementation Model for Antiterrorism Responsibilities

SOURCE: From David L. Carter and Richard N. Holden, "Terrorism and Community Security" in *Local Government Police Management*, 4th ed., edited by William A. Geller and Darrel W. Stephens (Washington, DC: International City/County Management Association, 2003) p.307. Reprinted by permission.

dard data exchange format is called Justice XML, sometimes referred to as the "Global Justice XML," "Data Model" or "GJXDM." Over 50 major JPS information-sharing projects are using the Justice XML standard, and the number is growing (Richey, p.35).

Withholding Information As Pilant (2004, p.34) explains: "Counterterrorism and antiterrorism are difficult tasks made even harder by the operational style that exists at almost every level of policing and in nearly every agency—that of withholding, rather than sharing, intelligence." According to White (2004, p.17): "On the surface it seems simple: Defense and intelligence communities gather information concerning possible terrorist activities in the United States. . . . Under the surface, however, a complex network of interagency rivalries, laws, security clearance issues and turf protection reduces the possibility of shared information." Polisar (p.8) echoes: "For far too long efforts to combat crime and terrorism have been handicapped by jurisdictional squabbles and archaic rules that prevented us from forging cooperative working relationships with our counterparts in local, regional, tribal and federal law enforcement. This must end."

Another federal effort aimed at preventing terrorism is the Terrorist Screening Center.

The Terrorist Screening Center (TSC)

Established by Homeland Security Presidential Directive 6 on September 16, 2003, the Terrorist Screening Center (TSC) has established a terrorist watch list and screening processes used at key points where terrorists seek to gain access to the United States, for example, visa applications, border crossings and airline travel. According to TSC Director Bucella (2006, p.14): "The TSC's vision is to establish a dynamic global screening network to support the detection of terrorists." Its number one priority is to help first responders safeguard America's citizens and communities.

Yet another federal initiative aimed at preventing terrorism is known as REAL ID.

REAL ID

Although originally intended over 100 years ago to certify a person was competent to operate a vehicle, today American driver's licenses are used every day as the most convenient, reliable document to authenticate a person's identity. More than 80 percent of citizens use their driver's license for other purposes than driving (*Improving Security and Protecting Privacy*, 2007, p.2). However, new technologies facilitate copying, forging, fabricating and exchanging fraudulent driver's licenses. The 9/11 terrorists had a total of 17 fraudulent driver's licenses. Recognizing this threat, in May 11, 2005, Congress enacted the REAL ID Act.

The REAL ID Act requires states to take new steps to verify the identity of applicants before issuing driver's licenses and other ID cards. By December 2009, states will have to verify and authenticate birth certificates, social security cards and other documents people use to obtain a driver's license. The act also requires states to make their driver's licenses and other IDs tamper-resistant and harder to forge. REAL ID will also require state authorities to share information with each other and to verify applicant data against existing federal databases.

The issue of privacy is always of concern when databases are being compiled. However, in its Notice of Proposed Rule Making (NPRM) the Department of Homeland Security clearly commits to privacy:

> DHS believes that protecting the privacy of the personal information associated with implementation of the REAL ID Act is critical to maintaining the public trust that government can provide basic services to its citizens while preserving their privacy. DHS recognizes the significant privacy issues that are associated with the act ("Notice of Proposed Rule Making," no date).

The Information Technology Association of America (ITAA) has called on Congress, the Department of Homeland Security and state governments to move forward with implementing the READL ID Act, with the ITAA president noting: "Today's system is the system that helped to bring us the terrorist attacks of September 11, 2001. We know the problem and we have the technology to fix it. The vast majority of Americans will applaud the government for closing this loophole for terrorists and criminals" (Kerber, 2007).

According to Stateline.org, 30 states are working on legislation to reject the mandatory license standards based on the cost, privacy concerns and fear that the new national standards will create a national ID card ("Montana and Washington First States to Opt Out of REAL ID," 2007, p.11).

A Homeland Security Initiative: The Center for Food Protection and Defense

In July 2004 the University of Minnesota was awarded a $15 million grant for a national Center for Food Protection and Defense. The school won the grant because it is one of only a few universities in the country with experts in agriculture, public health, veterinary medicine and medicine on the same campus. The university is partnering with General Mills, Cargill, 3M and Hormel. Frank Busta, professor emeritus of food science and nutrition, will direct the grant and has stated: "Our charge is to protect and defend safe food from intentional contamination. The vulnerability of food is immense. . . . We hope we can make it sufficiently difficult [so] if and when terrorists decide to look at [attacking the food supply], they will say, 'We'll try something else'" (Smetanka, 2004a, p.A4).

In announcing the new Center for Food Protection and Defense, at the time Homeland Security Secretary Tom Ridge noted: "Government can't do it alone. . . . Partnerships between government and our great research universities, businesses and scientists will produce together what would be impossible individually" (Smetanka, 2004b, p.B1).

Responding to Terrorist Attacks

America's first line of defense in any terrorist attack is the "first responder," the local police, firefighters and emergency medical professionals. Properly trained they have the greatest potential to save lives and limit destruction. As noted, key to their success is interoperability among those first responders. Lack of such interoperability was devastatingly obvious during the 9/11 attacks. However: "Five years after 9/11, we continue to turn a deaf ear to gaps in interoperable communications . . . the attacks of Sept. 11, 2001 revealed major problems in how well emergency agencies were able to talk to each other during a catastrophe. Many firefighters climbing the World Trade Center towers died when they were unable to hear police radio warnings to leave the crumbling buildings" (Barrett, 2007). When Hurricane Katrina hit the Gulf coast in August 2005, the lack of progress in addressing communication problems was again underscored, as radio transmissions were hindered because the storm's winds toppled towers.

Responses to specific threats such as chemical attacks and bomb threats have been discussed earlier in the chapter.

ASIS Guidelines Corresponding to the DHS Threat Advisory System

The *Threat Advisory System Response* is an ASIS guideline to provide private business and industry with possible actions that could be taken based on the alert levels of the DHS. The guidelines (p.6) note that threats move along a continuum of probability and that intervention with an appropriate level of security can harden a target, reducing the risk of an impending event. The threat levels and recommended responses for each are contained in Appendix B.

Militarized Attacks by International Terrorist Groups

Responding to a militarized attack is particularly challenging. Jones (2007a, p.34) explains: "The overall goal of an organized attack by a militarized terrorist group is to create terror among the populace of a community or a nation by inflicting horrific loss of life among innocents and responding police and security personnel." Such militarized terrorist attacks usually are either "decimation assaults" or "mass hostage sieges" (Jones, 2007b, p.44).

 Militarized attacks are usually either decimation assaults or mass hostage sieges.

The decimation assault makes for good publicity, which facilitates terrorist groups' fundraising and recruiting efforts (Jones). Such assaults typically involve a lone suicide bomber or a "gun-and-grenade" type attack and present a tactical problem for security forces, as opposed to a strategic problem: "Immediate interdiction by armed and properly trained security personnel is the best proven method for dealing with the perpetrators of a decimation assault who attempt to force access into a controlled building" (Jones, 2007c, p.30). Officers who try to interdict terrorists during the initial stage should expect to be targeted and, very likely, killed unless the officers go on the offense, as there will be no "negotiating" with terrorists: "It is the considered position of all counter-terrorism experts that trying to take an attacking terrorist alive, or warning him before employing deadly force to prevent the attack, is emphatically not feasible. Our police and security personnel must be specifically trained to deal swiftly and effectively with the mindset and tactics of militarized terrorists" (Jones, 2007c, p.31).

A mass hostage siege, the preferred type of attack for militarized terrorist groups, pays much greater dividends in human suffering and death, with a much greater terror impact (Jones, 2007b, p.45). The first goal of these terrorists is to establish contact with the news media, and security will be hard pressed to stop them from this. If denied such contact, they are likely to begin killing hostages. The second goal during a mass hostage siege is to turn the situation from a tactical problem for responding officers to a strategic and political problem for the local community. It is critical for security forces to keep the situation at a tactical level if they hope to have a positive outcome (Jones).

The third goal of such terrorists is to force surrounding officers to assault the building once it is wired with explosives and fully automatic weapons are prepositioned. To assault a fortified building held by militarized terrorists, police and security personnel need at least a 10 to 1 ratio in the assaulting force (Jones).

When attacks are not prevented, they must be thoroughly investigated.

Investigating Terrorist Acts

Fortunately, investigating terrorism has many similarities with investigating any other kind of criminal activity. In fact, several lessons learned from the war on drugs can help in the war on terrorism. For example, both "wars" involve covert illegal activities calling for sophisticated undercover operations. Both have domestic and international fronts. In addition, both require coordination among various agencies and information sharing not only with partners within this country, but also globally.

A documented "nexus" exists between traditional crime and terrorism, involving fraudulent identification, trafficking in illegal merchandise and drug sales as means to terrorists' ends (Loyka et al., 2005 p.7). Bratton (2006, pp.2–3) points out: "More and more of our organized crime investigations lead circuitously back to terrorism cases. We know that there is a confirmed link between counterfeit products and terrorism funding. . . . Today's organized crime entities have tentacles that extend internationally. In Los Angeles, we know that individuals involved in contraband cigarette trafficking, controlled substance trafficking, trademark violations, extortion, mail fraud, wire fraud, tax fraud, insurance fraud and money laundering are also significant fundraisers for known terrorist groups, including Hezbollah and Hamas."

Surveillance Cameras as Investigative Tools

When terrorists attacked London's transit system in 2005 four homemade bombs stuffed into backpacks did not fully explode. Only one person was injured. A day later, photographs of four suspects captured on surveillance cameras near the sites of the attempted attacks were broadcast on television. The remarkable speed of that investigation was repeated on July 7, 2007. British investigators, aided by surveillance cameras, tracked the suspects to Glasgow, Scotland, and arrested several suspects: "Police officials credited the 'Ring of Steel'—a network of thousands of surveillance cameras that line London's intersections and neighborhoods—for providing license plate numbers, suspects' images and other important clues" (Tanneeru, 2007). New York City, specifically lower Manhattan, the site of two terror attacks, will have a similar system in place by the decade's end if it can get the needed funding. The Lower Manhattan Security Initiative will require about $90 million to secure the 1.7 square miles, arguably one of the most valuable and sensitive pieces of real estate in the world (Tanneeru).

Not only are security professionals charged with being active participants in the war on terror, they must also be aware of and sensitive to concerns regarding individuals' rights and privacy.

Concerns Related to the War on Terrorism

The DHS recognizes the importance of preserving liberty and privacy in this country, but the public also expects law enforcement to deal with the terrorist threat: "Law enforcement must adapt and be practical to ensure we preserve what is the most basic civil right, which is the right not to be blown up" ("An Interview," p.18). Although not strictly held to the same constitutional constraints as public law enforcement officers, private security personnel should be sensitive to potential bias that may occur when balancing the need for safety with the right of citizens to be free from undue harassment and discrimination.

 Two concerns related to the "war on terrorism" are that civil liberties may be jeopardized and that people of Middle Eastern descent may be discriminated against or become victims of hate crimes.

The first guiding principle of the Department of Homeland Security is to protect civil rights and civil liberties:

We will defend America while protecting the freedoms that define America. Our strategies and actions will be consistent with the individual rights and liberties enshrined by our Constitution and the Rule of Law. While we seek to improve the way we collect and share information about terrorists, we will nevertheless be vigilant in respecting the confidentiality and protecting the privacy of our citizens. We are committed to securing our nation while protecting civil rights and civil liberties. (*Securing Our Homeland*, p.6)

Another concern is that some Americans may retaliate against innocent people of Middle Eastern descent, many of whom were either born in the United States or are naturalized citizens: "America's multicultural neighborhoods, particularly Arab and Muslim communities, were initially affected by backlash violence and hate crimes following the terrorist attacks" (Peed and Wexler, 2004, p.vii). Davies and Murphy (2004, p.1) likewise note: "Within hours of the Twin Towers' collapse and the attack on the Pentagon, U.S. residents and visitors, particularly Arabs, Muslims and Sikhs, were harassed or attacked because they shared—or were perceived to share—the terrorists' national background or religion." A study financed by the Justice Department found that following September 11th, Arab-Americans have a greater fear of racial profiling and immigration enforcement than of falling victim to hate crimes (A. Elliott, 2006).

Private security professionals can take the following steps to prevent racial profiling and discrimination against Arab-Americans (Henderson et al., 2006, p.25):

- Increase communication and dialogue.
- Develop person-to-person contact.
- Provide cultural awareness training.
- Recruit more Arab-Americans into the security profession.

As security professionals seek to build ties and trust with U.S. Muslim communities, they need to counter the idea that the war against terror is a war against Islam (Straw, 2007b, p.30). Experts say that Muslim-Americans' economic success and assimilation make their communities far less fertile breeding grounds for terror than their European counterparts and that they have more to lose in a case of a home-grown plot (p.32).

SUMMARY

- Security professionals' responsibilities related to homeland security include knowing the enemy, what to look for and being vigilant; taking all possible steps to prevent a terrorist attack; preparing themselves, their agencies/organizations for an attack, should one occur, through education and training; responding to an attack; and investigating the attack.

- Most definitions of terrorism have common elements, including the systematic use of physical violence, either actual or threatened, against noncombatants to create a climate of fear to cause some religious, political or social change.

- Three elements of terrorism are: (1) it is criminal in nature, (2) targets are typically symbolic and (3) the terrorist actions are always aggressive and often violent.

- As a result of 9/11 the Office of Homeland Security (later renamed the Department of Homeland Security) was established, reorganizing the departments of the federal government.

- The FBI is the lead agency for responding to terrorism. The Federal Emergency Management Agency (FEMA) is the lead agency for consequence management (after an attack).

- The FBI classifies terroristic acts as either domestic or international.
- Domestic terrorist groups include white supremacists, black supremacists, militia groups, other right-wing extremists, left-wing extremists, pro-life extremists, animal rights activists and environment extremists.
- The three-tiered model of al Qaeda terrorist attacks consists of sleeper cells attacking in conjunction with the group's leaders in Afghanistan, sleeper cells attacking on their own apart from centralized command and individuals supported by small cells.

- Most terrorist acts result from dissatisfaction with a religious, political or social system or policy and frustration resulting from an inability to change it through acceptable, nonviolent means.
- Terrorists may use arson, explosives and bombs, weapons of mass destruction (biological, chemical or nuclear agents) and technology.
- Militarized attacks are usually either decimation assaults or mass hostage sieges.
- Two concerns related to the "war on terrorism" are that civil liberties may be jeopardized and that people of Middle Eastern descent may be discriminated against or become victims of hate crimes.

APPLICATION

In 2006 President Bush signed the USA PATRIOT Improvement and Reauthorization Act. Go to http://www.whitehouse.gov.infocus/patriotact/ and outline the provisions of this act. Then read the speeches and news releases related to the act and add to your outline any additional information you learn.

DISCUSSION QUESTIONS

1. Which is the greater threat—domestic or international terrorism? Why?
2. Does your police department have a counterterrorism strategy in place? If so, what?
3. What type of terrorist attack would you fear most? Why?
4. Do you feel Americans have become complacent about terrorism?
5. Should American expect to give up some civil liberties to allow law enforcement officers to pursue terrorists?

REFERENCES

Barrett, Devlin. "6 of 75 Cities Get Top Disaster Rating." *Washington Post*, January 3, 2007.

Bratton, William J. "The Link between Organized Crime and Terrorism (and What We Need to Do about It." *Subject to Debate*, November 2006, pp.2–3.

Bucella, Donna A. "The Terrorist Screening Center." *The Police Chief*, August 2006, p.14.

Buhrmaster, Scott. "It's Not Over." *Law Officer Magazine*, July/August 2005, pp.42–45.

Chudwin, Jeff. "Homicide Bombers: Tactics for First-Responders." *Law Officer Magazine*, January 2007, pp.62–64.

Daniels, Rhianna. "Chemical Facilities Secure DHS Standards." *Security Director News*, February 2007, p.8.

Davies, Heather J. and Murphy, Gerard R. *Protecting Your Community from Terrorism: The Strategies for Local Law Enforcement Series Vol. 2: Working with Diverse Communities.* Washington, DC: The Office of Community Oriented Policing Services and the Police Executive Research Forum, 2004.

DeYoung, Karen. "Attempts Seen as Model for New Attacks on U.S. Soil." *Washington Post*, July 3, 2007, p.A01.

Dowle, Jim. "Homemade Explosives." *Law and Order*, October 2006a, pp.17–18.

Dowle, Jim. "Remain Vigilant." *Law and Order*, May 2006b, pp.22–24.

Dowle, Jim. Suspicious Packages." *Law and Order*, November 2006c, pp.10–14.

Edwards, Al. "DHS Reveals Chemical Guidelines." *Security Director News*, May 2007, p.1.

Elliott, Andrea. "After 9/11, Arab-Americans Fear Police Acts, Study Finds." *The New York Times*, June 12, 2006.

Elliott, Robert. "Hi-Tech Chemical Nose." *Security Management*, November 2006, pp.38–45.

"Emergency Procedures for Acts of Terrorism." *A Quick Reference Guide for Handling Disasters, Emergencies and Pandemics.* King of Prussia, PA: Allied Barton

Security Services (a supplement to *Security Management*), August 2006.

Faherty, Christopher. "Police Test Technology to Safeguard City from Nuclear Attacks." *The New York Sun*, April 2, 2007.

"FBI: Suicide Bombs a Big Concern." *The New York Times*, July 4, 2007.

Fusion Center Guidelines: Developing and Sharing Information and Intelligence in a New Era. Washington, DC: Department of Justice, April 2006.

Griffith, David. "Eyes Wide Shut." *Police*, June 2006a, p.10.

Griffith, David. "Get Real, America." *Police*, September 2006b, p.12.

Gural, Andrea. "State Security Directors Rank Communications Main Priority." *Security Director News*, May 2006, pp.2, 5.

Haber, Grant. "Facing the Threat of Improvised Explosives." *Law Enforcement News*, May 2004, pp.13–14.

Hall, Mimi. "State-Run Sites Not Effective vs. Terror." *USA Today*, July 23, 2007.

Hanson, Doug. "The Nation's Food and Water Supply: A New Target for Terrorists?" *Law Enforcement Technology*, January 2004, pp.18–24.

Harwood, Matthew. "Assessing Chlorine Gas Bombs." *Security Management*, June 2007, pp.18–19.

Heinecke, Jeannine. "Adding Another Layer to the Security Blanket." *Law Enforcement Technology*, March 2004, pp.78–85.

Henderson, Nicole J.; Ortiz, Christopher W.; Sugie, Naomi F.; and Miller, Joel. *Law Enforcement & Arab American Community Relations after September 11, 2001: Engagement in a Time of Uncertainty*. New York: Vera Institute of Justice, June 2006.

Horwitz, Sari. "Man's Best Terror Deterrent Still Somewhat-Reliable Dog." *Washington Post*, August 12, 2005, p.A01.

Hughes, Shawn. "Anxiety Attack." *Police*, September 2004, pp.32–36.

Improving Security and Protecting Privacy through REAL ID. Arlington, VA: Information Technology of America, May 6, 2007.

"An Interview with Homeland Security Secretary Michael Chertoff." *The Police Chief*, February 2007, pp.14–18.

Jackson, Derrick Z. "Tracking the Weapons of Homeland Terrorists." *The Boston Globe*, July 18, 2007.

Jones, Keith. "Terrorism Deterrence, Part I." *Tactical Response*, January/February 2007a, pp.34–36.

Jones, Keith. "Terrorism Deterrence, Part II." *Tactical Response*, March/April 2007b, pp.44–45.

Jones, Keith. "Terrorism Deterrence, Part III." *Tactical Response*, May/June 2007c, pp.30–31.

Keeney, Michelle; Kowalski, Eileen; Cappelli, Dawn; Moore, Andres; Shimeall, Timothy; and Rogers, Stephanie. *Insider Threat Study: Computer System Sabotage in Critical Infrastructure Sectors*. Pittsburgh, PA: CERT Program, Carnegie Mellon University, May 2005.

Kerber, Jennifer. *ITAA White Paper: Real ID Means Real Privacy*. Arlington, VA: Information Technology Association of America, May 10, 2007.

Linett, Howard. "Counter-Terrorism." *Police*, August 2005, pp.58–64.

Loyka, Stephan A.; Faggiani, Donald A.; and Karchmer, Clifford. *Protecting Your Community from Terrorism: Strategies for Local Law Enforcement. Volume 4: The Production and Sharing of Intelligence*. Washington, DC: Community Oriented Policing Services and the Police Executive Research Forum, February 2005.

Miller, Christa. "You Know It When You See It." *Law Enforcement Technology*, September 2006, pp.20–26.

"Montana and Washington First States to Opt Out of REAL ID." *Justice Bulletin*, May/June 2007, pp.11–12.

Morabito, Andrew and Greenberg, Sheldon. *Engaging the Private Sector to Promote Homeland Security: Law Enforcement–Private Security Partnerships*. Washington, DC: Bureau of Justice Assistance, September 2005. (NCJ 210678)

Morgenstern, Henry. "Suicide Terror: Is Law Enforcement Ready?" *Law Enforcement Technology*, September 2006, pp.32–41.

National Infrastructure Protection Plan. Washington, DC: Department of Homeland Security, 2006.

National Intelligence Estimate: The Terrorist Threat to the US Homeland. Washington, DC: National Intelligence Council, July 2007.

Notice of Proposed Rule Making, 4419-10, Department of Homeland Security, Office of the Secretary, 6 CFR Part 37, Docket No. DHS-2006–0030, RIN 1601-AA37, Minimum Standards for Driver's Licenses and Identification Cards Acceptable by Federal Agencies for Official Purposes, p.27.

Page, Douglas. "Dirty Bomb Detection: What's Hot." *Law Enforcement Technology*, August 2005, pp.124–129.

Peed, Carl R. and Wexler, Chuck. "Foreword." In *Protecting Your Community from Terrorism: The Strategies for Local Law Enforcement Series Vol. 2: Working with Diverse Communities*, edited by Heather J. Davies and Gerard R. Murphy. Washington, DC: The Office of Community Oriented Policing Services and the Police Executive Research Forum, 2004, pp.vii–viii.

Pilant, Lois. "Strategic Modeling: Los Angeles County's Counterterroism Program Is Being Duplicated Nationwide." *Police*, May 2004, pp.34–38.

Polisar, Joseph M. "The National Criminal Intelligence Sharing Plan." *The Police Chief*, June 2004, p.8.

Richey, Tom. "Connecting the Dots." *9-1-1 Magazine*, March 2007, pp.34–36, 64.

Sanow, Ed. "Vandalism? Terrorism." *Law and Order*, May 2002, p.5.

Savelli, Lou. *A Proactive Law Enforcement Guide for the War on Terrorism*. Flushing, NY: LooseLeaf Law Publications, Inc. 2004.

Securing Our Homeland. Washington, DC: Department of Homeland Security, no date.

Smetanka, Mary Jane. "'U' Studies Terrorism at Your Table." (Minneapolis/St. Paul) *Star Tribune*, July 6, 2004a, pp.A1, A4.

Smetanka, Mary Jane. "'U' Center Safeguards Food Supply." (Minneapolis/St. Paul) *Star Tribune*, July 7, 2004b, pp.B1, B4.

Spahr, Lisa L.; Ederheimer, Joshua; and Bilson, David. *Patrol-Level Response to a Suicide Bomb Threat: Guidelines for Consideration*. Washington, DC: Police Executive Research Forum, April 2007.

Straw, Joseph. "Interoperability Standards Stalled?" *Security Management*, August 2007a, pp.28–30.

Straw, Joseph. "Hearts, Minds and Homegrown Terror." *Security Management*, January 2007b, pp.30–32.

Straw, Joseph. "Q. What's Your Major? A. Homeland Security." *Security Management*, July 2007c, pp.34–37.

Tanneeru, Manav. "'Ring of Steel' Coming to New York." *CNN*, August 1, 2007.

The Terrorism Research Center. http://www.terrorism.com/index.php

Threat Advisory System Response Guideline. Alexandria, VA: American Society of Industrial Security, 2004.

Van Etten, John. "Impacts of Domestic Security on Law Enforcement Agencies." *The Police Chief*, February 2004, pp.31–35.

Wexler, Chuck. "Foreword." In *Patrol-Level Response to a Suicide Bomb Threat: Guidelines for Consideration*, by Lisa L. Spahr with Joshua Ederheimer and David Bilson. Washington, DC: Police Executive Research Forum, April 2007, pp.i–ii.

White, Jonathan R. *Defending the Homeland: Domestic Intelligence, Law Enforcement and Security*. Belmont, CA: Wadsworth Publishing Company, 2004.

White, Jonathan R. *Terrorism and Homeland Security*, 5th edition. Belmont, CA: Wadsworth Publishing Company, 2006.

Whitelaw, Kevin. "A Resurgent Menace." *U.S. News & World Report*, May 14, 2007, pp.32–33.

CHAPTER 14

Securing the Infrastructure

© AP/Wide World Photos

A security guard with Niscayah Group AB stands watch on a platform crowded with passengers as a Sound Transit commuter train arrives at Kent Station in Kent, Washington. The busy station serves train and bus passengers, particularly those commuting to and from Seattle, 25 miles to the north. Terrorist bombings of trains and buses overseas have raised concern over the security of mass transit systems in the United States.

Do You Know . . .

■ What types of losses are usually specific to industry and manufacturing?

■ How to protect against loss of tools?

■ What two special security concerns of industry and manufacturing are?

■ What threats to the food supply exist? What the greatest challenge to the food industry is?

■ What the Responsible Care® Security Code governs?

■ What overseas and domestic challenges U.S.-based oil companies face?

■ What the primary security problems at utility companies are? How utility companies can reduce loss?

■ What security measures have been used by the trucking industry?

■ What the primary security problems of the railroad industry are? What security measures have been taken by railroads?

■ What the prime concerns of the shipping industry are?

■ What major security problems mass transit systems face? What security measures mass transit systems have taken?

■ What the major security problems of airports and airlines are?

Can You Define?

espionage	ISTs	mission creep
intermodal	leakage	sabotage

Introduction

The lion's share of our critical infrastructures and key assets are owned and operated by the private sector. Customarily, private-sector firms prudently engage in risk management planning and invest in security as a necessary function of business operations and customer confidence. Moreover, in the present threat environment, the private sector generally remains the first line of defense for its own facilities. Consequently, private-sector owners and operators should reassess and adjust their planning, assurance and investment programs to better accommodate the increased risk presented by deliberate acts of violence (*The National Strategy for the Physical Protection of Critical Infrastructures and Key Assets*, 2003).[1]

Recall the *National Infrastructure Protection Plan* (NIPP) introduced in Chapter 13, the comprehensive risk management framework defining critical infrastructure protection roles and responsibilities of federal, state, local, tribal and private security partners. The goal of the NIPP is to: "Build a safer, more secure and more resilient America by enhancing protection of the nation's critical infrastructure and key resources (CI/KR) to prevent, deter, neutralize or mitigate the effects of deliberate efforts by terrorists to destroy, incapacitate or exploit them; and to strengthen national preparedness, timely response and rapid

[1]SOURCE: The National Strategy for the Physical Protection of Critical Infrastructures and Key Assets, 2003.

recovery in the event of an attack, natural disaster or other emergency" (*National Infrastructure Protection Plan*, 2006).[2] Clearly, the security of our national infrastructure has become a top priority in a post-9/11 world.

Although many of the security challenges faced by the companies and sectors discussed in this chapter remain the same as they have been for decades, changing technology and the threat of terrorism are relatively recent challenges. This chapter begins with a discussion of industrial and manufacturing security and the responsibilities of security directors at industrial and manufacturing facilities. This is followed by a look at common security concerns of food processing facilities, chemical plants and U.S.-based oil companies. Next is an explanation of utilities security, followed by a description of transportation security including moving cargo by truck, rail and ship. The chapter concludes with a discussion of mass transit security and airport security.

Industry and Manufacturing

Effective security can affect all aspects of industry and manufacturing, from selection of employees to distribution of finished products. Security is inseparable from good management and profits, and profits are vital to the national economy. Manufacturing includes a range of primary products, such as those related to food processing, textiles, metals, machinery, electrical products and heavy durable goods.

Security officers were first used on a large scale in manufacturing plants prior to World War I because of concern about sabotage and espionage. During World War II many manufacturing plants established proprietary security forces. More than two hundred thousand of these plant security officers were granted the status of auxiliary military police because their primary duties were to protect war goods and products, supplies, equipment and personnel. After the war, many larger manufacturers continued to maintain proprietary security forces, but more recently, as such programs have become increasingly expensive, many plants have begun using contractual security officers. Sometimes the contract security officers are supervised by a small proprietary security force.

As in any other type of establishment, the criteria for determining the expense and effort to be expended to protect a particular plant are based largely on the plant's importance and vulnerability. Especially vulnerable are plants whose products are small, valuable or particularly desirable, such as watches, calculators, small consumer electronics, television sets and jewelry. The incidence of theft is usually high in general merchandising warehouses and factories that manufacture such valuable articles. The incidence of theft is usually lower in heavy industrial plants, such as steel mills and furniture factories.

In addition, security needs generally increase as the size of the plant increases. Some plants cover many acres and have many buildings, such as Minnesota Mining and Manufacturing (3M) which, during the day, has more employees present than the population of many cities. When employees number in the thousands, it is extremely difficult to deter those who steal company property or break company rules.

---

[2]SOURCE: From "A Quantitative Tool" by William R. Floyd. © 1991 ASIS International, 1625 Prince Street, Alexandria, VA 22314. Reprinted by permission from the April 1991 issue of *Security Management* magazine.

Industrial and Manufacturing Security Responsibilities

The safety/security manager's role changed after 9/11, with many managers elevated from positions of secondary importance to major roles on corporate management teams: "No longer were they confined to training forklift operators by day and responding to burglar alarms at night. Now their scope of responsibilities encompassed an urgent need to protect the company's workforce, property and business continuity against a variety of threats" (Evenson, 2004, p.44). Table 14.1 provides a general security survey for industrial and manufacturing companies.

Table 14.1   Manufacturing Security Survey

Areas Evaluated and Grading Factors	Possible/ Assigned Raw Score*	Comments
1. Fences/barriers		
a. Gates secured and access controlled	4	
b. Routinely inspected	4	
c. Good state of repair	4	
d. Top guards/bottom rails	4	
e. Appropriate height	4	
	20	___
2. Building protection		
a. Windows protected	5	
b. Doors protected	5	
c. Unusual openings protected	5	
d. Hinge pins sealed	5	
	20	___
3. Security officers/alarms		
a. Officers are assigned or intrusion alarm system is installed	5	
b. Officer orders and procedures are in writing and adequately describe duties and system	5	
c. Clock rounds are made by officers; sprinkler alarm monitored by outside agency	5	
d. Officer training; alarms tested	5	
	20	___
4. Locking system/key control		
a. Key control records	3	
b. Distribution appropriate	3	
c. Master key system	2	
d. Changed as needed	2	
e. Lock type appropriate	2	
f. Key control officer	2	
g. Spare key protection	2	
h. Markings obliterated	2	
i. Good working order	2	
	20	___
5. Access controls		
a. Entry/exits designated	4	
b. Employees' access monitored	4	
c. Visitors controlled	4	
d. Contractors/vendors/service employees controlled	4	
e. Employee ID cards	4	
	20	___

(Continued)

Table 14.1   Manufacturing Security Survey (*Continued*)

Areas Evaluated and Grading Factors	Possible/ Assigned Raw Score*	Comments
6. Outside material storage		
a. Property protected and access controlled	5	
b. Stored or stacked	5	
c. Clear zones	5	___
	15	
7. Scrap/trash controls		
a. Contracts exist	3	
b. Supervision in effect	3	
c. Storage/staging adequate	3	
d. Inspections made	3	
e. Access controlled	3	___
	15	
8. Vehicle controls		
a. Away from buildings	3	
b. Out of dock areas	3	
c. Clear firelanes	3	
d. Employee parking adequate	3	
e. Access controlled	3	___
	15	
9. Exterior lighting		
a. Dock areas	2	
b. Parking lots	2	
c. Building perimeter	2	
d. Employee entrances	2	
e. Maintenance checks	2	___
	10	
10. Control signs		
a. Access point/perimeter	2	
b. Parking	2	
c. No trespassing signs	2	
d. Safety/security	2	
e. Restricted areas	2	___
	10	
11. Employee screening/verification		
a. Credit	3	
b. Criminal record check	3	
c. Previous employer	3	
d. Reference checks	3	
e. Other screening	3	___
	15	
12. Package/material control		
a. Written procedures in effect	3	
b. Forms adequate and controlled	3	
c. Authorizations defined	3	
d. Inspections made	3	
e. Accountability/verification	3	___
	15	
13. Security awareness		
a. Management attitude	9	
b. Program orientation	3	
c. Bulletins/newsletters	3	___
	15	

Table 14.1 Manufacturing Security Survey (*Continued*)

Areas Evaluated and Grading Factors	Possible/ Assigned Raw Score*	Comments
14. Proprietary information protection		
a. Designated and marked	2	
b. Filed and protected	2	
c. Formulas and microfiche protected	2	
d. Computers/computer software	2	
e. Destruction and disposal	2	__
	10	
15. General office security		
a. Funds (petty cash, etc.)	2	
b. Purchasing	2	
c. Payroll	2	
d. Negotiables	2	
e. Portable office equipment	2	
f. Prenumbered forms accounted for and protected	2	__
	12	
16. Shipping/receiving controls		
a. Double checks made	4	
b. Forms accountability/protection	3	
c. Seal accountability/protection	3	
d. Dock access restricted	3	
e. Drivers controlled	3	
f. Housekeeping	2	
g. Raw material protection	2	__
	20	
17. Tractor trailer theft prevention		
a. Kingpin locks used	5	
b. Loaded trailers sealed	5	
c. Trailers locked	5	__
	15	
18. Emergency planning/response		
a. Sprinkler system maintained	3	
b. Extinguisher equipment adequate	3	
c. Emergency plans implemented	3	__
	9	
19. Utility protection		
a. Water/steam	2	
b. Gas/electricity	2	
c. Generators/boilers	2	
d. Telephone equipment	2	__
	8	
20. Demographic/risk assessment		
a. Burglary	5	
b. Robbery	5	
c. Auto/vehicle theft	5	
d. Violent crime	5	__
	20	

*Risk probability is virtually certain—1; highly probable—2; moderately probable—3; improbable—4; unknown—5

SOURCE: William R. Floyd. "A Quantitative Tool." *Security Management*, April 1991, p.53. © 1995 American Society for Industrial Security, 1625 Prince Street, Alexandria, VA 22314–2818. Reprinted by permission.

Security managers must confront major challenges in a rapidly evolving global manufacturing environment. Plant security personnel coordinate their efforts with local, county and state law enforcement agencies in investigating internal theft and criminal incidents that occur on the premises. Defense-industry security personnel maintain liaison with the FBI and the Defense Investigative Service, Office of Industrial Security, and must report all security violations and theft of classified materials or products to the Defense Supply Agency.

The security linkage between the Department of Defense (DOD) and the industrial sector in the United States is not only massive but also complex. Strict regulations are spelled out in the DOD's *Industrial Security Manual* as well as in other security requirements specified by the military branches, NASA, the Atomic Energy Commission and the like.

Types of Losses

Although industry is susceptible to the same types of internal theft as any business, as well as to burglary and robbery, certain types of losses are more frequently encountered in industry than in other businesses.

 Industrial/manufacturing losses frequently include tools, materials, supplies, products, pallets, hand trucks, valuable scrap, uniforms, side-products, time and vital information.

Reported instances of internal theft from employees within the manufacturing sector include:

- Taking raw materials
- Taking company tools and equipment
- Getting paid for more hours than worked
- Getting excess expense reimbursement
- Taking finished products
- Taking precious metals

Some employees engage in three or four of these types of internal theft. The categories are *not* mutually exclusive.

In many types of industry, side-product control is important. Such items as metal shavings, wood scraps and reclaimable oil may be recovered and sold as salvage. Food scraps may be sold as hog feed. Therefore, policies should be developed regarding the handling of such potentially valuable by-products, and employees should be instructed on these policies. Then, the weighing, loading and disposing of valuable salvage should be carefully supervised.

A manufacturing company that provides uniforms should caution employees that personnel are expected to care for their uniforms and not take them for personal use. Pallets and hand trucks are also sometimes taken for personal use and never returned. In addition, these should be kept secured because burglars can transport stolen goods on pallets and hand trucks. Security officers should also be aware that intruders might use the company's own acetylene torches to open safes and that pry bars, cutting tools, ladders and forklifts should be secured so as not to make the task of a would-be thief easier.

Maintenance supplies such as cleaning liquids, paper towels, soap and even toilet paper are often stolen by employees and, consequently, should be kept secure. Proprietary gas pumps, too, may be used for personal vehicles and must be kept secured. Records should be kept of company vehicles' gas and oil use and mileage to further ensure that such supplies are not being transferred to personal vehicles. Another "big ticket" industrial security problem is theft of heavy equipment and machinery.

Finally, employees who are allowed to use company products or are given discounts when purchasing products may abuse this privilege by making purchases for friends or for selling such products at a profit, resulting in considerable loss to the employer.

Misuse or Theft of Tools   Tools constitute one of the most serious areas of loss. Losses can result either from the improper use of tools or from actual theft. Proper maintenance not only lengthens a tool's life, but also avoids merchandise damage and production slowdowns.

Hand power tools, drills, wrenches, hammers and pliers are highly susceptible to theft, especially if employees use their own tools as well as those belonging to the plant. All company tools should be checked into a tool room or a tool crib at the end of each shift.

 Tool loss can be reduced by having a tool room or tool crib with an attendant, a check-in and check-out procedure, distinctive markings on the tools, periodic inspections and inventories, metal detectors at gates and possibly a system for lending tools for personal use after hours.

Sabotage and Espionage

Although security measures were originally introduced into manufacturing companies to protect against sabotage and espionage during wartime, these two threats remain very real even during peacetime. They can be committed by competitors or by dissatisfied employees.

 Two special concerns of industry and manufacturing are sabotage and espionage.

Sabotage   The word *sabotage* originated in France during the Industrial Revolution when disgruntled factory workers threw their wooden shoes (sabots) into the machinery, thereby halting production. **Sabotage** is the intentional destruction of machinery or goods, or the intentional obstruction of production.

Methods of sabotage may be chemical, electrical, explosive, mechanical or psychological (strikes, riots and boycotts). Psychological sabotage has become more frequent in the last decade. In Minnesota, protestors against electrical power lines running through privately owned fields toppled several of the huge power line towers, each at a cost of hundreds of thousands of dollars. The costs were then passed on to the consumer in higher energy rates. Access control and inspections are two means to prevent sabotage.

Espionage   Traditionally espionage is associated with spying, especially spying to obtain military secrets. More recently the term has broadened considerably in meaning. Industrial **espionage** is the theft of trade secrets or confidential information.

Some well-intentioned executives may claim they are not concerned with espionage, that they have no secrets to hide. However, it is well known that competition is the "fuel" of the American economy and the heart of the free enterprise system. Nowhere does this manifest more clearly than in industries trying to reach the market with improvements on an established item. Most manufacturers have information they want to conceal from their competitors because lead time is so critical. Confidentiality of information buys time to "get a jump" on the market. All too often some executives delay until competition has driven them to near bankruptcy before they will acknowledge the need for protecting secrets, as discussed in Chapter 11.

In other instances, secret formulas are a company's primary source of profits. Although many products can be protected by patents, some cannot. Trade secrets such as formulas are much harder to protect than real property because, if they are stolen, the rightful owner still has possession, but not exclusive possession, thereby greatly diminishing the formula's value. Sometimes, in fact, the rightful owner may never realize the formula has been stolen. Trade secrets should be identified as such, be secured and be made known to the fewest people possible. A good example of protecting such a trade secret is the formula for Worcestershire sauce. It has been kept secret for more than 100 years because only two company officials know it at any one time.

Other types of information that may be stolen include new product research, production costs, sales figures, profit breakdowns, markups, salaries, reports on problems, merger plans, blueprints and the like. The minutes of executive committee meetings often contain such information and should be carefully guarded.

Manufacturing firms working under DOD contracts must protect classified information and materials and follow prescribed governmental regulations for safeguarding classified defense information, documents, materials, end products and storage and work areas. The security programs and policies at these manufacturing plants are mandated by DOD regulations, and the plants can be inspected at any time by the Office of Industrial Security of the U.S. Defense Supply Agency.

Employers should be suspicious of a break in security if competitors are consistently ahead of them, if they lose bids more often than usual or if their competition is hiring away key people. Prevent espionage through careful screening of personnel, document control and clear guidelines for personnel. Espionage is one result of the sharing of an IT network, discussed in Chapter 11. In fact: "The single largest issue bothering manufacturers now is the sharing of the IT network" (Freeman, 2005, p.20).

An Example: Security at the Montgomery Hyundai Manufacturing Plant

The security put into place at the Hyundai manufacturing plant in Montgomery, Alabama, was implemented during the construction phase, the best time to think about security (Martinez, 2005, pp.75–76). In addition to the usual security requirements, the Hyundai plant had to meet the standards of U.S. Customs and Border Protection because it is a foreign trade zone, with its home base in Korea. The requirement of having to answer to Customs instead of to local law enforcement makes Hyundai's security force somewhat like its own police force. The foreign-trade-zone status requires fencing and strict entrance and exit procedures. One hundred thirty-five doors are wired with access control using badges with encoded chips assigned to each worker. Each badge has specified access rights to prevent workers from going where they do not belong, helping prevent industrial espionage.

One important part of their security system is video saved to CD with a self-executing file so it can be played on any PC. Thirty-two pan/tilt cameras and 32 fixed cameras keep a "cyber-eye" on the 14 buildings situated on 500 of the 1,700 acres and 2 million square feet under roof. The video has a digital watermark, making any tampering obvious. When Customs agents spot check the plant, security protocol requires that incoming containers not be opened until the agents arrive. The video system not only records the containers' arrival but also runs continuously to show the containers remain untouched until agents arrive. The video system has allowed the security team to track down and identify a hit-and-run driver in the parking area.

Food Supply

Between August and mid-October of 2006, 199 people in 26 states became sick after eating fresh spinach contaminated with *E.coli*; 31 developed kidney failure, and 3 died (Straw, 2007a, p.64). Harowitz (2007, p.14) contends: "Compared to the world at large, our food sector's performance is exemplary. But we cannot afford to be complacent." According to the Centers for Disease Control (CDC), 76 million people fall ill each year in the U.S. from food-borne illnesses; 5,000 of them die. And that's without any tampering or terrorist intent to contaminate our food supply. Before 9/11 most food industry regulations focused on safety and preventing accidental or environmentally based contamination. However, since 9/11 the government has redirected its focus on protecting the nation's food supply (Sorrells, 2006, p.107).

 Threats to the U.S. food supply include disgruntled employees, hoaxes to elicit financial settlements, terrorist, criminals and subversives. The greatest challenge is detecting contamination.

The private sector has voluntarily boosted food security by improving access controls at food processing plants (Sorrells, p.107). In addition, many government regulations are made mandatory for companies in the effort to increase overall food security. For example, the Hazard Analysis Critical Control Points (HACCP) system is mandated across the seafood and juice sectors by the Food and Drug Administration (FDA) and throughout the meat and poultry areas by the U.S. Department of Agriculture. The following risk management principles are recommended for food security (Sorrells, p.102):

- Food security inspections of the facility should be conducted regularly by plant officials to verify key provisions of the risk management plan.
- All employees should be encouraged to report any sign of possible product tampering or break in the food security system.
- Integrity of the plant perimeter should be monitored for any signs of suspicious activity or unauthorized entry.
- Doors, windows, roof openings, vent openings, trailer bodies, railcars and bulk storage tanks should be secured (as by locks, seals and sensors) at all times.

- Entry into establishments should be controlled by requiring positive identification (such as picture IDs and sign-in/sign-out at security or reception).
- Truck deliveries should be verified against a roster of scheduled deliveries. Unscheduled deliveries should be held outside the plant premises, if possible, pending verification of shipper and cargo.
- Restricted areas inside the plant should be clearly marked as such and appropriately secured.
- Visitors, guests and other nonplant employees (such as contractors, salespeople or truck drivers) should be restricted to nonproduct areas unless accompanied by an authorized plant representative.
- A program should be in place to ensure the identification, segregation and security of all products involved in the event of deliberate product contamination.
- All outgoing shipments should be sealed with tamperproof, numbered seals that are included on the shipping documents.
- A system of positive identification of all plant employees should be in place.
- New hires (seasonal, temporary, permanent and contract workers) should have background checks before being hired.
- The plant should establish and enforce a policy on what personal items are and are not allowed inside the plant and within production areas.[3]

Chemical Plants

According to *Terrorism and the Chemical Infrastructure* (2006): "The chemical sector is a key part of the national economy and has been designated by the DHS as one of 17 sectors comprising the nation's critical infrastructure." Harwood (2007, p.89) notes: "One of the nightmare scenarios posited in our post-9–11 code-yellow world is that terrorists might attack chemical plants, turning the compounds used for commercial purposes into deadly weapons." As noted in Chapter 13, new regulations have hardened chemical sites deemed high-risk to prevent terrorists from gaining access to lethal chemicals. According to Homeland Security Secretary Michael Chertoff: "We are going to be more comprehensive than we have ever been in making sure we have a full picture of all the chemical-based risks out there, and making sure we are systematically driving down the risk of the most dangerous chemicals" (Hsu, 2007, p.A10).

Security at chemical facilities used to center on guards, gates and alarms, but now such facilities are using electronic technology to secure their sites with layers of protection (Kellogg and McGloon, 2005, p.94). Members of the American Chemistry Council (ACC) have taken aggressive measures since 9/11 to enhance security at their facilities, with ACC members self-imposing a series of mandatory security requirements. They have also worked with the Department of Homeland Security (DHS), the U.S. Coast Guard, the FBI and thousands of state and local emergency responders to develop their Responsible Care® Security Code (Durbin, 2005, p.53). All 2,040 ACC member facilities abide by this

---

[3]SOURCE: From "Recipe for Food Safety" by Eddie Sorrells. © 2006 ASIS International, 1625 Prince Street, Alexandria, VA 22314. Reprinted by permission from the August 2006 issue of *Security Management* magazine.

code and have completed vulnerability assessments and implemented training and security upgrades at a cost of more than $1 billion.

 The Responsible Care® Security Code sets forth security measures to be taken at chemical plants.

The security tools available to chemical producers have improved dramatically (Zunkel, 2005, p.50). Digital video recorders with motion detectors allow surveillance of critical areas, and security personnel can view events in real time, recreating events leading up to a critical point without time-consuming tape rewinding. Wireless access controls allow installing networked access controls on perimeter portals. Ram resistant fencing with integrated motion sensors gives early warning of intruders. And the list goes on.

Many plants are now switching to "inherently safer technologies" (ISTs). An example is seen at the Blue Plains Wastewater Treatment Facility in Washington, DC, which has switched to using sodium hypochlorite, or liquid bleach, to treat wastewater (Harwood). Liquid bleach is much safer than chlorine gas and easily contained if spilled. The Nottingham Water Treatment Plant in Cleveland, Ohio, now treats drinking water with liquid bleach instead of chlorine gas; some 1.1 million people are no longer at risk of a toxic gas release. The Wyandotte Wastewater Treatment Facility near Detroit, Michigan, switched from chlorine gas to ultraviolet light; more than 1 million people are no longer at risk of a toxic gas release. Manhattan Products, in Carlstadt, New Jersey, now produces household cleaning products with liquid ammonia instead of gaseous ammonia, removing the threat to 160,000 residents. Solae Company dba (doing business as) DuPont Soy Polymers in Louisville, Kentucky, switched from anhydrous sulfur dioxide to the safer sodium bisulfite for producing food products from soy; the change removed the threat to 37,000 residents. Wisconsin Power's Pulliam Plant in Green Bay switched from anhydrous to solid sulfur dioxide for pollution control, removing the threat to 180,000 residents. U.S. Filter Recovery Services, in Roseville, Minnesota, changed treatment chemicals for certain hazardous waste recovery processes; the change eliminated the threat of a gas release to 62,000 residents. Procter and Gamble has converted six manufacturing plants to ISTs despite the relatively high cost of switching: "Companies that still handle hazardous chemicals would be well advised to look beyond the up-front costs as these businesses have and take a second look at whether a move to IST makes good business and security sense for their own facilities" (Harwood).

Another way to reduce risks to citizens is to move a chemical facility out of a highly populated downtown area to a remote area, as the Hill Brothers Chemical Company did when it moved out of downtown Los Angeles, freeing 500,000 nearby residents from the risk of an ammonia gas release (Gips, 2006b, p.26). The Niklor Chemical Company moved from Carson, California, to a remote location near Mojave, removing a chlorine-gas danger from an area of 3.5 million residents.

The Center for American Progress conducted a survey to identify facilities that use hazardous substances and to spotlight successful practices. Key findings from the survey include the following (*Preventing Toxic Terrorism*, 2006):

- Some 284 facilities in 47 states have dramatically reduced the danger of a chemical release into nearby communities by switching to less acutely hazardous processes or chemicals or moving to safer locations.
- As a result of these changes, at least 30 million people no longer live under the threat of a major toxic gas cloud from these facilities.
- Eleven of these facilities formerly threatened more than one million people; another 33 facilities threatened more than 100,000; and an additional 100 threatened more than 10,000.
- Of respondents that provided cost estimates, roughly half reported spending less than $100,000 to switch to safer alternatives, and few spent over $1 million.
- Survey respondents represent a range of facilities small and large, including water utilities, manufacturers, power plants, service companies, waste management facilities and agricultural chemical suppliers.
- Facilities reported replacing gaseous chlorine, ammonia and sulfur dioxide, among other chemicals.
- The most common reasons cited for making changes included the security and safety of employees and nearby communities, as well as regulatory incentives and business opportunities.
- Facilities cut a variety of costs and regulatory burdens by switching to less hazardous chemicals or processes. These facilities need fewer physical security and safety measures and can better focus on producing valuable products and services.[4]

The facilities identified by the survey show that dramatic improvements are feasible if safety and security are given priority. Adopting safer alternatives, however, is the only certain way to prevent a catastrophic chemical release. Many chemical facilities have already taken this step, thereby protecting millions of Americans. Millions more could be taken out of harm's way with a concerted national effort to convert other high-risk facilities to safer chemicals and processes.

An Example: Security at Air Products and Chemicals, Inc.

The security at Air Products and Chemicals, Inc., a manufacturer of chemicals and chemical products, became a priority to senior management following the events of 9/11 (Kellogg and McGloon, p.96). Using the ACC's Responsible Care® Security Code as its guide, a team identified four areas or potential vulnerabilities: people, operations, transactions and information technology.

In looking at workforce risks, the team identified employee tracking as a vulnerability. The problem was addressed by developing a worldwide employee-tracking system that allows the company to locate and contact employees quickly in the event of a terrorist threat or other emergency. The team also found that better control over who entered the property was needed, so the company instituted a global ID card requirement for all employees, contractors and site visitors and also reduced the number of contractors it uses.

The team also examined vulnerabilities in operations, looking at manufacturing facilities, warehouses, transport vehicles and pipelines. Supplementing physical security in place—fences, gates, patrols and access controls—the com-

---

[4]SOURCE: *Preventing Toxic Terrorism* (Center for American Progress, April 24, 2006).

pany improved surveillance capabilities. In addition, a new incident-reporting system allowed any employee to report an incident on an electronic template and submit it by e-mail to the security department.

In addition to these measures, Air Products developed and implemented programs to assess who it sells dangerous chemicals to and to monitor everything from process controls and safety systems at plants to data systems that might be vulnerable to intellectual property intrusions and information theft.

U.S.-Based Oil Companies

According to Crocker (2007, p.86): "U.S.-based oil companies now face the more extreme security threats that energy sector operations in foreign countries have faced for decades."

 Overseas challenges for U.S.-based oil companies include corruption, political unrest and piracy. Domestic challenges include the regulatory environment, protecting against terrorist threats and tight budgets.

A major issue for U.S. oil operations is securing manned and unmanned off-shore oil platforms in the Gulf of Mexico (Crocker). Such platforms comprise hundreds of one-off design elements, meaning the loss of any one of these platforms could bring operations to a sudden, expensive halt: "The security systems for these facilities are inordinately sophisticated compared to security at other types of warehouses due to the cost associated with loss or damage of the items stored there" (Crocker).

An Example: Security at Shell Oil in Nigeria

Shell was the first large oil company to move into Nigeria and is still the largest with a 50 percent footprint in the market (Elliott, 2007, p.74). Nigeria is Africa's most populous country and its top oil producer, but it is also a chaotic, volatile, corrupt country currently experiencing an uncommonly intense time of kidnappings, corruption and attacks on major oil companies (Elliott). Shell is approaching the security problem and protecting its facilities and extensive pipelines with a three-pronged offense based on community relations, technology and human intelligence. Shell has focused on bettering its liaison with local communities by paying incentives for monitoring the oil ducts running through the villages and townships as well as building schools, clinics, hospitals and other facilities. Technologically, Shell is testing geoseismic sensors to thwart oil thieves who steal oil directly from the lines. Shell is also testing CCTV cameras, about 1,000 of which will be needed, as well as installing fencing around manifolds and flow stations. The security project is projected to cost about $1 million over the next few years.

Utilities

Everyone has contact with utility companies—water, gas, electric companies. We are heavily dependent on them daily. Yet, according to a *Security Management* survey, only about one-third of U.S. utilities reported having practiced a full-scale, utility-wide role-playing exercise simulating a terrorist attack (Gips, 2005a, p.99). The results of responses to whether such an exercise had been conducted are summarized in Figure 14.1.

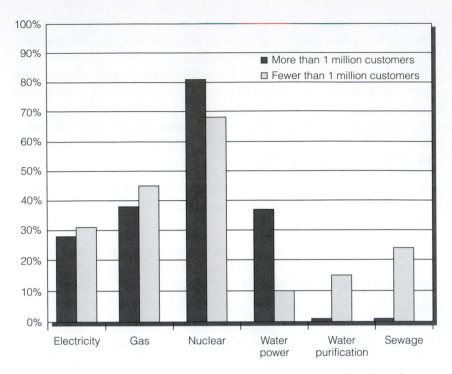

Figure 14.1 Utility Companies Practicing Response to Simulated Attacks

SOURCE: From "Survey Assesses Vital Services" by Michael A. Gips. © 2005 ASIS International, 1625 Prince Street, Alexandria, VA 22314. Reprinted by permission from the November 2005 issue of *Security Management* magazine.

This same survey found that nearly 80 percent of utilities had surrounded sensitive sites with fencing, 53 percent had protected sensitive facilities with vehicle barricades and 77 percent had upgraded procedures for screening prospective employees, contractors and vendors. In addition, 96 percent reported having conducted a vulnerability assessment since 9/11. The importance of vulnerability assessment is stressed by Goldsmith (2004, p.106) who differentiates between taking a gamble and taking a calculated risk: "Utilities that fail to undertake complete and accurate vulnerability assessments are truly gambling with assets and lives. By carefully examining and responding to risk, adverse actions can be avoided."

The need to protect the critical public utility infrastructure was recognized well before 9/11, and since that fateful day, efforts have accelerated to augment the traditional "three Gs" of protection: guns, guards and gates (Durstenfeld, 2005, p.16). In addition to armed guards, patrols, physical barriers and plant design, technology such as fence-line monitoring is playing a greater role in protecting U.S. utilities, taking a "far more aggressive, preventative and integrated approach" (Durstenfeld). According to Durstenfeld: "The threat to public utilities is asymmetrical. That is, it can happen anywhere at any time. Terrorists will choose the softest available target to achieve their ends, whether that target is symbolic, economic or political."

The potential of integrated public utility security is found in the ability to deploy hundreds, even thousands, of tiny sensors interconnected using wireless mesh networks or Internet technology for a complete, real-time picture of the environment, including radiation levels, temperature, humidity, air quality and oxygen levels, presence of toxic chemicals and gases, video verification of sensor anomalies before resources are dispatched, perimeter intrusion, as well as functioning of smoke detectors, power outlets and light switches (Durstenfeld, p.17). The conclusion: "Wireless integrated sensing networks will play a transformational role in keeping people safe, economic assets in production and symbolic targets protected. In addition to their life-saving capabilities, the role of these pervasive early warning systems makes sound business sense in minimizing the chaos and economic disruption of terrorist attacks" (Durstenfeld).

 Primary problems at utility companies include loss of stored items, trespassers and vandals at substations and distribution centers, security at construction sites, plans for emergencies and detection of resource diversion.

Utility service trucks are heavily equipped with supplies and tools that remain in the vehicles even when they are not in use. Consequently this equipment is highly vulnerable to theft. To counter this problem, inventory control and strict check-in and check-out procedures are needed. In addition, when the vehicles are at a service location, crew members often must leave the vehicle unattended and, again, vulnerable.

Another problem is encountered in utility companies' numerous unstaffed substations, frequently secured with chain-link fences and security lighting. Despite these measures, trespassers and vandals may pose serious problems. Additional problems include crews using the substations for beer parties and gambling; homeless individuals taking over the buildings; and contractors moving mobile homes onto a site and hooking up to the substation's electricity and water. Solutions to such problems might include alarms, guard dogs or roving patrols. Construction of major generating facilities presents additional security problems.

Like any other business, utility companies also have valuable records: subscriber credit histories, financial data and the like, often stored on computer. Controlling access to this information is the same as for any other business and might include locks, alarms, sign-in and sign-out procedures and guards.

Another area of concern is that of emergencies. Although utility companies are particularly accustomed to dealing with emergencies, crisis response such as handling fires, bombs and bomb threats must still be built into the overall security plan. As for any other type of establishment, procedures for evacuation should be determined and practiced.

Yet another area of concern, which lacks the high visibility of emergencies, is that of diversion of the resource provided by the utility, whether gas, electricity or water. The most usual means of diverting the resource is bypassing the meter that measures its use. For example, the owner of a large restaurant with an all-electric kitchen paid a utility employee to bypass the electric meter, leaving one light bulb connected to the meter to show some usage. The diversion was discovered when a new employee had an electrical problem and called the utility, whose service person discovered the crime. Such losses might be reduced by monitoring monthly usage and comparing it with predetermined norms.

 A utility company's losses can be reduced by careful access controls to tools and supplies, careful check-in and check-out procedures, alarms and surveillance cameras at substations and establishment of emergency plans.

Other measures that might be employed will vary from utility to utility.

An Example: Security at the Co-Mo Electric Cooperative

The Co-Mo Electric Cooperative in Tipton, Missouri, delivers electric power to 26,000 members in a 2,300-square-mile service area and maintains a 3,700-mile electricity distribution network (Anderson, 2006a, pp.34–36). The co-op's new security system has six digital cameras, with three cameras and a DVR at headquarters in Tipton and the remaining three with another DVR in the district office in Laurie. The cameras are positioned so security employees stationed in the back offices can watch the customer service counter and intervene if an employee is subjected to verbal or physical abuse. The director of operations and safety and several colleagues monitor the live video feeds from the front offices of both facilities and take action if any abusive or threatening behavior occurs. Disgruntled customers who have had their service cut off are the biggest security concern.

Cameras also monitor the front gates and night deposit boxes at both locations. To control access through the gates, employees and repair crews have fobs with an access control card that allows them to enter the co-op's fenced yards. Visitors must press a button to be allowed in. The button rings through to co-op staff, who check live video from the gate before remotely unlocking it. For additional safety, the front counters at both facilities are equipped with panic buttons linked to strobe lights that alert security staff in the back offices of a potential problem. If the light goes on, the first thing checked is the video. If an upset customer is observed on screen, one of the security staff goes out front and sits in the reception area. If the scene witnessed is something more serious, such as someone brandishing a weapon, the police are called. Police officers are equipped with fobs allowing them access to the back door so they can come in unseen and unheard to try to defuse the situation.

Security at Drinking Water Facilities

United States water systems consist of large networks of storage tanks, valves and pipes that transport clean water to customers over vast areas. By the very nature of their design, they provide multiple points for potential contamination—either accidental or intentional (Burroughs, 2006). The Environmental Protection Agency (EPA) is the lead agency for drinking water security. After 9/11 Congress appropriated over $100 million to help drinking water systems assess their risk of terrorist attacks as well as to develop response plans, since the vast majority of cities' security plans for water treatment and distribution facilities were originally designed to combat equipment theft and vandalism, not to deter bioterrorism (Jensen, 2004, p.6; Zunkel, 2004, p.47). Metropolitan water plans use fences extensively and some use advanced intrusion detection devices such as CCTV, fence sensors and buried cable sensors, but the majority rely on physical security products such as locks, barbed wire and ladder access controls (Zunkel).

Security experts recommend three general types of specific security-enhancing activities most deserving of federal support (Jensen, p.6):

■ Physical, technological upgrades—to improve security and research to develop technologies to prevent, detect or respond to an attack (real-time monitoring technologies to detect contaminants in treated drinking water)

- Education and training—simulation exercises in carrying out emergency response plans; training security staff and multidisciplinary consulting teams to assess utilities' security preparedness and to recommend improvements
- Strengthening key relationships—between water utilities and other agencies (e.g., the health department, law enforcement and security directors of neighboring drinking water systems) that may have key roles in an emergency response

Sandia researchers are working with the EPA, the University of Cincinnati and Argonne National Laboratory to develop contaminant warning systems that can monitor municipal water systems to quickly determine when and where a contamination occurs (Burroughs). From 2003 to 2006 a collaborative team created software to address water security issues. The software can aid in placing sensors during the design stage of a contaminant warning system. It can also determine when and where a contamination event happens, track changes and determine when the event is over.

The country's first guidelines for physical security of water and wastewater infrastructure systems were developed jointly by the American Society of Civil Engineers (ASCE) and the American Water Works Association with input from the Water Environment Federation (Daniels, 2007, p.1).

An Example: Security at Dallas's Water Utilities   Dallas, the seventh largest city in the United States and one of the top five largest water utilities, releases more than 440 million gallons of water on a normal day (Jensen). The water comes from surface water surrounding the city. Security at these lakes is provided by city police as well as security from the city water department and suburban cities making up 78 miles of shoreline at Lake Ray Hubbard, one of many lakes providing Dallas and suburbs with drinking water. The city continuously monitors water as it comes into its system as well as when it flows out, but the main security concern is physical security. Dallas completed a federally mandated vulnerability test of its assets, an ongoing process of upgrades and reinforcement, and currently spends $2 million annually on security measures. The physical facilities the city owns and operates are located behind fences, with posted security guards limiting access control.

Transportation

Shortly after the 9/11 terrorist attacks, the Transportation Security Administration (TSA) was formed. A component of the DHS, the TSA is responsible for overseeing security for our nation's highways, railroads, buses, mass transit systems, seaports and airports. More than 43,000 security officers, inspectors, directors, air marshals and managers are employed by the TSA to protect the nation's transportation systems so people and products can travel and move safely. Employees of TSA look for bombs at checkpoints in airports, inspect rail cars, patrol subways and work to make all modes of transportation safe.

Cargo Security: Transporting Goods by Truck, Rail and Ship

Our national economy depends on the movement of goods and merchandise by our transportation system, one of the largest industries in the United States. Manufacturing and industrial enterprises depend on the transportation system to supply them with raw materials for production and to then distribute the finished merchandise to consumers. Most materials and goods are transported by common carrier rather than by company-owned transportation fleets. Friedrick (2006, p.25) notes: "With people and products constantly on the move, the issue of where to focus transportation security efforts continues to be up for debate. From airports to seaports, school buses to mass transit, cruise lines to cargo ships, various security efforts have been implemented in greater or lesser degrees."

For this discussion *cargo* refers to anything that enters and is moved by the nation's transportation system, beginning at the shipper's loading platform and ending at a consignee's receiving dock. *Cargo theft* may involve entire shipments, containers and cartons, or pilferage of smaller amounts of merchandise. Commodities such as clothing, electrical appliances, automotive parts, food products, hardware, jewelry, tobacco products, scientific instruments and alcoholic beverages comprise about 80 percent of the total national losses.

The increasing popularity of cargo theft is due to two primary features: It is low risk (few thieves are apprehended, prosecuted or incarcerated), and it is extremely profitable. The direct cost of cargo theft in the United States is $12–15 billion annually ("Cargo Theft").

The illegal or unauthorized removal of cargo from the supply chain is called **leakage**, a concept similar to that of shrinkage. Cargo theft can occur from an 18-wheel trailer, a shipping container left on a dock or placed on a railway, or a warehouse. While some cargo thieves will take whatever commodity crosses their path, many groups steal to order. Common commodities targeted include consumer electronics, designer clothing and fragrances, alcohol and tobacco (Kennedy, 2005).

Methods used to steal cargo vary, and such crimes are generally extremely difficult to detect after they occur. In some cases, thieves break the locking mechanism off the back door of a trailer or container, or drill out a rivet holding the door in place, empty the cargo, and then shut the door again, sometimes taking the time to replace the rivet or otherwise visually disguise the theft so that nothing looks amiss to a passing security guard. Other times the driver is highjacked en route. These "driver give-ups" typically happen close to major interstate corridors (Bibb, 2005).

The millions of loaded cargo containers coming into the country present an opportunity for a terrorist to sneak a weapon of mass destruction into the United States (Anderson, 2005, p.62). A key first step to ensuring cargo security is to make sure the company designates a high-level person to take ownership of the issue internally. Background screening of staff is also critical as is building relationships with government and industry groups to leverage resources and share intelligence (Anderson).

Most security staffs have developed effective countermeasures against cargo theft, but common denominators can be seen. Measures that can be equally effective in all types of transportation to protect both shippers and carriers from losses due to theft and vandalism include personnel security, physical security, procedures for accepting cargo, secure packaging, documenting movement and delivery, periodic review of security procedures and prosecution of offenses.

Agencies that may assist with investigating cargo crime include the local police department, the United States Bureau of Customs and the FBI. Liaison with other carriers should be maintained to ensure mutual cooperation in all areas related to cargo security. Prosecution is of vital importance in deterring future thefts.

Numerous challenges face cargo theft investigators. One significant challenge is quantifying the problem, since cargo theft has historically not been designated a specific crime under the FBI's Uniform Crime Reports (UCR). Consequently such offenses are commonly reported as robbery, fraud, motor vehicle theft or grand theft: "Without a crime reporting code, it is difficult to show the impact of cargo theft. Without a way to show the impact, justifying the need for manpower to combat the crime is not available" (Callahan, 2008). Because cargo theft is variously classified under the UCR in several different ways, the result is that estimates of the annual dollar loss attributed to cargo theft differ wildly, from a few billion dollars to $120 billion (Gips, 2006a, p.28). Efforts are being made to overcome this inconsistency, with a provision in the law reauthorizing the USA PATRIOT Act requiring the attorney general to endow cargo theft with its own UCR code by the end of 2006. The law also calls for establishing a national cargo theft database. However, as of March 2008, this provision had yet to be implemented (Callahan).

Another problem centers on the mobile nature of the crime. Numerous jurisdictions around the country, particularly those close to major seaports and cargo distribution hubs, have developed cargo theft task forces to increase their effectiveness in conducting investigations. The success of these units has demonstrated that the surveillance and investigative abilities of a multijurisdictional team surpass those of any single agency. Examples of these teams include the California Highway Patrol's Cargo Theft Interdiction Program (CTIP), which from 1994 through 2004 recovered more than $148 million in stolen property and 1,245 cargo loads ("Cargo Theft"), and the Tactical Operations Multiagency Cargo Anti Theft Squad (TOMCATS) based in Miami–Dade County, Florida, comprising local, state and federal law enforcement agencies engaged in complex investigations of commercial vehicle and cargo theft by organized crime (OC) groups. TOMCATS recovers approximately $30 million in stolen property each year ("Commercial Motor Vehicle and Cargo Theft," 2005).

In the absence of a task force, experts recommend that an investigator work a cargo theft case backward, from the point of recovery to the initial loading of the product (Kennedy). The container or trailer carrier should be contacted for information on where the load should be. If the theft was from a refrigerated container, known as a *reefer*, the temperature chart should be collected as evidence. This chart will reveal a spike in temperature whenever the container was opened and will, presumably, indicate when the theft occurred (Kennedy).

Often discussed with cargo theft, particularly post-9/11, is the broader topic of supply chain integrity, which is concerned not only with those items taken out of the supply chain but also with those inserted into the chain. While cargo theft remains a concern, "of equal or even greater importance is the illicit introduction of things like weapons of mass destruction or bioterrorism into the supply chain" (Rogers et al., 2005, p.26). Furthermore, a proven nexus exists between organized retail crime, cargo theft and terrorism (Kennedy).

Although arresting thieves is still a goal, many agencies, including the FBI, are now focusing on finding the source—the OC groups and their front businesses—as approximately half of all domestic cargo thefts are the result of OC. Certain nontraditional OC groups who engage in cargo theft, such as Cuban and South American (Ecuadorian, Peruvian, etc.) groups, operate nationwide and are fairly sophisticated (Kennedy). These groups typically work in cells or crews of three or four, occasionally more, and lack the typical hierarchy found in more traditional OC groups, such as La Cosa Nostra. The modes of operation (MOs) do not vary much by group, except for the Asian and street gangs in Southern California who tend to be quite violent and will use guns to conduct armed hijackings.

The Trucking Industry   Nearly everything we wear, eat and use at home or work has, at some point, been on the back of a truck. The amount of cargo crisscrossing our country is mind-boggling and critical to daily life. A large portion of cargo theft occurs from commercial truck stops. Thieves know that truck drivers usually cannot offload their cargo over a weekend; thus, drivers who stop on a Friday evening are likely to drop their trailer and take only the tractor for transportation until Monday morning. During that time, the unsupervised trailer is extremely vulnerable to theft (Bibb). Other times, thieves wait at truck stops and, knowing that many drivers simply leave their truck running for the few minutes it takes them to grab some food or use a restroom, get in and drive the entire rig away.

Not uncommon are drivers who are part of the theft crew itself. For example, South American crews operating along the east coast, primarily in New York and New Jersey, commit "leakage theft," where one member works as a truck driver, picks up a legitimate load from a marine terminal or distribution center and then diverts the cargo before delivery. The thieves enter the container or trailer, leaving the manifested seal intact, take out a portion of the load and then close the container. When the load is delivered, it appears to be short-shipped, that is, that the mistake was made by the shipper (Kennedy).

The cargoes most frequently stolen from trucks include clothing and textiles, electrical and electronic supplies and components, foods, tobacco and liquor, appliances, automotive and other vehicle parts and paper, plastic and rubber products.

 Security measures in the trucking industry include use of proprietary and contract guards in shipping, receiving and storage areas; access control systems and perimeter fencing and lighting; CCTV systems and alarms; and special security seals and alarms on trucks.

The seal system is adapted from that initiated by the railroads several years ago. Under this system a numbered metal band is used to seal the door. Careful records should be kept of all seals. It is a federal crime for a nonauthorized person to break the seal on any interstate shipment. Therefore, if a seal is broken, the FBI and local police should be called to investigate.

Because employee theft accounts for such a large percentage of loss, a system of accountability with proper documentation from the purchase order to invoice and receiving slip is necessary. Although truckers have no control over the issuing of such documentation, drivers are responsible for carefully checking shipments as they are loaded and unloaded.

Another safeguard for trucking security is the law requiring drug and alcohol testing of drivers, which requires that each year 50 percent of potential drivers be tested for controlled substances and 25 percent be tested for alcohol. All such tests are to be strictly random.

Railroad Security   The freight rail system comprises more than 500 freight railroads operating along 200,000 miles of track (Gips, 2005b, p.56). In addition, the Association of American Railroads (AAR) has identified 1,308 critical facilities such as key bridges, tunnels, dispatch centers and storage facilities. The AAR (p.57) also notes that railroads ship about 1.7 million carloads of hazardous materials and hazardous waste annually.

Railroad security is provided by the oldest, perhaps most highly organized segment of the private security industry, the railroad police. The country's 3,500 railroad police work closely with local, state and federal law enforcement agencies. Although the railroad police are paid with corporate funds, at least 40 states have given them broad police powers. In these states, the railroad police have a dual responsibility to the rail industry and the public.

The Police and Security Section of the AAR describes the basic objectives of the railroad police as protecting life and property; preventing and suppressing crime; investigating criminal acts committed on or against the railroad, patrons or employees; arresting criminal offenders; supervising conduct on railroad property; and performing certain nonpolice services such as accident and claims investigation and safety management.

The security problems faced by railroads are immense—theft, vandalism and, increasingly, the threat of terrorism. Total losses incurred by these crimes cost railroad carriers millions of dollars every year.

 The primary security problems of the railroad industry are cargo theft, vandalism and theft of metals.

Theft of railroad cargo may occur on any point along a quarter million miles of track. It is one of the most important concerns of the railroad police. The areas most vulnerable to theft are tool rooms or tool cribs, warehouses, loading docks, shipping and receiving areas and distribution centers. The deliberate derailment of Amtrak's Sunset Limited in the Arizona desert during the fall of 1995 illustrates the vulnerability to terrorism of our 110,425-mile national railway system.

Railroad spur lines are also highly vulnerable. Ideally, the area around railroad spurs should be fenced, locked and kept lit at night. Railroad cars should be unloaded immediately. If this is not possible, they should be sealed until they can be unloaded.

 Security measures used by railroads include patrol, surveillance, undercover operations, CCTV monitoring, locking devices and gate controls and seals.

Railroad police prevent and control crime and enhance security by using such security measures as radio-equipped foot and vehicle patrol, canine patrol, and fixed-wing aircraft and helicopter patrol; fixed-surveillance stakeouts; undercover operations; exchange of intelligence information with public law enforcement agencies; employee security-consciousness programs; criminal investigations aimed at prosecuting those found responsible for crimes against the railroads; task forces moving many railroad police officers into a specific problem area to perform a tactical mission; public relations and education programs aimed at community awareness and support of railroad police activities; and installation protection, including CCTV, electronic security and sophisticated locking devices, gate controls and seals.

Most railroad security administrators believe engineering improvements to cars and trailers would help prevent cargo theft and vandalism, including improved door construction of boxcars and trailers, container locking mechanisms, boxcar and trailer locking devices and cable seals. They also suggest that further research is needed in such areas as:

- Night lighting (portable and permanent) for operational surveillance
- Helicopter patrol for theft and vandalism surveillance
- Canine units for trailer terminals and rail yard patrol
- CCTV in trailer terminal operations
- Photographic methods for trailer terminal operations
- Sensor devices used on rail car and trailer shipments
- Use of computers for determining claim and theft patterns
- Use of screened rail cars to protect auto shipments from vandalism and theft

Shipping Security The greatest security threat facing ships on the high seas is piracy, which the United Nations Convention on the Law of the Sea defines as "violence on the high seas," where "high seas" are waters beyond any state's 12-nautical-mile territorial marine border. Koknar (2004, p.75) contends: "Piracy and terrorism are joining forces and creating troubled waters for the maritime industry." Piracy attacks are not only costly, but often they are also deadly. Such hijackings are usually carried out by sophisticated syndicates with money, equipment, weapons, planning, experience and contacts with corrupt political officials or terrorist connections. The "loot" per vessel ranges from $20,000 to $8 million (Koknar).

Indonesia, Singapore and Malaysia are the most pirate-infested zones in the world, accounting for more than a quarter of all attacks: "Local villagers along the coasts of Indonesia, Malaysia and Africa welcome pirate business and provide the perpetrators with food and shelter. In many countries in Southeast Asia, Latin America and Africa, coast guard operatives, corrupt drug agents and other law enforcement officials moonlight as pirates" (Koknar).

 Piracy, terrorism and maritime insurance fraud perpetrated by pirate crews are prime concerns of the shipping industry.

In response to the 9/11 terrorist attacks and the growing threat of global terrorism, the International Maritime Organization (IMO), a United Nations specialized agency responsible for the safety and security of shipping and the prevention of marine pollution by ships, developed an amendment to the 1974 Safety of Life at Sea (SOLAS) Convention aimed at improving security on ships and at ship-port interface areas. The new chapter, which includes the International Ship and Port Facility Security (ISPS) Code, took effect July 1, 2004, and applies to passenger ships and cargo vessels weighing 500 gross tonnage (GT) or more, including mobile offshore drilling units. The amendment also designated the position of ship security officer (SSO) as the party responsible for security issues and for creating and updating the vessel's formal security plan. According to the IMO Web site ("SOLAS Amendments and ISPS Code . . .," 2004): "The ISPS Code contains detailed security-related requirements for implementation by Governments, port authorities and shipping companies in a mandatory section (Part A), together with a series of guidelines about how to meet these requirements in a second, non-mandatory section (Part B). It is the first ever internationally agreed regulatory framework addressing the crucial issue of maritime security and represents the international maritime community's contribution to the global resistance against terrorism."

While many SSOs are not security professionals but rather existing ship officers taking on this additional responsibility, beginning in 2008, individuals posted in the capacity of an SSO will be required to show evidence of being "qualified" to hold that position. Numerous training courses have been developed worldwide to meet this mandate; an online search will reveal scores of facilities providing training for SSOs.

Seaport Security   Scott (2006) contends that ports have a gaping hole in their security—one so big you could ride a truck through it, which is exactly what he did—several times: "Simply by riding along with truck drivers coming to drop

© Ed Kashi/Corbis

U.S. Customs and Border Protection officers scan containers at the Port of New York and New Jersey by using a VACIS® (Vehicle and Cargo Inspection System). On an average day in the Port of New York and New Jersey about 4,000 shipping containers are lifted off freighters and released into the arteries of American commerce.

off and pick up cargo, this reporter easily penetrated the security of ports in Los Angeles–Long Beach and Seattle, two of the nation's largest port complexes." He cited numerous examples of how he had free access to several seaports, noting that most ports lease their docks to private companies who develop their own security plans, which are approved by the Coast Guard who has overall security responsibility for seaports. Under the Maritime Transportation and Safety Act (MTSA) of 2002, each U.S. port is required to have a security officer. This officer may be responsible for each individual terminal or for the entire port, depending on the size of the operation and approval from the Coast Guard (Anderson, 2006b, p.72).

The security challenge at seaports is daunting, with about 11 million containers arriving by sea each year. United States Customs and Border Protection officials inspect closely fewer than 10 percent of them: "Many security analysts believe the smuggling of a nuclear weapon into the United States through a seaport is a very real possibility. The country's 361 commercial ports, meanwhile, have gotten so little funding in the past five years that experts routinely call them the 'soft underbelly' of America" (Marek, 2007, p.29). In September 2006 Congress passed the SAFE Ports Act, mandating that DHS provide the 22 largest U.S. seaports with enough radiation detectors to scan all containers by 2008: "Most security experts cite the SAFE Ports as the most substantial piece of maritime legislation in years" (Marek, p.30).

Activity on port security has surged since February 2007, when public anxiety was fueled by a proposed $6.8 billion business deal that would have given a firm run by the government of the United Arab Emirates leases to operate terminals in six U.S. ports.

Studying Intermodal Cargo Screening   The DHS is using the Port of Tacoma, the seventh largest container port in North America, as a testing site to detect radiation on cargo that comes off ships and is dispersed via rail (**intermodal**) for traces of radiation to determine the best methods to protect the country from potentially dangerous incoming cargo (Edwards, 2007, p.13). More than 70 percent of Tacoma's cargo is intermodal, making it an ideal site to test the radiation scanning technology. If the testing is successful, DHS hopes to replicate the technology at other ports throughout the country.

An Example: Security at the San Diego Port   Anderson (2006b, p.76) describes the San Diego Port as compact, housing various users in a small space. The port authority manages three terminals—a cruise line terminal and two marine terminals that deal primarily in break-bulk cargo and automobiles. The facility security officer is responsible for overseeing the physical security required under MTSA, including vulnerability assessments for each terminal, developing security plans and installing needed equipment such as fences and access control systems. The security officer is also responsible for hiring and managing contract guards who patrol the terminals and screen cruise ship passengers. To guard the two shipping terminals from water attack, the port has a floating fence of linked oblong balloons with steel cables running through them, the equivalent of concrete bollars. They may look harmless but can destroy the propeller of any vessel that tries to breach them.

Security of Imports from Foreign Countries   The security of commercial shipments imported into the United States has been upgraded through the Customs-Trade Partnership against Terrorism (C-TPAT) Program, the core principle of which is to secure supply chains from factory to shop (Lo et al., 2006, p.66). This voluntary program was launched in July 2002 and requires participating companies to comply with minimum security requirements and undergo audits to ensure that these requirements have been implemented. The requirements cover container security, physical security and access control, as well as preemployment screening practices, documentation of cargo security procedures, IT security and training. A drawback to participation is that small to medium-sized enterprises often know little about the requirements and hesitate to join the program because of the cost. While large enterprises have trained security staff who can carry out the tasks required by C-TPAT, the cost of hiring and training security staff and installing the proper equipment is frequently prohibitive. However, the companies that do join benefit by reduced number of inspections at customs, with a "fast lane" given to C-TPAT members to move their cargo expeditiously into the United States (Lo et al.).

A study of the supply line risk in 45 countries found that many companies are not properly assessing or countering vulnerabilities: "Most of the companies studied would only be 50 percent compliant with C-TPAT; some would be as low as 10 percent" (Purtell and Rice, 2006, p.82). Several common security gaps were identified across the study group: "Most companies failed to conduct container security inspections; containers often arrived at the seaport with no seals; there were no background investigations on employees; and there was no security or threat awareness training for workers. Most companies had no idea what, if any, security procedures had been adopted by their business partners" (Purtell and Rice, pp.78–80). Figure 14.2 summarizes the cargo theft and C-TPAT exposure ratings of high-growth countries.

Country	Corruption index	Supply chain theft exposures	Weighted C-TPAT risk
Brazil, Russia, India, and China			
Brazil	3.7	**Severe**	Low
Russia	2.4	**Severe**	Low
India	2.9	**Elevated**	**Elevated**
China	3.2	Guarded	Low
Other notable growth countries			
South Africa	4.5	**Severe**	Guarded
Poland	3.4	**High**	Low
Turkey	3.5	**Elevated**	**High**
Indonesia	2.2	**Severe**	**Severe**
Thailand	3.8	Guarded	Guarded
Nigeria	1.9	**Severe**	**Severe**
Malaysia	2.2	**Severe**	**Severe**

Figure 14.2   Cargo Theft and C-TPAT Exposure Ratings

SOURCE: From *Assessing Cargo Supply Risk* by Dan Purtell and James B. Rice, Jr. Used by permission of First Advantage Corporation.

Surprisingly, Russia and Brazil, which were among two of the highest-risk countries in terms of supply chain theft, were given a "low" threat rating in terms of C-TPAT; China represented a similar situation (Purtell and Rice, p.82). The reason for this incongruity is that although terrorism has high consequences, it has low probability in these regions; the more common risk in the countries studied is theft from organized crime: "The study indicated that, within the global supply chain, a cookie-cutter approach to security has led companies to overspend in low-risk countries such as China and underspend in high-risk countries such as Malaysia and Indonesia" (Purtell and Rice).

Mass Transit Security

Millions of Americans depend on mass transit systems for transportation. Our public transit system developed at the beginning of the nineteenth century as the need for moving large numbers of people within congested major cities became apparent. The first mass transit systems were horse-drawn streetcars. They were eventually replaced by cable and electric cars, buses and finally the rapid transit systems of today, including such systems as New York's subway, Chicago's El and San Francisco's BART. The early transit systems were not immune from the crime problems of the congested urban environment in which they operated. By the early 1900s, thieves, vandals, roving gangs of youths and pickpockets caused several states to authorize transit companies to establish security forces, some with full police authority. As crime increased nationally, it also increased at comparable levels in transit systems. As a result, most transit systems have established full-time security forces with full or limited police powers.

Hull, director of operations, safety and security at the American Public Transportation Association, notes that security for public transportation is based on several factors, beginning with training employees and informing the public. Personnel must be trained to understand their roles and responsibilities, including knowing what to look for and what to do if an event occurs. Security also involves educating the public to be aware of what is happening around them. As far as procedures are concerned, according to Hull, all transit systems have security plans in place and regularly review and test them through drills and tabletop operations. On the technology side, CCTV has been used since the 1970s, but today's surveillance equipment is vastly improved, providing both security in the form of intrusion detection and support for day-to-day operation (Friedrick).

 The major security problems faced by mass transit systems are robberies and assaults of operators, passengers and fare collectors; rapes and murders and theft of vehicles or their contents in park-and-ride areas as well as the potential for a terrorist attack.

Figure 14.3 summarizes the methods of rail-related attacks, with mechanical sabotage being the most common method.

Such incidents occur most often in the mass transit systems located in or near high-crime areas. People are most often victimized while waiting for transit vehicles, especially on platforms and in the rapid transit stations. Crime also occurs at station entrances and exits, stairwells, ramps and tunnels, and on the

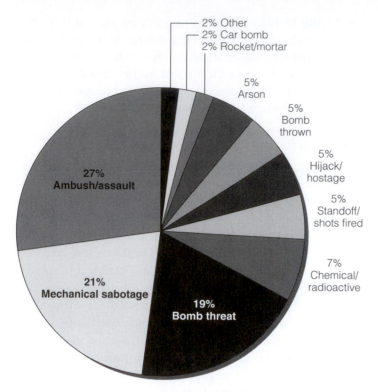

Figure 14.3 Methods of Rail-Related Attacks
SOURCE: Transportation Research Board.

vehicles themselves. A problem making rapid transit transportation unattractive to riders is the antisocial behavior of some riders—for example, drunkenness and the use of abusive conduct and language.

Roberts (2005, p.83) notes: "A multipronged approach that includes training programs, cutting-edge technology and K-9 units is the best way to secure mass transit. In today's energy-conscious society, a concerted national effort to promote use of rapid transit systems depends heavily on making such systems safe and attractive to the general public."

 Security measures for mass transit include security guards, CCTV in waiting areas and on vehicles, telephones and other emergency communications devices for riders, unbreakable glass as see-through barriers, high-intensity lighting and bomb-detection K-9s.

Installing such security equipment is expensive because of the large number of stations and vehicles in any given system, as well as the susceptibility of the equipment to vandalism. In addition, CCTV must be continuously monitored if it is to be effective, requiring more personnel than may be available.

One of the most advanced CCTV systems in the United States is being planned for the New York Metropolitan Transportation Authority (Roberts, p.88). The system, installed and monitored by Lockheed Martin, is part of a three-year, $212 million expansion that includes installing more than 1,000 cameras and more than 3,000 motion detectors and other sensors.

Hull contends that despite its high visibility and threats against it, public transportation lags behind aviation when it comes to funding. Although 16 times the number of travelers use publicly funded transit such as buses, light rail subways and commuter rail compared to domestic aircraft in the United States, the amount allocated to protecting public transportation is a fraction of what air travel has received—$500 million versus $20 billion (Friedrick).

Airport and Airline Security

The events of 9/11 forever changed the way we approach air travel. Despite this undeniable wake-up call regarding the gaping holes in aviation security, some contend we are still neglecting to consider the big picture regarding potential threats: "Over the years we have adopted a layered approach to aviation security. But all of our efforts are based on the assumption that the target is the aircraft. Given today's new threat model, where the explosion is the statement, attackers do not need to reach the aircraft to achieve their objective" (Raffel, 2007, p.58).

Skyjackings of commercial aircraft, bombings, bomb threats and extortion attempts involving aircraft and hostages have made the need for airport and airline security obvious. Terrorist groups have increasingly used such means to advance their causes, making some people afraid to travel by air because of these perceived dangers. Bomb threats can result in air traffic delays and in evacuation of entire sections of a terminal. Actual explosions result in extensive property damage, serious injuries and, often, deaths.

 Security problems of airports and airlines include skyjackings; bombs and bomb threats; air cargo theft; theft of passenger baggage, airline tickets, credit cards, merchandise from airport retail shops and items from vehicles in parking lots; crowd control; VIP escorts; traffic control; and the potential for large-scale disasters.

By 1972 the increasing frequency of skyjackings and bomb threats prompted the Federal Aviation Authority (FAA) to require certain security measures. The FAA requires:

- Screening of all persons and carry-on baggage before entering an airport's departure area
- The availability of a sworn law enforcement officer at the screening point within three to five minutes
- Development by both scheduled airline carriers and airport managers of security programs for FAA approval
- Development of an airport disaster plan

After 9/11 a new set of rules were implemented that experts have been recommending for decades, including requiring more stringent employee background checks and training as well as mandating that all checked baggage be scanned by sophisticated bomb scanning devices by 2014. Other security measures include banning curbside check-in or parking, forbidding nontravelers from accompanying passengers to the gate, having security personnel check all planes before passengers board, conducting random searches of flight crews and equipment, and prohibiting transporting cargo or mail on passenger jets.

Although skyjackings and bombings receive the most publicity, other serious security problems exist throughout our nation's vast network of 100 airports, a system through which 670 million passengers pass annually (Eisenberg, 2004). Losses from air cargo theft are estimated to be in excess of $100 million annually and are especially serious at the airports infiltrated by organized crime. Air cargo is different from other types of cargo because most is coordinated with passenger schedules. Also much air cargo is small and highly valuable, making it especially vulnerable to theft. In addition, because of the great number of people using airports, the maintenance of order and crowd control, VIP escorts and traffic control must be provided by airline and airport security personnel.

The responsibility for screening passengers and baggage rests with the air carriers. In most major airports, this is done by a contract security firm with a sworn law enforcement officer within minutes of the screening point to apprehend anyone who makes threats or tries to carry a dangerous weapon into the departure area. Although employees of contract security firms usually conduct the passenger checks, they maintain close cooperation with law enforcement agencies and airline and airport security personnel. Overall airport security is usually provided by law enforcement officers.

Becker (2005, p.38) recommends: "Older, proven technology with new state-of-the-art features and IP components is the answer to video security requirements." Intelligent video surveillance, a powerful, economical tool to enhance perimeter security at airports across the country, is able to run all objects in a camera's field of view against threat-specific, preprogrammed rules. If an object violates a rule, for example, a suspicious unattended bag, the software alerts security personnel by phone, pager or e-mail or by a display on a console. False alarms are almost totally eliminated (Baltazar, 2004, p.24).

Airports nationwide are training personnel of all types, from parking attendants to flight attendants, on behavioral detection method to help spot suspicious conduct by passengers. Personnel are given about four hours of training to help them know what to look for and where to report suspicious people or behavior. They are encouraged to report such observations and are assured they will not be criticized if their observations are wrong: "The crux of the program is that terrorists are human and give their motives away via stress-induced behavior. Often they are first-timers with no prior record of illicit activity, and they are aware that they will probably lose their lives in the attack" (Elliott, 2006, p.34). In addition, people concealing something on their body have distinct behavioral differences reflected in how they dress or walk.

Research being conducted on airport baggage screeners has found that screeners can spot specific items better if they see them frequently and that they are most effective when they search for a single type of threat such as guns or explosives, in contrast to searching for multiple threats at once (Straw, 2007b, p.26). The study suggests that, when feasible, different screeners should be looking for different items.

One major problem with providing more effective security at airports is the cost. An inherent conflict of interest exists between passenger security and the airline's interests, which an industry expert calls "the dirty little secret of aviation," namely, that profit-driven airlines are largely responsible for passenger safety, but the more airlines spend on security, the less profitable they become (Eisenberg). However, this same conflict can be seen in most profit-oriented businesses and organizations.

Screening of Passengers and Privacy Issues   The TSA is responsible for establishing the rules for screening passengers. The first such attempt was the Computer Assisted Passenger Prescreening System (CAPPS I), a system based on static rules against which passenger activities were checked, for example, buying a one-way ticket or paying in cash. It also flagged passengers whose names were similar to those of known terrorists. Its replacement, CAPPS II, is designed to assess and categorize passengers according to the risk they may pose and is based on identity verification. Efforts to work out the kinks of the latest passenger screening proposal seem "mired in the battle between privacy and security" (Gips, 2004, p.63).

A major concern of civil libertarians is **mission creep**, the fear that TSA will use the program for more than airline passenger profiling, extending to such venues as railroad stations and bus terminals. As one opponent stated: "It is no exaggeration to say that CAPPS II may represent the first step towards pervasive internal border controls that would subject all citizens to invasive government scrutiny every time they attempted to travel" (Gips, 2004, p.71).

Security at General Aviation Airports   Straw (2007c, p.28) also suggests: "The degree of risk posed by general aviation is set to increase in the coming years with the emergence of very light jets (VLJs)." For example, one manufacturer of a six-passenger jet received 2,500 orders last year. These small jets fly faster than their propeller-driven counterparts, the latter cruising at about 123 mph, while the former cruises between 400 and 610 mph (Straw, p.30). Anyone wanting to fly a VLJ into a building would give military jets much less time to get airborne and intercept it; a helicopter could not catch up.

In 2004 the TSA issued guidelines for general aviation airport security, recommending use of fencing, lighting, locks, alarms and signage, with measures and procedures scaled on the basis of current threat level and the airport's proximity to sensitive sites. However, their guidelines are voluntary.

SUMMARY

- Industrial/manufacturing losses frequently include tools, materials, products, pallets, hand trucks, valuable scrap, uniforms, side-products, time and vital information.

- Tool loss can be reduced by having a tool room or tool crib with an attendant, a check-in/check-out procedure, distinctive markings on the tools, periodic inspections and inventories, metal detectors at gates and possibly a system for lending tools for personal use after hours.

- Two special concerns of industry/manufacturing are sabotage and espionage.

- Threats to the U.S. food supply include disgruntled employees, hoaxes to elicit financial settlements, terrorists, criminals and subversives. The greatest challenge is detecting contamination.

- The Responsible Care® Security Code sets forth security measures to be taken at chemical plants.

- Overseas challenges for U.S.-based oil companies include corruption, political unrest and piracy. Domestic challenges include the regulatory environment, protecting against terrorist threats and tight budgets.

- Primary problems at utility companies include loss of stored items, trespassers and vandals at substations and distribution centers, security at construction sites, plans for emergencies and detection of resource diversion. A utility company's losses can be reduced by careful access controls to tools and supplies, careful check-in/check-out procedures, alarms and surveillance cameras at substations and establishment of emergency plans.

- Security measures in the trucking industry include use of proprietary and contract guards in shipping, receiving and storage areas; access control systems and perimeter fencing and lighting; CCTV systems and alarms; and special security seals and alarms on trucks.

- The primary security problems of the railroad industry are cargo theft, vandalism and theft of metals. Security measures used by railroads include patrol, surveillance, undercover operations, CCTV monitoring, locking devices and gate controls and seals.

- Piracy, terrorism and maritime insurance fraud perpetrated by pirate crews are prime concerns of the shipping industry.

- The major security problems faced by mass transit systems are robberies and assaults of operators, passengers and fare collectors; rapes and murders and theft of vehicles or their contents in park-and-ride areas as well as the potential for a terrorist attack. Security measures for mass transit include security guards, CCTV in waiting areas and on vehicles, telephones and other emergency communications devices for riders, unbreakable glass as see-through barriers, high-intensity lighting and bomb-detection K-9s.

- Security problems of airports and airlines include skyjackings; bombs and bomb threats; air cargo theft; theft of passenger baggage, airline tickets, credit cards, merchandise from airport retail shops and items from vehicles in parking lots; crowd control; VIP escorts; traffic control and the potential for large-scale disasters.

APPLICATION

As security director of a manufacturing company, you suspect a case of industrial espionage is occurring as your competitor always seems to have the jump on new developments that originate within your company. What steps would you take to investigate this suspicion? If the charge was well founded, what steps would you take? What resources would you use?

DISCUSSION QUESTIONS

1. What are some preventive measures a security director might apply to guard against espionage in a computer manufacturing company?

2. Name several effective ways to protect vital documents and records from destruction or theft.

3. What are some reasons employees engage in sabotage?

4. Which types of security discussed in this chapter seem most important to you? Why?

5. What features of your community's infrastructure are most vulnerable to terrorism? What, if anything, has been changed or implemented since 9/11 to address this vulnerability?

REFERENCES

Anderson, Teresa. "Containing Cargo Risk." *Security Management*, September 2005, pp.60–73.

Anderson, Teresa. "Digital Cameras Protect a Local Utility." *Security Management*, December 2006a, pp.34–36.

Anderson, Teresa. "Holding the Line." *Security Management*, September 2006b, pp.64–76.

Baltazar, Melchoir. "Smarter Software: The First Line of Defense." *Security Products*, December 2004, pp.24–25.

Becker, John. "Airports Look to Hybrid Video System." *Security Products*, January 2005, pp.38–39.

Bibb, Thomas. Marion County [Florida] Sheriff's Office, Interviewed August 11, 2005.

Burroughs, Chris. "Sandia Researchers Develop Contaminant Warning Program for EPA to Monitor Water Systems." Albuquerque, NM: Sandia National Laboratories Press Release, October 10, 2006.

Callahan, Joe. "Cargo Theft Will Get National Attention With Summit." *Ocala Star-Banner*, February 18, 2008. Online: http://www.ocala.com/article/20080212/NEWS/802120334/1025/NEWS .Accessed March 19, 2008.

"Cargo Theft Interdiction Program." California Highway Patrol Web site: http://www.chp.ca.gov/html/vtask.html. Accessed July 29, 2005.

"Commercial Motor Vehicle and Cargo Theft." Florida Department of Transportation Web site: http://www.dot.state.fl.us/mcco/cmv_cargo_theft.htm. Accessed July 29, 2005.

Crocker, Michael. "Platforms, Pipelines and Pirates." *Security Management*, June 2007, pp.77–86.

Daniels, Rhianna. "Rules on Tap for Water Utilities." *Security Director News*, February 2007, pp.1, 19.

Durbin, Marty. "Ensuring the Protection of the Nation's Chemical Sector." *Security Technology & Design*, April 2005, p.53.

Durstenfeld, Bob. "Public Utilities at Risk." *Security Products*, April 2005, pp.16–17.

Edwards, Al. "It's Test Time for Tacoma." *Security Director News*, July 2007, pp.13, 15.

Eisenberg, Daniel. "How Safe Can We Get? *Time, Inc.*, 2004.

Elliott, Robert. "Assessing Threats from Passengers." *Security Management*, September 2006, pp.32–40.

Elliott, Robert. "Crude Oil and Corruption." *Security Management*, June 2007, pp.67–74.

Evenson, Jon. "The Emerging Role of the Industrial Safety/Security Manager." *Security Technology & Design*, June 2004, pp.44–48.

Freeman, Joseph P. "The Case of the Barn Door." *Security Technology & Design*, March 2005, p.20.

Friedrick, Joanne. "On the Move: Transportation Security Takes Off." *Security Director News*, April 2006, p.25.

Gips, Michael A. "Passenger Screening in No-Fly Zone?" *Security Management*, June 2004, pp.63–72.

Gips, Michael A. "Survey Assesses Vital Services." *Security Management*, November 2005a, pp.91–99.

Gips, Michael A. "Tough Track for Railroads." *Security Management*, January 2005b, pp.56–66.

Gips, Michael A. "Cargo Security Getting Some Respect." *Security Management*, July 2006a, p.28.

Gips, Michael A. "Plants Find Right Security Chemistry." *Security Management*, August 2006b, p.26.

Goldsmith, Michael. "Awash in Risk." *Security Management*, April 2004, pp.103–106.

Harowitz, Sherry L. "Food Safety on the Back Burner." *Security Management*, April 2007, p.14.

Harwood, Matt. "New Chemical Solutions." *Security Management*, August 2007, pp.82–89.

Hsu, Spencer S. "U.S. Announces New Chemical Plant Security Rules." *Washington Post*, April 3, 2007, p.A10.

Jensen, Ralph C. "Securing Drinking Water." *Security Products*, February 2004, p.6.

Kellogg, Dorothy and McGloon, Kate. "Distilled Protection." *Security Management*, October 2005, pp.94–100.

Kennedy, Tim. Former security expert for New York Harbor and Target Corp., e-mail correspondence, August 3–4, 2005.

Koknar, Ali M. "Terror on the High Seas." *Security Management*, June 2004, pp.75–81.

Lo, Victor H.Y.; Szato, Matthew; Wong, William S.K.; and Kumaraswamy, Mohan. "Why the Weak Links?" *Security Management*, May 2006, pp.63–67.

Marek, Augia C. "Closing the Door at the Ports." *U.S. News & World Report*, January 8, 2007, pp.29–30.

Martinez, Liz. "Getting It in Gear." *Security Technology & Design*, September 2005, pp.74–76.

National Infrastructure Protection Plan. Washington, DC: Department of Homeland Security, 2006.

The National Strategy for the Physical Protection of Critical Infrastructures and Key Assets. Washington, DC: Department of Justice, February 2003.

Preventing Toxic Terrorism. Center for American Progress, April 24, 2006.

Purtell, Dan and Rice, James B., Jr. "Assessing Cargo Supply Risk." *Security Management*, November 2006, pp.78–87.

Raffel, Bob. "Suicide Bombers at the Gate." *Security Management*, October 2007, pp.54–60.

Roberts, Marta. "Keeping Mass Transit Ahead of the Curve." *Security Management*, November 2005, pp.83–89.

Rogers, King; Guffey, Ben; and Markle, Anne. "The Retail Loss Prevention Tool Bag." *Security Technology & Design*, February 2005, pp. 22–26.

Scott, Alwyn. "Piercing Port Security Easy as Hitching a Ride." *The Seattle Times*, July 25, 2006.

"SOLAS Amendments and ISPS Code Enter into Force on 1 July 2004." International Maritime Organization (IMO), June 30, 2004. Web site: http://www.imo.org/Circulars/mainframe.asp?topic_id=848&doc_id=3692. Accessed March 19, 2008.

Sorrells, Eddie. "Recipe for Food Safety." *Security Management*, August 2006, pp.98–107.

Straw, Joseph. "How Safe Is the Food Supply?" *Security Management*, April 2007a, pp.64–73.

Straw, Joseph. "Spotting IEDs Amid the IPods." *Security Management*, April 2007b, pp.26–27.

Straw, Joseph. "Very Light Jets: A Very Real Threat?" *Security Management*, March 2007c, pp.28–35.

Terrorism and the Chemical Infrastructure: Protecting People and Reducing Vulnerabilities. National Academy of Science, 2006.

Zunkel, Dick. "Protecting Our Water." *Security Technology & Design*, October 2004, pp.46–49.

Zunkel, Dick. "Protecting the Chemical Plant." *Security Technology & Design*, April 2005, pp.48–54.

Institutional Security

The potential for an armed robbery is ever present in financial institutions and other places where large sums of cash are on the premises. In this photo provided by the Little Rock Police Department, an unidentified man is seen wielding a gun inside a bank in Little Rock, Arkansas. A teller was shot dead during the robbery, and the suspect escaped with some money.

DO YOU KNOW . . .

- What security concerns exist at libraries? Museums and art galleries? Religious facilities? Financial institutions? Hospitals and healthcare facilities? Educational facilities?
- What the major losses in libraries are and how these losses might be reduced?
- What inherent conflict of interest exists between museum archivists and curators?
- What security measures can be taken at religious facilities to reduce risk and loss?
- What three areas financial institutions should consider to pass the IT exam?
- What the most frequent losses of financial institutions are?
- What conflicting needs hospitals and healthcare facilities face?
- How hospitals can mitigate their security concerns?
- What the most high-risk areas in a hospital are?
- What risks in long-term healthcare facilities are?
- What the primary means to reduce security problems in educational institutions are?
- What poses the greatest challenge in most institutions of higher education?

CAN YOU DEFINE?

ARTCENTRAL	critical wandering	INTERPOL	zero tolerance
bait money	foxing marks	photogrammetry	

Introduction

Most institutions discussed in this chapter are considered "open to the public." Because of this, they pose special challenges. Of course, these public places should follow the basic lines of defense against internal and external crime and against threats to safety that apply to most facilities. It is assumed that a facility's physical vulnerability has been minimized by adequate lighting, fencing, locks and alarms as appropriate and that basic procedural security controls have been established to minimize risk. Our country's institutions are now making use of private security concepts, equipment, procedures and personnel on an ever-increasing scale. Many facilities use the "twin force multipliers of training and technology to leverage the effectiveness of their uniformed security officers" (Potter, 2005, p.36).

Each institution has its own unique security concerns and challenges. This chapter focuses on institutions that may require special security including libraries, museums and art galleries, religious facilities, financial institutions, hospitals and other healthcare facilities, and educational institutions.

Libraries

Public and private libraries' unique, intrinsically valuable and irreplaceable archival collections of documents, referred to as special collections, are differentiated from the general circulating items in the library for security purposes (Schroeder, 2004, p.55). Books and manuscripts in the special collections should be carefully documented, making sure that any and all distinguishing features are recorded, including **foxing marks** (water or mold damage to pages), font or print oddities (e.g., a page printed off center) or any duplicated or missing pages. Usually valuable books and periodicals are kept in closed stacks, and their use is restricted and closely supervised. Libraries frequently use security personnel to deter disorderly behavior and vandalism during the hours they are open and to provide fire and security protection after hours.

Security Concerns

 The primary security concerns at libraries are theft of or damage to books, CDs and videos; disorderly behavior; and fire.

Motivations for archival collection theft is often the same as for other forms of theft—monetary gain (Schroeder, p.56). Sometimes thieves steal "on demand" for items desired by a specific individual. Some thieves want to embarrass the institution or point out problems in security. In other cases the theft is simply a crime of opportunity.

Although many libraries concentrate security efforts on theft, they should also be concerned about the threat of fire. Consider the destruction caused to Germany's Herzopin Anna Amalia Library, a sixteenth-century Renaissance structure, when fire broke out and flames threatened the shelves and walls crammed with priceless literature, musical composition and artworks. The heat reached 1,000 degrees Celsius (1,832 degrees Fahrenheit) in the topmost part of the building. Fire hoses fed off a supply pumped from the river behind the library: "While more than 300 firemen battled the blaze with the aid of 30 trucks, about 400 librarians, restoration specialists and local civilians formed a human chain and passed books and artworks hand-to-hand down three levels to a subterranean passageway leading to a newly built annex. The intrepid volunteers managed to salvage about 6,000 historical works, including a 1534 Bible belonging to Martin Luther. But by the time the two-hour fire was put out, about 50,000 books were torched and another 62,000 had been badly damaged by the flames, and by the more than 300,000 liters of water launched into the blaze. All together about one-tenth of the library's collection was incinerated, and more than 60 million euros of damage had been done" (Elliot, 2007, p.72).

Since that disaster, the library has taken steps to protect its contents, installing a state of the art fire suppression and detection system. The system features a misting unit because of its ability to put out blazes while inflicting minimal water damage on irreplaceable collections: "Other facets of the fire system include a smoke detection and aspiration system, emergency exit lights, rescue doors, a new elevator and rebuilt firewalls. In addition, within the stairwells of every floor is a dry uptake with an 80-millimeter diameter and connections for fire hoses" (Elliott, p.76).

Security Measures to Reduce Risk and Loss

 Library losses can be reduced by the electronic marking of books, by providing photocopy equipment and by having security personnel supervise the facility.

Using electronic markings on books and detection sensors at main exits can significantly reduce book theft. Book mutilation can be minimized by providing photocopying machines so material can be reproduced rather than torn from the books or periodicals. However, all reproductions should be done by library staff as books can be damaged if copied improperly. Some libraries have also instituted an annual or semiannual "amnesty" period during which overdue books can be returned without a fine.

Good record-keeping is another important preventive measure, as is keeping strict control over reading rooms and research areas. Credentials of those seeking entrance should be carefully checked. For example, Stephen Blumberg—a high-school graduate with no academic credentials and a history of mental illness—used a stolen identification card identifying him as a professor at the University of Minnesota to gain unrestricted access to some of the university's most valuable collections. Library security officials' failure to verify Blumberg's credentials led to his being able to steal more than $20 million worth of rare books and manuscripts from more than 140 universities in 45 states and Canada. He was eventually captured and convicted.

To avoid such embarrassing security breaches, the Folger Shakespeare Library in Washington, DC, limits access to the special collections to those with a PhD or equivalent degree or to graduate students writing a PhD thesis. Prospective researchers must apply for a reader's card by writing a letter of application and supplying two letters of reference (Schroeder, p.56).[1]

Another security measure adopted at many libraries is to restrict the size and type of notepads and notebooks that can be brought in, to require only pencils be used (no pens) and to limit readers on the number of items they have available at any one time. The more items lying on a table, the greater the probability that an item may be stolen or damaged.

Security personnel should also be aware of the methods thieves use to remove pages from books to sell. They may use a small tool that can be easily smuggled into a research space, such as a small metal or plastic ruler or an X-Acto knife. Using the "wet string" method, thieves soak a foot-long piece of cotton twine in the mouth and then place the twine inside a book to dampen the page's edge. Once damp, the page is easily broken from the book (Schroeder).

The ideal situation to prevent thieves from stealing pages or entire books is to have a staff member present at all times when people are using the research areas. Motivated, educated security personnel are critical in preventing damage to or theft of books. If security personnel cannot be continuously present, strategically placed CCTV cameras can supplement security. The challenge to security staff is to protect libraries' special collections from damage and theft while simultaneously allowing access to them by qualified individuals. They are also responsible for ensuring the library is secure after hours through implementation of locks, motion-activated CCTV cameras, alarms and, if feasible, an around-the-clock security force.

Many of the security issues faced by libraries, and their approaches to them, are the same as those at museums and art galleries.

---

[1]SOURCE: From "Special Protection for Special Collections" by Margaret Schroeder. © 2004 ASIS International, 1625 Prince Street, Alexandria, VA 22314. Reprinted by permission from the July 2004 issue of *Security Management* magazine.

Museums and Art Galleries

Ensuring that the material is accessible for those who need to consult it and keeping it safe are difficult objectives to reconcile. It has been said that museum registrars or archivists—whose primary job is chronicling and preserving the collections—would prefer to catalogue, preserve or stabilize the items, and then store away the material, never to be touched again. Conversely, the museum curator or circulation manager—whose primary job is circulating and making material available for public consumption—might relish the idea of having the object seen or used by as many people as possible. (Schroeder, p.55)

An inherent conflict of interest exists between museum archivists, who seek to preserve and store materials, and curators, who seek to make materials accessible to the public.

Security Concerns

Criminal problems most frequently encountered by museums and art galleries are theft of collection pieces and the inadvertent purchase of works of art fraudulently presented as authentic or that have been stolen. Museums also experience order-maintenance and vandalism problems, but the trend toward charging admission fees has reduced these problems.

Major security concerns of museums and art galleries include theft, fraud, vandalism and arson.

Many objects in museums are priceless and irreplaceable. Most frequently stolen are small items that can be easily concealed and sold for cash. Such items are often stolen while the museum is open to the public, but more valuable items are generally stolen at night. Sometimes precious metals and gems are removed from artifacts, reset and then sold. The primary areas of concern are vaults, reserve collections, study collections and public exhibition sections.

Motivations for stealing museum pieces are similar to those for theft from a library's special collection of books—selling for a profit or a personal desire for the object. In some rare instances an item is stolen for political purposes such as the theft of Edvard Munch's painting *The Scream*, which was stolen from the Oslo museum and held for ransom by an antiabortion group. In other instances, thieves want to embarrass an institution by showing defects in their security. For example, when thieves stole items from the Whitworth Art Gallery in the United Kingdom, the items were recovered safely a few days later next to a note stating the theft was done "to highlight the woeful security at your institution."

Art theft is an underground business driven by common criminals who walk into institutions in broad daylight and steal (Ozernoy, 2005, pp.42–43). Much of what is stolen is damaged or destroyed by the amateur thief, and in the United States only about 5 percent is ever recovered: "The rest—stolen paintings and icons, looted antiquities, and rare books—is a $4 billion to $6 billion industry estimated to be the third-largest black market in the world, after illegal drugs and illicit arms" (Ozernoy).

The biggest art heist to date in America happened March 18, 1990, when two thieves masquerading as police officers were ushered into Boston's Isabella Stewart Gardner Museum by a sleepy security guard on night duty. The thieves overpowered the museum's two guards, handcuffed them and then spent the next hour and a half stealing art valued at, at minimum, $300 million, including works by Rembrandt, Vermeer and Degas (Ozernoy, p.43).

Most people recall accounts of the vast looting that occurred in Iraq after U.S. troops entered Baghdad, with the Iraqi National Archeological Museum in Baghdad being overrun by both professional art thieves and local looters (Longmore-Etheridge and Faulk, 2004, p.80). Due to the cooperation of many international agencies, about 6,000 stolen artifacts have been recovered, and an amnesty program and tips by locals have netted more. However, some of the recovered artifacts were badly damaged.

Experts brought in to make security recommendations suggested intrusion detection, access control, fire suppression, smoke detection and a backbone for a small CCTV system to cover key interior and exterior locations. It was suggested that sound policies and procedures were more important than technology, implementing physical security and breaking the inertia of the psychologically traumatized staff. Inside buildings, all doors had to be replaced with solid core or metal doors with new locks. Display cases were rekeyed and had Plexiglas installed. Armed security guards were hired for additional protection.

Public exhibition sections are particularly vulnerable if a controversial exhibit is on display. Special security consideration must be given to displays having the potential to incite political or religious extremists.

Although theft is the marquee threat museums protect against, it is not the top menace many face. Fire and natural disasters often are more destructive in their impact, which may be large scale and irreversible (Keller, 2006, p.75). Stolen relics and artwork may be retrieved, but items destroyed are lost forever. Nonetheless, architects and museum directors often ignore natural disasters when planning their institutions. For example, many museums are built with insufficiently protective materials in areas prone to earthquakes, tornadoes, hurricanes and floods.

Museums that have proactively dealt with their locations in areas prone to natural disasters are the J. Paul Getty Museums in Malibu and Los Angeles, situated in the middle of earthquake and mudslide zones. In a technique currently used across the country, museum management has devised realistic drills and routinely practices them to keep employees trained on how to respond to natural disasters: "Proper planning, adequate use of technology, intelligent design and well-allocated resources give museums a fighting chance when disaster strikes" (Keller, p.76).

Traveling Exhibits   Exhibits that travel from museum to museum present additional security challenges: "Traveling exhibits have a range of security requirements that the hosting museum's security plans must accommodate. A thorough threat assessment must be taken of the host museum to determining the likelihood of theft and damage. A standard report designed by the American Association of Museums details everything about the museum, including size, age, fire protection equipment and security equipment. Once the report is received by the host museum, a panel of experts, including engineers, security experts and technicians reviews the document" (Turk, 2005, p.42).

Chapter 15: Institutional Security

In addition to protecting museum and gallery pieces while they are on display, security officers often play a role in ensuring the safe movement of pieces to and from the institution. Here security guards use video cameras to document the removal of art from Salander-O'Reilly Galleries in New York in October 2007.

For example, when the Einstein papers were to be put on display at the American Museum of Natural History in Michigan, a custom-made high-security case was constructed with built-in alarms for environmental conditions and theft. The case was designed to provide maximize visibility for viewers while protecting the pages from harsh light, humidity and accidental spills of liquids (Turk, p.40).

Security Measures to Reduce Risk and Loss

Museums and galleries can reduce losses by:

- Establishing a basic security system, including locks, alarms and security officers at stations and on patrol
- Maintaining detailed inventories
- Having each object professionally appraised and authenticated
- Positively identifying and registering each item

Most exhibits are rated as low-, medium- or high-risk, which determines the level of security needed: "A low-security exhibit, such as photographs that are reprints of the originals, may be sufficiently protected by roving patrols and CCTV cameras. High-level exhibits, however, require much more intensive and complicated security that often includes round-the-clock guards, sophisticated alarms systems, specialized exhibit enclosures and CCTV surveillance" (Turk, p.42).

ARTCENTRAL has been developed in New York by the International Association of Art Security, an organization that registers works of art using computer-oriented **photogrammetry**, a process comparable to fingerprinting. Photogrammetry provides a permanent, exact identification of works of art that is impossible to duplicate. This system is a deterrent to theft because the stolen objects are less marketable. It also greatly aids in recovery of stolen objects and their return to the rightful owner.

ARTCENTRAL's photogrammetry technology can identify two-dimensional works such as paintings, lithographs, wall hangings and tapestries, as well as three-dimensional works such as artifacts, antiques, silverware, porcelains and sculptures. All identified works are visibly and invisibly labeled, indicating that they are on file with **INTERPOL** (International Criminal Police Organization). A central file is located in New York, another at INTERPOL and a third at a secret, heavily guarded location. If a work registered with ARTCENTRAL is stolen, the theft is reported to INTERPOL, which in turn notifies state and local authorities as well as the FBI because it is assumed that interstate transportation of stolen goods will be involved. The FBI has established an Art Crime Team, a group of eight agents working in major art markets around the country supported by two assistant U.S. attorneys and several FBI analysts (*Art Theft Program*, 2005).

ARTCENTRAL is also available to individuals and to corporations. It is important for security directors of businesses and corporations to be aware of this because many corporations are now acquiring art collections. Security managers at these businesses may need to become familiar with the procedures for safeguarding artwork, including access control, CCTV and security patrols. Loss prevention is vital because once an art treasure is stolen, the chance of recovery is less than 5 percent.

An Example: Security at the Virginia Museum of Military Vehicles

The security system at the Virginia Museum of Military Vehicles (VMMV) is very elaborate and very apparent (Elliott, 2006, p.40). Fire is the greatest threat to the museum, as its buildings are constructed of wood, concrete block and steel. The buildings also house paint shops containing highly flammable materials. In addition, the collection itself, the largest in the country, adds to the fire risk because the vehicles are not just on display, but are regularly operated for private shows, movies and the like.

The system selected allows around-the-clock, off-site monitoring of the tucked away museum with its multiple warehouses. The system has 15 heat sensors, about 20 motion detectors, about 15 contact sensors covering the roll-up and boule-hinge doors and a handful of glass detectors for the complex's few windows. Motion detectors are in the hallways and in every bay area. In addition, there are two thermostats, seven cameras split between the two large buildings and aimed at entrances and the main areas, and cables to connect the sensing devices to the device interface units. Finally, software provides users with a graphical interface: "Everything, whether tied to fire or intrusion and regardless of which building it is in, feeds back to one central control room" (Elliott, 2006, p.40).

Religious Facilities

Religious institutions are no longer off-limits to criminals. The problem has become sufficiently widespread that few churches can leave their doors open, as was common in days past.

Security Concerns

Churches, synagogues, temples and other places of worship are in need of security. Historically, the church was considered relatively immune from criminal actions because of its special status in the community. Such is no longer the case. To hard-core criminals and even to many juvenile delinquents, the church has no special status. In fact, as businesses and private homes tighten their security, churches are perceived as an easy mark.

 Security concerns faced by religious institutions include the desire for easy accessibility at all times, their attractiveness to indigents and mental patients and the individuals included in their social outreach programs.

Many churches still pride themselves on being there for people 24 hours a day, seven days a week, including all holidays. Many churches have valuable religious relics, statues, money boxes and the like completely unprotected in their sanctuaries. Religious institutions may also be targets for hate crimes.

Numerous individuals from the disadvantaged segments of society are attracted by the religious institutions' social outreach programs—for example, soup lines, shelters for the homeless and food and clothing distribution outlets. Some of those seeking help may be mentally unbalanced or even violent, and it is not uncommon for those with criminal pasts to encounter such programs.

Another security challenge presents itself when religious institutions open their doors for use by outside groups, either free of charge or for a fee. The religious institution seldom has control over what these groups do within its facility.

Security Measures to Reduce Risk and Loss

Because religious institutions vary so greatly in size, basic philosophy regarding security measures and actual vulnerability, no one security system is applicable to all. Nonetheless, most might benefit from certain commonsense procedures.

 Security measures for religious institutions include perimeter protection, including lighting and fencing; safeguarding of valuables by such means as lighting, locks and alarms; and contingency plans for handling disruptive individuals.

If cemeteries are being vandalized, security measures might include improved lighting and decorative fencing, particularly protecting any historically significant graves.

An additional area of concern is to take precautions when money is being collected at special events, concerts, fundraisers and the like. Purse-snatchers and pickpockets may also be in attendance.

Financial Institutions

Financial institutions are highly attractive to robbers, burglars, embezzlers and other types of thieves. In addition, enormous losses are incurred yearly through fraudulent use of credit cards and checks. Added to these losses are an estimated $40 million in stock certificates and $25 million in government bonds that are lost or stolen annually: "Today's bank security directors have more on their minds than robbers, forgers—like terrorists and cyber thieves" (Friedrick, 2005a, p.19).

Government Regulations

Enhanced security measure requirements and new laws created to combat terrorism and fraudulent activities have forced financial institutions to devote unprecedented levels of resources to their compliance processes: "With fines of up to a million dollars for transactions that violate the Bank Secrecy Act (BSA), and several highly publicized incidents where a bank was fined tens of millions of dollars for violating provisions of the USA PATRIOT Act, pressure to meet federal requirements is intense, and regulatory scrutiny and enforcement are at all-time highs" ("Technology Eases Compliance Burden," 2006, p.3).

Security professionals need to be familiar with the Sarbanes-Oxley Act, which came into force in July 2002 and introduced major changes in regulating corporate governance and financial practice. In many respects security underpins the requirements of the act. It is important therefore to establish a credible, detailed security policy. In addition, examiners will want to see a business contingency plan that includes details on how the bank will respond to a disaster.

Johnston and Piazza (2005, p.84) note: "Every 12 to 18 months, a financial institution must be prepared to have its systems audited by the appropriate regulatory agency. Financial institutions must be prepared to pass these detailed IT exams, not only to avoid penalties from regulators but also to ensure that customer and member information remains secure, which will help to secure the organization's reputation."

 Three areas financial institutions must address to successfully pass the IT exam are technology management, personnel roles and multilayered protection.

Johnston and Piazza note: "Examiners will want to see whether the institution has clear and well-enforced policies in place to ensure system security and whether it keeps records of activities and enforcement actions that have been taken." Examiners will look for systems that keep records on a weekly, monthly and annual basis. Such records should be reported to executives and kept as proof of the institution's efforts to manage technology properly (Johnston and Piazza, p.88). Comprehensive security and performance-related reports covering both the perimeter and interior monitoring systems are needed to validate IT security.

Another vital component of the IT exam is demonstrating a clear division of labor between IT personnel: "For example, responsibilities of information security officers (ISOs) and security administrators (SAs) should be divided clearly. An ISO ensures that system security is managed and that employees correctly follow security policies, while the SA keeps systems running" (Johnston and Piazza, p.88).

The third area to consider is multilayered protection and evidence that systems are proactively monitored and controlled: "This includes ensuring that user rights are properly changed when an employee changes positions or is terminated; it should also include penetration testing by outside firms, as well as auditing by a CPA or other accredited auditors" (Johnston and Piazza).

Security Concerns

Marketing techniques such as electronic funds transfer systems, remote tellers, automatic bank machines and telephone transferring have had a major impact on the security concerns of financial institutions.

 The movement to make banking activities more accessible to citizens makes security more difficult. In addition, the large amounts of financial assets centralized in one location are extremely attractive to thieves.

The FBI's Financial Crimes Section's report covering 12 months ending September 30, 2006, explains in detail dozens of fraud schemes focusing on corporate fraud, healthcare fraud, mortgage fraud, identity theft, insurance fraud, mass marketing fraud and money laundering. The highest priority of the Financial Crimes Section (FCS) is corporate fraud, with a current active caseload of approximately 490 cases, of which 19 are so major as to have cost investors over $1 billion in combined losses. Investigations by the FCS have resulted in 171 indictments and 124 convictions, as well as over $1 billion in restitutions, $41 million in recoveries and $62 million in seizures.

 The most frequent losses involve theft of cash or stocks and bonds, check and credit-card fraud and embezzlement of funds.

A bank's security program is not limited to areas where money and valuables are exchanged or stored but rather is closely related to all aspects of the business operation. For example, embezzlement may account for more losses than burglary and robbery combined. In addition, fraud has increased. Phishing attacks, in which hackers use look-alike sites to trick customers into divulging confidential information, cost Americans nearly $3 billion in 2006 alone (Piazza, 2007, p.42). Banks with many branches face additional security challenges.

Automatic Teller Machines   Of special concern is the security of the automatic teller machine (ATM). Six categories of criminal activity involving ATMs are: unauthorized card use, fraudulent card use, insider manipulation, embezzlement, robbery and mugging, and physical attack on the ATM itself.

Unauthorized transfers can be initiated through ATM access cards. Unscrupulous users typically obtain these cards by stealing the holder's purse or wallet. Because many customers keep a written record of their personal identification number (PIN) with their card (although all financial institutions advise against it), access to the customer's account becomes all too simple.

Fraudulent card use can occur in many ways. Customers can defraud financial institutions by withdrawing more money than is actually in their accounts or by depositing worthless checks and then withdrawing the money before the scam is detected. Collusion is another way in which a customer can defraud a financial institution. In this case, ATM card holders dispute a transaction after knowingly giving their card and PIN to someone else and allowing that person to make a withdrawal from the account.

Bank employees can also be involved in fraudulent card use. Employees may establish fictitious accounts and order ATM cards for these accounts, or they may have access to legitimate cards and PINs through undelivered mail returned to the bank.

Adequate lighting is critical for ATMs because they may be used at any time, day or night. New technologies include a 911 button that can be pressed to summon the police immediately and a "Customer Awareness Monitor" placed above an ATM that allows the user to see the area behind them. High-resolution, wide-angle transaction and surveillance cameras, which are date and time stamped, are also used.

Security Measures to Reduce Risk and Loss

Significant increases in bank robberies, larcenies and burglaries, and the obvious absence of adequate protective measures, moved Congress to enact the Bank Protection Act in 1968. This act requires all federally insured banks, savings and loan institutions and credit unions to:

- Designate a security officer.
- Cooperate with and seek security advice from the FBI and other law enforcement agencies.
- Develop comprehensive security programs and implement protective measures to meet or exceed federal standards.
- Maintain **bait money**, currency whose serial numbers have been recorded. Sometimes this money is placed so that picking it up sets off a silent alarm.
- Periodically remove excess cash from tellers' windows and bank premises.
- Develop security-conscious opening and closing procedures and stringent security inspections.

In addition to developing and implementing a formal, written security plan and appointing a security officer, federally insured financial institutions must install and maintain vault area lighting systems, tamper-resistant exterior doors and window locks, cameras and alarm systems. Unfortunately, many small-town banks install poor-quality cameras that use fast film and have poor resolution. Consequently, the resulting pictures are often worthless. In addition, the cameras are sometimes installed at a six-foot level, making them susceptible to being blacked out with spray paint or shaving foam. Furthermore, many banks' alarm systems are outdated, leaving the institution vulnerable. Another area in which banks may be dated is in the use of signature cards to verify identification. Such cards take time and are highly unreliable.

The open design of many banks leaves tellers exposed and makes patrons' transactions quite public. The tellers' area should be protected by a standard door enclosed to the ceiling and controlled by a card reader. The customer area should be designed to prevent those standing in line from being able to listen to the transactions occurring in front of them or to watch as someone receives a large amount of cash.

Some banks are moving to *dual-factor authentication* to mitigate the risk of unauthorized users tapping into customers' accounts: "Dual-factor authentication combines something you know—your user name and password, with something you have" (Piazza, 2007, p.42). When customers enroll in the system, they choose a photo icon and a passphrase. When they log in the next time, they see the photo and passphrase so they can be sure they are at the right location rather than some fake site. This co-authenticates the bank to the customer and the customer to the bank.

To further enhance authentication, many banks are using *pattern analysis* to analyze customers' banking patterns in an effort to detect activity that falls outside the pattern and might, thus, be a potential flag for fraudulent transactions. Pattern analysis can detect intelligence-gathering activities related to identity theft and can detect multiaccount, cross-channel scams (Katz, 2005, p.60).

One valuable resource for financial institutions is the Financial Services Information Sharing and Analysis Center (FS/ISAC), a high-tech public-private group that allows the industry's security professionals to share threat and mitigation information (Piazza, 2004, p.57). One goal of the group is to bring security professionals from the physical and IT security world together to "bridge the schism between the two" (Piazza, 2004, p.61). This effort was introduced in Chapters 2 and 11.

An Example: Deterring Bank Robberies in Arkansas

The Arkansas Bankers Association has initiated a bank robbery prevention program that includes a "no hats, no hoods, no sunglasses" dress code for patrons along with a new reward program. The policy is highlighted in posters to make robbers worry they will be noticed. The program has been endorsed by the American Bankers Association and adopted in at least six other states. Missouri, one of the states adopting the program, reported bank robberies dropped 36 percent after the program was introduced. In fact, a rough survey shows that banks in states that did not use the posters were about four times more likely to be robbed than banks in participating states (Spadanuta, 2007, p.26).

Another Example: Merchants and Marine Bank Plans for Natural Disasters

When Hurricane Katrina battered businesses and homes with torrential winds, rain and water, Merchants and Marine Bank was ready and safeguarded the finances of thousands of customers. The $350 million community bank had sand, salt and even some jellyfish scattered throughout the facility. Much of their computer operations equipment was waterlogged, the safe had flooded and thousands of soggy dollars needed to be dried. An alert employee, however, had moved the bank's mainframe computer out of harm's way before the storm hit, preserving untold amounts of data. The bank relocated their data center to a branch outside of town, moving everything in half a day. The bank reopened three days later, and most of its 13 branches were fully operational. Fortunately, the bank had conducted mock disaster exercises prior to the hurricane and gone through the recovery process, preparation that obviously paid off when the real disaster struck ("Bank Recovers Quickly from Katrina," 2005, pp.4–5).

Hospitals and Other Healthcare Facilities

The United States has well over thirty thousand healthcare facilities, including publicly and privately owned hospitals, clinics, nursing homes, outpatient centers and physicians' office complexes. Of the healthcare facilities, hospitals have the most serious security challenges. They must maintain a safe environment for patients, visitors and employees, as well as protect physical assets such as medical equipment, supplies, buildings and personal property: "The general need to protect patients and staff, as well as the realization that hospitals and health care facilities may be possible terrorist targets, has heightened the awareness for security among health care providers" (Friedrick, 2005b, p.15).

Hospitals are big businesses, facing all the concerns of other institutions "open to the public." They are often spread over huge areas, causing even greater security problems. Further, because stress is often high, verbal abuse or threats of violence occur fairly regularly in hospitals (Longmore-Etheridge, 2007, p.52). Providing protection from violent crime to hospital users and employees is a major security challenge.

Nonetheless, many hospital administrators are unaware of their security risks or, if they are aware of such risks, think they are of low priority. The risks should be obvious, however. Hospitals present a stressful atmosphere for most patients and their visitors, as well as for many staff members. These locations also have a reputation as being a "magnet" for criminals, drug addicts and employee thieves. Security officers who work in hospitals and healthcare facilities must be able to interact with the medical staff—physicians, nurses, therapists—the clerical staff and the administration, as well as patients and visitors—frequently under emergency conditions. Public relations skills are vital in this position.

 Like most institutions, hospitals and healthcare facilities struggle with the conflicting needs of remaining open and accessible to the public while simultaneously protecting patients and staff and safeguarding property.

In addition, hospitals and healthcare facilities must comply with numerous government regulations.

The Health Insurance Portability and Accountability Act (HIPAA)

The Health Insurance Portability and Accountability Act (HIPAA) of 1996 requires medical service providers to implement security measures for all stored patient health information: "HIPAA is designed to provide greater confidentiality, integrity and authorized availability of protected electronic health information through the implementation of reasonable and appropriate administrative, physical and technical safeguards. In other words, patient information needs to be safe" (Curtin and Hazelton, 2004, p.32).

Issues related to this act include how to know when security measures are sufficient under the risk analysis and risk management sections of the regulation and how to respond when law enforcement demands patient information that privacy regulations protect: "Each organization must determine for its unique set of circumstances what specific steps would be reasonable and appropriate" (Tomes, 2005, p.76). The rule does offer possible solutions, called "addressable specifications," that include specific technologies such as encryption or specific procedures such as access control and controlling use of removable media from computers. Although hospital security is not required to adopt every possible security measure to protect against every imaginable harm, they are expected to implement reasonable and appropriate security measures: "The biggest problem for companies that must comply with HIPAA is that they can only guess at the meaning of terms such as 'reasonable and appropriate' until court cases set the boundaries. But with a good, well-documented risk analysis, they can be reasonably confident that their security measures are compliant" (Tomes, p.78).

Security Concerns

Most hospitals are very open, have few locked doors and cover large areas. They often include coffee shops, gift shops, flower shops, laundries, pharmacies and doctors' offices. The openness of most healthcare institutions makes access control more difficult. Any access controls must fit the institution's medical care objectives and its public relations program. Security restrictions that impede the primary goal of life preservation are unacceptable to administrative and medical staffs. For example, rigid procedures for checking out surgical equipment or supplies may hinder prompt medical treatment.

Security concerns of hospitals include the heavy daily flow of people, including patients, visitors, medical personnel, other employees and vehicle traffic; a substantial number of female employees; a high percentage of professional staff who often ignore security procedures and large quantities of consumable items such as drugs, linens, food, medical supplies and equipment, making property inventory and accountability extremely difficult.

 The major security concerns of healthcare facilities are visitor control, internal and external theft and the potential for fire.

Visitor control is a formidable security challenge. Yet most hospitals encourage visitors because patients usually benefit from visits. Visitors can also create problems, however, because often they are upset, frequently do not know their way around the hospital or may be tempted to steal. Most hospitals establish visiting hours in an attempt to control access during the hours when the hospital is not fully staffed and the corridors are not as well lit as usual. Some hospitals issue color-coded visitor passes that indicate the ward the wearer is authorized to visit. However, this system can cause lineups at the beginning of visiting hours and annoy visitors. Being told to wait in line to visit someone who may be gravely ill could understandably cause a visitor to become angry or hostile. In addition to having sign-in procedures and a pass system, many hospitals have security personnel patrolling the halls and regularly stopping visitors to offer help and make sure they are accessing only the hospital areas open to them.

A controversial approach is to allow friends and family to visit any time, a patient-centric philosophy supported by the nonprofit membership organization called Planetree, which consists of hospitals and healthcare organizations (Gips, 2007, p.16). Some security professionals, however, argue that such an approach thwarts effective security. While security staff at hospitals moving from an enforcement-oriented approach to the patient-centric model may find it difficult to adjust, one security director in a Planetree hospital states: "The atmosphere is nurturing and open, but security makes its presence known at every entrance" (Gips, 2007, p.18).

Many hospitals also use an employee identification badge system, color coded to indicate the person's position—for example, nurse, volunteer, receptionist. Employees and staff may be restricted to certain exits, and package inspections may be required. What can be locked should be.

Significant losses can result from inadequate control of services, cash and supplies. Services and supplies are especially difficult to monitor because of the emergency nature of many situations. Medications and services may be administered and never recorded or not charged to the appropriate patient. Failure to document medication dispensed can also result in the loss of accreditation by a hospital and endanger government funding.

Another major concern is internal theft. The items most frequently stolen are, in order, linens, patients' cash and personal effects, office supplies and equipment, food, radios and television sets and drugs. To reduce such losses, inventory controls must be established so that administration can identify problems and determine the significance of each. Theft from cars, especially physicians' cars, is another problem. Most hospitals encourage physicians to lock their medical bags in their cars' trunks.

Crimes against persons, including simple assaults as well as violent crimes such as rape and aggravated assaults on patients, nurses and visitors, are also frequently committed in and around medical centers. Historically, hospitals have attracted peeping Toms and sex criminals. Therefore, many hospitals provide escort services for women.

Hazardous wastes in hospitals and healthcare facilities pose additional security problems. An extremely important risk to guard against is the hazard of fire or explosions. Hospitals have large quantities of flammable chemicals, paper and oxygen, making them fire-loaded environments. Many patients in hospital settings are not ambulatory or are heavily sedated and, in the event of a fire or other incident, would require removal from the site via stretchers or litters. In addition, few patients or visitors know where the nearest stairs are because they customarily use the elevator.

Security Measures to Reduce Risk and Loss

Photo ID badges to control access may be used, and metal detectors might be used in emergency rooms. Duress buttons and CCTV cameras may be located in highly sensitive areas such as the nursery and pharmacy. These buttons may be tied into the access control system, allowing staff members to instantly alert a security officer in an emergency. The system can also alert security if a monitored door is open anywhere in the hospital.

 Hospital security concerns can be mitigated through recognition of the risks, careful inventory control, access control, training in fire prevention and evacuation procedures and surveillance.

The access control program at Children's Mercy Hospitals and Clinics stations security officers at public entrances and requires all visitors to sign in with these officers by showing valid identification. At sign-in, the visitor's arrival time and destination is recorded and they are issued a dated, color-coded sticker indicating the area(s) within the building that they are authorized to go (Gips, 2006a, p.76). The program also includes protocols for special restrictions and attention to situations that might create a risk of contamination. To lessen the risk of fire, smoking is restricted to designated areas. To avoid patient and visitor panic, a code word is established to alert the staff to the existence of a fire if one occurs.

Emergency response plans should include contingencies for dealing with domestic problems, crisis intervention and medical treatment support (Crumbley, 2004, p.93). In addition, because many patients cannot provide care for themselves in an emergency, security must be ready to assist with evacuations. Hospitals and healthcare facilities commonly work with local emergency management agencies to devise a plan for handling mass casualties.

Many hospitals have elaborate surveillance systems to monitor patients from the nurses' stations. These same systems may also be used to increase security. In addition, security officers stationed in the main lobby area as well as on patrol, equipped with radios or cell phones, can do much to increase security.

Special Security Considerations for the Most Vulnerable Areas

 The most high-risk areas in a hospital are the emergency room, the maternity ward, the psychiatric ward and the pharmacy.

To enter these areas, staff members usually must use their ID/access card in conjunction with a personal identification number (PIN) (Roberts, 2004, p.71). These areas are also usually protected by CCTV cameras and security patrols. The CCTV cameras are motion activated and continuously monitored.

Emergency Room (ER) Security   Hospital emergency rooms, especially in county hospitals, pose a serious challenge for security. Patients admitted to the emergency room are often drunk, disorderly and very combative. Some are victims of gunshot or knife wounds or of muggings. At times both a victim and an assailant are brought to the same emergency room, posing a great threat to the security of other patients and hospital personnel. Most county hospitals have a security officer on duty around the clock in the emergency room.

In some parts of the country, gang violence and domestic abuse have become security concerns for the local hospitals, and increasing numbers of security staff are required in the emergency room to handle the threats. Consider for example the scenario presented by the operations officer for security at Memorial Health Systems in Colorado Springs, Colorado: "A gang member is shot and his gang mates are in the emergency room waiting to see him, then the rival gang shows up to finish the job and it can be chaotic. It's our job to be proactive and not let the situation escalate" (Edwards, 2007, p.11).

Because emergency rooms are particularly high-risk areas, hospitals might enhance control levels by requiring all visitors to be escorted by a patient liaison (Roberts, 2004, p.71). In addition, a security guard should also be stationed in the area. Ambulance personnel may be required to key in a code to gain access to the ER, unless they are transporting a critical patient. In this instance security staff would be notified while the ambulance is en route to the hospital and be ready to open the entrance and clear the way to a trauma room.

In other hospitals, ambulance teams are given a key fob to take the place of an access control card. This fob is attached to a stand-alone proximity reader, allowing the ambulance team to rapidly enter with victims (Anderson, 2004, p.63).

Security staff at some facilities has been equipped with stun guns: "Taser International reports that the technology is in use by security departments at 72 hospitals" (Gips, 2006b, p.22). Every time a Taser is discharged, the security officer must complete a report and the incident is thoroughly investigated. Most such incidents occur in the ER, which is monitored by CCTV, so documentation is readily available.

A similar risk of violence exists when patients treated in the ER are transferred to the intensive care unit (ICU): "Hospital security has had to deal with several incidents in which visitors who were denied access to the ICU turned violent" (Anderson, 2004, p.62). Another risk in the ICU occurs when a life-threatening illness brings together estranged relatives who literally hate one another and may end up fighting violently over who has access to the ICU, which strictly limits the number of people who may be there at any one time.

A strategy some communities are using to reduce the violence often experienced in hospital emergency rooms by patients and visitors is to train the staff in violence prevention. Baystate Health in Springfield, Massasachusetts, is a three-hospital, multiple-treatment-center system with almost 10,000 employees that has taught nurses to spot signs of escalating aggression among visitors and defend against abusive behaviors (Longmore-Etheridge, 2007, p.52). Specifically nurses receive training in boundary setting, crisis intervention and the resources available to them in dealing with verbal abuse and threats of violence from visitors (p.56). Administrators should seek assistance from the police or other crime prevention and security specialists who can assess security issues.

Maternity Ward Security   Most maternity wards have some sort of infant protection systems to prevent baby switching and abductions. In addition to the human trauma of these crimes, such incidents can create liability and bad publicity for the hospital. The security in the maternity ward of Cape Cod Hospital is typical of many such wards across the country: "Every infant in the maternity ward is fitted with a leg band that will signal an alarm if taken too close to the sensors placed at doorways. The alarm will also sound if someone is manipulating or removing an active band" (Roberts, p.71). The alarms are triggered by sensors located in the ceiling throughout the ward. A training program that teaches nurses to use the infant protection bands also helps reduce false alarms, saving time and money (Roberts, p.72).

The maternity ward at Huntsville Hospital, the largest and oldest medical center in north Alabama, is an entire floor devoted to the mother/baby unit, so parents can go anywhere in the unit. However, if they try to get on the elevator with a child who is tagged, the doors will remain open and the elevator will not move (Blades, 2005, p.64). Similarly, stairwell doors will lock down if a tagged child is brought near them. If the doorway is opened somehow with a tagged child present, an alarm goes off. Additional security is provided by CCTV cameras in each area.

Psychiatric Ward Security   Violence is one of the biggest concerns for psychiatric wards (Friedrick, 2006, p.19). Security officers should be trained in both verbal and nonverbal skills for preventing acts of violence, as well as taught physical restraint techniques. For at-risk patients, some psychiatric wards use a bracelet system similar to that used in maternity wards.

Pharmacy Security   Roberts (2004, p.72) points out: "With prescription drug thefts on the rise in the last few years, arguably the greatest risk to a hospital is an underprotected pharmacy." She describes security at the Cape Code Hospital pharmacy as particularly tight: "A staff member needing to administer drugs will call in an order to the pharmacy. Outside the pharmacy is a door equipped with a videophone. The employee uses the phone to contact the pharmacy personnel inside. Once verified by the pharmacy staff, the employee is buzzed through the door and allowed to collect the order at the bulletproof prescription window. This area acts as a mantrap station and can be locked down, trapping the employee and the drugs inside." Monitored CCTV in the corridors surrounding the pharmacy enhances the security of the area.

In some cases, hospitals have moved the pharmacy from the ground floor to the second floor to make access more difficult to people walking in off the street. Many hospitals have also designed an access control system allowing entry to only those with legitimate needs and only during authorized hours.

Security in Nursing Homes and Other Long-Term Care Facilities

The U.S. Census Bureau projects that more than 40 million U.S. citizens will be of retirement age or older by 2010. By 2050 some 86.7 million citizens will be age 65 and older and 20.9 million will be 85 or older: "As the U.S. population ages, and more people reside in long-term-care (LTC) facilities, security professionals must learn to assess and address the unique risks of these facilities" (Boxerbaum and Donaldson, 2005, p.42).

The country currently has more than 20,500 nursing homes (Boxerbaum and Donaldson, p.44). Many of the elderly people living in these facilities bring their valuables with them, unlike in hospitals where patients are advised to leave their valuables at home. In addition, many are often weak, may have memory loss and may have no family members who visit.

 Among the risks in long-term care facilities are theft of personal property, abuse, physical assault, diversion of assets and extortion. Also of concern are elderly people who wander away.

When an elderly person with dementia strays from caregivers—a situation called **critical wandering**—they face many dangers (Longmore-Etheridge, 2006, p.102). Researchers have reported that one out of every 1,000 people age 65 or older, a total of more than 125,000 people annually, will become a critical wanderer: "Security and medical staff must work together to establish effective programs that safeguard these vulnerable patients. The prime elements of these programs are identifying patients with dementia, providing an environment that discourages wandering and supervising those with dementia effectively" (Longmore-Etheridge, p.106). Some institutions use a radio frequency (RF) antiwandering system, in which the patient wears a small RF transmitter as a bracelet or anklet that can trigger alarmed doors. Some hospitals have paid patient observers and a partnership with the police. Other care facilities have adapted existing infant monitoring technology as antiwandering systems, often supplementing these systems with sensor pads on beds or wheelchairs that trigger alarms when a patient gets up (Longmore-Etheridge).

One new technology that might address the critical wandering problem is a GPS-based wearable device to track residents both inside and outside of buildings (Boxerbaum and Donaldson, p.50). In addition to providing real-time information about the location of the resident, the device can also provide data on respiration and heart rate. Radio frequency and infrared technologies can also track residents as well as their valuables. The potential also exists to use behavioral recognition algorithms in conjunction with digital video recording technologies that would enable a CCTV system to identify behaviors associated with wandering residents (Boxerbaum and Donaldson).

Improving Security While Reducing Operating Expenses

Many institutions face mandates to improve security to comply with new regulations while, at the same time, trying to reduce operating expenses. Consider the example of an 800-bed hospital in dire need of a security upgrade but unable to justify the expense under a reduced operating budget (Schultz, 2005, p.52). The unit in most need of upgrading had special requirements: patient video monitoring and increased guard presence. Its video system had several analog cameras feeding into a large control room at the center of the wing with two guards monitoring the video.

When the decision was made to integrate this unit's security system, several other departments consolidated their control centers into a single point of command monitored by one guard from the wing's front desk. The result was that the hospital no longer needed a volunteer to staff the front desk. Because the video monitoring required only one guard, the other guard could patrol the wing's public areas, creating a visual security presence. The security upgrades not only improved safety but also saved the hospital about $450,000 annually in administrative and labor costs, paying for the upgrade and office retrofit (Schultz). In addition to enhancing security and saving money, a holistic, integrated approach to managing security can eliminate information silos that can slow response rates and blur the facts in emergency situations (Schultz).

Consider next how security is being provided in our country's educational institutions.

Educational Institutions

Pearl, Mississippi; West Paducah, Kentucky; Jonesboro, Arkansas; Fayetteville, Tennessee; Springfield, Oregon; Richmond, Virginia; Littleton, Colorado; Conyers, Georgia; Santee, California; Red Lake, Minnesota—these cities house schools that come to mind when school security is mentioned. In the fall of 2006, a 53-year-old drifter took six girls hostage at Platte Canyon High School in Bailey, Colorado, sexually assaulted them and fatally shot a 16-year-old girl before killing himself. Two days later, a 15-year-old former student allegedly shot and killed a principal at a school in Cazenovia, Wisconsin. During the same time frame, three teenagers were charged in Green Bay, Wisconsin, in an alleged plot to bomb and burn a high school and shoot students as they emerged. In Bart Township, Pennsylvania, Charles Carl Roberts IV, 32, shot and killed six young Amish girls and seriously injured four more after lining them up in their one-room school and shooting them "execution style." Roberts was armed with three guns, two knives and 600 rounds of ammunition (McCaffrey et al., 2006). More recently, a Virginia Tech student, Seung-Hui Cho, murdered two victims in a dormitory early in the morning and two hours later went to Norris Hall, an engineering building, and murdered 30 more before turning his gun on himself (Garrett, 2007, p.56).

Although school shootings capture headlines, they are rare. Nonetheless, educational institutions must be prepared for such incidents as well as for the more mundane security concerns. Educational institutions are responsible for providing a safe learning environment for staff and students, yet they are also subject to the same risks faced by business and industry.

 The major security concerns of educational institutions are safety of students and staff, violence, vandalism and theft, including burglary.

K–12 Programs

During the 2004–2005 school year, an estimated 54.9 million students were enrolled throughout the country in prekindergarten through grade 12 (*Indicators of School Crime and Safety: 2007*). Security needs of schools vary tremendously, depending on the size of the school system and the location of the facilities. For example, the New York City Public School System has 1,000 schools and 400 auxiliary buildings which cover more than one hundred million square feet. In contrast, some rural areas have one school that serves all grade levels for children living in communities as far as ten, fifteen or even more miles away from the school. Challenges faced by systems such as New York's will be more complex than those faced by small, rural schools. Nonetheless, crime and violence in schools is not limited to the large school systems. It has increased substantially in both suburban and rural school systems. Some school administrators place the blame on the open school concept, which they contend encourages an influx of idlers and dropouts who disrupt academic functions.

Security Concerns   Vandalism is a serious problem for the vast majority of schools, an issue compounded by general public apathy. People who live close to a school may see vandalism occurring at night, on weekends or during holidays, yet may do nothing and notify no one. One solution to this problem has been to use the school for community functions after school hours. This not only decreases the opportunity for undetected vandalism, but also improves community interest in protecting its facilities. Key findings of *Indicators of School Crime and Safety: 2007* include:

- Youths ages 5–18 were victims of 17 school-associated violent deaths from July 1, 2005, through June 30, 2006 (14 homicides and 3 suicides).

- Students ages 12–18 were victims of about 1.5 million nonfatal crimes at school, including about 868,100 thefts and 628,200 violent crimes.
- Violence, theft, drugs and weapons continue to be problems, with 25 percent of students in grades 9–12 reporting drugs were made available to them on school property.

Figure 15.1 summarizes the problems reported to the Safe Schools Helpline.

Security Measures to Reduce Risk and Loss   Increased violence, along with increases in burglaries, arson and vandalism coupled with the school's civil liability for its students' safety, have caused many school systems to develop a comprehensive security program, including intrusion-detection systems and nonbreakable windows. Some schools are even constructed without windows. The primary objectives of most school security programs are to protect staff and students and their personal property and to protect the school's facilities and equipment.

 Access control, lighting and security personnel are primary means to reduce risks at educational institutions.

Access control is always the first layer of security for K–12 schools (Grace, 2005, p.54). For example, the access control and visitor management system used in the Broward County (Florida) School District requires all visitors to

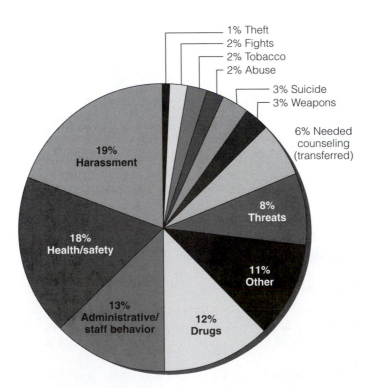

Figure 15.1   The Safe Schools Helpline Problems Reported 2004–2005
SOURCE: The Safe School Helpline, National Statistics 2004-2005.

present personal identification, such as a driver's license, to a school attendant when arriving at a school. The attendant swipes the ID through a reader, which automatically adds the ID information to the database and recognizes whether the ID is authentic or false. The attendant identifies the group to which the person belongs: parent, volunteer, vendor or contractor. The system then checks the name against offender databases. If no match is found, a badge is printed. If a match is found, a "deny" button appears at the bottom of the screen (Ritter and Fox, 2006, p.62).

New Jersey schools are using an iris recognition program to enhance security. The system, nicknamed T-PASS (Teacher-Parent Authorization Security System), links eye-scanning cameras with computers to identify people who have been preauthorized to enter the schools and, once their identity is confirmed, lets them in by unlocking the door (Cohn, 2006). Of the more than 9,400 times someone has attempted to enter the school using the iris scanner, there were no known false positives or other misidentifications. It is important to note that the system made staff members feel safer in the school. A significant loophole in the system occurs, however, when someone who is authorized to enter, hav-

Increasing numbers of schools across the country, particularly in urban districts, have installed metal detectors at entry points in an effort to reduce the number of weapons being brought into these educational facilities.

© Don Tremain/ Getty Images

ing passed the eye-scan check, holds the door open for others, who are then admitted.

School systems also use varying combinations of contract and proprietary personnel to establish security programs. In some states county and local ordinances give police powers to school security personnel. Many of these personnel have primary jurisdiction over criminal incidents that occur in the schools. Alarm systems are also commonly used. Other schools require all students to carry ID cards so that if they are involved in an incident, they can be easily identified. Educational programs are a key component of most school security programs.

Clear policies for expected behavior should be established for tardiness, absenteeism/class cutting, physical conflicts among students, student tobacco use, verbal abuse of teachers, drug use, vandalism of school property, alcohol use, robbery or theft, gangs, racial tensions, possession of weapons, physical abuse of teachers and sale of drugs on school grounds.

Many schools have adopted **zero tolerance** toward possession of guns, drugs or alcohol in schools—that is, no matter what the underlying circumstances, a student bringing a weapon, drugs or alcohol to school will be suspended or expelled. While no data suggest that zero tolerance policies reduce school violence, such policies have been shown to occasionally result in unreasonable suspensions and expulsions. Problems associated with zero tolerance policies were introduced in Chapter 12.

Behavior codes should be established and firmly and consistently enforced. These codes may include dress codes and bans on showing gang colors or using hand signals. Schools should also offer positive reinforcement to promote and reward friendliness and cooperation.

Graffiti removal should occur in schools immediately. Not only is graffiti unattractive, but it also enables gang members to advertise their turf and authority. In some instances photographs of the graffiti may aid investigations. As an alternative to graffiti, students might be encouraged to design and paint murals in locations where graffiti is most likely to occur.

Conflict prevention strategies are also important to address the problem of gangs in school. Teachers should be trained to recognize and deal with gang members in nonconfrontational ways. Staff should identify all known gang members.

Crisis management is another important part of dealing with gangs. Security and school officials should have a plan in place for dealing with crises that might arise. Teachers and students alike should know that most students who are violent "leak" their feelings and intentions in the weeks and months before committing a violent act. Such messages should never be ignored.

Tip lines can be a powerful proactive tool. However: "For any tip line to work, it must be truly anonymous, monitored around the clock and trusted to be free of bias. There should also be aggressive advertising of tip-line phone numbers through such mechanisms as student handbooks, special handouts, postcards and posters" (Connors, 2005, p.108).

The response to an "active shooter" situation became a topic of concern for educational institutions throughout the country following Columbine. The first responders in that crisis did what they had trained to do—control the scene, contain if able, try to contact the shooter and call in SWAT. Response protocol has changed since that incident with the development of Immediate Action Rapid Deployment or IARD. Under IARD protocol, rather than waiting for SWAT, officers "must charge into a situation—even if it means putting their own lives at stake" (Garrett, p.55). Armellino (2007) calls IARD an "effective aggressive tactic. In the case of a terrorist school takeover, any delay of the first responders to actively engage the intruders will guarantee that ultimately many innocents will die due to the delayed aggressive response."

"Someday in the near future, an American community—probably far from an urban center—will find that one of its schools has been taken over by Muslim terrorists who are holding the students hostage" (Giduck, 2006, p.29). Recommended preparation for this horrific scenario involves gathering drawings, blueprints, schematics, floor plans and walk-through videotapes of all schools in the community so as to know the target. Officer and other responder training is essential, since assaulting a school full of heavily armed terrorists holding hundreds of terrified hostages is not within most officers' experience. To adequately and effectively train for this situation, officers must approach it for what it is—war: "War in very cramped quarters with a lot of innocents in the way" (Giduck).

Colleges and Universities

 The greatest security challenge of most colleges and universities is their open environment.

In response to a *Security Director News* "Newspoll" (2007, p.23) asking for responses to the Virginia Tech shooting, almost two thirds of the directors surveyed thought open environments such as colleges and university can be effectively secured.

Security Concerns   The security concerns of colleges and universities are somewhat different from those of elementary and secondary school systems. A major difference is that some college and university facilities are used almost continuously (except at community colleges, which typically close by midnight). The 24-hour access commonly granted to areas such as student unions, which are heavily trafficked and usually have several entrances and exits, poses a major constraint in using electronic security. However, CCTV and alarm systems are often installed in bursars' and cashiers' offices and in the areas that serve as central collection points for all cash from campus facilities, such as student unions and cafeterias.

College campuses sustain significant losses from theft of college property. The items most frequently stolen include audiovisual and laboratory equipment, calculators, computers and educational materials such as books and art objects. Theft of examinations is also a major concern at colleges and universities, as is protecting the computer system, particularly against grade changing.

The large numbers of residential housing units for students and staff create a densely populated community. Some campuses are larger than many towns. Population density in high-rise dormitories makes it difficult to protect students and their personal property. The high concentration of students on larger campuses makes it unlikely, if not impossible, that residents will know all of the other residents of the dormitory; therefore, an intruder can easily pose as a student. Many colleges have installed extensive locking and access control systems to restrict access to student housing areas.

Besides dense population, the physical size of the campus may pose security problems. For example, the University of Houston campus covers 390 acres. Large campuses frequently provide motorcycle or foot patrols equipped with portable radios and emergency call boxes along pedestrian walkways.

A primary concern is safety of individuals. Armed robberies, assaults, muggings and rapes at college campuses are of concern throughout the country. On some campuses, students have organized rape crisis centers to counsel and assist rape victims. On other campuses, male students have formed protective night escort services for female students. One study found that approximately 22 percent of respondents reported being victims of at least one type of crime such as robbery, sexual assault, assault, battery, theft, burglary or fraud (Jennings et al., 2007, p.200). The same study also found that students did not engage in many changes in behavior to reduce their risk of being victimized (p.201).

Drinking and use of illegal drugs are major problems on some campuses. Special events on campus also challenge security. Alcohol intoxication seems to be a problem existing at most special events.

Security Measures to Reduce Risk and Loss   The Crime Awareness and Campus Security Act of 1990 and the Student Right-to-Know Act require institutions of higher education to gather and publish, at least annually, campus crime statistics for assault, burglary, criminal homicide, drug-abuse violations, forcible rape, liquor-law violations, motor vehicle theft, robbery and weapon possession. These figures must be available to all students and parents, faculty and current and prospective employees. These figures are also included in the FBI Uniform Crime Reports (UCR).

As in K–12 programs, *access control* is an important issue in security. The University of Pittsburg has implemented a solution that supports existing student ID cards. The system incorporates door alarms, glass-break alarms, burglar alarms and panic buttons; any of these devices can send a signal to the central monitoring system (Anderson, 2007a, p.40).

Like secondary schools, higher education institutions use a combination of contractual and proprietary *security personnel* and *security hardware* to protect their campuses, students and employees. The trend is to establish proprietary security forces and appoint directors of security for colleges and universities. Campus security officers can provide assistance to students seeking directions as well as help to ensure a safe, welcoming campus. At some larger institutions, security personnel are responsible for comprehensive law enforcement, traffic and fire safety and loss prevention functions. For example, the University of Connecticut Public Safety Division not only serves a police function, but also maintains a fire department, a mounted patrol, locksmith and key controls, an ambulance service and a campus transportation system. Increasingly, universities are instituting bicycle patrols. They are less expensive and more mobile than vehicles, are environmentally acceptable and provide a more efficient deterrent to crime on campus.

Locks and effective key control can significantly reduce such losses. The installation of electronic sensor detection devices in libraries has significantly reduced the number of stolen library books. Installation of photocopy equipment has likewise reduced the number of mutilated books and periodicals.

Improved lighting has also proved to be a sound security measure: "While specific lighting standards are not mandated, good lighting is a critical component of a university's program—and of its public image" (Roberts, 2005, p.96). Schools that neglect the importance of adequate lighting risk a negligence lawsuit if an incident occurs. Installing mercury vapor lamps, removing bushes and shrubs and adding a number of direct-ring emergency phones along all major walkways provide "corridors of security." The improved lighting acts as a psychological deterrent, allows people to see farther and thus to avoid would-be attackers, allows campus security to see potential trouble and, if a crime should occur, makes identification of the perpetrator easier. To meet energy conservation needs, after high-traffic periods are over, every other light is turned out for the remainder of the night.

Wichita State University used principles of Crime Prevention through Environmental Design (CPTED) to help solve problems with library security, which included materials being stolen, visitors viewing inappropriate materials on the library computers and some students being assaulted (Anderson, 2007b, p.92). One major problem was the library's 30 tall cabinets holding reference books were located between the main reference desk and the computers, so librarians at the reference desk did not have a clear line of sight. It was determined that the information in the cabinets was available electronically, so the cabinets were removed. With this change, the computer area and entrance could be seen from almost anywhere on the first floor. The reference desk was also relocated to be more central and more visible, giving the librarian a better view of the area. Computer use policies were also revamped. After these changes, security issues "all but disappeared."

A trend in campus security is the active involvement of students in crime prevention. On some campuses, students informally assist in crowd control and traffic direction at large public events such as sporting events. Other campuses have a more formal organization of student patrol or student marshal programs. At Syracuse University, students equipped with two-way radios and identified by arm patches as "student security services" patrol parking areas and general residence halls. The University of Georgia campus security department consists entirely of students with undergraduate degrees who are taking graduate programs in police science or criminal justice. Other universities offer incentives such as free tuition or tuition assistance to campus security workers.

The entire campus community, including campus security, faculty and administrators, needs to raise awareness and *promote prevention* of campus victimization. Among the crime prevention programs used in many colleges to reduce criminal activity are Operation Identification, Neighborhood Watch, security surveys, working with architects, rape awareness programs, office security, key control, escort services and orientation programs. These programs and any other crime prevention strategies for college campuses should involve students, employees and staff.

Unfortunately, not all crime and violence can be prevented, as evidenced by the tragedy at Virginia Tech. Several lessons can be learned from that incident, including giving greater consideration to the use of behavior threat assessment teams to identify students who might pose a threat to themselves or others (Harwood, 2007, p.62). The FBI's report, *The School Shooter: A Threat Assessment Perspective* (O'Toole, 2000), is one useful resource for such an undertaking. This report recommends that colleges and universities integrate their plans into the National Incident Management System and the Incident Command System so everyone responding uses the same terminology and coordinates their actions. Stephens (2007), executive director of the National School Safety Center, notes: "Living in a democratic society in which preeminence is given to individual freedoms propagates an underlying vulnerability." He notes that the Virginia Tech shooting emphasizes the need for colleges and universities to rethink their admissions and student screening policies as well as their supervision policies. They should train faculty to spot signs of depression and how to access mental health services for students.

Technology advances have made it easier for security to alert the campus and community through mass notification systems, although the rapidly unfolding events at Virginia Tech did bring to light some of the shortcomings of text message alert systems. Schools might consider installing stand-alone emergency phones on campus so students can notify security directly, or installing intercom systems that can immediately broadcast information to a single classroom or to the entire campus. Another recommendation is to use "smart" video cameras that rely on computer algorithms to detect suspicious activity.

Security should have virtual tours of the buildings on campus, have good crisis communications, be trained in the National Incident Management System and be armed: "Convincing college and university administrators that campus officers need to be armed is one of the major stumbling blocks in preparing schools to respond to the Cho Seung-Huis of the world" (Hamilton, 2007, p.48). And while school shootings are to be taken very seriously and certainly warrant attention in terms of advanced response planning, the threat of a shooter must be kept in perspective: "On-campus shootings are extremely rare; students are far more likely to die from drinking too much than at the hands of a fellow student" (Harwood).

SUMMARY

- The primary security concerns at libraries are theft of or damage to books, CDs and videos; disorderly behavior; and fire.
- Library losses can be reduced by the electronic marking of books, by providing photocopy equipment and by having security personnel.
- An inherent conflict of interest exists between museum archivists, who seek to preserve and store materials, and curators, who seek to make materials accessible to the public.

- The major security concerns of museums and art galleries include theft, fraud, vandalism and arson.
- Security concerns faced by religious institutions include the desire for easy accessibility at all times, their attractiveness to indigents and mental patients and the individuals included in their social outreach programs.
- Security measures for religious institutions include perimeter protection, including lighting and fencing; safeguarding valuables by such means as

- lighting, locks and alarms and contingency plans for handling disruptive individuals.
- Financial institutions face unique security problems. Three areas for financial institutions to consider to pass the IT exam are technology management, personnel roles and multilayered protection.
- The movement to make banking activities more accessible to citizens makes security more difficult. In addition, the large amounts of financial assets centralized in one location are extremely attractive to thieves.
- The most frequent losses in financial institutions involve theft of cash or stocks and bonds, check and credit-card fraud and embezzlement of funds.
- Like most institutions, hospitals and healthcare facilities struggle with the conflicting needs of remaining open, accessible to the public while simultaneously protecting patients and staff and safeguarding property.
- The major security concerns of healthcare facilities are emergency room security, visitor control, internal and external theft and the potential for fire.
- Hospital security problems can be mitigated through recognition of the risks, careful inventory control, access control, training in fire prevention and evacuation procedures and surveillance.
- The most high-risk areas in a hospital are the emergency room, the maternity ward, the psychiatric ward and the pharmacy.
- Among the risks in long-term care facilities are theft of personal property, abuse, physical assault, diversion of assets and extortion. Also of concern are elderly people who wander away.
- Major security concerns of educational institutions are safety of students and staff, violence, vandalism and theft, including burglary.
- Access control, lighting and security personnel are primary means to reduce risks at educational institutions.
- The greatest security challenge of most colleges and universities is their open environment.

APPLICATIONS

1. Develop a security checklist for three of the types of facilities discussed in this chapter.
2. The Quality Private Security Services Company has assigned you to the parking lot of the Interstate Manufacturing Company to assist in the flow of traffic and parking. At the end of the day, you are somewhat exhausted because of the sheer volume of paperwork and forms you were required to fill out, but also during the tour of duty you had to assist three employees by jump starting their cars, you assisted in changing two flat tires, you helped another two people who had locked their keys in their cars and you gave another person a ride to the bus stop because his car had a leaky radiator.

   You do not think that all these services you performed were part of your instructions to keep the flow of traffic and parking orderly. You complain to your supervisor about all this responsibility. What do you think your supervisor would say to you about parking lot management?

DISCUSSION QUESTIONS

1. Name several effective ways to protect vital documents and records from destruction or theft.
2. Which types of security discussed in this chapter seem most important to you? Why?
3. Do you have art galleries or museums in your community that might be at risk? If so, what kind of security do they have?
4. What kind of security is provided at your campus?
5. Does your campus involve students in their security program?

REFERENCES
Anderson, Teresa. "Technology Treats Hospital's Ailments." *Security Management*, 2004, pp.61–65.
Anderson, Teresa. "Campus Access Controlled." *Security Management*, July 2007a, pp.38–40.
Anderson, Teresa. "Great Plains, Great Plans." *Security Management*, June 2007b, pp.88–96.
Armellino, Rick. "When They Come to Kill the Kids." *PoliceOne.com*, 2007.

Art Theft Program. Washington, DC: Federal Bureau of Investigation, 2005.

"Bank Recovers Quickly from Katrina." *Directions*, Winter 2005, pp.4–5.

Blades, Marleah. "Fitting Solutions into the Big Picture." *Security Technology & Design*, September 2005, pp.60–64.

Boxerbaum, Elliot A. and Donaldson, Patrick F. "Respecting and Protecting Elders." *Security Management*, May 2005, pp.42–50.

Cohn, Jeffrey P. "Keeping an Eye on School Security: The Iris Recognition Project in New Jersey." *NIJ Journal*, July 2006.

Connors, David R. "Today's Lesson: Tip Lines." *Security Management*, November 2005, pp.100–108.

Crumbley, James R. "Diagnosis Security." *Security Management*, April 2004, pp.77–93.

Curtin, C. Matthew and Hazelton, Peter M. "The Road to HIPAA Security Rule Compliance." *Security Technology & Design*, November 2004, pp.32–38.

Edwards, Al. "Cooperation Critical in Healthcare Safety." *Security Director News*, August 2007, p.11.

Elliott, Robert. "Military Museum Guards against Fire." *Security Management*, January 2006, pp.40–42.

Elliott, Robert. "Fahrenheit 1,832." *Security Management*, March 2007, pp.70–78.

Friedrick, Joanne. "Financial Institutions Dive into New Realm of Risk." *Security Director News*, January 2005a, p.19.

Friedrick, Joanne. "Health Care Facilities Elevate Security Condition." *Security Director News*, June 2005b, p.15.

Friedrick, Joanne. "Managers Seek Balance between Personnel, Technology." *Security Director News*, July 2006, p.19.

Garrett, Ronnie. "Marching to the Sound of Guns." *Law Enforcement Technology*, June 2007, pp.54–64.

Giduck, John. "Responding to School Sieges." *Police*, September 2006, pp.28–34.

Gips, Michael A. "Hospital Safety Not Child's Play." *Security Management*, January 2006a, pp.71–77.

Gips, Michael A. "Hospitals Probing Stun Gun Use." *Security Management*, June 2006b, pp.22–24.

Gips, Michael A. "Challenges Posed by Patient-Centric Care." *Security Management*, February 2007, pp.16–22.

Grace, Guy. "Security for Schools Starts with Access Control." *Security Technology & Design*, May 2005, pp.54–57.

Hamilton, Melanie. "Can We Stop the Next Cho Seung-Hui?" *Police*, June 2007, pp.48–50.

Harwood, Matt. "Preventing the Next Campus Shooting." *Security Management*, August 2007, pp.54–64.

Indicators of School Crime and Safety: 2007. National Center for Education Statistics.

Jennings, Wesley G.; Gover, Angela R.; and Pudrzynska, Dagmar. "Are Institutions of Higher Learning Safe? A Descriptive Study of Campus Safety Issues and Self-Reported Campus Victimization among Male and Female College Students." *Journal of Criminal Justice Education*, July 2007, pp.191–208.

Johnston, Danny and Piazza, Peter. "Cramming for an IT Exam." *Security Management*, September 2005, pp.84–92.

Katz, Elzara. "Adapting to Automated Fraud." *Security Management*, February 2005, pp.59–65.

Keller, Steve. "Dealing Artfully with Disaster." *Security Management*, June 2006, pp.66–78.

Longmore-Etheridge, Ann. "Preventing Wanderlust in Patients." *Security Management*, June 2006, pp.102–108.

Longmore-Etheridge, Ann. "Nurses on Guard." *Security Management*, February 2007, pp.52–57.

Longmore-Etheridge, Ann and Faulk, Wilbur C. "Preserving the Lost Art of War." *Security Management*, August 2004, pp.80–87.

McCaffrey, Raymond; Duggan, Paul; and Wilgoren, Debbi. "Five Killed at Pa. Amish School." *Washington Post*, October 3, 2006.

"Newspoll." *Security Director News*, May 2007, p.23.

O'Toole, Mary Ellen. *The School Shooter: A Threat Assessment Perspective.* Washington, DC: Federal Bureau of Investigation, 2000.

Ozernoy, Ilana. "The Art of the Heist." *U.S. News & World Report*, October 10, 2005, pp.42–43.

Piazza, Peter. "Intelligence Is the Best Defense." *Security Management*, September 2004, pp.57–65.

Piazza, Peter. "Banks Prove Themselves to Customers—and Vice Versa." *Security Management*, February 2007, pp.42–44.

Potter, Anthony N. "Keeping the Program Healthy." *Security Technology & Design*, June 2005, pp.36–44.

Ritter, John R. and Fox, Jonathan. "Keeping Students Safe." *Security Management*, November 2006, pp.61–67.

Roberts, Marta. "Inoculating against Murphy's Law." *Security Management*, May 2004, pp.67–72.

Roberts, Marta. "Shedding Light on University Security." *Security Management*, May 2005, pp.91–96.

Schroeder, Margaret. "Special Protection for Special Collections." *Security Management*, July 2004, pp.55–62.

Schultz, Laura. "Integrated Building Security." *Security Products*, April 2005, pp.52–56.

Spadanuta, Laura. "Deterring Robberies." *Security Management*, August 2007, p.26.

Stephens, Ronald. "The Horror at Virginia Tech." *National School Safety Center News*, May 23, 2007.

"Technology Eases Compliance Burden for Bank of Utah." *Directions*, Winter 2006, pp.3–4.

Tomes, Jonathan P. "Prescription for Data Protection." *Security Management*, April 2005, pp.75–78.

Turk, Andrew. "Security in Motion." *Security Management*, August 2005, pp.40–46.

CHAPTER 16

Commercial Security

© Bill Aron/PhotoEdit

Commercial businesses rely on the public for financial success. In an effort to ease access and allow consumers to view merchandise before buying, some businesses trade away a degree of security. For example, shoplifting is a major source of loss for retail establishments. Shoplifters may work alone or in teams.

Do You Know . . .

■ What crimes are most frequently committed against retail establishments?

■ What preventive methods can be taken to curtail shoplifting?

■ What types of employee theft frequently occur in retail establishments and what preventive measures can be taken?

■ What the primary challenge for hotel security managers is?

■ What the major security concerns of the hotel/motel industry are?

■ What security concerns exist at racetracks? How these concerns are addressed?

■ What security concerns are common at sporting events?

■ What the major security concerns of office buildings include? What security measures are commonly used to address these concerns?

■ What the main security concerns of residential housing are?

■ What type of drug market poses the greatest threat in apartment complexes?

■ What the primary security concern is when providing security abroad?

Can You Define?

backstretch area	floor release limit	open drug market	shopping service
booster box	floorwalkers	prima facie evidence	skips
closed drug market	honesty shopping	probable cause	sliding
Dram Shop Acts	kleptomaniac	reasonable cause	zero floor release limit

Introduction

Commercial security encompasses a wide variety of enterprises, each with common challenges as well as unique challenges. Some of the businesses discussed in the previous two chapters might also have been included in this chapter. And most can benefit from the physical and procedural security measures discussed in Chapters 6 and 7.

This chapter begins with a discussion of retail security, including shopping centers and malls. This is followed by a discussion of security in lodging and hospitality enterprises, restaurants and bars, casinos, racetracks and at sporting events. Next security in office buildings as well as public and private housing security is discussed. The chapter concludes with a brief discussion of protecting individuals and businesses abroad.

Retail Security

It is a Friday evening. In the X Supermarket, a woman buys a dozen rolls from the bakery department. The rolls are placed in a white sack with the price marked on the outside. To this sack, the woman adds a pen and three cigarette lighters. She hurriedly pays the cashier the correct amount for the rolls in change and leaves without waiting for a receipt. The cashier pockets the money.

At the next counter a man is cashing a stolen government check. Across the street, the corner gas station is being held up. At a boutique just down the road, a woman is in a fitting room putting her street clothes on over an expensive bathing suit, another woman is switching prices on jewelry and an employee is marking down prices on items she is purchasing for herself.

Hourly, across the country, such actions result in tremendous losses to retailers. Retail establishments include general merchandise department stores, specialty and clothing stores, food and drug stores, appliance and furniture stores, radio and television stores, hardware stores, lumberyards, restaurants, fast-food shops, automobile dealers and gasoline service stations.

Whether located in a shopping mall, in a downtown business district or in isolation from other businesses, retailers face many common problems.

 Reported crimes committed against all types of retail establishments include shoplifting, burglary, vandalism, passing bad checks, fraudulent use of credit cards, employee theft and robbery.

"The retail industry is estimated to lose $30 billion annually to a wide spectrum of threats." Retail operations must develop loss prevention strategies to identify, quantify, prioritize and mitigate the potential causes of these losses at the local store level (Greggo, 2005, p.61).

The physical and procedural controls discussed in Chapters 6 and 7 are the most effective means of deterring robbery, burglary and vandalism in retail establishments. Proper lighting, locks, alarm systems and other measures are also appropriate in retail establishments. Of equal or greater importance, however, is safeguarding against losses from shoplifting, bad checks, fraudulently used credit cards and employee theft. The problem of shrinkage, loss of assets, has been discussed. The major sources of shrinkage are illustrated in Figure 16.1.

Shoplifting

Shoplifting is often considered the most widespread crime affecting retail stores. It is also generally considered to be a security problem rather than a law

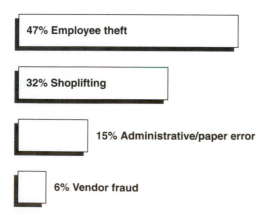

47% Employee theft

32% Shoplifting

15% Administrative/paper error

6% Vendor fraud

Figure 16.1   Sources of Inventory Shrinkage. Employee theft and shoplifting remain the two largest sources of shrinkage for retailers. The only changes from last year's survey were a 1 percent decrease in employee theft and a 1 percent increase in vendor fraud.
SOURCE: From the University of Florida's 2003 National Retail Security Survey by Dr. Richard Hollinger.

enforcement problem. Shoplifting[1] is the theft of retail merchandise by a person lawfully on the premises. Concealment of merchandise is **prima facie evidence**[2] of intent to shoplift. In many states price changing is also considered shoplifting.

Shoplifting is a form of larceny costing billions of dollars annually. Compounding the problem is public apathy. Many people have shoplifted at one time in their lives, and many have very little sympathy for big business. Thus, the responsibility for preventing shoplifting losses falls almost entirely on retail management.

The problem has many facets. Sales and security personnel must be familiar with the various types of shoplifters, methods they commonly use, signs indicative of shoplifting activity and means to prevent the crime. They must also be knowledgeable of the establishment's policies and procedures for apprehending, arresting, interrogating and deciding whether to prosecute offenders.

Types of Shoplifters Although anyone can be a shoplifter, it is helpful to recognize the most common types of shoplifters. Shoplifters can be classified as amateur—students, housewives, vagrants, alcoholics, drug addicts and kleptomaniacs—or as professional—those who steal for resale of merchandise. The great majority of shoplifting is done by amateurs, ordinary customers who give in to temptation. Most shoplifting incidences are impulsive.

Juveniles seldom steal from true need but rather for "kicks," as a dare or to be initiated into a club. They often enter stores in groups as a way to distract the sales staff. Some juveniles steal items they have been given money to purchase, using the money instead to purchase drugs or alcohol. Housewives are the next most common category of shoplifters. This may be partly because they frequently do most of the family's shopping and, therefore, are exposed to temptation more often than other individuals. They may also be trying to stretch their budget. Vagrants and alcoholics frequently are truly in need of food or liquor and steal to meet these needs. Drug addicts pose a very direct threat to the safety of store personnel and should always be approached cautiously. A **kleptomaniac** (compulsive thief) seldom needs the items stolen, but simply cannot resist. There are very few true kleptomaniacs.

Professional shoplifters are much more difficult to detect. For them shoplifting is a way of life, often their sole source of income. They usually steal to resell the items, either to a fence or on the black market.

Common Methods of Shoplifting Shoplifting methods include palming objects, dropping articles into a receptacle, placing items inside clothing, wearing items out of the store and switching price tags. Most amateur shoplifting thefts are simple and direct, with the items picked up and put into a pocket or purse. Professional shoplifters, on the other hand, may use sophisticated methods and devices. A favorite device of professional shoplifters is the **booster box,** a box whose top, bottom or end is hinged so that articles can be placed inside without actually opening the box. Adult shoplifters may have children un-

[1]Some states call shoplifting "retail theft."
[2]Evidence established by law; also called "direct evidence." For example, 0.1 percent ethanol in the blood is prima facie evidence of intoxication in some states.

knowingly carry out merchandise that has not been paid for. Some professional shoplifters claim items others have placed on layaway; they target those items with only a small amount left due, pay the small balance and walk away with someone else's potential purchase.

Shoplifters usually prefer crowded first floors, large sales and self-service establishments where they are less apt to be detected. A study of how thieves select stores in which to shoplift revealed that thieves found numerous blind spots within stores where employees were often disengaged, leaving opportunity open for thieves and losses (Daniels, 2007i, p.16). The study also found thieves targeted stores lacking effective exit controls.

Indicators of Possible Shoplifting   Knowing how shoplifters operate can be of great value in spotting the potential or actual shoplifter. Personnel can be trained to watch for certain characteristics and actions commonly associated with shoplifting. Actions that might be indicative of shoplifting include picking up and putting down items, frequently opening and closing a purse, continuously looking around, roaming while waiting for someone else to shop, walking aimlessly around the store, frequently using elevators or restrooms and sending clerks to get merchandise from back rooms.

Clothing, too, might be indicative of shoplifting, including bulky clothing in warm weather, a coat over an arm, a full skirt or a large hat. Individuals who carry many bags or boxes; briefcases, newspapers or umbrellas; or have an arm in a sling might be using these items to conceal shoplifted merchandise. Although any one or two of the preceding indicators could be very normal (e.g., having a briefcase and carrying a topcoat over the arm), a combination of several of the indicators may be regarded as suspicious.

Deterring Shoplifting   Numerous approaches to deter shoplifting are available to management. Commonly used preventive measures include training personnel, implementing antishoplifting merchandising techniques and using physical and procedural controls. Such deterrents discourage borderline thieves and help trap bold ones.

 The single most effective deterrent to shoplifting is surveillance by an alert, trained sales force. This may be supplemented by security officers or **floorwalkers**.

Clerical attention to customers may be the single most important factor in deterring shoplifting: "The first line of defense against shoplifters is floor employees—the eyes and ears of the store" (Martinez, 2004, p.58). Self-service establishments that save in personnel costs may simply be trading such savings for increased losses from shoplifting. Sales personnel should be trained in the characteristics that may indicate shoplifting as well as in the common methods of shoplifting.

In addition to being alert and observant, sales personnel should be trained to serve all customers promptly. Fast, efficient service will usually deter shoplifting, especially that committed by youths. True customers will appreciate this promptness; shoplifters will be aware that they are noticed. If the salesperson is busy with one customer when another enters, the salesperson should tell the customer, "I'll be with you in a minute." Salespeople should not turn their backs on customers, if possible. They should keep an eye on people who are "just looking" or wandering aimlessly around the store and should never leave the assigned area unattended.

Security officers, usually in uniform, may be positioned at entrances and exits and may also "float" around in a retail establishment, making their presence very obvious. Floorwalkers, on the other hand, pose as customers and seek to remain unnoticed so they can catch shoplifters "in the act." Thus, the goals of trained salespeople and those of floorwalkers are often in direct conflict. Salespeople who approach customers, believing they may be about to shoplift, thwart the objectives of the floorwalker. Whether the focus should be on prevention or on apprehension is a critical management decision.

Other deterrents to shoplifting that require little expense but that can result in great savings include merchandising techniques that thwart the would-be thief. Although modern merchandising rests on the premise that customers should be able to examine items, this also makes these items more susceptible to theft. Merchandising techniques to deter shoplifting include keeping displays orderly and not stacking merchandise too high; returning to the display any item looked at and not bought; keeping small, valuable items locked in display cases; placing identifying tags on all merchandise; displaying only one of a pair; not displaying expensive merchandise near exits and having small, easily stolen items located by the checkout.

Procedures such as keeping unused checkout lanes closed, locking the back door, having package checks, carefully checking price tags and bar codes, maintaining tight controls on fitting rooms and restrooms, issuing receipts, controlling refunds and establishing a communication system are important in deterring shoplifting.

Physical controls to deter shoplifting include changing the actual store layout, posting signs, installing locks and alarms and installing surveillance equipment such as convex mirrors and closed-circuit television (CCTV). One innovative approach is to enclose with floor-to-ceiling glass high-risk departments such as those with teenagers' trendy clothing—a frequent target of shoplifters—and provide only one entry/exit into the rest of the store. An increasing number of retailers are placing electronics and other high-priced, small items, such as video games, DVDs, CDs and the like, into a separate "bay" with a single electronically monitored entrance/exit through which customers must pass.

Electronically activated price tags are being used more and more. Such electronic article surveillance (EAS) is a cost-effective weapon against shoplifting. These tags set off an alarm if the item is taken from the store with the price tag still on it. These tags may be wafers, pellets or long plastic strips that are removed with a special instrument by sales personnel. Anyone attempting to remove the tags without the instrument will damage the article. There is a real danger, however, if sales personnel are not meticulous about removing the tags. Should a tag be left on carelessly, an innocent customer will set off the alarm. Such embarrassing episodes may prevent customers from coming back or, worse, lead to lawsuits. To avoid these negative outcomes, EAS tags should be made obvious and signs should indicate their presence (Gips, 2007, p.26).

Radio frequency identification (RFID) systems are an emerging technology being used by the Department of Defense as well as "giant" retailers like

Wal-Mart, Target and Albertsons (Page, 2004, p.128). The monitored device is housed in tiny tags, some smaller than a grain of rice, that give off unique identifying codes and enable tracking of items throughout an establishment. As mentioned in earlier chapters, RFID technology is used by some companies to track inventory, but its use as an asset management technique is often controversial (Daniels, 2006b, p.14). Nonetheless: "In the past five years, the radio identification tag industry has exploded into a $2 billion business" (DePass, 2006, p.D1).

Many other deterrents to shoplifting have been implemented in retail establishments. Some stores have an employee incentive program to reward personnel who assist in deterring or apprehending shoplifters. Others have encouraged customers to help detect shoplifting. For example, the General Mills Honesty Patrol encourages supermarket customers to report retail theft. Customers are given "Honesty Patrol" buttons and can report any retail thefts anonymously. They do not have to confront the suspect.

In addition, a careful system of inventory control, through which the magnitude of the problem is recognized and a written record of shoplifters detained (whether prosecuted or not) is kept, can help combat shoplifting. Such a list can be circulated to other merchants, provided it is marked "Confidential." Many cities have established a merchants' protective association to assist in maintaining and circulating a central list of shoplifters and bad-check passers.

Apprehending Shoplifters   It is critical to distinguish the thief from the absent-minded shopper who simply walks out of a department or store carelessly, but not fraudulently, without paying for an article. Shoplifters should be apprehended so that stolen merchandise can be recovered. This is a basic purpose of private security—to protect assets.

To apprehend a suspect for shoplifting, someone must actually see the item being taken and concealed or be reasonably certain an item has been taken. Apprehension may occur on or outside the premises, depending on state statute. Mere suspicion is not enough. There must be evidence of intent to steal, including such actions as leaving the department or floor without paying, concealing the property, taking off price tags or having no money to pay for items. The key to a lawful detention is **reasonable cause**, which is interpreted in the same way as probable cause by the courts. The Supreme Court has defined **probable cause** as "facts and circumstances within their knowledge and of which they had reasonable trustworthy information [that] were sufficient in themselves to warrant a man of reasonable caution in the belief that the suspect had committed a crime" (*Carroll v. United States*, 1925).

In many states, concealment is prima facie evidence of the intent to permanently deprive. In addition to seeing the item being taken, salespeople must provide continuous surveillance; otherwise, the suspect may pass the stolen merchandise to a confederate or simply get rid of it. The result would be "no case" and the risk of a false imprisonment suit.

A set procedure should be established for apprehending shoplifters. In most states it is no longer necessary for the shoplifter to leave the store, although prosecution is easier if the person has left the premises. In addition, apprehension outside the store causes less commotion and interference with the store's operation. However, if the merchandise is valuable and the thief may get away if allowed to leave the premises, the suspect should be apprehended inside the store.

Usually salespeople do *not* apprehend shoplifters. Rather, they notify the manager, security officer or floorwalker. It takes courage and confidence to confront a shoplifter and a strong personality to be able to withstand verbal and sometimes even physical abuse. The person who does the apprehending should first seek assistance because the suspect may have an accomplice who comes to the rescue. The apprehending employees should never call the suspect a thief or use the word *steal*, nor should they touch the suspect unless absolutely necessary.

The usual procedure is for the people making the apprehension to identify themselves, instruct the suspect to give up the merchandise, describe it specifically and state where it was taken from and then ask for the sales slip. If the suspect cannot produce a receipt, he or she is taken to the office. Force can be used if necessary. Courts have repeatedly ruled that requiring a suspected shoplifter to return to a store once outside constitutes an arrest, even if no physical force is used.

Managers, security officers, floorwalkers and sales personnel may make a citizen's arrest but must use extreme caution. It is usually better not to arrest until after questioning is completed.

A witness should be present when questioning a shoplifting suspect to avoid the charge that undue pressure was applied. Any involuntary confession is inadmissible, as is any confession given after prolonged questioning. The suspect should be treated courteously. If the suspect confesses, a written confession should be obtained to avoid civil lawsuits.

Detention has at least four very specific purposes: (1) to recover stolen merchandise, (2) to identify the suspect, (3) to learn the reasons for his or her action and (4) to decide whether to take criminal or civil action against the subject. People detained on suspicion of shoplifting are often asked to sign a standard release form such as the following:

> I hereby release the person(s) who detained me in connection with this incident and his or her employees, superiors, principals and customers from any claim or demand arising out of or in connection with the incident.

Such waivers often are not upheld in court, however. If items are taken from the suspect, they should be marked with the initials of the person obtaining the evidence, as well as the place and date. Careful records should be kept of all individuals apprehended, whether prosecuted or not.

Prosecuting Shoplifters Existing state statutes and the severity of punishment may be factors in whether prosecution is undertaken. In some states, punishment depends on the value of the item and how many times the person has been caught for a similar offense. Shoplifters may receive a fine and/or a jail sentence. In some states a civil suit can also be brought. Procedures for prosecuting juveniles must be especially well defined. In some states parents of minors are held civilly responsible for shoplifting offenses of their children.

Some managers believe all shoplifters should be prosecuted and that failure to prosecute even "first offenders" encourages shoplifting. They reason that the person who steals will also lie and may very well have shoplifted before but gotten away with it. Prosecution will serve as a deterrent to others, these managers argue. It will also help avoid false arrest suits and will improve security staff morale. Other managers, however, think that criminal prosecution is a law enforcement objective that does not meet security (prevention) objectives.

Even if a person has admitted guilt, the store does not always prosecute: "A policy of catching shoplifters and pushing for prosecutions may not be the best use of company resources" (Rosen, 2004, p.59). Reasons for nonprosecution include the fear of losing a good customer, the fear of damaging the store's reputation, the loss of time and the expense of testifying and the leniency of the courts to first offenders. Additionally, while security or sales personnel are in court testifying, the establishment is more vulnerable to other losses from shoplifting. Obviously, not all shoplifters will be prosecuted.

Reasonable guidelines should be established for prosecuting shoplifters. Factors to consider in establishing a policy on prosecuting shoplifters include the following:

- *Age*—Those 12 and under usually have their parents called and then are released to them. Those 13 to 16 are treated as juvenile offenders.
- *Monetary value*—Taking a 50-cent package of gum (a misdemeanor) differs from taking an $850 camera (a felony).
- *Past history*—A person with a past record of shoplifting is more likely to be prosecuted.
- *Attitude*—Is the suspect repentant and sorry or belligerent and hostile?
- *Strength of the case*—Are there witnesses, a confession, recovered property?

Illegal detention, malicious prosecution and slander suits should be guarded against.

Organized Retail Crime (ORC)

"While retail crime comes in many forms such as shoplifting, credit card fraud and internal theft, ORC is a different beat. Unlike shoplifting, ORC involves professional thieves operating as a network of 'boosters' and 'fences' who steal, repackage, and resell a staggering amount of stolen goods daily" (Thuermer, 2007, p.52). The most popular items on the organized retail crime (ORC) "shopping list" are electronics, DVDs, CDs, razor blades, liquor, over-the-counter medicine, baby formula, health and beauty care items and meat (Thuermer, p.58). A National Retail Federation (NRF) survey reports an increase in ORC despite the industry's best efforts to combat it, with 79 percent of respondents indicating their company has been a victim of ORC (see Figure 16.2).

Daniels (2007a, p.1) notes: "Although increased media attention and legislative action has been directed at organized retail crime, new research shows that additional action is needed to reduce the dollar amounts retailers lose to ORC gangs—an amount the FBI estimates at $30 billion a year."

Typically, an ORC member will scout a retail establishment during regular business hours and report back to other members regarding the location of high-end goods. The gang then either sends in a group of shoplifters to do a sweep of the expensive merchandise or returns after hours to burglarize the store (Martinez, 2005a, p.59). Profits from ORC are often funneled into terrorist

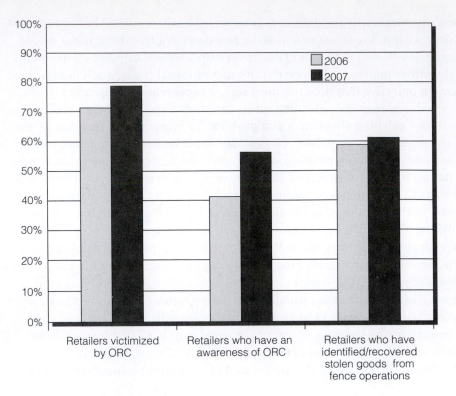

Figure 16.2   NRF Survey of Organized Retail Crime. According to the National Retail Federation's third annual Organized Retail Crime survey, ORC has increased despite the retail industry's best efforts to combat the situation. Leaders in the industry cite the complexity and sophistication of the crime and the perpetrators as part of the problem.

SOURCE: From the University of Florida's 2003 National Retail Security Survey by Dr. Richard Hollinger.

activities, "making this seemingly benign criminal activity [shoplifting] a serious national threat" (Martinez, 2005b, p.62).

According to Martinez (2005a, p.59): "Loss prevention professionals are not without a defense against organized retail theft. The first step toward successfully combating the problem is recognizing that it exists and acknowledging its gravity."

Technology and legislation are two vital tools in combating organized theft: "Retailers . . . are using antitheft devices as well as other technology to make it harder for boosters to hide the origin of stolen goods. They are also using software to help them spot connections in crimes. More recently, the Retail Industry Leaders Association and NRF joined forces to launch the Law Enforcement Retail Partnership Network (LERP-net), a Web-based computer database that will allow retailers to share ORC information with each other and with law enforcement" (Thuermer, p.58). LERP-net enhances private-public sector cooperation in the fight against organized theft and fraud (Friedrick, 2007b, p.17). Colorado has passed a new law aimed at cutting down organized retail theft. The legislation creates a task force to review ways to prevent and reduce ORC as well as to develop recommendations to enforce the law. The bill also requires dealers at flea markets and swap meets to show proof of ownership (Daniels, 2006a, p.14).

Losses from Bad Checks and Fraudulent Credit or Debit Cards

Most checks are cashed not in banks but in retail stores. Providing this service, however, creates the risk of loss through bad checks. To reduce losses from bad checks, retailers should:

- Teach personnel to recognize the different types of checks and the common types of bad checks.
- Establish a check-cashing policy and adhere to it.
- Train personnel to examine checks and identification.
- Record relevant information on the backs of all checks cashed.
- Reconcile identity documents with check passers' characteristics.

High-risk checks include second-party checks, illegible checks, postdated checks and out-of-town checks. In addition, a *money order* can be passed as a check. However, a money order is usually bought to send in the mail. Most stores should not accept money orders in face-to-face transactions.

Types of Bad Checks   Writing a "bad" check is a crime. It may be either forgery or fraud, depending on the type of check written. In either event, bad checks are of major concern to businesses. The most common types of bad checks are forged or altered checks, no-account checks and nonsufficient funds (NSF) checks.

Establishing Check-Cashing, Debit-Card and Credit-Card Policies
Every retail establishment should establish and post policies on how payment might be made. Some establishments do not accept checks. Others do not accept cash. Still others accept *only* cash.

Examining Checks, Debit Cards and Credit Cards   Personnel who accept payments should be taught how to examine what is presented as payment. Checks should be carefully examined, including the printed name and address, date, payee, numerical and written amount, and signature. Checks that are illegible, that are not written in ink or that contain erasures or written-over dates or amounts should not be accepted.

Individuals presenting payment other than cash should be required to produce identification containing a physical description (preferably a photograph) and a signature. Acceptable forms of identification include driver's licenses, military or government IDs and national credit cards.

Frequently stores have a **floor release limit**, meaning that any charge above a certain amount must be cleared through the credit-card company. Some stores have a **zero floor release limit**, meaning that all charges are cleared with the credit-card issuer.

Retail Employee Theft

Many losses assumed to be the result of customer shoplifting may actually be caused by employees. An estimated 30 percent of all business failures are the result of employee theft (Lamb, 2004, p.46). Employees have an easier time shoplifting because they know what security measures exist, and they are often in a department alone. In addition, turnover in personnel may be high, and extra personnel may be added during peak seasons when the risk of theft is known to be higher than usual.

Security measures previously discussed have special relevance to curbing retail losses. First, have effective preemployment screening so honest employees are hired. Next, establish the proper climate for honesty. Employees who are treated fairly and paid fairly are less likely to steal from their employers. A "zero shortage" attitude should be adopted, maintained and rewarded.

Just as people are key to detecting shoplifting, so people are key to detecting employee theft. Shopping services help detect employee dishonesty. Incentives to reduce employee theft include making certain each person is matched to his or her job, setting reasonable rules and enforcing them, setting clear lines of authority and responsibility, rewarding outstanding performance and removing the temptation to steal.

In addition, physical and procedural controls are essential. Limiting the number of employee exits, keeping storerooms locked and allowing entrance only by authorized personnel, checking lockers and packages, flattening trash and restricting access to assets, as feasible, should all be part of the retail security plan.

 Special employee security concerns in retail establishments include access to merchandise and cash. Specific pricing procedures, cash-handling procedures and refund procedures are essential. Personnel should be rotated periodically, and responsibilities should be separated.

Pricing   One major cause of inventory shrinkage is loosely controlled pricing procedures. Price switching or price altering can be done either by employees or by customers. Effective pricing procedures should thwart such actions. To deter employee theft by price alterations policies might allow only authorized employees to set prices and mark merchandise and might require periodic audits of prices recorded and prices changed.

A special risk is the salesperson who adds extra items to a customer's purchases to win the favor of that customer or who undercharges friends or relatives. Clerks who sell articles to friends and relatives at lower cost (called **sliding**) will find that once they start, they cannot stop without losing friends.

Employees who are allowed to make purchases at a discount may abuse the privilege by buying for friends and relatives, or sometimes even for resale at a profit. To thwart such actions, a manager or supervisor should make all employee sales and should keep a record to see that the cumulative amount is reasonable. In addition, employees should not shop until the end of the day and should leave the premises after their shopping is completed.

Cash Handling   Cash is particularly vulnerable to theft. The customer who hurriedly lays the correct change on the counter and leaves without waiting for a receipt presents an especially tempting situation for cash-handling personnel. All cash-handling personnel should be properly trained, supervised and rewarded for efficiency and honesty. However, the cashier position in most retail establishments is an entry-level position with low pay and high turnover. Consequently, many managers do not invest much in training their cashiers. This can be a costly mistake.

Several methods may be used to steal money from the cash register, often called "till tapping." Clerks may fail to ring up a sale and simply pocket the money. They may purposely shortchange people. They may deliberately under-ring a purchase and then "catch" the error, adding the charge manually to the customer's receipt and receiving the full price from the customer. The added amount would not show on the tape, and the clerk would be free to pocket the money. Clerks may also enter an over-ring, as though to correct an error, when they are actually pocketing the money. Supervisors should make periodic checks of the registers to ensure they balance. A clerk who is consistently over or under the correct amount should probably be given a job that does not involve handling money. Figure 16.3 illustrates one way to separate the functions of employees who deal with cash and how to trace transactions.

Honesty shopping, or a **shopping service**, tests the integrity of sales personnel who handle cash. Retailers frequently hire personnel from security firms who offer shopping services, that is, professional shoppers who pose as customers and who then check for violations of cash-handling procedures. Such services are often used in retail stores, bars, restaurants and other sales establishments. Typically, the honesty shopper makes a purchase using the correct change and leaves hurriedly (called a *put down*), the ideal situation for the till-tapping clerk. A second honesty shopper may observe whether the clerk rings up the sale, or the register tape may later be examined to see if that sale was recorded. Some honesty shoppers also use marked money. Remember, however, that employees may make an honest mistake, get busy and forget to ring up a sale. However, if it is an honest mistake, there will be an overage for that amount at the end of the day. When employees are informed that such a

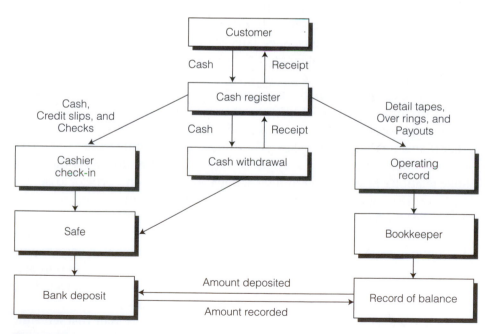

Figure 16.3   Retail Cash and Cash Flow Records

SOURCE: From the National Crime Prevention Institute. Reprinted by permission.

system is used, it will also act as a psychological deterrent to potentially dishonest employees.

Returns and Refunds   Retailers are combating return fraud with a unique fingerprint tool that uses UPC and serial numbers for products from participating manufacturers. When a product is scanned, the fingerprint is stored in an electronic database. If the product is returned, information on when and where the product was purchased can be pulled from the database (Beaulieu, 2005, p.16).

Exception-based reporting (EBR) can also help identify where losses are occurring (Daniels, 2007g, p.16). For example, Ann Taylor, a 900-store women's fashion chain, reviewed its return policy using the EBR system to examine the time between purchases and returns. The data indicated that nearly $500,000 worth of returns were reported to be three months after initial purchase or older, necessitating those items be marked down, which translated into loss.

It is easier for employees to abuse the return/refund system than it is for customers to do so. Therefore, the same policies regarding refunds should be rigidly applied to employees as well. Keep tight control of all credit documents, and match items to the return vouchers. Conduct periodic audits of return vouchers.

Shopping Center/Mall Security

A modern phenomenon is the large shopping mall, centralizing a large number of retail, entertainment, professional and business operations into one location, with ample parking and easy access for thousands of customers. Shopping center management has become such a specialized field that the International Council of Shopping Centers (ICSC) has begun to certify the qualifications of managers for shopping centers. Different combinations of local law enforcement personnel and proprietary and/or contractual guard forces provide security for these shopping centers. Most large shopping centers have a director of security, a proprietary security force, CCTV, a communications system and mobile patrols for parking lots.

Shopping centers and malls throughout the country pose special problems for security officers. The goal of these centers, like that of the individual establishments located within them, is profit. Because security represents a cost rather than a profit, it must make its contribution felt in other ways.

The primary objectives of shopping center security are loss prevention and public relations. Losses from criminal actions are not the only type of losses for which security personnel are responsible. They should be observant and watch for any fire or safety hazards that could ultimately result in a loss.

The second primary objective of shopping center security is to promote good public relations. Some shopping centers have experimented with having their officers wear blazers and slacks rather than the more traditional, military-type uniforms. While this does foster public relations, the deterrent effect of the highly visible, uniformed officer is often significantly diminished.

The December 5, 2007, shooting at Omaha's Westroads Mall that left nine dead and five injured brought home, once again, what security experts have known for decades: "Retail malls are 'soft targets'" (Davis, 2008, p.14). Large numbers of people, often carrying big packages, come and go through many entrances and exits. Research conducted by state homeland security advisors on the status of security at U.S. shopping malls found significant gaps in the emergency preparedness of malls:

- Very little money has been spent to upgrade security since 9/11.
- Training of mall security staff remains inadequate.
- Hiring standards have not changed substantially since 9/11.
- Risk assessments are rare. (Davis)

When asked to characterize the level of preparedness of large malls in their states, 31 percent said "poor," 24 percent said "fair," 27 percent said "good" and 18 percent said "very good." The most frequent reasons for the "poor" rating were inadequate training and equipment (Davis). Private mall security directors and state homeland security officials recommend the following to improve emergency preparedness:

- Conduct a formal risk assessment by experts.
- Curtail access to air circulation systems and other sensitive areas.
- Monitor deliveries.
- Use passive barriers to prevent cars with explosives from penetrating heavily populated areas.
- Develop and rehearse detailed and coordinated emergency response plans with first responders and mall tenants.
- Standardize antiterrorism training by setting minimum standards for frequency, material, learning methods and performance measures.
- Enhance partnerships with the public sector to maximize the expertise of state homeland security officials and first responders. (Davis)

Two separate studies suggest that malls can decrease their vulnerability by implementing relatively inexpensive security measures such as encouraging reporting of suspicious packages and daily searches of kiosks and pushcarts (Straw, 2007, p.30). According to a Rand study, the greatest risk for shopping centers is bombs placed by outsiders, followed by pedestrian suicide bombs. A study by the National Institute of Justice found that while most malls had emergency management plans, they often lacked input from police and first responders (Straw, p.32). This survey found that the most common measures implemented at malls were CCTV surveillance (50 percent), instructing staff to watch for suspicious dress and behavior (50 percent) and vehicle barriers (30 percent). The goal of mall security, after all, is to deter terrorists, not shoppers (Straw, p.30).

Assistance in Enhancing Retail Security

Retail security requires that merchandise and cash be protected from internal (employee) and external (customer, burglar or robber) theft. Advice, assistance and information on retail security can be obtained from merchants' protection associations, retail credit bureaus, better business bureaus, police departments and district attorneys' offices. In addition, a retail security checklist such as that shown in Figure 16.4 might be used to identify areas of weakness in the security system.

		1 2 3			1 2 3
I. Safe	a. Anchored b. Visible c. Lighted d. Decals e. Locks operable	_ _ _ _ _ _ _ _ _ _ _ _ _ _ _	VI. BLDG (front)	a. Doors b. Locks c. Windows d. Vents e. Lighting	_ _ _ _ _ _ _ _ _ _ _ _ _ _ _
II. Cash deposit	a. Excess in safe b. Excess in register c. Other locations d. Armored car e. Employee(s)	_ _ _ _ _ _ _ _ _ _ _ _ _ _ _	VII. BLDG (left side)	a. Doors b. Locks c. Windows d. Vents e. Lighting	_ _ _ _ _ _ _ _ _ _ _ _ _ _ _
III. Employee training	a. Shoplifting b. Robbery c. Till tap d. Short change e. Checks	_ _ _ _ _ _ _ _ _ _ _ _ _ _ _	VIII. BLDG (rear)	a. Doors b. Locks c. Windows d. Vents e. Lighting	_ _ _ _ _ _ _ _ _ _ _ _ _ _ _
IV. Employee screening	a. Previous employers b. Neighbors c. Fingerprints d. Police record e. Polygraph	_ _ _ _ _ _ _ _ _ _ _ _ _ _ _	IX. BLDG (right side)	a. Doors b. Locks c. Windows d. Vents e. Lighting	_ _ _ _ _ _ _ _ _ _ _ _ _ _ _
V. Employee access cntrl	a. No exterior keys b. No. ex-emp. w/keys c. Date comb. changed d. Date locks changed e. No. emp. opening and closing	_ _ _ _ _ _ _ _ _ _ _ _ _ _ _	X. BLDG (roof)	a. Doors b. Locks c. Skylights d. Vents and ducts e. Lighting	_ _ _ _ _ _ _ _ _ _ _ _ _ _ _

Crime Prevention Survey form — Page 1. Request / Routine; Retail business / Residential. Complaint number. Business name, Address, Manager's name, Business phone, Home phone, Survey date(s), Officer(s), Type of goods, Survey based on.

Additional comments _____

Note: 1–Adequate   2–Inadequate   3–Comments

Figure 16.4   Retail Security Checklist
SOURCE: Courtesy of the Chattanooga Police Department.

Lodging and Hospitality Establishments Security

The courts have held that hotels must take "a reasonable and prudent approach" to security (de Treville and Longmore-Etheridge, 2004, p.61). The president of the American Hotel and Lodging Association (AHLA) explains: "By common law, hotels are required to exercise 'reasonable care' for the safety and security of their guests." He recommends that an in-house security committee tour a selected hotel department each month looking for ways to improve security and safety (de Treville and Longmore-Etheridge).

According to the vice president—enterprise loss prevention for Marriott International, the challenge to the company in managing its 2,700 properties is balancing convenience and security (Friedrick, 2007a, p.18).

 The number one challenge for hotel CSOs is balancing security with customer convenience and freedom of movement.

Security Concerns in Hotels/Motels

In the effort to make hotels and motels more convenient for guests, management has increased the vulnerability to theft, vandalism and assault. Elevators and parking garages provide outside thieves, employees and guests with greater access to unprotected areas and less probability of detection while committing crimes.

 Major security concerns of the hotel/motel industry include both internal and external theft, vandalism, vice and fire.

Items most frequently stolen from hotels and motels include money, credit cards, jewelry, linens, silver, food, liquor and other easily concealed articles. The most significant internal theft losses result from inadequate procedures for cash handling, housekeeping activities, receiving and storing supplies, laundry services and restaurant/bar services.

Guests are vulnerable to theft not only by hotel/motel employees, but also by professional thieves and burglars who obtain access to guest rooms and loot them while the guests are away. Hotels and motels in resort areas encounter additional security problems because most guests are occupied with recreation or sightseeing and spend much time away from their rooms, often leaving large sums of cash, plane tickets, sporting equipment, cameras, credit cards, jewelry and expensive clothing in their rooms. Likewise, hotels and motels hosting large conventions and conferences face special security problems because the guests' schedules are easily predetermined and the times when rooms will be empty anticipated.

The long-term loss suffered from poor security can place a business in severe financial jeopardy. When a crime occurs on a property, a lodging and hospitality company's bottom line is threatened by loss of revenue as well as by increased insurance costs that can cause the establishment's insurance premiums to skyrocket by as much as 30 percent—for up to four years (Stover, 2006, p.76). As an example, one large hotel property in a resort area experienced a rash of car break-ins and thefts, with one incident escalating to an armed robbery of two elderly guests in their hotel room (Stover, p.71). As guests and conferences cancelled their reservations due to security concerns, the hotel experienced a revenue loss of more than $350,000. Not yet calculated are legal fees that will be incurred in defending the hotel against an inadequate security lawsuit and the potential increase in liability insurance premiums because of the hotel's adverse loss history. These costs could easily add several hundred thousand dollars to the bottom-line cost of the robbery.

Guests are not always the victims, however. Sometimes guests are the criminals, whether they consider their actions "criminal" or not. The American Hotel and Motel Association estimates that millions of dollars worth of property are lost each year because guests take items such as ashtrays and towels as souvenirs. Millions of dollars more are lost as the result of carelessness with hotel property and furnishings, as well as by intentional vandalism. Conventions pose an additional problem in that conventioneers can be extremely unruly. Further, some guests do not pay their bills, or they pay them with bad checks or invalid credit cards.

In addition to these losses, the hotel/motel industry must deal with problems such as prostitution and gambling, which frequently occur in semipublic establishments. The emphasis placed on this problem is determined by management.

Fire and ventilation are additional safety concerns. In the fall of 1990, the Hotel-Motel Fire Safety Act (HR94) was passed. This law requires federal employees who stay or meet in hotels or motels of three stories or more to use facilities that have sprinkler systems. Another safety hazard exists in facilities with indoor swimming pools: carbon monoxide poisoning. This deadly gas is given off by the pool's heater. Adequate ventilation is a necessity to prevent such hazards. The checklist in Figure 16.5 can be used to assess fire as well as pool safety in hotels and motels.

Security Measures in Hotels/Motels

Providing free movement and open facilities to guests must be balanced with implementing procedures to minimize criminal opportunities. Sound security measures not only increase the guests' safety, but also raise the profitability of the establishment. With huge losses sustained from employee theft and the growing frequency of guest-room theft and attacks on guests, increasing numbers of hotel and motel operators are turning to private security to reduce their losses.

The security practices of a particular hotel or motel are usually the responsibility of the individual owner or the franchise holder. Large, nationwide lodging chains often have corporate security staffs to provide support and guidance to the franchise owners. The corporate security staff conducts security surveys; investigates specific losses; establishes guidelines for security policies and staffing; makes recommendations on cash-handling procedures, preemployment screening and emergency plans; and maintains liaison with local law enforcement agencies.

Hotel/motel executives and security directors generally agree that security should be given a greater emphasis in training managers, owners and franchise holders. Specifically, degree programs in hotel and restaurant management should require courses in security, including civil liability issues.

Several specific policies and procedures not only improve security but can also reduce insurance premiums by 15 to 20 percent: "These include the appointment of a companywide risk manager, a claims-reduction program with attainable goals, incentives to meet the goal being tied to hotel managers' bonuses, written policies and procedures incorporated into an accessible employee manual, an active safety committee at each property and an injured-employee back-to-work program" (Stover, p.76).

CHECKLIST FOR FIRE AND POOL SAFETY

Here is a checklist of basics for evaluating hotel safety. Each group is different. If you have elderly or handicapped attendees, be sure to consider their special safety needs.

FIRE

☐ Do all areas of the hotel have sprinklers and fire alarms?
☐ Are fire-alarm systems regularly tested?
☐ Does the hotel have a *written* emergency plan?
☐ Does the plan include meeting and dining areas?
☐ Has the hotel staff been trained in evacuation procedures?
☐ Are there alarm switches on each floor?
☐ Do fire alarms alert the fire department directly?
☐ Are stairwells open to ground and roof?
☐ Do meeting rooms have at least two exits? (or more, if the room is large)?
☐ Does the hotel have emergency lighting?
☐ How far away is the fire department?
☐ When was the hotel last inspected by the fire department?
☐ What is the fire department's phone number?
☐ What is the hotel's security police phone number?
☐ Where are fire extinguishers located?
☐ Is the hotel in compliance with local fire codes?
☐ Are there any outstanding fire code violations?
☐ Are stairways and exits obstructed in any way?
☐ Are exits clearly marked with an exit sign?
☐ Are diagrams of emergency exits, stairways, and fire extinguisher locations posted in each room?

POOLS

☐ If pools are enclosed in hotel atriums, do rooms have a window that can be opened for ventilation?
☐ Are any of the rooms adjacent to the pool heating system?
☐ What codes of inspections apply to the pool heating system?
☐ Has the pool heating system been inspected and certified as safe?

Figure 16.5 Checklist for Fire and Pool Safety

SOURCE: Reprinted by permission from *Successful Meetings* magazine. © 1991 Bill Communications, Inc.

At the heart of the hotel/motel security system is adequate access control, which is a difficult procedure given the large number of employees and guests who have keys or access cards. This problem is compounded by the fact that the base population in most lodging establishments turns over 100 percent or more in a week. Most hotels and motels now use electronic locks opened by swiping a plastic card that bears no room number.

The increase in the number of armed robberies at motels has prompted many to follow the lead of hotels and install CCTV monitoring systems in lobby and cashier areas. Increasingly, hotels and motels are using monitoring systems in parking areas, ancillary lobbies and elevators.

Motels have generally avoided one problem that has traditionally plagued the hotel industry: **skips** or nonpaying guests. Most motels require guests to pay in advance or to establish valid credit. In most hotels, on the other hand, room charges and other costs incurred are accumulated and paid at checkout time. Guests may check out before all charges have been posted to the bill or, in some cases, not check out at all.

484 Section IV: Security Systems at Work

Although security usually requires the identification of items, an exception to this is the practice of identifying towels, ashtrays and any other items that tempt guests to "take" them as souvenirs. Unmarked towels and ashtrays have little sentimental value to travelers.

The safety and security of guests is every bit as important in economy hotels and motels as in the large or luxury hospitality chains, although economy hotels and motels may have limited capital resources with which to address security concerns.

Many lodging and hospitality enterprises also have restaurants and bars.

Restaurant and Bar Security

Restaurants and bars face many of the same security concerns as general retailers. In fact, many restaurants and bars also sell merchandise. In restaurants, unauthorized consumption of food and drink can result in tremendous losses. Policies establishing what employees can and cannot eat or drink while on the job should be clearly established. The fast-food industry faces some unique problems, including minimum wage employees and rapid turnover of employees.

The owner of Rosati's Pizza in Boulder, Colorado, says employee and external theft are a serious threat to his business: "There are thousands of dollars flowing into my store each day, and if 3 to 5 percent, which is the industry average, goes right into the pockets of my employees due to the theft and is not watched and not monitored, it can put me out of business quick" (Daniels, 2007f, p.14). To protect against such losses the business uses CCTV, which not only helps reduce losses, since employees know they are being watched, but can also be used to monitor productivity.

The Benihana restaurant chain has also implemented a video system at 20 locations, allowing management and the security staff to remotely monitor operations (Daniels, 2007b, pp.1, 16). The system provides recorded evidence in any incidents that could result in liability and is also used for more than security purposes. According to the system vendor: "We teach proactive use of video to manage stores and it has nothing to do with traditional security aspects of catching bad guys or loss issues. . . . We go on site to train their managers to influence employee behavior. It is very proactive and designed to train people how to do things the right way."

At a Hard Rock Café, a significant security problem existed in the retail store section with unpaid merchandise being lifted from two unenclosed areas at the sides of its main entrance. Store personnel found it difficult to monitor these areas; thus, enclosing the affected entrances with glass significantly reduced instances of theft. To further limit theft and fraud, the Hard Rock establishments use CCTV and also restrict the amount of cash they keep on hand (Daniels, 2007d, pp.15–16).

Many restaurants and bars also face the challenge of patrons who become inebriated. Concerning the problem of alcohol server liability, many states have enacted **Dram Shop Acts** making bartenders who continue to serve an obviously intoxicated patron liable for any harm that individual might do to others. Excessive drinking and other security problems may also be found in casinos, at racetracks and at sporting events.

Casino, Racetrack and Sporting Event Security

Only a few years ago, securing a public venue focused on the three "Gs": guards, guns and gates. However: "Now security officials are beginning to take far more aggressive, preventive and integrated approaches to protecting public venues, addressing seen and unseen threats, the integrity of critical computer networks, the quality of the air, and the potential presence of radiological material and toxic gases" (Durstenfeld, 2005, p.52). Casinos, racetracks and sporting events rely heavily on security officers to provide a safe environment and to protect assets. They also face the challenge of unruly patrons and large amounts of cash on hand.

Casino Security

The American Gaming Association contends that the $83.7 billion gaming industry is one of the most regulated, monitored and taxed U.S. industries: "Casinos promote games of chance, but when it comes to enhancing security, projecting a professional image, building customer loyalty and providing VIP treatment for frequent customers, casino owners and managers look for ways to keep the odds in their favor" (Wright, 2004, p.24).

Surveillance systems are vital to casino security: "A casino surveillance system can help the security team pinpoint cheaters, stamp out fraud and employee theft, keep patrons safe and document casino operations" (Longmore-Etheridge, 2007a, p.108). The Casino Royale and Hotel has added digital recording solutions to its entire property, with the technology monitoring the entire casino, including gaming tables, money exchange areas, exits and entrances, hotel common areas, parking areas and an off-site warehouse. Security staff can automatically stop and review a piece of video and e-mail the clip downstairs to the pit boss or to gaming officials if needed (Daniels, 2007c, p.17). Security can also print photos from video, enabling quick identification of regular offenders if they enter the casino.

Security staff at Atlanta City's Borgata Casino and Spa watches over the 135,000-square-foot gaming floor via a massive camera system consisting of 1,200 CCTV cameras that monitor all activities in the casino and other locations where cash is handled, such as the pit and the cage. A second nongaming system of 800 cameras monitors the 40-story, 2,000-room hotel tower, the in-house spa, a dozen restaurants, a 900-seat theater, a 2,900-seat entertainment complex and three parking lots (Longmore-Etheridge, 2004, p.103).

After 9/11 the ASIS International Council on Gaming and Wagering Protection surveyed 25 security professionals around the country and found physical security and surveillance to be more prevalent than in the past. The survey indicated live monitoring of property areas never before focused on, the use of proprietary explosives detection dogs and the use of employee awareness training programs. Additionally, security personnel were seeking ways to ensure more reliable and effective communications. Several properties had installed metal detectors at strategic or critical locations to screen for weapons. In addition, exterior HVAC boilers and other equipment accessible from low rooftops and doors leading to electric equipment, pool chemicals and other sensitive areas had been secured.

When casinos are located within hotels the security problems increase. Fifteen of the 25 largest hotels in the United States are part of gaming establishments located on the Las Vegas Strip (Boss and Longmore-Etheridge, 2006, p.78). Hundreds of thousands of guests and employees are concentrated in these areas on any given day or night.

In many states, casino-type gaming is combined with racing, posing additional challenges.

Racetrack Security

Racinos are dog and horse racing establishments that have casino features, such as card games and slot machines, as well. One such racino, the Mardi Gras Racetrack and Gaming Center in Hallandale Beach, Florida, has 700 high-quality, pan-tilt-zoom digital cameras strategically placed around the casino, count rooms and pari-mutuel betting area. Security staff can retrieve playback material in seconds by bringing up a specific camera number (Longmore-Etheridge, 2007a, p.116).

The aim of racetrack security is to protect the patrons, horses, jockeys/drivers, owners and grooms and to help the track meet the standards set forth by the various state racing commissions.

 Security concerns at a racetrack include access control, crowd control, parking security, vault security, alcohol control and fraud detection.

Some tracks use proprietary security guards in the **backstretch area**—the area where the horses, drivers and grooms are quartered. This is the most problematic area of the racetrack, with drinking, fighting and stealing being the major security issues.

The public areas of the racetrack such as the grandstand are usually protected by contract security officers who play an important public relations role as well as handle brawls and drunken patrons, personal injuries and protection of the big winners. They also frequently provide parking lot security. Other services provided by security personnel include guarding the vault and the runners conveying cash to and from the betting area, providing travel information, paging and handling lost-and-found articles.

 Security concerns at a racetrack can best be met by adequate access control, surveillance systems and by the presence of well-qualified, well-trained security personnel.

Security challenges and strategies at casinos and racetracks are similar to those found at large sporting events.

Sporting Event Security

Private security plays a significant role in maintaining order and controlling traffic at large public gatherings such as sporting events and trade shows. Many cities have built large, multipurpose facilities that they lease to organizations, such as professional football or baseball franchises, on a long-term seasonal basis, or for events such as auto, boat and home shows or concerts on a short-term basis.

© Reuters/CORBIS

A security guard sprays water on the crowd at a massive outdoor concert dubbed 'SARS-stock' at Downsview Park in Toronto, July 30, 2003. The day-long concert, headlined by the Rolling Stones, was organized to "bring back the energy" to the only area outside Asia to experience deaths from Severe Acute Respiratory Syndrome (SARS). A crowd of close to 430,000 people were expected to attend the 11-hour concert.

 Security concerns at sporting events include maintaining order, preventing admission of nonpaying people, preventing internal and external theft, providing first aid for injuries and regulating pedestrian and vehicle traffic.

The number of patrons at events can vary considerably. For example, a stadium may host a football game attracting eighty thousand people one night and a concert attracting only several thousand people the next night. Therefore most multipurpose stadiums maintain a small security force and then require the lessee or promoter of an event to provide additional security as the circumstances dictate. Security problems at large public gatherings were discussed in Chapter 3, which stressed the importance of private and public officers working together.

Office Building Security

Many contractual and proprietary security forces perform patrol, alarm and armored car/courier services at thousands of office buildings throughout the country as corporations seek to protect company assets as well as the lives and personal property of their employees. Some companies establish specific levels of security in their offices or buildings to meet requirements stipulated in government contracts. Others feel their corporation's work is highly sensitive, involving, for example, trade secrets, and thus view security as essential. In yet other instances, private developers build, own and manage inner-city office buildings and commercial industrial parks (frequently suburban office complexes that include nonmanufacturing businesses such as research laboratories, sales facilities, medical buildings and other professional offices situated along the front of the building with warehouses behind). These private developers may either provide security for the buildings and tenants in the complex or assign this responsibility to the prime tenant, the tenant who is leasing the most space in a particular building. Most private developers use the services of contract security firms to protect the entire complex.

Security Concerns of Office Buildings

"Open for Business" means open to the public. Most offices have a steady stream of outsiders. Among them may be people intent on committing such open-hour crimes as robbery or larceny. In addition, a would-be thief may "case" a particular office during business hours with the intent of returning for an after-hours burglary. Custodial personnel and tenants having keys to the building pose another after-hours threat. Further, employees can pilfer office supplies and petty cash during or after business hours.

 The major security concerns in office buildings include after-hours burglaries and theft; theft from a tenant by another tenant's employees; theft by service, maintenance and custodial employees; assaults, rapes and other crimes against persons; regulation and control of visitor traffic; bomb threats; protection of executive offices and personnel and fire watch.

The items most frequently stolen from office buildings include small office equipment such as calculators, duplicating and photocopying machines and computers and peripherals; office furnishings; securities and valuable documents; blank payroll checks and check-writing machines. Other corporate valuables that are often burglary targets include blank (unissued) stock certificates, the corporate seal, corporate minutes, office art and decorations and books. Many larger corporations maintain extensive professional libraries containing thousands of dollars worth of books, yet they often provide little or no control over access to them. And, as in any other type of business, office supplies and petty cash present another potential area for loss.

An additional challenge for office security is that some tenants may not perceive a need for security, thereby increasing the risk for other tenants in the same building who have security needs. As noted earlier, a nonsecure area adjacent to an area seeking security provides a vulnerable area for the "secure" office. Further, fire loading one tenant's office may pose a direct threat to other tenants, who may be completely unaware of such a threat. Compounding the problem is the fact that in office buildings having many different tenants, it is usually impossible to conduct fire or bomb evacuation drills.

Security Measures in Office Buildings

The amount of security devices and personnel required in an office building depends on the size and location of the building, the number and nature of tenant businesses and the crime rate of the area.

Primary security measures in office buildings are access control, proper authorization and documentation of the use of corporate assets by employees and periodic fire inspections and fire drills.

Many office buildings are constructed using the core concept, which has all elevators, restrooms, lobbies and service facilities located at the building's center, thus allowing more effective control of "public" areas while also permitting more flexible use of office space. Extra security measures to protect these public areas include CCTV, receptionists to monitor a visitor pass system and security officers. Elevators can be programmed to allow only authorized personnel to operate the elevators or to obtain access to specified floors after hours.

Internal losses can be minimized by requiring authorization and proper documentation of the use of company assets. For example, supplies should be obtainable only by requisition. The requisition forms should be checked periodically to ensure that the usage is reasonable. Petty cash is an easy target for internal loss unless a system of authorization and documentation is established. Vouchers are often required for all petty cash disbursed. However, the person responsible for disbursing petty cash might alter the amount on a voucher; for example, a voucher for $5 might be changed to read $35, with the person in charge pocketing $30. Therefore, vouchers should be periodically routed to the person signing for the cash to ensure that such changes have not occurred.

© AP/Wide World Photos

Most offices have a steady stream of outsiders. Security officers stationed at the entry points to thousands of office buildings throughout the country serve as gatekeepers to these businesses, helping the corporations protect company assets as well as the lives and personal property of their employees.

Vouchers should be canceled after they are recorded to prevent their reuse. In addition, unannounced audits of vouchers and petty cash ledgers should be made.

The mail room is another target for loss. Losses may occur because stamps are stolen or because mail-room personnel are not taught to weigh packages correctly or to determine the best postal rate and may be sending everything first class when third class or book rate might be more appropriate. Such practices, over time, can involve considerable financial loss for a business.

Houston's Greenway Plaza protects its 10 office buildings with CCTV, access control and well-trained security officers (Longmore-Etheridge, 2006, p.58). The average daytime population is about 12,000, mainly employees of tenant companies including financial, legal and a variety of other tenants. Each shift about 20 security officers patrol on foot, vehicles and bikes: "Not only are the bonds between tenants and security tight, but the security program also includes a 24/7 command center, a comprehensive, integrated access-control and badging system, a well-trained officer corps, carefully considered antiterrorism measures and a strong alliance with law enforcement and emergency services" (Longmore-Etheridge, p.60). This alliance is important because Greenway Plaza's security team responds to about 200 emergencies a year, mostly related to fire and medical situations (Longmore-Etheridge, p.63).

High-Rise Security

Owners of businesses in high-rise complexes must balance the need for secure individual floors with that of ensuring the safety of all tenants during an emergency (Evenson, 2005, p.40). Fire stairwells are often a key security concern for many high-rise office buildings because local fire codes may require that the stairwell doors be left unlocked. Two common options for effective stairwell re-entry systems are: (1) keeping the doors unlocked at all times or (2) installing an electrified lock release system connected directly to the building fire alarm panel and unlocked when the fire alarm panel is activated (Evenson, p.41). Installing crash-bars with alarms is another way to overcome this security problem.

In our post-9/11 world, the physical threat of terrorism to high-rise buildings has emerged as a significant concern. Lessons learned from the truck bombing of the Murrah Building in Oklahoma City in 1995 included the federal government re-examining their building's ability to withstand bomb blasts and developing mitigation concepts for window glass subjected to blasts. The government also implemented tighter building access controls for employees and visitors, and some commercial high-rise buildings placed additional restrictions on access to their underground parking lots (Aggleton, 2004, p.38).

Another result of the events of 9/11 is that new commercial high-rise buildings in New York City are required to have elevators that open onto a "smoke-stop vestibule" (Gips, 2005, p.44). Voluntary widening of stairwells is also being considered, not only to help the downward flow of building occupants during an evacuation but also to facilitate the counterflow of emergency responders trying to reach upper floors. An additional new requirement is that office buildings 100 feet tall or higher must have adequate sprinkler systems installed throughout the premises; however, owners have until July 1, 2019, to comply with this new standard. The tallest buildings (more than 780 feet) must designate a fire-safety director, deputy fire-safety directors, a building evacuation supervisor, fire wardens and an emergency-evacuation team (Gips, pp.45–47).

One extremely important lesson learned from the collapse of the World Trade Center (WTC) was the proven effectiveness of practice evacuations. According to a report by the National Institute of Standards and Technology (NIST), *Final Report on the Collapse of the World Trade Center Towers*, of the approximately 17,400 people in the two towers, 87 percent of the total building population and 99 percent of those located below the impact floors got out safely. A FEMA report stated that one principal reason the evacuation was so successful was the "conscientious implementation" of evacuation drills by the security team (Kitteringham, 2007, p.81).

The Sears Tower's Security   At 1,454 feet high, Chicago's Sears Tower is the tallest building in the United States. A team of security professionals at the Sears Tower oversees the safety and security of about 12,000 tenants employed by about 90 tenant companies, as well as the 8,000 to 13,000 visitors who come to visit the Skydeck, a top tourist attraction in Chicago (Longmore-Etheridge, 2007b, p.59).

After the collapse of the WTC, security was hardened accordingly. The number of security officers was increased, with security personnel wearing "hard" uniforms; the fronts of the lobbies were outfitted with x-ray machines; mandatory bag and briefcase screening were implemented for all employees and visitors; and customer service was not a priority. Many of these measures were not appreciated by the tenants, who felt they were working in a fortress-like, intimidating, unfriendly building.

When new management took over, security's approach became more subtle. Employees now flow in unimpeded, and visitors pass quickly through a metal detector and then use access-control cards at a series of decorative turnstiles to get to the elevators. Visitors can check in at a reception desk staffed with customer service agents in business suits (Longmore-Etheridge, 2007b, p.59).

Emergency notification service is an integral part of the Sears Tower's security and safety program. Tenants are contacted on several devices including phones, pagers, mobile phones and PDAs (Daniels, 2007h, pp.1, 10).

Burj Dubai Security   Burj Dubai is due to be the world's tallest skyscraper, 140 stories high with 55 elevators. The building will need hundreds of security personnel, both contract and proprietary, to staff check points, guard posts, control rooms, valet parking locations, concierge desks and other posts (Elliott, 2007, p.92). More than 200 full-time, specially trained security personnel will be on the property at any one time. Hundreds of sensors will be used throughout the building as well as a CCTV camera network of about 1,000 units. However: "Building design can only mitigate risk; it can't eliminate it. A disaster and crisis management plan and a crisis management team are being put together to deal with any situation that does occur due to natural or manmade incidents. Its members will liaise with the local police, civil defenses authorities, fire departments and others" (Elliott, p.93).

The discussion now returns to the United States for a look at an area of security often completely neglected—residential housing.

Security in Public and Private Housing

Although private security is usually thought to be solely involved with business and industry, it is becoming more important in residential units, where it is also needed. Burglaries of residential dwellings now account for hundreds of millions in property losses annually, a figure likely underreported. In addition, muggings and vandalism create problems for homeowners and renters.

 Security concerns of residential units include theft, vandalism and assaults, particularly muggings.

Although it would seem logical that expensive homes in exclusive neighborhoods would be the targets of thieves, often such is not the case. Studies by the U.S. Department of Housing and Urban Development (HUD) indicate that crime is considerably higher in public housing with low- and medium-income residents and with senior citizen residents than in other residential areas. In fact, crime rates in some public housing projects are two to four times higher, with higher rates of victimization per household or dwelling unit and substantially higher rates of multiple victimization of the same dwelling—that is, a large number of residences experiencing more than one burglary.

Anyone who has come home to find that his or her house or apartment has been burglarized may feel indignation, anger, rage and desire for revenge. It is, indeed, one of the most traumatic experiences a person can have. Knowing a stranger has gone through your most private possessions has an impact surpassed only by a personal assault or rape. Some steps individuals can take to deter burglars are given in a security checklist with the acronym STOP THIEF, shown in Figure 16.6.

Security consultants and firms can advise homeowners on security measures they might take. Many also offer around-the-clock monitoring of security systems installed within private homes. Such systems may include fire alarms connected directly with the fire department as well as sensors that will detect if the temperature drops below freezing. Increasing numbers of homeowners are installing special locks, floodlights and less expensive burglar alarms and/or buying safes and large dogs to protect their homes, valuables and families. Some homeowners' associations and exclusive residential developers hire security personnel to perform patrol services and to monitor central-gate entrances.

Access control, patrol by security officers and the provision of youth programs help to reduce residential losses. Access-control measures include door-keepers in vestibules, external door locks to interior hallways that tenants activate by remote control and monitoring of entrances with CCTV, sometimes connected so that tenants can view visitors seeking admittance. Some newer high-income apartment and condominium complexes have installed extensive alarm, monitoring and access-control systems monitored around the clock by a central console operator.

Many public housing authorities are implementing the same protective measures used by private apartment buildings in their high-rise complexes, includ-

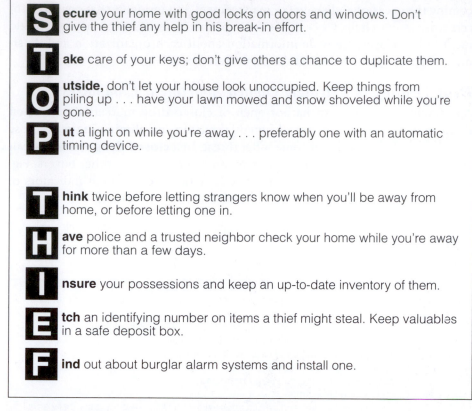

Figure 16.6 STOP THIEF

SOURCE: Reprinted by permission of State Farm Fire and Casualty Company.

ing CCTV monitoring and access control. Housing authorities in some large cities with many housing projects maintain armed proprietary or quasi-public security forces with limited or full police powers. Smaller housing authorities often organize tenant patrols or hire contract security firms to provide services. Although the inherent dangers in using tenant patrols must be acknowledged, they frequently do provide a good deal of security for residents in the building. Many public housing authorities have also established recreation programs and youth activities programs in an attempt to reduce the incidence of vandalism and crimes committed by juveniles.

As in business and industry, there is an architectural emphasis in designing neighborhoods and buildings that seeks to create safer environments that will minimize opportunities for the commission of crimes.

The Drug Problem in Public Housing

Various specific strategies have been used to tackle the drug problem in public housing. Often efforts focus on improving the physical environment, limiting entrances, improving lighting, erecting fences, requiring a pass card to gain entrance to the housing and keeping trash collected.

Another strategy for dealing with the drug problem in public housing projects is for security officers to acquire an understanding of the workings of the local public housing authorities or agencies (PHAs) that manage these complexes.

Officers need to work at establishing a relationship with the PHAs and at overcoming the occasional disbelief of management and residents that security officers truly want to help. Once this is accomplished, a fact-finding mission should identify key players, provide information about each organization and determine what programs exist and the participation level.

Drug Dealing in Privately Owned Apartment Complexes

Apartment complexes can harbor open or closed drug markets. In an **open drug market**, dealers sell to all potential customers, eliminating only those suspected of being police or some other threat. In a **closed drug market**, dealers sell only to people they know or who are vouched for by other buyers. Figure 16.7 presents some of the suspicious activities and common indicators of residential drug trafficking that security officers can be alert for.

 In apartment complexes open drug markets pose a greater threat than closed drug markets.

1. A high volume of foot and/or vehicle traffic to and from a residence at late or unusual hours.
2. Periodic visitors who stay at the residence for very brief periods of time.
3. Alterations of property by the tenants, including the following:
   a. Covering windows and patio doors with materials other than curtains or drapes;
   b. Barricading windows or doors;
   c. Placing dead bolt locks on interior doors; and
   d. Disconnecting fire alarms.
4. Consistent payment of rent and security deposits with U.S. currency, especially small denominations of cash. (Large amounts of 20 dollar bills are commonly seized from drug dealers.)
5. The presence of drug paraphernalia in or around the residence, including, but not limited to, glass pipes, syringes, propane torches, paper or tinfoil bundles, folded shiny-slick paper (snow seals), large quantities of plastic baggies, scales, money wrappers and small glass vials.
6. The presence of unusual odors coming from the interior of the residence, especially the odor of pungent chemical substances and/or burning materials.
7. The presence of firearms, other than sporting firearms, including fully automatic weapons, assault weapons, sawed-off shotguns, machine pistols, handguns and related ammunition and holsters.
8. The presence of tenant's possessions and furnishings which are inconsistent with the known income level of the tenant. This would include, but is not limited to, the following:
   a. New and/or expensive vehicles;
   b. Expensive jewelry and clothing; and
   c. Expensive household furnishings, stereo systems and other large entertainment systems.
9. Tenants who are overly nervous and apprehensive about the landlord visiting the residences.

Any of the indicators, by itself, may not be reason to suspect drug trafficking. However, when combined with other indicators, they may be reason to suspect drug trafficking. If you suspect drug trafficking in your neighborhood, please contact the police department at 555–5555.

Figure 16.7   Suspicious Activity and Common Indicators of Residential Drug Trafficking

SOURCE: *Drugs: A Municipal Approach, A Community Handbook* (Des Moines Police Department) p.26.

Protecting American Citizens and U.S. Business Interests Abroad

Many U.S. companies have offices abroad, often staffed by American citizens. Incidents such as the foiled terrorist bombings in London and the attack on Glasgow International Airport have propelled security directors to watch global operations closely (Daniels, 2007j, pp.1, 11). In most cases, security is even more critical in overseas branches than those in the United States because cultural factors influencing security may not be known.

Security Concerns

 The primary concern when providing security abroad is unfamiliarity with the language, local customs and expectations. Terrorism is also to be considered.

Security Measures

Corporate and business security concerns can be addressed by following the same procedures that would be followed in a hostile surrounding within the United States. Threats to personal safety can be reduced by following the procedures suggested for personal protection. In addition, the more that is known of the language, the culture and the political atmosphere, the greater the likelihood that the security plan will be effective. One of the greatest threats to security when abroad is the domestic help if they are not properly screened and trained.

SUMMARY

- Reported crimes committed against all types of retail establishments are shoplifting, burglary, vandalism, bad checks, fraudulent use of credit cards, employee theft and robbery.

- The single most effective deterrent to shoplifting is surveillance by an alert, trained sales force. This may be supplemented by security officers or floorwalkers.

- Another retail security problem is employee theft. Special risks in retail establishments include easy employee access to merchandise and cash. Specific pricing procedures, cash-handling procedures and refund procedures are essential. Personnel should be rotated periodically, and responsibilities should be separated.

- The number one challenge for hotel CSOs is balancing security with customer convenience and freedom of movement.

- Major security concerns of the hotel/motel industry include both internal and external theft, vandalism, vice and fire.

- Security problems at a racetrack include access control, crowd control, parking security, vault security, alcohol control and fraud detection. Security concerns at a racetrack can best be met by adequate access control, surveillance systems and by the presence of well-qualified, well-trained security personnel.

- Security concerns at sporting events include maintaining order, preventing admission of nonpaying people, preventing internal and external theft, providing first aid for injuries and regulating pedestrian and vehicle traffic.

- Major security problems in office buildings include after-hours burglaries and theft; theft from a tenant by another tenant's employees; theft by service, maintenance and custodial employees; assaults, rapes and other crimes against persons; regulation and control of visitor traffic; bomb threats; protection of executive offices and personnel and fire watch. Primary security measures in office buildings are access control, proper authorization and documentation of the use of corporate assets by employees and periodic fire inspections and fire drills.

■ Security problems of residential units include theft, vandalism and assaults, particularly muggings.

■ In apartment complexes, open drug markets pose a greater threat than closed drug markets.

■ The primary concern when providing security abroad is unfamiliarity with the language, local customs and expectations. Terrorism is also to be considered.

APPLICATIONS

1. Terry Benson, a private security officer, is working in a liquor store to prevent armed robberies and the purchase of liquor by juveniles. The store manager took into custody a man who presented a check for payment of liquor, but on being asked for identification, he ran out of the store with his purchase. The manager has caught him and brought him back to Officer Benson. What actions should Officer Benson now take?

2. The Riteway Department Store is being sued by a shoplifting suspect for destruction of his property. The suit is the result of the actions of a private security officer, Dawn Clough, who saw the suspect, a white male about 24 years old, palm a watch and put it in his jacket pocket. When Officer Clough approached the suspect to make inquiry, the suspect ran from the store to the parking lot, where he entered his car and then closed and locked the doors. Officer Clough ordered the suspect to open the car door. When he refused, Officer Clough broke the window and arrested the suspect. A search of the car revealed the stolen watch under the car's front seat.

   As security director for Riteway, would you recommend that management try to settle out of court or that it fight the charges? Why?

3. Evaluate the completeness of the retail security checklist in Figure 16.4. Are any important areas missing? If so, which ones?

DISCUSSION QUESTIONS

1. What are the advantages and disadvantages of prosecuting juvenile shoplifters? Adult shoplifters?

2. How can retail stores aid one another in preventing shoplifting? What is done in your area?

3. What are some legal requirements of hotels and motels that guests of the establishments should know?

4. Which types of security discussed in this chapter seem most important to you? Why?

5. What types of multipurpose stadiums or venues are in your area, and what types of security concerns are they likely to encounter on a routine basis?

REFERENCES

Aggleton, David G. "The Evolution of High-Rise Security." *Security Technology & Design*, September 2004, pp.34–39.

Beaulieu, Elizabeth. "Retailers Combat Return Fraud with 'Unique Fingerprint' Tool." *Security Director News*, March 2005, p.16.

Boss, Derk and Longmore-Etheridge, Ann. "Casinos Strengthen Their Security Hand." *Security Management*, September 2006, pp.78–86.

Daniels, Rhianna. "Colorado Approves ORT Bill." *Security Director News*, June 2006a, pp.14–15.

Daniels, Rhianna. "Levi Works with Retailers on RFID." *Security Director News*, June 2006b, pp.14–15.

Daniels, Rhianna. "Awareness of ORC Up in Past Year." *Security Director News*, 2007a, pp.1, 16.

Daniels, Rhianna. "Benihana Cooks Up New Solution." *Security Director News*, 2007b, pp.1, 16.

Daniels, Rhianna. "Casino Royale Trashes Tapes; Trades Up to Digital." *Security Director News*, July 2007c, pp.1, 17.

Daniels, Rhianna. "Hard Rock Cooks Up Standards." *Security Director News*, June, 2007d, pp.15–16.

Daniels, Rhianna. "Research Firm Identifies Ways to Reduce Risks at U.S-Based Shopping Centers." *Security Director News*, 2007e, pp.15–16.

Daniels, Rhianna. "Restaurant Owner Reduces Hours, Manages Operations, Safety Remotely." *Security Director News*, August 2007f, p.14.

Daniels, Rhianna. "Retailers Leverage EBR for ROI." *Security Director News*, July 2007g, pp.16–17.

Daniels, Rhianna. "Sears Tower's Tallest Order." *Security Director News*, July 2007h, pp.1–10.

Daniels, Rhianna. "Shoplifting Similar across the Globe." *Security Director News*, 2007i, pp.16–17.

Daniels, Rhianna. "Weighing Overseas Risk." *Security Director News*, August 2007j, pp.1, 11.

Davis, Robert C. "Shopping Malls: Are They Prepared to Prevent and Respond to Attack?" *NIJ Journal*, March 2008, pp.13–18. (NCJ 221500)

DePass, Dee. "RFID Comes of Age." (Minneapolis/St. Paul) *Star Tribune*, July 2, 2006, p.D1.

de Treville, Richard H. and Longmore-Etheridge, Ann. "Time to Check Out Liability Trends." *Security Management*, February 2004, pp.61–65.

Durstenfeld, Bob. "The Unseen Threats to Public Venue Security." *Security Technology & Design*, March 2005, p.52.

Elliott, Robert. "Towering Technology in Dubai." *Security Management*, April 2007, pp.86–93.

Evenson, Jon. "Integrating Life Safety and Security Systems." *Security Technology & Design*, March 2005, pp.38–43.

Friedrick, Joanne. "Hotels Juggle Security in Non-Stop Environment." *Security Director News*, March 2007a, p.18.

Friedrick, Joanne. "Retailers Are Counting on LERPnet to Combat Organized Theft, Fraud." *Security Director News*, June 2007b, p.17.

Gips, Michael A. "The Challenge of Making Safer Structures." *Security Management*, March 2005, pp.43–49.

Gips, Michael A. "EAS Not a Silver Bullet." *Security Management*, March 2007, p.26.

Greggo, Alan F. "Mission to Mitigate." *Security Management*, April 2005, pp.61–65.

Kitteringham, Glen. "Down and Out in Record Time." *Security Management*, September 2007, pp.78–90.

Lamb, John. "Employee Theft." *Security Products*, November 2004, pp.46–49.

Longmore-Etheridge, Ann. "No Gambling on Surveillance." *Security Management*, September 2004, pp.103–108.

Longmore-Etheridge, Ann. "Complex Protection Made Easy." *Security Management*, December 2006, pp.58–66.

Longmore-Etheridge, Ann. "Never Bet against Security." *Security Management*, September 2007a, pp.108–118.

Longmore-Etheridge, Ann. "Sears Tower's Well-Grounded Security." *Security Management*, May 2007b, pp.59–65.

Martinez, Liz. "CCTV in the Retail Environment." *Security Technology & Design*, March 2004, pp.58–62.

Martinez, Liz. "Combating Organized Retail Theft in 2005." *Security Technology & Design*, February 2005a, pp.58–59.

Martinez, Liz. "Enlisting Police and Prosecutors to Help Fight ORC." *Security Technology & Design*, April 2005b, pp.62–64.

Page, Douglas. "RFID Tags: Big Brother in a Small Device." *Law Enforcement Technology*, August 2004, pp.128–131.

Rosen, Mark B. "You Bagged the Shoplifter, Now What?" *Security Management*, April 2004, pp.59–65.

Sampson, Rana. *Drug Dealing in Privately Owned Apartment Complexes*. Washington, DC: Office of Community Oriented Policing Services.

Stover, James B. "Putting a Premium on Risk Reduction." *Security Management*, July 2006, pp.71–77.

Straw, Joseph. "Mall Security: Deterring Terrorists, Not Shoppers." *Security Management*, June 2007, pp.30–35.

Thuermer, Karen E. "Retailers Organize against Crime." *Security Management*, July 2007, pp.52–58.

Wright, Joe. "Strengthening Casino Security Also Enhances Marketing, Loyalty." *Security Products*, June 2004, p.24.

CASE CITED

Carroll v. United States, 267 U.S. 132 (1925).

Specific Crimes and Investigative Responsibilities

The following investigative background, responsibilities and tips are reprinted by permission from *Outline Guide for Private Security* (Stokes et al., pp.52–61).[1]

Assault

In most states, assault is defined as an unlawful attempt, coupled with the present ability, to commit a violent injury to another person.

The degrees and forms of assault vary widely from state to state. For example, assault can vary in degree from simple assault or assault with a deadly weapon or assault with great bodily injury. It can vary in form from simple assault of another to spousal abuse, child abuse, or elder abuse.

Responsibilities

- Call the police if company policy requires.
- Interview the victim for complete details of the event.
- Note injuries to the victim. Obtain photos, medical release, emergency room information, treatment.
- If a weapon is involved, consider photographing it in place.
- Obtain a complete description of the suspect, vehicle, weapon, etc.
- Obtain complete details of the incident: was there provocation, escalation, etc.
- Separate and interview witnesses.
- Locate and interview the suspect. Note any alibis. Photograph if appropriate.

Tips

- Denial or self-defense are common defenses.
- Determine if anyone was under the influence of alcohol or drugs.

Breach of Peace/Disturbing the Peace/ Disorderly Conduct

This refers to any conduct that puts fear into employees or citizens when committed, whether in public or private.

---

[1]Stokes, Floyd; Hess Kären; and Wrobleski, Henry. *An Outline Guide for Private Security*. Rosemount, MN: Innovative Systems-Publishers, 1993. Available at www.innsyspub.com

Responsibilities

- Call the police if company policy requires.
- Note the time security became involved in the incident.
- Assess any damages, property or personal, that may have occurred.
- Seek out and interview witnesses.
- Interview witnesses when possible.
- Determine if additional assistance should be obtained.
- If people are injured, see to it that they receive medical assistance.
- Seek out cause of incident.
- Determine disposition.

Burglary/Unlawful Entry/Breaking and Entering

The unauthorized or unlawful entry into a room or building by force or other means. The opening of a closed door or window will suffice whether it is locked or not. Anything that has been relied on to prevent intrusion constitutes a violation.

Responsibilities

- Call the police if company policy requires.
- Note the time security was made aware of the incident.
- Determine how entry was made.
- Determine who discovered the entry.
- Obtain a description of losses, including amount, brand names, manufacturers, model numbers, serial numbers, color, sizes, personal identifiers, unique marks, estimated value.
- Secure/protect the scene if necessary.
- Attempt to determine point of entry and point of exit. Thoroughly determine and examine those areas for physical evidence.
- Attempt to locate any witnesses.
- Interview witnesses if possible.
- Mark any physical evidence that may be found at the scene.
- Photograph and diagram the scene if possible.
- Determine appropriate disposition.

Theft

Theft is taking the personal property of another with the intent to permanently deprive that person of the property. Theft includes shoplifting, purse snatching, and pickpocketing.

Responsibilities

- Call the police if company policy requires.
- Interview the victim. Obtain a complete statement, including when the property was last seen, when it was discovered missing, and what the conditions were when the loss occurred.

- Obtain a complete description of property loss, including amount, brand names, manufacturer's number, model number, serial numbers, color, sizes, personal identifiers, unique marks, estimated value.
- Secure/protect the scene if appropriate.
- Conduct a thorough scene investigation including search for fingerprints, trace evidence, etc.
- Photograph/diagram the scene if necessary.
- Search the area for footprints, tire prints, other physical evidence.
- Attempt to locate and interview witnesses.
- If a suspect is identified, interrogate and obtain a statement, including alibis.
- Contact the insurance company if appropriate.

Trespass of Property

To invade the property of another without permission. In most incidents an individual is on the private property of another person without permission.

Responsibilities
- Call the police if company policy requires.
- Note the time security first observed the trespass.
- Note what called the person to the attention of security (actions, clothing, etc.).
- Determine if the person has any equipment with him such as a portable radio, beeper, or arson materials.
- Describe how the individual was confronted and the actions security took.
- Take statements from any witnesses.
- Determine appropriate disposition.

Vandalism/Criminal Mischief/Criminal Damage to Property

Vandalism is a harmful act whereby the usefulness or value of property is considerably diminished or destroyed. It includes vending machines, windows, motor vehicles, telephone coin boxes, fixtures, signs, construction equipment, walls, restrooms, etc. Graffiti is included in vandalism.

Responsibilities
- Call the police if company policy requires.
- Note the time security received the call or found the damage.
- Secure the scene if necessary.
- Seek out witnesses or individuals having knowledge of the incident.
- Conduct a thorough scene investigation.
- Photograph the scene if appropriate.
- Search for physical evidence.
- If a suspect is identified, interrogate for possible admissions.

Threat Advisory System Response (TASR) Guideline

Structure of the Threat Response Matrix

The TASR Guideline Matrix is divided into four major sections and further broken out by three subcategories as follows:

Category 1: Emergency Response—Business Continuity

Category 2: Personnel Protection

Category 3: Physical Protection

Please Note: For ease of understanding, steps outlined under "Considerations & Potential Actions" are additive. Each succeeding level incorporates all activities from the previous levels.

To use the matrix:
1. Identify the impending threat.[1]
2. Identify the National Threat Advisory Level released by the Department of Homeland Security and review actions identified with the corresponding advisory level.
3. Determine if the imposing threat can be considered against a critical infrastructure and/or at what level (National/Regional/State/Local) the threat applies.
4. Determine applicability of considerations and potential actions to personnel, assets, and facility(s).
5. Determine response to be taken.

---

[1] The Homeland Security Advisory System designates Green and Blue as two distinct levels. For ease of understanding and implementation of the ASIS Threat Advisory System Response Guideline, the Green and Blue levels have been combined into one.

13.0 Threat Level Matrix

(Developed from the Homeland Security Advisory System)

Threat Level	National (Including Critical Infrastructure)	Regional/State/Local
Red or Severe **R**	Declared when there is a severe risk of a terrorist attack or when an incident occurs or credible intelligence information is received by a critical infrastructure that a terrorist act is imminent.	Declared when a terrorist attack has occurred or credible intelligence indicates that one is imminent, that has prevention and response characteristics of a regional/state/local nature and that a specific target has been identified.
Orange or High **O**	Declared when there is a high risk of a terrorist attack or when a credible threat exists of terrorist activity against one of the critical infrastructures.	Declared when credible intelligence indicates that there is a high risk of a terrorist attack having prevention and response characteristics of a regional/state/local nature, but a specific target has not been identified.
Yellow or Elevated **Y**	Declared when there is a significant risk of a terrorist attack or when a general threat exists of terrorist activity against one of the critical infrastructures.	Declared when there is an elevated risk of terrorist attack, but a specific region of the U.S. or target has not been identified.
Blue or Guarded **B***	Declared when there is a general risk of terrorist attacks or when there is a general risk of terrorist attacks against one of the critical infrastructures.	Declared when there is a general risk of terrorist attacks.
Green or Low **G***	Declared when there is a low risk of terrorist attacks against one of the critical infrastructures.	Declared when there is a low risk of terrorist attacks.

*The Homeland Security Advisory System designates Green and Blue as two distinct levels. For ease of understanding and implementation of the ASIS Threat Advisory System Response Guideline, the Green and Blue levels have been combined into one.

14.0 Recommended Practice Advisory: Threat Response Matrix

Level 1					
Green/Blue Threat Levels					
Threat Level			Considerations & Potential Actions	Applies Y/N	Response Notes
Emergency Response—Business Continuity					
1	G	B	Develop/enhance organization Business Continuity Plan. (An organization should develop a business continuity plan that will address such topics as readiness, prevention, response, recovery/resumption, testing and training, and evaluation and maintenance.)		
2	G	B	Establish Crisis Management Team and other related Response Teams, such as an Emergency Response Team, Incident Response Team, Disaster Recovery Team, etc. and train as to their responsibilities relative to each threat level.		
3	G	B	Prepare to implement aspect of the Business Continuity Plan and contingency plan within the context of the current threat.		
4	G	B	Review and validate procedures for heightened alert status.		
5	G	B	Establish a central command (crisis management) center from which to direct contingency plans, response, and recovery/ resumption operations. Ensure appropriate communications equipment is installed and functioning including radios, cell phones, and Internet access.		
6	G	B	Prepare for the possibility of flooding or other destruction as a result of a bombing incident or other similar catastrophic events.		
7	G	B	Establish a prioritized roster of people to direct emergency response procedures.		
8	G	B	Review processes to support personnel who may be called to active military duty. Address return to work, benefits, leave procedures, etc.		
9	G	B	If possible, track locations of expatriate personnel on assignment and vacation in foreign countries and review contingency procedures for possible evacuation.		
10	G	B	Review budgets to support required security measures as costs increase due to a heightened threat level. Determine if partnerships can be leveraged with other organizations to reduce costs.		

(Continued)

	Threat Level		Considerations & Potential Actions	Applies Y/N	Response Notes
11	G	B	Develop tabletop exercises of procedures that may be appropriate.		
12	G	B	Plan for an alternate work site in the event of an evacuation, including the staging of nonperishable food, sleeping bags, medical supplies, water, miscellaneous supplies, etc. for key personnel needed to occupy the location. Be prepared to replicate critical company paper and electronic records (financial, personnel, legal, etc.), communications, and IT processing capabilities at relocation facility.		
13	G	B	Provide for the safekeeping of critical company records, i.e., financial, personnel, legal, etc.		
14	G	B	Perform emergency evacuation drills with all building staff to simulate actual conditions and practice response procedures.		
15	G	B	Develop rapport and maintain a liaison with local law enforcement, fire, and medical responders and develop communication methods and alternatives. Provide names and phone numbers for key contact personnel to the emergency response organizations. Ensure local agencies' familiarity with the physical layout and operational procedures. Designate arrival location for emergency response vehicles.		
16	G	B	Consult with local first responders and other government agencies regarding best actions to develop relative to "shelter in place."		
17	G	B	Invite local fire, police, EMS, and regulatory agencies in training exercises designed for the organization's Crisis Management Team and related Response Team(s).		
18	G	B	Work with local EMS first responders to establish pre-designated triage locations and backups.		
19	G	B	Develop a media relations and communications strategy, including a selected staging area for the media. In addition, provide additional media training for designated personnel.		
20	G	B	Make arrangements for mental health counselors for personnel should a devastating event occur.		
21	G	B	Establish a crisis hotline to take calls from and to provide information to personnel, family members, and others affected by an incident.		
22	G	B	If an organization has medical personnel associated with operations, verify response plans are current.		

(Continued)

	Threat Level		Considerations & Potential Actions	Applies Y/N	Response Notes
23	G	B	Ensure that the organization's first responders are certified in First Aid, Cardiopulmonary Resuscitation (CPR), and the use of Automatic External Defibrillators (AEDs).		
24	G	B	Develop relationships and documents (MOUs, MOAs), if appropriate, with state and federal agencies, including emergency management, law enforcement, and the military. Determine if partnerships can be leveraged with other organizations to reduce costs.		
25	G	B	Contact vendors and suppliers critical to the operation and confirm their emergency response plans.		
26	G	B	Establish a process for periodic monitoring of TV, radio, and news reports and incorporating this capability in the central command center.		
27	G	B	Develop canned messages (approved by organization's leadership) that can be disseminated to the workforce at the announcement of various alert levels. Determine when, by whom, and how those messages will be disseminated.		
28	G	B	Plan for alternate means of communications if phone lines are not available. Determine availability of satellite capability to support communications, if cell phone reception is not available.		
29	G	B	Maintain independent emergency lines separate from facility PBX. In addition, develop back up/alternate methods of communications.		
30	G	B	Determine the threats to existing/proposed information technologies. Establish an information/data security risk management program.		
31	G	B	Review and validate information/data security response plan, if established.		
32	G	B	Create an information technology security education and awareness program for technical administrators, key focal points, and the organization's general population.		
33	G	B	Establish comprehensive employee training program addressing information/data security.		
34	G	B	Refresh employees' knowledge of social engineering techniques designed to trick employees into divulging information that could be used to compromise data security.		
35	G	B	Review information posted to websites and be prepared to remove it if the information compromises security.		

(Continued)

Threat Level			Considerations & Potential Actions	Applies Y/N	Response Notes
36	G	B	Coordinate appropriate information technology security measures and programs with all key corporate, local, state, and federal security entities to ensure enhanced protection and response.		
37	G	B	Plan for and pre-position critical supplies of network, system, and other information technology hardware, firmware, and software so that during emergencies adequate levels of network and system access are not interrupted due to loss of any one component.		
Personnel Protection					
38	G	B	Provide key personnel, vendors, suppliers, and contractors a copy of the facility emergency procedures and other pertinent organizational guidelines.		
39	G	B	Develop training for employees, including alternate site employees, covering high risk/ critical functions, especially when functions are not conducted on a routine or daily basis.		
40	G	B	Develop emergency procedures and training for people with special needs.		
41	G	B	Train all personnel to raise their minimal level of security awareness to their surroundings and activities that may occur and the development of family plans. Determine training and guidelines for shelter in place plans and rationale.		
42	G	B	Determine placement/location of Automatic External Defibrillators (AEDs) to support timely response to emergencies. Require the development of AED protocols and training of Crisis Management Team and related Response Team(s) members.		
43	G	B	If established, validate that existing security access control/intrusion detection systems, i.e., cameras, alarms, locks, lighting, card access devices, etc., are in good working order. Have serviced, if needed.		
44	G	B	Establish a neighborhood watch program with surrounding communities.		
45	G	B	Establish a program to track employees' business travel and remote assignment locations.		
46	G	B	Encourage employees to volunteer at emergency organizations.		
47	G	B	Review and validate that basic training of response personnel is current and adequate in context of possible threat condition to the organization.		

(Continued)

	Threat Level		Considerations & Potential Actions	Applies Y/N	Response Notes
48	G	B	Be cognizant of current events. Monitor TV, radio, and newspaper reports.		
49	G	B	Prepare contingency plans for loss of water, heat, air conditioning, and electrical power.		
Physical Protection					
50	G	B	Review and verify availability of additional/ backup personnel to support security and facilities functions.		
51	G	B	Develop look-back and inwards surveillance plans ("watch who is watching you").		
52	G	B	Prepare and review risk assessments performed against facilities, assets, and personnel.		
53	G	B	Encourage the community to report suspicious activities, i.e., photographing the facility or government buildings, bridges, dams, water systems, power systems, interstate highway nodes, or asking detailed questions about security at these critical facilities.		
54	G	B	Train security personnel on acceptable and appropriate responses to civil disturbances, demonstrations, protests, etc.		
55	G	B	Make facility master keys available to appropriate personnel.		
56	G	B	Perform background checks on all full-time service contractor employees.		
57	G	B	Perform penetration tests of access control and intrusion detection systems.		
58	G	B	Install cameras for surveillance on equipment outside or adjacent to facilities, if not already in place.		
59	G	B	Develop procedures to perform inspections of items carried into the facility by personnel, contractors, and visitors.		
60	G	B	Develop plans and consider utilizing identified and unidentified security vehicles.		
61	G	B	Train security guards on special requirements unique to organization, e.g., vehicle inspection techniques.		
62	G	B	Install (or verify operation of) duress alarms from the receptionist desk and/or remote guard stations, executive offices, and key access points to the central command center.		
63	G	B	Equip receptionist phone with a notification to the central command center indicating a telephone off-hook situation.		

(Continued)

Threat Level			Considerations & Potential Actions	Applies Y/N	Response Notes
64	G	B	Develop plans for restricting vehicle access.		
65	G	B	As appropriate, install barricades, i.e., large flowerpots, cement stanchions, etc. to prevent vehicles from driving through facility entrance doors/gates.		
66	G	B	Know how to turn off power, gas, and water. Ensure procedures are ready for dealing with emergency shutdowns of HVAC systems in the event of a possible internal or external chemical release.		
67	G	B	Designate a "safe" interior location, which has a self-contained HVAC and filter system for personnel, in the event HVAC systems are shut down.		
68	G	B	Identify backup power sources and verify that they are operational. Ensure long-term availability of diesel fuel for emergency power generation through contractual obligations with suppliers, if appropriate. Further, determine priority of sequence of availability with other organizations, including government, as others may have precedence.		
69	G	B	Obtain and/or review facility maps, plans, as-built drawings, etc. for accuracy and secure in safe place for referencing.		
70	G	B	Determine secured storage alternatives if hazardous or other critical materials are present in or around facilities.		
71	G	B	Install emergency buzzers from dock ingress and egress to central command center.		
72	G	B	Designate limited locations for receipt of mail.		
73	G	B	Establish plans for an alternate emergency operations center at the organization's relocation facility from which to direct response and recovery operations if the primary facility is evacuated. Ensure appropriate communications equipment is installed and will be functioning including radios, cell phones, and Internet access.		
74	G	B	Ensure emergency exits are not obstructed and are clear of debris. Conduct periodic patrols to ensure compliance.		
75	G	B	Survey surrounding areas to determine those activities that might increase security risks, e.g., airports, government buildings, industrial facilities, pipelines, etc.		

Level 2				
Yellow Threat Level				
Threat Level		**Considerations & Potential Actions**	**Applies Y/N**	**Response Notes**
Emergency Response–Business Continuity				
1	Y	Ensure all business, emergency, and continuity/recovery plan documents are up to date, e.g., contact lists, notification/escalation procedures. Review and validate internal emergency communication plans for accuracy of names and numbers.		
2	Y	Conduct tabletop exercises of procedures that may be appropriate.		
3	Y	Convene Crisis Management Team and other related Response Teams to review emergency response and business continuity/recovery plans. Confirm functional responsibilities.		
4	Y	Review and refine emergency response processes within the context of the current threat information.		
5	Y	Verify cell phones and pagers are ready for distribution to the members of the Crisis Management Team and related Response Teams. Determine if cell phones should have text messaging capability.		
6	Y	If established, verify equipment, communications lists, and processes in the central command center.		
7	Y	Verify contacts and communicate with the law enforcement community and local outside emergency/medical, fire, and response personnel.		
8	Y	Obtain threat and intelligence updates from local, state, and federal authorities as well as private industry security sources.		
9	Y	Review the list of individuals notified by automatic alerts generated by security monitoring systems, e.g., network and IT intrusion detection systems, etc.		
10	Y	Reinforce user awareness in context of organizational requirements.		
11	Y	Review recovery plans to ensure they represent current situations/environments.		
12	Y	Implement procedures/software to stop potentially hostile/suspicious attachments at the email server. Create tighter levels of firewall, antivirus, and IDS filters so that they can readily be implemented in the event of an attack.		
13	Y	Review use of IT security filtering which may include upgrading firewalls and anti-virus software to ensure effectiveness of precluding electronic penetration of organizational systems.		

(Continued)

Threat Level		Considerations & Potential Actions	Applies Y/N	Response Notes
14	Y	Update checklists, focal points, and information technology inventories.		
15	Y	Perform penetration testing of individual organizational sites and encourage participation by vendors to validate cyber-security levels.		
		Personnel Protection		
16	Y	Implement employee training, including training of alternate site employees covering high-risk/critical functions, especially when functions are not conducted on a routine or daily basis.		
17	Y	Emphasize and elevate the importance of knowing planned absences, arrivals, and whereabouts of all personnel.		
18	Y	Be prepared to address sensitive issues relative to personnel expressing opinions either for or against threat prevention.		
19	Y	Ensure security-related information is communicated to personnel across the organization as approved by leadership.		
		Physical Protection		
20	Y	Ensure communication channels and processes are open, reliable, and consistent. Ensure alternative/backup forms of communications are available.		
21	Y	Periodically review actions taken to date against the stated threat conditions as they may rapidly change for either better or worse.		
22	Y	Perform inspections of items carried into the facility by employees, contractors, visitors, etc.		
23	Y	Implement any special security programs supported by trained personnel.		
24	Y	Review and verify vehicle inspection training for security personnel.		
25	Y	Maintain a high index of suspicion and remain alert to unusual activities, occurrences, and behavior.		
26	Y	Refresh employees' knowledge of the danger of malicious code delivered by email via worms, viruses, etc.		
27	Y	Provide daily summary to key management and security consoles.		
28	Y	Ensure security checks with other integrated security consoles.		
29	Y	Monitor news media and emergency and law enforcement bulletins.		
30	Y	Lock down access points after normal business hours and restrict access as appropriate.		

(Continued)

Threat Level		Considerations & Potential Actions	Applies Y/N	Response Notes
31	Y	Perform housekeeping of exterior grounds of facilities limiting the storage of items, i.e., crates and other objects, that would otherwise provide camouflage.		
32	Y	Enhance or provide manned coverage of dock areas, if not already doing so.		
33	Y	Verify truck driver's license, bill of lading, and other applicable paperwork relative to deliveries.		
34	Y	Physically inspect cargo as necessary.		
35	Y	Consider increasing screening activity of inbound packages.		
36	Y	File travel itineraries of all Crisis Management Team members and related Response Team members with appropriate management.		
37	Y	Review and file travel itineraries of high-level executives with security director or equivalent to evaluate risk and safety.		
38	Y	Validate all building alarms, access controls, intrusion detecting systems and building systems in accordance with threat conditions.		
39	Y	Evaluate off-site equipment storage.		

Level 3				
Orange Threat Level				
Threat Level		Considerations & Potential Actions	Applies Y/N	Response Notes
Emergency Response—Business Continuity				
1	0	Implement emergency and contingency plans as necessary.		
2	0	Increase frequency of threat intelligence updates.		
3	0	Restrict staff travel and vacation for Emergency Response/Crisis Management Team(s).		
4	0	Convene Emergency Response/Crisis Management Team(s) to review the more specific information that is available from law enforcement, the media, and other sources to assess the potential impact to the organization.		
5	0	Provide cell phones and pagers to the members of the Crisis Management Team and related Response Teams, if not already done.		
6	0	Verify alternate locations are valid and personnel supporting recovery operations are current in their obligations.		
7	0	Verify supplies are staged, secured, and complete to support recovery operations.		
8	0	Evaluate externally facing websites and, where necessary, close down nonessential services. For remaining sites, ensure all operating systems and related application software patches are applied. Ensure organizational security specialists have reviewed the organization's security definition for currency.		
9	0	Enhance monitoring of activity on essential services for externally facing websites to identify deviations from normal activity.		
10	0	Enhance monitoring of logging and intrusion detection for remaining sites, and review reporting mechanisms that are linked to an intrusion alert/notification system.		
11	0	Validate distributed-denial-of-service preparedness (Check with Internet service provider for capability to assist, e.g., block address ranges, etc).		
12	0	Increase alert status for IT security personnel consistent with the organization's Business Continuity Plan.		
13	0	Prepare for "cyber-isolation" of non-essential individuals' outside connections.		
Personnel Protection				
14	0	Be prepared to address issues related to personnel who serve in the military and may be called to serve.		

(Continued)

Threat Level		Considerations & Potential Actions	Applies Y/N	Response Notes
15	0	Be prepared to support personnel whose family members have been called to serve.		
16	0	Instruct personnel to report immediately suspicious activity, packages/articles, people, and vehicles to security personnel. Be cognizant of unattended packages/articles and vehicles.		
17	0	Instruct personnel to direct all press inquiries to the organization's Public Affairs office or equivalent.		
18	0	Review and validate that alternate travel arrangements are plausible in case modes of transportation are not available.		
19	0	Discuss risks associated with travel to foreign countries with the security director or equivalent.		
20	0	Cease travel to cities against which specific threats have been made.		
Physical Protection				
21	0	Review plans to address any redirection or constraint to transportation systems. Consult with local authorities about control of public roads and accesses that might make the facility more vulnerable if they were to remain open.		
22	0	Discuss and coordinate with facilities and building management other security controls for guests and vendors.		
23	0	Prepare for possible evacuation, closing, and securing of all individual organization facilities.		
24	0	Increase security patrols internally and externally. Determine increased officer requirements for extended periods. Possibly suspend holidays, etc. and hold discussions with contract security providers for increased human resources.		
25	0	Assign additional staff in the central command center to monitor existing security cameras in real time.		
26	0	Evaluate the use of special foot patrols, bicycle patrol, etc. Use canine patrols if appropriate (campus environments).		
27	0	Increase surveillance of all facilities and take increased precautions.		
28	0	Evaluate requiring special identification for day labor, i.e., special badges, colored wristbands, etc. Inspect government issued photo ID as proof of identification each time. Special access identification should be provided each time for entrance to the facility and retrieved upon departure.		

(Continued)

Threat Level		Considerations & Potential Actions	Applies Y/N	Response Notes
29	0	Evaluate vehicle inspection program to include checking beneath the undercarriage of vehicles, under the hood, and in the trunk.		
30	0	Approach all illegally parked vehicles in and around facilities. Question drivers and direct them to move immediately. If owner cannot be identified, have the vehicle towed.		
31	0	Implement random shift changes of security guards.		
32	0	Coordinate with facilities and building management and increase inspections in and around the facility to ensure utility and emergency systems are not tampered with, damaged, or sabotaged. This includes emergency generation and lighting, fire alarms, and perimeter protection.		
33	0	Evaluate arranging for security or law enforcement vehicles to be parked randomly near access points and exits.		
34	0	Prepare to restrict access to essential personnel only.		
35	0	Limit driveway and parking area access as appropriate.		
36	0	If feasible, discontinue, limit, or otherwise control inside perimeter parking. Evaluate eliminating underground parking at this threat level.		
37	0	Increase inspections on building systems and infrastructure, including HVAC systems. Review ability of facilities and building management to rapidly shut down HVAC equipment. Discuss conditions whereby HVAC is to be shut down and also restarted.		
38	0	Inspect and, if feasible, secure vacant rooms (e.g., meeting, guest, housekeeping, storage, etc.).		
39	0	If permissible, in compliance with fire code, restrict access to rooftops or, at a minimum, monitor with response.		
40	0	Evaluate restricting services provided by outside vendors/suppliers (e.g., cleaning crews, etc.) to possible non-sensitive areas.		
41	0	Coordinate security in non-organization owned locations to coordinate effective security enhancements.		
42	0	Enhance visibility in and around perimeters by increasing lighting and removing or trimming vegetation.		
43	0	If elevators are on premises, train staff in operation of the elevator and the correct response in the event of an emergency.		

(Continued)

Threat Level		Considerations & Potential Actions	Applies Y/N	Response Notes
44	0	Validate vendor lists for all routine deliveries and repair services.		
45	0	If conditions warrant, conduct heightened screening of all inbound mail. Direct attention to any packages or letters received without a return address or having indications of stains/powder.		
46	0	Visually and physically inspect all expected and unexpected deliveries.		
47	0	Coordinate operations relative to critical infrastructure concerns with armed forces, i.e., armed security, local law enforcement, or the military.		
48	0	Discontinue tours and cease other non-essential site visits.		
49	0	Staff central command center, if in existence, during normal operational hours and continue to review call lists for currency. Run call tests and verify all equipment operational.		

Level 4				
Red Threat Level				
Threat Level		**Considerations & Potential Actions**	**Applies Y/N**	**Response Notes**
Emergency Response—Business Continuity				
1	R	Convene Crisis Management Team and related Response Teams to manage and direct emergency response and/or business continuity/recovery plans in response to an imminent threat or actual event that impacts the organization, its employees, or third party vendors/suppliers, etc.		
2	R	Operate the central command center, if in existence, full staff 24/7.		
3	R	Notify law enforcement of facility evacuation and closings.		
4	R	Prepare to close the facility, protect assets, and shut down equipment and systems in the event of evacuation. Determine ahead of time who, if anyone, will remain behind to protect and monitor facility. Determine how and when facility will be reopened.		
5	R	Extract and maintain a pre-determined number of communication lines (telephone, fax, and Internet) for emergency purposes.		
6	R	Prepare to evacuate personnel and items needed to support recovery operations.		
7	R	Prepare for "manual evacuation" of essential computer hardware and systems, including support requirements necessary to an alternate location of operations.		
8	R	Restrict access to facilities, equipment and systems to essential personnel only.		
Personnel Protection				
9	R	Recommend personnel vary routes driven to work.		
10	R	Furlough nonessential personnel, institute flexible leave policy, or employee dispersal.		
11	R	Remind employees to direct all press inquiries to the Public Affairs department or equivalent.		
12	R	Eliminate travel into an area affected by a terrorist attack or an area that is a target of an attack.		
13	R	Cancel attendance at non-critical or off-site meetings, conventions, symposia, etc.		
14	R	Reinforce security awareness of surroundings at all times to avoid being a victim of a terrorist attack or a crime.		
15	R	Check emergency supplies, restock if necessary, and place in a handy place.		

(Continued)

Threat Level		Considerations & Potential Actions	Applies Y/N	Response Notes
16	R	Keep fuel tanks in vehicles full.		
17	R	Avoid passing on unsubstantiated information.		
18	R	Make available mental health counselors for employees as required and activate crisis hotline where appropriate.		
Physical Protection				
19	R	Cancel or postpone any individual organization-sponsored or hosted events.		
20	R	Pre-position specially trained teams or emergency response personnel.		
21	R	Implement plans to accommodate redirection or constraint of transportation.		
22	R	Redirect personnel to address critical emergency needs.		
23	R	Increase the number of security guards, guard postings, and roving guard visibility.		
24	R	Utilize alternate, enhanced methods of inspection at designated access points.		
25	R	Enhance monitoring of all buildings and access control/intrusion detection systems, i.e., cameras, alarms, locks, lighting, card access devices, etc. Ensure frequent checks with other integrated security consoles.		
26	R	Prepare to assist with evacuation and other emergency processes. Work in a coordinated effort with organizational security personnel and law enforcement as directed.		
27	R	Limit access points to minimal portals necessary to conduct operations.		
28	R	Inspect vacant buildings/rooms and use integrity seals, where possible, or lock down non-essential areas.		
29	R	Prepare to close facilities and shut down equipment in the event of evacuation and coordinate with security personnel. If warranted, disconnect organization's networks from the Internet.		
30	R	Confirm status and availability of any off-site equipment storage.		
31	R	Cancel or delay all non-vital facility work conducted by contractors, or continuously monitor their work with company personnel as applicable.		

Glossary

Note: The number in parenthesis at the end of each entry is the chapter number in which the glossary term appears.

access control—Properly located entrances, exits, fencing, landscaping and lighting can direct both foot and automobile traffic in ways that discourage crime. (6)

activity support—Encouraging legitimate functions in public spaces helps discourage crime. (6)

alarm respondent—Person employed by an organization to answer an alarm condition at a client's protected site, to inspect the protected site to determine the nature of the alarm, to protect or secure the client's facility until alarm system integrity can be restored and to assist law enforcement according to local arrangement. The alarm respondent may be armed and also may be a servicer. (1)

amphetamines—Stimulants taken orally as a tablet or capsule, or intravenously, to reduce appetite and/or relieve mental depression. (12)

andragogy—Adult learning. (2)

ARTCENTRAL—An organization in New York that registers works of art using computer-oriented photogrammetry, comparable to fingerprinting. (15)

assault—An attack on a person. (4)

asset—Anything of value to a business or organization, including people, equipment, computer hardware and software, and data and other information. (5)

assize of arms—A provision of the Statute of Westminster requiring every male between ages 15 and 60 to keep a weapon in his home as a "harness to keep the peace." (1)

asymmetric war—One in which a much weaker opponent takes on a stronger opponent by refusing to confront the stronger opponent head on. (13)

attack tree—Visually represents the goal of an attack on some asset as the trunk of the tree and possible/probable ways to accomplish it as branches. (5)

audit—An objective but critical on-site examination and analysis of a business, industrial plant, public or private institution or home to determine existing security, to identify deficiencies, to determine the protection needed and to recommend improvements to enhance overall security. (5)

authority—Right to give orders. (3)

backstretch area—The area of a racetrack where the horses, jockeys and grooms are quartered. (16)

bait money—Money in a bank, placed in such a way that when it is picked up an alarm sounds. (15)

barbiturates—Depressants or sedatives taken orally as a small tablet or capsule to induce sleep or to relieve tension. (12)

battery—The unconsented, offensive touching of another person, directly or indirectly. (4)

bench trial—A trial before a judge without a jury. (10)

biometrics—System that uses physical traits such as fingerprints, voice and even eyeballs to identify individuals. (6)

bioterrorism—Involves such biological weapons of mass destruction (WMD) as anthrax, botulism and smallpox. (13)

blind receiving—Going by the packing slip rather than actually counting a received shipment. (7)

bona fide occupational qualification (BFOQ)—Skill or knowledge that is reasonably necessary to perform a job and, consequently, may be a requirement for employment. (2)

booster box—A box whose top, bottom or end is hinged so that articles can be placed inside without actually opening the box. Apparatus of a shoplifter. (16)

bot—A type of malware that allows an attacker to gain complete control over the affected computer. (11)

Bow Street Runners—The first detective unit; established in London by Henry Fielding in 1750. (1)

Certified Protection Professional (CPP)—Program of the American Society for Industrial Security that provides certification for individuals who meet specific experience and educational requirements and pass a written examination. (2)

chain of custody—Documentation of who has had control of the evidence from the time it was found until presentation at trial. Also called the *chain of evidence.* (10)

chain of evidence—Documentation of who has had control of the evidence from the time it was found until presentation at trial. Also called the *chain of custody.* (10)

check kiting—A person makes simultaneous deposits and withdrawals using two or more banks to obtain credit before enough time has elapsed to clear the checks. (9)

citizen's arrest—The right of every citizen to arrest someone who is committing or has committed a crime, to be turned over to local authorities. (9)

closed drug market—Dealers sell only to people they know or who are vouched for by other buyers. (16)

commissioning—Inspecting and testing an installation to ensure that all expectations have been met. (6)

competitive intelligence—Consists of two overall facts: (1) the use of *public* sources to develop data (raw facts) on competitors and the market environment and (2) the transformation, by analysis, of that data into information (usable results). (11)

concentric zone theory—The more valuable an asset is, the more layers of protection it needs. (6)

conclusionary language—Assumptions or opinions, nonfactual. (10)

conditional threat—Warns that a violent act will happen unless certain demands or terms are met. (12)

connotative words—Words with strong emotional overtones. (10)

contextual integrity—Defines privacy using complex social principles expressed in algorithms written into software to monitor data use. (11)

contract services—Outside firms or individuals who provide security services for a fee. (1)

convergence—To come together and unite in a common interest or focus, a trend affecting security in many ways. (2)

copyright—"A property right in an original work of authorship (including literary, musical, dramatic, choreographic, pictorial, graphic, sculptural and architectural work; motion pictures and other audiovisual works; and sound recordings) fixed in any tangible medium of expression, giving the holder exclusive right to reproduce, adapt, distribute, perform and display the work" (*Information Asset Protection*, p.7). (11)

core concept—A style of building design in which all elevators, rest rooms, lobbies and service facilities are located at the building's center, allowing more effective control of public areas while also permitting more flexible use of office space. (16)

courier—A person assisting in the secured transportation and protection of items of value. (1)

crash bar—An emergency exit locking device. The door can be opened only from the inside, and if it is, an alarm sounds. Also called a *panic bar.* (6)

crime—An action that is harmful to another person and/or to society and that is punishable by law. (4)

crime prevention through environmental design (CPTED)—A theory proposing that the proper design and effective use of the built environment can reduce the incidence and fear of crime and make an improvement in the quality of life. (6)

criticality—Level of importance or seriousness of consequences. (5)

critical wandering—When an elderly person with dementia strays from caregivers. (15)

cross-examination—Questioning by the opposing side for the purpose of assessing the validity of the testimony. (10)

cybercrime—Computer crime. (9)

cyberspace—The artificial world created online in and between computer systems. (9)

dark figure of crime—The true number of crimes, including those never reported, is unknown. (9)

defamation—Injuring a person's reputation, such as by falsely inferring, by either words or conduct, in front of a third disinterested party, that a person committed a crime. (4)

defensible space—The name of a hypothesis developed by Oscar Newman holding that building designs that hinder crime give occupants a sense of security, thus encouraging them to guard themselves and their property. (6)

deliriants—Volatile chemicals that generally produce a "high" and loss of inhibition similar to that produced by alcohol. (12)

denotative words—Objective, nonemotional words. (10)

deposition—Where attorneys for both sides ask questions of an individual involved in a lawsuit and the questions and answers are recorded verbatim by a stenographer or court reporter. (10)

direct examination—The initial questioning of a witness or defendant by the lawyer who is using the person's testimony to further his or her case. (10)

direct threat—Identifies a specific act against a specific target and is delivered in a straightforward, clear and explicit manner. (12)

Dram Shop Acts—Make bartenders who continue to serve an obviously intoxicated patron liable for any harm that the individual might do to others. (16)

due diligence—The care a reasonable person exercises under the circumstances to avoid harm to other persons or their property. (2)

dynamic risk—Risk with the potential for both benefits and losses, for example, extending credit or accepting checks. (5)

empathy—Understanding where another person is coming from, whether you agree with it or not. (10)

encryption—The coding of a message. Used to thwart computer crime. (11)

enterprise risk management—Requires the convergence of traditional and information technology (IT) security to better define security risks and interdependencies between business functions and processes within an enterprise. (5)

enterprise security—Encompasses overseeing *all risks* an organization may face. (2)

envelope—A building's exterior; the first line of defense. (6)

espionage, industrial—Theft of trade secrets or confidential information. (14)

estimative language—Language based on analytical assessments and judgments rather than on facts or hard evidence. (13)

ethics—Deals with questions of right and wrong, of moral and immoral behavior. (4)

excessive force—More force than is reasonable to counteract the amount of resistance encountered. (4)

exclusionary rule—Makes inadmissible any evidence obtained by means violating a person's constitutional rights. (3)

exculpatory clauses—Clauses in a contract that limit liability, a disclaimer. (6)

exculpatory evidence—Information that may exonerate a suspect. (11)

felony—A serious crime such as murder, robbery or burglary that is punishable by death or by imprisonment in a state prison or penitentiary. (9)

FEMA—The Federal Emergency Management Agency, an independent federal agency charged with building and supporting the nation's emergency management system. (8)

fidelity bonds—Insurance protecting employers from losses suffered from dishonest employees. (7)

fire-loading—The amount of flammable materials within an area. (8)

fire triangle—The three elements necessary for burning: heat, fuel and oxygen. (8)

floor release limit—A value amount that cannot be exceeded with a check or credit/debit card unless the clerk clears it with the central office. (16)

floorwalkers—Employees who pose as customers and seek to remain unnoticed so as to catch shoplifters "in the act." (16)

foxing marks—Water or mold damage to pages in a book or document. (15)

fusion center—A mechanism to exchange information and intelligence, maximize resources, streamline operations and improve the ability to fight crime and terrorism by merging data from a variety of sources. (13)

gateway theory—Belief that using marijuana will lead to use of harder drugs. Also called the *stepping stone theory*. (12)

hacker—A computer enthusiast who engages in electronic snooping, software piracy and other types of high-tech illegal activities. (9)

hallucinogens—Drugs that may produce distortion, intensify sensory perception and lessen the ability to discriminate between fact and fantasy. (12)

honesty shopping—A procedure in which an individual, often a security officer, is hired to shop in such a way that will test the honesty of sales personnel who handle cash. Also called a *shopping service*. (16)

hot spot—An area that has a greater than average number of criminal or disorder events, or an area where people have a higher than average risk of victimization. (10)

hue and cry—The Anglo-Saxon practice whereby if anyone resisted the watchman's arrest, the watchman cried out and all citizens chased the fugitive and assisted in capturing him. (1)

hybrid services—Combine proprietary services and contract services. (1)

identity theft—A crime involving misappropriation of names, social security numbers, credit card numbers or other pieces of personal information for fraudulent purposes. (9)

igniter—Device to start a fire; includes matches, candles, cigarettes, explosives and the like. (9)

impeaching—Discrediting a witness's testimony. (10)

indemnity—The insurer agrees to pay no more than the actual amount of the loss; stated differently, the insured should not profit from a loss. (5)

indirect threat—Tends to be vague, unclear and ambiguous; the plan, the intended victim, the motivation and other aspects of the threat are masked or equivocal. (12)

intellectual property rights (IPR)—"A category of intangible rights protecting commercially valuable products of the human intellect. The category comprises primarily trademark, copyright and patent rights, but also includes trade secret rights, publicity rights, moral rights and rights against unfair competition." (*Information Asset Protection*, p.7). (11)

intentional tort—An illegal act committed on purpose. (4)

intermodal—Cargo that comes off ships and is dispersed via rail. (14)

interoperability—The ability to exchange information seamlessly. (13)

INTERPOL—International Criminal Police Organization. (15)

interrogatories—Written list of questions to which the defendant is asked to respond in writing. May be several pages long and may include questions attempting to obtain information that might be damaging to the defendant. (4, 10)

ISTs—Inherently safer technologies. (14)

jargon—Specialized language of a field, for example, *unsub* for unknown subject. (10)

jihad—A call to a holy war. (13)

kleptomaniac—A compulsive thief. (16)

law of large numbers—States that the more statistical information is available, the better the prediction as to what will happen in the future. (5)

leakage—Occurs when a person intentionally or unintentionally reveals clues to feelings, thoughts, fantasies, attitudes or intentions that may signal an impending violent act. (12)

Also refers to the illegal or unauthorized removal of cargo from the supply chain. (14)

liability without fault—The employer is held absolutely liable for job-related accidents and disease regardless of fault. (7)

libel—Generally refers to written defamatory remarks. (4)

licensing—Permission from a competent authority to carry out the business of providing security services on a contractual basis. (1)

malware—Malicious software; includes Trojan horses, viruses and worms, adware, spyware and bots. (11)

mesh network—A wireless communications technology that allows each radio to function as a router, meaning data can be sent to or through any other radio in the network to reach the intended destination, providing radios communicate on a peer-to-peer level. (11)

meta-analysis—A quantitative tool to evaluate several separate but similar experiments to test the pooled data for statistical significance. It is a way to combine the results from multiple experimental studies into one analysis of whether a program works or not. (6)

methamphetamine—Or "meth"; also known as *speed*, *ice* and *crystal*. A potent central nervous system stimulant. (12)

misdemeanor—A minor crime punishable by a fine and/or a relatively short jail sentence. (9)

mission creep—When an agency uses a program for more than originally intended. (14)

moral—That which is right or virtuous. (4)

narcotics—Drugs that produce sleep, lethargy or relief of pain and include heroin, cocaine and crack. (12)

natural surveillance—Placing physical features, activities and people in ways that maximize the ability to see what is going on to discourage crime. (6)

negligence—Occurs when a person has a duty to act reasonably but fails to do so and, as a result, someone is injured. (4)

noncompete agreements—Agreements preventing employees from quitting and going to work for competitors. (11)

nondelegable duty—One for which authority can be given to another person, but responsibility for it cannot. Civil liability remains with the person who has the legal duty to act. (4)

nondisclosure agreements—Agreements prohibiting employees from revealing sensitive information to outsiders. (11)

nonverbal communication—Includes the eyes, facial expressions, posture, gestures, clothes, tone of voice, proximity and touch. In writing, it includes neatness, paper quality, copy quality, binding and the like. (10)

nystagmus—An uncontrolled bouncing or jerking of the eyeball when the intoxicated person looks to the extreme right or left, and up or down. (12)

Occupational Safety and Health Act of 1970 (OSH Act)—Makes employers responsible for providing a safe workplace. (8)

Occupational Safety and Health Administration (OSHA)—Enforces the Occupational Safety and Health Act of 1970. (8)

open drug market—Dealers sell to all potential customers, eliminating only those suspected of being police or some other threat. (16)

OSHA—The Occupational Safety and Health Administration. (8)

outsourcing—Contracting of security services by private corporations and government agencies. (1)

pandemic—A disease occurring over a wide geographic area and affecting an exceptionally high proportion of the population. (8)

panic bar—An emergency exit locking device that can be opened only from the inside; if it is opened, an alarm sounds. Also called a *crash bar*. (6)

patent—The government grant of a right, privilege or authority to exclude others from making, using, marketing, selling, offering for sale or importing an invention for a specified period (20 years from the date of filing). (11)

pedagogy—Youth learning. (2)

perpetual inventory—A policy of keeping track of supplies/merchandise on hand almost daily; this is in contrast to an annual inventory, that is, taking stock only once a year. (7)

phishing—Attempts by fraudsters to trick people into revealing their personal information, such as passwords, by creating fake Web sites that look very much like the sites of legitimate financial institutions. (9)

photogrammetry—A process comparable to fingerprinting; provides a permanent, exact identification of works of art that is impossible to duplicate. (15)

physical security footprint—The mark left during or after a security action; what the public sees and lets them know that security is present. (6)

plaintiff—An individual who has been wronged and who files suit against the person committing the offense. (4)

power—The *force* that can be used to carry out one's authority. (3)

predication—The total set of circumstances that would lead a reasonable, prudent and professionally trained person to believe that an offense has occurred, is occurring or will occur. (10)

prerequisites—The background necessary to master a skill. (2)

prima facie evidence—Evidence that establishes a fact if not contested, for example, the specific blood alcohol level for intoxication is stated in state laws. (16)

private security—A profit-oriented industry that provides personnel, equipment and/or procedures to *prevent* losses caused by human error, emergencies, disasters or criminal actions. (1)

private security services—May be proprietary, contract or hybrid. Include guards, patrols, investigators, armed couriers, central alarm respondents and consultants. (1)

privatization—Duties normally performed by sworn personnel (e.g., police officers) are performed by others, often private security officers. (3)

probability—The likelihood of something occurring. (5)

probable cause—The situation in which individuals have facts and circumstances within their knowledge and of which they have reasonable trustworthy information that are sufficient in themselves to warrant a person of reasonable caution in the belief that the suspect has committed a crime *(Carroll v. United States)*. The same as *reasonable cause*. (16)

proprietary information—A property right or other valid economic interest in data resulting from private investment. (11)

proprietary services—In-house security services, directly hired, paid and controlled by the company or organization, usually for a salary rather than a fee. (1)

psychosocial—Individual psychological characteristics such as temperament and self-identity. (12)

punitive damages—Award made to punish a defendant who is deemed to have behaved in such an abhorrent manner that an example must be made to keep others from acting in a similar way. (4)

pure risk—Risk with the potential for injury, damage or loss with no possible benefits, for example, crimes and natural disasters. (5)

qualitative risk assessment—Assigns relative values to assets, risks, controls and effects. (5)

quantitative risk assessment—The goal is to calculate objective numeric values for each component gathered during the risk assessment and cost-benefit analysis. (5)

racinos—Dog and horse racing establishments that have card games and slot machines as well. (16)

reasonable cause—The situation in which individuals have "facts and circumstances within their knowledge and of which they had reasonable trustworthy information [that] were sufficient in themselves to warrant a man of reasonable caution in the belief that the suspect had committed a crime" (*Carroll v. United States*, 1925). The same as *probable cause*. (16)

registration—Permission from a state authority before being employed as an investigator or detective, guard, courier, alarm system installer or repairer, or alarm respondent. (1)

respondent superior—A concept that implies that employers are held liable for wrongful acts or negligence by an employee acting within the scope of his or her duties or in the employer's interest. (4)

restitution—Making up for a crime, a payment of some form. (4)

RFID—Radio frequency identification. (7)

risk—A known threat that has effects that are not predictable in either their timing or their extent. (3, 5)

risk assessment—The process of identifying and prioritizing risks to a business. (5)

risk management—Anticipating, recognizing and appraising a risk, initiating some action to remove the risk or reduce the potential loss from it to an acceptable level, and evaluating the results. (5)

sabotage—The intentional destruction of machinery or goods, or the intentional obstruction of production. (14)

Sarbanes-Oxley legislation—Requires as one of its corporate governance provisions that companies give employees a way to report financial irregularities anonymously. (11)

secrecy agreements—Agreements directed at individuals who come into contact with vital trade secrets of a business—for example, technicians called in to repair a vital piece of machinery. Such individuals may be asked to sign an agreement to keep such information confidential. (11)

Section 1983—Part of the Civil Rights Act which says that anyone acting under the authority of local or state law who violates another person's constitutional rights—even though they are upholding a law—can be sued. (4)

security survey—An objective, critical, on-site examination and analysis of a business, industrial plant, public or private institution or dwelling to determine its existing security, to identify deficiencies, to determine the protection needed and to recommend improvements to enhance overall security. (5)

shopping service—See *honesty shopping*. (16)

shrinkage—Loss of assets. (7)

sinsemilla—A highly potent form of home-grown marijuana obtained from unpollinated female plants. (12)

skips—Nonpaying guests. (16)

slander—Verbal derogatory statements. (4)

sleeper cell—A group of terrorists who blend into a community. (13)

sliding—The practice in which a clerk sells articles to friends or relatives at lower cost. (16)

SMART objectives—Objectives that are specific, measurable, attainable, relevant and trackable. (2)

spam—Electronic junk mail; technically termed unsolicited commercial e-mails. (9)

Statute of Westminster—A law issued by King Edward I that formalized England's system of criminal justice and apprehension. Established the *watch and ward, hue and cry* and *assize of arms* (1285). (1)

stepping stone theory—Belief that use of marijuana leads to use of harder drugs; also called the *gateway theory*. (12)

strict liability—Refers to instances when the person is held liable to the injured party even though the person may not have knowingly done anything wrong—for example, using explosives or keeping wild animals as pets. Also called *liability without fault.* (4)

subrogation—Substitution of the insurer in place of the insured for the purpose of claiming indemnity from a third person for a loss covered by insurance. (5)

substantive damages—Refers to actual damages a judge or jury feels the plaintiff is entitled to. (4)

surety bond—Usually provides monetary compensation if the bonded party fails to perform certain promised acts, for example, when an overextended contractor is unable to complete a construction project. (7)

technology escrow—Like an insurance policy for intellectual property; required when two or more parties negotiate a license for technology, such as mission-critical software or other proprietary information. (11)

telecommunications—The science of communication by the transmission of electronic impulses—for example, telegraph, telephone, fax. (11)

territoriality—People protect places they feel are their own and have a certain respect for the territory of others. (6)

terrorism—The use of force or violence against persons or property in violation of the criminal laws of the United States for purposes of intimidation, coercion or ransom. (13)

tithings—In Anglo-Saxon England, a unit of civil administration consisting of 10 families; established the principle of collective responsibility for maintaining law and order. (1)

tort—Civil wrong for which the court seeks a remedy in the form of damages to be paid. (4)

tort law—Civil law defining citizens' responsibilities to each other and providing for lawsuits to recover damages for injury caused by failing to carry out these responsibilities. (3)

toxic work environment—A hostile workplace. Indicatorsof such an environment include highly authoritarian management styles, supervision that is changeable and unpredictable, management methods that are invasive of privacy and extreme secrecy. (12)

trademark—"A word, phrase, logo or other graphic symbol used by a manufacturer or seller to distinguish its product or products from those of others." (*Information Asset Protection*, p.8). (11)

trailers—Paths of paper or accelerant that spread fire from one location to another. (9)

Trojan horse—Installs malicious software while under the guise of doing something else. (11)

Uniform Crime Reports (UCR)—Statistics on crime, compiled annually by the FBI. (9)

universal precaution—States that all blood and other bodily fluids must be treated as if infectious. (8)

veiled threat—One that strongly implies but does not explicitly threaten violence. (12)

vetted—Approved to share information with assuredness that sensitive need-to-know information will be handled appropriately. (3)

vicarious liability—The legal responsibility for the acts of another person because of some relationship with that person—for example, the liability of an employer for the acts of an employee. (2, 4)

vulnerability—An organization's susceptibility to risks. (5)

watch and ward—A custom that provided town watchmen to patrol the city during the night and the ward to patrol the city during the day. (In Middle English, *wardien* meant to keep watch.) (1)

watch clock—A seven-day timepiece. Keys are located at various stations in a facility; the security officer simply inserts the key into the watch clock at each station, and a record is automatically made of the time the location has been checked. (6)

well, the—The area between the lawyers and the judge, intended for the judge's protection. No one is allowed there unless invited by the judge. (10)

white-collar crime—Business-related crime, such as embezzlement, bribery and receiving kickbacks. (9)

zero floor release limit—All charges are cleared with the credit-card issuer. (16)

zero tolerance—Any behavior in a prohibited category, regardless of mitigating circumstances, results in the same usually harsh punishment such as termination of employment. (12, 15)

Name Index

Subject Index

on liability associated with armed security personnel, 103
on malicious prosecution, 100–101
on negligence, 101–102
on negligent liability, 95
on nondelegable duty *versus* vicarious liability, 96
on reasonable standard of care and proximate result, 96
recap of, 109–111
on reducing liability, 106
on security liability, 103
on use of force, 102
legal counsel, 293
legal investigators, 20
liability
of armed security personnel, 103
checklist for, 110
exculpatory clauses and, 162
to injured bystander, 102
lawsuits involving, trends in, 103
negligent, 95
reducing, 106
strict, 95
in United States, 94
vicarious, 96
without fault, 207
libel, 98
library security, 436–438
concerns about, 437
electronic marking for, 437
foxing marks for, 436
measures for, 437
and removal of book pages, 438
wet string method and, 438
licensing, 27–29
lie detector tests, 21
lighting, 161, 173, 461
as barrier, 169
perimeter, 168
Lincoln, Abraham, 11, 12
listening, 282
Little Rock, Arkansas, bank robbery, 435
Local Area Networks (LANS), 305
lockers, for employees, 205
locks, 157, 204, 461
card-operated, 157, 173
combination, 157, 204, 461
computer-managed (CM) systems of, 157
key-operated, 157
keypads for, 157
pushbutton, 157
time, 173
lodging establishment security, 480–484. See also hotel security
log
incident report, 283, 284
OSHA requirements for, 213
London
Metropolitan Police of, 9
transit system attack of 2005 in, 397
long-term care facilities security, 453
Los Angeles
airport security in, 370

private security in, 18
riots in, 224
security in, 63
loss events, 137
identifying, 136
loss exposure, 123
loss prevention, 41, 56, 57, 130
from accidents, emergencies, and natural disasters, 211–244
incident response *versus*, 125
loss prevention specialist, responsibilities of, 41, 56, 57
losses
from criminal actions, 245–272
by fire, 230–234
in industrial security, 408, 409
investigation of, 279
Lower Manhattan Construction Command Center, 257
Lower Manhattan Security Initiative, 397
ludes. *See* depressants
lysergic acid diethlyamide (LSD), 345
common symptoms, signs, and dangers of, 347

M resources, 144
mace, 103
magstripe cards, 158
mailrooms, 193, 490
malicious prosecution, 100–101
mall security, 478–479
malware, 313, 315, 316, 332
management, 45
versus leadership, 40
by objectives, 45
Management and Training Corporation, 81
manager, 45, 55
Manhattan Products, Carlstadt, New Jersey, 413
manufacturing security, 404–411
global environment of, 408
responsibilities of, 404
survey for, 405–407
mapping, 283
marijuana abuse, 342, 343, 344
common symptoms, signs, and dangers of, 347
history of, 339
in workplace, 341
Maritime Transportation and Safety Act (MTSA), 426
Mark Jackson v. Rohm & Hass Co., 98
Marshall v. Barlow's Inc., 213, 214
Marxist cabals, 14
Maryland, 166
Maslow, Abraham, 3
Maslow's hierarchy of needs, 3
mass transit security, 428
material safety data sheet (MSDS), 222
maternity ward security, 452. *See also* hospital security
mayhem, 353
McClernand, John A., 11
McDermott, Michael, 356

McGruff, crime dog, 262
McVeigh, Timothy, 188, 374
MDMA (Ecstasy), 341, 343
common symptoms, signs, and dangers of, 347
MediaDefender, Inc., 319
medical emergencies, 220–221
carbon monoxide poisoning as, 221
hepatitis B as, 220
HIV and AIDS as, 220
pandemic, 220
universal precautions and, 220
Memorial Health Systems, Colorado Springs, Colorado, 451
mentor, 45
merchandise
blind receiving of, 199
delivery of, 199
purchasing of, 199
receiving of, 199
Merchants and Marine Bank, and Hurricane Katrina, 447
mesh networks, 310
meta-analysis, 161
metal detectors, 175, 457
metal seal bars, 199
methamphetamine, 341, 342, 345
Meyers v. Ramada Inn of Columbus, 101
Miami–Dade County, Florida, Tactical Operations Multiagency Cargo Anti Theft Squad (TOMCATS), 421
Microsoft
guidelines of, for implementing security recommendations, 146–148
incident response at, 125
qualitative and quantitative risk assessment at, 135
risk management at, 123
Middle Ages
in England, 6
security during, 4
Miles, David, 127
military, Operational Risk Management (ORM) strategy, 124
Mill, James, 112
Minnesota
discarded information in, 322
electric power lines in, 409
Miranda v. State of Arizona, 281
Miranda warning, 71, 281
mirror, 174
mischief, criminal, investigative responsibilities for, 502
misdemeanor, 247
mission creep, 432
mitigation, 130, 137
mobs. *See* crowd control
Molotov cocktails, 226
money order, 475
moonlighting, 69
Morabian, Albert, 299
moral, defined, 111
morale, 45
morphine. *See* narcotics
motel security, 480–484
checklist for fire and pool safety, 483

U.S. Department of Transportation (USDOT), hazardous materials incidents and, 221, 222
U.S. Filter Recovery Services, Roseville, Minnesota, 413
U.S. General Accounting Office (GAO), 307
U.S. Government Accountability Office, 312
U.S. Justice Department, 200, 398
  and IT piracy, 319
  National Drug Intelligence Center (NDIC) of, 341
  Office of Community Oriented Policing Services (COPS) of, 86
  Office of National Drug Control Policy (ONDCP) of, 342
  Operation Site Down of, 319
U.S. Nuclear Regulatory Commission (NRC), 388
U.S. Secret Service
  hackers and, 263
  on information asset protection, 328
  on terrorism, 389, 390
U.S. v. Ziegler, 98
USA PATRIOT Act, 376, 444
  and cargo security, 421
utilities security, 415–419
  guns, guards, and gates for, 416
  IT for, 416
  losses in, 417
  role-playing exercises for, 416
  at substations, 417
  and utility trucks, 417
  at water facililties in Dallas, Texas, 419

Valium. *See* depressants
valuables, transporting, 206
vandalism, 255
  investigative responsibilities for, 502
  at schools, 455
vaults, 173
vehicle barriers, 169
vehicle cargo inspection system (VACIS), 425
vehicle control, 185
vehicle-borne improvised explosive devices (VBIEDs), 226, 227
vendors, as visitors, 189
very light jets (VLJs), 432
vetted, 85
vetting, 257
vicarious liability, 46
video equipment, restricting use of, 197
video security systems, 411
  intelligent, 165
  intelligent surveillance, 431
  Internet protocol (IP), 164, 309
Vietnam War, and drug use, 339
violence
  biological factors in, 352
  causes of, 351

desensitization to, 351
domestic (*See* domestic violence)
leakage of, 356, 357
macrosocial factors of, 351, 352
matrix for, 352
microsocial factors of, 351, 352
psychosocial factors in, 351, 352
school (*See* school violence)
in United States, 350, 351
workplace (*See* workplace violence)
violent crime, increase in, 350
VIPs, protecting, 77
Virginia Museum of Military Vehicles (VMMV), 442
Virginia Tech shootings, 337, 455
  lessons learned from, 462
viruses, 314
visitor management systems, 187
  capabilities of, 188
visitors
  contractors as, 189
  to hospitals, 449
  nonbusiness access request for, 188
  photo ID with barcode for, 187
  in tour groups, 189
  vendors as, 189
voice biometrics, 159
voice over Internet protocol (VoIP), 165, 310
  during emergency, 219
vulnerability, 193–195
  employee tracking as, 414
  in hospitals, 451
  industrial, 404
  in office building security, 490
  in risk analysis, 128
  at utilities, 416
  and workplace violence, 357
vulnerability assessment (VA), 140

Wackenhut, George R., 13
Wackenhut Corporation, 13
Wackenhut Corrections Corporation, 81
war
  asymmetric, 376
  on drugs, 348
  holy, 381
ward, 7
warehouses, 193
warez, 318
warning, before natural disasters, 235
Washington, D.C. security, 188
watch, before natural disasters, 235
watch and ward, 7
watch clock, 175
Water Environment Federation, 419
water facilities security, 418–419
  Dallas, Texas, 419
watermark technology, 320
Watkins, William, 12
Watts riot of 1965, 224
weapons of mass destruction (WMDs), 387–389
weather, watches and warnings in, 235

weather alert radio, 235
Weingarten rights, 71
Weingarten rules, 72
Welch, David, 321
well, in courtroom, 296
Wells, Henry, 10
Wells Fargo and Company, 10
Westroads Mall shooting, Omaha, Nebraska, 478
wet string method, 438
Wheed, Ammunition, 13
whistleblower, retaliation against, 321
White Out. *See* inhalants
white-collar crime, 257–259
  fraud as, 257
  identity theft as, 258
Whitworth Art Gallery, 439
Wichita State University, 461
Wide Area Networks (WANS), 305
Wild Bunch, 9
Wild West, 9
Wildermuth, Terry, 127
Wisconsin, 166
  Pulliam Plant, Green Bay, 413
witnesses, 293
  impeaching, 292
  rebuttal, 295
  strategies for excelling as, 296
  surrebuttal, 295
work order, sample, 194
workplace
  culture of, 349
  emergency management in, 215
  impact of domestic violence on, 362
workplace accidents
  investigations of, 276
  prevention of, 214, 215
  three cause levels of, 277
workplace alcohol abuse, 348–350
workplace drug abuse, 337–369
  introduction to, 338
  problem of, 341–343
  recognizing, 346–348
workplace violence, 337–369
  alcohol abuse and, 350
  categories of, 354
  classification of, 353, 354
  continuum of, 354
  dealing with, 361–362
  defined, 352
  drug testing and, 358
  extent and impact of, 354, 355
  HARM model of, 353
  ineffective approaches to, 361
  introduction to, 338
  legal issues in, 366–367
  lost work-time (LWT) due to, 355
  management process for, 362
  motivations for, 355
  no threats, no violence policy regarding, 359
  peer review and, 360
  persons vulnerable to, 357

Photo Credits

This page constitutes an extension of the copyright page. We have made every effort to trace the ownership of all copyrighted material and to secure permission from copyright holders. In the event of any question arising as to the use of any material, we will be pleased to make the necessary corrections in future printings. Thanks are due to the following authors, publishers, and agents for permission to use the material indicated.

Chapter 1. 1: © Cengage Learning/Heinle Image Resource Bank 6: © EARL S. CRYER/UPI/Landov 6: © Keren Su/Danita Delimont Agency/drr.net 11: © Bettmann/CORBIS

Chapter 2. 32: © Kim Kulish/Corbis 54: © SCHIFRES LUCAS/CORBIS SYGMA

Chapter 3. 63: © Michael Newman/PhotoEdit 80: © AP/Wide World Photos

Chapter 4. 93: © AP/ Wide World Photos 104: © Roger Ressmeyer/CORBIS

Chapter 5. 119: © Colin Anderson/Jupiterimages 129: © Ed Kashi/CORBIS

Chapter 6. 151: © Tim Wright/CORBIS 160: © AP/Wide World Photos 174: © Alvis Upitis/Brand X Pictures/Photolibrary

Chapter 7. 181: © Stephen Chernin/Getty Images 185: © Tim Rue/Corbis 204: © Joe Raedle/Getty Images

Chapter 8. 211: © AP/Wide World Photos 225: © AP/Wide World Photos 226: © Jim Beckel/*The Oklahoman*/Corbis 233: © Image Source/Corbis

Chapter 9. 245: © Roy McMahon/Corbis 251: © AP/Wide World Photos

Chapter 10. 273: © Michael Newman/PhotoEdit 295: © AP/Wide World Photos

Chapter 11. 303: © AP/Wide World Photos 319: © AP/Wide World Photos

Chapter 12. 337: © AP Photo/*The Roanoke Times*, Matt Gentry 358: © Michael Newman/PhotoEdit

Chapter 13. 370: © David McNew/Getty Images 385: © BILL CAHIR/ Newhouse News Service/Landov

Chapter 14. 402: © AP/Wide World Photos 425: © Ed Kashi/Corbis

Chapter 15. 435: © AP/Wide World Photos 441: © Chip East/Bloomberg News/Landov 457: © Don Tremain/Getty Images

Chapter 16. 465: © Bill Aron/PhotoEdit 487: © Reuters/CORBIS 489: © AP/ Wide World Photos